Rexx Programmer's Ref

Howard Fosdick

Wiley Publishing, Inc.

Rexx Programmer's Reference

Published by
Wiley Publishing, Inc.
10475 Crosspoint Boulevard
Indianapolis, IN 46256
www.wiley.com

Copyright © 2005 by Wiley Publishing, Inc., Indianapolis, Indiana

Published simultaneously in Canada

ISBN: 0-7645-7996-7

Manufactured in the United States of America

10 9 8 7 6 5 4 3 2 1

1MA/ST/QS/QV/IN

About the Author

Howard Fosdick

Howard Fosdick has performed DBA and systems support work as an independent consultant for 15 years. He's coded in Rexx for nearly two decades and has worked in most other major scripting languages. Fosdick has written many technical articles, founded two database users' groups, and is known as the originator of such concepts as "hype cycles" and "open consulting."

Credits

Senior Acquisitions Editor
Debra Williams Cauley

Development Editor
Eileen Bien Calabro

Production Editor
Felicia Robinson

Technical Reviewer
Mark Hessling

Copy Editor
Publication Services

Editorial Manager
Mary Beth Wakefield

Vice President & Executive Group Publisher
Richard Swadley

Vice President and Publisher
Joseph B. Wikert

Project Coordinator
Erin Smith

Graphics and Production Specialists
Jonelle Burns
Carrie Foster
Lauren Goddard
Denny Hager
Joyce Haughey
Jennifer Heleine

Quality Control Technicians
John Greenough
Leeann Harney
Jessica Kramer
Carl William Pierce

Proofreading and Indexing
TECHBOOKS Production Services

To Kate, my parents, and Phoebe Jane.

Foreword

Rexx is a very underrated programming language; elegant in design, simple syntax, easy to learn, use and maintain, yet as powerful as any other scripting language available today.

In 1979, Mike Cowlishaw, IBM fellow, designed a "human-centric" programming language, Rexx. Cowlishaw's premise was that the programmer should not have to tell the interpreter what the language syntax was in each program they wrote; that was the job of the interpreter. So unlike most other programming languages, Rexx does not suffer from superfluous, meaningless punctuation characters throughout the code.

Since the release of Rexx outside of IBM, Rexx has been ported to virtually all operating systems and was formally standardised with the publishing of the ANSI Standard for Rexx in 1996. In late 2004, IBM transferred their implementation of Object REXX to the Rexx Language Association under an Open Source license. This event signalled a new era in the history of Rexx.

This book provides a comprehensive reference and programming guide to the Rexx programming language. It shows how to use the most popular implementations of Rexx and Rexx external function packages and is suited to both the programmer learning Rexx for the first time as well as the seasoned Rexx developer requiring a single, comprehensive reference manual.

Rexx has had a major influence on my life for the past 20 years since I wrote my first XEDIT macro in Rexx. In the last 10 years I have maintained the Regina Rexx interpreter, ably assisted by Florian Große-Coosmann, and in my remaining spare time have developed several Rexx external function packages (and my XEDIT-like text editor, THE). However, like many developers of open source products, I have never quite documented the products as completely as they deserve.

This is the book I would have liked to write if I had had the time. I'm glad Howard had the time!

Mark Hessling
Author of Rexx/SQL, Rexx/gd, Rexx/DW, Rexx/CURL,
Rexx/Curses, Rexx/Wrapper, Rexx/Trans,
The Hessling Editor (THE), Maintainer of Regina,
Rexx/Tk, PDCurses, http://www.rexx.org/

Acknowledgments

Special thanks are due to Mark Hessling, who writes and maintains Regina Rexx and a wide variety of open source Rexx tools and interfaces. As the technical reviewer for this book, Mark was an invaluable source of recommendations for improvement as well as (oops!) corrections. His expertise and helpfulness were critical to improving this book.

Special gratitude is also due to the inventor of Rexx, Michael Cowlishaw. His advice and feedback were very much appreciated.

In the process of developing this book, I wrote inquiries to many people without any prior introduction. Each and every one of them responded helpfully. It was a great pleasure to meet people with such an interest in Rexx, who so kindly answered questions and who greatly improved this book with their suggestions.

I would like to give heartfelt thanks to María Teresa Alonso y Albado, W. David Ashley, Gil Barmwater, Dr. Dennis Beckley, Alex Brodsky, Frank Clarke, Steve Coalbran, Ian Collier, Les Cottrell, Michael Cowlishaw, Chip Davis, Prof. Rony Flatscher, Jeff Glatt, Etienne Gloux, Bernard Golden, Bob Hamilton, Henri Henault , Stéphane Henault, Mark Hessling, Jack Hicks, IBM Corporation, René Vincent Jansen, Jaxo Inc., Kåre Johansson, Kilowatt Software, Les Koehler, Laboratorios Bagó S.A., Joseph A. Latone, Henri LeFebure, Michael Lueck, Antoni Levato, Dave Martin, Rob McNair, Patrick TJ McPhee, Dr. Laura Murray, Walter u. Christel Pachl, Lee Peedin, Priscilla Polk, the Rexx Language Association, Pierre G. Richard, Peggy Robinson, Morris Rosenbaum, Dr. Elizabeth Rovelli, David Ruggles, Roger E. Sanders, Thomas Schneider, Theresa Stewart, UniForum Chicago, Vasilis Vlachoudis, Stan Wakefield, Keith Watts, Dr. Sandra Wittstein, and Claudio Zomparelli.

Beyond those who provided technical advice and input for this book, I wish to thank my editors at John Wiley and Sons, Inc. Eileen Bien Calabro greatly improved the readability of this book through her writing recommendations. Debra Williams Cauley provided insightful perspective and guidance on the preparation and organization of the book. Finally, I thank Richard Swadley. I appreciate his confidence and hope this book fulfills its promise both in the quality of its material and in its sales and distribution.

Special thank you to the following developers for permission to reprint or refer to their code (most of these items fall under various open source licenses):

W. David Ashley—IBM Corporation, project leader of the Mod_Rexx project for scripts appearing in the chapter on Apache programming with Mod_Rexx

Les Cottrell and the Stanford Linear Accelerator Laboratory—Authors of Rexx/CGI library for a script illustrating their Rexx/CGI library

Henri Henault & Sons—Authors of the Internet/REXX HHNS WorkBench for a script and screen shot illustrating the Internet/REXX HHNS WorkBench.

Acknowledgments

Mark Hessling—Developer/maintainer of Regina Rexx and many open source Rexx tools for material on Rexx/gd and the reference tables of Rexx/Tk functions

Patrick TJ McPhee—Developer of RexxXML for the example program appearing in the chapter on RexxXML

Pierre G. Richard, Joseph A. Latone, and Jaxo Inc.—Developers of Rexx for Palm OS for example scripts appearing in the chapter on Rexx for Palm OS

Contents at a Glance

Contents at a Glance

Contents

Contents

Contents

Contents

Contents

Contents

Contents

Contents

Contents

Introduction

Of all the free scripting languages, why should you learn Rexx? Rexx is unique in that it combines *power* with *ease of use*. Long the dominant scripting language on mainframes, it is definitely a "power" language, yet it is also so easy to use that its popularity has expanded to every conceivable platform. Today the vast majority of Rexx developers use the language on Windows, Linux, Unix, and dozens of other systems . . . and, there are nine free and open source Rexx interpreters available.

Here's the Rexx story in a nutshell:

❑ Rexx runs on *every* platform under nearly every operating system.

So, your skills apply anywhere . . . and your code runs everywhere.

❑ Rexx enjoys a strong international standard that applies to every Rexx interpreter . . .

from handhelds to PCs to servers to mainframes.

❑ Rexx is as easy as BASIC, yet about as powerful as Perl.

❑ Rexx's large user community means:

❑ Many free interpreters optimized for different needs and environments

❑ A vast array of free interfaces and tools

❑ Good support

❑ Rexx comes in object-oriented versions as well as a version that is Java-compatible (and even generates Java code!)

You may be wondering why ease of use is so important in a programming language—especially if you are a high-end developer. First, understand that a truly "easy" language is easy to use, learn, remember, maintain, and code. The benefits to beginners are obvious. With Rexx, you can start coding almost immediately. There are no syntax tricks or language details to memorize before you begin. And, since Rexx is also a powerful language, you can rest assured that you won't run out of power as you learn and grow in the language. Read the first few chapters in this book, and you'll be scripting right away. Continue reading, and you'll mature into advanced scripting before you finish.

If you are a highly experienced developer, Rexx offers more subtle benefits. You will be wildly productive, of course, as you free yourself from the shackles of syntax-driven code. More important is this: Simplicity yields reliability. Your error rate will decline, and you'll develop more reliable programs. This benefit is greatest for the largest systems and the most complicated scripts. Your scripts will also live longer because others will be able to understand, maintain, and enhance them. Your clever scriptlets and application masterpieces won't die of neglect if you leave the company and continue your career elsewhere.

Few easy languages are also *powerful*. Now, how does Rexx do *that*?

Rexx surrounds its small instruction with an extensive function library. Scripts leverage operating system commands, external interfaces, programs, and functions. Rexx is a "glue" language that ties it all together. Yet the language has few rules. Syntax is simple, minimal, flexible. Rexx doesn't care about uppercase or lowercase or formatting or spacing. Rexx scripts don't use special symbols and contain no punctuation.

> **Power does not require coding complexity!**

If you've worked in the shell languages, you'll breathe a sigh of relief that you've found a powerful language in which you can program now and then without trying to recall arcane language rules. If you've struggled with the syntax of languages such as Bash, Korn, Awk, or the C-shell, you'll enjoy focusing on your programming problem instead of linguistic peculiarities. And if you've ever had to maintain someone else's Perl code, well . . . you might *really* be thankful for Rexx!

This book contains everything you need to know to get started with Rexx. How to freely download and install the product. How to program in standard Rexx and object-oriented Rexx. How to program handhelds. How to program Windows, Linux, Unix, and mainframes. How to program in the Java environment in a Rexx-based language called NetRexx. How to script operating system commands, control Web servers and databases and graphical user interfaces (GUIs) and Extensible Markup Language (XML) and Apache and . . . you name it.

Everything you need is in this one book—it's virtually a "Rexx encyclopedia." It teaches standard Rexx so that your skills apply to any platform—from handhelds to PCs and laptops to midrange servers running any operating system to mainframes. Yet it goes beyond the basics to cover interface programming and advanced techniques. The book starts out easy, and is based on coding examples throughout to make learning fast, simple, and fun. But it's comprehensive enough to go the distance and cover advanced scripting as well. And, you can freely download all the Rexx interpreters, tools, and interfaces it covers. Welcome to the world of free Rexx !

Who This Book Is For

This book is for anyone who wants to learn Rexx, or who already works with Rexx and wants to expand his or her knowledge of the language, its versions, interfaces, and tools. How you use this book depends on your previous programming or scripting knowledge and experience:

❑ If you are a complete beginner who has heard about Rexx and have come this far, you've come to the right place. Rexx is easily learned, and this book tells you everything you need to know. It's a progressive tutorial that won't let you get lost. And if you stick with it, you'll be able to handle almost any programming problem by the end of the book.

❑ If you are an experienced programmer in some other scripting or programming language, then you too have come to the right place. You can learn Rexx very quickly simply by reading the early chapters in this book. You'll be able to program in Rexx immediately. As the book progresses into tutorials on interfaces to databases, Web servers, GUIs, and the like, you'll learn how to program Rexx in the context of the larger environment to meet your programming needs.

❑ If you are a systems administrator or support person, you'll be able to grow your knowledge of a language that applies to a very wide variety of situations and can be a great tool. This book covers the interfaces, tools, and varieties and implementations of Rexx you'll need to know about. It doesn't stop with the basics, but plows right on ahead into the advanced features you'll want to learn and use.

❑ If you already use Rexx, you will be able to expand your knowledge through this book. You can learn about free Rexx interfaces and tools with which you may not be familiar. You'll learn about Rexx programming in new environments, such as scripting handhelds, object-oriented Rexx, and scripting in the Java environment with NetRexx. You'll also find the complete reference in the appendices a useful source of consolidated information. This is the only Rexx reference you'll need on your desk.

What This Book Covers

This book teaches standard Rexx, quickly and simply. It teaches you what you need to know to work with Rexx on any platform. You'll know a language that runs anywhere—from handheld devices such as personal digital assistants, pocket PCs, Palm Pilots, and mobile and smart phones to desktop and laptop PCs, with operating systems like Windows, Linux, and others, to midrange servers from all the major vendors—right on up to the world's largest mainframes. Rexx applies to almost any programming problem.

Beyond the Rexx language proper, this book covers all the major interfaces into Web servers, databases, GUIs, XML, and the like. It describes many of the free tools that are available to make scripting with Rexx easier and more productive.

The book covers nine free Rexx interpreters. Eight of them meet the international standards for Rexx, yet each adds its own special features and extensions. The book tells where to download each interpreter, shows how to install it, and demonstrates how to make the most of its advantages and extensions.

All the Rexx interpreters, tools, and interfaces this book covers are free or open source. The one exception is IBM mainframe Rexx, which comes bundled with IBM's operating systems.

In the end, this book covers not only Rexx scripting, but also the whole world of Rexx programming across all environments and interfaces, and with all Rexx interpreters. It is truly a Rexx encyclopedia.

How This Book Is Structured

Take a quick look at the table of contents, and you will see that this book is broken down into three broad sections:

❑ The book begins with a progressive tutorial and examples that cover all the basic aspects of the Rexx language. These eventually lead into more advanced scripting topics, such as how to write portable code and using optimal coding style. The last chapters of this section (Chapters 15 through 18) cover the most common Rexx interfaces and tools. These introduce and demonstrate how to code Rexx in interfacing to operating systems, SQL databases, Web servers, GUIs, XML, and other tools.

- ❑ The chapters of the second section of the book describe the different Rexx interpreters and the unique advantages of each. These chapters apply Rexx to different environments, such as handhelds, mainframes, and various other platforms. They include tutorials on object-oriented Rexx, handheld scripting, and how to program in the Java environment with NetRexx.

- ❑ Finally, the book has a detailed and comprehensive reference section in the form of a series of appendices. This reference section is a complete stand-alone reference. You won't need any other tome on your desk to write Rexx scripts.

How you decide to progress through the book really depends on your current skill level with regard to Rexx and scripting and what you want to do. You can use this book as a tutorial by working with it straight through, or you can dive into particular chapters and topics that interest you. Or, just use the appendices as your complete Rexx reference. Any approach is fine—use the book in the way that is best for you.

What You Need to Use This Book

You need nothing besides this book to get started. While this book is an "encyclopedia of Rexx," its examples were all run using freely downloadable Rexx interpreters, tools, and interfaces. The chapters all tell you where to download any interpreters, tools, and interfaces the book demonstrates, as well as how to set up and install them. The examples in this book were run and tested under Windows and/or Linux, but you can work with this book with Rexx running any operating system you like.

Conventions

To help you get the most from the text and keep track of what's happening, we've used a number of conventions throughout the book.

> **Boxes like this one hold important, not-to-be-forgotten information that is directly relevant to the surrounding text.**

Concerning styles in the text:

- ❑ We *italicize* important words when we introduce them.
- ❑ We show keyboard strokes like this: Ctrl-A.
- ❑ We show filenames, URLs, variable names, and code within the text like this: my_file.txt.
- ❑ We present code in two different ways:

```
In code examples we highlight new and important code with a gray background.
```

```
The gray highlighting is not used for code that's less important in the present
context, or that has been shown before.
```

The Rexx language is not case-sensitive, so its instructions and functions can be encoded in uppercase, lowercase, or mixed case. For example, the `wordlength` function can be encoded as `wordlength`, `WordLength`, or `WORDLENGTH`. This book uses capitalization typical to the platforms for which its sample scripts were written, but you can use any case you prefer.

Due to the typesetting software used in preparing this book, single quotation marks may appear as vertical, forward-leaning, or backward-leaning. All are simply single quotation marks to Rexx. For example, these two coding examples are exactly equivalent, even though the quote marks slant in different directions:

```
say `Hello`
```

```
say 'Hello'
```

Source Code

As you work through the examples in this book, you may choose either to type in code manually or to use the source code files that accompany the book. The source code in this book is available for free download at www.wrox.com. Once at the site, simply locate the book's title (either by using the Search box or by using one of the title lists) and click the `Download Code` link on the book's detail page to obtain the source code for the book.

> Because many books have similar titles, you may find it easier to search by ISBN; for this book the ISBN is 0764579967.

Once you have downloaded the code, just decompress it with your favorite compression tool. Alternatively, you can go to the main Wrox code download page at www.wrox.com/dynamic/books/download.aspx to see the code available for this book and all other Wrox books.

Errata

We make every effort to ensure that there are no errors in the text or in the code. However, no one is perfect, and mistakes do occur. If you find an error in one of our books, such as a spelling mistake or faulty piece of code, we would be very grateful for your feedback. By sending in errata, you may save another reader hours of frustration and at the same time you will be helping us provide even higher-quality information.

To find the errata page for this book, go to www.wrox.com and locate the title using the Search box or one of the title lists. Then, on the book details page, click the `Book Errata` link. On this page, you can view all errata that has been submitted for this book and posted by Wrox editors. A complete book list, including links to each book's errata, is also available at www.wrox.com/misc-pages/booklist.shtml.

If you don't spot "your" error on the Book Errata page, go to www.wrox.com/contact/techsupport .shtml and complete the form there to send us the error you have found. We'll check the information and, if appropriate, post a message to the book's errata page and fix the problem in subsequent editions of the book.

p2p.wrox.com

For author and peer discussion, join the P2P forums at p2p.wrox.com. The forums are a Web-based system for you to post messages relating to Wrox books and related technologies and interact with other readers and technology users. The forums offer a subscription feature to email you on topics of your choosing when new posts are made to the forums. Wrox authors, editors, other industry experts, and your fellow readers are present on these forums.

At http://p2p.wrox.com you will find a number of different forums that will help you not only as you read this book, but also as you develop your own applications. To join the forums, just follow these steps.

1.   Go to p2p.wrox.com and click the Register link.

2.   Read the terms of use and click Agree.

3.   Complete the required information to join as well as any optional information you wish to provide and click Submit.

You will receive an email with information describing how to verify your account and complete the joining process.

> **You can read messages in the forums without joining P2P; but in order to post your own messages, you must join.**

Once you join, you can post new messages and respond to messages other users post. You can read messages at any time on the Web. If you would like to have new messages from a particular forum emailed to you, click the Subscribe to this Forum icon by the forum name in the forum listing.

For more information about how to use the Wrox P2P, read the P2P FAQs for answers to questions about how the forum software works as well as many common questions specific to P2P and Wrox books. To read the FAQs, click the FAQ link on any P2P page.

Part I

Introduction to Scripting and Rexx

Overview

Before learning the Rexx language, you need to consider the larger picture. What are scripting languages? When and why are they used? What are Rexx's unique strengths as a scripting language, and what kinds of programming problems does it address? Are there any situations where Rexx would *not* be the best language choice?

This chapter places Rexx within the larger context of programming technologies. The goal is to give you the background you need to understand how you can use Rexx to solve the programming problems you face.

Following this background, the chapter shows you how to download and install the most popular free Rexx interpreter on your Windows, Linux, or Unix computer. Called *Regina*, this open-source interpreter provides a basis for your experiments with Rexx as you progress in the language tutorial of subsequent chapters. Note that you can use *any* standard Rexx interpreter to learn Rexx. So, if you have some other Rexx interpreter available, you are welcome to use it. We show how to download and install Regina for readers who do not already have a Rexx interpreter installed, or for those who would like to install an open-source Rexx on their PC.

Why Scripting?

Rexx is a *scripting language*. What's that? While most developers would claim to "know one when they see it," a precise definition is elusive. Scripting is not a crisply defined discipline but rather a directional trend in software development. Scripting languages tend to be:

❑ *High level* — Each line of code in a script produces more executable instructions — it does more — than an equivalent line encoded in a lower-level or "traditional" language.

❏ *Glue languages* — Scripting languages stitch different components together — operating system commands, graphical user interface (GUI) widgets, objects, functions, or service routines. Some call scripting languages *glue languages*. They leverage existing code for higher productivity.

❏ *Interpreted* — Scripting languages do not translate or *compile* source code into the computer's machine code prior to execution. No compile step means quicker program development.

❏ *Interactive debugging* — Interpreted languages integrate interactive debugging. This gives developers quick feedback about errors and makes them more productive.

❏ *Variable management* — Higher-level scripting languages automatically manage variables. Rexx programmers do not have to define or "declare" variables prior to use, nor do they need to assign maximum lengths for character strings or worry about the maximum number of elements tables will hold. The scripting language handles all these programming details.

❏ *Typeless variables* — Powerful scripting languages like Rexx even relieve the programmer of the burden of declaring data types, defining the kind of data that variables contain. Rexx understands data by usage. It automatically converts data as necessary to perform arithmetic operations or comparisons. Much of the housekeeping work programmers perform in traditional programming languages is automated. This shifts the burden of programming from the developer to the machine.

Figure 1-1 contrasts scripting languages and more traditional programming languages.

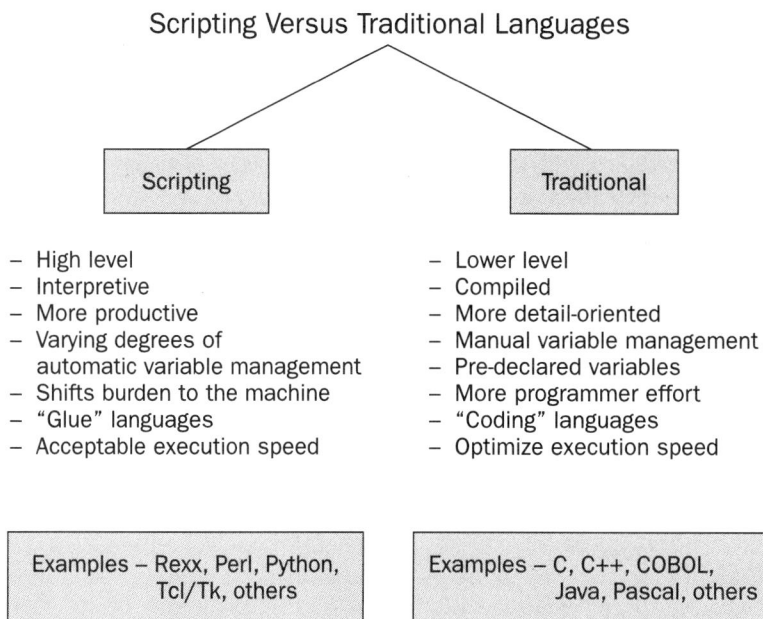

Scripting Versus Traditional Languages

Scripting	Traditional

- – High level
- – Interpretive
- – More productive
- – Varying degrees of automatic variable management
- – Shifts burden to the machine
- – "Glue" languages
- – Acceptable execution speed

- – Lower level
- – Compiled
- – More detail-oriented
- – Manual variable management
- – Pre-declared variables
- – More programmer effort
- – "Coding" languages
- – Optimize execution speed

Examples – Rexx, Perl, Python, Tcl/Tk, others	Examples – C, C++, COBOL, Java, Pascal, others

Figure 1-1

On the downside, scripting requires greater machine resources than hand-coded programs in traditional, compiled languages. But in an era where machine resources are less expensive than ever and continue to decline in price, trading off expensive developer time for cheaper hardware makes sense.

> Hardware performance increases geometrically, while the performance differential between scripting and compiled languages remains constant.

Here's how hardware addresses scripting performance. The original IBM PC ran an 8088 processor at 4.77 MHz. It executes less than a hundred *clauses* or statements of a Rexx script every second. Current Pentiums execute several million Rexx clauses per second.

Just for fun, this table shows how much faster a standard Rexx benchmark script runs on typical PCs at 5-or 6-year intervals. Later in this chapter, we'll show you how to benchmark your own computer against the numbers in this table:

Year	Make	Processor	Speed	Memory	Operating System	Rexx	Clauses per Second
1982	IBM PC	8088	4.77 Mhz	320 KB	DOS 6.2	Mansfield	70
	Zenith	8088-2	8 Mhz	640 KB	DOS 6.2	Mansfield	95
1988	Clone	386/DX	25 Mhz	2 MB	DOS 6.2	BRexx	3,600
1993	Clone	486/SX	25 Mhz	8 MB	Windows 3.1	BRexx	6,000
	Clone	486/DX2	66 Mhz	8 MB	Windows 3.1	BRexx	8,200
	IBM	486/SX2	50 Mhz	20 MB	Windows 95	BRexx	11,500
1998	Gate-way	Pentium II	266 Mhz	512 MB	Red Hat 8	Regina	180,000
	Gate-way	Pentium II	266 Mhz	512 MB	Windows 98SE	Regina	225,000
	Gate-way	Pentium II	266 Mhz	512 MB	Windows 98SE	BRexx	325,000
2005	Clone	Celeron	2.6 Ghz	1 GB	Windows XP	Regina	1,100,000
	Clone	Celeron	2.6 Ghz	1 GB	Windows XP	BRexx	1,800,000
	IBM	Pentium IV	2.2 Ghz	768 MB	Windows 2000	Regina	1,800,000
	Clone	Pentium IV	3.4 Ghz	1 GB	Windows 2003	Regina	2,400,000

Source- author's hands-on tests (yep, even on the old IBM PC model 1!).

The bottom line is that the program that consumes over an hour on the 8088 runs in a second on a modern Pentium. While the table ignores subtle factors that affect performance, the trend is clear. For most programming projects, trading machine cycles for labor costs makes sense. Why not use a more productive tool that shifts the burden to the machine?

Labor-saving benefits extend beyond program development to maintenance and enhancement. Experts like T. Capers Jones estimate that up to 75 percent of IT labor costs are devoted to program maintenance. An easy-to-read, easy-to-maintain scripting language like Rexx saves a great deal of money.

Sometimes, you'll hear the claim that scripting languages don't support the development of large, robust, "production-grade" applications. Years ago, scripting languages were primitive and this charge rang true. But no longer. IT organizations routinely develop and run large applications written in Rexx and other scripting languages. For example, the author has scripted two production business applications of over 10,000 lines. You can run an entire enterprise on scripts.

Why Rexx?

The distinguishing feature of Rexx is that it combines *ease of use* with *power*. Its goal is to make scripting as easy, fast, reliable, and error-free as possible. Many programming languages are designed for compatibility with older languages, the personal tastes of their inventors, the convenience of compiler-writers, or machine optimization. Rexx ignores extraneous objectives. It was designed from day one to be powerful yet easy to use.

One person invented Rexx and guided its development: Michael Cowlishaw of IBM's UK laboratories. Cowlishaw gave the language the coherent vision and guiding hand that ambitious software projects require to succeed. Anticipating how the Internet community would cooperate years later, he posted Rexx on the 'net of its day, IBM's VNET, a network of tens of thousands of users. Cowlishaw solicited and responded to thousands of emailed suggestions and recommendations on how people actually used early Rexx. The feedback enabled Cowlishaw to adapt Rexx to typical human behavior, making Rexx a truly easy-to-use language.

Ease of use is critical — even to experienced developers — because it leads to these benefits:

❑ *Low error rate* — An easy-to-use language results in fewer bugs per program. Languages that rely on arcane syntax, special characters and symbols, and default variables cause more errors.

❑ *Reliability* — Programs are more reliable due to the lower error rate.

❑ *Longer-lived code* — Maintenance costs dictate the usable life span of code. Rexx scripts are much easier to maintain than scripts written in languages that rely on special characters and complex syntax.

❑ *Reduced cost* — Fast program development, coupled with a low error rate and high reliability, lead to reduced costs. Ease of maintenance is critical because up to three-quarters of IT professionals engage in maintenance activities. Code written by others is easier to understand and maintain if it is written in Rexx instead of syntax-driven languages like the shell languages or Perl. This reduces labor costs.

❑ *Higher productivity* — Developer productivity soars when the language is easy to work with. Scripting in Rexx is more productive than coding in either lower-level compiled languages or syntax-based shell languages.

❑ *Quicker testing* — Interpretive scripting languages lend themselves to interactive testing. Programmers get quick feedback and can easily trace program execution. Combined with the low error rate of an easy-to-use language, this means that less test time is required.

❑ *Easy to learn* — An easy-to-use language is easier to learn. If you have programmed in *any* other programming or scripting language, you can pick up Rexx very quickly.

- ❏ *Easy to remember* — If you write only the occasional program, Rexx is for you. Languages with special characters and quirky syntax force you to review their rules if you only script now and then.

- ❏ *Transfer skills* — Since Rexx is easy to work with, developers find it easy to adapt to platform differences or the requirements of different interfaces. Rexx has a strong platform-independent standard. As well, many Rexx interfaces and tools are themselves cross-platform products.

Power and Flexibility

That Rexx is easy to learn and use does *not* mean that it has limited features or is some sort of "beginner's language." Rexx competes, feature for feature, with any of the other major scripting languages. If it didn't, it certainly would not be the primary scripting language for mainframes, nor would it have attained the widespread use it enjoys today on so many other platforms. Nor would there be many hundreds of thousands of Rexx users distributed around the world.*

Ease of use and power traditionally force language trade-offs. It is easy to get one without the other, but difficult to achieve both. Rexx is specifically designed to combine the two. It achieves this goal through these principles:

- ❏ *Simple syntax* — Some very powerful languages rely extensively on special symbols, nonobvious default behaviors, default variables, and other programming shortcuts. But there is no rule that power can only be achieved in this manner. Rexx eschews complex "syntax programming" and encourages simpler, more readable programming based on English-language keyword instructions and functions.

- ❏ *Small command set, with functions providing the power* — Rexx has a small core of only two dozen instructions. This simplicity is surrounded by the power of some 70 built-in functions. A well-defined, standard interface permits Rexx to call upon external function libraries. This allows you to extend the language yourself, and it means that many open-source extensions or libraries of routines are freely available. Rexx scripts also wield the full power of the operating system because they easily issue operating system commands.

- ❏ *Free-form language* — Rexx is not case-sensitive. It is a *free-form language* and is about as forgiving concerning placement of its source text as a programming language can be. This permits programmers to self-describe programs by techniques such as indentation, readable comments, case variations, and the like. Rexx relieves programmers from concern about syntax and placement, and lets them concentrate on the programming problem they face.

- ❏ *Consistent, reliable behavior* — Rexx behaves "as one would assume" at every opportunity. Its early user community provided feedback to one "master developer" who altered the language to conform to typical human behavior. As the inventor states in his book defining Rexx: "The language user is usually right." Rexx was designed to encourage good programming practice and then enhanced by user feedback to conform to human expectations.

- ❏ *Modularity and structured programming* — Rexx encourages and supports *modularity* and *structured programming*. Breaking up large programming problems into discrete pieces and restricting program flow to a small set of language constructs contributes greatly to ease of use and a low error rate when developing large feature-full applications. These principles yield simplicity without compromising power.

❏ *Fewer rules* — Put the preceding points together, and you'll conclude that Rexx has fewer rules than many programming languages. Developers concentrate on their programming problem, not on language trivia.

❏ *Standardization* — While there are at least nine free Rexx interpreters, eight adhere to the Rexx standards. This makes your scripts portable and your skills transferable. A standardized language is easier to use than one with numerous variants. Rexx has two strong, nearly identical standards. One is defined in the book *The Rexx Language*, or *TRL-2*, by Michael Cowlishaw (Prentice-Hall, 1990, second edition). The other is the 1996 standard from the American National Standards Institute, commonly referred to as *ANSI-1996*.

Universality

Rexx is a *universal language*. It runs on every platform, from handheld devices, to laptops and PCs, to servers of all kinds, all the way up to the largest mainframes. Here are the major platforms on which free Rexx interpreters run:

Operating System Family	Operating Systems
Windows	Windows 2003/2000, Windows XP, Windows ME/98SE/98/95, Windows CE, Windows 3.1, all others
Linux	Red Hat, SuSE, UnitedLinux, Debian, Mandrake, Fedora, all others
Unix	Sun Solaris, IBM AIX, HP HP/UX, IRIX, Sun OS, Digital Unix, all others
BSD	OpenBSD, FreeBSD, NetBSD, others
Mac OS	Mac OS X, Mac OS 9, Mac OS 8, others
DOS	MS-DOS, PC-DOS, all others including free versions; both 32- and 16- bit versions
OS/400	All versions, including i5/OS*
OS/2	OS/2 Warp, eCS (eComStation), osFree*
Mainframes	VM, OS, VSE*
VM	z/VM, VM/ESA, VM/XA, VM/SP, VM/CMS, CMS, others*
OS	z/OS, OS/390, MVS/ESA, MVS/XA, MVS/SP, MVS, TSO, others*
VSE	z/VSE, VSE/ESA, VSE/XA, DOS/VSE, DOS/VS, others*
Handhelds	Runs natively under Windows CE, Palm OS, and Symbian/EPOC32; also runs under DOS emulators (such as PocketDOS, XTM, and all others)

Operating System Family	Operating Systems
Windows CE	Windows CE .Net, Windows Pocket PC, Windows Mobile, Windows Handheld/PC or H/PC, and Windows for Pocket Personal Computer or Windows P/PC, Pocket PC Phone Edition, Microsoft Smartphone, others
Symbian OS	Symbian OS, EPOC32
Palm OS	All versions

*Rexx comes bundled with the operating system.

Free or open-source Rexx also runs on OpenVMS, OpenEdition, BeOS, Amiga OS, AROS, AtheOS/Syllable, QNX (QNX4/QNX6), SkyOS, and others. Object-oriented Rexx interpreters run under Windows, Linux, Solaris, AIX, and OS/2.

The benefits of a universal language are:

❑ Your skills apply to any platform.

❑ Scripts run on any platform.

Here's an example. A site that downsizes its mainframes to Unix machines could install free Rexx on the Unix machines. Rexx becomes the vehicle to transfer personnel skills, while providing a base for migrating scripts.

As another example, an organization migrating from Windows to object-oriented programming (OOP) under Linux could use free Rexx as its cross-platform entry point into OOP. Rexx runs under both Windows and Linux and standard, procedural Rexx is a subset of object-oriented Rexx.

A final example: a company runs a data center with mainframes and Unix servers, uses Windows on the desktop, and programs "pocket PC" handhelds for field agents. Rexx runs on all these platforms, making developers immediately productive across the whole range of company equipment. Rexx supports the platform range that allows a mainframer to program a handheld, or Windows developer to script under Unix.

A standardized scripting language that is freely available across a wide range of systems yields unparalleled skills applicability and code portability.

Typical Rexx Applications

Rexx is a general-purpose language. It is designed to handle diverse programming needs. Its power gives it the flexibility to address almost any kind of programming problem. Here are examples.

❑ *As a "glue" language* — Rexx has long been used as a high-productivity "glue" language for stitching together existing commands, programs, and components. Rexx offers a higher-level interface to underlying system commands and facilities. It leverages services, functions, objects, widgets, programs, and controls.

❑ *Automating repetitive tasks* — Rexx scripts automate repetitive tasks. You can quickly put together little scripts to tailor the environment or make your job easier. Rexx makes it easy to issue commands to the operating system (or other environments or programs) and react to their return codes and outputs.

❑ *Systems administration* — Rexx is a high-level, easy-to-read, and easy-to-maintain way to script system administration tasks. By its nature, systems administration can be complex. Automating it with an easily understood language raises system administration to a higher, more abstract, and more manageable level. If you ever have to enhance or maintain systems administration scripts, you'll be thankful if they're written in Rexx instead of some of the alternatives!

❑ *Extending the operating system* — You typically run Rexx scripts simply by typing their name at the operating system's command prompt. In writing scripts, you create new operating system "commands" that extend or customize the operating system or programming environment.

❑ *Application interfaces* — Rexx scripts can create flexible user interfaces to applications programmed in lower-level or compiled languages.

❑ *Portable applications* — Rexx's standardization and extensive cross-platform support make it a good choice for applications that must be ported across a range of systems. Its readability and ease of maintenance make it easy to implement whatever cross-platform enhancements may be desired. For example, while Rexx is the same across platforms, interfaces often vary. Standardizing the scripting language isolates changes to the interfaces.

❑ *Prototyping and exploratory programming* — Since Rexx supports quick development, it is ideal for developing prototypes, whether those prototypes are throw-aways or revisable. Rexx is also especially suitable for exploratory programming or other development projects apt to require major revision.

❑ *Personal programming* — An easy-to-use scripting language offers the simplicity and the speedy development essential to personal programming. PCs and handheld devices often require personal programming.

❑ *Text processing* — Rexx provides outstanding text processing. It's a good choice for text processing applications such as dynamically building commands for programmable interfaces, reformatting reports, text analysis, and the like.

❑ *Handheld devices* — Small devices require compact interpreters that are easy to program. Rexx is quite useful for PDAs, Palm Pilots, Pocket PCs and handheld PCs, and mobile and smart phones.

❑ *Migration vehicle* — Given its cross-platform strengths, Rexx can be used as a migration vehicle to transfer personnel skills and migrate legacy code to new platforms.

❑ *Macro programming* — Rexx provides a single macro language for the tools of the programming environment: editors, text processors, applications, and other languages. Rexx's strengths in string processing play to this requirement, as does the fact it can easily be invoked as a set of utility functions through its standardized application programming interface, or API.

❑ *Embeddable language* — ANSI Rexx is defined as a library which can be invoked from outside applications by its standard API. Rexx is thus a function library that can be employed as an embeddable utility from other languages or systems.

❏   *Mathematical applications* — Rexx performs computations internally in decimal arithmetic, rather than in the binary or floating-point arithmetic of most programming languages. The result is that Rexx always computes the same result regardless of the underlying platform. And, it gives precision to 999999 decimal places! But Rexx is not suitable for all mathematical applications. Advanced math functions are external add-ins rather than built-in functions for most Rexx interpreters, and Rexx performs calculations slowly compared to other languages.

What Rexx Doesn't Do

There are a few situations where Rexx may not be the best choice.

Rexx is not a *systems programming language*. If you need to code on the machine level, for example, to write a device driver or other operating system component, Rexx is probably not a good choice. While there are versions of Rexx that permit direct memory access and other low-level tasks, languages like C/C++ or assembler are more suitable. Standard Rexx does not manipulate direct or relative addresses, change specific memory locations, or call PC interrupt vectors or BIOS service routines.

Rexx is a great tool to develop clear, readable code. But it cannot force you to do so; it cannot save you from yourself. Chapter 12 discusses "Rexx with style" and presents simple recommendations for writing clear, reliable code.

Scripting languages consume more processor cycles and memory than traditional compiled languages. This affects a few projects. An example is a heavily used transaction in a high-performance online transaction processing (OLTP) system. The constant execution of the same transaction might make it worth the labor cost to develop it in a lower-level compiled language to optimize machine efficiency. Another example is a heavily computational program in scientific research. Continual numeric calculation might make it worthwhile to optimize processor cycles through a computationally oriented compiler.

Our profession has reached the consensus that for most applications, scripting languages are plenty fast enough. Yet they are also much more productive. This is why scripting is one of the major software trends of the decade.

If you're interested in reading further about the trend towards scripting, these authoritative sources summarize it. The last one listed is a formal study that compares productivity and resource usage for Rexx, C, C++, Java, Perl, Python, and Tcl:

John Ousterhout, "Scripting: Higher Level Programming for the 21st Century," *IEEE Computer*, March 1998.

David Barron, *The World of Scripting Languages*, NY: Wiley, 2000.

Lutz Prechelt, "An Empirical Comparison of Seven Programming Languages," *IEEE Computer* (33:10), 2000.

Figure 1-2 summarizes the kinds of programming problems to which Rexx is best suited as well as those for which it may not be the best choice.

When to Use Rexx

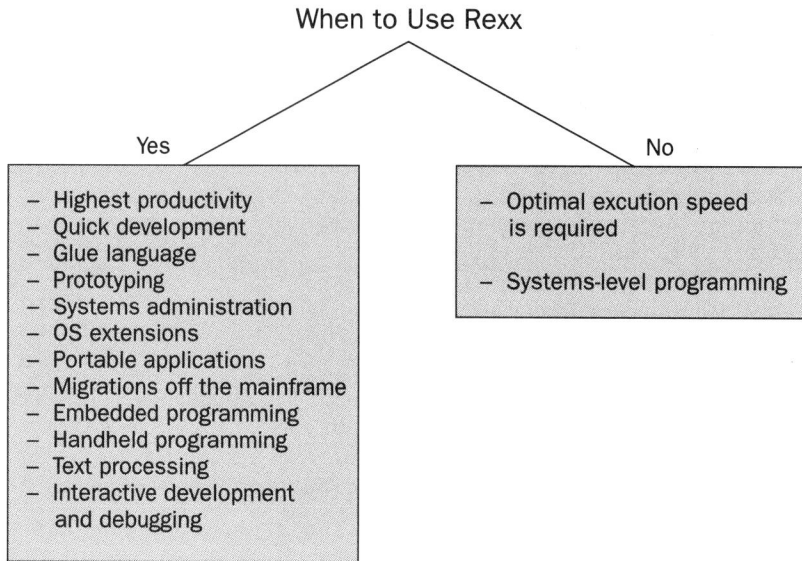

Figure 1-2

Which Rexx?

There are at least six free implementations of what we refer to as standard or *classic* Rexx. This is Rexx as defined by the TRL-2 standard mentioned earlier. There are also two object-oriented supersets of classic procedural Rexx. And, there is NetRexx, the free Rexx-like language that runs in a Java Virtual Machine and presents an alternative to Java for developing applets and applications. Which Rexx should you use?

The first half of this book teaches classic Rexx. *It applies to any standard Rexx interpreter on any platform.* Once you know standard Rexx you can easily pick up the extensions unique to any Rexx interpreter. You can also easily learn interface programming, how to use Rexx tools and packages, object-oriented Rexx, NetRexx, or any Rexx variant. After all, the whole point of Rexx is ease of learning!

This table summarizes the free Rexx interpreters.

Rexx Interpreter	Platforms	Cost and Licensing	Distribution
Regina	All platforms	Free. Open source. GNU Library General Public License or Lesser General Public License (LGPL)	Binaries or Source
Rexx/imc	Unix, Linux, BSD	Free. Copyrighted freeware. No warranty, distributed as is.	Binaries or Source

Rexx Interpreter	Platforms	Cost and Licensing	Distribution
Brexx	Windows, Win CE, DOS (32- and 16- bit), Linux, Unix, Mac OS, Amiga, others	Freeware. Free for personal and nonprofit use, fee for commercial use.	Binaries or Source
Reginald	Windows	Freeware. No warranty, distributed as is.	Windows Installer Binaries
r4	Windows	Freeware. Limited warranty.	Binaries
Rexx for Palm OS	Palm OS	Shareware. Free for personal use, fee for commercial use.	Binaries
Open Object Rexx (formally known as Object REXX or IBM Object REXX)	Linux, Windows, Solaris, AIX	Free. Distributed under the Common Public License. Previously developed and supported by IBM. Today enhanced and maintained by the Rexx Language Association. See Chapter 27 for full information.	Binaries or Source
roo!	Windows	Freeware. Limited warranty.	Binaries
NetRexx	Any platform running a Java Virtual Machine (JVM)	Free. IBM License Agreement for IBM Employee-Written Software. No warranty, distributed as is.	Binaries

All these interpreters meet the TRL-2 Rexx language standard. The single exception is NetRexx, which is best termed a "Rexx-like" language. Any standard Rexx you have installed can be used for working with the sample code in the first half of this book. This includes all the previously listed interpreters (except NetRexx), as well as standard Rexx interpreters bundled with mainframe or other operating systems.

To get you up and programming quickly, we defer closer consideration of the unique strengths of the various Rexx interpreters and the differences between them. If you need to know more right now, skip ahead to Chapter 19. That chapter discusses the evolution of Rexx and the roles it plays as a prominent scripting language. It describes all the free Rexx interpreters listed above and presents the strengths of each. Chapters 20 through 30 then show how and where to download and install each Rexx product. They describe the unique features of each interpreter and demonstrate many of them in sample scripts.

If you're new to Rexx, we recommend starting with Regina Rexx. Regina Rexx is a great place to start for several reasons:

❑ *Popularity* — Regina is the most widely used free Rexx. Its large user community makes it easy to get help on public forums. More interfaces and tools are tested with Regina than any other Rexx implementation.

- ❏ *Runs anywhere* — Rexx is a platform-independent language, and Regina proves the point. Regina runs on almost any operating system including those in these families: Windows, Linux, Unix, BSD, 32-bit DOS, Mac OS, and Symbian/EPOC32. It also runs on many important "second-tier" systems, including BeOS, OpenVMS, OpenEdition, Amiga OS, AROS, AtheOS/Syllable, QNX (QNX4/QNX6), OS/2, eCS, osFree, and other systems.

- ❏ *Meets all standards* — Regina meets all Rexx standards including the TRL-2 and ANSI-1996 standards.

- ❏ *Documentation* — Regina comes with complete documentation that precisely and fully explains the product.

- ❏ *Open source* — Regina is open source and distributed under the GNU Library General Public License. Some Rexx interpreters are free but not open source, as shown in the preceding table.

The code examples in this book all conform to standard Rexx and were tested using Regina Rexx under Windows and /or Linux. Run these scripts under any standard Rexx in any environment. A few scripts require a specific operating system. For example, those in Chapter 14 illustrate how to issue operating system commands and therefore are system-specific. Other scripts later in the book use specific open-source interfaces, tools, or interpreters. Where we present examples that run only in certain environments, we'll point it out.

To get you ready for the rest of the book, the remainder of this chapter shows you how to download and install Regina under Windows, Linux, and Unix. You need only install Regina if you don't already have access to a Rexx interpreter.

Downloading Regina Rexx

Regina Rexx can be freely downloaded from the SourceForge Web site at `http://sourceforge.net`. SourceForge is the hugely popular download site for free and open-source products. Find the Regina interpreter at `http://regina-rexx.sourceforge.net`. Of course, Web addresses sometimes change. In this case, just enter the keywords `Regina Rexx` into any Internet search engine such as Google or Yahoo! and the current download Web site will pop up.

Download sites list various files or downloads for different platforms. Regina is available for many operating systems in either executable or source forms. Download file types include the self-extracting executable `.exe` for 32-bit Windows platforms, `.zip` files, `.rpm` files for the Red Hat Linux package manager, `.gz` or `.tar.gz` files for Linux, Unix, or BSD, and other file formats for other operating systems. Pick the appropriate file type for your operating system and download that file. In the detailed instructions that follow, we downloaded the `.exe` file for Windows, and the `.tar.gz` and `.rpm` files for Linux and Unix.

You'll also see the product documentation at the Web site. This documentation includes the *release notes*, short memos that summarize the changes to Regina in each release. You would normally download the latest official release of Regina. But if you're interested in the exact differences among different releases, the release notes describe them.

The Web site also offers the complete Regina documentation manual. This is a separate file available in either `.zip` or `.pdf` formats. We highly recommend downloading the product documentation.

Installing Regina varies slightly by the file type you download and the target operating system into which you're installing. In the sections that follow we describe typical installs under Windows, Linux, and Unix. These instructions enable any desktop user to install Regina and test the examples presented in subsequent chapters.

Installing Regina under Windows

Assuming you download an .exe file for Windows, all you have to do to install Regina is to double-click on that file. The file is self-extracting. It automatically starts the Install Wizard to guide you in installing Regina. Installation is then the same as for any other Windows product.

After you double-click on the .exe file, the Install Wizard prompts you to agree to the licensing terms. After selecting a folder into which to install the product, you are asked which file extensions to associate with Regina (.rexx, .rex, .rx, and .cmd). Minimally, be sure to associate Regina with its default extension of .rexx. If the install process asks whether to install the "Regina Stack Service," reply no. This is an advanced Regina feature that supports capabilities that go beyond standard Rexx.

Windows installation may provide slightly different prompts or questions across releases, but in all cases the install process is quite simple and looks like what you're familiar from all other Windows products.

Test to make sure that the installation succeeded. Assuming that you've associated the file extensions of the Rexx source code files with the Regina interpreter, you can just double-click on a Rexx script to run it. Let's start by running a non-GUI Rexx script from the command-line prompt.

To get to the Windows command prompt, select Start | Run and then enter either command or cmd into the Run box (depending on your version of Windows) to get a command prompt window. Once at the command prompt, change the current directory to the Regina directory that contains the demo programs. For example, if you installed Regina on the C: drive under the directory Regina, its demo programs are probably under the directory Regina\demo. So, enter these commands into the command window:

```
c:
cd  \Regina\demo
```

Once in the directory where the source code of the Rexx program you want to run resides, just enter the script's name to execute it. For example, let's benchmark your system by running the demo program used in the first table in this chapter, called rexxcps.rexx. You can compare your system's performance to those listed in the first table. To run the program, enter:

```
rexxcps.rexx
```

Results from program execution appear on the command prompt screen. It is very unlikely you'll encounter an error. If you do, the most common error message looks similar to this:

```
'rexxcps.rexx' is not recognized as an internal or external command, operable
program or batch file
```

This means that either you have not entered the correctly spelled name of the Rexx program at the command prompt, or the demo program is not in the current or "working" directory. Check to ensure that the demo program resides in the current directory and that you entered its name accurately. Another possibility is that you did not associate files with the extension of .rexx with Regina when installing the product. In this case, you need to establish the proper Windows *file association* between Regina and files of type .rexx. Go to Windows file association panel to ensure this association exists. On most versions of Windows, you get to the file association panel through the file Explorer, then access the options Tools | Folder Options | File Types. Or just enter the keywords `associating files` to Windows help to find the proper panel.

When you enter only the name of the Rexx script to run to the command prompt, as in the preceding example, you run the script *implicitly*. Double-clicking on the script file also executes it implicitly. An alternative way to run Regina Rexx scripts is to *explicitly* invoke the interpreter against the script you wish to run. From the directory in which the script resides, enter this command to the command line:

```
regina   rexxcps.rexx
```

or

```
regina   rexxcps
```

You should see the program's output on the command prompt screen. If you did not associate files of type .rexx with Regina, you will have to explicitly invoke Regina on the Rexx script in order to run it.

Try creating your own first Rexx script. Enter this two-line script via the Notepad editor and save it under filename testme.rexx:

```
/*  a simple Rexx test program  */
say 'hello'
```

From the same directory that the newly entered program resides in enter:

```
testme.rexx
```

or

```
regina   testme
```

You should see the program output `hello` on the screen. The Rexx `say` instruction writes it to the display.

Windows installation is simple and automated. Problems are extremely rare. If you do experience a problem, check that files of extension .rexx are associated with the Regina executable, and that the directory in which the Regina executable resides is in the Windows PATH environmental variable. If all else fails, just reinstall the product. Regina includes an "uninstaller" you should run first, before trying to reinstall it. The uninstall program is available from the Windows' menu at Start | Programs | Regina Rexx, or in Regina's main installation directory under the filename uninstall.exe.

Installing Regina under Linux and Unix

There are several ways to install Regina Rexx on Linux, Unix, or BSD systems. This section describes a simple, generic approach that will work for almost any Unix-derived operating system. Where slight differences exist, the Regina *Install Notes* that download with the product point them out. If you have the automated-install tool called the Red Hat Package Manager available, you may wish to follow the alternative install procedures in the section that follows entitled "Installing Regina with Red Hat Package Manager." But we ask that you read this section first so that you understand how to test your install and run Rexx scripts.

To install Regina under any Linux, Unix, or BSD family operating system, use the `root` user ID and download the source `.tar.gz` file into an empty directory. In this example, we downloaded the file named `Regina-REXX.3.3.tar.gz` into an empty directory we created named: `/regina`. Switch into that directory so that it is your working directory:

```
cd  /regina
```

Uncompress the file by entering the `gzip` command, naming the file you just downloaded as its operand:

```
gzip  -d   Regina-REXX-3.3.tar.gz
```

This produces an uncompressed archive or `.tar` file. In this example, this output file would be named:

```
Regina-REXX.3.3.tar
```

Extract all the files from the archive or `.tar` file into a subdirectory of the current directory by issuing the `tar` command:

```
tar  xvf  Regina-REXX.3.3.tar     # Most Linuxes and Unixes
```

or

```
tar  -xvf  Regina-REXX.3.3.tar    # some OS's require a dash before the options
```

In this example, the files were automatically extracted from the archive file and placed into a directory named `/regina/Regina-3.3`.

Change your current directory to the directory to which the files were extracted and read the Install Notes. They are usually in a file named `INSTALL*` or `README.*`. The filename may be either upper- or lowercase, but in any case it will be similar to one of these.

For example, these two commands would change to the proper directory and allow you to view the Install Notes assuming they are in a file named `INSTALL`:

```
cd  Regina-3.3
more INSTALL
```

17

Now, do what the Install Notes tell you to do, and you will have successfully installed Regina. If you logged in as the `root` user ID to Linux or most Unixes, all you have to do to complete the install is enter these two commands to the operating system:

```
./configure
make install
```

These commands configure and install Regina. Since they compile source code, they require a C compiler to run. Almost all Linux, Unix, and BSD machines will have a C compiler present. In the rare event that your system does not have one installed, download a free compiler from any of several sites including www.gnu.org.

Now, test that the installation succeeded by running one of the Regina-provided demo scripts in the `demo` subdirectory. Let's benchmark your system by running the benchmark program used in the first table of this chapter. You can compare your system's performance to the examples listed in the table. The program to run is called `rexxcps.rexx`. To run it, enter:

```
./regina   demo/rexxcps.rexx
```

or

```
./regina   demo/rexxcps
```

The characters `./`   tell Linux to look for the interpreter program `regina` in the current directory. You can eliminate the need for these two characters by adding that directory to your PATH environmental variable. Then, you can enter:

```
regina   demo/rexxcps
```

In the unlikely event you get a message similar to the following, you need to set an environmental variable so that the Regina interpreter can locate its library file. See the Regina's Install Notes for a simple solution to this problem:

```
regina: error while loading shared libraries: libregina.so:
cannot open shared object file: No such file or directory
```

Now, let's create our own first sample script. Access a text editor such as `vi` or `emacs`, and enter these two lines into a file:

```
/*  a simple Rexx test program  */
say 'hello'
```

Save the file under the name `testme.rexx`. After exiting the editor, make the Rexx script file executable. To do this, change its permissions to "executable" with the operating system's `chmod` command:

```
chmod  +x  testme.rexx
```

Now you can run the script by this command and view its output. The script writes the single word, `hello`, to your display screen through Rexx's `say`   instruction:

```
regina  testme.rexx
```

On Linux, Unix, and BSD platforms, it is common to code the first line of the Rexx script to tell the operating system which interpreter should execute that script. This allows you to run the script *implicitly*, by specifying only the name of the script to run to the operating system's command line:

```
testme.rexx
```

To set this up, the first line of the script must start with the characters #!, encoded starting in the first position of the first line. These two characters are then immediately followed by the fully qualified path name of the Rexx interpreter executable. For example, for our version of Regina, the name of the executable was `regina` and it was installed it into the default directory named /usr/bin. The sample script would then be entered like this:

```
#!/usr/bin/regina

/*  a simple Rexx test program  */
say 'hello'
```

That's all there is to installing Regina under Linux, Unix, or BSD. Our example assumes a simple approach. We used the `root` user ID and left all Regina files in the subdirectory into which the archive extract command (`tar xvf`) placed them. For a personal computer, this is all you need to do. On shared servers, procedures can sometimes be more complicated. For example, you might want to install the product under some user ID other than `root`, or you might be a systems administrator who must follow your organization's product install standards. Read the Install Notes that download with Regina to handle these more complicated situations. Chapter 19 covers several more advanced aspects of Rexx installs in its section entitled "Multiple Rexx Interpreters on One Computer." Chapters 20 through 30 address specific Rexx interpreters and tell how to download and install them.

Installing Regina with Red Hat Package Manager

There's also a simpler way to install Regina on many Linux and some Unix systems. As described here, this procedure works only for Intel- or clone-based computers and does not require a C compiler. The *Red Hat Package Manager*, or *RPM*, is a tool that automates product installation. Check to see if you have RPM available to you by entering this command to your operating system's command prompt. It lists all the RPM *packages* or products installed on your computer:

```
rpm  -qa
```

To install Regina using the RPM, log in as the `root` user ID and download the Regina file with the filename extension .i386.rpm. Then enter the `rpm` command to the operating system's prompt to install Regina:

```
rpm  -ivv   Regina-REXX-3.3-1.i386.rpm        # install with feedback
```

The switches -ivv tell the `rpm` command to install the product and issue verbose comments on what it does. These describe any errors (unlikely) as well as informational messages and the directories used for the product installation. The name of the download file will vary slightly by release, of course. For more detailed information on RPM installs, see Chapter 21.

Summary

This chapter lists the advantages of scripting in Rexx and suggests where Rexx is most useful. Given its power, flexibility, portability, and ease of use, Rexx is suitable for addressing a wide range of programming problems. The only situations where Rexx does not apply are those oriented toward "systems programming" and programs that demand totally optimized machine utilization.

Rexx distinguishes itself among scripting languages by combining ease of use with power. Rexx uses specific interpreter design techniques to achieve this combination. Rexx has simple syntax, minimal "special variables," no "default variables," a case-insensitive free-format combined with a small, easily learned instruction set. Its many built-in functions, extensibility, and the ability to issue commands to the operating system and other external interfaces give Rexx power while retaining ease of use.

Ease of use is important even to highly experienced computer professionals because it reduces error rates and determines the life span of their code. Experienced developers leverage a quickly coded language like Rexx to achieve outstanding productivity.

The final part of this chapter showed how to download and install Regina Rexx under Windows, Linux, and Unix. This popular Rexx interpreter is a free, open-source product you can use to learn Rexx in the tutorial of the following chapters. Any other standard Rexx interpreter could be used as well. The next several chapters get you quickly up and running Rexx scripts through an example-based tutorial.

*IBM Corporation estimates that there are up to one million Rexx users worldwide, as posted on their Web site on February 2004.

Test Your Understanding

1. In what way is Rexx a *higher-level* language than compiled languages like C or C++ ? What's a *glue language*? Why is there an industry-wide trend towards scripting languages?

2. Are developers required to code Rexx instructions starting in any particular column? In upper- or lowercase?

3. If you're an expert programmer, why is ease of use still important?

4. What are names of the two object-oriented Rexx interpreters? Will standard or *classic* Rexx scripts run under these OO interpreters without alteration?

5. Does Rexx run on Palm Pilots? How about cell phones? Mainframes?

6. What are the two key Rexx standards? Are these two standards almost the same or significantly different?

7. Traditionally there is a trade-off between ease of use and power. What specific techniques does Rexx employ to gain both attributes and circumvent the trade-off?

2

Language Basics

Overview

This chapter describes the basic elements of Rexx. It discusses the simple components that make up the language. These include script structure, elements of the language, operators, variables, and the like. As a starting point, we explore a simple sample script. We'll walk through this script and explain what each statement means. Then we'll describe the language components individually, each in its own section. We'll discuss Rexx variables, character strings, numbers, operators, and comparisons.

By the end of this chapter, you'll know about the basic components of the Rexx language. You'll be fully capable of writing simple scripts and will be ready to learn about the language features explored more fully in subsequent chapters. The chapters that follow present other aspects of the language, based on sample programs that show its additional features. For example, topics covered in subsequent chapters include directing the logical flow of a script, arrays and tables, input and output, string manipulation, subroutines and functions, and the like. But now, let's dive into our first sample script.

A First Program

Had enough of your job? Maybe it's time to join the lucky developers who create computer games for a living! The complete Rexx program that follows is called the Number Game. It generates a random number between 1 and 10 and asks the user to guess it (well, okay, the playability is a *bit* weak. . . .) The program reads the number the user guesses and states whether the guess is correct.

```
/* The NUMBER GAME - User tries to guess a number between 1 and 10  */

/* Generate a random number between 1 and 10                        */

the_number = random(1,10)

say "I'm thinking of number between 1 and 10. What is it?"
```

```
pull the_guess

if the_number = the_guess then
   say 'You guessed it!'
else
   say 'Sorry, my number was: ' the_number

say 'Bye!'
```

Here are two sample runs of the program:

```
C:\Regina\pgms>number_game.rexx
I'm thinking of number between 1 and 10. What is it?
4
Sorry, my number was: 6
Bye!

C:\Regina\pgms>number_game.rexx
I'm thinking of number between 1 and 10. What is it?
8
You guessed it!
Bye!
```

This program illustrates several Rexx features. It shows that you document scripts by writing whatever description you like between the symbols /* and */. Rexx ignores whatever appears between these *comment delimiters*. Comments can be isolated on their own lines, as in the sample program, or they can appear as *trailing comments* after the statement on a line:

```
the_number = random(1,10)   /* Generate a random number between 1 and 10 */
```

Comments can even stretch across multiple lines in *box style*, as long as they start with /* and end with */:

```
/*********************************************************************
 *   The NUMBER GAME - User tries to guess a number between 1 and 10    *
 *   Generate a random number between 1 and 10                          *
 *********************************************************************/
```

Rexx is *case-insensitive*. Code can be entered in lowercase, uppercase, or mixed case; Rexx doesn't care. The if statement could have been written like this if we felt it were clearer:

```
IF the_number = the_guess THEN
   SAY 'You guessed it!'
ELSE
   SAY 'Sorry, my number was: ' the_number
```

The variable named the_number could have been coded as THE_NUMBER or The_Number. Since Rexx ignores case it considers all these as references to the same variable. The one place where case *does* matter is within *literals* or hardcoded character strings:

```
         say 'Bye!'      outputs:     Bye!
```

while

```
        say 'BYE!'      displays:     BYE!
```

Character strings are any set of characters occurring between a matched set of either single quotation marks (`'`) or double quotation marks (`"`).

What if you want to encode a quote within a literal? In other words, what do you do when you need to encode a single or double quote as part of the character string itself? To put a single quotation mark within the literal, enclose the literal with double quotation marks:

```
    say "I'm thinking of number between 1 and 10. What is it?"
```

To encode double quotation marks within the string, enclose the literal with single quotation marks:

```
    say 'I am "thinking" of number between 1 and 10. What is it?'
```

Rexx is a *free-format language*. The spacing is up to you. Insert (or delete) blank lines for readability, and leave as much or as little space between instructions and their operands as you like. Rexx leaves the coding style up to you as much as a programming language possibly can.

For example, here's yet another way to encode the `if` statement:

```
    IF the_number = the_guess THEN  SAY 'You guessed it!'
                              ELSE  SAY 'Sorry, my number was: ' the_number
```

About the only situation in which spacing is *not* the programmer's option is when encoding a Rexx *function*. A function is a built-in routine Rexx provides as part of the language; you also may write your own functions. This program invokes the built-in function `random` to generate a random number between 1 and 10 (inclusive). The parenthesis containing the function argument(s) must immediately follow the function name without any intervening space. If the function has no arguments, code it like this:

```
    the_number = random()
```

Rexx requires that the parentheses occur *immediately after* the function name to recognize the function properly.

The sample script shows that one does not need to *declare* or predefine variables in Rexx. This differs from languages like C++, Java, COBOL, or Pascal. Rexx variables are established at the time of their first use. The variable `the_number` is defined during the assignment statement in the example. Space for the variable `the_guess` is allocated when the program executes the `pull` instruction to read the user's input:

```
    pull  the_guess
```

In this example, the `pull` instruction reads the characters that the user types on the keyboard, until he or she presses the <ENTER> key, into one or more variables and automatically translates them to uppercase. Here the item the user enters is assigned to the newly created variable `the_guess`.

All variables in Rexx are variable-length character strings. Rexx automatically handles string length adjustments. It also manages numeric or data type conversions. For example, even though the variables the_number and the_guess are character strings, if we assume that both contain strings that represent numbers, one could perform arithmetic or other numeric operations on them:

```
their_sum  =  the_number  +  the_guess
```

Rexx automatically handles all the issues surrounding variable declarations, data types, data conversions, and variable length character strings that programmers must manually manage in traditional compiled languages. These features are among those that make it such a productive, high-level language.

Language Elements

Rexx consists of only two dozen *instructions*, augmented by the power of some 70 *built-in functions*. Figure 2-1 below pictorially represents the key components of Rexx. It shows that the instructions and functions together compose the core of the language, which is then surrounded and augmented by other features. A lot of what the first section of this book is about is introducing the various Rexx instructions and functions.

Elements of Rexx

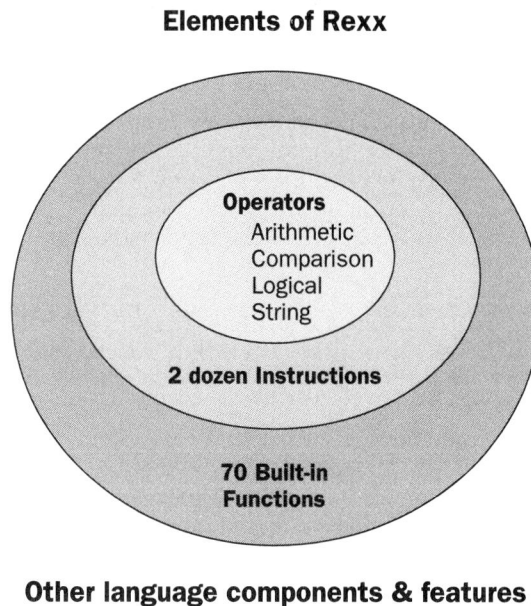

Operators
Arithmetic
Comparison
Logical
String

2 dozen Instructions

70 Built-in Functions

Other language components & features

Figure 2-1

Of course, this book also provides a language reference section in the appendices, covering these and other aspects of the language. For example, Appendix B is a reference to all standard Rexx instructions, while Appendix C provides the reference to standard functions.

The first sample program illustrated the use of the instructions `say`, `pull`, and `if`. Rexx instructions are typically followed by one or more *operands*, or elements upon which they operate. For example, `say` is followed by one or more elements it writes to the display screen. The `pull` instruction is followed by a list of the data elements it reads.

The sample script illustrated one function, `random`. Functions are always immediately followed by parentheses, usually containing function *arguments*, or inputs to the function. If there are no arguments, the function must be immediately followed by empty parentheses `()`. Rexx functions always return a single result, which is then substituted into the expression directly in place of the function call. For example, the random number returned by the `random` function is actually substituted into the statement that follows, on the right-hand side of the equals sign, then assigned to the variable `the_number`:

```
the_number = random(1,10)
```

Variables are named storage locations that can contain values. They do not need to be declared or defined in advance, but are rather created when they are first referenced. You can declare or define all variables used in a program at the beginning of the script, but Rexx does not require this. Some programmers like to declare all variables at the top of their programs, for clarity, but Rexx leaves the decision whether or not to do this up to you.

All variables in Rexx are internally stored as variable-length strings. The interpreter manages their lengths and data types. Rexx variables are "typeless" in that their contents define their usage. If strings contain digits, you can apply numeric operations to them. If they do not contain strings representing numeric values, numeric operations don't make sense and will fail if attempted. Rexx is simpler than other programming languages in that developers do not have to concern themselves with data types.

Variable names are sometimes referred to as *symbols*. They may be composed of letters, digits, and characters such as . ! ? _ . A variable name you create must not begin with a digit or period. A *simple variable name* does not include a period. A variable name that includes a period is called a *compound variable* and represents an *array* or *table*. Arrays will be covered in Chapter 4. They consist of groups of similar data elements, typically processed as a group.

If all Rexx variables are *typeless*, how does one create a numeric value? Just place a string representing a valid number into a Rexx variable. Here are *assignment statements* that achieve this:

```
whole_number_example            =   15
decimal_example                 =   14.2
negative_number                 =  -21.2
exponential_notation_example    =   14E+12
```

A *number* in Rexx is simply a string of one or more digits with one optional decimal point anywhere in the string. Numbers may optionally be preceded by their sign, indicating a postive or a negative number. Numbers may be represented very flexibly by almost any common notation. Exponential numbers may be represented in either engineering or scientific notation (the default is scientific). The following table shows examples of numbers in Rexx.

Number Type	Also Known As	Examples
Whole	Integer	'3' '+6' '9835297590239032'
Decimal	Fixed point	'0.3' '17.36425'
Exponential	Real --or--	'1.235E+11' (*scientific*, one digit left of decimal point)
	Floating point	'171.123E+11' (*engineering*, 1 to 3 digits left of decimal)

Variables are assigned values through either assignment statements or input instructions. The assignment statement uses the equals sign (=) to assign a value to a variable, as shown earlier. The input instructions are the `pull` or `parse` instructions, which read input values, and the `arg` and `parse arg` instructions, which read command line parameters or input arguments to a script.

If a variable has not yet been assigned a value, it is referred to as *uninitialized*. The value of an uninitialized variable is the name of the variable itself in uppercase letters. This `if` statement uses this fact to determine if the variable `no_value_yet` is uninitialized:

```
if  no_value_yet = 'NO_VALUE_YET'  then
     say 'The variable is not yet initialized.'
```

Character strings or *literals* are any set of characters enclosed in single or double quotation marks (' or ").

If you need to include either the single or double quote within the literal, simply enclose that literal with the other *string delimiter*. Or you can encode two single or double quotation marks back to back, and Rexx understands that this means that one quote is to be contained within the literal (it knows the doubled quote does not terminate the literal). Here are a few examples:

```
literal= 'Literals contain whatever characters you like: !@#$%^&*()-=+~.<>?/_'
need_a_quote_mark_in_the_string = "Here's my statement."
same_as_the_previous_example    = 'Here''s my statement.'
this_is_the_null_string = ''  /*two quotes back to back are a "null string" */
```

In addition to supporting any typical numeric or string representation, Rexx also supports *hexadecimal* or base 16 numbers. *Hex strings* contain the upper- or lowercase letters A through F and the digits 0 through 9, and are followed by an upper- or lowercase X:

```
twenty_six_in_hexidecimal = '1a'x  /*  1A is the number 26 in base sixteen    */
hex_string = "3E 11 4A"X           /*  Assigns a hex string value to hex_string */
```

Rexx also supports *binary*, or base two strings. Binary strings consist only of 0s and 1s. They are denoted by their following upper- or lowercase B:

```
example_binary_string = '10001011'b
another_binary_string = '1011'B
```

Rexx has a full complement of functions to convert between regular character strings and hex and binary strings. Do not be concerned if you are not familiar with the uses of these kinds of strings in programming languages. We mention them only for programmers who require them. Future chapters will explain their use more fully and provide illustrative examples.

Operators

Every programming language has *operators*, symbols that indicate arithmetic operations or dictate that comparisons must be performed. Operators are used in calculations and in assigning values to variables, for example. Rexx supports a full set of operators for the following.

❑ Arithmetic

❑ Comparison

❑ Logical operators

❑ Character string concatenation

The arithmetic operators are listed in the following table:

Arithmetic Operator	Use
+	Addition
-	Subtraction
*	Multiplication
/	Division
%	Integer division — returns the integer part of the result from division
//	Remainder division — returns the remainder from division
**	Raise to a whole number power
+ (as a prefix)	Indicates a positive number
- (as a prefix)	Indicates a negative number

All arithmetic operators work as one would assume from basic high-school algebra, or from programming in most other common programming languages. Here are a few examples using the less obvious operators:

```
say (5 % 2)    /* Returns the integer part of division result. Displays: 2   */
say (5 // 2)   /* Returns the remainder from division.      Displays: 1   */
say (5 ** 2)   /* Raises the number to the whole power.     Displays: 25  */
```

Remember that because all Rexx variables are strings, arithmetic operators should only be applied to variables that evaluate to valid numbers. Apply them only to strings containing digits, with their optional decimal points and leading signs, or to numbers in exponential forms.

Numeric operations are a major topic in Rexx (as in any programming language). The underlying principle is this — *the Rexx standard ensures that the same calculation will yield the same results even when run under different Rexx implementations or on different computers.* Rexx provides an exceptional level of machine- and implementation-independence compared with many other programming languages.

If you are familiar with other programming languages, you might wonder how Rexx achieves this bene-fit. Internally, Rexx employs decimal arithmetic. It does suffer from the approximations caused by languages that rely on floating point calculations or binary arithmetic.

The only arithmetic errors Rexx gives are *overflow* (or *underflow*). These result from insufficient storage to hold exceptionally large results.

To control the number of significant digits in arithmetic results, use the `numeric` instruction. Sometimes the number of significant digits is referred to as the *precision* of the result. Numeric precision defaults to nine digits. This sample statement illustrates the default precision because it displays nine digits to the right of the decimal place in its result:

```
say  2 / 3              /* displays  0.666666667  by default     */
```

This example shows how to change the precision in a calculation. Set the numeric precision to 12 digits by the `numeric` instruction, and you get this result:

```
numeric digits  12      /*  set numeric precision to 12 digits   */
say  2 / 3              /*  displays:  0.666666666667            */
```

Rexx preserves trailing zeroes coming out of arithmetic operations:

```
say  8.80 - 8           /*  displays: 0.80  */
```

If a result is zero, Rexx always displays a single-digit `0`:

```
say  8.80 - 8.80        /*  displays: 0     */
```

Chapter 7 explores computation further. It tells you everything you need to know about how to express numbers in Rexx, conversion between numeric and other formats, and how to obtain and display numeric results. We'll defer further discussion on numbers and calculations to Chapter 7.

Comparison operators provide for numeric and string comparisons. These are the operators you use to determine the equality or inequality of data elements. Use them to determine if one data item is greater than another or if two variables contain equal values.

Since every Rexx variable contains a character string, you might wonder how Rexx decides to perform a character or numeric comparison. The key rule is: *if both terms involved in a comparison are numeric, then the comparison is numeric.* For a numeric comparison, any leading zeroes are ignored and the numeric values are compared. This is just as one would expect.

If either term in a comparison is other than numeric, then a *string comparison* occurs. The rule for string comparison is that leading and trailing blanks are ignored, and if one string is shorter than the other, it is padded with trailing blanks. Then a character-by-character comparison occurs. String comparison is case-sensitive. The character string ABC is not equal to the string Abc. Again, this is what one would normally assume.

Rexx features a typical set of comparison operators, as shown in the following table:

Comparison Operator	Meaning
=	Equal
\= ¬=	Not equal
>	Greater than
<	Less than
>= \< ¬<	Greater than or equal to, not less than
<= \> ¬>	Less than or equal to, not greater than
>< <>	Greater than or less than (same as not equal)

The "not" symbol for operators is typically written as a backslash, as in "not equal:" \=   But sometimes you'll see it written as ¬ as in "not equal:" ¬=   Both codings are equivalent in Rexx. The first representation is very common, while the second is almost exclusively associated with mainframe scripting. *Since most keyboards outside of mainframe environments do not include the symbol ¬ we recommend always using the backslash.* This is universal and your code will run on any platform. The backslash is the ANSI-standard Rexx symbol. You can also code "not equal to" as: <>   or >< .

In Rexx comparisons, if a comparison evaluates to TRUE, it returns 1. A FALSE comparison evaluates to 0. Here are some sample numeric and character string comparisons and their results:

```
'37'  = '37'    /*  TRUE  - a numeric comparison */
'0037'= '37'    /*  TRUE  - numeric comparisons disregard leading zeroes */
'37'  = '37 '   /*  TRUE  - blanks disregarded    */
'ABC' = 'Abc'   /*  FALSE - string comparisons are case-sensitive      */
'ABC' = '  ABC  ' /* TRUE- preceding & trailing blanks are irrelevant  */
' '   = '     '   /* TRUE- null string is blank-padded for comparison  */
```

Rexx also provides for *strict comparisons* of character strings. *In strict comparisons, two strings must be identical to be considered equal* — leading and trailing blanks count and no padding occurs to the shorter string. Strict comparisons only make sense in string comparisons, not numeric comparisons. Strict comparison operators are easily identified because they contain doubled operators, as shown in the following chart:

Strict Comparison Operator	Meaning
==	Strictly equal
\== ¬==	Strictly not equal
>>	Strictly greater than
<<	Strictly less than
>>= \<< ¬<<	Strictly greater than or equal to, strictly not less than
<<= \>> ¬>>	Strictly less than or equal to, strictly not greater than

Here are sample strict string comparisons:

```
'37' == '37 '   /* FALSE - strict comparisons include blanks       */
'ABC' >> 'AB'   /* TRUE - also TRUE as a nonstrict comparison       */
'ABC' == '  ABC '  /* FALSE - blanks count in strict comparison     */
' '  == '  '    /* FALSE - blanks count in strict comparison        */
```

Logical operators are sometimes called *Boolean operators* because they apply *Boolean logic* to the operands. Rexx's logical operators are the same as the logical operators of many other programming languages. This table lists the logical operators:

Logical Operator	Meaning	Use
&	Logical AND	TRUE if both terms are true
|	Logical OR	TRUE if either term is true
&&	Logical EXCLUSIVE OR	TRUE if either (but not both) terms are true
¬ or \ (as a prefix)	Logical NOT	Changes TRUE to FALSE and vice versa

Boolean logic is useful in `if` statements with multiple comparisons. These are also referred to as *compound comparisons*. Here are some examples:

```
if ('A' = var1) & ('B' = var2) then
    say 'Displays only if BOTH comparisons are TRUE'

if ('A' = var1) | ('B' = var2) then
    say 'Displays if EITHER comparison is TRUE'

if ('A' = var1) && ('B' = var2) then
    say 'Displays if EXACTLY ONE comparison is TRUE'

if \('A' = var1)  then say 'Displays if A is NOT equal to var1'
```

Concatenation is the process of pasting two or more character strings together. Strings are appended one to the end of the other. *Explicitly* concatenate strings by coding the *concatenation operator* `||` . Rexx also automatically concatenates strings when they appear together in the same statement. Look at these instructions executed in sequence:

```
my_var = 'Yogi Bear'
say 'Hi there,' || ' ' || my_var    /* displays: 'Hi there, Yogi Bear'   */
say 'Hi there,'my_var               /* displays: 'Hi there,Yogi Bear'
                                              no space after the comma */
say 'Hi there,'  my_var             /* displays: 'Hi there, Yogi Bear'
                                              one space after the comma */
```

The second `say` instruction shows *concatenation through abuttal*. A literal string and a variable appear immediately adjacent to one another, so Rexx concatenates them without any intervening blank.

Contrast this to the last `say` instruction, where Rexx concatenates the literal and variable contents, but with one blank between them. If there are one or more spaces between the two elements listed as operands to the `say` instruction, Rexx places exactly one blank between them after concatenation.

Given these three methods of concatenating strings, individual programmers have their own preferences. Using the concatenation operator makes the process more explicit, but it also results in longer statements to build the result string.

Rexx has four kinds of operators: arithmetic, comparison, logical, and concatenation. And there are several operators in each group. If you build a statement with multiple operators, how does Rexx decide which operations to execute first? The order can be important. For example:

4 times 3, then subtract 2 from the result is 10

Perform those same operations with the same numbers in a different order, and you get a different result:

3 subtract 2, then multiple that times 4 yields the result of 4

Both these computations involve the same two operations with the same three numbers but the operations occur in different orders. They yield different results.

Clearly, programmers need to know in what order a series of operations will be executed. This issue is often referred to as the operator *order of precedence*. The order of precedence is a rule that defines which operations are executed in what order.

Some programming languages have intricate or odd orders of precedence. Rexx makes it easy. Its order of precedence is the same as in conventional algebra and the majority of programming languages. (The only minor exception is that the prefix *minus operator* always has higher priority than the exponential operator).

From highest precedence on down, this lists Rexx's order of precedence:

❏	Prefix operators	`+    -    \`
❏	Power operator	`**`
❏	Addition and subtraction	`+    -`
❏	Concatenation	by intervening blanks `||` by abuttal
❏	Comparison operators	`=    ==    >    <    >=    <=` ...and the others
❏	Logical AND	`&`
❏	Logical OR	`|`
❏	EXCLUSIVE OR	`&&`

If the order of precedence is important to some logic in your program, an easy way to ensure that operations occur in the manner in which you expect is to simply enclose the operations to perform first in parentheses. When Rexx encounters parentheses, it evaluates the entire expression when that term is required. So, you can use parentheses to guarantee any order of evaluation you require. The more deeply nested a set of parentheses is, the higher its order of precedence. The basic rule is this: *when Rexx encounters expressions nested within parentheses, it works from the innermost to the outermost.*

To return to the earlier example, one can easily ensure the proper order of operations by enclosing the highest order operations in parentheses:

```
say  (4 * 3)  - 2        /* displays: 10 */
```

To alter the order in which operations occur, just reposition the parentheses:

```
say  4 * (3 - 2)         /* displays: 4  */
```

Summary

This chapter briefly summarizes the basic elements of Rexx. We've kept the discussion high level and have avoided strict "textbook definitions." We discussed variable names and how to form them, and the difference between simple variable names and the compound variable names that are used to represent tables or arrays. We discussed the difference between strings and numbers and how to assign both to variables.

We also listed and discussed the operators used to represent arithmetic, comparison, logical, and string operations. We gave a few simple examples of how the operators are used; you'll see many more, real-world examples in the sample scripts in the upcoming chapters.

The upcoming chapters round out your knowledge of the language and focus in more detail on its capabilities. They also provide many more programming examples. Their sample scripts use the language elements this chapter introduces in many different contexts, so you'll get a much better feel for how they are used in actual programming.

Test Your Understanding

1. How are comments encoded in Rexx? Can they span more than one line?

2. How does Rexx recognize a function call in your code?

3. Must variables be declared in Rexx as in languages like C++, Pascal, or Java? How are variables established, and how can they be tested to see if they have been defined?

4. What are the two instructions for basic screen input and output?

5. What is the difference between a *comparison* and *strict comparison*? When do you use one versus the other? Does one apply strict comparisons to numeric values?

6. How do you define a numeric variable in Rexx?

3

Control Structures

Overview

Program logic is directed by what are called *control structures* or *constructs* — statements like if-then-else, do-while, and the like. Rexx offers a complete set of control structures in less than a dozen instructions.

Rexx fully supports *structured programming*, a rigorous methodology for program development that simplifies code and reduces programmer error. Structured programming restricts control structures to a handful that permit single points of entry and exit to blocks of code. It encourages *modularity* and reduces complex spaghetti code to short, readable, sections of self-contained code. Small, well-documented routines mean greater clarity and fewer programmer errors. While developer convenience sometimes leads to unstructured code ("Well... it made sense when I wrote it!"), structured, modular code is more readable and maintainable.

We recommend structured programming; nearly all of the examples in this book are structured. But we note that, as a powerful programming language, Rexx includes instructions that permit unstructured coding if desired.

This chapter discusses how to write structured programs with Rexx. We start by listing the Rexx instructions used to implement structured constructs. Then, we describe each in turn, showing how it is used in the language through numerous code snippets. At appropriate intervals, we present complete sample scripts that illustrate the use of the instructions in structured coding.

The latter part of the chapter covers the Rexx instructions for unstructured programming. While we don't recommend their general use, there are special situations in which these instructions are highly convenient. Any full-power scripting language requires a full set of instructions for controlling logical flow, including those that are unstructured.

Structured Programming in Rexx

As we've mentioned, structured programming consists of a set of constructs that enforce coding discipline and organization. These are implemented in Rexx through its basic instructions for the control of program logic. The basic constructs of structured programming and the Rexx instructions used to implement them are listed in this table:

Structured Construct	Rexx Instruction
PROCESS	Any set of instructions, executed one after another. The `exit` or `return` instructions end the code composing a program or routine.
IF-THEN. IF-THEN-ELSE	`if`
DO. DO-WHILE	`do`
CASE	`select`
CALL	`call`

Figure 3-1 illustrates the structured constructs.

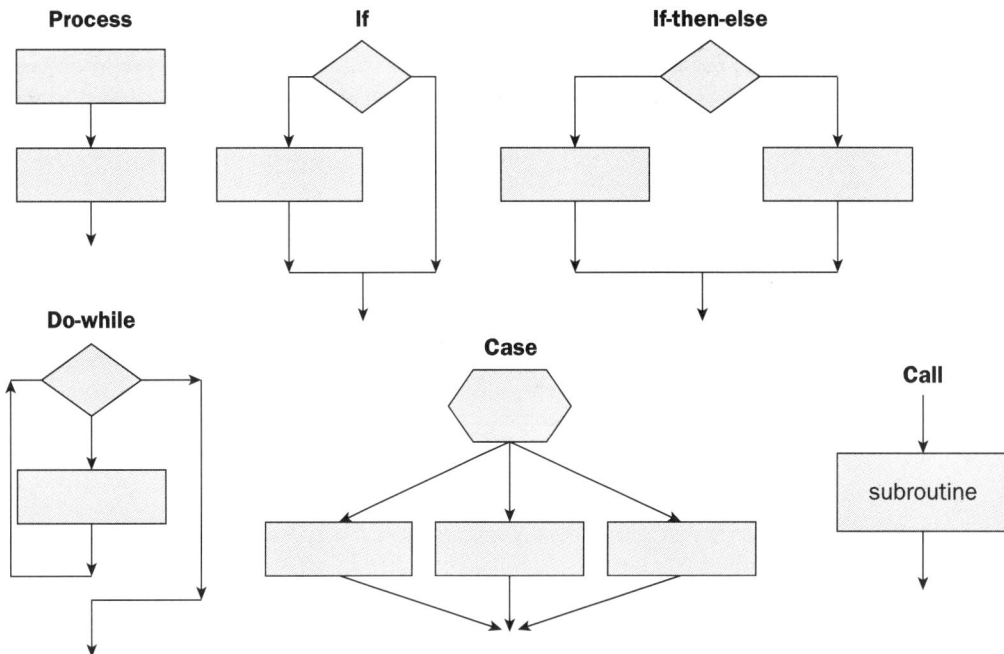

The Structured Control Constructs

Figure 3-1

IF Statements

if statements express conditional logic. Depending on the evaluation of some condition, a different branch of program logic executes. if statements are common to nearly all programming languages, and they represent the basic structured instruction for conditional logic. The two basic formats of the Rexx if instruction are:

```
IF   expression   THEN   instruction
```

and

```
IF   expression   THEN   instruction   ELSE   instruction
```

Rexx evaluates the *expression* to 1 if it is TRUE, and 0 if it is FALSE. Here are sample if statements:

```
/* A simple IF statement with no ELSE clause */

if  input = 'YES' then
   say 'You are very agreeable'

/* In this example the IF statement tests a two-part or "compound" condition. The
   SAY instruction executes only if BOTH conditions are TRUE, because of the
   AND (&) operator */

if input = 'YES' &  second_input = 'YES' then
   say 'You are doubly agreeable today'

/* This compound IF is true if EITHER of the two expressions are TRUE */

if input = 'YES' |  second_input = 'YES' then
   say 'You are singly agreeable today'

/* Here's a simple IF statement with an ELSE clause.
   The DATATYPE function verifies whether the variable INPUT contains a NUMBER */

if  datatype(input,N) then
   say 'Your input was a number'
else
   say 'Your input was not numeric'

/* This coding is NOT recommended in Rexx, though it is popular in languages
   like C or C++ or many Unix shell languages...
   Variable VAR must be exactly 1 or 0  -- or else a syntax error will occur! */

if (var) then
   say 'VAR evaluated to 1'
else
   say 'VAR evaluated to 0'
```

To execute more than a single instruction after either the then or else keywords, you *must* insert the multiple instructions between the keywords do and end. Here is an example:

```
if datatype(input,N) then do
   say 'The input was a number'
   status_record = 'VALID'
   end
else do
   say 'The input was NOT a number'
   status_record = 'INVALID'
end
```

The do-end pair groups multiple instructions. This is required when you encode more than one instruction as a logic branch in an if instruction. Notice that you must use the do-end pair for either branch of the if instruction when it executes more than a single statement. In other words, use the do-end pair to group more than a single instruction on either the then or the else branches of the if instruction.

You can nest if statements, one inside of another. If you nest if statements very deeply, it becomes confusing as to which else clause matches which if instruction. *The important rule to remember is that an else clause is always matched to the nearest unmatched if.* Rexx ignores indentation, so how you indent nested if statements has no effect on how Rexx interprets them.

The following code includes comments that show where the programmer sees the end of each if instruction. He or she includes these for documentation purposes only, since Rexx ignores comments (regardless of what the comments may say).

```
if age => 70 then
   say 'Person MUST start taking mandatory IRA distributions'
else
   if age >= 65 then
      say 'Person can receive maximum Social Security benefits'
   else
      if  age >= 62 then
         say 'Person may elect reduced Social Security benefits'
      else
         say 'Person is a worker bee, not a beneficiary'
      /* end-if */
   /* end-if */
/* end-if */
```

Here's another style in which to code this example. This series of nested if statements is sometimes referred to as an *if-else-if ladder*. The first logic branch that evaluates to TRUE executes:

```
if age => 70 then
   say 'Person MUST start taking mandatory IRA distributions'
else if age >= 65 then
   say 'Person can receive maximum Social Security benefits'
else if  age >= 62 then
   say 'Person may elect reduced Social Security benefits'
```

Some languages provide special keywords for this situation, but Rexx does not. (For example, some Unix shell languages provide the elif keyword to represent Rexx's else if pair). Remember to code a do - end pair whenever more than one instruction executes within a branch of the if instruction.

The if-else-if ladder embodies another structured construct often referred to the *CASE construct*. In a CASE construct, a set of conditions are tested, then one logic branch is selected from among several.

Rexx provides the `select` instruction to create CASE logic, as will be explained later. In Rexx you can either choose an if-else-if ladder or the `select` instruction to encode CASE logic.

Sometimes, you'll encounter a coding situation where you want to code a logic branch that performs no action. In this case, code the Rexx nop instruction. "nop" is a traditional computer science abbreviation or term that means "no operation." The `nop` instruction is a placeholder that results in no action. Here is an example. The `nop` instruction in this code ensures that no action is taken when the `if` statement condition evaluates to TRUE:

```
if case_is_undetermined = 'Y' then
    nop       /* No action is taken here. NOP is a placeholder only. */
else do
    say 'Case action completed'
    status_msg = 'Case action completed'
end
```

DO Statements

The `do` instruction groups statements together and optionally executes them repetitively. It comes in several forms, all of which we'll explore in this chapter. do instructions permit repetitive execution of one or more statements. They are the basic way you code program "loops" in Rexx.

You are already familiar with the simple `do-end` pair used to group multiple instructions. Here is the generic representation of how this is coded:

```
DO
      instruction_list
END
```

Use the `do-end` group when you must execute multiple instructions in a branch of the `if` instruction, for example. Here's another form of the `do` instruction that repetitively executes a group of instructions while the condition in the `expression` is TRUE:

```
DO  WHILE expression
      instruction_list
END
```

This coding example shows how to use this generic format. It employs a `do while` to call a subroutine exactly 10 times:

```
j = 1
do while j <= 10
    call sub_routine
    j = j + 1
end
```

The `do` instruction is flexible and offers other formats for devising loops. The preceding loop could also be coded with a simpler form of the `do` instruction:

```
do   10
    call sub_routine
end
```

Or, the example could be coded using a *controlled repetitive loop*:

```
do  j = 1  to  10  by 1
    call sub_routine
end
```

The phrase `by  1` is unnecessary because Rexx automatically increases the `do` loop *control variable* by 1 if this phrase is not coded. But the keyword `by` could be useful in situations where you want to increase the *loop counter* by some other value:

```
do j = 1 to 20 by 2
    call sub_routine
end
```

In addition to the `to` and `by` keywords, `for` may be used establish another limit on the loop's execution if some other condition does not terminate it first. `for` is like `to`, in that Rexx checks it prior to each iteration through the loop. `to`, `by`, and `for` may be coded in any order. In this example, the `for` keyword limits the `do` loop to three executions:

```
do j = 1 to 100 by 1 for 3
    say 'Loop executed:'   j  'times.'   /* Ends with: 'Loop executed: 3 times.' */
end
```

You may alter the loop control variable yourself, directly, while inside of the `do` loop, but this is not a recommended programming practice. It is confusing, and there is always an alternative way to handle such a situation from the logical standpoint. We recommend always using the loop control variable only for controlling an individual loop, and only altering that variable's value through the `do` instruction condition test.

Rexx also contains unstructured loop control instructions such as `leave`, `iterate`, and `signal`, which we cover later in the section of this chapter on unstructured control constructs. At that time we also cover the `do  until` and `do  forever` forms of do loops, which also fall outside the rules of structured programming.

A Sample Program

This program prompts the user to input a series of words, one at a time. The program identifies words that are four characters long, and concatenates them into a list, which it then displays. The program illustrates a basic do loop, using it to read input from the user. It also shows how to use the `if` instruction in determining the lengths of the words the user enters.

If you were to enter this sentence to the program (one word at a time):

```
now is the time for all good men to come to the aid of their country
```

the program's output would be:

```
Four letter words:  time good come
```

Here's the sample program:

```
/*  FOUR LETTER WORDS:                                            */
/*                                                                */
/*      This program identifies all four letter words in the     */
/*      input and places them into an output list.               */

four_letter_words  = ''         /* initialize to no 4 letter words found yet */

say "Enter a word: "        /* prompt user to enter 1 word        */
parse pull wordin .         /* the period ensures only 1 word is read in   */
do while wordin \= ''
   if length(wordin) = 4  then
      four_letter_words  = four_letter_words  wordin

   say "Enter a word: "     /* read the next word in              */
   parse pull wordin .
end

say 'Four letter words:'  four_letter_words       /* display output      */
```

The do while loop in this script provides the control structure for the program to prompt the user and read one word after that prompt. The do while loop terminates when the user declines to enter a word — after the user just presses the <ENTER> key in response to the program's prompt to Enter a word: When the user presses the <ENTER> key without entering a word, this statement recognizes that fact and terminates the do while loop:

```
do while wordin \= ''
```

Recall that the pull instruction reads an input and automatically translates it to uppercase. This program uses parse pull to read an input *without* the automatic translation to uppercase:

```
parse pull wordin .
```

The period ensures that only the first word is accepted should the user enter more than one. This use of the period is a convention in Rexx, and it's about the only example of *syntax-based coding* in the entire language. You could achieve the same effect by coding:

```
parse pull wordin junk
```

The first word entered by the user is parsed into the variable wordin, while any remaining words entered on the input line would be placed into the variable named junk.

The program uses the `length` function to determine whether the word the user entered contains four letters. If so, the next statement concatenates the four letter word into a list it builds in the variable named `four_letter_words`.

```
if length(wordin) = 4  then
   four_letter_words  = four_letter_words  wordin
```

The assignment statement relies on the fact that Rexx automatically concatenates variables placed in the same statement, with one space between each. An alternative would have been to use the explicit concatenation operator:

```
four_letter_words  = four_letter_words  ||  wordin
```

But in this case the output would have been:

```
Four letter words:  timegoodcome
```

Explicit concatenation requires explicitly splicing in a blank to achieve properly spaced output:

```
four_letter_words  = four_letter_words  ||  ' '  ||  wordin
```

After the user is done entering words, the program displays the output string through the following statement. Since this is the last statement coded in the program, the script terminates after issuing it:

```
say 'Four letter words:'  four_letter_words      /* display output      */
```

SELECT Statements

The CASE construct tests a series of conditions and executes the set of instructions for the first condition that is TRUE. Rexx implements the CASE construct through its `select` instruction. The `select` instruction tests expressions and executes the logic branch of the first one that evaluates to TRUE. Here is the generic format of the `select` instruction:

```
SELECT  when_list   [ OTHERWISE  instruction_list ]  END
```

The `otherwise` branch of the `select` instruction executes if none of the prior `when_list` conditions are found to be TRUE. Note that it is possible to code a `select` instruction without an `otherwise` keyword, but if none of the `when_list` conditions execute, an error results. We strongly recommend coding an `otherwise` section on every `select` statement.

The Rexx `select` instruction provides more control than the same CASE construct in some other programming languages because you can encode any expression in the `when` clause. Some languages only permit testing the value of a specified variable.

Here's a simple coding example using `select`:

```
select
   when gender = 'M' then
      say 'Gender is male'
```

```
      when gender = 'F' then do
         say 'Gender is female'
         female_count = female_count + 1
         end
      otherwise
         say 'Error -- Gender is missing or invalid'
         say 'Please check input record'
   end    /* this END pairs with the SELECT instruction itself */
```

If the value in the variable gender equals the character M, the first logic branch executes. If the value is F, the group of instructions associated with the second when clause runs. If neither case is true, then the instructions following the otherwise keyword execute.

Notice that an instruction_list follows the otherwise keyword, so if you code more than one statement here you do not need to insert them in a do-end pair. Contrast this to the when groups, which *do* require a do-end pair if they contain more than a single instruction. Don't forget to encode the final end keyword to terminate the select statement.

CALL Statements

All programming languages provide a mechanism to invoke other scripts or routines. This allows one script, referred to as the *caller*, to run another, the *subroutine*. Rexx's call instruction invokes a subroutine, where the subroutine may be one of three kinds:

- ❏ *Internal* — Consists of Rexx code residing in the same file as the caller.

- ❏ *Built-in* — One of the Rexx built-in functions.

- ❏ *External* — Code residing in a different file than the invoking script. An external subroutine may be another Rexx script, or it may be written in any language supporting Rexx's interface.

The subroutine may optionally return one value to the caller through the Rexx *special variable* named result. (Rexx has only a handful of special variables and result is one of them). Of course, you can have the subroutine send back one or more results by changing the values of variables it has access to. We'll explore all the ways in which caller and subroutines or functions can communicate in detail in Chapter 8, which is on subroutines and modularity. For now, we'll just focus our discussion on the call instruction.

Subroutines and *functions* are very similar in Rexx. The one difference is that a function *must* return a value to the caller by its return instruction, where a subroutine may elect do so.

The following sample program illustrates the call instruction by invoking an internal routine as a subroutine. The subroutine is considered *internal* because its code resides in the same file as that of the program that calls it. The program subroutine squares a number and returns the result.

The main program reads one input number as a *command-line argument* or *input parameter*. To run the program and get the square of four, for example, you enter this line to specify the command-line argument:

```
   square.rexx  4
```

Or, you may start the program by entering a line like this:

```
regina  square  4
```

Recall that the first example given earlier *implicitly* invokes the Rexx interpreter, while the second example *explicitly* invokes it. The command-line argument follows the name of the Rexx script you want to run. Here it's a single value, 4, but other programs might have either many or no command-line arguments.

The program responds to either of the above commands with:

```
You entered: 4    Squared it is: 16
```

Here's the program code:

```
/*   SQUARE:                                               */
/*                                                         */
/*     Squares a number by calling an internal subroutine  */

arg number_in .                  /* retrieve the command-line argument    */

call square_the_number number_in
say 'You entered:' number_in '  Squared it is:' result

exit 0


/*   SQUARE_THE_NUMBER:                                    */
/*                                                         */
/*     Squares the number and RETURNs it into RESULT       */

square_the_number: procedure

    arg the_number
    return  the_number * the_number
```

The main program or *driver* uses the `arg` instruction to read the command-line argument into variable number_in. As with the `pull` and `parse pull` instructions, encode a period (`.`) at the end of this statement to eliminate any extraneous input:

```
arg number_in .                  /* retrieve the command-line argument */
```

The `call` instruction names the internal routine to invoke and passes the variable number_in to that routine as its input. The subroutine uses the `arg` instruction to read this parameter (exactly as the main routine did). Here is the encoding of the `call` instruction. The first parameter names the subroutine or function to run, while each subsequent parameter is an input argument sent to the subroutine. In this case, the `call` instruction passes a single argument named number_in to the subroutine named square_the_number:

```
call square_the_number number_in
```

The first line of the subroutine identifies it as the routine named square_the_number. Notice that a colon follows its name on the first line of the subroutine — this identifies a *label* in Rexx. An internal subroutine starts with the routine's name in the form of a label. The `procedure` instruction on the first line of the subroutine ensures that only the arguments passed to the subroutine will be accessible from within it. No other variables of the calling routine are viewable or changeable by this subroutine. Here is the first executable line of the subroutine:

```
square_the_number: procedure
```

The subroutine reads the number passed into it from its caller by the `arg` instruction. Then, the subroutine returns a single result through its `return` instruction. Here is how this line is encoded. Notice that Rexx evaluates the expression (squaring the number) before executing the `return` instruction:

```
return  the_number * the_number
```

The caller picks up this returned value through the *special variable* named `result`. The main routine displays the squared result to the user through this concatenated display statement:

```
say 'You entered:' number_in '  Squared it is:' result
```

This displays an output similar to this to the user:

```
You entered: 2    Squared it is: 4
```

The driver ends with the instruction `exit   0`. This unconditionally ends the script with a *return code,* or returned value, of 0. The last statement of the internal subroutine was a `return` instruction. `return` passes control back to the calling routine, in this case passing back the squared number. If the subroutine is a function, a `return` instruction is required to pass back a value.

There is much more to say about subroutines and modular program design. We leave that discussion to Chapter 8. For now, this simple script illustrates the structured CALL construct and how it can be used to invoke a subroutine or function.

Another Sample Program

Here's a program that shows how to build menus and call subroutines based on user input. This program is a fragment of a real production program, slimmed down and simplified for clarity. The script illustrates several instructions, including `do` and `select`. It also provides another example of how to invoke internal subroutines.

The basic idea of the program is that it displays a menu of transaction options to the user. The user picks which transaction to execute. The program then executes that transaction and returns to the user with the menu. Here is how it starts. The program clears the screen and displays a menu of options to the user that looks like this:

```
Select the transaction type by abbreviation:

    Insert = I
    Update = U
    Delete = D
      Exit = X

Your choice => _
```

Based on the user's input, the program then calls the appropriate internal subroutine to perform an Insert, Update, or Delete transaction. (In the example, these routines are "dummied out" and all each really does is display a message that the subroutine was entered). The menu reappears until the user finally exits by entering the menu option 'x'.

Here's the complete program:

```
/*   MENU:                                                         */
/*                                                                 */
/*      This program display a menu and performs updates based     */
/*      on the transaction the user selects.                       */

'cls'                               /* clear the screen (Windows only)  */
tran_type = ''
do while tran_type \= 'X'          /* do until user enters 'X'          */
   say
   say 'Select the transation type by abbreviation:'
   say
   say '    Insert = I '
   say '    Update = U '
   say '    Delete = D '
   say '      Exit = X '
   say
   say 'Your choice => '
   pull tran_type .
   select
      when tran_type = 'I' then
         call insert_routine
      when tran_type = 'U' then
         call update_routine
      when tran_type = 'D' then
         call delete_routine
      when tran_type = 'X' then do
         say
         say 'Bye!'
         end
      otherwise
         say
         say 'You entered invalid transaction type:' tran_type
         say 'Press <ENTER> to reenter the transaction type.'
         pull .
      end
end
exit 0


/* INSERT_ROUTINE goes here                                        */
INSERT_ROUTINE: procedure
   say 'Insert Routine was executed'
   return 0

/* UDPATE_ROUTINE goes here                                        */
UPDATE_ROUTINE: procedure
```

```
    say 'Update Routine was executed'
    return 0

/* DELETE_ROUTINE goes here                                    */
DELETE_ROUTINE: procedure
    say 'Delete Routine was executed'
    return 0
```

The first executable line in the program is this:

```
'cls'                          /* clear the screen (Windows only)  */
```

When the Rexx interpreter does not recognize a statement as part of the Rexx language, it assumes that it is an operating system command and passes it to the operating system for execution. Since there is no such command as cls in the Rexx language, the interpreter passes the string cls to the operating system for execution as an operating system command.

cls is the Windows command to "clear the screen," so what this statement does is send a command to Windows to clear the display screen. Of course, this statement makes this program *operating-system-dependent*. To run this program under Linux or Unix, this statement should contain the equivalent command to clear the screen under these operating systems, which is clear:

```
'clear'                        /* clear the screen (Linux/Unix only) */
```

Passing commands to the operating system (or other external environments) is an important Rexx feature. It provides a lot of power and, as you can see, is very easy to code. Chapter 14 covers this topic in detail.

Next in the program, a series of say commands paints the menu on the user's screen:

```
    say
    say 'Select the transation type by abbreviation:'
    say
    say '   Insert = I '
    say '   Update = U '
    say '   Delete = D '
    say '     Exit = X '
    say
    say 'Your choice => '
```

A say instruction with no operand just displays a blank line and can be used for vertically spacing the output on the user's display screen.

The script displays the menu repeatedly until the user finally enters 'x' or 'X'. The pull command's automatic translation of user input to uppercase is handy here and eliminates the need for the programmer to worry about the case in which the user enters a letter.

The select construct leads to a call of the proper internal routine to handle the transaction the user selects:

```
select
    when tran_type = 'I' then
        call insert_routine
    when tran_type = 'U' then
        call update_routine
    when tran_type = 'D' then
        call delete_routine
    when tran_type = 'X' then do
        say
        say 'Bye!'
        end
    otherwise
        say
        say 'You entered invalid transaction type:' tran_type
        say 'Press <ENTER> to reenter the transaction type.'
        pull .
    end
```

The `when` clause where the user enters 'x' or 'x' encloses its multiple instructions within a `do-end` pair. The `otherwise` clause handles the case where the user inputs an invalid character. The final `end` in the code concludes the `select` instruction.

Remember that the logic of the `select` statement is that the first condition that evaluates to TRUE is the branch that executes. In the preceding code, this means that the program will call the proper subroutine based on the transaction code the user enters.

Following the `select` instruction, the code for the main routine or driver ends with an `exit 0` statement:

```
exit 0
```

This delimits the code of the main routine from that of the routines that follow it and also sends a return code of 0 to the environment when the script ends. An `exit` instruction is required to separate the code of the main routine from the subroutines or functions that follow it.

The three update routines contain no real code. Each just displays a message that it ran. This allows the user to verify that the script is working. These subroutines cannot access any variables within the main routine, because they have the `procedure` instruction, and no variables are passed into them. Each ends with a `return 0` instruction:

```
return 0
```

While this sample script is simple, it shows how to code a menu for user selection. It also illustrates calling subroutines to perform tasks. This is a nice modular structure that you can expand when coding menus with pick lists. Of course, many programs require graphical user interfaces, or GUIs. There are a variety of free and open-source GUI interfaces available for Rexx scripting. GUI programming is an advanced topic we'll get to in a bit. Chapter 16 shows how to program GUIs with Rexx scripts.

Unstructured Control Instructions

Rexx is a great language for structured programming. It supports all the constructs required and makes structured programming easy. But the language is powerful and flexible, and there are times when unstructured flow of control is necessary (or at least highly convenient). Here are the unstructured instructions that alter program flow in Rexx:

Instruction	Use
do until	A form of the do instruction that implements a *bottom-drive loop*. Unlike do-while, do-until will always execute the code in the loop at least one time, because the condition test occurs at the bottom of the loop.
do forever	Creates an *endless loop*, a loop that executes forever. This requires an *unstructured exit* to terminate the loop. Code the unstructured exit by either the leave, signal or exit instruction.
iterate	Causes control to be passed from the current statement in the do loop to the bottom of the loop.
leave	Causes an immediate exit from a do loop to the statement following the loop.
signal	Used to trap *exceptions* (specific program error conditions). Can also be used to unconditionally transfer control to a specified label, similarly to the GOTO instruction in other programming languages.

Figure 3-2 below illustrates the unstructured control constructs.

The do until and do forever are two more forms of the do instruction. do until implements a bottom-driven loop. Such a loop always executes at least one time. In contrast, the do while checks the condition *prior* to entering the loop, so the loop may or may not be executed at least once. do until is considered unstructured and the do while is preferred. Any logic that can be encoded using do until can be coded using do while — you just have to think for a moment to see how to change the logic into a do while.

Let's look at the difference between do while and do until. This code will not enter the do loop to display the message. The do while tests the condition prior to executing the loop, so the loop never executes. The result in this example is that the say instruction never executes and does not display the message:

```
ex = 'NO'
do while ex = 'YES'
   say 'Loop 1 was entered'    /* This line is never displayed.    */
   ex = 'YES'
end
```

The Un-Structured Control Constructs

Do-until

Do-Forever

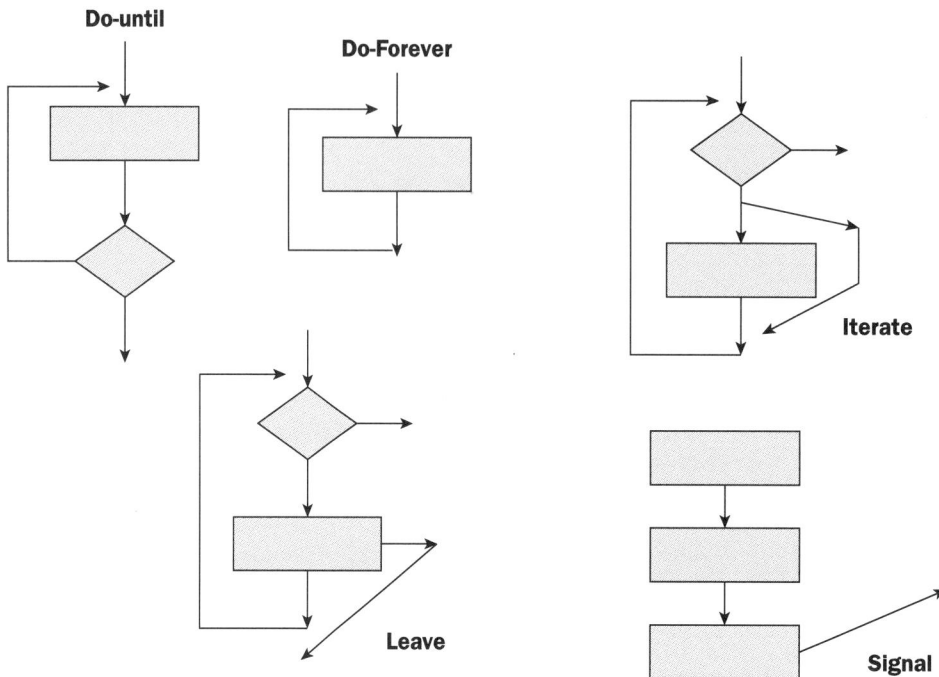

Iterate

Leave

Signal

Figure 3-2

If we replace the do while loop with a do until loop, the code will execute through the loop one time, printing the message once. This is because the condition test is applied only at the bottom of the loop. A do until loop will always execute one time, even if the condition test on the do until is false, because the test is not evaluated until after the loop executes one time. The result in this example is that the say instruction executes once and displays one output line:

```
ex = 'NO'
do until ex = 'YES'
    say 'Loop 2 was entered'    /* This line is displayed one time. */
    ex = 'YES'
end
```

do forever creates an *endless loop*. You *must* have some unstructured exit from within the loop or your program will never stop! This example uses the leave instruction to exit the endless loop when j = 4. The leave instruction transfers control to the statement immediately following the end that terminates the do loop. In this example, it breaks the endless loop and transfers control to the say statement immediately following the loop:

```
j = 1
do forever
    /* do some work here */
    j = j + 1
    if j = 4 then leave      /* exits the DO FOREVER loop */
```

```
end
say 'The above LEAVE instruction transfers control to this statement'
```

Another way to terminate the endless loop is to encode the `exit` instruction. `exit` ends a program unconditionally (even if a subroutine is executing or if execution is nested inside of a do loop). Control returns to the environment (the operating system) with the optional string encoded on the `exit` statement passed up.

What return code you can pass to the environment or operating system using the `exit` instruction depends on what that operating system accepts. Some systems accept only return codes that are numeric digits between 0 and 127. If your script returns any other string, it is translated into a 0. Other operating systems will accept whatever value you encode on the `exit` instruction.

Here's an example. The following code snippet is the same as the previous one, which illustrates the `leave` instruction, but this time when the condition $j = 4$ is attained, the script unconditionally exits and returns 0 to the environment. Since the script ends, the `say` instruction following the do forever loop never executes and does not display its output:

```
j = 1
do forever
   /* do some work here */
   j = j + 1
   if j = 4 then
      exit  0   /* unconditionally exits and passes '0' back to the environment */
end
say 'this line will never be displayed'   /* code EXITs, never reaches this line
*/
```

Another instruction for the unstructured transfer of control is `signal`. The `signal` instruction acts much like the GOTO statement of other programming languages. It transfers control directly out of any loop, CASE structure, or `if` statement directly to a Rexx label. A *label* is simply a symbol immediately followed by a colon. This sample code snippet is similar to that we've seen earlier, except that this time the `signal` instruction transfers control to a program label. So, once $j = 4$ and the `signal` instruction execute, control is transferred to the program label and the `say` instruction displays its output line:

```
j = 1
do forever
   /* do some work here */
   j = j + 1
   if j = 4 then
      signal  my_routine   /* unconditionally go to the label MY_ROUTINE */
end

/*  other code here gets skipped by the SIGNAL instruction */

my_routine:
   say 'SIGNAL instruction was executed, MY_ROUTINE entered...'
```

`signal` differs from the GOTO of some other languages in that it terminates all active control structures in which it is encoded. You could not transfer control to another point in a loop using it, for example.

Duplicate labels are allowed within Rexx scripts, but control will always be transferred to the one that occurs first. We recommend that all labels in a program be unique within a program for the sake of readability.

In an entirely different role, the `signal` instruction is also used to capture or "trap" errors and special conditions. Chapter 10 discusses this in detail. This is a special mechanism within the Rexx language designed to capture unusual error conditions or "exceptions."

The last unstructured instruction to discuss is the `iterate` instruction. The `iterate` instruction causes control to be passed from the current statement in the `do` loop to the bottom of the loop. In this example, the `iterate` instruction ensures that the `say` instruction never executes. The `if` instruction's condition evaluates to TRUE every time that statement is encountered, so the `iterate` instruction reruns the `do` loop and the `say` instruction never runs:

```
j = 1
do until j = 4
    /* do some work here */
    j = j + 1
    if j > 1 then iterate
        say 'This line is never displayed!'   /* this line will never execute */
end
```

Summary

This chapter summarizes Rexx's structured and unstructured control constructs. These include the `if`, `do`, `select`, `call`, `exit`, and `return` instructions for structured programming, and the unstructured `iterate`, `leave`, and `signal` instructions. The `do until` and `do forever` forms of the `do` instruction are also unstructured.

Use the instructions this chapter covers to direct conditional logic as in most other programming languages. This chapter presented many small code snippets to illustrate how to use the instructions that control program logic. Subsequent chapters will provide many more examples of the use of these instructions. These upcoming examples demonstrate the instructions in the more realistic context of complete programs. They will make the use of the instructions for the control of logical flow much clearer.

Test Your Understanding

1. Why is structured programming recommended? What Rexx instructions implement structured programming? How do subroutines and functions support the benefits of structured programming?

2. How does Rexx determine which `if` instruction each `else` keyword pairs with?

3. Name two ways that a script can test for the end of user input.

4. What are the differences between *built-in*, *internal*, and *external* subroutines? What is the difference between a *function* and a *subroutine*?

5. What are the values of TRUE and FALSE in Rexx?

6. What is the danger in coding a do forever loop? How does one address this danger?

7. What are the two main functions of the signal instruction? How does the signal instruction differ from the GOTO command of many other programming languages?

8. What is the difference between the do-while and do-until instructions? Why use one versus the other? Are both allowed in structured programming?

4

Arrays

Overview

Every programming language provides for *arrays*. Sometimes they are referred to as *tables*. This basic data structure allows you to build lists of "like elements," which can be stored, searched, sorted, and manipulated by other basic programming operations.

Rexx's implementation of arrays is powerful but easy to use. Arrays can be of any *dimensionality*. They can be a one-dimensional *list*, where all elements in the array are of the same kind. They can be of two dimensions, where there exist pairs of entries. In this case, elements are manipulated by two subscripts (such as I and J). Or, arrays can be of as many dimensions as you like. While Rexx implementations vary, the usual constraint on the size and dimensionality of array is memory. This contrasts with other programming languages that have specific, language-related limitations on array size.

Rexx arrays may be *sparse*. That is, not every array position must have a value or even be initialized. There can be empty array positions, or *slots*, between those that do contain data elements. Or arrays can be *dense*, in which consecutive array slots all contain data elements. Figure 4-1 below pictorially shows the difference between sparse and dense arrays. Dense arrays are also sometimes called *nonsparse* arrays.

Arrays may be initialized by a single assignment statement. But just like other variables, arrays are defined by their first use. You do not have to predefine or preallocate them. Nor must you declare a maximum size for an array. The only limitation on array size in most Rexx implementations is imposed by the amount of machine memory.

Dense versus Sparse Arrays

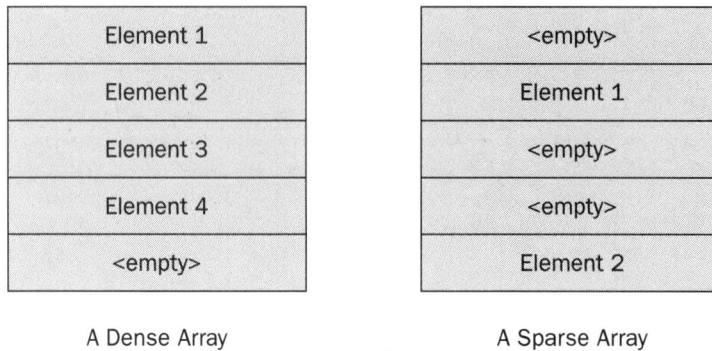

A Dense Array	A Sparse Array
Element 1	<empty>
Element 2	Element 1
Element 3	<empty>
Element 4	<empty>
<empty>	Element 2

A Dense Array   A Sparse Array

Figure 4-1

You can refer to individual elements within a Rexx arrray by numeric subscripts, as you do in other programming languages. Or, you can refer to array elements by variables that contain character strings. Rexx then uses those character strings as indexes into the array. For this reason, Rexx arrays are sometimes termed *content addressable*. They can be used as a form of *associative memory*, in that they create an association between two values. This permits innovative use of arrays in problem solving. We'll explain what these terms mean and why are they important in more detail later in the chapter. We'll even give several examples of how content addressable memory structures are useful in resolving programming problems. For now, remember that the subscripts you encode to access individual array elements can be either numeric or string variables.

Like many scripting languages, Rexx lacks complex data structures such as lists, trees, records, and the like. These are unnecessary because by understanding content-addressable arrays it is easy to build these structures. Rexx arrays provide the foundation to build any imaginable data structure. We'll show you how later in this chapter. First, let's explore the basics of how to code arrays and process their data elements.

The Basics

To approach the subject of arrays, let's review the way variable names are created. The basis for Rexx arrays are compound variable names or *symbols*. So far we've seen several kinds of symbols within Rexx:

- ❑ *Constants* — Literal strings or other values that cannot be changed.

- ❑ *Simple symbols* — Variable names that do not begin with a digit and do not contain any embedded period(s).

- ❑ *Compound symbols* — The basis for arrays. Like simple symbols, they do not begin with a digit. However, they contain one or more periods.

Simple symbols are synonymous with variable names, as we have known them thus far, while *compound symbols* contain one or more periods. Compound symbols are the basis for arrays.

In compound symbols, the *stem* is the part of the name up to and including the first period. The stem is sometimes called a *stem variable*. The *tail* comprises one or more symbols separated by periods.

Here are a few examples:

❑   list.j — list is the name of an array or table.

❑   list.j — list. is the stem of the array. Note that the stem name includes the period.

❑   books.j.k — books. is the stem, j.k is the tail. j and k are two subscripts.

In these examples, Rexx substitutes in the value of the variables j and k before referencing into the arrays. These values can be numbers, but they do not have to be. Rexx allows indexing into an array based on any variable value you encode, whether it is numeric or a string value.

Here is a sample series of statements that refer to an array element based on a string value in a variable. The first line below initializes all elements in an array to the null string (represented by two back-to-back quotation marks). The second line assigns a value to a specific array element. The last two statements show how a character string provides a subscript into the array to retrieve that data element from the array:

```
fruit. = ''               /* initialize all array elements to the null string */
fruit.cherry = 'Tasty!'   /* set the value of an array element                */
subscript_string = cherry /* establish an index into the array                */
say fruit.subscript_string /* displays: Tasty!                                 */
```

It is probably worth noting that Rexx uppercases the string cherry into CHERRY in the subscript assignment statement above because that character string is not enclosed in quotation marks. Rexx also uppercases variable names such as fruit.cherry into FRUIT.CHERRY internally. Had we coded subscript_string = 'cherry' as the third line in the sample code, it would not work properly. The array tail is uppercased internally by Rexx so the subscript string used for finding the data element must also be uppercase.

What happens if you accidentally reference an array with a subscript that is not yet initialized? Recall that in Rexx an uninitialized variable is always its own name in uppercase. So, if my_index has not yet been assigned a value, my_array.my_index resolves to MY_ARRAY.MY_INDEX. Oops! This is probably not what the programmer intended.

Initialize the array as a whole by referring to its stem. The dimensionality of the array does not matter to this operation. We saw one example of initializing an entire array in one line of the sample code. Here are some more examples:

```
list. = 0    /* initialize all possible entries in the array LIST to 0        */
books. = ''  /* initialize all possible entries in BOOKS array to null string */
```

You *cannot* perform other kinds of operations on entire arrays by single statements — in most Rexx implementations. For example, these statements *are invalid* and result in errors:

```
numbers. = numbers. + 5    /* add 5 to each entry in the NUMBERS array */
lista. = listb.          /* move all contents of array LISTB
                            into the array LISTA */
```

To process all the elements in an array, use a do loop. This works as long as the array is indexed or sub-scripted by numeric values, and each position, or slot, in the array contains a value. To process all the elements in the array, you must keep track of the maximum subscript you use. There is no Rexx function that returns the largest numeric subscript you've used for an array. Here is an example that shows how to process all the elements of an array. In this code, each contiguous array position contains an element, and the array subscript is numeric:

```
array_name. = ''          /* initialize all elements to some nonoccurring value   */

number_of_elements = 5   /* initialize to the number of elements in the array     */

/*  place elements into the array here */

/*  This code processes all elements in the array. */
do  j = 1  to number_of_elements
    say  "Here's an array element:" array_name.j
end
```

Another technique for array processing is to initialize the array to zeroes for numeric values, or to the empty string or *null string* for character string entries (represented by two back-to-back quotation marks ' '). Then process the array starting at the beginning until you encounter an entry set to the initialization value. Here's sample code that processes all elements of an array based on this approach:

```
array_name. = ''   /* initialize all array elements to some nonoccurring value */

/*  place elements into the array here */

/*  This code processes all elements in the array. */
do  j = 1  while array_name.j <> ''
    say  "Here's an array element:" array_name.j
end
```

If you take this approach, be sure that the value used for initialization never occurs in the data you place into the array!

This approach also assumes a *nonsparse*, or *dense, array* — one in which the positions in the array have been filled consecutively without skipping array slots or positions. For a sparse array, we recommend storing the largest numeric subscript you use in a variable for future reference. Obviously, you cannot simply process a sparse array until you encounter the array initialization value because some positions within the array may not contain data items. In processing a sparse array, your code will have to be able to distinguish between array positions that contain valid values and those that do not. For this reason, it is useful to initialize all sparse array elements to some unused default value (such as the null string or zeroes) prior to using the array.

In many programming languages, you must be concerned with what the subscript of the first entry in a table is. Is the first numeric subscript 0 or 1? In Rexx, the first subscript is whatever you use! So, input the first array element into position 0 or 1 as you prefer:

```
array_name.0  = 'first element'
```

or

```
array_name.1 = 'first element'
```

Just be sure that whatever choice you make you remember and that you remain consistent in your approach. This flexibility is a handy feature of content-addressable arrays.

As an informal convention, many Rexx programmers store the number of array elements in position 0, then start storing data elements in position 1:

```
array_name.0  = 3       /* store number of elements in the array here */
array_name.1 = 'first element'
array_name.2 = 'second element'
array_name.3 = 'last element'
```

Assuming that the array is not sparse and the index is numeric, process the entire array with code like this:

```
do  j = 1  to array_name.0
    say  "Here's an array element:" array_name.j
end
```

Placing the number of array elements into position 0 in the array is not required and is strictly an informal convention to which many Rexx programmers adhere. But it's quite a useful one, and we recommend it.

A Sample Program

This sample program illustrates basic array manipulation. The program defines two arrays. One holds book titles along with three descriptors that describe each book. The other array contains keywords that will be matched against the three descriptors for each book.

The user starts the program and inputs a "weight" as a command line parameter. Then the program lists all books that have a count of descriptors that match a number of keywords at least equal to the weight. This algorithm is called *weighted retrieval*, and it's often used in library searches and by online bibliographic search services.

Chapter 4

Here's the entire program. The main concepts to understand in reviewing it are how the two arrays are set up and initialized at the top of the program, and how they are processed in the body. The do loops that process array elements are similar to the ones seen previously.

```
/*  FIND BOOKS:                                                 */
/*                                                              */
/*     This program illustrates basic arrays by retrieving book */
/*     titles based on keyword weightings.                      */

keyword. = ''            /* initialize both arrays to all null strings */
title. = ''

/* the array of keywords to search for among the book descriptors   */

keyword.1 = 'earth'    ;    keyword.2 = 'computers'
keyword.3 = 'life'     ;    keyword.4 = 'environment'

/* the array of book titles, each having 3 descriptors         */

title.1 = 'Saving Planet Earth'
  title.1.1 = 'earth'
  title.1.2 = 'environment'
  title.1.3 = 'life'
title.2 = 'Computer Lifeforms'
  title.2.1 = 'life'
  title.2.2 = 'computers'
  title.2.3 = 'intelligence'
title.3 = 'Algorithmic Insanity'
  title.3.1 = 'computers'
  title.3.2 = 'algorithms'
  title.3.3 = 'programming'


arg weight . /* get number keyword matches required for retrieval  */

say 'For weight of' weight 'retrieved titles are:'  /* output header */

do j=1 while title.j <> ''                    /* look at each book   */
   count = 0
   do k=1 while keyword.k <> ''               /* inspect its keywords */
      do l=1 while title.j.l <> ''
         if  keyword.k = title.j.l  then count = count + 1
      end
   end

   if count >= weight then   /* display titles matching the criteria */
      say title.j
end
```

The program shows that you can place more than one Rexx statement on a line by separating the statements with a semicolon. We use this fact to initialize the searchable keywords. Here's an example with two statements on one line:

```
keyword.1 = 'earth'   ;   keyword.2 = 'computers'
```

To implement the weighted-retrieval algorithm, the outermost do loop in the script processes each book, one at a time. This loop uses the variable j as its subscript:

```
do j=1 while title.j <> ''                    /* look at each book    */
```

The do loop could have included the phrase by 1, but this is not necessary. Rexx automatically defaults to incrementing the loop counter by 1 for each iteration. If we were to encode this same line and explicitly specify the increment, it would appear like this. Either approach works just fine:

```
do j=1 by 1 while title.j <> ''               /* look at each book    */
```

The loop that processes each book, one at a time, is the outermost loop in the code. The next, inner loop uses k as its control variable and processes all the keywords for one book:

```
    do k=1 while keyword.k <> ''              /* inspect its keywords */
```

The innermost loop uses l for loop control and inspects the three descriptors for each book title. This code totals how many of each book's descriptors match keywords:

```
        do l=1 while title.j.l <> ''
            if  keyword.k = title.j.l  then count = count + 1
        end
```

If the count or *weight* this loop totals is at least equal to that input as the command line argument, the book matches the retrieval criteria and its title is displayed on the user's screen.

This script is written such that the programmer does not need to keep track of how many variables any of the arrays contain. The while keyword processes items in each do loop until a null entry (the null string) is encountered. This technique works fine as long as these two conditions pertain:

❑   The script initializes each array to the null string.

❑   Each position or slot in the arrays is filled consecutively.

Its approach to array processing makes the program code independent of the number of books and keywords it must process. This flexibility would allow the same algorithm to process input from files, for example. So, it would be easy to eliminate the static assignment statements in this program and replace them with variable input read in from one or more input files. You can see that the approach this script takes to array processing provides great flexibility.

The script demonstrates that nested array processing and simple logic can provide sophisticated *weighted retrieval* by applying search terms to item descriptors. From the standpoint of Rexx arrays, it shows how to nest array-processing do loops and terminate those loops when all items in the arrays have been processed.

Associative Arrays

The sample program indexed its tables by numeric subscripts. The script processed the arrays simply by incrementing the numeric subscripts during do loops. But Rexx also allows subscripts to be variables that contain character strings. Let's discuss this approach now.

Associative arrays subscript entries by character strings. You can use them to create *key-value pairs*. Here's an example. We've created an array of months called the month array. In initializing this array, we've placed multiple assignment statements per line. We accomplish this by separating individual statements by semicolons:

```
month.1  = january   ;   month.2  = february  ;   month.3 = march     ;
month.4  = april     ;   month.5  = may       ;   month.6 = june      ;
month.7  = july      ;   month.8  = august    ;   month.9 = september ;
month.10 = october   ;   month.11 = november  ;   month.12 = december ;
```

This array associates months with their ordinal positions in the calendar. For example, if you want to know what the 12th month is, referencing month.12 returns DECEMBER. We've established a group of keys that return specific values.

Combined with the previous array, the following code returns the calendar position of any given month:

```
say 'Enter the calendar position of the month you want displayed...'
pull monthly_position .
say 'Month number' monthly_position 'is' month.monthly_position
```

If you enter 4, the script returns APRIL:

```
Enter the calendar position of the month you want displayed...
4
Month number 4 is: APRIL
```

Notice that the month is returned in uppercase letters. This is because the month names were not enclosed in quotation marks when the array values were initialized. So Rexx uppercased them. To retain lowercase alphabetics for the month names, simply enclose the initialization strings in quotation marks (as was done in the sample program that performed the weighted-retrieval algorithm). Here's how to initialize data elements to retain the lowercase month names:

```
month.1  = 'january'  ;   month.2  = 'february'  ;   month.3 = 'march'    ;
```

The month array in this problem represents a set of *key-value pairs*. A key-value pair is a simple data structure that can be used to resolve a wide range of programming problems. Let's take a look at a complete sample script that illustrates their use.

A Sample Associative Array Program

Here's a simple sample script that uses an associative array. It is a telephone area code lookup program. The user enters the name of a town in the Chicago area, and the program returns the area code of that suburb. Here's what interaction with the script looks like:

```
D:\Regina\pgms>regina code_lookup.rex
For which town do you want the area code?
Chicago
The area code for CHICAGO is 312
For which town do you want the area code?
Homewood
The area code for HOMEWOOD is 708
For which town do you want the area code?
Cincinnati
Town CINCINNATI is not in my database
For which town do you want the area code?
Zion
The area code for ZION is 847
For which town do you want the area code?
<user presses <ENTER> key and leaves the program>
```

Here's the program code:

```
/* CODE LOOKUP:                                          */
/*                                                       */
/*      Looks up the areacode for the town the user enters.   */

area. = ''       /* preinitialize all entries to the null string */

area.Chicago  = 312   ;   area.Wrigleyville = 773
area.Homewood = 708   ;   area.Geneva       = 630
area.Zion     = 847   ;   area.Schaumburg   = 847

do while town <> ''
   say 'For which town do you want the area code?'
   pull town .
   if town <> '' then do
      if area.town = ''
         then  say 'Town' town 'is not in my database'
         else  say 'The area code for' town 'is' area.town
   end
end
```

The program first initializes the entire `area` array to the null string by the single assignment statement. It sets all entries in that array to the null string (represented by two back-to-back single quotation marks `' '`):

```
area. = ''        /* preinitialize all entries to the null string */
```

Next, six assignment statements set the area codes for specific towns. This will be the *lookup table* for the area codes. This lookup table could be considered a list of key-value pairs:

```
area.Chicago  = 312   ;   area.Wrigleyville = 773
area.Homewood = 708   ;   area.Geneva       = 630
area.Zion     = 847   ;   area.Schaumburg   = 847
```

The program prompts the user to enter the name of a town:

```
say 'For which town do you want the area code?'
pull town .
```

If the array element `area.town` is equal to the null string, then this array slot was not assigned a value – the program tells the user that the town is not in the area code database. Otherwise, `area.town` represents an area code value that the script reports to the user:

```
if area.town = ''
    then  say 'Town' town 'is not in my database'
    else  say 'The area code for' town 'is' area.town
```

The program reports the desired area codes until the user enters the null string to the prompt to terminate interaction. The user enters the null string simply by pressing the <ENTER> key without entering anything.

As in the previous programming example, be sure that you understand the use of case in this sample script. The town is returned in uppercase because the tail of each array element is uppercased by Rexx. Rexx views variable names internally as uppercased. The comparison with the town name the user types in works properly because the `pull` instruction automatically translates the city name he or she enters into all uppercase letters.

To summarize, this script shows how arrays can be subscripted by *any* value (not just numeric values). This supports *content-addressable* or *associative arrays*, a data structure concept that applies to a wide range of programming problems. Here we've used it to implement a simple lookup table based on key-value pairs. Associative memory can also be applied to a wide range of more complex programming problems. The next section discusses some of these applications.

Creating Data Structures Based on Arrays

The Code Lookup program creates a *lookup table*, a simple data structure implemented as a one-dimensional array. By a *one-dimensional array* we mean that the table is accessed using only a single subscript. An array's *dimensionality* is defined by the number of subscripts coded to it.

- ❏   `array_name.1` — A one-dimension array
- ❏   `array_name.1.1` — A two-dimension array
- ❏   `array_name.1.1.1` — A three-dimension array

Arrays can have any number of dimensions to create more detailed associations. This forms the basis for creating complex data structures. Subscript strings essentially become *symbolic pointers*, access points that allow you to create content-addressable data structures. Scanning a table for a value becomes unnecessary because content-addressability provides direct access to the desired entry. Using these principles you can create data structures such as lists, trees, records, C-language *structs*, and symbolic pointer-based data structures.

In the sample program that retrieved book titles, the array named `keywords` is one-dimensional (it uses just a single subscript). The data structure it represents is a *list*. The script implements its algorithm through *list processing*.

In that script, the array named `title` has elements that are referred to either by one subscript (the book title) or by two (the descriptors associated with each title). There is a hierarchical relationship — each book has a set of descriptors. The data structure represented here is a *tree*. The logic that searches the three descriptors for a specific book performs *leaf-node processing*.

Each *root node* has the same number of *leaves* (descriptors), so we have a *balanced tree*. But Rexx does not require developers to declare in advance the number of elements an array will hold, nor that the tree be balanced. We could have any number of descriptors per book title, and we could have any number of leaves per tree. The algorithm in the program easily processes a variable number of array items and handles data structures composed of unknown numbers of elements. The Find Books program manages a *balanced tree*, or *B-tree*, but could as well handled an *unbalanced*or *skewed tree*.

In the sample program that retrieved area codes, towns and their area codes were associated by means of *key-value pairs*. This kind of data structure is widely used, for example, in lookup tables, "direct access" databases, and Perl programming. It forms the conceptual basis of the popular embedded open source database Berkeley DB. Even such a simple association can underlie high-powered application solutions.

Figure 4-2 pictorially illustrates some of the basic data structures that can easily be created by using arrays. That Rexx supports such a wide range of data structures, without itself requiring complex syntax, shows how a "simple" language can implement sophisticated processing. This is the beauty of Rexx: power based on simplicity.

Example Data Structures Based on Arrays

Element 1
Element 2
Element 3

A Simple List
or Look-up Table

Key 1	Value 1
Key 2	Value 2
Key 3	Value 3
Key 4	Value 4

Key-value Pairs

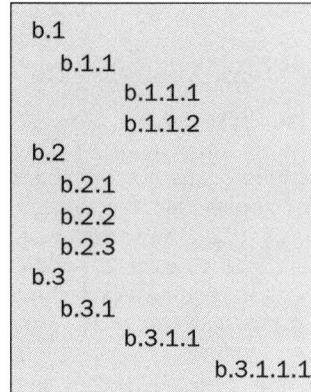

```
b.1
    b.1.1
    b.1.2
b.2
    b.2.1
    b.2.2
b.3
    b.3.1
    b.3.2
```

Balanced Tree

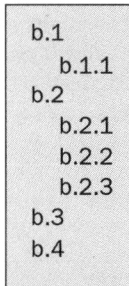

```
b.1
    b.1.1
b.2
    b.2.1
    b.2.2
    b.2.3
b.3
b.4
```

Un-Balanced Tree

```
b.1
    b.1.1
        b.1.1.1
        b.1.1.2
    b.2
        b.2.1
        b.2.2
        b.2.3
    b.3
        b.3.1
            b.3.1.1
                b.3.1.1.1
```

A Multi-level Tree
(unbalanced)

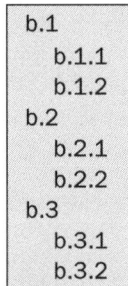

Figure 4-2

Summary

Rexx supports content-addressable arrays that can be of any dimensionality. These arrays can be initialized as an entity by referring to the array stem. However, other kinds of whole-array manipulation based on the stem are not permitted in standard Rexx. Array sizes do not have to be declared or defined prior to use, and sizes are limited only by the size of memory in most Rexx implementations.

Arrays provide a way to build the more powerful data structures that compiled languages sometimes offer and scripting languages like Rexx "lack." Symbolic pointers form the basis of content-addressable data structures. Using- content-addressable arrays, you can easily build lists, trees, records, structures, and other variable-length and variably sized data structures. Rexx simplifies the programmer's task because no complicated language elements are necessary to implement advanced data structures. The syntax remains clean and simple, even while the data structures one builds become powerful and flexible.

Test Your Understanding

1. How many subscripts can be applied to an array? How many dimensions may an array have? Must array subscripts be numeric values?

2. What operations can you perform on a group of variables by referring to an array stem? What operations are not permitted on a stem?

3. Describe two ways to process all the elements in an array. Does Rexx keep track of the number of elements in an array?

4. What kinds of data structures can be defined based on arrays? Describe three and explain how to create each.

Input and Output

Overview

Input/output, or *I/O*, is how a program interacts with its environment. Input may come from what a user types in, an input file, or another program. Program output might be written to the display, to an output file, or to a communication mechanism such as a pipe. These are just a few of the possibilities.

Rexx provides a simple-to-use, high-level I/O interface. At the same time, Rexx aims for standardization and portability across platforms. Unfortunately, this latter goal is difficult to achieve — I/O is inherently *platform-dependent*, because it relies upon the file systems and drivers the operating system provides for data management. These vary by operating system.

This chapter describes the Rexx I/O model at a conceptual level. Then it explores examples and how to code I/O. The last part of the chapter discusses some of the problems that any programming language confronts when trying to standardize I/O across platforms, some of the trade-offs involved, and how this tension has been resolved in Rexx and its many implementations.

Rexx provides an I/O model that is easy to use and as portable as possible. Section II explores the I/O extensions that many versions of Rexx offer for more sophisticated (but less portable) I/O. Chapter 15 illustrates database I/O and how to interface scripts to popular database management systems such as SQL Server, Oracle, DB2, and MySQL.

The Conceptual I/O Model

Rexx views both input and output as *streams* — a sequence of *characters*, or *bytes*. The characters in the stream have a sequence, or order. For example, when a Rexx script reads an input stream, the characters in that stream are presented to the script in the order in which they occur in the stream.

A stream may be either *transient* or *persistent*. A transient stream could be the characters a user enters through the keyboard. They are read; then they are gone. A persistent stream has a degree of permanency. Characters in a file, for example, are stored on disk until someone deletes the file containing them. Files are persistent.

For persistent streams only, Rexx maintains two separate, independent *positions:* a *read position* and a *write position.* The type of access to the persistent stream or file determines which of these positions make logical sense. For example, for a file that a script reads, the read position is important. For a file that it writes, the write position is important.

The read and write positions for any one file may be manipulated by a script independently of one another. They might be set or altered *explicitly.* Normally, they are altered *implicitly* as the natural result of read or write operations.

Programs can process streams in either of two *modes:* character by character or line by line. Rexx provides a set of functions to perform I/O in either manner. These are typically referred to as *character-oriented I/O* and *line-oriented I/O.* Figure 5-1 summarizes these two basic I/O modes.

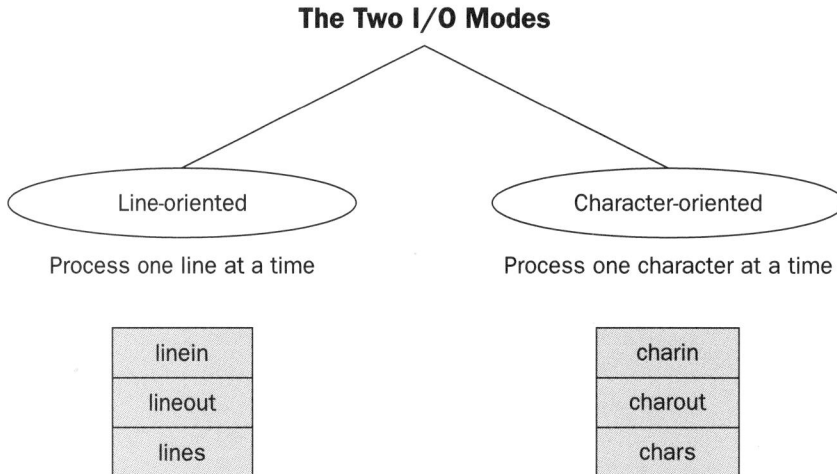

The Two I/O Modes

Line-oriented	Character-oriented
Process one line at a time	Process one character at a time

linein	charin
lineout	charout
lines	chars

Figure 5-1

A stream is typically processed in either one of the two I/O modes or the other. However, it is possible to intermix character- and line- oriented processing on a single stream.

Like many programming languages, Rexx recognizes the concept of *standard input* and *standard output.* The former is the default location from which input is read, and the latter is the default location to which output is written. These defaults are applied when no specific name is encoded in a Rexx statement as the target for an I/O operation. Standard input is normally the keyboard, and standard output is the display screen. Standard Rexx does not include the concept of a *standard error stream.*

As with variables, Rexx files are defined by their first use. They are not normally predefined or "declared." In standard Rexx, one does not explicitly "open" files for use as in most programming languages. Files do not normally need to be closed; they are closed automatically when a script ends. For most situations, this high level of automation makes Rexx I/O easy to use and convenient. For complex programs with many files, a situation in which memory is limited, or when a file needs to be closed and reopened, Rexx provides a way to explicitly close files.

Line-Oriented Standard I/O

With this conceptual background on how input/output works in Rexx, we can describe standard Rexx I/O. Let's start with I/O that considers the stream to consist of *lines*, or line-oriented I/O. Here the three basic functions for standard line I/O:

❏   linein — Reads one line from an input stream. By default this reads the line from default standard input (usually the keyboard).

❏   lineout — Writes a line to an output stream. By default this writes to standard output (usually the display screen). Returns 0 if the line was successfully written or 1 otherwise.

❏   lines — Returns either 1 or the number of lines left to read in an input stream (which could be 0).

This sample script reads all lines in an input file, and writes those containing the phrase PAYMENT OVERDUE to an output file. (A form of this simple script actually found a number of lost invoices and saved a small construction company tens of thousands of dollars!):

```
/*  FIND PAYMENTS:                                         */
/*                                                         */
/*  Reads accounts lines one by one, writes overdue payments */
/*  (containing the phrase PAYMENT OVERDUE) to an output file. */

parse arg filein fileout              /* get 2 filenames          */

do while lines(filein) > 0            /* do while a line to read */
   input_line = linein(filein)        /* read an input line       */
   if pos('PAYMENT OVERDUE',input_line) >= 1 then      /* $ Due?  */
      call lineout fileout,input_line  /* write line if $ overdue */
end
```

To run this program, enter the names of its two arguments (the input and output files) on the command line:

```
regina   find_payments.rexx   invoices_in.txt   lost_payments_list_out.txt
```

In this code, the parse arg instruction is to arg as parse pull is to pull. In other words, it performs the exact same function as its counterpart but does not translate input to uppercase. arg and parse arg both read input arguments, but arg automatically translates the input string to uppercase, whereas parse arg does not. This statement reads the two input arguments without automatically translating them to uppercase:

```
parse arg filein fileout              /* get 2 filenames          */
```

This statement:

```
do while lines(filein) > 0
```

shows how Rexx programmers often perform a read loop. The `lines` function returns a positive number if there are lines to read in the input file referred to. It returns 0 if there are none, so this is an easy way to test for the end of file. The `do` loop, then, executes repeatedly until the end of the input file is encountered.

The next program statement reads the next input line into the variable `input_line`. It reads one *line* or record, however the operating system defines a *line*:

```
input_line = linein(filein)              /* read an input line     */
```

The `if` statement uses the string function `pos`, which returns the position of the given string if it exists in the string `input_line`. Otherwise, it returns 0. So, if the character string PAYMENT OVERDUE occurs in the line read in, the next line invokes the `lineout` function to write a line to the output file:

```
if pos('PAYMENT OVERDUE',input_line) >= 1 then     /* $ Due? */
    call lineout fileout,input_line      /* write line if $ overdue */
```

There are two ways to code the `lineout` function:

```
call  lineout  fileout,input_line
```

or

```
feedback  = lineout(fileout,input_line)
```

The recommended approach uses the `call` instruction to run the `lineout` function, which automatically sets its return string in the special variable `result`. If the variable `result` is set to 0, the line was successfully written, and if it is set to 1, a failure occurred. The sample script opts for clarity of illustration over robustness and does not check `result` to verify the success of the write.

The second approach codes `lineout` as a function call, which returns a result, which is then assigned to a variable. Here we've assigned the function return code to the variable `feedback`. You'll sometimes see programmers use the variable `rc` to capture the return code, because `rc` is the Rexx *special variable* that refers to return codes:

```
rc  = lineout(fileout,input_line)
```

Now, here's something to be aware of. This coding *will not work*, because the return string from the `lineout` function has nowhere to go:

```
lineout(fileout,input_line)     /*  Do NOT do this, it will fail!  */
```

What happens here? Recall that the return code from a function is placed right into the code as a replacement for the coding of the function. So after this function executes, it will be converted to this if successful:

```
0
```

A standard rule in Rexx is that whenever the interpreter encounters something that is not Rexx code (such as instructions, expressions to resolve, or functions), Rexx passes that code to the operating system for execution. So, Rexx passes 0 to the operating system as if it were an operating system command! This causes an error, since 0 is not a valid operating system command.

We'll discuss this in more detail in Chapter 14, when we discuss how to issue operating system commands from within Rexx scripts. For now, all you have to remember is that you should either call a function or make sure that your code properly handles the function's returned result.

The lines function works slightly differently in different Rexx implementations. It always returns 0 if there are no more lines to read. But in some Rexx interpreters it returns 1 if there are more lines to read, while in others it returns the actual number of lines left to read. The latter produces a more useful result but could cause Rexx to perform heavy I/O to determine this value.

The ANSI standard clarified this situation in 1996. Today ANSI-standard Rexx has two options:

❑   lines(file_name,C) — Count. Returns the number of lines left to read.

❑   lines(file_name,N) — Normal. Returns 1 if there are lines left to read.

For backward compatibility, the second case is the default. A true ANSI-standard Rexx will return 1 if you encode the lines function without specifying the optional parameter, and there are one or more lines left to read in the file. However, some Rexx implementations will return the actual number of lines left to read instead of following the ANSI specification.

Standard Rexx does not permit explicitly opening files, but how about closing them? Rexx closes files automatically when a script ends. For most programs, this is sufficient. The exception is the case where a program opens many files and uses an exceptional amount of memory or system resources that it needs to free when it is done processing files. Another example is the situation in which a program needs to close and then reopen a file. This could happen, for example, if a program needed to sequentially process the same file twice.

How a file is closed or how its buffers are flushed is implementation-dependent. Most Rexx interpreters close a file by encoding a lineout function without any parameters beyond the filename. Just perform a write operation that writes no data:

```
call  lineout  'c:\output_file'      /* flushes the buffers and closes the file -
                                        in most Rexx implementations            */
```

The stream function is another way to close files in many implementations. stream allows you to either:

Check the state of a file

or

Issue various commands on that file

The status check is ANSI standard, but the specific commands one can issue to control a file are left to the choice of the various Rexx implementations. Here's how to issue an ANSI-standard status check on a file:

```
status_string = stream(file_name)        /* No options defaults to a STATUS check */
```

or

```
status_string = stream(file_name,'S')  /* 'S' option requests return of
                                          file STATUS                  */
```

The status values returned are those shown in the following table:

Stream Status	Meaning
READY	File is good for use.
NOTREADY	An I/O operation attempt will fail.
ERROR	File has been subjected to an invalid operation.
UNKNOWN	File status is unknown.

The commands you can issue through the stream function are completely dependent on which Rexx interpreter you use. Regina Rexx allows you to open the file for reading, writing, appending, creating, or updating; to close or flush the file, and to get its status or other file information. Regina's stream function also allows scripts to manually move the file pointers, as would be useful in directly accessing parts of a file.

The file pointers may be moved in several ways. All Rexx scripts that perform input and/or output do this *implicitly*, as the result of normal read and write operations. Scripts can also move the file pointers *explicitly* . . . but these operations are implementation-specific. Some Rexx interpreters, such as Regina, enable this via stream function commands, while others provide C-language-style seek and tell functions that go beyond the Rexx standard. Read your Rexx's documentation to see what your interpreter supports. Part II goes into how specific Rexx interpreters provide this feature and offers sample scripts.

The lineout, charout, linein, and charin functions provide the most standardized way to explicitly control file positions, but care is advised. Most scripts just perform standard read and write operations and let Rexx itself manage the file read and write positions. Later in this chapter we discuss alternatives for those cases where you require advanced file I/O.

Character-Oriented Standard I/O

The previous section looked at line-oriented I/O, where Rexx reads or writes a line of data at a time. Recall from the introduction that Rexx also supports *character-oriented I/O*, input and output by individual characters. Here the three basic functions for standard character I/O:

❑   charin — Returns one or more characters read from an input stream. By default this reads one character from default standard input (usually the keyboard).

❑ charout — Writes zero or more characters to an output stream. By default this writes to standard output (usually the display screen). Returns 0 if all characters were successfully written. Or, it returns the number of characters remaining after a failed write.

❑ output (usually the display screen) — Returns 0 if all characters were successfully written. Or, it returns the number of characters remaining after a failed write.

❑ chars — Returns either 1 or the number of characters left to read in an input stream (which could be 0).

This sample program demonstrates character-oriented input and output. It reads characters or *bytes*, one by one, from a file. It writes them out in hexadecimal form by using the charout function. The script is a general-purpose "character to hexadecimal" translator. Here is its code:

```
/*   TRANSLATE CHARS:                                          */
/*                                                             */
/*   Reads characters one by one, shows what they are in hex format */

parse arg filein fileout .     /* get input & output filenames    */
out_string = ''                /* initialize output string to null */

do j=1 while chars(filein) > 0      /* do while a character to read */
    out_string = ' ' c2x(charin(filein))      /* convert it to hex    */
    call charout ,out_string                  /* write to display     */
    call charout fileout,out_string           /* write to a file too */
end
```

The script illustrates the use of the chars function to determine when the input file contains no more data to process:

```
do j=1 while chars(filein) > 0      /* do while a character to read */
```

This character-oriented chars function is used in a manner similar to the line-oriented lines function to identify the *end-of-file* condition. Figure 5-2 below summarizes common ways to test for the end of a file.

Testing for End of File

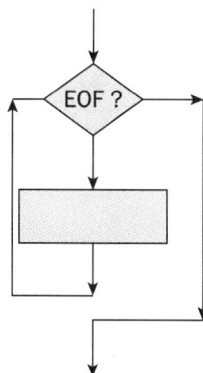

Common end of file tests –

· The "lines" function
· The "chars" function

Less common end of file tests –

· Scan for a known value
  (eg, user enters a null line to the script,
  or a value like "END" or "EXIT")
· The "stream" function
· SIGNAL ON NOTREADY error condition trap

Figure 5-2

73

The script uses the conversion function `c2x` to convert each input character into its hexadecimal equivalent. This displays the byte code for these characters:

```
out_string = '  ' c2x(charin(filein))        /* convert it to hex   */
```

This script illustrates the `charout` function twice. The first time it includes a comma to replace the output filename, so the character is written to the default output device (the display screen). The second `charout` function includes an output filename and writes characters out to that file:

```
call charout ,out_string                     /* write to display    */
call charout fileout,out_string              /* write to a file too */
```

Let's take a look at some sample output from this script. Assume that the input file to this script consists of two lines containing this information:

```
line1
line2
```

The hexadecimal equivalent of each character in the character string `line1` is as follows:

```
  l    i    n    e    1
 6C   69   6E   65   31
```

With this information, we can interpreter the script's output. The script output appears as shown, when run under Linux, Unix, Windows, DOS, and the MacOS. Linux, Unix, and BSD terminate each line with a line feed character (x'0A'). This character is also referred to as the *newline* character or sometimes as the *linefeed*. Windows ends each line with the pair of characters for carriage return and line feed (x'0D0A'). DOS does the same as Windows, while the Macintosh uses only the carriage return to mark the end of line:

```
Linux:    6C  69  6E  65  31  0A  6C  69  6E  65  32  0A
Unix:     6C  69  6E  65  31  0A  6C  69  6E  65  32  0A
Windows:  6C  69  6E  65  31  0D  0A  6C  69  6E  65  32  0D  0A
DOS:      6C  69  6E  65  31  0D  0A  6C  69  6E  65  32  0D  0A  1A
MacOS:    6C  69  6E  65  31  0D  6C  69  6E  65  32  0D
```

Some operating systems mark the end of the file by a special *end-of-file character*. This byte occurs once at the very end of the file. DOS is an example. It writes its end-of-file character Control-Z or x'1A' at the very end of the file. Windows operating systems may optionally contain this character as the last in the file (for compatibility reasons) but one rarely sees this anymore.

This example shows two things. First, what Rexx calls *character I/O* is really "byte-oriented" I/O. Bytes are read one by one, regardless of their meaning to underlying operating system and how it may use *special characters* in its concept of a file system. Rexx character I/O reads every byte in the file, including the end-of-line or other special characters.

Second, character I/O yields platform-dependent results. This is because different operating systems manage their files in different ways. Some embed *special characters* to denote line end, others don't, and the characters they use vary. Character I/O reads these special characters without interpreting their meanings. Line-oriented I/O strips them out. If you want only to read lines of data or I/O records in your script, use line-oriented I/O. If you need to read *all* the bytes in the file, use character I/O.

Character I/O is easy to understand and to use. But it is often platform-dependent. If you're concerned about code portability, be sure to reference the operating system manuals and code to handle all situations. Or, stick to line-oriented I/O, which is inherently more portable.

Conversational I/O

A user interaction with a script is termed a *conversation* or *dialogue*. The interactive process is called *conversational I/O*. When writing a Rexx script that interacts with a user, one normally assumes that the user sees program output on a display screen and enters input through the keyboard. These are the default input and output streams for Rexx.

To output information to the user, code the `say` instruction. As we've seen, the operand on `say` can be any expression (such as a list of literals and variables to concatenate). `say` is equivalent to this call to `lineout`, except that `say` does not set the special variable `result`:

```
call  lineout  , [expression]
```

The comma indicates that the instruction targets *standard output*, normally the user's display screen.

Use `pull` to read a string from the user and automatically translate it to uppercase, or use `parse pull` to read a string without the uppercase translation. Both instructions read user input into a *template*, or list of variables. Discard any unwanted input beyond the variable list by encoding a period (sometimes referred to as the *placeholder variable*).

This statement reads a single input string and assigns the first three words of that string to the three variables. If the user enters anything more than three words, Rexx discards it because we've encoded the period placeholder variable at the end of the line:

```
parse  pull  input_1  input_2  input_3  .
```

Redirected I/O

I/O *redirection* means you can write a program using conversational I/O, but then redirect the input and/or output to other sources. Without changing your program, you could alter its input from the keyboard to an input file. The `pull` or `parse` instructions in the program would not have to be changed to make this work. Similarly, you could redirect a script's `say` instructions to write output to a file instead of the display screen, without changing your program code.

Here is how to redirect I/O. Just run the script using the redirection symbols shown in this table:

Redirection Symbol	Meaning
>	Redirects output to a new file. Creates a new file or overwrites an existing file if one exists with that filename.
>>	Appends (adds on to) an existing file. Creates a new output file if one does not already exist having the filename.
<	Redirects input from the specified file

How's how to invoke the Four-Letter Words program of Chapter 3 with input from a file instead of the keyboard:

```
regina  four_letter_words.rexx  <four_letter_words.input
```

The file `four_letter_words.input` consists of one word per line (so it conforms to the program's expectation that it will read one word in response to each prompt it gives). Here's how to give the script input from a file and redirect its output to a file named `output.txt` as well:

```
regina  four_letter_words.rexx  <four_letter_words.input  >output.txt
```

Redirected I/O is a very powerful concept and a useful testing tool. You can write programs and change their input source or output destination *without changing the script*!

But redirection is operating-system-specific. Operating systems that support redirected I/O include those in the Linux, Unix, BSD, Windows, and DOS families.

A warning about Windows — members in the Windows family of operating systems do not handle I/O redirection consistently. Different versions of Windows handle I/O redirection in slightly different ways. This has long been an issue for programmers who want their programs to run across many Windows versions. This is not a Rexx issue, but rather an inconsistency in the behavior of Windows operating systems. If you rely on redirection under Windows, you will have to test your scripts on each version of the operating system they run on to ferret out any Windows inconsistencies.

I/O Issues

I/O is operating system dependent and thus presents a difficult issue for any programming language. The reason is the inherent tension between an I/O model that is easy to use, easy to understand, and portable — versus the desire to take advantage of operating-system-specific features for file system manipulation.

Rexx always promotes ease of use and portability. Fitting with this philosophy, simplicity trumps OS-specific features and maximizing I/O performance. So, the ANSI standard Rexx I/O model is simple and portable. It does not take advantage of OS-specific I/O features or optimize I/O by platform.

Standard Rexx recognizes the trade-off between I/O portability and OS-specific I/O features by including functions such as `stream` and the `options` instruction, which are open ended and permit operands beyond the ANSI standard. This allows Rexx interpreters to add I/O extensions within the context of the ANSI standard that go beyond the standard to leverage OS-specific features.

The second section of the book describes the I/O extensions that different Rexx interpreters provide to leverage OS- specific I/O features. *Remember that all Rexx interpreters, whatever addtional I/O extensions they offer, still provide the standard Rexx line-oriented and character-oriented I/O described in this chapter.*

This chapter assumes the user interface to consist of a screen display and keyboard, and that disk I/O means manipulating data residing in files. Of course, many programs require more advanced I/O and different forms of user interfaces. Upcoming chapters cover these topics. Chapters 15 and 16, for example, describe and illustrate both database I/O and screen I/O using various GUI packages. Chapter 17 discusses Web interfaces for Rexx scripts. Section II illustrates the I/O extensions in many Rexx interpreters that provide more sophisticated file processing.

Summary

This chapter provides an overview of the Rexx I/O model and how it is implemented in standard functions for line- and character-oriented I/O. We discussed conversational I/O and how to redirect I/O under operating systems that support it. Redirection is a powerful debugging tool and provides great flexibility, because the source of input and target for output for scripts can be altered *without changing* the scripts themselves. The flexibility that redirection provides is very useful during script testing and debugging.

Two I/O related topics will be covered in upcoming chapters. The *external data queue* or *stack* is an area of memory that can be used to support I/O operations. The second important topic is I/O error handling. Both are covered in future chapters.

Upcoming chapters also cover I/O through interface packages, such as databases, GUI screen handlers, Web server interfaces, and similar tools.

Test Your Understanding

1. What are the two basic kinds of standard Rexx input/output? Why would you use one approach versus the other? Which is most portable across various operating systems?

2. What kinds of file control commands can you issue through the `stream` function? Do these vary by Rexx implementation? What file statuses does the `stream` function return?

3. Describe the two ways in which you can invoke an I/O function like `linein` or `charout`. How do you capture the return code from I/O functions? What happens if you fail to?

4. Do you need to close a file after using it? Under what conditions might this be appropriate? How is it done?

5. If you require very powerful or sophisticated I/O, what options does Rexx offer?

String Manipulation

Overview

String manipulation means parsing, splicing, and pasting together *character strings*, sets of consecutive characters. Rexx excels at string manipulation. This is important for a wider variety of reasons than may be apparent at first. Many programming problems are readily conceived of as operations on strings. For example, building commands to issue to the operating system is a really a string-concatenation exercise. Analyzing the feedback from those commands once they are issued means text analysis and pattern matching. Much of the data formatting and reporting that IT organizations perform requires string processing. Data validation and cleansing require text analysis.

In a broad sense, many programming problems are essentially exercises in "symbol manipulation." *String processing* is a means to achieve generic symbol manipulation.

List processing is another example. Entire programming languages (such as LISP) have been built on the paradigm of processing lists. A list can be considered simply a group of values strung together. Manipulating character strings thus becomes a vehicle for list processing.

The applications that these techniques underlie are endless. Everything from report writing, to printing mailing labels, to editing documents, to creating scripts for systems administration, to scripts that configure the environment, rely on string manipulation.

This chapter introduces Rexx's outermost operators, functions, and pattern-matching capabilities. We show you the features by which Rexx supports string processing so that you will combine them in new ways to address the programming problems you face.

Concatenation and Parsing

Concatenation is the joining together of strings into larger strings. *Bifurcation* refers to splitting a string into two parts. *Parsing* is the inspection of character strings, to analyze them, extract pieces, or break them into components. For example, parsing a U.S. telephone number could separate it into its constituent parts—a country code, an area code, the prefix and suffix. *Pattern matching* is the scanning of strings for certain patterns. Together, these operations constitute *string manipulation* or *text processing*. Figure 6-1 summarizes the major string operations.

Basic String Operations

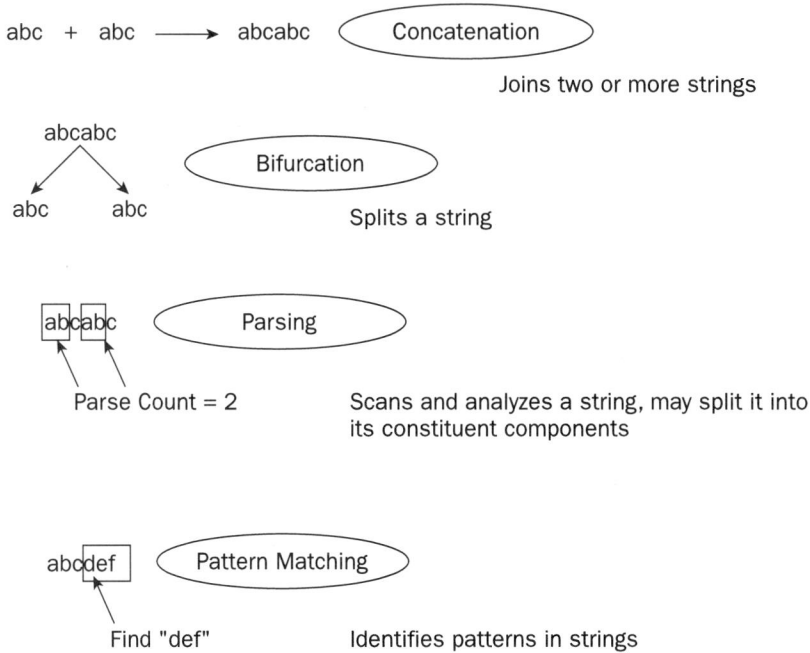

abc + abc ⟶ abcabc   (Concatenation)

Joins two or more strings

abcabc

abc   abc   (Bifurcation)

Splits a string

abcabc   (Parsing)

Parse Count = 2   Scans and analyzes a string, may split it into its constituent components

abcdef   (Pattern Matching)

Find "def"   Identifies patterns in strings

Figure 6-1

We've already seen that Rexx supports three ways of concatenating strings. These are:

❑   *Implicit concatenation* with one blank between the symbols

❑   *Abuttal,* in which immediately adjacent symbols are concatenated without an intervening blank

❑   *Explicit concatenation* via the concatenation operator, ||

The three styles of concatenation can be intermixed within statements. Concatenation may occur wherever expressions can be coded. Here are some sample statements run in sequence:

```
apple='-Apple'
say  'Candy' || ' ' || apple || ' ' || 'Rodeo'
                              /* displays: 'Candy -Apple Rodeo'        */
say  'Candy'apple             /* displays: 'Candy-Apple'               */
say  'Candy' apple            /* displays: 'Candy -Apple'              */
say  'Candy'apple apple 'Rodeo'  /* displays: 'Candy-Apple -Apple Rodeo  */
```

We've also seen several simple examples of string parsing. The arg instruction retrieves the arguments sent in to a program or internal function and places them into a list of variables. Its general format is:

```
arg  [template]
```

The *template* is a list of symbols separated by blanks and/or patterns. The pull instruction operates in the same manner as arg, reading and parsing a string input by the user into a list of variables. The input string is parsed (separated) into the variables in the list, positionally from leftmost to rightmost, as separated by one or more spaces. The spaces delimiting the strings are stripped out, and the variables do not contain any leading or trailing blanks.

There are two special cases to consider when a script reads and parses input by the arg or pull instructions. The first is the situation in which more arguments are passed in to the routine than the routine expects. Look at this case:

```
user input:   one  2  three  '4'
program:      pull a b c

a contains: ONE
b contains: 2
c contains: THREE  '4'
```

The last (rightmost) variable c in the variable list contains all remaining (unparsed) information. The rule is: *If you code too few input variables to hold all those that are input, the final variable in the input list contains the extra information.* Remember that you could just ignore this extra information by coding a period:

```
program:      pull  a  b  c  .
```

Now the variables will contain:

```
a contains: ONE
b contains: 2
c contains: THREE
```

The '4' is simply eliminated from the input by the *placeholder variable*, the period at the end of the pull instruction input list or *template*.

The second situation to consider is if too few arguments are passed in to the receiving routine. Say that the script issues a pull instruction to read input from the user. If too few elements are input by the user, any variables in the list that cannot be assigned values are set to null:

```
user input: one  2
program:    pull a b c

a contains: ONE
b contains: 2
c contains: ''         /*  c is set to the null string  */
```

Variable c is set to the null string (represented by back-to-back quotation marks, ' '). This is different from saying that the variable is uninitialized, which would mean its value is its own name in uppercase. If the last variable were uninitialized, it would be set to 'C'.

pull is short for the instruction:

```
parse  upper  pull  [template]
```

The *template* is a list of symbols separated by blanks and/or patterns. upper means uppercase translation occurs. Its presence is optional on the parse instruction. To avoid uppercase translation, just leave the upper keyword out of the parse instruction.

Let's look at the parse instruction in more detail. This form of the instruction parses an expression:

```
parse  [upper]  value  [expression]  with  [template]
```

The *expression* evaluates to some string that is parsed according to the *template*. The template provides for three basic kinds of parsing:

❑   By words (character strings delimited by blanks or spaces)

❑   By pattern (one character or a string other than blanks by which the expression string will be analyzed and separated)

❑   By numeric pattern (numbers that specify column starting positions for each substring within the expression)

Figure 6-2 below illustrates these three parsing methods.

Parsing by Template

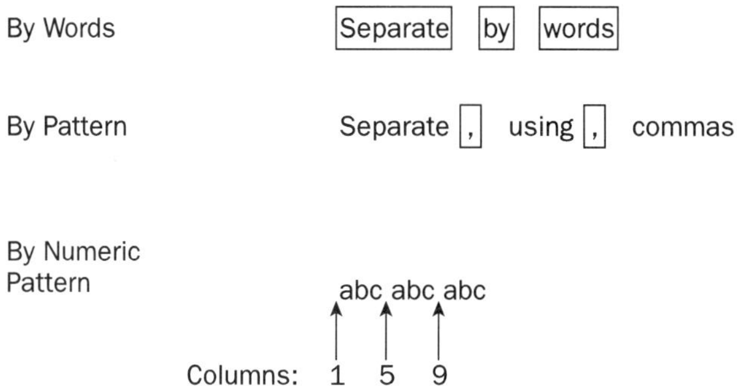

Figure 6-2

You are already familiar with parsing by words. This is where we use parse to separate a list of elements into individual components based on intervening blanks. Let's parse an international telephone number as an example.

```
phone = '011-311-458-3758'
parse  value  phone  with  a   b
```

This is a parse by *words* or blank separators. Since there are no blank separators anywhere within the input string, the results of the `parse` instruction are:

```
a = 011-311-458-3758
b = ''                 /* b is assigned the null string. */
```

Obviously, the dash (-) here is the separator, not the blank. Let's try parsing by *pattern*, using the dash (-) as the separator or *delimiter*:

```
parse value phone with country_code  '-'  area_code  '-'  prefix  '-'  suffix
```

The results are:

```
country_code = 011
area_code = 311
prefix = 458
suffix = 3758
```

If there were more information in the input variable, regardless of whether or not it contained more dash delimiters, it all would have been placed into the last variable in the list, `suffix`. If there are too few strings in the input variable list, according to the parsing delimiter, then extra variables in the variable list are assigned null string(s).

The *pattern* can be supplied in a variable. This yields greater programmability and flexibility. In this case, enclose it in parentheses when specifying it in the template:

```
sep = '-'         /* the dash will be the delimiter ... */
parse value phone with country_code (sep) area_code (sep) prefix (sep) suffix
```

This `parse` instruction gives the same results as the previous one with the hardcoded delimiter dashes. The advantage to placing the separator pattern in a variable is that we can now parse a different, international designation for this phone number using the same `parse` instruction, just by changing the separator inside the pattern variable:

```
phone = '011.311.458.3758'
sep = '.'         /* The period is the Swiss delimiter for phone numbers  ... */
parse value phone with country_code (sep) area_code (sep) prefix (sep) suffix
```

The same `parse` instruction properly separates the constituent pieces of the phone number with this different delimiter. So, supplying the separator pattern in a variable gives scripts flexibility in parsing operations.

Now parse by *numbers*. These represent *column positions* in the input. Run:

```
phone = '011-311-458-3758'
parse  value  phone  with country_code 5 area_code  9 prefix 13 suffix
```

Here are the results from this statement:

```
country_code = 011-
area_code = 311-
prefix = 458-
suffix = 3758
```

Oops! You can see that parsing by numbers goes strictly by column positions. Delimiters don't count. Add these extra columns positions to eliminate the unwanted separators:

```
parse value phone with country_code  4  5  area_code  8  9 prefix  12  13  suffix
```

This gives the intended results because it parses out the unwanted separators by column positions:

```
country_code = 011
area_code = 311
prefix = 458
suffix = 3758
```

These are *absolute* column positions. Each refers to an absolute column position, counting from the beginning of the string.

Placing a plus (+) or minus (–) sign before any number makes its position *relative* to the previously specified number in the list (or 1 for the first number). You can mix absolute and relative positions together in the same template, and even use negative numbers (which move the relative position backwards to the left) but be careful. Unless you have a situation that really requires it, jamming all the parsing into one complex statement is rarely worth it. Just code a series of two or three simpler statements instead. Then others will be able to read and understand your code.

This example properly parses the phone number with both absolute and relative column numbers. The plus signs (+) indicate relative numbers. In this case, each advances the column position one character beyond the previous absolute column indicator:

```
parse value phone with country_code 4  +1 area_code 8  +1 prefix 12  +1 suffix
```

This statement produces the desired result:

```
country_code = 011
area_code = 311
prefix = 458
suffix = 3758
```

With this background, you can see that the `parse` instruction provides real string-processing power. This example assigns the entire telephone number in the variable `phone` to three new variables (kind of like a three-part assignment statement):

```
parse value phone with phone_1  1  phone_2  1  phone_3
```

Now the variables `phone_1`, `phone_2`, and `phone_3` all contain the same value as `phone`:

```
phone   = '011.311.458.3758'

phone_1 = '011.311.458.3758'
phone_2 = '011.311.458.3758'
phone_3 = '011.311.458.3758'
```

In all the examples thus far, the input string was not changed. But it can be if encoded as part of the variable list. Here's an example. Say that we have this variable:

```
employee_name = 'Deanna Troy'
```

This statement simply translates the employee's name into uppercase and places it back into the same variable:

```
parse  upper  value  employee_name  with  employee_name
```

This statement strips off the employee's first name and places it into the variable `first_name`. Then it puts the remainder of the name back into the `employee_name` variable:

```
parse  value  employee_name  with  first_name  employee_name
```

The `value` keyword refers to any expression. You may also see the keyword `var` encoded when referring specifically to a variable. In this case, you should not code the `with` keyword. This statement using `var` gives the exact same results as the previous example with `value` and `with`:

```
parse  var employee_name  first_name  employee_name
```

A Sample Program

With this introduction to parsing, here's a sample program to illustrate parsing techniques. This script preprocesses the "load file" used to load data into a relational database such as DB2, Oracle, SQL Server, or MySQL. The script performs some simple data verification on the input file prior to loading that data into the database. This "data-cleansing" script ensures the data we load into the database is clean before we run the database load utility. A script like this is useful because the data cleansing that database utilities typically perform is limited.

Here's how the data will look after it's loaded into the relational table:

EMP_NO	FNAME	LNAME	DEPT_NO
10001	George	Bakartt	307
10002	Bill	Wall	204
10003	Beverly	Crusher	305

Databases like DB2, Oracle, and SQL Server accept input data in several different file formats. Two of the most popular are *comma-delimited files* and *record-oriented* or *column-position files*. Here's an example of a *comma-delimited file*:

```
10001,"George","Bakartt","307"
10002,"Bill","Wall","204"
10003,"Beverly","Crusher","305"
1x004,"joe","Zip","305"
10005,"Sue","stans","3x5"
```

Commas separate the four input fields. In this example, all character strings are enclosed in double quotation marks. Under operating systems that employ a file type, the file type for comma-delimited ASCII files is typically `*.del`. This input file is named `database_input.del`.

Here is the other kind of file, a *record file*. Data fields start in specific columns. Fields are padded with blanks, as necessary, so that the next field starts in its required column. Where file types are used this file is typically of extension `*.asc`, so we've named this file `database_input.asc`:

```
10001George Bakartt307
10002Bill   Wall   204
10003BeverlyCrusher305
1x004joe    Zip    305
10005Sue    stans  3x5
```

The program reads either of these two input file types. It determines which kind of file it is processing by scanning the input text for commas. If the data contains commas, the program assumes it is dealing with a comma-delimited ASCII file.

Then the program performs some simple data verification. It ensures that the EMP_NO and DEPT_NO data items are numeric, and that the first and last names both begin with capital letters. The script writes any errors it finds to the display. Here's the program:

```
/*  DATABASE INPUT VERIFICATION:                                */
/*                                                              */
/*      Determines type of database input file (*.del or *.asc). */
/*      Reads the input data as appropriate to that file type.  */
/*      Verifies EMP_NO and DEPT_NO are numeric, names are cap alpha. */

arg input_file .                /* read input filename from user */
c = ','                         /* variable C contains one comma */

do while lines(input_file) > 0
   input_line = linein(input_file)    /* read a line from input file   */

   /* get EMP_NO, FNAME, LNAME, DEPT_NO from *.DEL or *.ASC file        */

   if pos(c,input_line) > 0 then do      /* File is delimited ASCII.   */
      parse value input_line with emp_no (c) fname (c) lname (c) dept_no
      fname   = strip(fname,B,'"')
      lname   = strip(lname,B,'"')       /* remove quote " marks       */
      dept_no = strip(dept_no,,'"')
      end
```

```
      else do
         parse value input_line with emp_no 6 fname 13 lname 20 dept_no
         fname  = strip(fname)
         lname  = strip(lname)                  /* remove trailing blanks  */
      end

      say 'Input line:' emp_no fname lname dept_no

      /* Ensure EMP_NO & DEPT_NO are numeric */

      if datatype(emp_no) \= 'NUM'  |  datatype(dept_no) \= 'NUM' then
         say 'EMP_NO or DEPT_NO are not numeric:' emp_no dept_no

      /* Ensure the two names start with a capital letter */

      if verify(substr(fname,1,1),'ABCDEFGHIJKLMNOPQRSTUVWXYZ') > 0 then
         say "First name doesn't start with a capital letter:" fname
      if verify(substr(lname,1,1),'ABCDEFGHIJKLMNOPQRSTUVWXYZ') > 0 then
         say "Last name doesn't start with a capital letter:" lname

   end
```

So that we can easily feed it either kind of file to process, the script accepts the filename as an input parameter. This technique of reading the name of the file to process from the command line is common. It offers more flexibility than "hardcoding" the filename into the script.

To start off, the script reads the first line of input data and determines whether it is processing a comma-delimited input file or a record-oriented file by this code:

```
   if pos(c,input_line) > 0 then do      /* file is delimited ascii */
```

The pos built-in function returns the character position of the comma (represented by the variable c) within the target string. If the returned value is greater than 0, a comma is present in the input line, and the program assumes that it is dealing with comma-delimited input. If the script finds no comma in the input line, it assumes that it is dealing with a record-oriented input file.

If the program determines that it is working with a comma-delimited input file, it issues this parse instruction to split the four fields from the input line into their respective variables:

```
   parse value input_line with emp_no (c) fname (c) lname (c) dept_no
```

This parse statement strips data elements out of the input string according to comma delimiters. But there is a problem. The second, third, and fourth data elements were enclosed in double quotation marks in the input file. To remove these leading and trailing quotation marks, we use the built-in strip function:

```
   fname    = strip(fname,B,'"')
   lname    = strip(lname,B,'"')               /* remove quote " marks    */
   dept_no  = strip(dept_no,,'"')
```

The B operand stands for Both—strip out *both* leading and trailing double quotation marks. Other strip function options are L for *leading* only and T for *trailing* only. Both is the default, so as the third line in the previous example shows, we don't need to explicitly code it. Instead, we just show that parameter is missing by coding two commas back-to-back. The final parameter in the `strip` function encloses the character to remove within quotation marks. Here we enclosed the double quotation marks (") within two single quotation marks, so that `strip` will remove double quotation marks from the variable's contents.

If the script does not find a comma in the input line, it assumes that it is dealing with a file whose data elements are located starting in specific columns. So, the script employs a *parse by number* statement, where the numbers specify column starting positions:

```
parse value input_line with emp_no 6 fname 13 lname 20 dept_no
```

If you program in languages like COBOL or Pascal, you might recognize this as what is often referred to as *record I/O*. Languages like C, C++, and C# call this an I/O *structure*, or *struct*. Chapter 5 showed that Rexx's stream I/O model is simple, yet you can see that it is powerful enough to easily perform record I/O by parsing the input in this manner. Part of the beauty of Rexx is that it is so easy to perform such operations, without needing special syntax or hard-to-code features in the language to accomplish them.

After the parsing by number, the record input may contain trailing blanks for the two names, so these statements remove them:

```
fname   = strip(fname)
lname   = strip(lname)                  /* remove trailing blanks  */
```

Now that it has decoded the file and normalized the data elements, the program can get to work and verify the data contents. This statement uses the `datatype` built-in function to verify that the EMP_NO and DEPT_NO fields (the first and last data elements in each input record) are numeric. If `datatype` does not return the character string NUM, then one of these fields is not numeric and an error message is displayed:

```
if datatype(emp_no) \= 'NUM'  |  datatype(dept_no) \= 'NUM' then
    say 'EMP_NO or DEPT_NO are not numeric:' emp_no dept_no
```

The `logical or` (|) is used to test both data elements in one `if` instruction. If either is not numeric, the error message is displayed.

Finally, the script uses the `verify` built-in function to ensure that the two names both start with a capital letter. First, this nested use of the `substr` built-in function returns the first letter of the name:

```
substr(fname,1,1)
```

Then the `verify` function tests this letter to ensure that it's a member of the string consisting of all capital letters:

```
if verify(substr(fname,1,1),'ABCDEFGHIJKLMNOPQRSTUVWXYZ') > 0 then
    say "First name doesn't start with a capital letter:" fname
```

The *nesting* of the `substr` function means that we have coded one function (`substr`) within another (`verify`). Rexx resolves the innermost function first. The result of the innermost function is then plunked right into the code at the position formerly occupied by that function. So, the `substr` function returns the first letter of the variable `fname`, which then becomes the first parameter within the parentheses for the `verify` function.

Pretty nifty, eh? Rexx allows you to nest functions to an arbitrary depth. We do not recommend nesting beyond a single level or else the code can become too complicated. We'll provide an example of deeper nesting (and how it becomes complicated!) later in this chapter.

It's easy to code for *intermediate results* by breaking up the nesting into two (or more) statements. This example shows how to eliminate the nested function to simplify the code. It produces the exact same result as our nested example:

```
first_letter = substr(fname,1,1)
if verify(first_letter,'ABCDEFGHIJKLMNOPQRSTUVWXYZ') > 0 then
```

After the script runs, here is its output for the sample data we viewed earlier:

```
D:\Regina\hf>regina database_input.rexx database_input.asc
Input line: 10001 George Baklarz 307
Input line: 10002 Bill Wong 304
Input line: 10003 Beverly Crusher 305
Input line: 1x004 joe Zip 305
EMP_NO or DEPT_NO are not numeric: 1x004 305
First name doesn't start with a capital letter: joe
Input line: 10005 Sue stans 3x5
EMP_NO or DEPT_NO are not numeric: 10005 3x5
Last name doesn't start with a capital letter: stans
```

The last two lines of the input data contained several errors. Parsing techniques and string functions together enabled the program to identify these errors.

String Functions

The `parse` instruction provides syntactically simple, but operationally sophisticated parsing. You can resolve many string-processing problems with it. Rexx also includes over 30 string-manipulation functions, a few of which the sample script above illustrates.

This section describes more of the string functions. A later section in this chapter discusses the eight outermost functions that are *word-oriented*. The *word-oriented functions* process strings on the basis of words, where a *word* is defined as a character string delimited by blanks or spaces. For example, this string consists of a list of 16 words:

```
now is the time for all good men to come to the aid of their country
```

Before we proceed, here is a quick summary of Rexx's string functions (see Appendix C for full coding details of these and all other Rexx functions):

❑   `abbrev` — Tells if one string is equal to the first characters of another

❑   `center` — Centers a string within blanks or other *pad* characters

❑   changestr — Changes all occurrences of one string within another to a specified string

❑   compare — Tells if two strings are equal (like using the = operator)

❑   copies — Returns a string concatenated to itself n times

❑   countstr — Counts how many times one string appears within another

❑   datatype — Verifies string contents based on a variety of "data type" tests

❑   delstr — Deletes a substring from within a string

❑   insert — Inserts one string into another

❑   lastpos — Returns the last occurrence of one string within another

❑   left — Returns the first n characters of a string, or it can left-justify a string

❑   length — Returns the length of a string

❑   overlay — Overlays one string onto another starting at a specified position in the target

❑   pos — Returns the position of one string within another

❑   reverse — Reverses the characters of a string

❑   right — Returns the last n characters of a string, or it can right-justify a string

❑   strip — Strips leading and/or trailing blanks (or other characters) from a string

❑   substr — Returns a substring from within a string

❑   translate — Transforms characters of a string to another set of characters,
                as directed by two "translation strings"

❑   verify — verifies that all characters in a string are part of some defined set

❑   xrange — Returns a string of all valid character encodings

The changestr and countstr functions were added by the ANSI-1996 standard. Rexx implementations that meet the TRL-2 standard of 1990 but not the ANSI-1996 standard may not have these two functions. This is one of the few differences between the TRL-2 and ANSI-1996 standards (which are fully enumerated in Chapter 13). Regina Rexx fully meets the ANSI-1996 standard and includes these two functions.

Here's a simple program that demonstrates the use of the abbrev, datatype, length, pos, translate, and verify string functions. The script reads in four command-line arguments and applies data verification tests to them. The script displays any inaccurate parameters.

```
/*   VERIFY ARGUMENTS:                                            */
/*                                                                */
/*      This program verifies 4 input arguments by several criteria.  */

parse arg first  second  third  fourth  .   /* get the arguments    */

/* First parm must be a valid abbreviation for TESTSTRING         */

if abbrev('TESTSTRING',first,4) = 0 then
```

```
    say 'First parm must be a valid abbreviation for TESTSTRING:' first

/* Second parm must consist only of digits and be under 5 bytes long */

if datatype(second) \= 'NUM' then
    say 'Second parm must be numeric:' second
if length(second) > 4 then
    say 'Second parm must be under 5 bytes in length:' second

/* Third parm must occur as a substring somewhere in the first parm  */

if pos(third,first) = 0 then
    say 'Third parm must occur within the first:' third first

/* Fourth parm translated to uppercase must contain only letters ABC */

if fourth = '' then
    say 'You must enter a fourth parameter, none was entered'
uppercase = translate(fourth)     /* translate 4th parm to uppercase */
if verify(uppercase,'ABC') > 0 then
    say 'Fourth parm in uppercase contains letters other than ABC:' fourth
```

Here's an example of running this program with parameters it considers correct:

```
c:\Regina\pgms> regina verify_arguments TEST 1234 TEST abc
```

Here's an example where incorrect parameters were input:

```
c:\Regina\pgms>regina verify_arguments TEXT 12345 TEST abcdef
First parm  must be a valid abbreviation for TESTSTRING: TEXT
Second parm must be under 5 bytes in length: 12345
Third parm must occur within the first: TEST TEXT
Fourth parm in uppercase contains letters other than ABC: abcdef
```

Let's discuss the string functions this code illustrates.

The first parameter must be a valid abbreviation for a longer term. Where would you use this function? An example would be a program that processes the commands that a user enters on a command line. The system must determine that the abbreviation entered is both valid and that it uniquely specifies which command is intended. The abbrev function allows you to specify how many characters the user must enter that match the beginning of the target string. Here, the user must enter at least the four letters TEST for a valid match:

```
if abbrev('TESTSTRING',first,4) = 0 then
    say 'First parm must be a valid abbreviation for TESTSTRING:' first
```

The second parameter the user enters must be numeric (it must be a valid Rexx number). The datatype function returns the string NUM if this is the case, otherwise it returns the string CHAR:

```
if datatype(second) \= 'NUM' then
    say 'Second parm must be numeric:' second
```

`datatype` can also be used to check for many other conditions, for example, if a string is alphanumeric, binary, lowercase, mixed case, uppercase, a whole number, a hexadecimal number, or a valid symbol.

Using the `length` function allows the program to determine if the second parameter contains more than four characters:

```
if length(second) > 4 then
    say 'Second parm must be under 5 bytes in length:' second
```

The third parameter must be a substring of the first parameter. The `pos` function returns the starting position of a substring within a string. If the substring does not occur within the target string, it returns 0:

```
if pos(third,first) = 0 then
    say 'Third parm must occur within the first:' third first
```

This code ensures that the user entered a fourth parameter. If a fourth parameter was not entered, the argument will have been set to the null string (represented by the two immediately adjacent single quotation marks):

```
if fourth = '' then
    say 'You must enter a fourth parameter, none was entered'
```

Finally, when translated to uppercase, the fourth parameter must not contain any letters other than A, B, or C. Using the `translate` function with a single parameter translates the fourth argument to uppercase:

```
uppercase = translate(fourth)        /* translate 4th parm to uppercase */
```

Use the `verify` function to ensure that all characters in a string are members of some set of characters. This `verify` statement ensures that all the characters in the string named `uppercase` are members of its second parameter, hardcoded here as the literal string ABC. If this is not the case, the `verify` function returns the position of the first character violating the rule:

```
if verify(uppercase,'ABC') > 0 then
    say 'Fourth parm in uppercase contains letters other than ABC:' fourth
```

The Rexx string functions are pretty straightforward. This script shows how easy it is to use them to perform data verification and for basic string processing.

The Word-Oriented Functions

A *word* is a group of printable characters surrounded by blanks or spaces. A word is a blank-delimited string. Rexx offers a group of *word-oriented functions*:

❑   `delword`—Deletes the *n*th word(s) from a string

❑   `space`—Formats words in a string such that they are separated by one or more occurrences of a specified pad character

- ❏   `subword` — Returns a *phrase* (substring) of a string that starts with the *n*th word
- ❏   `word` — Returns the *n*th word in a string
- ❏   `wordindex` — Returns the character position of the *n*th word in a string
- ❏   `wordlength` — Returns the length of the *n*th word in a string
- ❏   `wordpos` — Returns the word position of the first word of a phrase (substring) within a string
- ❏   `words` — Returns the number of words in a string

These functions can be coupled with the outermost functions to address any number of programming problems in which symbols are considered as strings of words. One such area is *textual analysis* or *natural language processing*. An example of a classic text analysis problem is to confirm the identity of the great English playwright Shakespeare. Were all his works written by one person? Could they have been written by one his better-known contemporaries?

One way to answer these questions is to analyze Shakespeare's works and look for word-usage patterns. Humans tend to use words in consistent ways. (Some experts claim they can analyze word usage to the degree that individuals' *linguistic profiles* are unique as their fingerprints). Analyzing Shakespeare's texts and comparing them to those of contemporaries indicates whether Shakespeare's works were actually written by him or someone else.

Special-purpose languages such as SNOBOL are particularly adept at natural language processing. But SNOBOL is premodern; it lacks good control constructs and robust I/O. Better to use a more mainstream, portable, general-purpose language like Rexx that offers strong string manipulation in the context of good structure.

Text analysis is a complex topic outside the scope of this book. But we can present a simple program that suggests how Rexx can be applied to textual analysis. The script named Poetry Scanner reads modern poetry and counts the number of articles and prepositions in the input. It produces a primitive form of "sophistication rating" or *lexical density*. In our example, this rating comprises two ratios: the ratio of the number of longer words to the number of shorter words, and the ratio of prepositional words to the total number of words in the text.

To perform these operations, the script translates the input text to all uppercase and removes punctuation, because punctuation represents extraneous characters that are irrelevant to the analysis.

For this input poem:

```
"The night was the darkest,
for the byrds of love were flying. And lo!
I    saw    them    with the eyes of the eagle.
above
    the cows    flew    in the cloud pasture.
below
    the   earthworms   were   multiplying ...
god grant that they all find their ways home."
```

. . . the program produces this output:

```
THE NIGHT WAS THE DARKEST
FOR THE BYRDS OF LOVE WERE FLYING AND LO
I SAW THEM WITH THE EYES OF THE EAGLE
ABOVE
THE COWS FLEW IN THE CLOUD PASTURE
BELOW
THE EARTHWORMS WERE MULTIPLYING
GOD GRANT THAT THEY ALL FIND THEIR WAYS HOME

Ratio long/short words:  0.40625
Number of articles:     8
Number of prepositions: 5
Ratio of preps/total words: 0.111111111

Press ENTER key to exit...
```

Here is the program:

```
/*   POETRY SCANNER:                                     */
/*                                                       */
/*      This program scans text to perform primitive text analysis.  */

list_of_articles = 'A AN THE'
list_of_preps    = 'AT BY FOR FROM IN OF TO WITH'

big_words       = 0   ;   small_words  = 0
number_articles = 0   ;   number_preps = 0

do while lines('poetry.txt') > 0
   line_str = linein('poetry.txt')  /* read a line of poetry       */
   line_str = translate(line_str)   /* translate to uppercase      */
   line_str = translate(line_str,'      ',',.,!:;"') /* remove punc.  */
   call lineout ,space(line_str)    /* display converted input line */

   do j=1 to words(line_str)        /* do while a word to process  */
      if wordlength(line_str,j) >= 5 then
         big_words = big_words + 1             /* count big words   */
      else
         small_words = small_words + 1         /* count small words */
      word_to_analyze = word(line_str,j)       /* get the word      */
      if wordpos(word_to_analyze,list_of_articles) > 0 then
         number_articles = number_articles + 1 /* count the articles*/
      if wordpos(word_to_analyze,list_of_preps) > 0 then
         number_preps = number_preps + 1       /* count prep phrases*/
   end
end
say
say 'Ratio long/short words: ' (big_words/small_words)
say 'Number of articles:    ' number_articles
say 'Number of prepositions:' number_preps
say 'Ratio of preps/total words:' (number_preps/(big_words+small_words))
```

The program demonstrates several of the word-oriented functions, including `words`, `word`, `wordlength`, and `wordpos`. It also uses the `translate` function in two different contexts.

After it reads a line of input, the program shows how the `translate` function can be used with only the input string as a parameter to translate the contents of the string to all uppercase letters:

```
line_str = translate(line_str)              /* translate to uppercase      */
```

Then `translate` is used again, this time to replace various punctuation characters with blanks. In this call, the third parameter to `translate` contains the characters to translate, and the second parameter tells what characters to translate them to. This example translates a various punctuation characters into blanks:

```
line_str = translate(line_str,'        ','.,!:;"')        /* remove punc. */
```

The `do` loop processes the individual words in each input line. It executes while there is a word to process in the current input line:

```
do j=1 to words(line_str)              /* do while a word to process      */
```

The `words` function returns the number of blank-delimited words in the input line, `line_str`.

The `wordlength` function tells the length of the word. The script uses it to determine whether the word is longer than 4 bytes:

```
if wordlength(line_str,j) >= 5 then
    big_words = big_words + 1              /* count big words   */
```

The script needs to get an individual word in order to determine if that word is an article or preposition. To parse out one word from the input string, the script invokes the `word` function:

```
word_to_analyze = word(line_str,j)              /* get the word */
```

To identify articles in the text, the program initializes a string containing the articles:

```
list_of_articles = 'A AN THE'
```

Then it uses the `wordpos` function to see if the word being inspected occurs in this list of articles. `wordpos` returns the starting position of the word in a string if it occurs in the string. If it returns 0, we know that the word is not an article:

```
if wordpos(word_to_analyze,list_of_articles) > 0 then
    number_articles = number_articles + 1              /* count the articles*/
```

What this line of code really does is *list processing*. It determines if a given element occurs in a list. String processing is easily used to emulate other kinds of processing techniques and various data structures, such as the *list*. As mentioned in the chapter introduction, string manipulation is powerful because it is a generic tool that can easily be used to implement other processing paradigms.

The program ends with several `say` instructions that show how output can be dynamically concatenated from the results of expressions. The last line of the program calculates a ratio and displays it with an appropriate label:

```
say 'Ratio of preps/total words:' (number_preps/(big_words+small_words))
```

Rexx evaluates the expression in parentheses prior to executing the `say` instruction and displaying the output line. Remember that in evaluating expressions, Rexx always works from the innermost set of parentheses on out. The script uses the parentheses to ensure that this expression is resolved first:

```
(big_words+small_words)
```

The result of this expression feeds into the division:

```
(number_preps/(big_words+small_words))
```

To summarize, this simple program illustrates a number of the word and string functions. More importantly, it demonstrates that these features can be combined to create powerful string-processing scripts. Rexx offers excellent string-processing facilities.

The Bit String Functions and Conversions

The TRL-2 standard added support for *bit strings*, strings that represent binary values. Bit strings are composed solely of 0s and 1s. They are represented as a string of 0s and 1s immediately followed by the letter b or B:

```
'11110000'b          /* represents one character (or "byte") as a bit string */
```

This encoding parallels that used to represent *hexadecimal* (or *hex*) strings. Hex is the base-16 arithmetic system by which computer bits are represented. Each character or byte is represented by two hex digits. Hex strings are composed of the digits 0 thru 9 and letters A thru F, immediately followed by the letter x or X:

```
'0D0A'x              /* the two byte end-of-line indicator in Windows and DOS */
```

Binary strings find several uses. For example, use them to specify characters explicitly, bit by bit. This helps you store and manipulate unprintable characters, for example. The relationship of bit strings to characters is described by the table called a *character map*. Sometimes this is referred to as the *character encoding scheme*.

Want to see your system's entire character map? Just enter the `xrange` function:

```
say  xrange()     /* displays the character map */
```

Or display some portion of the character map by specifying a range of starting and ending points. The range can be expressed in binary, hex, or character. You'll see the entire map, just as shown earlier, if you enter the entire range of the map explicitly:

```
say xrange('00'x,'FF'x)                          /* displays the character map */
```

This statement also displays the entire character range:

```
say xrange('00000000'b,'11111111'b)              /* displays the character map */
```

Display the same character map in hex (base-16) by using the c2x (character-to-hex) conversion function:

```
say  c2x(xrange())                       /* displays the character map in hex */
```

Want to see it as a bit string? You'll have to do two conversions: character to hex, then hex to binary. Nest the character-to-hex (c2x) function within the hex-to-binary (x2b) function to do this. Remember, Rexx always evaluates the expression nested in the innermost parentheses first and works its way outward from there. In this example, Rexx first performs the xrange function; then it executes c2x, and finally it runs x2b, giving us the binary map in the end:

```
say  x2b(c2x(xrange()))                  /* displays the character map in binary */
```

Bit strings have many applications. For example, database management systems manipulate *bit map indexes* to provide quick access to data having a low variety of possible values (*low cardinality*) by ANDing bit strings representing the data values. Another use for bit strings is in the technique called *key folding*. This develops a key for direct (random) data access based on character string key fields. A logical or bit operation is applied to the character field(s) to develop a key that is evenly distributed across direct access slots or positions in the database or on disk. A similar technique called *character folding* is used to map similar characters to a common target, for example, to eliminate certain distinctions between strings. This would be useful when you want similar strings to be compared as equal.

Rexx provides three *binary string functions* that perform logical operations on binary strings:

❏   bitand — Returns the string result of two strings logically AND'd together, bit by bit

❏   bitor — Returns the string result of two strings logically OR'd together, bit by bit

❏   bitxor — Returns the string result of two strings logically EXCLUSIVE OR'd, bit by bit

Here are examples that apply these binary operations on bit strings. The binary string functions return their results in the form of a character string (comprising one character, since 8 bits make a character and the input strings we supply are one character long). Therefore, we use the character-to-hex (c2x) and hex-to-binary (x2b) functions to interpret the result back to a displayable bit string:

```
say  x2b(c2x(bitand('11110000'b,'11001100'b)))   /* displays: 11000000 */
say  x2b(c2x(bitor('11110000'b,'11001100'b)))    /* displays: 11111100 */
say  x2b(c2x(bitxor('11110000'b,'11001100'b)))   /* displays: 00111100 */
```

The bitand operation sets bits to TRUE (1) in the result, only if they are TRUE in *both* strings. bitor sets bits to TRUE (1) if they are TRUE in *either* string. The bitxor function sets bits to TRUE only if they are TRUE *in exactly one* input string or the other.

The next chapter covers data conversions in further detail and includes an sample program that demonstrates folding a two-part character key. It illustrates the bitand function and the c2x (character-to-hexadecimal) and x2b (hexadecimal-to-binary) conversion functions.

Summary

This chapter introduces string processing. It describes the basic techniques for concatenation and parsing in Rexx and lists the many built-in functions for string and word processing. The sample programs demonstrate some of these techniques and functions.

The techniques we explored included concatenation, or the joining together of strings, and parsing, the analysis and splitting of strings into their constituent substrings. We looked at a sample script that performed input data validation and saw how string analysis and parsing applied to this problem. Then we looked at string functions, including those that analyze *words*, or discrete groups of letters surrounded by spaces or blanks. Finally, we discussed bit strings. These can be used in a wide variety of applications, such as database bit indexes and key folding. We discussed the major bit manipulation functions and how bit strings are converted to and from other forms by using conversion functions.

Chapter 8 illustrates more string manipulation. It includes a script that can tell whether parentheses are balanced (for example, as they might be coded within a Rexx statement). There is also a function called Reverse, which reverses the characters in an input string, just like the Rexx built-in reverse function. This new Reverse script does its work in an interesting way — it calls itself as its own subroutine. Stay tuned!

Test Your Understanding

1. What is *string processing*, and why are outermost features important in a scripting language?

2. What are the three methods of string concatenation? How is each different?

3. What are the three methods of parsing with the parse instruction, and how does each operate?

4. Which built-in function would you use for each of the following tasks:

   ❏ Checking that all characters in one string occur as members in another

   ❏ Verifying the data type of a user-input data item

   ❏ Finding the position of a substring with a string

   ❏ Removing all occurrences of a specified character from a string

   ❏ Right- and left- justifying a string for printing in a report

   ❏ Removing leading and/or trailing pad characters from a string

5. What is the difference between the wordindex and wordpos functions?

6. How are printable characters, hex characters, and bit strings related? What are some of the conversion functions used to convert values between them?

7. What are some of the uses of bit strings in applications?

7

Numbers, Calculations, and Conversions

Overview

The second chapter gives the barest definition of what numbers are and how they are used. Rexx is designed to handle arithmetic in as natural as manner as possible. It conforms to the basic rules of computation that people absorb in high school or college. For most programs, you'll need no special knowledge of how Rexx handles numbers. Rely on its automatic numeric conversions and rounding, and your scripts will work just fine.

Rexx differs from languages that place the burden of cross-system consistency on the developer. *Its language definition ensures that calculations provide the same outputs, regardless of language implementation or the platform on which it is run.*

Rexx achieves this cross-platform consistency by employing decimal arithmetic internally. This contrasts with the floating-point or binary arithmetic used by most other programming languages, which produce calculation results that can vary by platform. Rexx's natural or human-oriented approach to computation is part of its appeal as an easy-to-use, portable scripting language.

Even with this high level of automation, there will be situations where you require some knowledge of how Rexx handles calculations and how you can affect them. This chapter probes a little more deeply so that you'll be able to handle these situations appropriately. More specifically, we'll look at the ways in which you can express numeric values within scripts. We'll discuss the numeric functions for manipulating numbers, as well as the conversion functions that transpose numbers to other forms. We'll also look at how to manage precision in calculations, and ways to print or display numbers in the appropriately. The last part of the chapter focuses on the conversion functions that convert between numbers, character strings, bit strings, and hexadecimal values. A sample script demonstrates several conversion functions in illustrating a programming technique called key folding.

The Basics

All Rexx variables are character strings. Numbers are just character strings whose contents are considered numeric. Numbers are strings of one or more digits, optionally preceded by plus or minus sign (+ or –), and optionally containing a single period to represent a decimal point. Extending Rexx's flexible treatment of numbers, numbers may optionally have preceding or trailing blanks (which Rexx ignores when calculating).

Numbers may also be expressed in two forms of exponential notation: *scientific* and *engineering*. Scientific notation has one digit to the left of the decimal place, followed by fractional and exponential components. Engineering notation expresses the integer component by a number between 1 and 999. The E that precedes the exponential portion of the number in either notation can be either uppercase or lowercase. Spaces may not be embedded within the exponential portion of a number.

Here are some valid Rexx numbers:

```
3          /* a WHOLE number - often called an INTEGER in other languages  */
'  3  '    /* the same number- leading and trailing blanks don't matter    */
   -33     /* a negative number                                            */
'   -33'   /* the same numeric value- leading blanks are inconsequential   */
12.000     /* a decimal number - the internal period represents a decimal point*/
.33        /*  another decimal number                                      */
'  +   3.3 '     /* valid - the blanks are ignored                         */
5.22e+22   /* scientific exponential number                                */
5.22E+22   /* the same number - either 'E' or 'e' is fine                  */
14.23E+7   /* engineering notation                                         */
```

Here are a few *invalid* numbers:

```
'3  3'   /* Internal spaces are not allowed.                              */
3.3.3    /* More than one period is not allowed.                          */
'333b'   /* This contains the letter b. Alphanumeric strings are not numeric.  */
333(33   /* contains an invalid internal character, the left parenthesis  */
```

A string containing one of these forms of valid numbers will be recognized by Rexx as a number when appropriate. For example, when two values are compared, Rexx implements a *numeric comparison* if both values are numeric. Otherwise, it employs a *character comparison*. The way Rexx performs the numeric comparison internally is to subtract one number from the other. A result of 0 means that the two numbers are the same; any other value indicates their difference.

The basic rules of calculation in Rexx are:

❑   Results are determined up to the number of significant digits (which defaults to 9).

❑   Trailing zeroes are retained (except when using the power and division operators).

❑   A result of 0 is represented as a single-digit 0.

❑   Results are expressed in scientific exponential notation if either the number of digits prior to the decimal point exceeds the setting for significant digits or the number of digits following the decimal point exceeds twice the number of significant digits.

The term *significant digits* refers to how many digits are retained during a calculation. This is often termed the *precision* to which results are carried. Beyond this number of significant digits, or precision, Rexx rounds off the number.

The default number of significant digits is 9. Remember the Poetry Scanner program in the previous chapter? This is why it printed this output:

```
Ratio of preps/total words: 0.111111111
```

in response to this calculation:

```
say  'Ratio of preps/total words:'  (number_of_preps/(big_words/small_words))
```

The nine digits to the right of the decimal point are the default number of significant digits (the default precision). Use this simple command to alter the number of significant digits:

```
numeric  digits  [expression]
```

For example, set the precision to four digits:

```
numeric  digits  4
```

If you placed this statement prior to the calculations in the Poetry Scanner script, that same `say` instruction would display:

```
Ratio of preps/total words: 0.1111
```

This shows the power of the `numeric digits` instruction. With it you can alter or carry out accuracy to any desired point.

`numeric digits` also determines whether your output appears in exponential notation. If you expect a nonexponential result but Rexx gives you an exponential one, increasing the precision is one way to change this.

The `numeric` instruction also has the `fuzz` keyword to indicate how many significant digits less than that set by `numeric digits` will be involved during numeric comparisons. `numeric fuzz` *only* applies to comparisons. It has the effect of temporarily altering the number of significant digits for comparisons only. Its value must be less than the setting of `numeric digits`. Its default is 0.

`fuzz` essentially controls the amount by which two numbers may differ before being considered equal. For example, if `numeric digits` = 5 and `numeric fuzz` = 1, then numeric comparisons are carried out to four significant digits.

Here's a series of statements to demonstrate the effects of `numeric digits` and `numeric fuzz`. You can see how their settings determine the precision of comparisons:

```
numeric digits 4    /* set down to 4 from the default of 9    */
numeric fuzz   0    /* leave at its default of 0              */
say 2.998 = 2.999   /* Displays: 0                            */
say 2.998 < 2.999   /* Displays: 1                            */
```

```
numeric fuzz   1     /* set up to 1 from 0 to alter comparisons */
say 2.998 = 2.999    /* Displays: 1                              */
say 2.998 < 2.999    /* Displays: 0                              */
```

`numeric form` allows you to dictate which form of exponential notation is used. The default is `scientific`. To change this to engineering notation, enter:

```
numeric  form  engineering
```

Use the built-in functions `digits`, `fuzz`, and `form` to retrieve or display the current settings of `numeric digits`, `numeric fuzz`, and `numeric form`, respectively. For example, assuming that you haven't changed the defaults, here's what these functions return:

```
say  digits()      /* displays setting for NUMERIC DIGITS: 9       */
say  fuzz()        /* displays setting for NUMERIC FUZZ:   0       */
say  form()        /* displays setting for NUMERIC FORM:   SCIENTIFIC  */
```

The only two errors Rexx gives from calculations are *overflow/underflow* and *insufficient storage*. The first occurs when the exponential part of a number becomes too large or too small for the language interpreter, while the second means Rexx ran out of memory.

Chapter 10 discusses and illustrates how to set up error or exception routines to handle or "trap" certain kinds of error situations. One error you can manage by exception routines is the unintended loss of significant digits. This is achieved through the LOSTDIGITS condition, a feature added to Rexx by the ANSI-1996 standard. Chapter 10 gives full details on the LOSTDIGITS condition and how to use it.

To control the display style of numbers, use the `format` built-in function:

```
format(number_string,before,after)
```

`format` rounds and formats a number. `before` indicates how many characters appear in the integer part and `after` indicates how many characters appear in the decimal part.

If `before` is too small to contain the number, an error results. If `after` is too small, the number is rounded to fit.

If `before` is larger than the integer requires, blanks precede the number. If `after` is larger than the decimal part requires, extra zeroes are added on the right.

With this information, another option in the Poetry Scanner script would have been to leave `numeric digits` alone (letting it default it to 9 for all calculations), then format the output to reduce the number of digits to the right of the decimal point:

```
outratio = number_preps/(big_words+small_words)
say 'Ratio of preps/total words:'  format(outratio,1,4)
```

This yields the same result we got earlier from changing the value of `numeric digits` to 4:

```
Ratio of preps/total words: 0.1111
```

Here are a few more examples of the `format` function:

```
say format(13,8)      /* displays: '      13'
                         -- use to right-justify a number */

say format(1.11,4,0) /* displays: '   1'
                         -- rounded and right-justified  */

say format(1.1,4,4)  /* displays: '   1.1000'
                         -- extended with zeroes           */

say format(1.1,4)    /* displays: '    1.1'
                         -- right-justified                */

say format(1234,2)   /* error - not enough room for the integer part  */
```

`format` can also be used to control the display of exponential numbers. This is the template for this version of `format`:

```
format(number [,[before] [,[after] [,[expp] [,expt]]]])
```

`expp` and `expt` control the formatting of the exponential part of the result. `expp` is the number of digits used for the exponential part, while `expt` sets the trigger for the use of exponential notation. Here are a few examples:

```
format('12345.67',,,2,3)    ==    '1.234567E+04'
format('12345.67',,,4,4)    ==    '1.234567E+0004'
format('12345.67',,2,,0)    ==    '1.23E+4'
format('12345.67',,3,,0)    ==    '1.235E+4'
```

The `format` function is useful for generating reports with numbers nicely aligned in columns. Use it to right-justify numbers and ensure that a consistent number of decimal places appear. Also use it to round off numbers to any point of precision.

More Numeric Functions

To this point, we've discussed functions that determine precision in calculations and comparisons, and we've demonstrated how to format numbers for printing and display. Beyond `digits`, `form`, `format`, and `fuzz`, Rexx offers several other built-in functions designed to manipulate numbers. Here are these additional numeric functions:

❑   `abs` — Returns the absolute value of a number

❑   `max` — Returns the largest number from a list of numbers

❑   `min` — Returns the smallest number from a list of numbers

❑   `random` — Returns a random number within the range given (inclusive)

❑   `sign` — Returns 1 if number is greater than 0, or 0 if the number is 0, or -1 if the number is less than 0

❑   `trunc` — Truncates a number

Appendix C contains complete coding information for all these functions. Here, we will cover some of their common uses.

Here are a few examples of the functions:

```
say  abs(-4.1)          /* displays: 4.1       */
say  abs(4.1)           /* displays: 4.1       */
say  abs(-0.11)         /* displays: 0.11      */
say  abs(-0)            /* displays: 0         */

say  max(3,2,88)        /* displays: 88        */
say  max(0,-1,-17)      /* displays: 0         */
say  max(-7.0000,-8)    /* displays: -7.0000   */

say min(-1,14,-7.0000)  /* displays: -7.0000   */
say min(50,13)          /* displays: 13        */

say  sign(-12)          /*  displays: -1       */
say  sign(1)            /*  displays: 1        */
say  sign(0)            /*  displays: 0        */

say  trunc(11.11)    /* displays: 11     -Returns whole number after truncation */
say  trunc(11.11,2)  /* displays: 11.11
                        -Returns number truncated to 2 decimal places */
say  trunc(11.11,1)  /* displays: 11.1
                        -Returns number truncated to 1 decimal place  */
```

The random function takes this form:

```
random(min, max, seed)
```

It generates a random number between min and max (inclusive), based on the seed value. If you don't provide a seed, Rexx generates its own random number (usually based on the system time-of-day clock). If min and/or max are not specified, they default to 0 and 999, respectively. Here are a couple examples:

```
random(1,2)  /* simulate a coin toss, returns Heads or Tails */
random(1,6)  /* simulate rolling a single die,
                result is between 1 and 6 inclusive */
```

Many Rexx implementations offer extensions for transcendental mathematical functions. These include tangent, sine, cosine, and the like. Section II covers these implementation-specific extensions to standard Rexx when it discusses the features of the various open-source Rexx interpreters. Also, Appendix H lists a few dozen of the many free and open-source Rexx tools and interfaces that are available. Among them are several external function libraries that support advanced mathematics.

Conversions

Rexx variables contain values representing character, decimal, hexadecimal, and binary strings. Obviously, there will be occasions when you need to convert variables from one of these representations to another. Rexx provides a set of *conversion functions* that allow you to convert data between the different formats. Here is a list of these conversion functions:

Function	Converts
b2x	Binary to hexadecimal
c2d	Character to decimal
c2x	Character to hexadecimal
d2c	Decimal to character
d2x	Decimal to hexadecimal
x2b	Hexadecimal to binary
x2c	Hexadecimal to character
x2d	Hexadecimal to decimal

The datatype function is useful in testing variables to see what kind of data they contain. datatype without an option returns either the character string NUM or CHAR to indicate whether the operand is numeric or character:

```
say  datatype('12345')    /* displays: NUM   */
say  datatype('abc')      /* displays: CHAR  */
say  datatype('abc123')   /* displays: CHAR  */
```

Or, you can specify an option or "type" of test to perform:

```
say  datatype('12','W')   /* displays: 1   -the string contains a Whole number */
```

As always, options to functions can be specified in either uppercase or lowercase. Here is the complete set of options or tests for the datatype function:

datatype Option	Use
A	Alphanumeric — returns 1 if the string contains only characters in the ranges 'a'–'z', 'A'–'Z', and '0'–'9'.
B	Binary — returns 1 if the string contains only 0s and 1s.
L	Lowercase — returns 1 if string contains characters only in the range 'a'–'z'.
M	Mixed case — returns 1 if string contains characters only in the ranges 'a'–'z' and 'A'–'Z'.

Table continued on following page

105

datatype Option	Use
N	Number — returns 1 if string is a valid Rexx number.
S	Symbol — returns 1 if string comprises a valid Rexx symbol.
U	Uppercase — returns 1 if string contains only characters in range 'A'–'Z'.
W	Whole number — returns 1 if string represents a whole number under the current setting for numeric digits. In many programming languages, a whole number is referred to as an integer.
X	Hexadecimal — returns 1 if string represents a valid hex number (consists only of letters 'a'–'f', 'A'–'F', and digits '0'–'9').

The string that datatype inspects can be of any representation: character, hex, or binary. The sample program Verify Arguments in Chapter 6 showed how to use datatype in testing the values of user-input parameters.

A Sample Program

Here's a sample program that uses the data conversion functions and the bitand bit string function. This script takes two character fields and folds (logically ANDs) the bit representation of these character fields together to create a direct access key. As mentioned in Chapter 6, this technique is called *key folding* and can be used in developing a file manager or database system. It permits direct access to records based on randomizing character keys. Here's the program:

```
/*  FOLDED KEY:                                             */
/*                                                          */
/*     This program folds a character key from two input fields.     */

char_key1        = 'key_field_1'                /* the original string */
char_key_hex1    = c2x(char_key1)               /* the string in hex   */
char_key_bin1    = x2b(char_key_hex1)           /* the string in binary*/

char_key2        = 'key_field_2'                /* the original string */
char_key_hex2    = c2x(char_key2)               /* the string in hex   */
char_key_bin2    = x2b(char_key_hex2)           /* the string in binary*/

folded_key = bitand(char_key_bin1, char_key_bin2)         /* fold keys */

say 'First key   :' char_key1                   /* display all results */
say 'In hex      :' char_key_hex1
say 'In binary   :' char_key_bin1

say 'Second key  :' char_key2
say 'In hex      :' char_key_hex2
say 'In binary   :' char_key_bin2

say 'Folded key  :' folded_key
```

The program output looks like this:

```
First key   : key_field_1
In hex      : 6B65795F6669656C645F31
In binary   : 0110101101100101011110010101111101100110011010010110010101101100011
001000101111100110001
Second key  : key_field_2
In hex      : 6B65795F6669656C645F32
In binary   : 0110101101100101011110010101111101100110011010010110010101101100011
001000101111100110010
Folded key  : 0110101101100101011110010101111101100110011010010110010101101100011
001000101111100110000
```

The program shows how to use built-in functions for conversions between data types. This statement converts the original character string key to its hexadecimal equivalent through the c2x function:

```
char_key_hex1   = c2x(char_key1)                    /* the string in hex   */
```

Then, the x2b function converts that hex string to a binary string:

```
char_key_bin1   = x2b(char_key_hex1)                /* the string in binary*/
```

After both original character strings have been converted to binary, this statement logically ANDs the two bit strings together to produce the folded key:

```
folded_key = bitand(char_key_bin1, char_key_bin2)   /* fold keys */
```

The original input fields the script folded contained the character strings key_field_1 and key_field_2.

The last line in the output shows that ANDing these values together on the bit level only changes the few bits at the end of the folded key string. These two key values require more differentiation than just a single different final character! (We've used similar input values here to make the operation of the script more clear.) In a real environment, we would expect the key fields to hold more diverse data to make this algorithm useful. Nevertheless, the program shows how simple it is to perform useful operations with the bit manipulation and conversion functions. We've implemented a simple algorithm to create keys out of arbitrary character strings with just a few lines of code.

Summary

Rexx guarantees that the results of arithmetic operations will be the same regardless of the platform or the Rexx interpreter. This is an important advantage over many other programming languages, which place this burden on the developer. It makes Rexx code more reliable and portable with little effort on the programmer's part.

The only differences in calculations come in where implementations support different maximums (for example, different maximum precision) or when they have differing amounts of total memory with which to work.

One downside to Rexx's approach to numeric computations is its relatively slow speed. All variables contain strings values that must be converted internally prior to computation. The result is that computations are slower than they are in languages that carry numeric values in internal formats optimized to perform calculations. Given modern computer hardware, this downside only matters when programs are computationally bound. For the typical program, this "downside" matters not at all.

Rexx transparently handles issues with numeric conversions as necessary to perform numeric operations. Nevertheless, there are times when knowing a little more about how Rexx handles numbers is useful; this chapter provides that detail. We discussed ways to represent numbers in Rexx variables, how to control the precision to which calculations are carried out, techniques to format numbers for display, the use of exponential notation, and the built-in functions that manipulate numbers.

The `datatype` function is the basic means by which the kinds of data held within variables may be ascertained. Rexx provides a full set of functions for converting strings between data types. These are usually referred to as the *conversion functions*. Appendix C provides a full coding reference for all Rexx functions, including the conversion functions.

Test Your Understanding

1. Describe the relationship between `numeric digits` and `numeric fuzz`. How do their settings affect precision and numeric comparisons? Why would you set `fuzz` rather than just altering `digits`?

2. What's the difference between scientific and engineering exponential notations? To which does Rexx default? How do you display and/or change the default?

3. What functions are used to right-justify numeric output in reports?

4. What kinds of data conditions does the `datatype` function help identify?

5. Which of the following are valid numbers?

```
-22
'    -22    '
2.2.
2.2.2
222b2
2.34e+13
123.E  -2
123.2  E  + 7
```

8

Subroutines, Functions, and Modularity

Overview

Rexx fully supports structured programming. It encourages *modularity*—breaking up large, complex programs into a set of small, simple, interacting components or pieces. These components feature well-defined interfaces that render their interaction clear. Modularity underlies good program structure. Modularity means more easily understood and maintained programs than ill-designed "spaghetti" code, which can quickly become unmaintainable on large programming projects. Structured programming practices and modularity together reduce error rates and produce more reliable code.

Rexx provides the full range of techniques to invoke other programs and to create subroutines and functions. The basic concept is that there should be ways to link together any code you create, buy, or reuse. This is one of the fundamental advantages to using a "glue" language like Rexx.

With Rexx, you can develop large, modular programs that invoke routines written in Rexx or other languages, which issue operating system commands and utilize functions packaged in external function libraries. This chapter describes the basic ways in which one writes modular Rexx programs.

This chapter investigates how to write internal subroutines and functions, and how to call them from within the main program. Passing arguments or values into subroutines is an important issue, as is the ability to pass changed values back to the calling program. Variable *scoping* refers to the span of code from within which variables can be changed. This chapter explores the rules of scoping and how they affect the manner in which scripts are coded. Finally, we introduce the idea of *recursion*, a routine that calls itself as its own subroutine. While this may at first seem confusing, in fact it is a simple technique that clearly expresses certain kinds of algorithms. Not all programming languages support recursion; Rexx does. The chapter includes a brief script that illustrates how recursion operates.

The Building Blocks

As Figure 8-1 shows, any Rexx script can invoke either *internal* or *external* routines. *Internal* means that the code resides in the same file as the script that *calls* or invokes the routines. Those routines that are *external* reside in some file other than that of the invoking script.

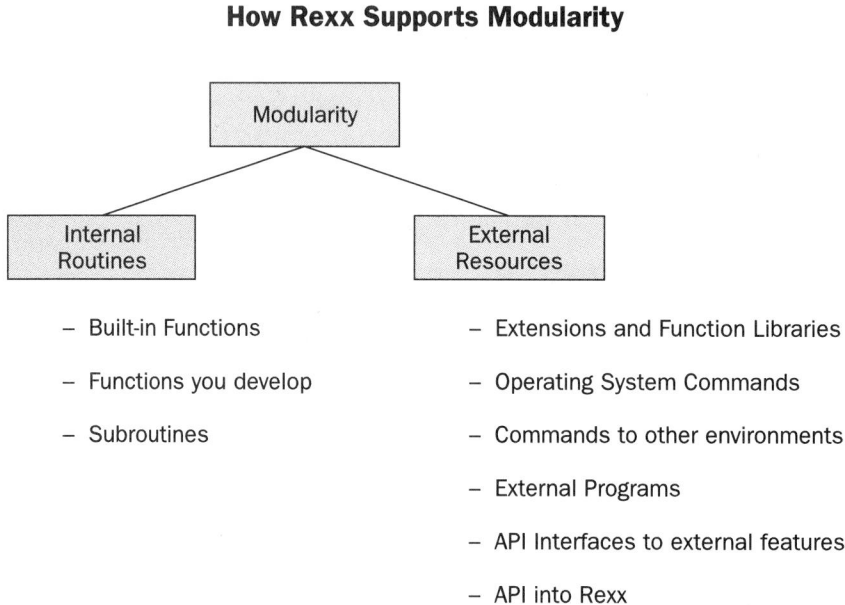

How Rexx Supports Modularity

```
                        ┌──────────────┐
                        │  Modularity  │
                        └──────────────┘
                         /            \
            ┌──────────────┐      ┌──────────────┐
            │   Internal   │      │   External   │
            │   Routines   │      │  Resources   │
            └──────────────┘      └──────────────┘
```

– Built-in Functions   – Extensions and Function Libraries

– Functions you develop   – Operating System Commands

– Subroutines   – Commands to other environments

                                – External Programs

                                – API Interfaces to external features

                                – API into Rexx

Figure 8-1

Internal routines are classified as either *functions* or *subroutines*. Functions include those that are provided as part of the Rexx language (the *built-in functions*) and those that you write yourself (*user-defined functions*). Functions are distinct from subroutines in that functions *must* return a single result string to the caller through the `return` instruction with which they end. Rexx replaces the function code in any statement with the returned value from the function. Subroutines may or may not send back a value to their caller via their `return` instruction. The returned value from a subroutine, if there is one, is placed into the special variable named `result`.

External routines can be functions, too. Often, these come in the form of a package designed to support a particular functionality and are called *extensions* or *function libraries*. External routines might also be the equivalent of internal subroutines, written in Rexx, except that they reside in a different file than that of the caller.

Rexx makes it easy to invoke external programs from your script, regardless of the language in which they are written. If the Rexx interpreter encounters a string in a script that does not correspond to its instruction set, it evaluates that expression and then passes it to the operating system for execution. So, it is simple to run operating system commands or other programs from a Rexx script. Chapter 14 illustrates how to do this. One of Rexx's great strengths is its role in issuing, controlling, and coordinating operating system commands. It is also easy to direct commands to other outside "environments" such as text editors or other tools. Rexx is called a *macro language* because it is often used to provide programmability for various tools. For example, on mainframes Rexx is used as the macro language to program the widely used editors, XEDIT and the ISPF Editor.

There are a large variety of Rexx extensions and packages. For example, the open-source *Rexx/SQL* package provides an interface to a variety of relational databases from within Rexx scripts. Other examples include interfaces to *curses*, the text-screen control package; to *RexxXML*, for XML programming; to *ISAM*, the indexed sequential access method; to *TK* and *DW*, for easy GUI programming; to *gd*, for graphics images; *RxSock*, for TCP/IP sockets, and many other interfaces. Chapters 15 through 18 discuss and demonstrate some of these free and open-source packages. Chapter 29 discusses a few of the many interfaces to mainframe Rexx and how Rexx offers a high-level macro and interface language for mainframe interfaces and facilities. Appendix H lists several dozen of the many free and open-source interfaces that are available and tells how to locate them for downloading.

Internal Functions and Subroutines

Functions must always return exactly one result to the caller. Use the `return` instruction to do this. *Subroutines* may or may not send a result back to the caller via `return`, but they, too, end with the `return` instruction.

Functions may be invoked in either of two ways. One method codes the function name, immediately followed by arguments, wherever one might encode an expression:

```
returned_string  =  function_name(parameter_1, parameter_2)
```

The function is resolved and the string it returns is plunked right into the expression where it was coded. In this case, the assignment statement then moves that value to the variable `returned_string`. Since you can code a function anywhere you can code an expression, nesting the function within an `if` or `do` instruction is common:

```
if ( balanced_parentheses(string_in) ) = 'YES' then
```

Here the call to the function `balanced_parentheses` is nested within an `if` instruction to provide a result for the comparison. After the function `balanced_parentheses` has been run, its result is plunked right where it was encoded in the `if` instruction.

You can nest functions within functions, as shown in this `return` instruction from one of the sample scripts we discuss later in this chapter:

```
return substr(string,length(string),1) || ,
reverse(substr(string,1,length(string)-1))
```

Recall that the comma is the *line continuation character*. So, both of these lines constitute a single statement.

This `return` instruction features a complex expression that returns a single character string result to the caller. The first part of the expression nests the `length` function within the `substr` function; the second part nests `length` within `substr` within `reverse`. Yikes! Nesting is very powerful, but for the sake of clarity we don't recommend getting too fancy with it. Deeply nested expressions may show cleverness but they become unintelligible if too complex. When complex code is developed for corporate, governmental, or educational institutions, the value of that code drops the moment the programmer who wrote it leaves the organization.

The second basic way to invoke a function is through the `call` instruction:

```
call  function_name   parameter_1, parameter_2
```

For example, to duplicate the code we looked at earlier where the invocation of the `balanced_parentheses` routine was nested within an `if` statement, we could have alternatively coded:

```
call  balanced_parentheses  string_in
if result = 'YES' then   /* inspect the result returned from the function call */
```

The result string from the function is automatically placed into the special variable named `result` and may be accessed from there.

Special variable `result` will be set to uninitialized if not set by a subroutine. In this case its value will be its own name in capitals: `RESULT`.

Subroutines may only be invoked by the `call` instruction. Encode this in the exact same manner as the second method for invoking functions:

```
call subroutine_name  parameter_1,  parameter_2
```

The special variable `result` contains a value *if* the subroutine passed back a value on its `return` instruction. Otherwise `result` will be set to uninitialized (the value `RESULT`). All uninitialized variables are their own names set to uppercase, so use this test to see if `result` was not set:

```
if result = 'RESULT'  then say 'RESULT was not set by the subroutine.'
```

The built-in function `symbol` can also be used to see if any variable is uninitialized or whether it has been assigned a value. It returns the character string `VAR` if a variable has a value or the string `LIT` otherwise. We can apply it to see if `result` was assigned a value:

```
if symbol('RESULT')  == 'VAR'  then say 'A result was returned'
if symbol('RESULT')  == 'LIT'  then say 'No result was returned'
```

To summarize, here's a code snippet that shows how to organize a main routine (or *driver*) and its subroutine. The code shows that the `call` to the internal subroutine did not set special variable `result`:

```
/* Show whether RESULT was set by the CALL */

call  subroutine_name

if result = 'RESULT'
   then  say 'No RESULT was returned'
   else  say 'A RESULT was returned'

if symbol('RESULT')  == 'VAR'
   then say 'A RESULT was returned'
```

```
if symbol('RESULT')  == 'LIT'
   then say 'No RESULT was returned'

exit 0

subroutine_name:
   return
```

The `return` instruction ends the subroutine, but does not include an operand or string to send back to the calling routine. The code snippet displays these messages when it returns from the subroutine:

```
No RESULT was returned
No RESULT was returned
```

Now change the last statement in the code, the `return` instruction in the subroutine, to something like this:

```
return 'result_string'
```

Or, change it to this:

```
return 0
```

Either encoding means that the special variable `result` is set to the string returned. After invoking the internal routine, the code snippet now displays:

```
A RESULT was returned
A RESULT was returned
```

When encoding subroutine(s) and/or functions after the main routine or driver, code an `exit` instruction at the end of the code for the main routine. This prevents the flow of control from rolling right off the end of the main routine and going into the subroutines.

Here is another example that is the exact same as that seen in the preceding example. However, we have coded it incorrectly by commenting out the `exit` instruction that follows the main routine. We have also added a statement inside the subroutine that displays the message: `Subroutine has been entered`.

Here's the code:

```
/* Show whether RESULT was set by the CALL */

call  subroutine_name

if result = 'RESULT'
   then  say 'No RESULT was returned'
   else  say 'A RESULT was returned'

if symbol('RESULT')  == 'VAR'
   then say 'A RESULT was returned'
if symbol('RESULT')  == 'LIT'
   then say 'No RESULT was returned'
```

```
/* exit 0 */                              /* now commented out */

subroutine_name:
   say 'Subroutine has been entered'      /* new line of code  */
   return 0
```

This script displays this output:

```
Subroutine has been entered
A RESULT was returned
A RESULT was returned
Subroutine has been entered     <=  this line results from no EXIT instruction!
```

This shows you must code an `exit` instruction at the end of the main routine if it is followed by one or more subroutines or functions. The last line in the sample output shows that the subroutine was entered incorrectly because an `exit` instruction was not coded at the end of the main routine. As with the subroutine's `return` instruction, it is optional whether or not to code a return string on the `exit` statement. In the preceding example, the `exit` instruction passed a return code of 0 to the environment.

What if we place the code of subroutines *prior* to that of the main routine? Here we located the code of the subroutine prior to the driver:

```
/* Shows why subroutines should FOLLOW the main routine */

subroutine_name:
   say 'Subroutine has been entered'
   return 0

call  subroutine_name

if result = 'RESULT'
   then  say 'No RESULT was returned'
   else  say 'A RESULT was returned'

if symbol('RESULT')  == 'VAR'
   then say 'A RESULT was returned'
if symbol('RESULT')  == 'LIT'
   then say 'No RESULT was returned'
exit 0
```

Running this script displays just one line:

```
Subroutine has been entered
```

What happened was that Rexx starts at the top of the file and proceeds to interpret and execute the code, line by line. Since the subroutine is first in the file, it executes first. Its instruction `return   0` caused exit from the program before we ever got to the main routine! Oops. Always place the code for any internal subroutines or functions *after* the main routine or driver.

We'll cover program structure in more detail later. For now, here are some basic rules of thumb:

- ❏ End each subroutine or function with the `return` instruction.
- ❏ Every function *must* have an operand on its `return` instruction.
- ❏ Subroutines may optionally have a result on their `return` instruction.
- ❏ Encode the `exit` instruction at the end of the code of the main routine or driver.
- ❏ Place subroutines and functions after the main routine or driver.

We saw that Rexx uninitializes special variable `result` when a called subroutine does not pass back a result string. If you ever need to uninitialized a Rexx variable yourself, code the `drop` instruction:

```
drop  my_variable
```

This sets a variable you may have used back to its uninitialized state. It is now equal to its own name in all uppercase.

You can drop multiple variables in one instruction:

```
drop   my_variable_1   my_variable_2   my_variable_3
```

Passing Parameters into a Script from the Command Line

Passing data into a script is important because this provides programs with flexibility. For example, a script that processes a file can retrieve the name of the file to process from the user. You can pass data elements into scripts by coding them on the same command line by which you run the script. Let's explore how this is accomplished.

Data passed into a script when it is invoked are called *command-line arguments* or *input parameters*. To invoke a Rexx script and pass it command-line arguments or parameters, enter something like this:

```
c:\Regina\pgms> script_name  parameter_1  2  parameter_3
```

The script reads these three input strings `parameter_1`, 2, and `parameter_3` with the `arg` instruction. `arg` automatically translates the input parms to uppercase. It is the equivalent of the instruction `parse upper arg`. If no uppercase translation is desired, use `parse arg`. Remember that a period following either of these instructions discards any more variables than are encoded on the `arg` or `parse arg` instruction. This example discards any arguments beyond the third one, if any are entered:

```
arg input_1 input_2 input_3  .     /* read 3 arguments, translate to capitals   */
```

Here is the same example coded with the parse arg instruction:

```
parse arg input_1 input_2 input_3 . /* read 3 arguments, no upper translation   */
```

By default, the `arg` and `parse arg` instructions splice the input parameters into pieces based on their separation by one or more intervening spaces. If you ran the program like this:

```
c:\Regina\pgms> script_name  parameter_1  2  parameter    _3
```

You'd want to code this statement in the script to pick up the input arguments:

```
parse arg  input_1  input_2  input_3  input_4  .
```

The resulting variable values would be:

```
input_1  =   parameter_1
input_2  =   2
input_3  =   parameter
input_4  =   _3
```

As per the basic rules of parsing, encoding too many input parameters puts all the overflow either into the *placeholder variable* (the period) or into the last specified input variable on the `parse arg` instruction.

Entering too few input parameters to match the `parse arg` statement means that the extra variables on the `parse arg` will be set to uninitialized. As always, an uninitialized variable is equal to its own name in uppercase.

Passing Parameters into Subroutines and Functions

Say that our sample script needs to run a subroutine or function, passing it the same three input parameters. Code the subroutine or function call as:

```
call  sub_routine  input_1, input_2, input_3
```

Code a comma between each of the parameters in the `call` instruction. The string (if any) sent back from the `call` will be available in the special variable named `result`.

Code a function `call` just like the `call` to the previous subroutine. Or encode it wherever you would an expression, as illustrated earlier, in the form:

```
result_string =  function_name(input_1, input_2, input_3)
```

Inside the function or subroutine, use either `arg` or `parse arg` to retrieve the arguments. The function or subroutine picking up the input parameters should encode commas that parallel those of the `call` in its `arg` or `parse arg` instruction:

```
arg input_1,  input_2,  input_3  .
```

or

```
parse arg  input_1,  input_2,  input_3  .
```

The period or placeholder variable is optional. Presumably, the subroutine or function knows how many input parameters to expect and does not need it.

These examples illustrate the `arg` *instruction* retrieving the argument string passed to a script and splicing it apart into its individual pieces. There is also an `arg` *built-in function*. The `arg` function returns information about input arguments to the routine. For scripts called as functions or subroutines, the `arg` function either:

❑ Tells how many argument strings were passed in

❑ Tells whether a specific-numbered argument was supplied

❑ Supplies a specified argument

Let's look at a few examples. To learn how many arguments were passed in, code:

```
number_of_arguments  =  arg()
```

To retrieve a specific argument, say the third one, code:

```
get_third_argument  =  arg(3)
```

To see if the third argument exists (was passed or encoded in the call), write:

```
if (arg(3) == '')  then say 'No third argument was passed'
```

or

```
if arg(3,'O')  then say 'No third argument was passed'
```

The first of the two sample lines show that an input argument read by an internal routine will be the null string if it is not supplied to the routine. This differs from a command-line input argument that is read but not supplied, which is set to uninitialized (its own name in uppercase).

The second sample line shows one of the two options that can be used with the `arg` function:

❑ E (Exists) — Returns 1 if the *n*th argument exists. Otherwise returns 0.

❑ O (Omitted) — Returns 1 if the *n*th argument was Omitted. Otherwise returns 0.

The `arg` function *only* supplies this information for scripts that are called as functions or subroutines. For scripts invoked from the operating system's command line, the `arg` function will always show only 0 or 1 argument strings. In this respect Rexx scripts invoked as commands from the operating system behave differently than scripts invoked as internal routines (functions or subroutines). This is one of the very few Rexx inconsistencies you'll have to remember: the `arg` function tells how many arguments are passed into an internal routine, but applied to the command-line arguments coming into a script, it always returns either 0 or 1.

A Sample Program

To see how parameters are passed into programs, and how code can be modularized, let's look at a couple sample programs. The first sample program consists of a brief script that reads information from the command line. This main routine or "driver" then turns around and calls a subroutine that performs the real work of the program. Then the driver displays the result from the subroutine on the user's screen.

Of course, the driver could actually be part of a larger application. For example, it might be a "service routine" shared among programs in the application. Whatever its use, the important principles to grasp are how code can be modularized and how information can be passed between modules.

The first sample program tells whether parentheses in a string are *balanced*. A string is said to be balanced if:

❑   Every left parenthesis has a corresponding closing right parenthesis

❑   No right parenthesis occurs in the string prior to a corresponding left parenthesis

Here are some examples. These input strings meet the two criteria and so are considered balanced:

```
(())
() () ()
return (qiu(slk) ())
((((((()()))))))
if (substr(length(string,1,2)))
```

These are unbalanced strings. Either the numbers of left and right parentheses are unequal, or a right parenthesis occurs prior to its corresponding left parenthesis:

```
)alkjdsfkl(              /* right paren occurs before its left paren */
((akljlkfd)              /* 2 left parens, only 1 right paren        */
if (substr(length(string,1,2))  /* 3 left parens, only 2 right parens        */
```

The last example shows that a script like this could be useful as a syntax-checker, or as a module in a language interpreter. You can actually use it to verify that your scripts possess properly encoded, balanced sets of parentheses.

To run the program, enter the string to verify as a command-line argument. Results appear on the next line:

```
C:\Regina\pgms> call_bal.rexx  · if(substr(length(string,1,2))
Parentheses are NOT balanced
```

Try again, this time adding one last right parenthesis to the input string:

```
C:\Regina\pgms> call_bal.rexx  if(substr(length(string,1,2)))
Parentheses are balanced!
```

Here's the code for the caller. All it does is read the user's command-line input parameter and pass that character string to a function named `balanced_parens` that does the work. The function `balanced_parens` may be either internal or external—no change is required to its coding regardless of where you place it. (However, you must be sure the operating system knows where to locate external functions. This often requires setting an environmental variable or the operating system's search path for called routines. We'll discuss this in detail later.)

```
/*  CALL BAL:                                                    */
/*                                                               */
/*     Determines if the parentheses in a string are balanced.   */

arg  string .         /* the string to inspect                  */

if  balanced_parens(string) = 'Y' then   /* get answer from function */
    say 'Parentheses are balanced!'       /* write GOOD message ..or..*/
else
    say 'Parentheses are NOT balanced'    /* write INVALID message   */

exit 0
```

Here's the internal or external function that figures out if the parentheses are balanced. The algorithm keeps track of the parentheses simply by adding 1 to a counter for any left parenthesis it encounters, and subtracting 1 from that counter for any right parenthesis it reads. A final counter (ctr) equal to 0 means the parentheses are balanced — that there are an equal number of left and right parentheses in the input string. If at any time the counter goes negative, this indicates that a right parenthesis was found prior to any possible matching left parenthesis. This represents another case in which the input string is invalid.

```
/*  BALANCED PARENS:                                             */
/*                                                               */
/*     Returns Y if parentheses in input string are balanced,    */
/*     N if they are not balanced.                               */

balanced_parens:

arg  string .         /* the string to inspect                  */

ctr = 0                      /* identifies right paren BEFORE a left one */
valid = 1
endstring = length(string)          /* get length of input string */

do j=1  to endstring  while (valid)
   char = substr(string,j,1)           /* inspect each character   */
   if char = '(' then ctr = ctr + 1
   if char = ')' then ctr = ctr - 1
   if ctr < 0   then valid = 0
end

if ctr = 0 then return 'Y'
         else return 'N'
```

Another way to code this problem is for the subroutine to return 1 for a string with balanced parentheses, and 0 if they are unbalanced. Then you could code this in the caller:

```
if balanced_parens(string)  then
   say  'Parentheses are balanced!'
else
   say  'Parentheses are NOT balanced'
```

119

This allows coding the function as an *operatorless condition test* in a manner popular in programming in languages like C, C++, or C#. But remember that the expression in an if instruction must evaluate to 1 (TRUE) or 0 (FALSE) in Rexx, so the function *must* return one of these two values. A nonzero, positive integer other than 1 will not work in Rexx, unlike languages in the C family. A positive value other than 1 results in a syntax error in Rexx (we note, though, that there are a few Rexx interpreters that are extended to allow safe coding of operatorless condition tests).

Coding operatorless condition tests also runs counter to the general principle that a function or subroutine returns 0 for success and 1 for failure. Wouldn't balanced parentheses be considered "success"? This coding works fine but contravenes the informal coding convention.

The Function Search Order

Given that Rexx supports built-in functions, internal functions, and external functions, an important issue is how Rexx locates functions referred to by scripts. For example, if you write an internal function with the same name as a built-in function, it is vital to understand which of the two functions Rexx invokes when some other routine refers to that function name.

This issue is common to many programming languages and is called the *function search order*. In Rexx the function search order is:

1. *Internal function* — The label exists in the current script file.

2. *Built-in function* — Rexx sees if the function is one of its own built-in functions.

3. *External function* — Rexx seeks an external function with the name. It may be written in Rexx or any language conforming to the system-dependent interface that Rexx uses to invoke it and pass the parameter(s).

Where Rexx looks for external functions is operating-system-dependent. You can normally place external functions in the same directory as the caller and Rexx will find them. On many platforms, you must set an *environmental variable* or a *search path* parameter to tell the operating system where to look for external functions and subroutines.

The function search order means that you could code an internal function with the same name as a Rexx built-in function and Rexx will use *your* function. You can thus replace, or override, Rexx's built-in functions.

If you want to avoid this, code the function reference as an uppercase string in quotation marks. The quotation marks mean Rexx skips Step 1 and *only* looks for built-in or external functions. Uppercase is important because built-in functions have uppercase names.

With this knowledge, you can override Rexx functions with your own, while still invoking the built-in functions when you like. You can manage Rexx's search order to get the best of both worlds.

Recursion

A *recursive* function or routine is one that calls itself. Any recursive function could be coded in traditional nonrecursive fashion (or *iteratively*), but sometimes recursion offers a better problem solution. Not all programming languages support recursion; Rexx does.

Since a recursive function invokes itself, there must be some end test by which the routine knows to stop *recursing* (invoking itself). If there is no such end test, the program recurses forever, and you have effectively coded an "endless loop!"

Figure 8-2 pictorially represents recursion.

How Recursion Works

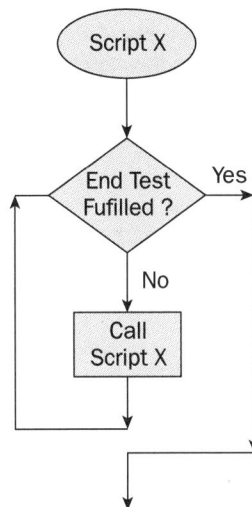

Figure 8-2

This sample recursive function reverses the characters within a given string—just like Rexx's `reverse` built-in function. If you feed it the character string `abc`, it returns the string `cba`.

The function calls itself to process each character in the input string and finds its "end test" when there are no more characters left in the string to process. Each time the function is entered, it returns the last character in the string and recurses to process the remaining string.

```
/*   REVERSE:                                                        */
/*                                                                   */
/*      Recursive routine that reverses the characters in a string.  */

reverse: procedure

parse arg string           /* read the string to reverse            */

if string == ''            /* here's the 'end recursion' condition   */
```

```
      then return ''
   else
      return substr(string,length(string),1) || ,
            reverse(substr(string,1,length(string)-1))
```

The `reverse` function uses the *strictly equal* operator (`==`). This is required because the regular "equals" operator pads item with blanks for comparisons, something that might not work in this function. The line that uses the strictly equal operator compares the input string to the *null string*, the string that contains no characters, represented by two back-to-back quotation marks (`''`). This is the "end test" that tells the function to return, because it has processed all the characters in the original input string:

```
if string == ''           /* here's the 'end recursion' condition      */
   then return ''
```

The last two lines of the function show how to continue a statement across lines. Just code a comma (`,`) and the `return` instruction's expression spans into the next line. The comma is Rexx's *line continuation character*. Code it at any natural breakpoint in the statement. Between parts of a statement is fine; within the middle of a character string literal would not work. This is valid:

```
say  'Hi '   ,
     'there!'                 /*  valid line continuation */
```

But this will fail with a syntax error, because the line continuation character appears in the middle of a quoted literal:

```
say  'Hi        ,
     there!'                  /* invalid line continuation, syntax error! */
```

Of course, the trick to this program to reverse character strings is this one, heavily nested line of code:

```
      return substr(string,length(string),1) || ,
            reverse(substr(string,1,length(string)-1))
```

The first portion of this statement always returns the last character in the substring being inspected:

```
substr(string,length(string),1)
```

An alternative way to code this is to use the `right` function, as in: `right(string, 1)`.

The second portion of the `return` statement recursively invokes the `reverse` function with the remaining substring to process. This is the original string passed in, minus the last character (which was just returned to the caller):

```
reverse(substr(string,1,length(string)-1))
```

To test a program like this, you need a simple *driver* or some "scaffolding" to initially invoke the new `reverse` function. Fortunately, the rapid development that Rexx enables makes this easy. Coding a driver to test the new `reverse` function is as simple as coding these few lines:

```
/*    Simple "test driver" for the REVERSE function.           */

parse arg string .
call reverse string                 /* call the REVERSE function  */
say 'The reversed string is:' result  /* display the RESULT        */
exit 0
```

This code reads an input string from the user as an input command-line argument. It invokes the recursive, user-written `reverse` function and displays the result to the user.

The `say` instruction in this code uses the special variable `result` to display the string returned from the `reverse` function on the user's display screen:

```
say 'The reversed string is:' result  /* display the RESULT        */
```

Our new `reverse` function has the same name and functionality as Rexx's own, built-in `reverse` function. Which will Rexx run? The *function search order* tells us. Assuming that the `reverse` function we coded is internal, Rexx invokes it, because user-written internal functions have priority over Rexx's built-in functions in the function search order. If we want to use the built-in Rexx reverse function instead, we would code the name of the function in quoted uppercase letters. These two lines show the difference. This line invokes our own `reverse` function:

```
call reverse   string      /* call our own REVERSE function        */
```

In contrast, this statement runs Rexx's built-in `reverse` function:

```
call 'REVERSE' string      /* use the Rexx built-in REVERSE function */
```

More on Scoping

Developers place internal functions and subroutines after the main routine or driver in the script file. Here's the basic prototype for script structure where the main script has subroutines and/or functions:

```
main_routine:
    call  my_function      parameter_in
    call  my_subroutine    parameter_in
    exit 0

my_function: procedure
    return  result_string

my_subroutine: procedure
    return
```

Rexx does not require any label for the main routine or driving portion of the script, but we recommend it as a good programming practice. A Rexx *label* is simply a name terminated with a colon. In this script, we've identified the driver routine with the label `main_routine:`. This is good programming practice in very large programs because it may not always be obvious where the logic of the driver really starts. In other words, if there is a long list of variable declarations or lots of initialization at the top of a script, identifying where the "real" work of the main routine begins can sometimes be helpful.

A key issue in any large program is *scoping* — which of the caller's variables are available for reading and/or updating by a called function or subroutine. In Rexx, the `procedure` instruction is the basic tool for managing variable scoping. `procedure` is encoded as the first instruction following the label in any function or subroutine for which it's used.

The `procedure` instruction protects all existing variables by making them unknown to any instructions that follow. It ensures that the subroutine or function for which it is encoded cannot access or change any of its caller's variables. For example, in the `reverse` function, we coded this first line:

```
reverse: procedure
```

This means the `reverse` routine cannot read or update any variables from its caller — they are protected by the `procedure` instruction. This is a good start on proper modularity, but of course, we need a way to give the `reverse` routine access to those variables it *does* need to access. One approach is to pass them in as arguments or parameters, as we did in calling the `reverse` function, with this general structure:

```
calling routine:
    parse arg parm_1 parm_2 .  /* get command-line arguments from the user  */
    call function_name parm_1, parm_2       /* pass them to the internal routine */
    say 'The function result is:'  result  /* retrieve RESULT from the routine */
    exit 0

function_name: procedure
    parse arg parm_1, parm_2                 /* get parameters from the caller  */
    return result_string                     /* return result to caller         */
```

The `procedure` instruction protects all variables from the function or subroutine. This function cannot even read any of the caller's variables. It knows only about those passed in as input parameters, `parm_1` and `parm_2`. It can read the variables that are passed in via `arg`, and it sends back *one* result string via the `return` instruction. *It cannot change the value of any of the arg variables in the caller.* These are passed in on a read-only basis to the function or subroutine, which can only pass back one string value by a `return` instruction.

Another approach to passing data items between routines is to specify *exposed variables* on the `procedure` instruction. These variables are available for both reading *and updating* by the invoked routine:

```
function_name: procedure  expose  variable_1  array_element.1
```

In this case the function or subroutine can read and manipulate the variable `variable_1` and the specific array element `array_element.1`. The function or subroutine has full read and update access to these two `expose`'d variables.

With this knowledge, here's an alternative way to structure the relationship between caller and called routine:

```
calling_routine:
    parse arg parm_1 parm_2 .  /* get command-line arguments from the user  */
    call subroutine_name               /*  call the subroutine (or function) */
    say 'The function result is:'  result  /* retrieve RESULT from the routine */
    say 'The changed variables are:' parm_1 parm_2  /* see if variables changed */
```

```
    exit 0

subroutine_name: procedure  expose  parm_1  parm_2
   /* refer to and update the variables parm_1  and parm_2 as desired        */
   parm_1 = 'New value set by Sub. '
   parm_2 = '2nd new value set by Sub.'
   return  result_string                             /* return result to caller   */
```

The output from this code demonstrates that the subroutine changed the values the caller originally set for variables parm_1 and parm_2:

```
The function result is: RESULT_STRING
The changed variables are: New value set by Sub. 2nd new value set by Sub.
```

The procedure instruction limits variable access in the called function or subroutine. Only those variables specifically named on the procedure expose instruction will be available to the called routine.

To summarize, there are two basic approaches to making caller variables available to the called routine. Either pass them in as input arguments, or code the procedure expose instruction followed by a variable list. The called function or subroutine cannot change input arguments — these are read-only values passed by the caller. In contrast, any variables listed on the procedure expose statement can be both read and updated by the called function or subroutine. The calling routine will, of course, "see" those updated variable values.

Two brief scripts illustrate these principles. This first demonstrates that the called routine is unable to change any variables owned by its caller because of the procedure instruction coded on the first line of the called routine:

```
/* This code shows that a PROCEDURE instruction (without an EXPOSE         */
/* keyword) prevents a called function or subroutine from reading          */
/* or updating any of the caller's variables.                              */
/*                                                                         */
/* Argument-passing and the ARG instruction gives the called              */
/* function or subroutine READ-ONLY access to parameters.                  */

calling_routine:

   variable_1 = 'main'
   variable_2 = 'main'

   call my_subrtn(variable_1)

   say 'main:' variable_1 variable_2              /* NOT changed by my_subrtn */
   exit 0

my_subrtn: procedure

   arg variable_1                                 /* provides read-only access */

   say 'my_subrtn:' variable_1  variable_2        /* variable_2 is not set     */

   variable_1 = 'my_subrtn'
```

```
    variable_2 = 'my_subrtn'

    say 'my_subrtn:' variable_1  variable_2
    return
```

This is the output from this script:

```
my_subrtn: MAIN  VARIABLE_2
my_subrtn: my_subrtn  my_subrtn
main: main  main
```

The first output line shows that the subroutine was passed a value for `variable_1`, but `variable_2` was not passed in to it. The subroutine accessed the single value passed in to it by its `arg` instruction. The second line of the output shows that the called routine locally changed the values of variables `variable_1` and `variable_2` to the string value `my_subrtn` — but the last line shows that these assignments did not affect the variables of the same names in the caller. The subroutine could not change the caller's values for these two variables. This is so because the `procedure` instruction was encoded on the subroutine but it did not list any variables as `expose`'d.

This next script is similar but illustrates coding the `procedure expose` instruction to allow a called routine to manipulate the enumerated variables of its caller:

```
/*  This code shows that ONLY those variables listed after EXPOSE      */
/*  may be read and updated by the called function or subroutine.      */

calling_routine:

    variable_1      = 'main'
    array_name. = 'main'                 /* The called routine can update    */
    array_element.1 = 'main'                  /* array elements if desired.   */
    not_exposed     = 'main'

    call my_subrtn                       /* don't pass parms, use EXPOSE  */

    say  'main:'  variable_1  array_name.4  array_element.1  not_exposed
    exit 0

my_subrtn: procedure expose  variable_1  array_name. array_element.1

    say 'my_subrtn:' variable_ 1 array_name.4  array_element.1  not_exposed

    variable_1   = 'my_subrtn'           /* These will be set back in the */
    array_name.4 = 'my_subrtn'           /* caller, since they were       */
    array_element.1 = 'my_subrtn'        /* on the PROCEDURE EXPOSE.      */

       say 'my_subrtn:' variable_1  array_name.4  array_element.1 not_exposed
    return
```

The output from this script is:

```
my_subrtn: main main main  NOT_EXPOSED
my_subrtn: my_subrtn  my_subrtn  my_subrtn  NOT_EXPOSED
main: my_subrtn  my_subrtn  my_subrtn  main
```

The first output line shows that the subroutine accessed the three caller's variables listed on the `procedure expose` instruction. This shows the three variables set to the string value `main`. The fourth variable shows up as `NOT_EXPOSED` because the subroutine did not list it in its `procedure expose` statement and cannot access it.

The second output line shows that the subroutine set the value of the three variables it can change to the value `my_subrtn`. This line was displayed from within the subroutine.

The last output line confirms that the three variables set by the subroutine were successfully passed back to and picked up by the caller. Since only three variables were passed to the subroutine, the fourth variable, originally set to the string value `main` by the caller, still retains that same value.

What about external routines? Invoke them just like internal routines, but the Rexx interpreter always assigns them an implicit `procedure` instruction so that all the caller's variables are hidden. You cannot code a `procedure expose` instruction at the start of the external routine. Pass information into the external routine through input arguments. Code a `return` instruction to return a string from the external routine. Or, you can code an `exit` instruction with a return value.

For internal routines, if you code them without the `procedure` instruction, *all* the caller's variables are available to the internal routines. All the caller's variables are effectively *global variables*. Global variables are values that can be changed from any internal routine. Global variables present an alternative to passing updatable values into subroutines and functions via the `procedure expose` instruction.

Developers sometimes like using global variables because coding can be faster and more convenient. One does not have to take the time to consider and encode the correct `procedure expose` instructions. But global variables are not considered a good programming practice because they violate one of the key principles of modularity — that variables are explicitly assigned for use in specific modules. So that you recognize this scenario when you have to maintain *someone else's* code, here is the general script structure for using global variables:

```
/* Illustrate that Global Variables are accessible to ALL internal routines */
main_routine:
    a = 'this is a global variable!'
    call  my_subroutine
    say  'Prove subroutine changed the value:' a
    feedback = my_function()
    say 'Prove the function changed the value:' a
    exit 0

my_subroutine:
    /* all variables from MAIN_ROUTINE are available to this routine for
       read and or update */
    a = 'this setting will be seen by the caller'
    return

my_function:
    /* all variables from MAIN_ROUTINE are available to this routine for read
       and or update */
    a = 'this new value will be seen by the caller'
    return 0
```

The program output shows that the two internal routines are able to change any variable values in the calling routine at will. The two output lines are displayed by the driver. The latter portion of each line shows that the subroutine and function were able to change the value of the global variable named a:

```
Prove subroutine changed the value: this setting will be seen by the caller
Prove the function changed the value: this new value will be seen by the caller
```

All you have to do to use global variables is neglect to code the procedure instruction on subroutines on functions. This is convenient for the developer. But in large programs, it can be extremely difficult to track all the places in which variables are altered. *Side effects* are a real possibility, unexpected problems resulting from maintenance to code that does not follow the principles of structured programming and modularity.

To this point, we've discussed several ways to pass variables into and back from functions and subroutines. This chart summarizes the ways to pass information to and from called internal subroutines and functions:

Technique	Internal Routine's Variable Access	Comments
Pass arguments as input parameters	Read-only access to the passed variables *only*	Standard for passing in read-only values
procedure expose	Read and update access to expose'd variables *only*	Standard for updating some variables while hiding others
procedure (*without* expose)	Hides *all* the caller's variables	Standard for hiding all caller's variables
Global variables	Read and update access to *all* the caller's variables	Violates principles of modularity; works fine but not recommended
return expression	Send back one string to the caller	Standard for passing back one item of information

Whichever approach(es) you use, consistency is a virtue. This is especially the case for larger or more complex programming applications.

Another Sample Program

This next sample script illustrates a couple of the different ways to pass information into subroutines. One data element is passed in as an input argument to the routine, while the other data item is passed in via the procedure expose instruction.

This program searches a string and returns the rightmost occurrence of a specified character. It is a recursive function that duplicates functionality found in the built-in `lastpos` function. It shows how to pass data items to a called internal routine as input parameters and how to use the `procedure expose` instruction to pass in updateable items.

```
/*   RINDEX:                                                        */
/*                                                                  */
/*      Returns the rightmost position of a byte within a string.   */

rindex: procedure expose search_byte

parse arg string                                /* read the string */

say string search_byte                 /* show recursive trace for fun */

string_length   = length(string)       /* determine string length    */
string_length_1 = length(string) -1    /* determined string length - 1 */

if string == ''              /* here's the 'end recursion' condition    */
    then return 0
else do
    if substr(string,string_length,1) == search_byte then
        return string_length
    else
        new_string_to_search = substr(string,1,string_length_1)
    return rindex(new_string_to_search)
end
```

This script requires two inputs: a character string to inspect for the rightmost occurrence of a character, and the character or "search byte" to look for.

When invoked, the function looks to see if the last character in the string to search is the search character. If yes, it returns that position:

```
    if substr(string,string_length,1) == search_byte then
        return string_length
```

If the search character is not found, the routine calls itself with the remaining characters to search as the new string to search:

```
        new_string_to_search = substr(string,1,string_length_1)
        return rindex(new_string_to_search)
```

The end condition for recursion occurs when either the character has been found, or there are no more characters in the original string to search.

The function requires two pieces of input information: the string to inspect, and the character to find within that string. It reads the string to inspect as an input parameter, from the `parse arg` instruction:

```
parse arg string                          /* read the string */
```

The first line in the function gives the program access to the character to locate in the string:

```
rindex: procedure expose search_byte
```

The two pieces of information are coming into this program in two different ways. In a way this makes sense, because the character to locate never changes (it is a global constant), but the string that the function searches is reduced by one character in each recursive invocation of this function. While this program works fine, it suggests that passing in information through different mechanisms could be confusing. This is especially the case when a large number of variables are involved.

For large programs, consistency in parameter passing is beneficial. Large programs become complicated when programmers mix internal routines that have `procedure expose` instructions with routines that do not include this instruction. Rexx allows this but we do not recommend it. Consistency underlies readable, maintainable code. Coding a `procedure` or `procedure expose` instruction for *every* internal routine conforms to best programming practice.

Summary

This chapter describes the basic mechanisms by which Rexx scripts are modularized. Modularity is a fundamental means by which large programs are rendered readable, reliable, and maintainable. Modularity means breaking up large, complex tasks into a series of smaller, discrete modules. The interfaces between modules (the variables passed between them) should be well defined and controlled to reduce complexity and error.

We covered the various ways to pass information into internal routines and how to pass information from those routines back to the caller. These included passing data elements as input arguments, the `procedure` instruction and its `expose` keyword, and using global variables. We discussed some of the advantages and disadvantages of the methods, and offered sample scripts to illustrate each approach. The first sample script read a command-line argument from its environment and passed this string as an input argument to its subroutine. The subroutine passed a single value back up to its caller by using the `return` instruction. The last sample script was recursive. It invoked itself as a subroutine and illustrated how the `procedure expose` instruction could be used to pass values in recursive code. This latter example also suggests that consistently encoding the `procedure expose` instruction on *every* routine is a good approach for large programming projects. This consistent approach reduces errors, especially those that might otherwise result from maintenance on large programs that use global variables.

Test Your Understanding

1. Why is modularity important? How does Rexx support it?

2. What's the difference between a subroutine and function? When should you use one versus the other?

3. What is the difference between internal and external subroutines? How is the `procedure` instruction used differently for each?

4. What is the function search order, and how do you override it?

5. What are the basic ways in which information is passed to/from a caller and its internal routines?

6. What happens if you code a `procedure` instruction without an `expose` keyword? What's the difference between parameters passed in to an internal subroutine and read by the `arg` instruction versus those that are exposed by the `procedure expose` instruction?

7. In condition testing, TRUE is 1 and FALSE is 0. What happens when you write an if instruction with a condition that evaluates to some nonzero integer other than 1?

9

Debugging and the Trace Facility

Overview

Where scripting languages really shine is in the fast, easy program development they make possible. Their interpretive nature leads to built-in tools that make debugging much easier.

Rexx offers tremendous power in its *tracing facility*. Implemented by its `trace` instruction, the `trace` built-in function, and a variety of supporting functions and features, the tracing facility enables you to quickly and easily step through your code as it executes. Rexx will display the results of expression evaluation, variable contents, lines of code as they are translated and run, program position . . . indeed, almost anything going on in the script. You can *single-step* through your code, allowing Rexx to pause before or after each line of the source code. You can execute Rexx statements while your script is paused, for example, to inspect or alter the values of variables. At anytime, you can easily turn tracing on, off or to some different level of granularity. The trace facility makes debugging even the most complex logic a simple affair. This chapter describes the trace facility and how to use it in detail.

The say Instruction

Figure 9-1 shows three basic approaches to debugging Rexx scripts.

Debugging Options

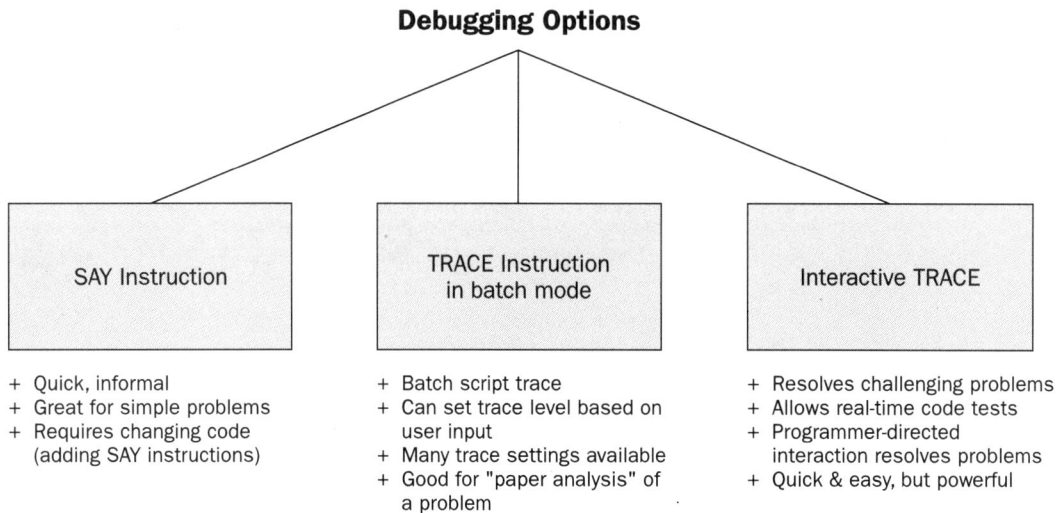

SAY Instruction	TRACE Instruction in batch mode	Interactive TRACE
+ Quick, informal + Great for simple problems + Requires changing code (adding SAY instructions)	+ Batch script trace + Can set trace level based on user input + Many trace settings available + Good for "paper analysis" of a problem	+ Resolves challenging problems + Allows real-time code tests + Programmer-directed interaction resolves problems + Quick & easy, but powerful

Figure 9-1

Let's start with the most basic approach to debugging. This simple technique temporarily adds extra `say` statements to the code to display variable values. Rexx makes this easy because of the manner in which the `say` instruction automatically concatenates expressions.

Take as an example the `rindex` program in the previous chapter. Recall that this script returns the rightmost position of a given character within a string. When first written and run, this program displayed this output as its answer regardless of the input search string:

```
The rightmost byte position is: 0
```

Clearly, something was wrong. Simply adding one line with a `say` instruction at the start of the routine made the problem evident:

```
say string search_byte
```

When the program ran with this debugging aid, here were the results from the `say` instruction:

```
D:\Regina\pgms>regina rindex.rexx abc b
abc SEARCH_BYTE
ab SEARCH_BYTE
a SEARCH_BYTE
SEARCH_BYTE
The rightmost byte position is: 0
```

The value of the byte to search for, entered in the command line as the character b, was not being picked up by the routine. Instead of the character string SEARCH_BYTE, we should have seen the input parameter string b repeated on each output line.

After adding the `expose search_byte` keywords to the `procedure` instruction, the program result was what we would expect:

```
D:\Regina\hf>regina rindex.rexx abc b
abc b
ab b
The rightmost byte position is: 2
```

So, the problem was improperly passing a value to a subroutine. The `say` instruction is ideal for this quick debugging because it automatically concatenates operands for instant output.

The trace Instruction

While quickly adding a `say` instruction to display some variable values or to trace execution of a program works well, many debugging situations require more powerful techniques. The `trace` instruction provides information at any level of detail and fulfills the need for both power and flexibility.

Typical encoding of the trace instruction is simple:

```
trace  [setting]
```

where the *setting* is any one of the following values:

Trace Setting	Name	Function
A	All	Traces all clauses before execution.
C	Commands	Traces all host commands before execution. This allows you to ensure that the command you're sending to the operating system (or other external environment) is correct. It's especially useful if the script dynamically creates or prepares those commands. If the command causes error or failure, its return code also appears.
E	Error	Traces any host command that results in error or failure after it executes.
F	Failure	Traces any host command that fails along with its return code.
I	Intermediates	Traces all clauses before their execution, including intermediate results during expression evaluation.
L	Labels	Traces labels as execution runs through them.
N	Normal	Nothing is traced except that host commands that fail are traced after their execution, along with their return codes.
O	Off	Nothing is traced.
R	Results	Traces clauses before their execution along with the final results of expression evaluation. Displays values assigned from `pull`, `arg`,and `parse` instructions.

When is each of these trace settings most useful? This setting is the default:

```
trace n
```

It traces nothing except failed host commands. It is minimally intrusive and is a good default value for working programs.

`trace r` is recommended for general-purpose debugging. It traces clauses before they execute and the final results of expression evaluation. It also shows when values change by `pull`, `arg`, and `parse` instructions. When you need to run a trace, `trace r` is usually where to start. If problems persist, `trace i` gives fuller detail. It gives everything that `trace r` does plus includes the details of intermediate expression evaluation.

If you're unsure about what routines are being entered and executed, try `trace l`. This lists all labels program execution passes through and shows which internal routines are entered and run. It's an easy way to determine if a subroutine or function you coded is being entered and executed at the proper time.

If the problem is that commands to the host operating system are failing, `trace c` will trace all host commands before their execution. For any that cause an error or fail, it also shows the return code from the command. `trace e` and `trace f` are weaker forms of `trace c` that trace host command errors and failures, respectively. We recommend `trace c` as simplest and most complete if problems are occurring in executing host commands.

Where does one code the `trace` instruction? Anywhere in the code you like. A simple approach is to code one `trace` instruction near the very top of the program. It can be set to `trace n` (the default), and then changed to any other value desired during debugging. Just remember to set it back to `trace n` once debugging is completed. This approach is simple and consistent but does require changing the code to change the trace setting.

Another approach is to code a `trace` instruction at the start of the program, then have the program read the `trace` option dynamically, from the outside environment. For example, the program could prompt the user to enter the trace setting. Or, it might accept it as an optionally coded command-line argument to the program. Or, the program could even read this information from a "control file" or configuration file that dictates program behavior. For example, under Windows you could use an `.ini` file to configure tracing. Under Unix or Linux, you might use a `config` file.

However you set the trace option, you can code as many `trace` instructions as you like in a single script. These can flip the trace off or on, or set different levels of trace detail appropriate to different routines or sections of code. Scripts can dynamically control their trace levels themselves.

The `trace` instruction accepts the setting as a constant (a string literal or symbol), or it can be encoded as a variable or even as an expression to evaluate with the optional `value` keyword. These are the two basic formats for the `trace` instruction:

```
trace   [setting]
```

or

```
trace   value   [expression]
```

Here's how to set the trace level by using a variable:

```
trace_variable = 'r'
trace  value  trace_variable
```

The trace instruction can be coded multiple times in a program, and you can turn tracing on or off (by trace o) as desired. This is mainly of use in very large programs, where you really want to zero in only on problems occurring in a newly added routine or better understand the effects of newly changed or problem code.

Let's look at some examples. Here is the output that results from placing a trace r instruction in the rindex function immediately after the 1st line of code (after the procedure instruction):

```
D:\Regina\hf>regina rindex.rexx ab b
   16 *-*  parse arg string                   /* read the string               */
      >>>     "ab"
   18 *-*  say string search_byte             /* show recursive trace for fun  */
      >V>     "ab"
      >V>     "b"
ab b
   20 *-*  string_length   = length(string)   /* determine string length       */
      >V>     "ab"
   21 *-*  string_length_1 = length(string) -1 /* determined string length - 1 */
      >V>     "ab"
   23 *-*  if string == ''                    /* Here's the 'end recursion' condition. */
      >V>     "ab"
   25 *-*  do
   26 *-*  if substr(string,string_length,1) == search_byte then
      >V>     "ab"
      >V>     "2"
      >V>     "b"
   27 *-*  return string_length
      >V>     "2"
The rightmost byte position is: 2
```

With trace r, line 16 shows how the parse arg instruction assigns values on entry to this function. Every expression appears *prior* to execution, then the result to which it evaluates. The listing shows that this trace setting resolves most debugging needs handily.

If you continue to have trouble, change the trace r to trace i and see the intermediate results of expression evaluation as well. This makes for longer, more complex output that you'll want to see only if you're having real trouble in debugging.

Let's take out the trace instruction in the rindex function, and instead place a single trace l at the top of the driver program. This traces all the labels the script execution passes. In this case, it verifies that the driver routine invokes the rindex function:

```
D:\Regina\hf>regina rindex abc a
   14 *-*  rindex:
```

The `trace 1` *label trace* is great for automatically displaying which internal routines are called during a large program. It gives more concise output than `trace r` when you're just worried about which routines are being called and when. Use it for those situations in which you're not sure if a routine is being called or if it is not clear how often a routine is invoked.

To debug scripts that issue operating system commands, `trace c` is a good choice. It traces host commands *prior* to execution, and it gives the return code from any command that results in error or failure. To check its output, here's a simple test program that we ran under Windows. This program intends to issue the `dir` (list directory) command to Windows, but the command was misspelled as `dri`:

```
/*  Script to test tracing output for a failed operating system command */
trace c
'dri'                   /* Mistake - this should have been coded as: dir    */
```

Running this script gives this output:

```
      3 *-*   'dri'
'dri' is not recognized as an internal or external command,
operable program or batch file.
        +++ RC=1 +++
```

The output clearly shows the problem with the operating system command that was issued.

`trace e` shows any host command that results in error or failure and its return code, while `trace f` shows host commands that result in failure and their return code. We recommend `trace c` because it always lists the command that caused the problem.

Reading Trace Output

Trace output is designed to be easy to read. The preceding example shows that lines are numbered for easy identification. Right after the line number is the identifier *-* and the source line of code from the program. The symbol >>> identifies the value assigned to variables as a result of parsing or a value returned from an internal routine. For example, look at these two lines from the trace of the preceding `rindex` function:

```
     16 *-*   parse arg string                     /* read the string            */
        >>>      "ab"
```

The trace output on the second line shows that this string was assigned to the variable `string` as a result of the `parse arg` instruction.

When the trace shows the contents of a variable, it precedes with this symbol >V>. These two statements show that the string sent back via the `return` instruction is "2":

```
     27 *-*   return string_length
        >V>      "2"
```

Notice how the trace is indented to convey more information. The strings displayed on the screen by the `say` instruction start on the left, while program statements and variable contents are indented. This sample code is pretty linear, but where nesting is more involved, indentation makes the trace output much easier to follow.

For many programs, just these simple rules are all that is required to interpret trace output. Here are the trace output identifiers you might encounter:

Trace Output Identifier	Meaning
_	A source line or clause
+++	A trace message
>>>	The result of an expression (for `trace r`), a value assigned to a variable from parsing, or the string returned by an internal function or subroutine
>.>	Identifies a what is assigned to a placeholder(the period) during parsing

These output prefixes appear only if trace intermediates (`trace i`) is in effect:

Trace Output Identifier	Meaning
>V>	Identifies variable contents
>L>	Identifies a literal string
>F>	The result of a function call
>P>	The result of a prefix operation
>O>	The result of an operation on two items
>C>	Contents of a compound (array) variable after substitution and before use

The trace Function

The `trace` instruction enables scripts to dynamically turn the trace facility off and on, and to specify the level of detail provided by the trace. In addition to the `trace` instruction, there is also a `trace` built-in function. The `trace` function returns the current value of the trace, and optionally sets the trace level to a new value.

When coded without an input parameter, the `trace` function returns the current trace setting:

```
say  trace()                  /* display current trace setting */
```

An input argument can be coded to set the trace:

```
current_trace = trace('O')    /* turns the trace setting off    */
```

The allowable values for the `trace` function are the exact same as those for the `trace` instruction. The following table lists the possible `trace` function values. Since these values are the same as those for the `trace` instruction, you can review the `trace` instruction table near the beginning of this chapter for a full explanation of each setting. This table lists the one-word meanings of the options for easy recall:

Trace Setting	Meaning
A	All
C	Commands
E	Errors
F	Failure
I	Intermediates
L	Labels
N	Normal
O	Off
R	Results

When the `trace` function includes an operand, it returns the current `trace` setting; *then* it alters the trace level to the new setting. Look at these three instructions run in sequence:

```
say   trace()      ==  N    /* displays the default setting                */
say   trace('C')   ==  N    /* returns current trace setting, then alters it */
say   trace()      ==  C    /* displays the current trace setting           */
```

Interactive Tracing

So far we have discussed the trace setting as if it is something one turns on or off (multiple times if desired). Then you read its output after the script executes. This is a "batch" approach to debugging. In fact, one of the biggest benefits of tracing is the potential to pause the script at desired points and perform real-time operations, called *interactive tracing*.

To start interactive tracing, code the `trace` instruction with a question mark (?) preceding its argument. For example, this statement starts interactive tracing for results:

```
trace   ?r      /* turn on interactive tracing for Results */
```

Here's another example. This statement turns interactive tracing on for commands:

```
trace   ?c      /* turn on interactive Command trace */
```

The ? is a toggle switch. If tracing is off, this it turns on; if tracing is on, this turns it off. The first `trace` instruction or function you execute with ? encoded turns tracing on. The next one that executes with the question mark will turn it off.

When in *interactive mode*, the Rexx interpreter pauses after each statement or clause. Or, to be more precise, the Rexx interpreter pauses after executing each statement and displays the next statement to execute. At this point, you can perform any one of three actions listed in the following table:

Your Action	Result
Press the <ENTER> key (also referred to as entering a null line)	The interpreter continues until the next point at which it should pause.
Enter an equals sign =	The interpreter reexecutes the last clause. This allows you to "go back" one clause, make changes, and allow it to be rerun. For example, you could alter the value of a variable or change how an if instruction might be evaluated.
Enter any Rexx clause or expression or statement	Rexx immediately executes what you've entered.

The last option listed in this table bears some explanation. When the interpreter pauses, you can enter any valid Rexx clause, expression, or statement. The interpreter then immediately executes what you've entered. This allows you to change the value of variables to see how the program will respond. For example, you could enter an executable statement like this to alter a variable's value and see how this alters the script's execution:

```
my_variable = '123'
```

As another example, you could enter statements to display the contents of an array. This would allow you to verify that the array contains what you think it should at that point in your program:

```
do j = 1 to 5; say array_name.j ; end ;
```

You can even enter a statement to change the level of detail in the trace output, or you can run any other valid Rexx statement.

Interactive tracing lets you *single-step* through a script, inspecting and then running that code one clause at a time. You can inspect or change variables at will, see how code changes would affect execution, change various aspects of the environment, and alter the trace level itself.

Settings for the trace instruction are saved and restored across internal routines. If you enter an internal routine of no interest, merely turn off the trace:

```
trace o      /* turn trace off */
```

The original trace setting will be restored when the caller is reentered.

Trace options are one of the few places in which Rexx uses abbreviations. Normally, the language uses full words for enhanced readability. The reason the trace instruction is an exception is that interactive tracing allows terse input from the keyboard so that the developer does not have to type so much and can work with simple mnemonic abbreviations when debugging.

Sometimes during a trace, its useful to be able to "skip ahead" a number of clauses with the interactive trace temporarily turned off. To do this, code a negative number on the `trace` instruction. This tells the interpreter to skip tracing a certain number of clauses, and then to resume as before. For example, this statement skips tracing the next 50 clauses, after which tracing resumes:

```
trace -50
```

You can also code a positive number on the `trace` instruction to skip a specified number of interactive pauses. For example, this instruction skips the next five interactive pauses, then resumes tracing as before:

```
trace  5
```

Some Rexx implementations allow turning on the trace externally, so you do not have to alter your script to trace it. An example is mainframe Rexx, described in detail in Chapter 29. Mainframe Rexx under operating systems such as VM and OS permits *immediate commands*, which can alter the trace level from outside the script while the script executes. All standard Rexx interpreters support internally changing the trace through the `trace` instruction and `trace` function.

Summary

As an interpreted scripting language, Rexx offers superior debugging facilities. Chief among them is interactive tracing, by which you can dynamically inspect and even alter your script's variables and its execution.

In most cases a simple batch approach to turning on the trace quickly resolves any programming problem. But when called for the full power of a completely interactive tracing facility is available. Using it, there are very few logic and programming errors you cannot quickly rectify. The trace facility is a big advantage of Rexx scripting versus programming in traditional compiled programming languages. Interacting tracing can dramatically reduce the time spent in debugging and resolving logic errors.

Test Your Understanding

1. What is the default setting for the `trace` instruction? What settings are recommended for:

   ❑ General-purpose debugging

   ❑ Seeing which subroutines and internal functions are being entered and executed

   ❑ Viewing intermediate results of all clauses

2. Your script issues commands to the operating system, but they are failing. What do you do?

3. How do you turn interactive tracing on? Off?

4. How do you single-step through the code of a script as it executes?

10

Errors and Condition Trapping

Overview

Full-featured programming languages require a mechanism through which programmers can catch, or *trap*, exceptions or errors. In Rexx, this is often referred to as *exception handling* or *condition trapping*.

Rexx offers a simple, but serviceable, means for trapping exceptional conditions. When an exception occurs, control is transferred to a routine to address the error. After the error routine handles the condition, execution of the primary script can resume.

This chapter explores Rexx's exception-trapping mechanism and the way in which you can use it in scripts to identify, capture, and manage errors. First, we'll discuss the specific kinds of errors that Rexx can trap. We'll discuss how to set up, or *enable*, error trapping. Then we'll take a look at a program that illustrates the exception-trapping mechanism. We'll progressively improve this program to expand its error-trapping capabilities and demonstrate different approaches to managing errors. We conclude by mentioning some of the limitations of exception conditions in standard Rexx, and how some Rexx interpreters extend beyond the ANSI standards to provide more generalized error trapping.

Error Trapping

When an error condition occurs, it is considered to be *raised*. Rexx interpreters that adhere to the TRL-2 standard allow the raising of six different error conditions, while the ANSI-1996 standard adds a seventh error condition. The table below lists all the error conditions:

Error Condition	Use
ERROR	Raised when a host command indicates an error upon return.
FAILURE	Raised when a host command indicates failure.
HALT	Raised by an external interrupt to a program. Example: the user presses Control-C (aka Ctrl-C).
NOVALUE	Raised when a variable that is to be used has not been assigned a value. The invalid variable reference could occur in an expression, in a parse template, or in a procedure or drop instruction.
NOTREADY	Raised by an input/output (I/O) error on a device unable to handle the I/O request.
SYNTAX	Raised by a syntax or runtime error in the script.
LOSTDIGITS	Raised when an arithmetic operation would cause the loss of digits. Significant digits in the result exceed the number of significant digits currently set by numeric digits or the system default of nine significant digits. (This trap was added in the ANSI-1996 standard and may not be present in Rexx implementations that adhere to the earlier TRL-2 standard.)

How to Trap Errors

The procedure to manually trap errors is simple. First, code either a signal or call statement in your script to identify the error you wish to intercept. This instruction can optionally specify the name of the routine to transfer control to when the error occurs. Second, code the routine to handle the error. Rexx transfers control to this trap routine based on the label encoded in the signal or call statement that refers to that error condition.

If the signal or call statement does not the specify the name of the error routine to which to transfer control, by default Rexx transfers control to a routine with the same name as that of the error. For example, say you code:

```
signal on novalue
```

This statement enables the NOVALUE error condition without specifically naming the error routine to handle it, so Rexx assumes that it will find an error routine named NOVALUE to handle the condition.

Here's the basic coding template for how to enable and code for error conditions:

```
main_routine:

    signal  on  novalue  name  novalue_handler

    /*  main_routine's code goes here. */
```

```
    exit

novalue_handler:

    /* Code to handle the NOVALUE error goes here. */

    signal main_routine     /* go back to the main_routine after error-handling */
```

Figure 10-1 shows the basic logic of conditions or error handling diagrammatically.

Condition Trapping

signal on *condition* name *label_name*

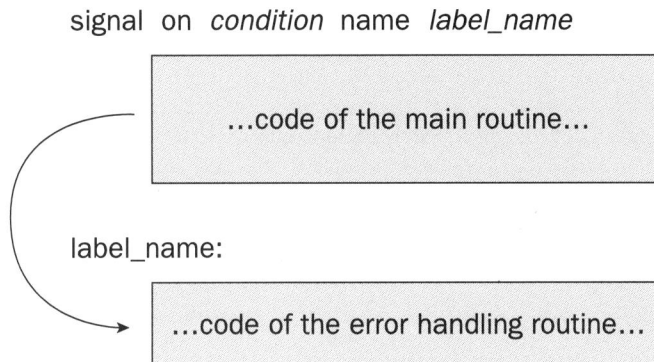

Figure 10-1

Remember that we previously saw the signal instruction used in a manner similar to an unconditional GOTO statement. This is a new form of the signal statement that sets up and enables a condition trap.

In the sample code, this line enables the trap for the NOVALUE condition and names the routine that will handle this error:

```
signal  on  novalue  name  novalue_handler
```

This line does *not* immediately transfer control to the routine to which it refers; it only *enables* the trap so that the error routine will be invoked when and if the exception condition named on the signal statement (the NOVALUE condition) occurs.

The name keyword is followed by the name of the error routine for that condition. In this example, the name of the routine that will be run when the NOVALUE condition occurs is novalue_handler. Somewhere later in the code there *must* be a label that identifies the routine that handles the error condition. This error-handling code performs any appropriate processing for the specified condition. In most cases, error routines return control to the point of invocation after printing an error message or performing other corrective action. But they could end the script or take any other action desired.

The `signal` or `call` instructions can be coded without explicitly specifying the name of the trap routine. In this case, the label of the error routine must be the same as the condition that is raised. Here are examples:

```
signal on error    /* enables ERROR trap to be handled by routine named ERROR: */
signal on novalue  /* NOVALUE condition requires a routine labeled NOVALUE:    */
call on failure     /* FAILURE errors are handled by a routine labeled FAILURE: */
```

We'll get into the differences between `signal` on and `call` on later. For now, note that `signal` can be coded with all seven conditions but that `call` cannot be coded with the SYNTAX, NOVALUE, and LOSTDIGITS errors. `call` enables a smaller set of error-condition routines.

A Sample Program

Here's a simple script that illustrates how to trap syntax or runtime errors. The program prompts the user to enter a Rexx expression or statement. Then it executes the `interpret` instruction to evaluate that expression and execute it. The prompt/interpret loop continues indefinitely until the user enters the letters `exit`. At that point the `interpret` instruction executes the `exit` instruction the user entered, which terminates the program.

Besides showing how to trap an error condition, this is a useful script because it allows you to interactively test various Rexx statements. You can purposely enter a statement with invalid syntax and read the error message with which Rexx responds. The script provides a handy "statement tester." It also shows how the `interpret` instruction can be used to dynamically interpret and execute Rexx statements. Here's the script:

```
/* REXX TRY1                                          */
/*                                                    */
/*      Reads user-input Rexx statements and interprets them.  */

say "Type: 'exit' to end this program"

start_loop:
   signal on syntax                 /* establish error trap  */

   do forever
      call charout ,"==> "          /* prompt/read on 1 line */
      parse pull expression$
      interpret expression$         /* INTERPRET user's input */
   end

end_start_loop: exit 0

SYNTAX:
   say 'SYNTAX:' errortext(rc) '(error' rc')'     /* write error*/
   signal start_loop                /* return to processing   */
```

Here's a sample interaction with the program:

```
C:\Regina\pgms>regina rexx_try1.rexx
Type: 'exit' to end this program
==> say 3+2
```

```
5
==> if a=3 then
SYNTAX: Incomplete DO/SELECT/IF (error 14)
==> if a=3
SYNTAX: THEN expected (error 18)
==> exit
```

The sample interaction shows that the user starts the program and it prompts him or her to enter a Rexx statement. He or she enters: say 3+2. The interpret instruction evaluates and executes this instruction, so the script displays the result: 5. Next the user enters an invalid if instruction. The interpret instruction runs it, which raises the SYNTAX exception.

In the script, this line enabled the syntax condition trap. The error routine it enables must be labeled SYNTAX: since no other explicit label was specified:

```
    signal on syntax                    /* establish error trap    */
```

All the error handler does in this script is write an error message and send control back to a label in the main routine. Here is the code for the exception handler:

```
SYNTAX:
    say 'SYNTAX:' errortext(rc) '(error' rc')'    /* write error         */
    signal start_loop                             /* return to processing */
```

rc is one of Rexx's *special variables* (others include result and sigl). rc contains the error code associated with the syntax error. The line that displays the error message applies the built-in function errortext to the error code in special variable rc to display the complete text of the syntax error message to the user. (In the cases of ERROR and FAILURE conditions, rc is set to the return code from the failed host command.)

At the end of the SYNTAX error routine, the signal start_loop instruction transfers control back to the main routine. When using signal to enable the error routine, the trap routine must explicitly direct execution back to the main program, if desired. This return of control from the exception routine is not automatic when the trap is invoked by the signal instruction.

Note the sample code transfers control back to a point *at which it will reexecute the signal statement that enables the ERROR trap*:

```
start_loop:

    signal on syntax                    /* establish error trap    */
```

Whenever a trap is enabled by signal, then processed, it *must* be reenabled again to reestablish it. In other words, processing a trap by signal turns off that trap and the condition must be reenabled if it is to be captured again later. So, typically, the first thing a script does after processing an error condition is reenable that condition by reexecuting the signal statement that set it up.

If we do not reexecute the signal on syntax statement to reenable the error condition, the *default action* for that error condition occurs if the error condition is raised again. The default action is what happens whenever an error condition is *disabled* or has not yet been enabled at all within the script.

A `signal on` or `call on` instruction has not been executed to enable the error trap. The default action for a syntax error is for Rexx to write an appropriate error message and stop executing the script.

These are the default actions for all untrapped conditions:

Condition	Default Action
SYNTAX and HALT	Rexx writes an appropriate error message and ends the program.
ERROR, FAILURE, NOVALUE, NOTREADY, LOSTDIGITS	The condition is ignored and the program continues.

You can *dynamically* enable and disable trap routines from your code. To turn a condition on, code `signal on` or `call on`. To disable it, use `signal off` or `call off`. Here is an example:

```
call on error    /* enable ERROR error trap */

/* some code might go here */

call off error   /* disable ERROR error trap, accept default action for error */

/* some code might go here */

call on error    /* enable ERROR error trap again */
```

You can also code multiple routines to handle a single error condition, then dynamically determine which one will be enabled at any time. This code first enables one error routine, then another:

```
signal on notready name notready_routine_1  /* enable NOTREADY error handler */

/* some code might go here */

signal off notready                          /* enable a different NOTREADY   */
signal on notready name notready_routine_2  /*    error handling routine      */
```

Of course, *only one* routine should be enabled at any time. If you code statements that try to enable more than one routine, Rexx simply uses the last one enabled. In the following code sequence, Rexx would run the second routine when the SYNTAX error is raised:

```
signal  on syntax  name routine_1
signal  on syntax  name routine_2
```

An Improved Program

Let's improve the preceding program to manage all the conditions Rexx can raise for traps. This version uses `signal` to set traps for all seven conditions. You can enter various expressions to see which the program identifies through its error conditions. Here's the script:

```
/* REXX TRY2:                                              */
/*                                                         */
/*     Reads user-input Rexx statements and interprets them. */

say "Type: 'exit' to end this program"

start_loop:
   signal on syntax    name syntax_rtn /* establish error traps */
   signal on error     name error_rtn
   signal on failure   name failure_rtn
   signal on halt      name halt_rtn
   signal on notready  name notready_rtn
   signal on novalue   name novalue_rtn
   signal on lostdigits name lostdigits_rtn

   do forever
      call charout ,"==> "             /* prompt/read on 1 line  */
      parse pull expression$
      interpret expression$            /* INTERPRET user's input */
   end

end_start_loop: exit 0

SYNTAX_RTN:
   say 'SYNTAX:' errortext(rc) '(error' rc')'
   signal start_loop

ERROR_RTN:
   say 'ERROR: The comand entered returned an error, rc=' rc
   say 'The command was:' sourceline(sigl)
   signal start_loop

FAILURE_RTN:
   say 'FAILURE: Uninitialized variable or failure in system service'
   signal start_loop

HALT_RTN:
   say 'HALT: External interrupt identified and captured'
   signal start_loop

NOTREADY_RTN:
   say 'NOTREADY: I/O error occurred'
   signal start_loop

NOVALUE_RTN:
   say 'NOVALUE: Variable was not assigned a value:' expression$
   signal start_loop

LOSTDIGITS_RTN:
   say 'LOSTDIGITS: arithmetic operation lost significant digits'
   signal start_loop
```

This script operates the same as the simpler version but traps more error conditions. Here's a sample interaction:

```
D:\Regina\pgms>regina rexx_try2.rexx
Type: 'exit' to end this program
==> say 3+4
7
==> say a
NOVALUE: Variable was not assigned a value: say a
==> a=4
==> say a
4
==>                             /* Á user entered CTRL-C on this line  */
HALT: External interrupt identified and captured
==> 'dri'                       /* user incorrectly enters DIR command */
'dri' is not recognized as an internal or external command,
operable program or batch file.
    19 *-*  interpret expression$       /* INTERPRET user's input            */
        +++ RC=1 +++
ERROR: The command entered returned an error, rc = 1
The command was:   interpret expression$       /* INTERPRET user's input       */
==>
```

The interaction shows that the `say a` instruction was intercepted by the NOVALUE condition, because the variable a had not yet been assigned a value. The blank input line is where the user entered the key combination Control-C. The HALT condition routine caught this and displayed its message.

Lastly, the user tries to enter a Windows `dir` (list directory) command, but mistypes it as: `dri`. The Error-condition trap gains control. It displays the value returned by the failed command, its *condition code*, available in Rexx special variable `rc`. Rexx also sets the value of special variable `sigl` whenever transfer of control is effected to an internal subroutine or by raising a condition. `sigl` is set to the line in the source code where the transfer occurred. It can be used to identify the line that caused the problem by a trap routine. This script uses it as an input to the `sourceline` built-in function, which then displays the source code of the line that caused the condition to be raised:

```
say 'The command was:' sourceline(sigl)
```

This line in the code resulted in this display output:

```
The command was:   interpret expression$       /* INTERPRET user's input */
```

This correctly identifies the `interpret` instruction as the line in the script from which the condition was raised.

We should note in passing that the `sourceline` function also has another use. Coding `sourceline` without any arguments returns the number of lines in the script:

```
script_line_count = sourceline()     /* determine number of lines in the script */
```

In this script, the seven `signal on` statements enable all the trap conditions. These instructions specify the names of the trap routines. If not explicitly named, the routine names default to the name of the condition which they trap. For example, the ERROR condition would require the label ERROR: in the script if the `signal on` instruction does not specifically name some other error routine.

Each trap routine ends with this statement:

```
signal  start_loop
```

The label `start_loop` occurs *before* the cascade of `signal on` instructions, so that after any trap routine executes, the program reenables it. If the script did not do this, then each error condition would be disabled after one execution of its corresponding error routine. The default action would then apply to any error condition that was subsequently raised.

One more word about this sample program: It is somewhat system-dependent. For example, different operating systems handle the Control-C entry in slightly different ways. An entry of Ctrl-C on one system was immediately trapped in the program, while in another, it was necessary to enter Ctrl-C, then press the Enter key. Your operating system may give slightly different results. When trapping error conditions, it is very important to test the script on the system on which it will run.

With this improved version of this script, we have a truly useful program. Use it to interactively test any Rexx statement and also learn about any of Rexx's error conditions by trapping them. The script is a generic Rexx "statement tester and verifier." Its exception handling allows it to display good error messages to the user when a statement does not check out.

Special Variables

In this chapter, we've identified two more special variables, `rc` and `sigl`. In the TRL-2 standard, Rexx has but three *special variables* — variables identified by a hardcoded keyword, into which Rexx places information at certain times. This chart summarizes the special variables:

Special Variable	Meaning
rc	The return code from a host command, or a Rexx SYNTAX error code.
sigl	The line number that caused control to jump to a label. This could be set by the transfer of control caused by a trapped condition, or simply by a regular call to an internal routine or invoking an internal function.
result	The string sent back to a calling routine by the `return` instruction. If `return` is coded without an operand result is set to uninitialized.

All special variables are uninitialized until an event occurs that sets them. While we won't go into them here, it is probably worth noting that the ANSI-1996 standard adds several more special variables to the language.

signal versus call

So far, our sample code has used the `signal` instruction. Rexx also permits enabling error conditions through the `call` instruction. Let's discuss the differences between `signal` and `call`.

First, `signal` applies to all seven error conditions. `call` does *not* apply to SYNTAX, NOVALUE, and LOSTDIGITS errors. *These are invalid and cannot be coded:*

```
call on syntax        /* Invalid ! */
call on novalue       /* Invalid ! */
call on lostdigits    /* Invalid ! */
```

Second, recall that `signal` forces an *abnormal change* in the flow of control. It terminates any `do`, `if`, or `select` instruction in force and unconditionally transfers control to a specified label. `call` provides for normal invocation of an internal subroutine to handle an error condition. It offers a more "normal" way to implement trap routines through the commonly used subroutine mechanism. Control is automatically transferred from the error routine back to the main program when the `return` instruction in the trap routine executes (as with any `called` routine).

There is one wrinkle. The `result` special variable is not set when returning from a called condition trap; any value coded on the `return` instruction is ignored.

To illustrate the use of `call`, here is a script that asks the user to input an invalid operating system command. This raises the ERROR condition and starts the ERROR: routine. The trap routine puts the user into Rexx's interactive debugging mode, from which he or she can enter various diagnostics. When the user turns off the trace, the script continues. Here is the code:

```
/* REXX TRY3:                                            */
/*                                                       */
/*     Shows how CALL traps a command ERROR.             */
/*     Places user into interactive debugging mode.      */

say "Type: 'exit' to end this program"

start_loop:

   call on error                      /* establish error trap */

   do forever
      call charout ,"Enter bad command ==> "      /* prompt   */
      parse pull expression$
      interpret expression$          /* INTERPRET user's input */
   end

end_start_loop: exit 0

ERROR:
    say 'ERROR: The line entered returned an error, rc=' rc
    say 'ERROR MESSAGE:' errortext(rc)
    say 'ERROR LINE:'    sourceline(sigl)
    trace '?'                /* put user in interactive trace mode */
    say 'Interactive Trace'
    return
```

At the program prompt, the user should enter an operating system (OS) command. For example, under Windows he or she could enter the directory (`dir`) command:

```
Enter bad command ==> dir
```

This command executes normally. The error condition is raised when the user enters an incorrect operating system command:

```
Enter bad command ==> dri
```

In this case, the user mistyped the command. When the error is raised, the trap routine displays the error message by the built-in function `errortext`. It also displays the source line that caused the problem by using the `sourceline` function with the `sigl` special variable as an input parameter. Finally, it places the user in interactive trace mode through this instruction:

```
trace  '?'
```

Once inside the interactive trace, the user could interactively enter whatever statements might be useful to gather information and solve the problem. Since the user entered an invalid command, perhaps he or she would ask the operating system for help by entering:

```
help dir
```

This would execute the Windows `help` command and display more information about the `dir` command to the user. Since the trace facility allows entering any valid statement, the user could also enter any other command that he or she believes might be helpful to understand the situation.

When the user finishes with interactive debugging mode, he or she just turns off the interactive trace by issuing this instruction, and the script resumes:

```
trace off
```

This script shows how to identify errors and place users into interactive sessions to fix them. This could be useful during program development or in certain kinds of system administration scripts. The ability to dynamically place the user into an interactive session with the interpreter is a feature unique to Rexx scripting that should only be used with knowledgeable users but that is very powerful where applicable.

Recall that when Rexx encounters a command that is not part of the Rexx language, by default it passes it to the operating system for execution. In this case, the Rexx `interpret` instruction ultimately passed the OS command the user entered to the operating system for execution. This is how the `dir` command got sent to Windows for execution.

This sample script is operating-system-dependent because the commands it asks the user to enter are OS-specific. For example, the `dir` (list directory) command is common to all versions of Windows, while the `help dir` command is only common to some versions of Windows. Both commands fail under Linux, Unix, BSD, and other operating systems. (Since this script captures failed operating system commands, perhaps that's okay!)

One other consideration specific to Windows ME/98SE/98/95 and DOS is that these operating systems *always* send back a return code of 0 from all OS commands. Running this program on these systems will not properly trap the error code. This is a defect of those operating systems, not of Rexx or its error handling.

For example, running this program under Windows 98SE failed to trap the error and instead just reflected back the OS error message:

```
Enter bad command ==> dri
Bad command or file name
Enter bad command ==> exit
D:\Regina\pgms> _
```

The cause of this behavior is that the underlying operating system does not issue a return code indicating that the OS command failed. So, there is no bad return code for Rexx to capture. This is not a Rexx issue, but you need to be aware of this behavior if you code under older Windows or DOS operating systems.

The condition Function

The built-in `condition` function offers a trap routine another means of obtaining information about the circumstances under which it was invoked. `condition` takes a single input argument, which may be any of the following:

Condition Argument	Full Name	Meaning
C	Condition name	Returns the name of the trapped condition (e.g., ERROR, FAILURE, HALT, NOVALUE, NOTREADY, SYNTAX, or LOSTDIGITS)
D	Description	A system-dependent description or reason for the condition
I	Instruction	Returns either CALL or SIGNAL to tell how the condition was trapped
S	State	The current state of the trapped condition (not the state at the time when the condition was trapped). May be one of the following: ON — the condition is enabled OFF — the condition is disabled DELAYED — any new occurrence of the condition will be delayed (ignored)

What if an error condition is executing and the same condition is raised again? This is the purpose of the DELAYED state. This state prevents a second trap from being invoked while an error-condition routine is executing.

A Generic Error-Trap Routine

To this point, we have discussed error trapping by progressively refining a single program. The program gives users the ability to discover error numbers and messages for various Rexx errors by interactively submitting error-prone statements to the script. One version of the script, in the earlier section entitled "An Improved Program," trapped all seven ANSI-1996 standard error conditions. Each condition was handled by its own separate trap routine.

Now, here's a twist. This sample script also handles the seven ANSI-1996 standard error conditions. But this program sends all errors to a single, consolidated, generic error-handling routine. The trap routine obtains orientation information about the error that occurred through the condition function by issuing that function with various parameters. Here is the code for the script:

```
/* REXX TRY4:                                           */
/*                                                      */
/*    Shows how to use the CONDITION function to get    */
/*    information in the trap routine.                  */

say "Type: 'exit' to end this program"

start_loop:
   signal on syntax    name who_am_i   /* establish all raised  */
   signal on error     name who_am_i   /* conditions to the     */
   signal on failure   name who_am_i   /* same trap routine     */
   signal on halt      name who_am_i
   signal on notready  name who_am_i
   signal on novalue   name who_am_i
   signal on lostdigits name who_am_i

   do forever
      call charout ,"==> "               /* prompt for user input  */
      parse pull expression$
      interpret expression$              /* INTERPRET user's input */
   end

end_start_loop: exit 0

WHO_AM_I:
   say 'Name of trapped condition:' condition('C')
   say 'Description:' condition('D')
   say 'Method of invocation:' condition('I')
   say 'Current state of the trapped condition:' condition('S')
   signal start_loop
```

The trap routine named WHO_AM_I invokes the condition function several times to learn information about its environment and invocation. Here is sample output for this script:

```
C:\Regina\pgms\regina rexx_try4.rexx
Type: 'exit' to end this program
==> hi
Name of trapped condition: NOVALUE
Description: HI
Method of invocation: SIGNAL
```

```
Current state of the trapped condition: OFF
==> if a=b then
Name of trapped condition: SYNTAX
Description: Error 14.3: THEN requires a following instruction
Method of invocation: SIGNAL
Current state of the trapped condition: OFF
==> exit
```

This script highlights a basic design decision when trapping errors. Do you write one trap routine to handle all conditions, as in this script, or should you trap each error separately, as in the previous examples in this chapter?

What determines your approach is likely how much you care about error trapping in the program and how specific you want the code to be for each error condition. If generic error handling is acceptable, one routine to manage all errors will be suitable and faster to develop. If the program needs very specific, tight control of errors, then taking the time to write a separate routine for each anticipated condition is probably justified. The trade-off is between the specificity of the error routines and the time and effort required to develop them.

Some sites adopt sitewide standards for error handling. These sites supply a common error routine you invoke from your code to manage errors. Sitewide standards promote standardized exception handling and also reduce the workload because each programmer does not have to define and code his or her own error routines.

Limitations

There are two downsides to error trapping in Rexx. First, there are seven error conditions but no provision to add or define more yourself. Unlike some programming languages, ANSI-standard Rexx does not provide a generalized mechanism by which you can define and raise your own error conditions. Second, standard Rexx offers no way to explicitly raise conditions. All conditions are only raised by the interpreter when the specific condition events occur.

To handle conditions outside the scope of the seven Rexx provides you'll have to write code to identify and invoke them yourself.

How is this done? It depends on the errors you wish to trap, but the general technique is for the script to simply check status after attempting a task. For example, say you wish to manage error codes from a relational database or SQL calls. Simply check the return code and status from these calls in your program, and invoke the internal routine you've written to manage specific return codes. Other interfaces can be controlled in much the same manner. Check the return code from any call to the interface; then manage errors through an error-handler in your script. Chapters 15 through 18 explore interface programming and error handling for interfaces in detail.

A few Rexx interpreters go beyond the TRL-2 and ANSI-1996 standards to support enhanced error handling within the interpreter. Reginald Rexx, described in Chapter 23, allows developers to define their own error conditions and manually raise them if desired. Open Object Rexx also provides enhanced error-trapping features. Chapters 27 and 28 describe Open Object Rexx.

Summary

This chapter discussed the basic mechanism through which special errors or exceptions are captured and addressed. Standard Rexx supports seven error conditions, two of which are specifically oriented toward handling host command errors.

Error conditions are enabled by either the `signal` or `call` instructions. Error routines can be given unique names or coded under the default name of each error condition. If appropriate, be sure to reenable a condition once it has been raised and its error routine executed.

Depending on how concerned you are with trapping and addressing errors, you may take the simpler, more generic approach, and handle all errors from within one error routine, or you may wish to write a detailed routine for each condition.

This chapter provides several generic error-handling routines. You can take them and adapt them to your own needs. We progressively evolved the sample script to give a good idea of the different ways in which exceptions can be handled. Two of the scripts took diametrically opposed approaches to enabling and trapping all seven kinds of error conditions. One coded a separate routine for each exception, while the other coded one generic routine to handle all error conditions. Take these examples as a starting point in determining which approach works best for your own projects.

Test Your Understanding

1. What is the purpose of error trapping? What are the seven kinds of condition traps, and what error does each manage? Which error condition was added by the ANSI-1996 standard?

2. How do you capture an external interrupt from within a script?

3. What are the differences between `signal on` and `call on`? Are their conditions for which `call` is invalid?

4. What instruction is used to dynamically evaluate and run expressions?

5. How do you enable an error condition? Can you have multiple error routines to handle the same error condition in the same program?

6. What should you always do after executing an error-condition routine?

7. Is it better to write one generic error routine to handle all errors, or should you write a different routine to manage each kind of error?

The External Data Queue, or "Stack"

Overview

Most Rexx interpreters support an in-memory data structure called the *external data queue*, or *stack*. It is a general-purpose mechanism for passing data — between routines, programs, scripts and the operating system, and other entities.

A number of instructions and built-in functions manipulate the stack: `pull`, `parse pull`, `push`, `queue` and the `queued` built-in function. This chapter covers those instructions.

The stack evolved from Rexx's mainframe origins. Mainframe operating systems supported the stack as an integral feature of the environment, so it was only natural that Rexx support this key operating system feature. If you use mainframe Rexx you employ the stack to send commands to the operating system, to retrieve the results from those commands, for interprogram communication, and for other purposes.

Few operating systems other than those on mainframes support a stack. Rexx interpreters, therefore, come with their own "stack service" that mimics how Rexx operates with the mainframe stack.

Depending on your operating system and your Rexx interpreter, you may or may not end up using the stack. Nevertheless, it is important to know about it for several reasons. First, much Rexx documentation mentions the stack. If you don't know about it or understand it, understanding Rexx documentation becomes difficult. Second, the stack is a built-in feature of Rexx interpreters that has some good uses. For example, it's pretty common to use the stack as a vehicle to send input to operating systems commands and retrieve their output.

This chapter provides the necessary introduction to the stack that developers on all platforms require.

What Is the Stack?

The stack is sometimes called the *external data queue*, but we follow common usage and refer to it as *the stack*. It is a block of memory that is logically external to Rexx. Instructions like push and queue place data into the stack, and instructions like pull and parse pull extract data from it. The queued built-in function reports how many items are in the stack.

The stack is a general-purpose mechanism. The manner in which it is implemented within any particular Rexx interpreter varies. Different Rexx interpreters support the stack by different internal mechanisms. The goal is to support a stack that mimics that of mainframe Rexx, as defined in the various Rexx standards.

Computer scientists define a *stack* as a particular kind of data structure, diagrammed in Figure 11-1.

Stack: a Last-In-First-Out data structure

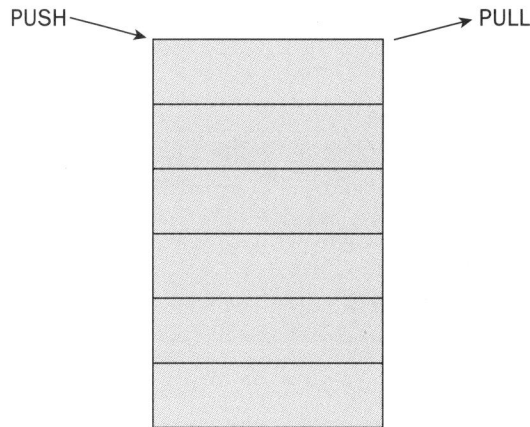

Figure 11-1

The *push* operation places data onto the stack; the *pull* operation removes data from the stack. The most-recently pushed data is retrieved first by the pull operation. Therefore, data that was most recently placed on the stack is retrieved first. This is referred to as a *last-in, first-out* (or *LIFO*) data structure because of the order in which data is stored and retrieved.

Computer scientists define the data structure called a *queue* in a similar manner. As visualized in Figure 11-2, the *queue* operation puts data into the queue, and the *pull* operation removes it. The oldest data in the queue is removed first, so a queue structure is a *first-in, first-out* (or *FIFO*) mechanism.

Queue: a First-In-First-Out data structure

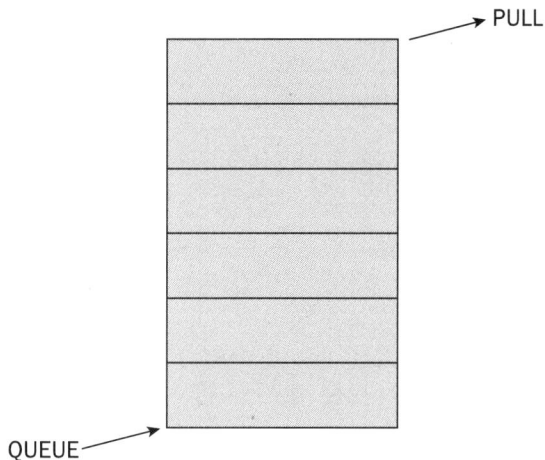

Figure 11-2

What we call "the stack" in Rexx actually functions as *either* a stack or a queue. Figure 11-3 shows that data is placed into the Rexx stack by either push or queue operations (by the push and queue instructions, respectively). Then the pull or parse pull instructions retrieve data from the Rexx stack.

The Rexx "Stack" is both a _Stack_ and a _Queue_

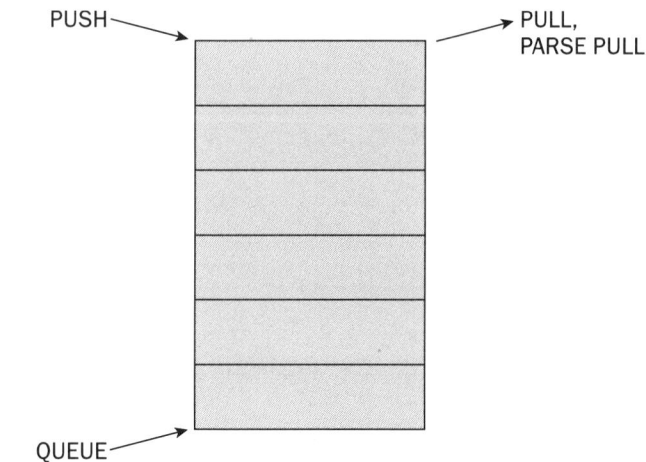

Figure 11-3

Whether the Rexx stack functions as a stack or queue data structure is dictated simply by whether one uses the push or queue instruction to place data into the stack. (Of course, you can intermix push and queue instructions, but then it's up to you to keep track of how you've placed data on the stack.) The Rexx stack can be used either as a stack or queue data structure (or both), depending on the instructions you use to manipulate it.

The data in the stack is always manipulated in terms of character strings. push or queue instructions place a string in the stack, and pull or parse pull retrieves that character string from the stack. The strings are typically referred to as *lines*. Place a line onto the stack; retrieve a line of data later. Stack access and retrieval is strictly *line-oriented*. There is no concept of "character-oriented" stack I/O.

The size of the stack is implementation-dependent. Many Rexx interpreters allow the stack to grow to the size of available memory. The stack is always implemented as an in-memory facility.

An Example — Placing Data into the Stack and Retrieving It

This first sample script was tested under Regina Rexx, which comes with its own built-in stack. But the program will work with almost any Rexx interpreter, because most come with built-in stack facilities. This sample script places three lines of data into the stack and retrieves and displays them in LIFO order. Then it places three lines into the stack and retrieves and displays them in FIFO order. The program illustrates how to populate the stack and retrieve lines from it, as well as how to use the stack in its role as either a stack or queue data structure.

Here is sample program output. It shows that the first three lines of data placed in the stack were retrieved in LIFO, or reverse order. Then three more lines were placed into the stack. These were retrieved and displayed in FIFO order.

```
C:\Regina\hf>regina stack.rexx
STACK: LINE #3
STACK: LINE #2
STACK: LINE #1
QUEUE: LINE #1
QUEUE: LINE #2
QUEUE: LINE #3
```

Here is the script:

```
/*   STACK:                                            */
/*                                                     */
/*      This program shows how to use the Rexx Stack as either a   */
/*      stack or a queue.                               */

do j=1 to 3
   push 'Stack: line #'  || j        /* push 3 lines onto the stack */
end

do j=1 to queued()                   /* retrieve and display LIFO   */
```

```
      pull line
      say line
   end

   do j=1 to 3
      queue 'Queue: line #'  ||  j      /* queue 3 lines onto the stack */
   end

   do queued()                          /* retrieve and display FIFO    */
      pull line
      say line
   end

   exit 0
```

The first do loop in the program places three lines of data onto the stack. It uses the push instruction to do this. We number the lines so that when they are retrieved in *the*LIFO order their order is apparent. Items placed into the stack by the push instruction are retrieved in LIFO order:

```
   do j=1 to 3
      push 'Stack: line #'  ||  j      /* push 3 lines onto the stack */
   end
```

The next code block shows the use of the queued built-in function to discover the number of lines on the stack, as well as a loop to retrieve all the lines from the stack:

```
   do j=1 to queued()                   /* retrieve and display LIFO    */
      pull line
      say line
   end
```

Since the three items were placed on the stack via push, they are retrieved in LIFO order. Their retrieval and display on the user's screen appear like this:

```
   STACK: LINE #3
   STACK: LINE #2
   STACK: LINE #1
```

After this do group, the three lines placed into the stack have all been removed. If we were to test queued() at this point, it would return a value of 0.

The next do group uses the queue instruction to place three new lines into the stack. These three lines will be retrieved in FIFO order, because the queue instruction placed them onto the stack:

```
   do j=1 to 3
      queue 'Queue: line #'  ||  j      /* queue 3 lines onto the stack */
   end
```

This retrieval do group shows a better way of retrieving lines from the stack. It uses the queued function to determine how many items are in the stack, and the interpreter only needs to resolve this value one time. At the end of the loop, the stack is again empty. queued() would return 0 if run again at that time:

```
do queued()                        /* retrieve and display FIFO   */
   pull line
   say line
end
```

Since the three lines were placed on the stack by the `queue` instruction, they are retrieved and displayed in FIFO order:

```
QUEUE: LINE #1
QUEUE: LINE #2
QUEUE: LINE #3
```

Thus the mechanism in Rexx we refer to as the stack really functions as either a queue or a stack data structure, depending on which instructions are used to place data into it.

At this point you are likely to have a key question — aren't `pull` and `parse pull` used to get data from standard input (the keyboard)? How does Rexx know whether these two instructions should retrieve data from the keyboard or from the stack?

The rule is this — `pull` and `parse pull` *will retrieve data from the stack, if there is any data in the stack. If there is no data in the stack, then these two instructions retrieve data from standard input (or the specified input stream).*

The stack is thus the priority input for these two instructions. But for any script that does not place data into the stack, the stack is empty and it is essentially ignored. In this case (which is what you see most often), the `pull` and `parse pull` instructions get their data from an input stream in the standard manner.

Say we coded this:

```
do j=1 to 3
   push 'Stack: line #' || j      /* push 3 lines onto the stack */
end

do j=1 to 4                        /* retrieve and display LIFO    */
   pull line
   say line
end
```

We've placed *three* lines onto the stack, but the retrieval loop tries to `pull` *four* lines. What happens? Rexx reads and displays the three lines from the stack. Now there are no lines on the stack. So the fourth `pull` instruction reads from its default input stream, the keyboard. In other words, after displaying the three lines in the stack on the display screen, this script suddenly falls silent and waits for the user to input one line from the keyboard. Assuming that the user enters a line, the script then immediately displays it back to the user by the `say` instruction that follows the `pull` instruction in the last iteration of the do loop.

If you use the stack you need to be cognizant of this behavior. Address it simply by understanding how many lines you have on the stack at all times. Use the `queued` function to manage this, because it tells you how many lines are on the stack.

If you do not use the stack, your scripts retrieve data from the input stream (standard or specified) as they always do through the `pull` and `parse pull` instructions. Unless the program places lines into the stack, you can generally pretend it doesn't exist.

If you have lines in the stack but want specifically to read the next line from default standard input, use the instruction `parse linein`. `parse linein` is a short form of:

```
parse value linein() with [template]
```

Use this statement only if you have lines in the stack and want specifically to avoid them and read from standard input. If there is no standard input to read (for example, from the keyboard), this instruction pauses until a line is input.

Another Example — The Stack for Interroutine Communication

The stack has several common uses. Here we see another one. This sample script uses the stack to pass data to an internal routine. It allows passing a variable number of parameters to the internal routine without worrying about how many there are or having to name them on the `procedure expose` instruction. Here is the code:

```
/*   STACK PARMS:                                          */
/*                                                         */
/*      This program shows how pass an arbitrary list of parameters  */
/*      to an internal subroutine by using the stack.      */

number_of_parms = 5                /* define number of parms to pass */

do j=1 to number_of_parms
   queue 'Parm: line #' || j    /* queue the parms onto the stack */
end

call get_parms number_of_parms
exit 0


get_parms: procedure          /* no variables need be EXPOSE'd  */

   do j = 1 to arg(1)         /* retrieve and display all the  */
      parse pull line         /* input parms passed in via     */
      say line                /* the stack                     */
   end
   return
```

In this script, the driver simply queues several lines of input parameters in the stack. The use of `queue` is important — this ensures that parameters will be retrieved in the proper order by the subroutine. Using `push` would create a FIFO structure, in which the `parse pull` instruction in the subroutine would retrieve the input parameters in the reverse order by which they were placed in the stack — probably not what is intended.

The subroutine uses the `arg(1)` built-in function to control the `do` loop which retrieves and displays all the input parameters. Recall that `arg(1)` retrieves the value of the first argument to the internal subroutine. In this case, this value will be that in the variable `number_of_parms`, which is 5.

Output from this script shows that the passing and retrieval of the parameters between the two routines and looks like this:

```
C:\Regina\hf>regina stack_parms.rexx
Parm: line #1
Parm: line #2
Parm: line #3
Parm: line #4
Parm: line #5
```

Practical Use of the Stack

As mentioned earlier, Rexx has a stack because this was a feature of the mainframe operating system under which it was first developed, VM (also referred to as CMS or VM/CMS). The goal was to take advantage of the operating system's stack as a feature of the Rexx language.

Unfortunately, few operating systems beyond those on the mainframe support a stack. The upshot is that a platform-dependency worked its way into the Rexx language definition. How does Rexx support a stack when running on operating systems that do not offer one?

The developers of Rexx interpreters have several choices:

❑   Add a stack facility to the operating system

❑   Create a stack "service" or "daemon" to provide this feature

❑   Build the stack into the interpreter itself

The first two approaches have the advantage that the stack becomes a more generic feature with expanded features. It could be used, for example, for communication between two programs (in a manner similar to how *piping* is used on many operating systems). But the downside is that the Rexx interpreter has to include and be distributed with an external component.

The last approach, building a stack into the interpreter itself, is simpler and more self-contained but provides more limited functionality. For example, even two Rexx scripts run by the same interpreter could not use the stack to communicate between them, because running under two invocations of the interpreter means that they each have their own stacks.

The ANSI-1996 standard does not resolve these internal complexities. It refers to the use of the stack as an I/O mechanism for commands through the address instruction as an allowable extension rather than as an integral part of the standard.

Mainframe Rexx includes commands, instructions, and functions to manipulate the stack beyond the Rexx standards. For example, you can create your own memory area (or *buffer*) to provide a "private stack" for the use of your scripts. Buffers are created by the makebuf command, and eliminated by the dropbuf and desbuf commands. The qbuf function tells how many buffers are in the stack.

There is even the ability to work with more than one stack. Commands such as `newstack` create another stack, while `delstack` deletes a stack, and `qstack` returns the number of stacks in use. When using multiple stacks, the idea is that, at any one time, one stack called the *current stack* will be used.

Figure 11-4 diagrams the relationships between buffers and stacks. Each stack can contain a number of buffers, and each buffer can contain a number of lines.

The Relationship Between Stacks and Buffers

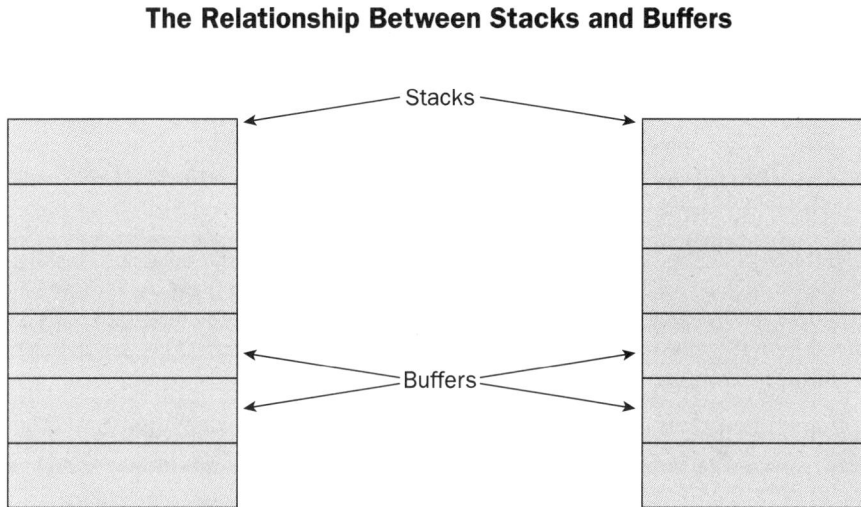

**Each Stack can contain multiple Buffers,
and each Buffer can contain multiple lines.**

Figure 11-4

In mainframe Rexx, the stack is a critical communication area through which commands are passed to the operating system for execution, and through which the results of those commands are read by the script. Chapter 29 on mainframe Rexx explores this in further detail.

Most free and open-source Rexx implementations include extensions that mimic the mainframe Rexx stack features. Regina, for example, includes VM-like built-in functions to create a new stack buffer (`makebuf`), remove a buffer from the stack (`dropbuf`), and remove all strings and buffers from the stack (`desbuf`). Most Rexx implementations simulate IBM mainframe Rexx in that they allow the sending of commands to the operating system and the retrieving of the results of those commands via the stack. These extensions to standard Rexx offer greater capability in using the stack at the possible price of less standardization and reduced code portability. The chapters in Section II on the various Rexx interpreters describe the stack-handling features of the different interpreters.

Some Rexx interpreters on some platforms permit the stack to be used as an interprocess communication vehicle. In other words, multiple, separate processes on one machine use the stack to communicate among themselves. This is rather like the manner in which pipes or sockets can be used for communication between different processes on the same machine. Examples of Rexx interpreters that support this are Regina and VM mainframe Rexx.

167

Some Rexx interpreters go so far as to allow the stack to be used for communication between different processes on different machines. Regina is one example. Its rxqueue executable and rxqueue built-in function support this feature. The stack thus becomes a generic, machine-independent vehicle for inter-process communications. It can even be used for communications between different processes across the Internet. See the documentation for your specific Rexx interpreter to determine what uses it supports for interprocess communcation using the stack or its stack service.

Summary

This chapter explains the role and function of the stack within Rexx. It shows how the stack could be used as if it were either of two different in-memory data structures: a stack or queue. Stacks are LIFO data structures. The last-in data is the first retrieved. Queues are FIFO data structures, where the first item put in the queue is also the first item retrieved.

We covered the instructions and built-in functions that place data on the stack and retrieve it from the stack. These include the push, queue, and pull instructions, and also the queued function. Two sample programs illustrated use of the stack. The first merely demonstrated how items are placed on the stack and retrieved from it, while the other showed how the stack could be used to pass an arbitrary list of parameters to an internal subroutine.

Finally, we discussed how and why the stack came to be part of Rexx. We mentioned that some Rexx interpreters on some platforms permit multiple processes on the same machine to access the same stack, while others even support using the stack for communications across different machines. These advanced facilities are interpreter-dependent and platform-dependent, so check your documentation to see what features are available to you.

The goal of this chapter is to arm you with the background you need so that when you encounter documentation referring to the stack, or a Rexx implementation that relies on the stack, you'll know what you need to be functional.

Test Your Understanding

1. Do all Rexx implementations have a stack? Look in your specific documentation. How does your interpreter implement the stack?

2. What's the difference between the stack and queue data structures? How do you use the Rexx stack to mimic the behaviors of both? What is the role of the queued function?

3. How much information can you place into the stack?

4. Should you use the stack if your goal is to develop code that can be ported across platforms?

5. Can you have more than one stack? What are buffers, and how do you create and destroy them?

Rexx with Style

Overview

One of the primary advantages to Rexx is its ease of use. This leads to programs that are easier to read, enhance, and maintain. But as with any programming language, whether these benefits are truly attained depends on how scripts are written. Developers who design and build clear programs create work that has a longer life; those who develop cryptic or overly clever programs create scripts that will prove less useful after they change jobs. For this reason, we've offered recommendations throughout this book regarding Rexx best coding practices.

This chapter consolidates guidelines for writing clear, maintainable Rexx scripts. While some of the rules of thumb it offers might be considered personal preferences, there is value in attempting to list some of the techniques that lead to the most useful code having the greatest longevity. Figure 12-1 lists some of the techniques we'll discuss in this chapter.

Sometimes developers downplay readable style because it does not appeal to their desire to create "clever" programs. But good programming style is important even to the best developers. It directly affects the reliability of one's code and how many mistakes are made in developing and enhancing that code. This should convince even the advanced, hard-core developer of its value.

Readers are urged to consider how they might write Rexx in the most readable style possible. Whatever approach one adopts, consistency is a virtue. A program that passes variables between routines in a consistent manner, for example, is relatively easy to understand and change compared to a program that uses different means to communicate between different routines. From this comes the first rule of thumb for large programs — whatever stylistic or readability conventions you adopt, apply them throughout and your program will prove much easier for others to enhance and maintain. With this said, here are suggested points of style for good Rexx programming:

The Steps to Good Programming Style

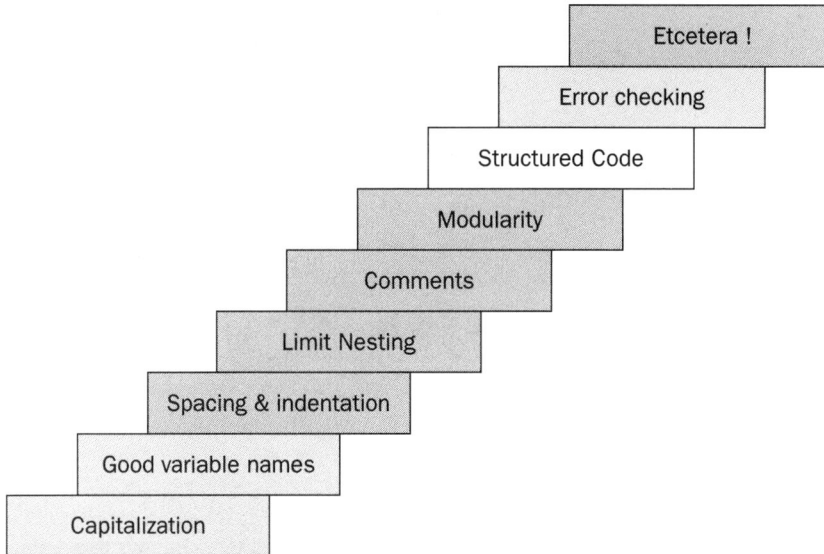

Figure 12-1

Capitalize on Capitalization

The data that Rexx scripts manipulate is *case-sensitive*. As are the literal strings you code within your Rexx program. A literal string such as This is mine differs from the string THIS IS MINE.

But the Rexx language itself – its instructions and functions — are *case-insensitive*. You can code the if instruction as if or IF or If. It's all the same to Rexx. This gives programmers the flexibility to use capitalization as a tool for clarity. Perhaps the most readable style capitalizes Rexx instructions and leaves everything else in lowercase. Here's a sample code snippet that embodies this style. Notice how it leverages capitalization as a vehicle for greater readability:

```
IF social_security_payments > maximum_yearly_contribution THEN DO
   payments = 'completed'
   stop_payments = 'YES'
   END
ELSE DO
   call payment_routine
   stop_payments = 'NO'
END
```

It's not unusual to see older or mainframe scripts in all uppercase. This harkens back to the days when all coding was uppercase (as in COBOL coding on green-bar paper) and does not take full advantage of Rexx's case-flexibility to enhance readability:

```
IF SOCIAL_SECURITY_PAYMENTS  > MAXIMUM_YEARLY_CONTRIBUTION THEN DO
   PAYMENTS = 'COMPLETED'
   STOP_PAYMENTS = 'YES'
   END
ELSE DO
   CALL PAYMENT_ROUTINE
   STOP_PAYMENTS = 'NO'
END
```

Scripting in all lowercase is often popular with those from Linux, Unix, or BSD backgrounds. The author confesses to an all-lowercase preference (probably the result of too much C/C++ programming in his squandered youth).

Good Variable Naming

In Rexx (or almost any programming language), taking advantage of long variable names allows the use of much more meaningful descriptors. The preceding sample `if` statement uses nice long variable names. This is far superior to cryptic abbreviations, such as those in this version of the same code:

```
IF ssp > mx_yrly_cntrb THEN DO
   p = 'completed'
   stp_p = 'YES'
   END
ELSE DO
   call pymnt_routine
   stp_p = 'NO'
END
```

In this example, the variable `maximum_yearly_contribution` is abbreviated as the much-less-memorable variable name, `mx_yrly_cntrb`. Imagine the confusion as one misremembers this abbreviated variable name as `max_yrly_cntrb` or mistypes it as `mx_yrly_contrib`. While it is easy to overlook the value of full variable names when coding, during maintenance, enhancements or other activities the value of good variable names becomes evident.

Most Rexx programmers string portions of the variable names together with the underscore character. But this is not required. Sometimes you'll see scripts written by Visual Basic or Java programmers, or those from other object-oriented programming backgrounds, that mix case in their variable names:

```
SocialSecurityPayments
```

This variable-naming style is sometimes called *upper camel case* or just *camel case*. Another style you might encounter strings together capitalized words with underscores to create full variable names. Here is an example of this style:

```
Social_Security_Payments
```

For some, the use of capitals without intervening underscores (`SocialSecurityPayments`) leads to more typing errors due to the need to toggle the "shift" key while typing the variable name. But any of these naming conventions works fine, so long as it is applied consistently throughout the program.

Even though Rexx does not require declaring variables, it can often be useful to do so. For example, in a large program, defining variable names and their initial values provides useful documentation. With good spacing, it's readable as well:

```
auto_list.       =  ''          /* list of cars to process  */
auto_to_find     =  ''          /* car to locate for query  */
total_queries    =  0           /* queries per cookie       */
debug_flag       =  'OFF'       /* turn ON if debugging     */
```

Predefining variables in this fashion is also useful in that you can also use the `signal on novalue` condition to trap the use of any variable that has not been initialized.

In large programs using global variables, some developers like to distinguish their global variables from those local to individual routines by prefacing them with a common stem. This is yet another use for compound variables. Here is a sample code snippet from a operating system utility written in Rexx that shows how global variables have been uniquely identified by a common stem:

```
global.number_of_current_block =  1    /* block on the pass list    */
global.blocks_processed        =  0    /* blocks processed so far   */
global.split_blocks            =  0    /* blocks split due to update overflow */
```

The use of the stem `global.` makes it easy to spot any global variables within the script.

Use Spacing and Indentation

The preceding sample `if` statement makes obvious a fundamental principle of program readability: *Make indentation parallel the logic of the program.* Remember the rule that an `else` keyword pairs with the nearest unmatched `if` instruction? Indentation that follows this rule makes the logic obvious to anyone reading the program. But indentation that violates program logic makes it much harder to read (and safely update) scripts.

Here's an example. To Rexx, this is the same `if` instruction as the one encoded earlier. But to a human this is clearly inferior to the original:

```
IF  social_security_payments > maximum_yearly_contribution THEN DO
payments = 'completed';    stop_payments = 'YES'
END;    ELSE DO
call payment_routine ;   stop_payments = 'NO'
END
```

As well as indentation, spacing is another tool for enhancing readability. This line is generously spaced and easily read:

```
if ( answer = 'YES'  |  answer = 'Y' )  then
```

Change the spacing in this statement, and it becomes less easy to decifer:

```
if (answer='YES'|answer='Y')  then
```

Take advantage of Rexx's *free format* nature to add extra spaces in your code wherever it might render the code more readable.

Remember that the one place Rexx will *not* allow a space is immediately after a function and before the parentheses that follow it. This is correct:

```
feedback = function_name(argument1, argument2)
```

But this incorrect coding means that Rexx will not recognize the function:

```
feedback = function_name  (argument1, argument2)    /* Invalid ! */
```

The function `function_name` must immediately be followed by the left parenthesis. The set of parentheses contain its argument(s). If there are no function arguments, just code an empty set of parentheses, like this:

```
feedback = function_name()     /* no arguments to pass means empty parentheses */
```

Another aspect of readability is how statements are continued across lines. Place the line continuation character, the comma (,), at a natural breakpoint between phrases in a statement to enhance readability. This example:

```
address environment   command  WITH INPUT   STREAM   filename_1  ,
                                OUTPUT STREAM   filename_2  ,
                                ERROR   STREAM   filename_3
```

reads easier than this:

```
address environment   command  WITH INPUT   STREAM,
filename_1   OUTPUT STREAM   filename_2      ERROR,
STREAM     filename_3
```

Both work fine as far as Rexx is concerned. Placing a few spaces prior to the comma increases its visibility. Vertical alignment works wonders in enhancing readability.

Rexx permits coding more than one statement per line by encoding the *line separation character*, the semicolon (;). Generally, putting more than one statement per line is not recommended. It makes code denser and therefore harder to read. But there are two situations in which this might make sense:

❑   Initializing variables

❑   Initial assignment of values to array variables

Consistent vertical spacing makes multiple statements per line much more readable. For example, in Chapter 4 this code initialized several array elements in the sample script named Find Book:

```
keyword.1 = 'earth'   ;   keyword.2 = 'computers'
keyword.3 = 'life'    ;   keyword.4 = 'environment'
```

This is preferable to jamming as many statements as possible on each line:

```
keyword.1='earth';keyword.2='computers';keyword.3='life';keyword.4='environment'
```

More than one statement per line can be readable only if done in the proper circumstances and with appropriate spacing.

Limit Nesting

Like most expression-based languages, Rexx allows you to nest expressions to almost any depth. This provides great flexibility, but in practice, once expressions become too nested, they become unintelligible to anyone other than their original author. (And even the original developer will have trouble decoding his or her complex statements when maintaining the program after an absence!).

Functions often form part of expressions, because they can return a result string right into the point in the expression in which they are coded. Nesting functions too deeply is tempting to many programmers. It's fun and it's clever. But ultimately the downside of difficult maintenance outweighs this personal value. Unless you *know* no one will ever have to enhance or change your script, it's a real disservice to the next developer to stick him or her with code made more complex by dense expressions or deeply nested functions.

The way to clarity, of course, is to simplify. Break up that complex expression to a series of simpler ones. Break apart deeply nested functions into a series of simpler statements. It makes the code a bit longer, but much more readable.

Here's an example. Remember the `rindex` program from Chapter 8? This function found the rightmost occurrence of a search byte within a given string. Here is the code for that function:

```
/*   RINDEX:                                              */
/*                                                        */
/*      Returns the rightmost position of a byte within a string.   */

rindex: procedure expose search_byte

parse arg string                              /* read the string */

say string search_byte              /* show recursive trace for fun */

string_length   = length(string)       /* determine string length     */
string_length_1 = length(string) -1  /* determined string length - 1 */

if string == ''            /* here's the 'end recursion' condition     */
   then return 0
else do
   if substr(string,string_length,1) == search_byte then
      return string_length
   else
      new_string_to_search = substr(string,1,string_length_1)
   return rindex(new_string_to_search)
end
```

This version of the same function eliminates the statements that determine the string length and the length of the string minus 1. It takes out these two statements and instead nests these expressions within the body of the code:

```
string_length   = length(string)       /* determine string length     */
string_length_1 = length(string) -1  /* determined string length - 1 */
```

Here's the same function with more nesting:

```
/*  RINDEX:                                                    */
/*                                                             */
/*     Returns the rightmost position of a byte within a string.   */

rindex: procedure expose search_byte

parse arg string                                /* read the string */

say string search_byte              /* show recursive trace for fun */

if string == ''            /* here's the 'end recursion' condition    */
   then return 0
else do
   if substr(string,length(string),1) == search_byte then
      return length(string)
   else
      new_string_to_search = substr(string,1,(length(string)-1))
   return rindex(new_string_to_search)
end
```

The code works just as well but is a little harder to decipher. You could nest the functions in this script even further, but nesting is a trend you can get carried away with. It makes for more compact code. But for the benefit of reducing the length of this function by a few lines of code, the nested functions make this routine tough to understand.

Comment Code

Code comments are English-language explanations interspersed among Rexx statements that provide explanation of the script. They are valuable in describing what a program does and explaining how it does it. While many programmers resist writing comments in their code, without comments the longevity of their code is reduced. For example, a very clever program may look like gibberish without comments that explain its operations.

We've seen several styles for program commentary. Comments "blocks" can look like this:

```
/*************************************************************************/
/*  RINDEX: This program finds the rightmost position of a byte in a string.   */
/*************************************************************************/
```

Or, they can be coded like this, as a single long comment statement:

```
/*************************************************************************
 *    RINDEX: This program finds the rightmost position of a byte in a string.    *
 *************************************************************************/
```

Individual comments may appear on a line of their own:

```
/* This routine finds the rightmost position of a byte in a string.   */
```

Or they can be *trailing comments*, appearing on the line of code they explain:

```
square = a_number  *  a_number      /* find the square of the number */
```

The main point of comments is: *that you use them!* So many programmers severely minimize program commentary that it compromises the value of what they develop. While their code was obvious to them when they developed it, without some English explanation those who maintain that code in the future are left clueless. Document while you program, or do it after you're done. Just be sure you do it.

For significant industrial programs, we minimally recommend a comment block with this information at the top of the program:

```
/**************************************************************************/
/* Program: fin_1640                            Date:   08/06            */
/*                                              By:    H. Fosdick        */
/*                                                                       */
/* Purpose:    Kicks off the nightly batch financial system.            */
/*                                                                       */
/* Usage: fin_1640                                                       */
/* Parms: none                                                           */
/*                                                                       */
/* Inputs:  (1) financial scheduler track  (2)  previous nite txn list  */
/* Outputs: none directly, but 3 history files through called subroutines */
/*                                                                       */
/* Calls: all "fin_" package programs (14 of them, see Nightly Run List) */
/*                                                                       */
/* Maintenance: __Date___    ___By____  ____Fix_____           */
/*                08/06        HF       Created.                         */
/*                08/14        HF       Updated DB2 error processing     */
/*                09/12        BC       Added job fin_1601 on abend       */
/**************************************************************************/
```

Every time a programmer changes the code he or she should be sure to add a comment on the change(s) made, to the "Maintenance" section of this comment block.

Each internal or external function or subroutine should also have its own leading comment block. On one hand, assuming that the subroutines are small, this may be no more than a brief statement of purpose for the routine. On the other hand, if subroutines are large, or if they involve complicated interactions with other routines, their documentation should be correspondingly more detailed. In this case, documentation should detail input and output variables, file updates, and other changes the routine makes to the environment.

Good comments carry intelligence. Poor comments do not add to the information already available in the program. Cryptic, codelike comments offer little value. Here are a few favorites, collected verbatim from production programs at IT sites:

```
/* Obvious to the casual observer */

/*yew, move the ting over there */

/* Add to the mess already created! */

/* Do NOT show this code to any manager !! */

/*   not sure what this does, but suggest that you don't mess with it    */

/* Don/t blame me I didnt write. it I just work here */

/*Think this is bad you should c my java.*/
```

While there is no way to scientifically assess the value of commentary, clearly some comments are more useful than others.

Write Modular Code

Modularity is fundamental to large programming systems that are maintainable and flexible. Monolithic code is almost always difficult to change or improve. Modularity limits the "breakage" that occurs from an incorrect enhancement because each module is small and performs a single, limited task. The unintended consequences or side effects of code changes are minimized.

Modules also lend themselves to easier, more exhaustive testing than monolithic systems. A large program that consists of many small, well-defined routines is almost always a better program going forward than one that has fewer lines of code but less clear-cut interfaces between its larger, more complex modules.

How does one best define modules? Some favor top-down methodologies which progressively refine the functionality of the modules. Others use any of the many automated design tools, such as AllFusion, Oracle Designer, the Information Engineering Facility, IBM's Rationale tools, or others. Automated tools tend to enforce good design discipline and often embed guidelines for optimal program design or best practices.

All internal routines (functions and subroutines) follow the main routine or driver in the source code file. The main routine should be clearly marked as such. The internal routines should optimally appear in the file in the same order in which they are initially referred to by the main routine. Subroutines that are invoked from within subroutines should appear in the source code listing immediately below the subroutine that invokes them. Widely shared subroutines can be collected in their own documented area.

Beyond good modular design, variable scoping across routines is a major area for good program design that affects program reliability.

The best approach is to code the `procedure expose` instruction at the start of each internal routine. This protects all variables that are not specifically listed from inadvertently being changed by the subroutine. It also ensures that you know exactly which variables each subroutine requires, and documents this list for anyone maintaining the program in the future.

Should you use any global variables? Best practice says no. The risk is not to the programmer who first develops the code, but rather to any who must later maintain or modify it. The risk of breakage or unintended side effects rises exponentially when a large program uses many global variables, especially in languages like Rexx that allow variables to be defined by first use (rather than requiring declarations). This is because the person doing maintenance cannot be sure what variable names have previously been used or where.

If you must use global variables, here are some suggestions:

❑   Define (declare) all of them in a single block at the top of the code.

❑   These variable definitions should initialize each variable.

❑   Precede all global variables with a common stem, such as `global`.

❑   Include a comment block to specifically identify this set of global variable declarations.

Another approach is to pass information between all routines by a global stack. Essentially the stack becomes a control block or in-memory `*.ini` or configuration file that defines behavior and passes information.

However you pass information between routines (`procedure expose`, input arguments, global variables, or a global stack), be consistent across all routines in the program. Mixing modes in information passing almost guarantees future error during program maintenance. Our best recommendation is to code `procedure expose` for each internal routine, listing all variables used by that routine.

Write Structured Code

Structured programming requires only one entry point and one exit from any code block. The benefit is increased clarity and easier code enhancement and maintenance. Studies also show that structured coding results in fewer errors. Writing structured, modular code provides a big payback and really helps you script Rexx with style.

Chapter 3 discussed the control constructs used in Rexx for structured programming. Let's review them here. These are the instructions you should use in your code in order to write structured programs:

Structured Control Constructs
if-then
if-then-else
do-end group
do-while
do n times
do initialize-loop-counter to limit by increment
select

Structured Control Constructs
call
return
exit

As a powerful general-purpose programming language, Rexx also supports unstructured control constructs. Their use is not recommended as they fall outside the principles of structured programming. If you use any of the following instructions, as described in the following table, your code is unstructured:

Unstructured Control Constructs		
Instruction	**Unstructured Use**	**Use Instead**
signal	Used as an unconditional GOTO	if-then-else
do-until	Bottom-driven loop	do-while
do forever	Endless loop requiring an unstructured exit	do-while
iterate	By-passes statement(s) within a loop	if-then-else
leave	Unstructured exit from a loop	if-then-else, do-while

The column on the right-hand side of this table shows the structured constructs that should be used to replace the unstructured ones on the left side. We recommend that you replace any instances of the unstructured instructions in the leftmost column in your code with their structured equivalents from the right-most column.

> Any unstructured control construct can be replaced by a structured one. Any program logic that can be written as unstructured code can also be written in structured form.

Handle Errors

Error-handling code greatly increases the robustness of an application. Scripts that omit the small amount of code it takes to include good error checking are greatly inferior to those that include it.

Identifying and handling common errors allow an application to better adjust to its environment. It saves application users both time and confusion when scripts, at the very least, display a descriptive error message that explains unexpected conditions or failures.

Why don't all scripts check for and handle errors? Quite simply, it is quicker for most developers to program without including such "extraneous" coding. Unfortunately, developers do not often go back and add error checking to their scripts after the initial script is up and working.

The errors that scripts should check for fall into several categories. Here are the major categories of problems for which your scripts should check and manage:

❏ Command results

❏ Interpreter-raised error conditions

❏ Return codes from interfaces

❏ I/O results

Chapter 14 goes into how to issue operating system commands and verify that they worked. Scripts can check return codes from the commands and even parse their message outputs for further information. The condition traps for ERROR and FAILURE also capture errant commands.

Remember that there are several other exception conditions scripts can trap, including HALT, NOVALUE, NOTREADY, SYNTAX, and LOSTDIGITS. Chapter 10 covers Rexx's condition-trapping mechanism and how scripts use it to manage errors.

Many scripts interface to external packages, for example, for graphical user interfaces (GUIs) or database storage. Always check the return codes from functions or commands that control external interfaces. A program that fails to recognize an interface error and blithely continues could cause a *hard failure*, a failure that stops an application and leaves no clue as to what happened.

Be sure to check the return string from the stream I/O functions. As listed in Chapter 5, some of these functions and their return strings are:

❏ charin — Returns number of characters read (0 if none were read).

❏ charout — Returns number of characters *not* successfully written (0 means success).

❏ chars — Returns a nonzero value if characters remain to be read.

❏ linein — Returns a line read from a file, or the null string if no line exists to read.

❏ lineout — Return value varies by requested operation. For writing one line, a return value of 0 means the line was successfully written, 1 means it was not.

❏ lines — Returns a nonzero value if there is at least one line left to be read.

Failure during charin or linein can result in raising the NOTREADY condition if some problem occurs. As shown in Chapter 10, this can be trapped by an appropriate error routine.

And now, a mea culpa. The scripts in this book do not include robust error checking because we limit the size of the scripts for clarity. Including good error handling in all the scripts would be redundant and detract from what the scripts illustrate. If you're coding in the workplace, we urge you not to take the easy way out but to code strong error checking. Industrial-strength programming requires complete error checking and a fail-safe coding approach.

Additional Suggestions

There are many other suggestions to make for producing the most readable, maintainable, error-free code. In the sections that follow, we briefly discuss a few of the more widely accepted. Following these suggestions will make your code much more readable, maintainable, and reliable. Good programming practices are as much a part of the value of scripts as are the algorithms those scripts embody.

Subscripts

For looping control variables, use common subscript names like i, j, and k. These should always be set explicitly at the start of the loop: don't make assumptions about whether a loop control variable has been used previously in the code or what its value is. Also, do not use these subscripts for other purposes. Limit their use to subscripting and use more descriptive variable names for other purposes.

A classic scripting error is to use one of these common variables as a loop control variable, and then assign it another value for another purpose inside the loop! While this may sound like silly mistake to make, it indeed happens in large programs or in situations where many developers maintain a single program. Another classic error is to use the same subscripting variable for an outer loop and for an inner loop nested within the outer loop. This produces "interesting" results in the behavior of the outer loop!

To summarize, our recommendations for loop-control subscripts are:

❑ Explicitly initialize them at the top of each do loop in which they are used.

❑ Do not alter them within the loop (let the do instruction increment them).

❑ Use your set of subscripting variables only for subscripting.

Quotation marks for commands

Chapter 14 explores in detail how to issue operating system commands from within scripts. That chapter demonstrates how to issue OS commands, how to send them input and retrieve their output, how to recognize and identify commands that fail, and a host of other important related topics. This section summarizes a few rules of thumb for limiting errors in scripts that issue operating system commands or commands to other external interfaces.

Some programmers always enclose the operating system commands within their scripts within quotation marks. This readily identifies where OS commands occur within scripts. Other developers prefer not to enclose operating system commands in quotation marks, unless they must in order to avoid Rexx's evaluation of the expression before passing it to the operating system. This produces readable code because it is less cluttered with quotation marks. Either approach works fine. We recommend consistency with whichever you choose.

Try to avoid double-nesting quotation marks. Especially in mainframe scripting, you'll sometimes see complex nesting of quotation marks that is really not necessary.

It is better to build a command string through several simple statements than to dynamically concatenate a complex command in a single statement. Also, it is easier to debug commands that are built within variables: Simply display the variable's contents to the screen and see if it appears as a valid command.

Here is an example. This statement builds a character string that will be an input argument to a function:

```
sqlstr = "insert into phonedir values('" || lname || "'",
          ",'" || phone "')"
```

The string concatenated into the variable is syntactically complex. If we want to ensure that it is correct, we could issue a simple `say` statement to display the value on the screen:

```
say  sqlstr              /* display string on screen to verify accuracy */
```

Here's the interface command in which this character string is used. You can see that building the command component separately is *way* easier than if we had actually nested it within this statement:

```
if SQLCommand(i1,sqlstr) <> 0 then sqlerr('During insert')
```

To summarize, our recommendations for building commands and function strings are:

❏ Build them in several simple steps, not in one complicated statement.

❏ Build them in a variable, which can easily be displayed and verified.

❏ Avoid cluttering command statements with superfluous quotation marks.

Consider declaring all variables

Some developers find it clear to define or declare all variables in advance and initialize them at that time. In large programs, it can otherwise be difficult to locate the first use of a variable or tell what it was initialized to.

This code snippet illustrates this principle. Here we assume that we have a very large script, and the declaration of all global variables at the top of the program helps document and explain their use. Separating the global variable definitions from the start of program logic segments the program into more readily understood components. Each variable in the program is initialized to some value, which makes it easy to find the initial setting for any variable:

```
/**************************************************************************/
/* Variable Declaration and Initialization Section                       */
/**************************************************************************/
global.number_of_current_block =  1     /* block on the pass list         */
global.blocks_processed         =  0     /* blocks processed so far        */
global.split_blocks             =  0     /* blocks split due to update overflow */

/*   further variable declarations appear here . . .                      */

/**************************************************************************/
/* Main Routine:                                                          */
/**************************************************************************/
if global.memory_blocks_allocated >= (global.seg_count * global.block_size) . . .
```

By splitting out the definition and initialization of all variables prior to the "main routine," the programmer makes the entire program clearer and better modularizes program activity.

Rexx-aware editors

Some editors are Rexx-aware. They highlight elements of the language in different colors and assist in indenting code. Rexx-aware editors make your job easier because they highlight the structure of scripts by color-coding and indentation. We recommend using these editors if you have the opportunity, because they tend to reduce error rates and make coding quicker and easier.

Examples of Rexx-aware editors include:

- ❑ THE (The Hessling Editor) for Linux, Unix, Windows, and other platforms
- ❑ The Rexx Text Editor (or RexxEd), which is distributed along with Reginald Rexx
- ❑ The Interactive System Productivity Facility, or ISPF, on the mainframe
- ❑ XEDIT on the mainframe

Publish site standards for coding style

Consistency within a program is key to its readability. Consistency across all programs at a site extends this virtue to the code asset owned by the company or organization. Many organizations consider developing, disseminating, and enforcing such standards fundamental to the value of their code base.

The keys to the viability of site coding standards are that they are easily accessed by the developers and that management holds the developers accountable to scripting to the standards. Standards can be made readily accessible by publishing them on a corporate intranet or placing them on a shared local area network drive. Programmers should be able to access the standards in the normal course of their work with little or no extra effort.

Developers can be held accountable to corporate standards by several means. Two of them, automated checking tools and code reviews, are discussed in the following sections.

Consider automated tools to ensure standards compliance

Consider purchasing or developing automated tools to enforce good program documentation and style. Simply promulgating site standards is of little value unless those standards are adhered to. Automated tools are one means to ensure that this happens.

Here is a very simple example of "automation" in the service of standards. One site keeps a set of documentation templates on a shared departmental disk drive. Programmers copy each template, and fill in the blanks to document their applications. This ensures developers provide all the required documentation elements, and at the same time, makes it easier on the developers because they do not have to worry about designing the structure of the documents. By completing what is already provided, programmers both meet the documentation standards and do so with the least effort.

Consider code reviews

In the absence of automated tools, *code reviews* (having one's code looked over by a peer) can be a way of administratively enforcing good programming practice or sitewide programming standards. Several formal methodologies optimize code reviews, including *structured walk-throughs* and *joint application development* techniques. A quick Web search on either of these terms will give you good beginning information about what they entail.

While many programmers don't care to have their code checked in this manner, code reviews are a proven technique to ensure conformance to site standards and more reliable code. The "egoless programming" promoted by code reviews tends to render applications more maintainable and prolong their life.

Avoid Common Coding Errors

Some of the most common coding errors in any programming language derive from odd or hard-to-remember syntax and coding detail. Fortunately, using Rexx results in fewer errors of this nature than many languages because of its spare, clean style.

Nevertheless, a few coding errors are common among Rexx programmers, especially those new to the language. This brief section lists the more common errors you'll encounter.

Failing to end a comment

Each comment starts with the two characters /*. Be sure to code the corresponding ending characters */. Otherwise, the rest of your script becomes one long comment! Also, the two characters /* and */ must be immediately adjacent one another with no intervening blank.

Failing to end a literal string or parenthetical expression

For each single or double quotation mark, there must be a corresponding end quotation mark. This rule applies to parentheses as well. For each left parenthesis, there must appear a corresponding right parenthesis later in the code.

Improper coding of functions

When invoking functions without the `call` instruction, the left parenthesis must immediately follow the function name:

```
fd = function_name(argument1, argument2) /* No space prior to first paren ( */
```

Forgetting that functions return a string

A function returns a value. If you code the function as the only item on a line:

```
function_name(argument1)          /* nowhere for the result string to go ! */
```

the value it returns has to go somewhere. Where Rexx will send it is to the default command environment. Thus if the function above returns a value of 1, this string will be sent to the operating system for execution!

One solution is to capture the result string in a variable:

```
feedback = function_name(argument1)        /* result string goes into FEEDBACK */
```

Another approach is to invoke the function by the `call` instruction so that the special variable `result` can capture the result string:

```
call function_name  argument1             /* RESULT contains the result string */
```

Using parentheses on call

Do not enclose arguments to the `call` instruction in parentheses. This statement is incorrect:

```
call subroutine(argument1, argument2)     /*  Á INCORRECT ! */
```

Here is the correct way to code this statement:

```
call subroutine  argument1,  argument2   /* correct         */
```

This is an easy mistake to make because when you encode an embedded function you always immediately follow it by parentheses. A `call` is different in this respect.

Failure to use commas on call or in parse arg

While parentheses are not needed, commas to separate input arguments to a routine are (see the above). Commas must also be coded between the arguments referred to in the `parse arg` instruction:

```
parse  arg  argument1 ,  argument2
```

Confusing command-line arguments with internal routine arguments

As in the preceding example, retrieve arguments passed in to internal routines by using the `arg` or `parse arg` instruction and variables separated by commas. Contrast this to *command-line arguments,* which are retrieved into a routine by the same instructions *but without separating commas*:

```
parse  cmd_line_arg_1  cmd_line_arg_2  .
```

The `arg()` function tells how many parameters were passed into an internal routine. It only returns 0 or 1 when applied to command-line arguments.

Global variables

Global variables are convenient when first developing a large program but significantly reduce reliability as that program undergoes enhancements and maintenance. Code `procedure expose` for each internal function or subroutine.

Forgetting return or exit

Remember to code the `return` instruction when a subroutine ends to send control back to the caller. Functions *must* return a string to the caller; subroutines may optionally do so. Be sure to encode the `exit` statement at the end of the main routine and prior to any subroutines and functions that follow it, so that the flow of control does not inadvertently "roll off" the end of the program into the internal routines placed after it.

Forgetting about automatic uppercase conversion

Instructions `pull` and `arg` automatically convert input to uppercase. This is convenient but must be kept in mind when later using those strings in comparisons; compare those strings to their uppercase equivalents. If uppercase translation is *not* desired, code `parse pull` and `parse arg` instead.

Uppercase translation can be particularly tricky when reading in filenames. Under operating systems like Windows or DOS, filenames are not case-sensitive. However, operating systems like Linux, Unix, and BSD use case-sensitive names. Having the user input these filenames when running under Linux, Unix, or BSD means that your program must use `parse arg` or `pull arg` to read them. `arg` or `pull` alone translates the filenames to uppercase, which likely produces incorrect filenames.

Another place to remember about automatic uppercase translation by the interpreter is with variable names and values. Rexx uppercases variable names internally, and it will also uppercase character strings that are not enclosed in quotation marks. Several sample scripts in Chapter 4 relied on these facts to work properly.

Incorrectly continuing a statement

Rexx uses the line continuation character, the comma (,), to separate items in a list as well as for line continuation. Rexx interprets this coding:

```
a = max(1, 3, 5,
          7, 9)
```

as:

```
a = max(1, 3, 5 7, 9)
```

Correct this by recognizing that you need one comma to separate every item in the list as well as an extra comma for line continuation:

```
a = max(1, 3, 5, ,
          7, 9)           /* correct */
```

We suggest surrounding commas with spaces or blanks for enhanced readability.

Failing to use strict comparisons

Remember that in a character string comparison, Rexx ignores leading and/or trailing blanks and blank-pads the shorter item in the comparison as necessary. Use the strict comparison operators like *strictly equals* (= =) when strings must be precisely compared on a character-by-character basis, without Rexx making assumptions concerning spaces or padding.

Incorrectly coding strict comparisons for numbers

Strict comparisons make sense only in comparing strings and should not mistakenly be coded when comparing numeric values.

Summary

Good coding style is often a matter of preference. Nevertheless, there are a few rules of thumb that render scripts more readable and maintainable. We've discussed some of the generally accepted ones in this chapter. These include the proper use of capitalization, good variable naming, proper spacing and indentation, extensive code commentary, structuring and modularizing code, and robust error and exception handling.

We also listed a few common coding errors and how to avoid them. Learning to avoid these errors in your coding will quickly reduce the time you spend in debugging and testing your scripts. Some of the most common errors include incorrectly coding the invocation or return from routines and functions, improperly passing or reading arguments or parameters, and failing to terminate comment blocks or encode line continuations.

While many developers style themselves as "heavy-duty techies"—and write obscure code to prove it—the best programmers write the most readable code. Their scripts feature lower error rates, are easier to enhance and maintain, and remain useful longer. We urge readers to take the stylistic concerns highlighted in this chapter to heart and write code that conforms to best practice.

Test Your Understanding

1. What is "the virtue of consistency" when applied to programming practice?

2. Why do some programmers deeply nest functions? What is the downside of this practice?

3. What makes a "good" comment in a script? What are the three styles of commenting scripts?

4. What are the basic principles of modularity? Of structured programming?

5. What's wrong with `do-until` loops and the `signal` instruction used as a GOTO? With what should you replace these two constructs?

6. What makes a "good" variable name? Why is good variable-naming important?

7. Should you use global variables? Why, or why not?

13

Writing Portable Rexx

Overview

One of the great advantages to Rexx is that it runs on every available *platform*, or hardware/operating system combination. Rexx scripts run on handheld devices, laptops, PCs, midrange servers of all kinds, all the way up to the largest mainframes.

This book covers the major Rexx interpreters. All are either free or open source or come bundled with an operating system. All support *classic Rexx*, the form of the language standardized by TRL-2 and later by the ANSI-1996 standard. Additionally, there are Open Object Rexx and roo!, true object-oriented supersets of classic Rexx, and NetRexx, a Rexx-like language for developing applications and applets in the Java environment. Figure 13-1 below shows how object-oriented Rexx interpreters and NetRexx evolved from classic Rexx. Beyond these free implementations and variations, there exist several commercial implementations as well.

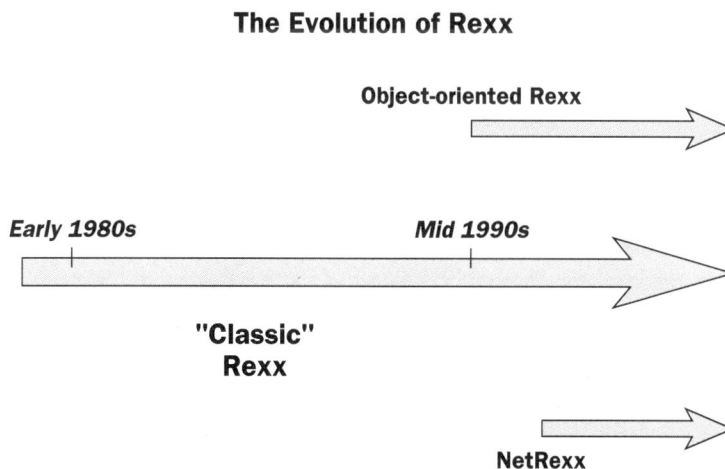

The Evolution of Rexx

Object-oriented Rexx

Early 1980s   *Mid 1990s*

**"Classic"
Rexx**

NetRexx

Figure 13-1

Rexx's ubiquity and standardization have two implications. First, this means that your knowledge applies to a broad range of platforms. If you know how to code Rexx scripts on a PC, you can do it on a mainframe. If you program Rexx under Windows, you can do it under Linux, Solaris, VM, or any of dozens of other operating systems. In learning Rexx, you acquire a broadly applicable skill portable across numerous environments.

The second advantage to ubiquity and standardization is *code portability*. For example, a script could be developed under Windows and then run under Unix. Code can be designed to be platform-independent, leading to savings for organizations that support diverse platforms. Different kinds of problems can be addressed by scripts hosted on different platforms. One could develop scripts in one environment and run them in another.

Code portability is not a given. Regardless of language standards, there are still different platform-unique characteristics that intrude upon this goal. This chapter points out some of the factors affecting code portability and how to address them when writing Rexx scripts.

Whether code portability is desirable depends on your goals. In most cases, creating scripts that are compatible across many operating systems, platforms, and Rexx interpreters restricts the use of the language to its standard capabilities. It forgoes the power of language extensions and OS-unique features beyond the Rexx language standards. Writing and testing portable code also typically involves extra effort. This chapter does not argue for code portability — whether portability is desirable depends on your own needs. The purpose here is simply to offer guidance where portability is a goal.

To provide this guidance, the chapter covers several key topics. First, we discuss some of the factors that affect code portability. These orient you as to how easy (or difficult) it may be to achieve portability in different application projects. Next, we discuss the various Rexx standards. Understanding what these standards contain and their slight differences helps you achieve portable scripts because you'll know better what it means to "code to the standard" if you know what the standards define.

After this, we discuss how scripts learn about their environment. This underlies portability. Only the environmentally aware script can act in ways that support its portability. We start by reviewing various functions and features of Rexx that the book has already covered, but this time we view them through a new lense — how can they aid portability? We also introduce new instructions and functions whose main purpose is environmental awareness. Then, we demonstrate some of the principles of portability with a script that intelligently determines the platform and interpreter it runs under. This is the core requirement of a portable application: the ability to query and understand the environment in which it executes.

We conclude the chapter with a more detailed discussion of the techniques and challenges of portable code. This addresses Rexx tools and interfaces, and the manners in which they can enhance (or detract) from portable scripting.

Factors Affecting Portability

Your knowledge of Rexx is widely applicable across platforms because humans have the ability to discern (and allow for) minor differences. Programs, of course, have no such capability unless it is explicitly recognized and coded for.

There are several factors that affect code portability.

First is whether the code stays within the Rexx standards. Code that remains within the ANSI-1996 standard will be most portable. Better yet, code within the slightly more narrow TRL-2 standard definition, since many Rexx implementations were designed for TRL-2 and do not address the minor ANSI-1996 improvements. Later in this chapter we summarize the evolution of Rexx standards and the minor differences between them.

The second factor that affects the portability of Rexx scripts across platforms is whether the developer considers code portability a goal during program design and development. Sometimes it is quite possible to make choices that provide a higher degree of code portability without any extra effort — all that is required is that the developer recognize the nuances of code portability in his or her program and address them up front.

Take, for example, file I/O. Recall that Chapter 5 illustrated both line-oriented and character-oriented I/O. Both are implemented through a set of instructions and functions that are all well within all Rexx standards. Yet scripts making certain assumptions when using character-oriented I/O will be less portable than those using line-oriented I/O (since character I/O reads the line-ending and file-ending characters that vary across operating systems). This is a simple example where code can be made much more portable at the mere price of understanding platform differences.

Perhaps the biggest factor affecting code portability is the degree to which the script issues operating system commands. This is one of the major uses of Rexx, of course, and operating system commands vary by the OS.

Recognize that the OS's under which the script is to run affect how portable that script can be. For example, Windows is a family of like operating systems. It is easier to write a script to run under different versions of Windows and to issue Windows commands than it is to write a script that issues both Windows and Linux commands and runs under both Windows and Linux, for example. Cross-platform portability is always easier when the operating systems involved are similar, such as those within a single operating system family. Portability across all forms of Windows or across all varieties of Linux is easier than achieving portability across Windows and Linux.

The nature of the commands the script issues affect its portability. If you write a script that runs under the three major varieties of Unix (Sun Solaris, IBM AIX, and HP HP/UX), the higher-level commands are common across these three OSs. By *higher-level*, we mean Unix commands that meet generally accepted Unix System standards. The *lower-level commands* diverge among these three versions of Unix. They become unique and system-dependent. Lower-level commands include, for example, those of the proprietary volume managers used in these three systems. Another example is parameters that configure the Unix kernel.

Foreknowledge of the environments in which a script will run is a key determinant in how much effort it costs to make the code portable. The developer can design and modularize code to address the target operating systems. He or she can isolate OS-specific code to certain places within the program, and avoid literal command strings in favor of building them within variables, for example. Retroactively trying to impose code portability on a working script that was designed without this goal in mind is always more difficult and always costs more.

How many operating system commands a script issues (and how OS-specific those commands are) determine how portable code is and how much effort portability takes. A script that performs a generic task independent of operating system should be highly portable. The scripts in this book provide examples. Up to this chapter, only one executed an operating system command (the Windows `cls` command to clear the display screen). It was easy to test these scripts under both Windows and Linux. The next chapter goes into more detail about how to issue commands from Rexx scripts to the operating system. Since these scripts are oriented toward issuing OS commands, they are much more bound to the platform for which they were developed and run. The rule of thumb is: *generic tasks can be coded to be run anywhere, whereas OS-specific tasks will always present a challenge if code portability is a goal.*

Finally, many Rexx programs interface to outside packages, for example, for user interaction through a GUI or data storage via a database management system. The following chapters describe and illustrate some of these interfaces. Interfaces present another portability challenge. Some interfaces are themselves designed to be platform-independent, so they make scripts more portable. Other interfaces are platform-dependent and so render scripts that use them platform-specific. Consider the costs as well as the benefits of any interface before deciding to use it in your scripts.

Rexx Standards

Outside of limiting the operating system commands your script issues and sticking to cross-platform interfaces, the biggest action you can take to develop portable code is to code within the Rexx standards. This section describes these standards in more detail as well as the manner in which they evolved and the differences between them. Understanding the standards and their differences enables you to code for greatest portability.

Figure 13-2 shows the evolution of Rexx and its standards.

Rexx Standards

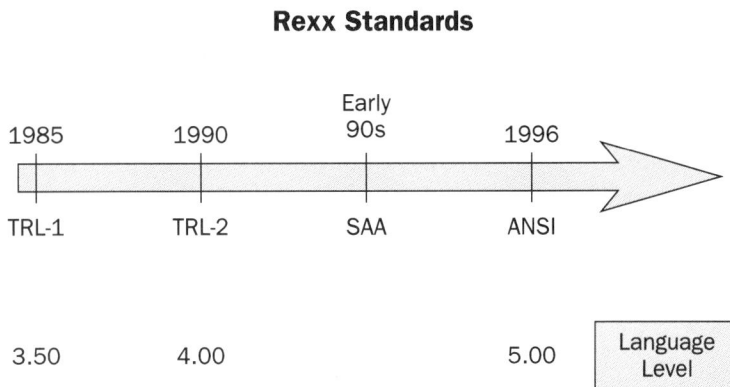

Figure 13-2

This table summarizes the four Rexx key standards and when each was promulgated:

Standard	Date	Language Level
TRL-1	1985	3.50
TRL-2	1990	4.00
SAA	1992	--
ANSI	1996	5.00

Michael Cowlishaw, the inventor of Rexx, wrote his definitive book *The Rexx Language: A Practical Approach to Programming* in 1985. He produced this book after several years of feedback on Rexx from the thousands of users connected to IBM's VNET network (an internal IBM network that presaged the Internet). The result was that the original Rexx language definition embodied in TRL-1 was remarkably complete, mature and stable.

Mr. Cowlishaw issued the second edition to his book, called TRL-2, in 1990. TRL-2 lists the changes it makes over TRL-1 in an appendix. There are 33 changes that take only four pages to describe. Many of the changes are highly specific "minor additions" more than anything else. The major improvements are summarized below.

Major TRL-2 Standard Additions to TRL-1

Input/output — The `stream` function is added for greater control over I/O, and it and the `NOTREADY` condition offer greater control over I/O errors.

Condition trapping — In addition to the `NOTREADY` condition, the `condition` function provides more information to error routines. The `signal` and `call` instructions can refer to named trap routines (previously the names of the trap routines were required to be the same as the name the condition they handled).

Binary strings — Binary strings are added as well as several conversion functions that apply to them: `b2x` and `x2b`.

More specific definitions — TRL-2 tightens up the definitions of TRL-1 where necessary, providing a more accurate language definition for interpreter writers. There are also many very small miscellaneous changes.

Rexx interpreters that conform to the language definition of TRL-1 are said to be of *language level* 3.50. Those conforming to TRL-2 are at language level 4.00.

IBM defined and published its *Systems Application Architecture* standard, or *SAA*, in the early 1990s. The goal of SAA was to increase code and skills portability across IBM's diverse operating systems. As part of this effort, IBM identified Rexx as its *common procedures language* across all its operating systems. This had two effects. First, IBM ensured that Rexx was available and came bundled with all its operating systems. This not only included mainframe operating systems in the OS, VM, and VSE families, but also included systems such as OS/400 and OS/2. The second effect of SAA was that IBM converged the features of its Rexx implementations across its platforms. TRL-2 (and its VM/CMS implementation) formed the common base.

An *American National Standards Institute*, or *ANSI*, committee embarked on standardization of Rexx beyond that of TRL-2 in the early 1990s. The committee completed its work in 1996 with the publication of the Rexx standard X3.274-1996. This standard is commonly referred to in Rexx circles as *ANSI-1996*. The ANSI-1996 standard makes only minor language additions to the TRL-2 standard. The primary contributions of the ANSI-1996 standard to Rexx are below. The language level of ANSI-1996 is 5.00.

Major ANSI-1996 Standard Additions to TRL-2

ANSI legitimacy — Confers the prestige and imprimatur of an international standard upon Rexx. ANSI is the main organization for standardization of programming languages.

A few new features — ANSI-1996 adds a few language features where they are nondisruptive to existing scripts and earlier standards. These include, for example, the new built-in string manipulation functions `changestr` and `countstr`, and the new trap condition `LOSTDIGITS`. The `date` and `time` functions are enhanced to perform conversions in addition to just reporting the date and time. A few more special variables are added (`.rc`, `.rs`, `.result`, `.mn`, `.sigl`).

Data left to read — The `chars` and `lines` functions previously returned the number of characters or lines left to read on the input stream. Determining these values could consume much time for large files. ANSI-1996 allows the returning of 1, meaning "some undetermined number of characters or lines are left to read." The `lines` function has two options: `C`, which returns the number of lines left to read in the file, and `N`, which allows a return of 1 for one or more lines left to read and 0 if there are no lines left to read. For backward compatibility, `N` is the default.

Command I/O — ANSI-1996 more accurately defined how input is sent to commands and how command output and errors are captured. These are reflected in enhancements to the `address` instruction and `address` function. The `address` instruction now includes keywords `input`, `output` and `error` to manage communication to/from the operating system or other external command execution environment. The `address` function can return the setting of these three new keywords. Chapter 14 illustrates how to use the `address` instruction and `address` function.

More precise language definition — Provides a more precise definition of Rexx beyond that provided by TRL-2. TRL-2 defines Rexx in book form, readable by the typical software developer or IT programmer. The ANSI-1996 standard is written in a format designed for those who need the precise definition necessary to create a Rexx interpreter or assess whether a specific interpreter meets international standards. The ANSI-1996 standard is more rigorous than TRL-2 but less readable for the average developer.

Nearly all Rexx implementations meet the TRL-2 standard. Many also either meet the ANSI-1996 standard or are being enhanced to meet it. To rephrase this in terms of the "language level," nearly all Rexx implementations meet or exceed language level 4.00 and some achieve 5.00. The main exceptions to this rule would be those Rexxes that were purposely designed as "language variants," for example, NetRexx. Rexx thus features a strong, well-defined and widely adhered to language standard. Coding to it greatly increases code portability.

All the programs appearing to this point in this book conform to the TRL-2 and ANSI-1996 standards. In the upcoming section of this book on "Rexx Implementations" we cover some of the implementation- and platform-specific aspects of various Rexx interpreters. Subsequent chapters on interfaces to outside packages (like databases, the Tk GUI, XML and the like) also go beyond the Rexx standard, because they are not part of the language.

One big factor in Rexx's success as a widely used scripting language is that it was defined rigorously by a highly readable book, TRL-2, relatively early in its history. Yet this language definition was published *after* the language had reached a full, stable state. Compared to many programming languages, Rexx was lucky in this regard. The popularity of some programming languages suffers because they become widely implemented before a standard solidifies; other languages quickly gain a standard but this occurs before the language gains all the necessary features. Rexx programmers benefit from this happy history with much more standardized and portable code than many other languages.

The bottom line is that to render your scripts as standardized and as portable as possible, all you need do is code to the TRL-2 and ANSI-1996 standards. This section spells out exactly the differences between the major Rexx standards. Combined with information from your Rexx interpreter's manual, this knowledge makes it much more possible to code portable scripts.

How a Script Learns about Its Environment

We've mentioned a few factors that affect code portability. Underlying this is the script's ability to learn about its environment. To issue operating system commands in a cross-system manner, for example, the script needs to be able to determine under which operating system it runs. The script might also need to know about how it was invoked, the version and language level of Rexx running it, the date and time, and other bits of environmental information. This section addresses this need. First we'll repeat (but consolidate) instructions and functions that provide information to scripts that have been discussed in previous chapters. Then we'll get into new material showing how scripts retrieve environmental information critical to their knowledgeable interaction with their environment in a cross-platform manner.

As covered earlier in Chapter 8, a script learns its input arguments or parameters through these two key instructions:

- ❑ `parse arg` — Access input parameters (without automatic uppercase translation)
- ❑ `arg` — Access input parameters (with automatic uppercase translation)

`arg` is just the "short form" of the instruction:

```
parse upper arg  [template]
```

The `arg` function can:

- ❑ Tell how many input arguments were passed — Coded as `arg()`
- ❑ Tell if the nth argument exists — Coded as `arg(n, 'E')`
- ❑ Return the nth argument (assuming it exists) — Coded as `arg(n)`

A number of built-in functions allow scripts to access environmental information. Scripts that issue these functions without any arguments retrieve environmental information:

Function	Environmental Information Returned
address	Returns current default command environment, or, returns the current `input`, `output`, and `error` redirections.
date	Returns the date in any of a variety of formats based on the input parameter.
digits	Returns numeric precision.
fuzz	Returns precision for numeric comparisons (the *fuzz factor*).
form	Returns whether current format for exponential numbers is `SCIENTIFIC` or `ENGINEERING`.
sourceline	Returns the total number of lines in the source script, or returns a specific line if a line number is supplied as an argument.
time	Returns local time in 24-hour clock format. A variety of options allow the time to be returned in any desired format. Can also be used to measure elapsed time (as an *interval timer*).
trace	Returns the current trace level.

Many of these functions can also be used to set operational characteristics by supplying input arguments. We've seen examples of all these functions except for `date` and `time`.

The `stream` function is also useful for retrieving information about I/O operations and the I/O environment. Most Rexx interpreters provide for a much broader use of the `stream` function than the Rexx standards minimally require. This transforms the `stream` function into a general-purpose mechanism for retrieving I/O information, controlling I/O devices, and issuing I/O commands. All interpreters minimally support these two `stream` options:

❑   `D` (Description) — An implementation-dependent description of I/O status

❑   `S` (Status) — The state of the stream: `ERROR`, `NOTREADY`, `READY`, or `UNKNOWN`

Individual I/O operations return values that indicate whether the I/O operation was successful. Take a new look at the I/O functions from the perspective of their return values and the information these carry:

I/O Function	I/O Information Returned
charin	Returns the number of characters read (0 if none were read).
charout	Returns the number of characters *not* successfully written (0 means success).
chars	Returns a nonzero value if at least one character remains to be read.
linein	Returns a line read from a file or the null string if no line exists to read.
lineout	Return value varies by requested operation. For writing one line, a return value of 0 means the line was successfully written, 1 means it was not.
lines	Returns a nonzero value if there is at least one line left to be read.

The `chars` and `lines` functions may return either the exact number of characters or lines left to be read, or 1, indicating that some unspecified number of characters or lines remain to be read. The ANSI-1996 standard permits the interpreter flexibility in this regard. The trade-off is between providing precise information about the amount of data left to be processed in the file versus the performance overhead of calculating this value.

Trap or *exception routines* help script writers managed I/O errors raised by the NOTREADY and SYNTAX conditions. `signal on` or `call on` instructions enable trap routines you write in the program. Trap routines can be used to handle these error conditions: SYNTAX, HALT, ERROR, FAILURE, NOVALUE, NOTREADY, and LOSTDIGITS. These built-in functions provide useful information to trap routines:

Function	Feedback to the Error Routine
condition	Returns the name of trapped condition, a textual description of the condition, how the trap routine was invoked (`call` or `signal`), and the current state of the trapped condition (ON, OFF, or DELAY)
errortext	Returns the textual error message for a given Rexx error number
sourceline	Returns the number of lines in the source script, or a specific line if a line number is supplied as an argument
trace	Returns the current trace level, or can be used to alter it

All these functions can be coded anywhere in Rexx scripts except for `condition`, which specifically returns information about the current trapped condition and is thus not likely to be useful outside of a trap routine.

Several important Rexx *special variables* provide information both to trap routines and throughout Rexx scripts. The three special variables in the TRL-2 standard are uninitialized until an event occurs that sets them:

Special Variable	Meaning
rc	The return code from a host command, or a Rexx SYNTAX error code.
sigl	The line number that caused control to jump to a label. This could be set by the transfer of control caused by a trapped condition, or simply by a regular `call` to an internal routine or invoking an internal function.
result	The string sent back to a calling routine by the `return` instruction. If `return` is coded without an operand, `result` is set to uninitialized.

Previous chapters in this book have mentioned most of these sources of information for Rexx scripts. Our intent here is to consolidate this information, then build upon it and combine it with new features to show how you can write portable scripts. Now, let's move on to adding new sources of environmental information: the `parse source` and `parse version` instructions.

Chapter 13

The `parse source` instruction provides three information elements. They are listed in this table:

parse source Information Element	Meaning
system	A single word for the platform on which the script is running. Often cites the operating system.
invocation	One word that indicates how the script was invoked. Often returns COMMAND, FUNCTION or SUBROUTINE.
filename	The name of the file containing the Rexx script that is running. Usually this is a fully qualified file name conforming to the conventions of the operating system on which the script is running.

Here's sample code that shows how to retrieve this system information:

```
parse  source  system  invocation  filename .
say 'System:' .system  'Invocation:'  invocation  'Filename:'  filename
```

The output of this code, of course, depends on the platform on which it is run. Here's an example of the output generated when this code runs under Regina Rexx on a Windows XP system:

```
System: WIN32  Invocation: COMMAND  Filename: C:\Regina\pgms\parseenv.rexx
```

The same statements run under Red Hat Linux with Regina yield:

```
System: UNIX  Invocation: COMMAND Filename: /regina/parseenv.rexx
```

This output is system-dependent (which is the entire point!). By retrieving it the script can understand on which platform it is running. The script also knows the filename containing its own code and the manner in which it was invoked. Of course, the filename will represent the file-naming conventions of the operating system on which the script runs. For example, Windows filenames will have backslashes between directory levels, while Linux, Unix, and BSD will contain forward slashes between directory names.

The `system` or platform keyword is most significant. Table L-1 in Appendix L lists common values for the `system` data element for popular Rexx interpreters running on various platforms. The appendix gives you an idea of what many environments return. Of course, inside your scripts you should not rely on this chart but rather run the preceding two lines on any platform on which you intend to run your script. This is necessary because you could find slight or unexpected differences across platforms. Using this code cues your script into these differences.

The `parse version` instruction tells the script about the Rexx interpreter that is running it. While `parse source` yields basic platform information, `parse version` supplies basic interpreter information. This can be used, for example, to figure out in real time which Rexx features will be supported or which version of an interpreter is being used. Here are the `parse version` data items:

parse value Information Element	Meaning
language	Interpreter name and version
level	The *language level* this interpreter supports, according to the Rexx language levels described earlier in this chapter (e.g., 3.50, 4.00, 5.00, or similar identifier)
date	Along with `month` and `year`, describes the release date for the interpreter
month	See `date`
year	See `date`

Here's an example of how to code to retrieve this information:

```
parse version language level date month year .
say 'Language:' language 'Level:' level 'Date:' date 'Month:' month 'Year:' year
```

When run under Windows XP with Regina Rexx, here is sample output:

```
Language: REXX-Regina_3.2(MT)  Level: 5.00  Date: 25 Month: Apr Year: 2003
```

Running the statements under Red Hat Linux with Regina yields this output:

```
Language: REXX-Regina_3.3RC1(MT)  Level: 5.00  Date: 16 Month: Nov Year: 2003
```

The `level` is especially important because it tells the script what Rexx features it can expect to see. The script could execute different code appropriate to the particular interpreter under which it runs to fulfill its tasks.

The `language` allows the script to dynamically adapt to any known peculiarities or extensions offered by specific Rexx interpreters. Chapters 20 through 30 describe many of these extended features and how to use them.

After collecting information from `parse source` and `parse version`, a script usually knows enough about its environment that it can issue operating system commands appropriate to the platform on which it is running. By running different statements or modules based on the platform, scripts can be rendered platform-independent.

Another step is often useful. Based on the `parse source system` feedback, issue an operating system command appropriate to the OS that provides more information on its version and release level. For example, under Windows and DOS systems, execute the `ver` (version) command. For all forms of Linux, Unix, and BSD, run the `uname` command (such as `uname -a`). The script can capture the feedback from these commands and know exactly what operating system it is working with. (An error return code from the command shows that the script was not on track with the command it executed!) This can be trapped by an exception condition routine if desired or simply addressed by analyzing the command return code.

A Sample Program

To this point, we have discussed a variety of instructions and functions that can aid in writing portable code. Some of these functions were introduced in earlier chapters in different contexts, while others are newly introduced in this chapter. All are useful to writing portable code because all supply environmental information to scripts. Now, we need to look at an example program that shows how to synthesize this information into portable code.

This example program determines the Rexx interpreter under which it runs and the Rexx standards for that interpreter. This is a key ability portable scripts must have: the ability to determine how they are being run and under which interpreter. In this instance, the script expects to see the Regina interpreter. If not, it displays a message.

The script also determines whether it is running under Windows or Linux. It issues an OS command to determine the OS version and release (either `ver` for Windows or `uname -a` for Linux). Then it displays the OS version and release information to the user.

```
/* WHERE AM I:                                            */
/*                                                        */
/*    This script learns about its environment and determines  */
/*    exactly which Windows or Linux OS it runs under.    */

parse version language level     date     month year .
parse source  system   invocation filename .

language = translate(language)        /* ensure using Regina Rexx */
if pos('REGINA',language) = 0 then
   say 'ERROR: Interpreter is not Regina:'  language

say 'Interpreter version/release date:' date month year
say 'Language standards level is:    ' level
say 'Version information from an OS command follows...'

/* determine operating system, get its version/release info      */

select
   when system = 'WIN32' then
       'ver'
   when system = 'UNIX' |  system = 'LINUX' then
       'uname -a'
   otherwise
      say 'Unexpected SYSTEM:' system
end

if rc <> 0 then             /* write message if OS command failed */
   say 'Bad return code on OS Version command:' rc
```

Here is sample output for this script on Windows XP running Regina Rexx:

```
Interpreter version/release date: 25 Apr 2003
Language standards level is:     5.00
Version information from an OS command follows...

Microsoft Windows XP [Version 5.1.2600]
```

Here is output from the script when run under Red Hat Linux with Regina:

```
Interpreter version/release date: 16 Nov 2003
Language standards level is:       5.00
Version information from an OS command follows...
Linux localhost.localdomain 2.4.18-14 #1 Wed Sep 4 13:35:50 EDT 2002 i686 i686 i386
GNU/Linux
```

Let's discuss the program code. In the program, these two lines retrieve all the necessary environmental information:

```
parse version language level     date     month year .
parse source  system   invocation filename .
```

Following these statements, the `select` instruction issues either the `ver` command for Windows systems, or the `uname -a` command for Linux and Unix systems. The following code snippet shows how scripts can dynamically tailor any operating system dependent commands they issue. The `select` statement keys off of the environmental feedback previously retrieved by the `parse source` instruction:

```
select
    when system = 'WIN32' then
        'ver'
    when system = 'UNIX' | system = 'LINUX' then
        'uname -a'
    otherwise
        say 'Unexpected SYSTEM:' system
end
```

In this manner, the script interacts intelligently with its environment. The Where Am I? script could easily be turned into a generic function or subroutine which returns environmental information depending on its input parameters. It then becomes a generalized *service routine*, which can be incorporated into any larger script. In this manner, a script can learn about its environment and adapt its behavior and the commands it issues to become portable and platform-independent.

Techniques for Command Portability

To this point, we have summarized the various instructions and functions that aid in making code portable, and we have synthesized several of them into a sample program that determines critical facts about its environment. Now we can discuss various approaches for designing portable scripts that issue operating system commands.

The first rule is simple and sometimes applicable: minimize the use of OS commands. This eliminates the case in which a script casually issues an OS command which really is not necessary, thereby compromising its portability.

Where equivalent OS commands exist and their results can be handled generically, simple `if` instructions can issue the appropriate OS command. For example, the script named Menu in Chapter 3 issued the Windows `cls` (clear screen) command to clear the display screen before writing its menu for the user. The direct equivalent command under Linux and Unix is `clear`. Since these two commands are equivalent in function, the program could easily be made portable simply by determining which operating system the script runs on, and then issuing the proper command to clear the display screen through a simple `if` instruction.

Of course, return codes from commands are just as system-dependent as the commands themselves. Generally, a return code of 0 means success, while anything else means failure. This example shows that the situation is vastly simplified if the script does not need to inspect or react to return codes.

What if the OS command produces output the script needs to process? This is a more complicated case. For example, say that the program issues the `dir` command under Windows or the `ls` command under Linux or Unix to display a file list to the user. The outputs of these two commands are close enough that if the goal is merely to display the file listing to the user, the script can use the same technique as with the `cls` and `clear` commands—just encode an `if` statement to issue the appropriate command for the operating system and display its output to the user. But if the script processes the command outputs, the situation becomes much more complicated. Output formats from `dir` and `ls` are significantly different. Here the approach might be to invoke an appropriate internal function specific to each operating system to issue the file list command and perform the analysis of its output. This is another common technique — code a different OS-dependent module to handle each operating system's commands.

A third technique is to determine the platform, then invoke an entirely different script depending on which operating system is involved. Here the top-level, or driving, script is only a small block of code at the very highest level of the program. It does little more than identify the operating system. After this determination, it calls an OS-dependent script.

Which technique is best depends on the tasks the script performs and the numbers and kinds of operating system commands it issues. The *binding* or degree to which the code depends on the operating system determines which approach makes sense for a given situation. In all cases, identifying the platform on which the script is running is the first step, and isolating OS-dependent code (by `if` logic or into separate modules or routines) is the key.

Foreknowledge of the need for portability and the operating systems that will be supported vastly reduces the effort involved in developing portable code. The similarity (or differences) among the supported platforms is another critical factor in determining the effort required. For example, it is relatively easy to develop a script that is portable across all versions of Windows, or to test a script across all major Linux distributions. It's quite another matter to port a script that issues a lot of OS commands from Windows to Linux or vice versa.

Issues in Code Portability

At the beginning of this chapter, we discussed a few factors that affect the portability of code. Now that we've described the instructions, functions, and coding techniques that pertain to portability, we can revisit the earlier discussion with greater specificity. Let's explore these issues in greater detail. Here are a number of issues of which to be aware when writing portable scripts:

❑ *Retrieving platform and interpreter information* — The earlier sample script demonstrates how to retrieve operating system and Rexx interpreter information. Implemented as a callable service routine, such code can be used by any Rexx script to get the information it needs to run as a cross-platform program. A service routine that determines operating system, platform, interpreter, and other environmental information forms the basis of platform-independent code in many large applications.

❑ *Screen interfaces* — Input/output to the display screen is a major area of incompatibility among many platforms. Using a cross-platform user interface like the Rexx/TK or Rexx/DW libraries are one way to get around this problem — assuming that these interfaces are portable across the platforms on which the scripts will run. Chapter 16 discusses GUI interfaces in some detail.

❑ *Database interfaces* — Databases can mask I/O differences across platforms. For example, interfacing your Rexx script to Oracle makes the I/O interface between Windows and Linux the same because Oracle calls are the same in both environments. Just ensure that the database itself can be relied upon for portability across the platforms you target. From this standpoint, major databases like Oracle and DB2 offer the best portability among the major databases (SQL Server only runs under Windows family operating systems). Among open-source databases, MySQL, PostgreSQL, and Berkeley DB offer great portability. Chapter 15 discusses database programming in detail and shows how to accomplish it with sample scripts.

❑ *Other interfaces* — We mention GUI and database interfaces specifically because these issues pertain to so many programs. But the principles apply to many other packages and interfaces as well — they may be useful as levers to gain more code portability, or they may hamper portability by their own isolation to certain environments. If portability is a goal, the key is to consider the impacts of any external packages with which your scripts will interface. Careful thought will allow you to leverage interfaces for greater application portability and avoid having them limit the portability of your scripts.

❑ *Character sets and code pages* — Different platforms use different character-set-encoding schemes. For example, Windows, Linux, Unix, BSD, and DOS systems use ASCII, whereas mainframes use EBCDIC. Scripts that manipulate characters as hexadecimal or bit strings need to be aware of these different encodings. Related issues include *collating* (or sort) order and *code pages* or character sets.

❑ *Interpreter differences* — We've already mentioned how scripts retrieve interpreter information. Code within the lowest common denominator language level to ensure the widest portability of your scripts. We might call this *interpreter portability* — Rexx scripts that can be run under any Rexx interpreter. This trades off the convenience and power of using implementation-specific built-in functions, for example, for the benefit of code portability.

❑ options *Instruction* — The options instruction issues interpreter-specific instructions to the Rexx interpreter. Its format is:

```
options  expression
```

Here's an example that instructs a Rexx interpreter to conform to language level 5.00 and ensure that the trace is off:

```
options  '5.00 Notrace'
```

The options that can be set are unique to each Rexx interpreter. Check your language manual to see what your version of Rexx supports. *If the interpreter does not recognize any the items, it ignores them without issuing an error.* This means that if it is important to know whether the options were set properly, your code will have to perform this task. (Wouldn't it be nice to have a corresponding options *function* by which your script could retrieve the options in effect? There is none.) Using options may force interpreter-dependent code unless its use is carefully controlled.

❏ *Capturing errors by conditions* — The ability to trap conditions and process them through error routines can be a tool to gain greater cross-platform portability. NOTREADY might help with handling I/O issues while LOSTDIGITS can manage concerns with significant digits.

❏ *Universal "not" sign* — Use the ANSI-standard symbol for the "not" sign, which is the backslash (\). For example, for "not equals" you should code \= or <> or >< instead of the mainframe-only symbols ¬=. See Figure 13-3.

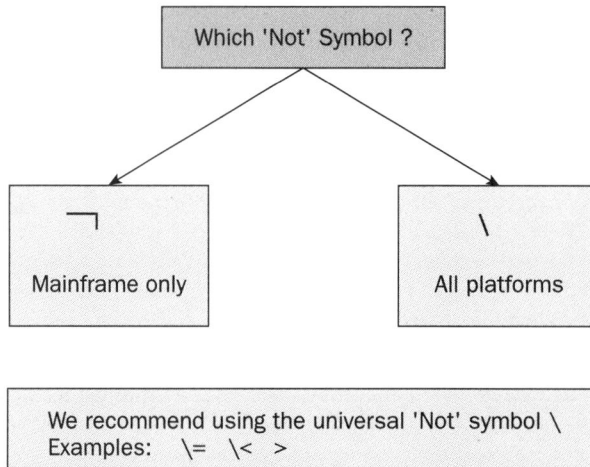

Figure 13-3

❏ *First line of the script* — For greatest portability, do *not* code a Linux/Unix/BSD interpreter-location line as the first line of the script, as in this example:

```
#!/usr/local/bin/rexx
```

Without this line, you'll typically have to run Rexx scripts explicitly. Instead code this as the first line of the script for maximum portability, starting in column 1 of line 1:

```
/* REXX  */
```

This ensures that the script will run properly on mainframes running VM or OS, and it's still compatible with almost every other platform, as long as the script runs explicitly.

❏ *The* address *instruction* — The address instruction sends input to OS commands and captures their output. The ANSI-1996 address instruction standard provides for the new keywords input, output, and error to manage command I/O. The alternatives are to use the stack for command I/O when using the address instruction, or to avoid the address instruction entirely by using redirected I/O.

Many Rexx interpreters still emphasize the stack for command I/O, yet this feature is not central to the ANSI-1996 standard. The ANSI-1996 address keywords for I/O are the true standard, yet many Rexx interpreters still do not support them. You'll have to investigate what interpreter(s) and platform(s) your portable code is to run on to decide which approach to use. Chapter 14 covers the address instruction in detail.

❑ *Stay within the ANSI-1996 standard for the stack* — On the mainframe and in some other environments, the stack is not only used for command processing, it is used for many other purposes as well. For greatest portability, stay strictly within the stack definition provided by the ANSI-1996 standard. Or better, use standard language features other than the stack to accomplish the work.

❑ *Use only standard operands* — The Rexx standards define certain instructions and functions and allows them to have implementation-specific (nonstandard) operands. Examples include the `options` instruction (to issue directions to the interpreter) and the `stream` function (to issue I/O commands). If portable code is a goal it is prudent not to use nonportable operands for these instructions and functions.

I/O and Code Portability

File input/outout is a major area in which operating systems differ. This is because the I/O routines, or *I/O drivers*, are different for every operating system. Whether you code in Rexx or some other scripting language, you may encounter I/O incompatibilities when scripts are run on different platforms. I/O should be *encapsulated* (or placed in separate routines or modules) to isolate this platform-specific code within large Rexx scripts.

OS differences lead to minor differences in Rexx implementations. Check your release-specific documentation to understand these differences.

Generally, line-oriented I/O is more portable than character-oriented I/O because character I/O may read OS-dependent characters (representing line or file end) as part of the input stream. Scripts can be written to rationalize the differences in character-oriented file I/O across platforms if they recognize this.

To stay within the strictest standards, assume that the `chars` and `lines` functions return 0 if there is no more data to read, or some nonzero value otherwise. The nonzero value might be the number of characters or lines left to read in a persistent stream, or it could simply be 1, indicating more data to read. These two functions should only be applied to *persistent streams* (files), not to *transient streams* (like keyboard input).

To explicitly flush the output buffers and close a file, code the `lineout` function without a string to write. Almost all Rexx implementations follow this TRL-2 standard. If program logic permits, the most standard, portable way to close a file is to simply let Rexx close it without instruction from the script.

The earlier section titled "How a Script Learns about Its Environment" discussed standard return codes from the I/O functions: `charin`, `charout`, `chars`, `lines`, `linein`, and `lineout`. Given that I/O varies across operating systems, this is one area in which many Rexx interpreters still do have minor differences. The reader is advised to check his specific interpreter documentation for details. When coding across platforms or developing code that runs under more than one Rexx implementation, check the documentation for all interpreters involved. And also, *test the script* under all the operating systems under which it will run!

Portable scripts should avoid explicitly positioning the read and write positions within files. Some Rexx interpreters provide good advanced facilities in this regard that are outside the Rexx standards. Part II discusses these extended features for file positioning and direct data access.

Interfaces for Portability — RexxUtil

We've previously mentioned that interfaces can aid in code portability. Let's discuss the popular *RexxUtil* package as an example. The RexxUtil package is an external function library that enhances code portability across the platforms on which it runs. These include operating systems in the Windows, Unix/Linux/BSD, mainframe, DOS, and OS/2 families. Instead of issuing operating-system-dependent commands, scripts can invoke routines in the RexxUtil package. These then translate the script's requests into OS-specific commands. The effect is to buffer the script from issuing operating-system unique commands.

Figure 13-4 shows how this works. A script invokes a RexxUtil service, and the RexxUtil function performs the appropriate operating system calls. Since RexxUtil runs on a number of platforms, it effectively shields the script from issuing OS-specific calls in order to access OS features and facilities. Instead, the script interfaces with the portable RexxUtil package.

**Using an Interface Package to
Increase Script Portability**

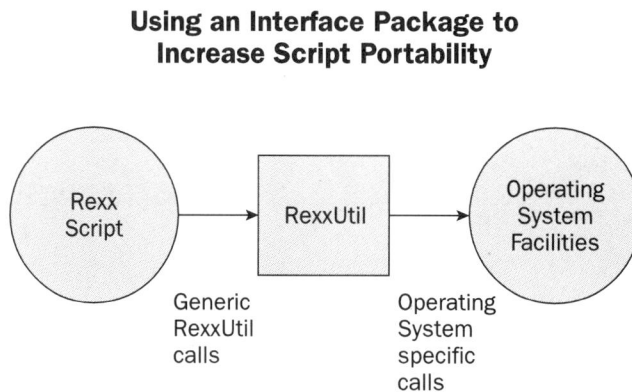

Figure 13-4

There have been various versions of the RexxUtil library over the years, tailored and adapted to a range of platforms, Rexx interpreters, and products. It might be useful to describe the kinds of functions that the library contains to give an idea of the system-specific requests from which it buffers scripts. This list enumerates and describes the major categories of functions in RexxUtil packages:

❑ *Housekeeping* — These functions load the RexxUtil library and make it accessible, or drop it from use and memory.

❑ *File system management* — These functions manage, manipulate, search, and control operating system files and directories.

❑ *System interaction* — These functions retrieve operating system, environmental, configuration, and hardware information.

❑ *Macro-space control* — These functions manage the macros available for execution. Macros can be loaded, cleared, dropped, initialized, stored, and so on.

❑ *Console I/O* — These functions support basic screen and keyboard I/O.

❑ *Stem manipulation* — These functions manipulate arrays via their stems. To give one example, the do over function processes an entire array in a simple loop, even for sparse arrays or arrays with non-numeric indexes or subscripts.

❑ *Semaphores* — These functions manage semaphores (flags used for synchronization), including *mutexes* (semaphores designed to single-thread critical code sections).

❑ *Character-set Conversions* — These functions convert to and from Unicode and support file encryption and decryption.

RexxUtil is not the only interface package which can be used to enhance code portability. Various database, GUI, and server-scripting packages provide the same platform-independence as the RexxUtil package. Chapters 15 through 18 describe a number of these interface packages and how to use them. Just be sure that the interface ports across all the platforms on which your scripts are to run!

Summary

This chapter discusses issues of code portability and offers some suggestions on how to write portable scripts. For some projects, code portability is a key goal. The ideas in this chapter may help achieve it. For other projects, portability is irrelevant and one doesn't need to spend time or effort on it. Always understand your project goals thoroughly before making these choices and coding a scripting solution.

Where code portability is a goal, understand the Rexx standards, the differences between them, and how the interpreter you are using fits with the standards. Coding to the standards is an important means to achieving portable code.

This chapter also listed many functions and instructions through which scripts can derive environmental information. We discussed a brief program that interrogated its environment to determine the interpreter running it as well as the operating system platform. Such a program can be expanded into a more robust, generic "service routine" to provide intelligence to other routines about their environment. The first step any portable script must take is understanding the environment in which it runs.

We discussed a list of issues developers face when striving to make their code portable. Hopefully, the discussion brought up points that stimulate your own thinking on how you can write code that is portable across the platforms with which you are concerned.

The next chapter goes into detail on how to issue commands from within scripts to the operating system (or other outside interface). It addresses how to send input to OS commands, how to check their return codes, how to capture their output, and how to capture their error messages.

Test Your Understanding

1. Is code portability always a virtue?

2. What instructions might a script issue to learn about its environment?

3. What is the difference between `arg` and `parse arg`?

4. What is the `sourceline` function used for?

5. Where can you find a list of the differences between the TRL-1 and TRL-2 standards?

14

Issuing System Commands

Overview

One important use of Rexx is to develop *command procedures*. These are scripts that issue operating system commands. The ability to create command procedures is one of Rexx's great advantages. You can automate repetitive tasks, create scripts for system administration, and customize or tailor the operating system to your preferences.

Command procedures must manage many aspects of interaction with the operating systems, such as building and issuing the proper OS commands and handling bad return codes and errors.

Many refer to command procedures as *shell scripts*, although technically this is not quite accurate because Rexx is not a shell. Rexx is a scripting language interpreter that runs outside of the *shell* or OS command interpreter. (There is one exception: a version of Regina runs within the zsh shell and provides true shell scripting capability. With it you can permanently change the current environment and perform tasks that can only be accomplished from within a shell, such as setting environmental variables and changing the working directory).

Command procedures are useful for a wide variety of reasons. Scripting operating system commands allows you to:

❑   *Automate repetitive tasks* — Ever been faced with entering a lengthy list of commands to get something done? Scripting allows you to automate these tasks, whether they are for system administration or simply for individual users.

An example is an "install script." For one site the author developed a simple install script that, once developed, ran on hundreds of desktops to install a relational database management system. Performing this task without automation would have been unthinkably time-consuming. The users themselves could not have done it because they did not have the expertise, and the tasks would have been too error-prone. Command scripting presented a time-efficient way to get this work done.

❑ *Save keystrokes* — Creating simple scripts eliminates mundane typing and saves keystrokes. You can create "shortcuts" for command sequences and save time.

❑ *Eliminate error* — Many system commands are complicated. Scripting them eliminates the need to remember (and correctly enter) various cryptic switches and options.

❑ *Embed intelligent interaction in the script* — Error handling, special cases, and other unusual situations — these are not what you want to face when you interact with an operating system to perform some complex system administration task. Scripting allows you to embed intelligent interaction with the operating system in a portable, sharable form. Someone with less experience can run a script and perform a job without having the same level of expertise that was required to develop the script.

❑ *Run scheduled tasks* — Once commands are encoded in a script, that procedure can be run in off-hours or scheduled to run whenever desired. This is referred to as a *batch command* or *batch procedure*.

An example from the author's experience is scripting the `create database` command in a database system that *single-threaded* that task (only one such command could run at one time). We strung together the dozen `create database` commands we needed to issue in a simple Rexx script and let it run overnight. Had we performed this work interactively, it would have taken us over 14 hours. Running it during the day would have also meant developers could not use the server that day. Running the command script at night saved a day's work for the entire programming staff.

❑ *Document procedures* — The `create database` script provided us with an historical activity log, a file that we kept to document the parameters used in creating the databases. Performing the same work interactively often means that the actual commands that were issued and their output messages are lost or forgotten. Scripting can produce log files that later can be inspected or analyzed to understand what happened or to recall exactly what was done.

❑ *Extend the operating system* — Under most environments one can execute a Rexx script simply by entering its name. To the world, the script appears as if it were a new operating system command. Rexx thus provides a way to extend, enhance, customize or tailor the environment to either personal preference or corporate standard.

❑ *Speed* — In terms of elapsed or "wall clock" time, it is *way* faster to run a "batch" script than to interactively perform some set of tasks via a graphical user interface (GUI). GUIs are great for simplifying tasks that need to be performed interactively (read: manually). But scripted automation is always faster. Moreover, it is sometimes difficult to reduce complex tasks to simple repeatable procedures using GUIs because of their context-driven nature. GUIs and command scripts work together to handle interactive and automated tasks in an effective way.

While writing scripts to automate operating system commands is very useful, there are some downsides. The big one is that any script that issues OS commands becomes platform-dependent. In most cases, this is fine. The whole point of a command script is to issue commands specific to the platform on which it runs. But don't issue operating-system-specific commands in a script you intend to port. If you do, think carefully about how this can be done in a modularized, portable way. It is not unusual to see scripts which issue just a few system commands and become system-dependent, only to mount an effort to port them later to some other platform. A little forethought can minimize porting effort. Chapter 13 covered this issue in its discussion of how to develop portable Rexx code.

Issuing Operating System Commands

Let's look at how to issue operating system commands from within scripts. We'll start with a very simple, one-line sample script; then we'll progress through various techniques that yield better flexibility and programmability. In the next section, we'll look closely at how scripts read feedback from the commands to ensure they ran properly. There are several techniques to accomplish this and you'll want to understand them all.

For a first example, here is a complete, one-line script that issues an operating system command. The script issues the Windows `dir` (directory) command:

```
dir              /* this script issues the DIR command */
```

The output to this script depends on the files in the current directory. Here's an example:

```
Volume in drive D is WD_2
Volume Serial Number is 1E20-1F01
Directory of D:\Regina

    .      <DIR>            03-24-04 11:47p .
    ..     <DIR>            03-24-04 11:47p ..
REXX     EXE      344,064  04-25-03  5:20p rexx.exe
REGINA   EXE       40,960  04-25-03  5:21p regina.exe
REGINA   DLL      385,024  04-25-03  5:21p regina.dll
```

First, we need to understand how the Rexx interpreter knows to send this command to the operating system for execution. The basic rule is this: Rexx evaluates the expressions in any line it reads. If it ends up with a string that it does not recognize (a string that is not a Rexx instruction, label, or assignment statement), Rexx passes the string to the *active environment* for execution.

By default, the active environment is the operating system. Sometimes this is called the *default environment*. Rexx does not "understand" or recognize operating system commands. Rexx evaluates expressions, ends up with a character string outside the Rexx language definition, and passes it to the active environment for execution.

After the command executes, control returns to the script line that immediately follows the command (exactly the same as if the script had called an internal or external routine). The special variable `rc` will contain the return code issued by the operating system command. What this value is depends on the command, the operating system, and the command's success or failure.

This example executes the Windows `dir` or `directory` command, captures the return code the operating system issues for that command, and displays an appropriate message:

```
dir                        /* this script issues the DIR command */
if  rc = 0 then
    say 'DIR command execution succeeded'
else
    say 'DIR command failed, return code ='   rc
```

It is important to remember two key rules when building commands. First, you are just building a character string (a string that represents a valid command), so you can leverage all the power of Rexx's string manipulation facilities to do this.

Here's an example that issues the `directory` command with two *switches* or options to the Windows command window. The Windows command we want to build lists files in the current directory sorted by size:

```
dir /OS
```

The coding to build this command uses automatic concatenation (with one blank) for pasting together the first two elements, and explicit concatenation by the concatenation operator to splice in the last item without any intervening space:

```
dir '/O' || 'S'
```

So, you can dynamically build character strings that represent commands to issue to the operating system in this fashion. You can even programmatically build arbitrarily complex commands using Rexx's expression evaluation. Here's a "gibberish generator" that ultimately builds and issues the exact same command:

```
dir_options = 'ABCDLNOPQSTWX4'      /* list of all options for the DIR command */
                                    /* build the DIR command with options       */
'dir /'  ||  substr(dir_options,7,1) || substr(dir_options,10,1)
```

Use whatever coding you want (or have to) to build operating system commands. It's all the same to the Rexx interpreter. You can leverage the flexibility inherent in the interpreter's evaluation of expressions prior to passing the resulting character string to the operating system for command execution.

Sometimes building the command string becomes complicated enough that developers prefer to build the string inside a variable, then issue the command by letting Rexx interpret that variable's contents:

```
command = dir  '/O'  ||  'S'   /* build the operating system command  */
command                        /* issues the command string to the OS */
```

This approach also makes it easy to verify that the command string is built correctly because you can just display it on the screen:

```
say  command                   /* display the command to ensure correctness */
```

The second important rule to remember is that Rexx evaluates the expression *before* passing it to the operating system for execution. Say we directly coded the above dir command in the script, exactly like this:

```
dir  /OS
```

The results are not what we expect:

```
Error 41 running "C:\Regina\pgms\dir_test.rexx", line 2: Bad arithmetic conversion
```

What happened? Rexx evaluates the expression *before* passing results to the outside command environment, the operating system, for execution. Rexx sees the slash as the division symbol, and recognizes that operands were not encoded correctly to evaluate the attempt at division. To avoid evaluating the expression, do what you always do in Rexx: enclose the command in quotation marks and make it a string literal. This line gives the expected result of a directory listing because the single quotation marks prevent Rexx from evaluating the string before sending it to the OS for execution:

```
'dir  /OS'
```

Feedback from OS Commands

Of course, a script that issues an operating system command must ensure that the command executed properly. Most scripts need to verify the command by feedback they receive after it executes. Feedback from OS commands comes in several forms:

- ❏ The command return code
- ❏ Error condition traps
- ❏ The command's textual output. This potentially includes an error message

To view the command *return code*, simply view the value of special variable `rc`. Rexx sets this special variable for your script to inspect after the command has been issued. Since command return codes are both OS- and command- specific, refer to the operating system's documentation or online help system to see possible values.

Robust code handles all possible error codes. A typical approach is to identify and directly address the most common ones in the script, such as "success" and "failure." Unexpected or highly specific return codes can be handled by displaying, printing, and logging them.

One occassionally sees scripts that ignore command return codes. This mistake leads to scripts that cannot even tell if the OS commands they issue succeeded or failed. We strongly recommend that any script check whether the OS commands it issues succeed. In return for the small amount of time you save in not checking command return codes, the user is left absolutely clueless when an error occurs. Design scripts to *fail safe*, so they at least display appropriate error messages when commands they issue fail.

Error or *exception routines* are another way to manage OS commands that result in error. Chapter 10 demonstrated how command errors and failures can be trapped and addressed in special routines by coding an error trap routine. Enable that routine through these instructions:

```
signal on error
signal on failure
call on error
call on failure
```

If `call on failure` and `signal on failure` are not active, the ERROR condition is raised instead. So, you could handle both situations without distinguishing between them simply by coding `call on error` or `signal on error`.

The last form of command feedback is the textual output the command issues. This could be valid command output, such as the list of filenames that result from the `dir` command. Or it could be an error message. For example, a `dir` command might result in a textual error message such as:

```
File Not Found
```

Your script can capture and analyze the OS command output. It can take special actions if the text output is an error or warning message of some kind.

Let's look at a simple way to capture output from an operating system command. Most operating systems permit *I/O redirection*, the ability to direct an input stream into a command and the ability to direct its output to a file. Operating systems that support redirection include all forms of Linux, Unix, BSD, Windows, and DOS.

One simple way to capture command output is to redirect the output of that command to a file, then read the file's contents from within the Rexx program. This complete script issues the `dir` command and redirects its output to a file named `diroutput.txt`. The `do` loop then reads all lines from this file and displays them on the screen:

```
'dir > diroutput.txt'          /* issue DIR command, redirect output to a file */
do while lines(diroutput.txt) > 0   /* show the Rexx script can access all      */
    say linein(diroutput.txt)        /* lines of DIR output by reading the file */
end
```

The `lines` and `linein` functions refer to the file named `diroutput.txt`. This filename may or may not need to be coded in quotation marks depending on which operating system the script runs under. Unix-derived systems like Linux use case-sensitive filenames, so you will typically encode filenames in quotation marks. Windows and related systems do not require quoting filenames; they are not case-sensitive.

Of course, the point of redirecting command output is to capture it so that the script can analyze it. Instead of displaying the output, as above, the script might parse it looking for messages that indicate specific errors, for example. Then it could intelligently identify and respond to those errors.

In the following table, you can see the three redirection symbols most operating systems support.

Redirection Symbol	Use
<	Input comes from the named file.
>	Output is written to the specified file. If the file does not exist it is created. If the file does exist, it is over-written.
>>	Output is appended (added on to the end of) the specified file. If the file does not exist it is created. Use this symbol to preserve existing file contents and add to it.

In the Rexx script above, we have surrounded the entire `dir` command with single quotation marks. This prevents Rexx from becoming confused by the output redirection symbol (>) during expression evaluation. Otherwise Rexx interprets *the carrot* (>) as its "greater than" symbol. The single quotation marks prevent Rexx from evaluating the expression, so it passes the entire string, including the redirection symbol to the default command environment (the operating system) for execution.

Here's an example in which a Rexx script redirects both input and output for an operating system command. This is a `sort` command, as issued from within the Rexx script:

```
'sort <sortin.txt >sortout.txt'
```

The script directs that the `sort` command take its input to sort from the file `sortin.txt`, and that it send the sorted list to the output file `sortout.txt`. If the input file `sortin.txt` contains these lines:

```
python
rexx
perl
php
```

The output file `sortout.txt` contains the same items in sorted order:

```
perl
php
python
rexx
```

The script can set up the input file to the sort by creating it, if desired. The script accesses the output file simply by reading its contents. The script could then perform any desired analysis of the command output. For example, it could parse the output to recognize and respond to common error messages. It could recognize error messages from the `sort` command such as these examples:

```
Invalid switch.
```

```
Input file not found
```

Of course, the script needs to know from where to read the error messages. On some operating systems, error messages will appear concatenated to or in place of the results when an error occurs. On others, they may go to a default output device with a standard name, such as `stderr`. `stderr` may or may not be directed by default to the same place as command output, depending on the operating system and the command redirection syntax you encoded. For example, for a Windows script to intercept error messages through the same location as it reads correct command output, the `sort` command would need to be changed to the following:

```
'sort  <sortin.txt  >sortout.txt 2>&1'
```

This Windows-specific form of the command directs standard error output (`stderr`) to the same output file as the `sort` command's output. So, if an error occurs, the phrase `2>&1` directs the textual error messages to the output file named `sortout.txt`. Here, the script can read, parse, and analyze any error messages that appear. Different operating systems have different conventions and syntax that dictate where and how scripts access command error messages. This example and its syntax were tested under Windows XP and works under Windows server. Most Unix-derived operating systems employ a similar syntax.

The more sophisticated the script, the better it will be at these two tasks:

❑ Recognizing textual error messages

❑ Responding to them intelligently

You must consider how comprehensive and fail-proof you want your script to be. It might just report any unexpected output to the user and stop, or it could be intelligent enough to identify and react to every possible command error. Different levels of coding will be appropriate for different situations. There is clearly a trade-off between effort and the robustness of a script. The choice is yours. We recommend minimally recognizing that an error has occurred and informing the user with a descriptive message.

Rexx provides other ways to feed input to operating system commands and to capture their output. These offer flexibility and address operating systems and other command environments that do not support redirection. We discuss them next.

Controlling Command I/O

With this introduction to issuing operating system commands, several questions pop up. For operating systems that do not support redirection, or in cases where we want to control these operations more closely from within the script, we must address these issues:

❑   How to direct input lines to a command

❑   How to capture command outputs

❑   How to capture command error messages

❑   How to issue commands to environments other than the operating system

The `address` instruction fulfills all these needs. It allows you to specify an origin for command input and targets for command output and command error output. The `address` instruction refers to command input, output and error messages by the following keywords:

Command I/O	address Keyword
Command input	`input`
Command output	`output`
Command error output	`error`

The `input`, `output`, and `error` parameters can be specified in either of two ways, as character streams or arrays. This is the basic format for the `address` instruction that redirects the command's input, output and error information via three *character streams*:

```
address environment  command  WITH INPUT   STREAM    filename_1 ,
                              OUTPUT  STREAM    filename_2 ,
                              ERROR   STREAM    filename_3
```

The `with` clause and its keywords `input`, `output`, and `error` were added to Rexx as part of the ANSI-1996 standard. Here is the same command with input, output, and error information directed to and from three different *arrays*:

```
address environment  command  WITH  INPUT   STEM    array_name_1. ,
                              OUTPUT  STEM    array_name_2. ,
                              ERROR   STEM    array_name_3.
```

The keywords `stream` and `stem` redirect to files or arrays, respectively, when using the `address` instruction. The period is a required part of the array names because the `address` instruction refers to what are properly termed *stem variables*.

The *environment* appears immediately after the `address` keyword. The *environment* is the target to which commands are sent. In all examples we've presented thus far this is the operating system. But it also could be a variety of other programs or interfaces, for example, a text editor or a network interface. What environments are available depend on the platform on which the script runs and which tools or interfaces are installed on that platform. The available environments are platform-dependent.

In Regina Rexx, the string SYSTEM refers to the operating system. To maximize portability, this string is the same regardless of the platform on which the Regina script runs. Other Rexx interpreters refer to the operating system by other keywords. Table L-2 in Appendix L lists some of the popular ones and shows the instruction you run to determine its default for your system.

The *command* is the string to send to the *environment* for execution. It is evaluated *before* being sent to the *environment* for execution, so consider whether it should be enclosed in quotation marks to prevent evaluation. You can either create the command string in advance and refer to the variable holding it in the address instruction, or allow Rexx to dynamically create the command for you by its expression evaluation.

The keyword with is followed by one, two or three redirection statements. The three redirection statements are identified by the three keywords input, output, and error. Any one or all three of these redirections can occur; those not listed take defaults. They may be coded in any order.

input refers to the source of lines that will be fed into the *command* as input. This essentially redirects input for the *command*. output collects the *command* output, and error collects what the *command* sends to "standard error."

Using the keyword stream, as in the first example, means that input, output or error is directed to/from operating system files. For input, each line in the file is a line directed to the command's standard input. Command output and error are directed to the named output and error files.

The alternative to using streams for command input/output is arrays. The keyword stem permits coding an array name for the three redirections. Be sure to code the *stem name* of the array as shown earlier (the name of the array immediately followed by a single period).

When using array input, you are required to first set array element 0 to the number of lines that are in the input. Using the preceding example, if the input has 10 lines, set it like this *before* issuing the address instruction:

```
array_name_1.0 = 10
```

You would also move the 10 input lines into the array before issuing the operating system command. In this example, this means setting the values of array_name_1.1 through array_name_1.10 with the appropriate command input lines.

After the command executes, array element 0 for output contains the number of lines output, and array element 0 for error contains the number of error lines output. For example, this statement displays the number of output lines from the command:

```
say array_name_2.0        /* display number of output lines from the command  */
```

Display all the output lines from the command simply by coding a loop like this:

```
do j = 1 to array_name_2.0
    /* process array elements here */
end
```

This is the preferred technique for displaying or processing the command output. Another technique is to set the array to the null string before issuing the command:

```
array_name_2. = ''       /* all unused array values are now the null string */
```

Process all elements in the output array by checking for the null string:

```
do j = 1 while array_name2.j  <>  ''
    /* process array elements here  */
end
```

You can intermix stream and array I/O in one `address` instruction. For example, you could present command input in an array, and direct the command output and error to files. Or, you could send file input to the command, and specify that its outputs and error messages go into arrays. There is no relationship among the three specifiers; use whatever fits your scripting needs.

One can even code the same names for `input`, `output`, and `error`. Rexx tries to keep them straight and not intermix their I/O. This practice becomes complicated and confers no particular advantage. It is not recommended.

A Few Examples

To this point, we have described the basic ways in which scripts control and access command I/O. The `address` instruction underlies these techniques. Since the `address` instruction is easier to demonstrate than it is to describe, we need to look at a few more examples.

Remember how we redirected input to the `sort` command earlier and redirected its output? We did this through the redirection operators supported in operating systems like Windows, Linux, Unix, BSD, and DOS through this command:

```
'sort  <sortin.txt  >sortout.txt'
```

This `address` instruction achieves the same result. We've enclosed the input and output filenames in single quotation marks to prevent uppercasing:

```
address  SYSTEM  sort  WITH  INPUT  STREAM  'sortin.txt'  ,
                              OUTPUT  STREAM 'sortout.txt'
```

We code the keyword `SYSTEM` because Regina Rexx defines this string as its standard identifier for the operating system (regardless of what the underlying OS may be). Other Rexx interpreters may require other strings under various operating systems (see Table L-2 in Appendix L).

The keyword `with` tells Rexx that one, two or three redirections will follow, identified by the keywords `input`, `output`, and `error`. These three keywords may appear in any order. Those that are not coded take defaults. Since we want to send input to the `sort` command from a file, we coded keyword `stream`, followed by the filename, `sortin.txt`.

Coding `output stream` tells Rexx to send the command output to the file named `sortout.txt`. Rexx is case-insensitive, so the case of keywords like `with input stream` is irrelevant to the interpreter. We used mixed case here simply to clarify the `address` instruction keywords.

output and error streams can either replace or be appended to the named files. Use the keywords replace or append to denote this. replace is the default. Here is the same example that was given earlier, but with the provision that the output stream will be added (appended) to, instead of replaced:

```
address  SYSTEM  sort  WITH  INPUT  STREAM  'sortin.txt'  ,
                              OUTPUT APPEND  STREAM  'sortout.txt'
```

Recall that the comma (,) is the *continuation character*. We've coded it here simply to continue this long instruction across lines. We also placed single quotation marks around the filenames. The instruction works without them but then the filenames will be altered to uppercase. Whether this is desirable depends on the operating system. Operating systems like Linux, Unix, and BSD are case-sensitive in their file-naming convention; operating systems like Windows and DOS are not.

Since we've specified append on the address instruction's output stream, if no output file named sortout.txt exists, running this instruction results in an output file containing:

```
perl
php
python
rexx
```

Running the command a second time appends to the output file for this result:

```
perl
php
python
rexx
perl
php
python
rexx
```

The replace option would always give the same result that is listed first in this example. In other words, the replace option replaces any existing file with the results, while append will add results to the end of an existing file.

You can mix file I/O and array I/O in the same address instruction. This example provides input via an array but writes the output to a file to give the same results as the previous examples:

```
in_array.0 = 4              /* REQUIRED- place number of input lines in element 0 */

in_array.1 = 'python' ;   in_array.2 = 'rexx' ;
in_array.3 = 'perl'   ;   in_array.4 = 'php'

address  SYSTEM  sort  WITH  INPUT STEM  in_array. OUTPUT STREAM  'sortout.txt'
```

You *must* place the number of input array lines in element 0 of that array *prior* to executing the address instruction or it will fail. Of course, you also place the elements to pass in to the command in the array. If you specify array output, Rexx communicates to your program how many output and error lines are produced by filling in array element 0 with that value.

Discovering Defaults — the address Function

Many Rexx instructions have corresponding functions. For example, the `arg` instruction reads input arguments while the `arg` function returns information about input arguments. In like manner, the `address` built-in function complements the `address` instruction. Use the `address` function to find out what the default command environment is. This statement displays the default command environment:

```
say  address()   /* displays default command environment. Example:  SYSTEM */
```

The ANSI-1996 standard added several parameters you can specify on the `address` function to retrieve specific `address` instruction settings. The following table lists the `address` function options:

address Function Option	Option Stands For...	Meaning
I	Input	Returns the `input` default
O	Output	Returns the `output` default
E	Error	Returns the `error` default
N	Normal	Returns the current default environment

Here is an example. This `say` instruction displays the defaults for each source or target:

```
say    'Input source: ' address('I')  ,
       'Output target:' address('O')  ,
       'Error target: ' address('E')
```

What this displays will be system- and interpreter-dependent. Here's an example of output for Regina Rexx version 3.4 running under Windows XP:

```
Input source: INPUT NORMAL Output target: REPLACE NORMAL Error target: REPLACE NORMAL
```

The `address` function, then, is the basic means through which a script can get information about where its commands will be issued and how their I/O is controlled.

Issuing Commands to Other Environments

In addition to redirecting command I/O, the `address` instruction is the basic mechanism by which you direct commands to environments other than the operating system. To do this, simply code a different environment on the `address` instruction:

```
address  KEDIT   'set autosave 5'
```

This example sends a command to the KEDIT program, a text editor. Of course, what environments are available (and how you refer to them in the *environment* string), strictly depends on your platform and the available interfaces. Typical command interfaces are for program and text editors, network control, teleprocessing monitors, and the like.

There are two basic ways to tell Rexx where to send commands to. We've seen one — code the *environment* string on the `address` instruction. Another way is to issue the `address` instruction with an *environment* specified but lacking a command. *This sets the command target for all subsequent commands.* Look at these commands run in sequence:

```
address SYSTEM    /* all commands now will go to SYSTEM for execution  */

'dir'             /* list all files in the directory                  */
'ver'             /* see what version of Windows we're running        */

address KEDIT     /* all commands will now go to KEDIT for execution  */

'set autosave 5'  /* issue a command to KEDIT                         */

address SYSTEM    /* all subsequent commands go to SYSTEM again       */

'help'            /* get a list of commands for which Windows offers Help */
```

Using this form of the `address` instruction has the advantage that you can code shorter, more intelligible commands. But explicitly coding a command on the `address` instruction along with its environment better documents where the commands are sent for execution. Personal preference dictates which to use.

You might also see the `address` instruction coded without any target:

```
address
```

In this case, the instruction causes commands to be routed to the environment specified prior to the last time it was changed. In other words, repeated coding of `address` without any environment operand effectively "toggles" the target for commands back and forth between two target environments.

While this could be appropriate and convenient for certain situations, we do not recommend this approach. It becomes confusing; we prefer one of the two more self-documenting approaches described previously.

Remember that you can always code the `address` function to determine the target environment for commands:

```
say  address()      /* displays the default command environment. */
```

Finally, we mention that the `address` instruction requires that the *environment* must be a symbol or literal string. It cannot be a variable. As in certain other Rexx instructions, code the `value` keyword if you need to refer to the *environment* as a value contained in a variable:

```
environment_variable = 'SYSTEM'
address  value  environment_variable         /* sets the environment to SYSTEM */
```

Sending a variable parameter into the `address` instruction provides greater flexibility than hardcoding and allows scripts to dynamically change the target of any commands.

A Sample Program

You now know the basic techniques for issuing operating system commands and managing their results. Let's look at a sample program that shows some of these techniques in action.

This program provides command help information for Windows XP. First it issues the Windows `help` command to the operating system without any operands. Under Windows XP, the command would be issued like this:

```
help
```

This command outputs a list of operating system commands with one line of description for each. The output looks similar to this:

```
ASSOC   Displays or modifies file extension associations.
AT      Schedules commands and programs to run on a computer.
ATTRIB  Displays or changes file attributes.
BREAK   Sets or clears extended CTRL+C checking.
          ... etc ...
```

The script captures this output and places it into an array. The command name is the index; the command description is stored in the array at that position. For example, the subscript ASSOC holds the line of help information on that command, the array element with subscript AT contains a line of information on that command, and so on.

(Under Windows XP, the `help` command returns more than one line of description for a handful of the commands. This program ignores the second line for those few commands.)

After building the array of command help information, the script prompts the user to enter an operating system command. In response, the script displays the one-line description for that command from the array. It also asks the user if he wants more detailed command information. If the user responds yes or y, then the program issues the help command for the specific command the user has chosen to the operating system. For example, if the user wants more information on the `dir` command, the script issues this Windows command on the user's behalf:

```
help  dir
```

This OS command displays more extensive information about the command and its use. Several lines of command help information appear as well as a listing of command options or switches.

After the user views the verbose help information on the command, the program prompts him to enter another command about which he needs information. The user either enters another OS command seeking help information, or he enters `quit` and the program terminates.

Here is example interaction with this script:

```
C:\Regina\pgms> regina  command_help.rexx
Enter Command you want Help on, or QUIT: ver
VER          Displays the Windows version.
Want detailed information? n
```

```
Enter Command you want Help on, or QUIT: vol
VOL          Displays a disk volume label and serial number.
Want detailed information? y
Displays the disk volume label and serial number, if they exist.

VOL  [drive:]
Enter Command you want Help on, or QUIT: ls
LS    No help available.
Enter Command you want Help on, or QUIT: quit
```

Here is the script:

```
/*  COMMAND HELP:                                              */
/*                                                             */
/*     (1)  Gets HELP on all OS commands, puts it into an array.  */
/*     (2)  Lets user get HELP info from the array or the OS.     */

trace off                    /* ignore HELP command return code of '1'*/

cmd_text_out. = ''           /* array to read HELP output into       */
cmd_help. = ''               /* array to build with command HELP info */

address SYSTEM 'help' WITH OUTPUT STEM cmd_text_out.

/* read contents of CMD_TEXT_OUT, build help array CMD_HELP      */

do j=1 to cmd_text_out.0
   parse var cmd_text_out.j  the_command  command_desc
   cmd_help.the_command = command_desc
end

/* allow user to query CMD_HELP array & issue full HELP commands   */

call charout ,"Enter Command you want Help on, or QUIT: "
pull cmd_in .
do while cmd_in <> 'QUIT'
   if cmd_help.cmd_in = '' then
      say cmd_in '   No help available.'
   else do
      say cmd_in cmd_help.cmd_in
      call charout ,"Want detailed information? "
      pull answer .
      if answer = 'Y' | answer = 'YES' then
         address SYSTEM 'help' cmd_in
   end

   call charout ,"Enter Command you want Help on, or QUIT: "
   pull cmd_in .
end
```

This script first sets the trace off, because issuing a valid `help` command under Windows XP sends back a return code of 1. This contravenes normal operating system convention and means that if the script does not mask the trace off, the user will view error messages after the script (correctly) issues Windows XP `help` commands.

Then the script initializes all elements in its two arrays to the null string:

```
cmd_text_out. = ''          /* array to read HELP output into    */
cmd_help.  = ''             /* array to build with command HELP info */
```

The subsequent `address` instruction gets output from the Windows `help` command into the array named `cmd_text_out`:

```
address SYSTEM 'help' WITH OUTPUT STEM cmd_text_out.
```

This instruction does not specify input to the `help` command because it intends to issue the `help` command without operands or any input. The output from the `help` command goes into the array `cmd_text_out`. Each element in this array contains an OS command and one line of help information.

The script needs to break apart the OS command from its single line of help information. The following code does this and builds the new array `cmd_help`.

```
/* read contents of CMD_TEXT_OUT, build help array CMD_HELP  */

do j=1 to cmd_text_out.0
   parse var cmd_text_out.j  the_command  command_desc
   cmd_help.the_command = command_desc
end
```

The `cmd_help` array contains one description line per Windows command. Its index is the command itself — it is an *associative array*, as explained in Chapter 4. Once the array is built, the next step is to prompt the user to enter the operating system command about which he wants help. This statement causes the prompt to appear on the user's screen:

```
call charout ,"Enter Command you want Help on, or QUIT: "
```

The program then uses the command the user enters as an index into the `cmd_help` array. This statement applies that command as the index into the array and displays the associated line of help information to the user:

```
say cmd_in cmd_help.cmd_in
```

Now, the script presents the user with a choice. Either he can ask for full information about the OS command about which he is inquiring, or he can say "no more" and ask about some other OS command. These statements prompt the user as to whether he wants more information about the current command:

```
call charout ,"Want detailed information? "
pull answer .
```

If the user answers YES to this prompt, the script then issues the Windows XP `help` command with the OS command of interest as its operand. The generic format for this Windows `help` command is this:

```
help command
```

For example, if more information were desired about the Windows `dir` (directory) command, the script would issue this command to Windows:

```
help  dir
```

As another example, if more information were needed about the `ver` (version) command, the script would issue this Windows command:

```
help  ver
```

This form of the `help` command prompts Windows XP to display several lines of detailed help information on the screen. This is the line in the program that actually issues the extended `help` command:

```
address SYSTEM 'help' cmd_in
```

The variable `cmd_in` is the command the user wants detailed information about. So, if the user requests information on the `dir` command, this statement resolves to:

```
address SYSTEM 'help' dir
```

Since SYSTEM is Regina Rexx's *default command environment*, the program did not need to explicitly encode the `address` instruction. This line would have given the same result:

```
'help'  cmd_in
```

This statement is less cluttered than coding the full `address` instruction, but one must know what the default command environment is to understand it. Some developers prefer to code the `address` instruction in full to better document their code. Others prefer to issue operating system commands without it for the sake of brevity.

Using the Stack for Command I/O

The manner in which commands are sent input and their outputs and errors are captured varies between Rexx interpreters. This chapter describes the ANSI-1996 standard, which specifies the `input`, `output`, and `error` keywords on the `address` instruction. Rexx interpreters increasingly comply with this standard, but not all do. Some Rexx interpreters have not yet upgraded to support the new ANSI-1996 forms of the `address` instruction. The ANSI-1996 standard ultimately should offer more portability, so this approach is recommended where possible.

For many years in mainframe Rexx, the external data queue or *stack* was used for communications between Rexx scripts and the commands they executed. (You'll recall that Chapter 11 discussed the stack and its use in some detail and presented several sample scripts that make use of it.) Because mainframe Rexx was the first available Rexx, and because the ANSI-1996 standard was devised rather late in the Rexx evolution, most Rexx interpreters also support the stack for command I/O.

Regina Rexx is typical in this regard. It fully supports the ANSI-1996 standard `address` instruction with its ANSI keywords for stream and stem I/O. But in recognition of the historical importance of mainframe Rexx, it alternatively allows you to use the stack for command I/O. This fits with Regina's philosophy of supporting all major standards, both de facto and de jure.

Using the stack for command I/O via its keywords `FIFO` and `LIFO` is an "allowed extension" to the ANSI-1996 standard. `FIFO` and `LIFO` stand for first-in, first-out and last-in, first-out, respectively. Chapter 11 introduced these concepts along with their common uses for the stack.

Remember the example of how to code the sort using redirected input and output? The OS command we originally coded within a script was:

```
'sort  <sortin.txt  >sortout.txt'
```

This code implements the same result by using the stack in Regina Rexx:

```
/* Show use of the Stack for Command input and output */

queue  'python'                 /* place 4 unsorted items into the stack       */
queue  'rexx'
queue  'perl'
queue  'php'
address SYSTEM sort WITH INPUT FIFO ''  OUTPUT FIFO ''
do queued()
    parse pull  sorted_result  /* retrieve & display the 4 items off the stack */
    say  sorted_result
end
```

The code places four unsorted items into the stack through the `queue` instruction. The `address` instruction uses the keywords `input fifo` to send those four items in unsorted order to the `sort` command. The `output fifo` keywords retrieve the four sorted items from the `sort` command in FIFO order. The two back-to-back single quotation marks that appear in these clauses mean that the default stack will be used:

```
WITH INPUT  FIFO ''
WITH OUTPUT FIFO ''
```

Rexx clears or *flushes* the stack between its use as an input to the command and its role as a target to collect the command output. The interpreter endeavors to keep command input and output accurate (not intermixed).

The `do` loop at the bottom of the script displays the four sorted items on the user's screen:

```
perl
php
python
rexx
```

We recommend using the ANSI-1996 standard `address` instruction and its keywords `with`, `input`, `output`, `error`, `stream` and `stem`. This is more portable than using the stack and is becoming more widely used. But either approach will work just fine.

Summary

Operating system commands bring great power to Rexx scripts, while scripting brings programmability and flexibility to operating systems. This chapter describes how Rexx scripts issue commands to the operating system and other target environments. It shows how to verify success or failure of these commands by checking their return codes, as well as other techniques to analyze command results. It also describes the several methods by which input can be sent to those commands, and through which command output and errors are captured.

Rexx implementations traditionally use the stack for command I/O, but developers increasingly favor the ANSI-1996 standard approach. This chapter illustrates both methods and showed several code examples.

We looked at the ways in which operating system commands can be assembled and submitted to the OS for execution. We investigated how scripts know whether commands succeed, and ways to inspect their error output. Then we explored the `address` instruction, the basic vehicle by which command I/O can be intercepted, managed, and controlled, and the `address` function, which returns information about the command execution environment. Finally, we showed how to use the stack for controlling command I/O. Many Rexx scripts use the stack for command I/O instead of the ANSI-1996 compliant `address` instruction.

Test Your Understanding

1. When does Rexx send a command string to an external environment? What is the default environment?

2. Why and under what conditions should you encode OS commands in quotation marks? Describe one method to prepare an entire command before coding it on the line that will be directed to the OS for execution. How would you print this command?

3. What are the three basic ways to get feedback from OS commands within scripts. Where do you look up return code information for OS commands?

4. Name two different ways to redirect OS command input and output in a script. Which should you use when?

5. What are the two kinds of sources and targets you can specify with the address command? Can the two be intermixed within a single address command?

6. How do you code the `address` command to tell Rexx to send all subsequent commands to a particular target environment? How do you "toggle" the `address` target between two different environments?

15

Interfacing to Relational Databases

Overview

Many scripts are only useful when the scripting language interfaces to a wide variety of packages. For example, scripts need to control *graphic user interfaces*, or *GUIs*, perform database I/O, serve up customized Web pages, control TCP/IP or FTP connections for communications, display and manipulate images, and perform many other tasks that require interfaces to outside code.

Rexx offers a plethora of free and open-source interfaces, packages, and function libraries for these purposes. Appendix H lists and describes many of the more popular ones. This chapter explores how scripts interface to databases. Then Chapters 16 through 18 explore other free interfaces for Rexx scripts, including GUIs, graphical images, programming Web servers, and Extensible Markup Language (XML).

Databases are among the most important interfaces. Few industrial-strength programs can do without the power and data management services of modern *database management systems*, or *DBMS*.

Most database systems are *relational*. They view data in terms of *tables* composed of rows and columns. Relational DBMSs typically provide complete features for data management, including transactional or concurrency control, backup and recovery, various utilities, interfaces, query languages, programming interfaces, and other features for high-powered data management.

Several packages enable Rexx scripts to interface with databases. These allow the scripts to interface to almost any DBMS, including both open-source and commercial systems. This chapter focuses on the most popular open-source database interface, Rexx/SQL. Rexx/SQL interfaces Rexx scripts to almost any database. Among them are open-source databases like MySQL, PostgreSQL, Mini SQL, mSQL, and SQLite, and commercial databases like Oracle, DB2 UDB, SQL Server, and Sybase. A full list follows in the next table.

Rexx/SQL has been production tested with several different Rexx interpreters, including Regina and Open Object Rexx. The examples in this chapter were all run using Regina Rexx with Rexx/SQL. Rexx/SQL supports two types of database interface: custom, or *native*, *interfaces* and *generic database interfaces*. Native interfaces are DBMS-specific. They confer performance advantages but work with only one database. Generic database interfaces work with almost any database and offer greater standardization and more portable code — but at the possible cost of lesser performance and the exclusion of non-standard features.

We cover Rexx/SQL in this chapter because it is:

❏   Widely used

❏   Open source

❏   Interfaced to all major databases

❏   Conforms to database standards

The sample scripts in this chapter all run against the MySQL open-source database. MySQL is the most widely used open-source database and we used it for the database examples because it fits with the book's emphasis on free and open-source software. While the sample scripts use the MySQL interface, they could run against databases other than MySQL with very minor modifications. In most cases, only the first database function call (SqlConnect) would have to be altered in these sample scripts to run them against other databases. The latter part of this chapter explains how to connect scripts to other popular databases, including Oracle, DB2 UDB, and Microsoft SQL Server. The chapter's sample scripts were tested on a Windows server running MySQL.

Rexx/SQL Features

The Rexx/SQL database interface follows the two major database standards for a *call-level interface*, or *CLI*. These two interface standards are the *Open Database Connectivity Application Programming Interface*, or *ODBC API*, and the *X/Open CLI*.

Rexx/SQL supports all expected relational database operations and features. It executes all kinds of SQL statements, including *Data Definition Language*, or *DDL*, and *Data Manipulation Language*, or *DML*. Data definition statements create, alter, and remove database objects. They include, for example, create table or drop index. Data manipulation statements operate on rows of data, and include such statements as select, insert, update, and delete.

Rexx/SQL provides all the features and functions with which you may be familiar from the call-level interface of any database. If you are familiar with the CLI used by Oracle, DB2 UDB, MySQL, or any almost any other database, you will find Rexx/SQL easy and convenient. Rexx/SQL supports features such as cursor processing, dynamic statement preparation, bind variables and placeholders, SQL control structures such as the *SQL Communications Area* (*SQLCA*), SQL error messages, null processing, auto-commit options, concurrent database connections, and the retrieval and setting of database interface behaviors.

If you have no experience with call-level database processing, this chapter offers an entry-level tutorial. It will help you download and install Rexx/SQL and write simple Rexx scripts that process the database. Ultimately, you may want to pursue the topic of database processing further by reading about the ODBC or X/Open CLIs.

Downloading and Installing Rexx/SQL

Information on Rexx/SQL is available at `http://rexxsql.sourceforge.net`. If Web site addresses change, enter the keyword `Rexx/SQL` into any search engine and download sites will pop up.

Both source and binaries appear as downloadable for various platforms. For example, Windows users can download a `*.zip` file. Decompressing that file effectively installs the product. Linux, Unix, and BSD users can download `*.tar.gz` files. Source is available in `*src.zip` files.

Download the file specific to the database to which your Rexx scripts will connect, or download the generic ODBC driver. Look for these keywords within the download filename to tell you which database it supports, as outlined in the that follows.

Keyword	Supports
ORA	Oracle
DB2	DB2 UDB
SYB	Sybase
SAW	Sybase SQL Anywhere
MIN	Mini SQL (mSQL)
MY	MySQL
ODBC	Generic ODBC driver
UDBC	Openlink UDBC interface
SOL	Solid Server
VEL	Velocis (now Birdstep)
ING	Ingres
WAT	Watcom
INF	Informix
POS	Postgres and PostgreSQL
LITE	SQLite
PRO	Progress

Rexx/SQL uses these abbreviations throughout the product whenever there is a need to provide a standard moniker for a database. Of course, updates and changes may occur to the list so check the Rexx/SQL home page documentation to determine which databases are fully supported.

As an example, let's interface Rexx to a MySQL database under Windows. Download either a file named `rxsql__odbc_w32.zip` or one named `rxsql__my_w32.zip`. Some of the underscores in these sample filenames are replaced by the version number of the product. For example, depending on the version number, a real filename might be something like `rxsql24_odbc_w32.zip`. The filenames also show which database the driver supports. For example, `rxsql24_odbc_w32.zip` supports the generic ODBC driver, while `rxsql24_my_w32.zip` supports MySQL. We chose the native MySQL interface for the examples in this chapter, but either works fine and provides the same results.

Under Windows, if you use an ODBC driver, you must use Windows' *ODBC Data Sources Administrator Tool* to register the ODBC driver with Windows. On Windows XP, access this panel through Start | Settings | Control Panel | Administrative Tools | Data Sources (ODBC). If you have a different Windows version and have trouble locating this panel, simply use the Help function and search for keyword `ODBC`.

If you're not using Windows, or if you're on Windows but are using a native interface, registering the driver via the ODBC Data Sources Administration Tool is not necessary. Since we use the native MySQL interface for the examples in this chapter, we did not have to use the ODBC Data Sources Administrator Tool.

The Rexx/SQL download will decompress to include files with names starting with the letters `README`. For example, in downloading the ODBC driver for Windows, we saw the two files `README.odbc` and `README.rexxsql` among the extracted files. *Read these files!* They tell you all you need to know about setting up Rexx/SQL for your particular platform.

On some platforms, you may need to finish the installation by setting a couple of environmental variables. The `PATH` variable on many operating systems might need to include the directory where Rexx/SQL is installed. The `README` file will tell you if any other actions are required.

For example, on Windows systems, the `PATH` should be set to include the folder in which the Rexx/SQL Dynamic Link Library, or DLL, file resides, named `rexxsql.dll`. For Linux, Unix, and BSD systems, the directory in which the shared library file for Rexx/SQL resides must be pointed to by the environmental variable that references library files. On Linux this environmental variable is named `LD_LIBRARY_PATH`. See the `README` file for this name for other Unix-derived operating systems.

Once Rexx/SQL is installed, run the product's test script named `simple.cmd`. It resides in the directory in which Rexx/SQL installs. This test program simply connects, then disconnects, from the database for which you installed Rexx/SQL. It lists descriptive error messages in the event of any problem.

Next run the product test script named `tester.cmd`. This is a more ambitious test script that creates some tables, makes multiple database connections and disconnections, and runs a wide variety of common SQL statements on the database. The documentation at the top of this script gives you advice about how to run it. You must set an environmental variable or two, the nature of which varies by the database you use. Read the documentation at the top of the script for all the details — *prior* to running the script.

If the two test scripts work, Rexx/SQL is installed successfully on your system. Incidentally, the two test scripts provide excellent examples of how to code for Rexx/SQL in your scripts. Along with the sample scripts in this chapter, you can use them as coding models to get started with Rexx/SQL and database scripting.

The Basics

The Rexx/SQL database interface follows the two major database standards for a CLI: the *ODBC API* and the *X/Open CLI*. Interfacing with the database via the CLI means issuing a series of database or *SQL calls*. Rexx/SQL supplies these as a set of functions. The series of calls a script issues depends on the type of database activity the script performs.

Let's discuss the Rexx/SQL database functions organized by functional area. Our goal here is to give you an overview of what these functions are, what they do, and how to apply them. (Appendix F describes all the functions in full detail. The appendix lists the functions alphabetically along with their full coding formats and coding examples.)

Database Connections. These functions enable scripts to connect to a specified database, manage that connection, and disconnect from the database when SQL processing is completed.

❑   `SqlConnect` — Connects to a SQL database

❑   `SqlDisconnect` — Disconnects from a SQL database

❑   `SqlGetInfo` — Retrieves Rexx/SQL information about a connection

❑   `SqlDefault` — Switches the default connection to another open connection

Environmental Control. While there is but a single function for environmental control, it has an important role in database programming. This function allows scripts to either query or set various runtime values that affect their interactions with the database.

❑   `SqlVariable` — Retrieves or sets default runtime values

Issuing SQL Statements. These functions enable scripts to issue all kinds of database calls, including data definition and data manipulation statements. SQL statements can be executed by a single Rexx statement, or they can be prepared in advance and executed repeatedly and with optimal efficiency. These functions also allow scripts to process multiple-row result sets either with cursors or other techniques for multi-row processing.

❑   `SqlCommand` — Issues a SQL statement to the connected database

❑   `SqlPrepare` — Allocates a work area for a SQL statement and prepares it for processing

❑   `SqlExecute` — Executes a prepared statement

❑   `SqlDispose` — Deallocates a work area for a statement

❑   `SqlOpen` — Opens a cursor for a prepared `select` statement

❑   `SqlClose` — Closes a cursor

❑   `SqlFetch` — Fetches the next row from a cursor

❑   `SqlGetData` — Extracts part of a column from a fetched row

❑   `SqlDescribe` — Describes expressions from a `select` statement

Transaction Control. The two transaction control statements permit scripts to dictate when data changes are permanently applied to the database. Transaction control is fundamental to how databases guarantee data integrity and their ability to recover a database, if necessary.

❑   `SqlCommit` — Commits the current transaction

❑   `SqlRollback` — Rolls back the current transaction

We'll see examples of many of these SQL functions in the sample scripts that we will now discuss.

Example — Displaying Database Information

As explained previously, scripts interface to databases by issuing a series of Rexx/SQL function calls. The previous lists describe what these functions are named and what they do. Now we need to see how to put them together in real programs.

The first sample database script performs several "startup" and "concluding" actions that are common to all database scripts. The only real action it takes once it connects to the database is to report some environmental information it retrieves about the databaase. Here is what this first sample database script does:

1. Loads the Rexx/SQL function library for use

2. Connects to the MySQL database

3. Retrieves and displays environmental information about the database

4. Disconnects from the database

Figure 15-1 describes these actions diagrammatically as a flowchart. With the addition of database processing logic, this is the skeletal structure of most SQL scripts.

Typical Database Interaction

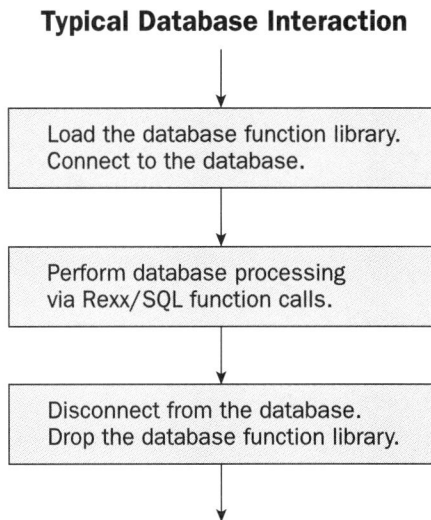

Figure 15-1

Here's what the output from the first sample script looks like. You can see it just displays some basic version information about the Rexx/SQL interface along with environmental information it retrieved from the database:

```
The Rexx/SQL Version is: rexxsql 2.4 02 Jan 2000 WIN32 MySQL
The database Name is: mySQL
The database Version is: 4.0.18-max-debug
```

Here's the script:

```
/********************************************************************/
/* DATABASE INFO:                                            */
/*                                                           */
/*    Connects to MySQL, displays database information.      */
/********************************************************************/
signal on syntax                 /* capture SQL syntax errors  */


/* load all SQL functions, make them accessible to this script  */

if RxFuncAdd('SQLLoadFuncs','rexxsql', 'SQLLoadFuncs') <> 0 then
   say 'rxfuncadd failed, rc: ' rc

if SQLLoadFuncs() <> 0 then
   say 'sqlloadfuncs failed, rc: ' rc


/* connect to the MySQL database, use default user/password      */

if SQLConnect(,,,'mysql') <> 0 then call sqlerr 'On connect'


/* get and display some database information                 */

say 'The Rexx/SQL Version is:' SQLVariable('VERSION')

if SQLGetinfo(,'DBMSNAME','desc.') <> 0
   then call sqlerr 'Error getting db name'
   else say 'The database Name is: ' desc.1

if SQLGetinfo(,'DBMSVERSION','desc.') <> 0
   then call sqlerr 'Error getting db version'
   else say 'The database Version is: ' desc.1


/* disconnnect from the database and drop the SQL functions    */

if SQLDisconnect() <> 0 then call sqlerr 'On disconnect'

if SQLDropFuncs('UNLOAD') <> 0 then
   say 'sqldropfuncs failed, rc: ' rc

exit 0


/* capture any SQL error and write out SQLCA error messages    */

sqlerr: procedure expose sqlca.
   parse arg msg
   say 'Program failed, message is: ' msg
   say sqlca.interrm              /* write SQLCA messages */
   say 'SQL error is:' sqlca.sqlerrm    /* write SQLCA messages */
```

```
        call SQLDropFuncs 'UNLOAD'
        exit 99

syntax: procedure                    /* capture any syntax errors */
        say 'Syntax error on line: ' sigl    /* identify syntax error*/
        return
```

The first step in this program is to load the Rexx/SQL external function library and make its functions available for the use of this script. Regina uses the *Systems Application Architecture*, or *SAA*, standard functions to achieve this. Here is one way of coding them:

```
if RxFuncAdd('SQLLoadFuncs','rexxsql', 'SQLLoadFuncs') <> 0 then
    say 'rxfuncadd failed, rc: ' rc

if SQLLoadFuncs() <> 0 then
    say 'sqlloadfuncs failed, rc: ' rc
```

The RxFuncAdd function first loads or *registers* the SqlLoadFuncs function. The middle parameter specifies the name of the file in which SqlLoadFuncs can be found. In Windows, this external library is a *Dynamic Link Library*, or *DLL*, file. It is named rexxsql.dll. The directory in which this file resides should be part of Windows' PATH environmental variable so that Regina can locate it.

Under Linux, Unix, and BSD, the equivalent of a Windows DLL is a *shared library file*. An environmental variable specifies the directory in which this shared library file resides. Different versions of Unix use different environmental variable names for this purpose, so check the README* file for the details for your Unix version. On most systems, it will be named LD_LIBRARY_PATH or LIBPATH. On Linux systems, this environmental variable is LD_LIBRARY_PATH.

To reiterate, the RxFuncAdd statement registers the function SqlLoadFuncs, which is part of the Rexx/SQL external library. The call to SqlLoadFuncs then loads the remainder of the Rexx/SQL external library. Now all its functions are available for the use of this script. See Chapter 20 if you want more detail on the functions to access external libraries.

Since all scripts that interface to databases use this code, consider placing it in a Rexx script function or subroutine. This takes it out of line for the main body of the code and simplifies your program.

Once the script loads the Rexx/SQL external function library, it can connect to the database. Here we connect to the MySQL database named mysql (one of the two databases MySQL creates by default when installed):

```
if SQLConnect(,,,'mysql') <> 0 then call sqlerr 'On connect'
```

The SqlConnect statement can take several other parameters, as shown in its template diagram:

```
SQLCONNECT([connection name], [username], [password], [database], [host])
```

The required parameters for this statement vary by the database with which you are trying to connect. Our example only supplies the name of the database to which the script wishes to connect. SqlConnect is just about the only statement in Rexx/SQL whose coding is database-dependent. The section entitled "Working with Other Databases" later in this chapter discusses and illustrates how to code the SqlConnect function for systems like Oracle, DB2 UDB, SQL Server, and ODBC connections.

After connecting, the script executes the `SqlVariable` function to retrieve and display the version of Rexx/SQL:

```
say 'The Rexx/SQL Version is:' SQLVariable('VERSION')
```

Then the script invokes the `SqlGetInfo` function twice, with different parameters, to retrieve the DBMS name and version:

```
if SQLGetinfo(,'DBMSNAME','desc.')    <> 0
if SQLGetinfo(,'DBMSVERSION','desc.') <> 0
```

Rexx/SQL places the results into the stem variable named in the call. Here this stem variable is `desc.`, so the output strings we want are in the variable named `desc.1`. The full statements show how these values are retrieved and displayed:

```
if SQLGetinfo(,'DBMSNAME','desc.') <> 0
    then call sqlerr 'Error getting db name'
    else say 'The database Name is: ' desc.1

if SQLGetinfo(,'DBMSVERSION','desc.') <> 0
    then call sqlerr 'Error getting db version'
    else say 'The database Version is: ' desc.1
```

Its work done, the script disconnects from the database and drops the Rexx/SQL function library from memory. Scripts typically perform these two steps as their final database actions. Here is the code that implements these two terminating actions:

```
if SQLDisconnect() <> 0 then call sqlerr 'On disconnect'

if SQLDropFuncs('UNLOAD') <> 0 then
    say 'sqldropfuncs failed, rc: ' rc
```

We've nested the functions inside of `if` instructions in order to check their return codes. When performing database processing, we recommend *always* checking return codes from the database functions. If not for this little bit of extra code, the application could otherwise behave in ways that completely mystify its users, even when the problem is something so simple as a database that needs to be started up. It is standard practice in the database community to check the return code from every SQL statement in a program.

When database function errors occur, this script executes this internal routine:

```
sqlerr: procedure expose sqlca.
    parse arg msg
    say 'Program failed, message is: ' msg
    say sqlca.interrm                       /* write SQLCA messages */
    say 'SQL error is:' sqlca.sqlerrm       /* write SQLCA messages */
    call SQLDropFuncs 'UNLOAD'
    exit 99
```

Here's an example of the kind of error message this routine might output. In this case, the `SqlConnect` function failed because an incorrect database name was supplied. The database name was incorrectly specified as `mysqlxxxx` instead of as `mysql`:

```
Program failed, message is: On connect
REXX/SQL-1: Database Error
SQL error is: Unknown database 'mysqlxxxx'
```

In this example, the error routine displays the SQL error message and stops the program (the last statement in the error routine is an `exit` instruction). You could write the routine to take any other appropriate action, as you see fit, and continue the program. You might even choose whether to end the program or continue it, depending on the nature and severity of the error the error routine encounters.

The error routine shows how to retrieve and display various error messages from the database. Its first line gives its full access to the *SQL Communications Area*, or *SQLCA*:

```
sqlerr: procedure expose sqlca.
```

The SQLCA is the basic data structure by which the DBMS passes status information back to the program. The status values in the SQLCA set by database activity include the following:

❑ `SQLCA.SQLCODE` — SQL return code

❑ `SQLCA.SQLERRM` — SQL error message text

❑ `SQLCA.SQLSTATE` — Detailed status string (N/A on some ports)

❑ `SQLCA.SQLTEXT` — Text of the last SQL statement

❑ `SQLCA.ROWCOUNT` — Number of rows affected by the SQL operation

❑ `SQLCA.FUNCTION` — The last Rexx external function called

❑ `SQLCA.INTCODE` — The Rexx/SQL interface error number

❑ `SQLCA.INTERRM` — Text of the Rexx/SQL interface error

Database scripts can either handle SQL errors in the body of the code (*inline*), or they can consolidate error handling into one routine, such as the `sqlerr` routine in the sample script. In large projects consolidating code is advantageous because it leads to code reuse, standardizes error handling, and reduces the size and complexity of the inline code.

The `SYNTAX` error condition trap fits right in with the `sqlerr` routine in capturing and handling SQL syntax errors. It is very easy to make syntax errors when coding to the SQL CLI because the character strings one issues to the database become complicated. The `SYNTAX` error condition trap manages this challenge:

```
syntax: procedure                    /* capture any syntax errors */
   say 'Syntax error on line: ' sigl    /* identify syntax error*/
   return
```

For large applications, we recommend writing a single SQL error-handling routine and having all SQL errors sent to that routine. The SYNTAX trap routine can also call the SQL error handler, if desired. This sample script simplifies error handling for clarity of illustration. The test scripts distributed with Rexx/SQL provide a fuller and more robust SQL error handler. Review those scripts if you want to develop a more comprehensive, generalized SQL error handler.

Example — Create and Load a Table

Now we know how scripts connect to and access relational databases. The next step is to develop examples that issue data manipulation language statements to manage the data in databases, and data definition language statements to manage database objects like relational tables. To illustrate basic SQL programming, let's create a simple telephone number directory. Each entry (row) has only two columns: the person's last name and his or her telephone number.

This program creates a phone directory. It does this by creating a database table named phonedir, then loading it with data. The "data load" is simply an interactive loop that prompts the user to enter people's names and their phone numbers. When the user enters the character string EXIT, the program ends.

Here is the script:

```
/****************************************************************/
/* PHONE DIRECTORY:                                             */
/*                                                              */
/*     Creates the phone directory and loads data into it.      */
/****************************************************************/
signal on syntax                  /* capture SQL syntax errors  */
call sql_initialize               /* load all Rexx/SQL functions*/

if SQLConnect(,,,'mysql')    <> 0 then call sqlerr 'On connect'
if SQLCommand(u1,"use test") <> 0 then call sqlerr 'On use'


/* drop the table if it exists, and create the table a-new      */

rc = SQLCommand(d1,"drop table phonedir") /* dont care about rc */

sqlstr = 'create table phonedir (lname char(10), phone char(8))'
if SQLCommand(c1,sqlstr) <> 0 then call sqlerr 'On create'

say "Enter last name and phone number ==> "
pull lname phone .


/* this loop collects data from user, inserts it as new rows    */

do while (lname <> 'EXIT')
    sqlstr = "insert into phonedir values('" || lname || "'",
           ",'" || phone "')"
    if SQLCommand(i1,sqlstr) <> 0 then call sqlerr 'On insert'
```

```
      say "Enter last name and phone number ==> "
      pull lname phone .
end

call sql_pgm_end                    /* disconnect, drop functions */
exit 0
```

The first line of the program enables the SYNTAX error condition:

```
signal on syntax                    /* capture SQL syntax errors  */
```

Since the previous sample script, Database Info, already showed the code for the SYNTAX error handler, we have not shown it again in the above program. Similarly, the next line in the script invokes a new subroutine called sql_initialize:

```
call sql_initialize                 /* load all Rexx/SQL functions*/
```

This routine registers and loads the Rexx/SQL interface. It contains exactly the same code as the previous program (using the RxFuncAdd and SqlLoadFuncs functions). We do not duplicate this code in this example, in order to keep it as short and readable as possible.

After connecting to the database, the script tells MySQL which database it wants to use. It issues the MySQL use test database command through a single call to the SqlCommand function:

```
if SQLCommand(u1,"use test") <> 0 then call sqlerr 'On use'
```

For purposes of initialization, the script drops the phonedir table if it already exists. If the phonedir table does not exist and this statement fails, that's okay. We're only dropping it to ensure that the subsequent create table statement will not fail because the table already exists. (The pairing of drop table / create table statements in this manner is a common technique in database processing.) Here is the drop table statement:

```
rc = SQLCommand(d1,"drop table phonedir") /* dont care about rc */
```

The statements that create the database table phonedir come next:

```
sqlstr = 'create table phonedir (lname char(10), phone char(8))'
if SQLCommand(c1,sqlstr) <> 0 then call sqlerr 'On create'
```

As this code shows, the new table has only two columns: one for the person's last name and one for their phone number. The first statement builds the SQL create table statement in a variable, while the second statement executes that command. The second statement also references the sqlerr routine, because we consolidated all SQL error processing in a single routine. Since this routine contains the exact same code as the previous sample program, we have not included it in the program's code here.

The script now enters a do loop where it prompts for the user to enter names and their associated phone numbers. These two statements build and issue the SQL insert statement that adds each record to the database:

```
sqlstr = "insert into phonedir values('" || lname || "'",
         ",'" || phone "')"
if SQLCommand(i1,sqlstr) <> 0 then call sqlerr 'On insert'
```

Instead of building the SQL statement separately, in the first statement, it could be nested inside of the `SqlCommand` function call. We use a separate statement to build this string because of its syntactical complexity. This makes for more readable code. A large percentage of SQL programming errors involve statement syntax, and this approach makes it easy to verify the SQL statement simply by displaying the string. We generally recommend building SQL statements in variables like this rather than dynamically concatenating them within the actual SQL function encoding.

To end the program, we need to issue the `SqlDisconnect` and `SqlDropFuncs` calls. Since this code is the same as the previous program, we've isolated it in its own routine called `sql_pgm_end`:

```
call sql_pgm_end                    /* disconnect, drop functions */
```

We don't include this code in the example because it duplicates the same lines as the previous sample script. You can see that using common routines for database connection, disconnection, and error handling is a very sensible approach. It both reduces the code you must write for each script and reduces errors.

In database programming, scripts must `commit` (make permanent) any database changes. In this script, the data is *auto-committed* to the database by disconnecting from the interface. Auto-commit automatically commits the data to the database if the script ends normally. Alternatively, the script could explicitly issue the SQL `SqlCommit` statement:

```
if SQLCommit() <> 0 then call sqlerr 'On commit'
```

The Rexx/SQL interface allows scripts to control the auto-commit feature. Use the `SqlVariable` function to retrieve and/or set this and other behaviors of the database interface. Simple programs like this sample script tend to rely on auto-commit to apply changes to the database upon their termination. More advanced database scripts require explicit control of commit processing. We'll see an example of the `SQLCommit` function later in this chapter in a script that updates the phone numbers in the database.

Example — Select All Results from a Table

Okay, we've created a table in the database and inserted a few rows in it. The preceding sample script shows how these tasks can be accomplished. The logical question now is: How do we view the rows in the table?

This script shows one easy way:

```
/******************************************************************/
/* PHONE DIRECTORY LIST:                                          */
/*                                                                */
/*     Displays the phone directory's contents.                   */
/******************************************************************/
signal on syntax                    /* capture SQL syntax errors  */
call sql_initialize                 /* load all Rexx/SQL functions*/

if SQLConnect(,,,'mysql')    <> 0 then call sqlerr 'On connect'
if SQLCommand(u1,"use test") <> 0 then call sqlerr 'On use'

sqlstr = 'select * from phonedir order by lname'
```

```
if SQLCommand(s1,sqlstr) <> 0 then call sqlerr 'On select'


/* This loop displays all rows from the SELECT statement.      */

do j = 1 to sqlca.rowcount
    say 'Name:'  s1.lname.j  'Phone:'  s1.phone.j
end

call sql_pgm_end                    /* disconnect, drop functions */
exit 0
```

This script uses some of the same *database service routines* as the previous example:

❑   syntax—Error routine that handles SYNTAX errors

❑   sql_initialize—Registers and loads Rexx/SQL external functions

❑   sqlerr—Consolidates SQL statement error handling

❑   sql_pgm_end—Disconnects from the database and drops Rexx/SQL functions

The code for these routines is in the first sample program and is not repeated here. The basic problem in this script is this: how do we execute a SQL select statement to retrieve and display the rows in the table? Here is the code that builds and executes the select statement:

```
sqlstr = 'select * from phonedir order by lname'
if SQLCommand(s1,sqlstr) <> 0 then call sqlerr 'On select'
```

This statement retrieves the data of the rows in the phonedir table. To display it, we need a do loop:

```
do j = 1 to sqlca.rowcount
    say 'Name:'  s1.lname.j  'Phone:'  s1.phone.j
end
```

The data elements in each row are referred to by this syntax:

```
Statement_name.Column_name.Row_identifier
```

In the example, for the person's name, this resolves to:

```
s1.lname.j
```

This neat Rexx/SQL syntax makes multiple row retrieval easy. Just put this row reference inside a do loop and display all the data. Later we'll see another way to display data from a SQL select statement via standard ODBC-X/Open programming, called *cursor processing*.

The variable sqlca.rowcount was set by the interface as feedback to the select statement. It tells how many rows were retrieved by the select, so we use it as the loop control limit. Another way to get this same information is to inspect element 0 in the returned rows. s1.lname.0 and s1.phone.0 also contain a count of the number of rows retrieved. Instead of referring to `sqlca.rowcount`, as does the preceding code, we could also have coded the display loop as:

```
do j = 1 to s1.lname.0
   say 'Name:' s1.lname.j 'Phone:' s1.phone.j
end
```

Either approach to controlling the number of do loop iterations works fine. Once retrieval and display of the rows is complete, the script calls its internal routine `sql_pgm_end` to disconnect from the database and drop the Rexx/SQL functions. This terminates the database connection and releases resources (memory).

Example — Select and Update Table Rows

We've created a database table, inserted rows, and viewed the rows. Time to update the data.

This simple script updates the phone numbers. Its do loop prompts the user to enter a person's name. If the person exists in the table, the program prompts for a phone number, and updates that person's phone number in the `phonedir` table. If the person does not exist in the table, the script displays a "not found" message and prompts for the next person to update. The script ends when the user enters the character string EXIT.

Here is the script:

```
/****************************************************************/
/* PHONE DIRECTORY UPDATE:                                      */
/*                                                              */
/*    Updates rows in the phone directory w/ new phone numbers. */
/****************************************************************/
signal on syntax               /* capture SQL syntax errors   */
call sql_initialize            /* load all Rexx/SQL functions */

if SQLConnect(,,,'mysql')    <> 0 then call sqlerr 'On connect'
if SQLCommand(u1,"use test") <> 0 then call sqlerr 'On use'

say "Enter name or 'EXIT':"     /* prompt for person for whom  */
pull lname .                    /* we'll update the phone      */

do while (lname <> 'EXIT')

    /* retrieve the phone number for the person to update       */

    sqlstr = 'select phone from phonedir where lname ="' ,
       || lname || '"'
    if (SQLCommand(s1,sqlstr) <> 0) then call sqlerr 'On select'

    /* if we retrieved one row, we retrieved the person given    */
    /* go ahead and update that person's phone # in the database */

    if sqlca.rowcount <> 1 then
```

```
          say 'This person is not in the database:' lname
      else do
          say lname 'Current phone:' s1.phone.1
          say 'Enter new phone number:'
          pull new_phone .
          sqlstr = 'update phonedir set phone ="' || new_phone || '"',
                   || ' where lname ="' || lname || '"'
          if SQLCommand(u1,sqlstr) <> 0 then call sqlerr 'On update'
      end

      /* commit to end the interaction, get the next person's name */

      if SQLCommit() <> 0 then call sqlerr 'On commit'
      say "Enter name or 'EXIT':"
      pull lname .
  end

  call sql_pgm_end                    /* disconnect, drop functions */
  exit 0
```

Much of the code of this program is similar to what we've seen in previous examples. Among the new statements, this is the `select` statement that tries to retrieve the phone number of the person the user enters:

```
sqlstr = 'select phone from phonedir where lname ="' ,
         || lname || '"'
if (SQLCommand(s1,sqlstr) <> 0) then call sqlerr 'On select'
```

If the variable `sqlca.rowcount` is not 1 after this call, we know that we did not retrieve a row for the name. The person (as entered by the user) does not exist in the table:

```
if sqlca.rowcount <> 1 then
   say 'This person is not in the database:' lname
```

The script assumes that each person's name is unique, so the statement will either retrieve 0 or 1 rows. Of course, in a real database environment, some unique identifier or *key* other than the person's name would likely be used.

If we do retrieve a row, this code prompts the user to enter the person's new phone number and updates the database:

```
say lname 'Current phone:' s1.phone.1
say 'Enter new phone number:'
pull new_phone .
sqlstr = 'update phonedir set phone ="' || new_phone || '"',
         || ' where lname ="' || lname || '"'
if SQLCommand(u1,sqlstr) <> 0 then call sqlerr 'On update'
```

After the SQL `update` statement, the program commits any changes made to apply them permanently to the database through the `SqlCommit` function:

```
if SQLCommit() <> 0 then call sqlerr 'On commit'
```

Example — Cursor Processing

In the programs thus far, we've relied on a very useful feature of the Rexx/SQL interface: the ability to execute any SQL statement in one function call. The Rexx/SQL SqlCommand function lets scripts issue either data definition or data manipulation statements, including select's. The Rexx/SQL interface does not limit which SQL statements are allowed, unlike some call-level database interfaces.

Some interfaces do not allow SQL select statements that return more than one row to be run through a single statement. If a select statement returns more than one row, it requires *cursor processing*. A *cursor* is a structure that allows processing multiple-row result sets, one row at a time.

These are the major steps in processing multi-row results sets using a cursor:

1.   A SqlPrepare statement prepares the cursor for use. This allocates a work area and "compiles" the select statement associated with the cursor.

2.   The SqlOpen function opens the cursor.

3.   A program do loop retrieves rows from the cursor, one by one, through the SqlFetch function.

4.   When done, the script closes the cursor by a SqlClose, and deallocates the work area by a SqlDispose call.

Figure 15-2 illustrates this process pictorially.

Database Cursor Processing

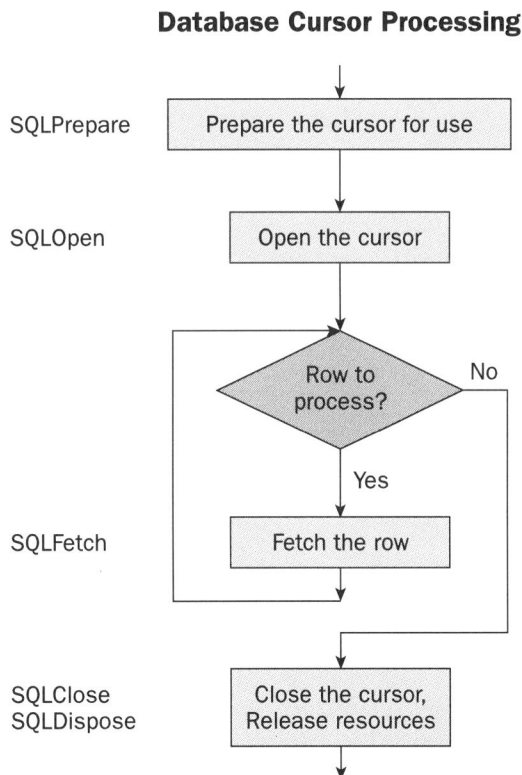

Figure 15-2

This script implements the logic of cursor processing:

```
/*****************************************************************/
/* PHONE DIRECTORY LIST2:                                        */
/*                                                               */
/*    Displays the phone directory's contents using a cursor.    */
/*****************************************************************/
signal on syntax                   /* capture SQL syntax errors */
call sql_initialize                /* load all Rexx/SQL functions*/

if SQLConnect(,,,'mysql')    <> 0 then call sqlerr 'On connect'
if SQLCommand(u1,"use test") <> 0 then call sqlerr 'On use'

sqlstr = 'select * from phonedir order by lname'
if SQLPrepare(s1,sqlstr) <> 0 then call sqlerr 'On prepare'

if SQLOpen(s1) <> 0 then call sqlerr 'On open'

/* this loop displays all rows from the SELECT statement        */

do while SQLFetch(s1) > 0
    say 'Name:'  s1.lname  'Phone:'  s1.phone
end

if SQLClose(s1)   <> 0 then call sqlerr 'On close'
if SQLDispose(s1) <> 0 then call sqlerr 'On dispose'

call sql_pgm_end                   /* disconnect, drop functions */
exit 0
```

In this program, the `SqlPrepare` function allocates memory and internal data structures and readies the SQL statement (here a `select`) for subsequent execution:

```
sqlstr = 'select * from phonedir order by lname'
if SQLPrepare(s1,sqlstr) <> 0 then call sqlerr 'On prepare'
```

Next, open the cursor by a `SqlOpen` statement. Cursors must always be explicitly opened, as this next statement shows. In this respect, cursors are not like Rexx files, which are automatically opened for use:

```
if SQLOpen(s1) <> 0 then call sqlerr 'On open'
```

Once the cursor is open, fetch and display rows from the cursor, one at a time, by using the `SqlFetch` call. This `do` loop shows how individual rows may be processed, one after another:

```
do while SQLFetch(s1) > 0
   say 'Name:'  s1.lname  'Phone:'  s1.phone
end
```

After all the rows have been processed, end by closing the cursor and freeing any resources. Use the `SqlClose` and `SqlDispose` functions for this:

```
if SQLClose(s1)   <> 0 then call sqlerr 'On close'
```

```
if SQLDispose(s1) <> 0 then call sqlerr 'On dispose'
```

Statement preparation can be used for other SQL statements besides `select`. While this approach may seem more cumbersome, it offers a performance benefit if the script executes the SQL statement more than once. This is because the `SqlPrepare` function places SQL statement compilation into a separate step. Executing the SQL statement is then a separate, more efficient, repeatable step. If you prepare a SQL statement one time, then execute it repeatedly, this multi-step approach yields better performance.

SQL `insert`, `update` and `delete` statements can also be prepared in advance. Use the `SqlExecute` function after the `SqlPrepare` function to execute the SQL `insert`, `update` or `delete` statement. End the process by `SqlDispose`. Use the same sequence of statements for data definition statements: `SqlPrepare`, `SqlExecute`, `SqlDispose`. (One DDL statement, `describe`, requires this sequence: `SqlPrepare`, `SqlDescribe`, `SqlDispose`).

Rexx/SQL gives you the choice whether to opt for convenience with the single-statement processing of the `SqlCommand` function, or to go for performance with `SqlPrepare` and `SqlExecute`. The trade-off between the two approaches is one of coding convenience and simplicity versus optimal performance.

Bind Variables

Structured Query Language, or SQL, permits the kinds of database queries illustrated by the sample programs above. But if SQL statements were always hardcoded, the language would not offer the programmability or flexibility scripts require. Bind variables provide the required flexibility. *Bind variables* are placeholders within SQL statements that allow scripts to dynamically substitute values into the SQL statement.

Here's an example. In the phone directory update script, we prompted the user to enter a person's name; then we retrieved the phone number based on that name. We then dynamically concatenated that person's name into the SQL `select` statement the script issued. The statements worked fine but the dynamic concatenation made for some complex syntax. Here's a simpler way to write the same statements using a *parameter marker* or *placeholder variable* that represents the bind variable

```
sqlstr = 'select phone from phonedir where lname = ? '
if (SQLCommand(s1,sqlstr,lname) <> 0) then call sqlerr 'On select'
```

The question mark (?) is the placeholder variable. The `SqlCommand` function includes an extra parameter that supplies a value that will be dynamically substituted in place of the placeholder variable prior to SQL statement execution. In this example, the value of `lname` will replace the placeholder variable before execution.

Bind variables can be a more efficient way to process SQL statements. They also are a little easier or cleaner to code. Rexx/SQL fully supports them. But different DBMSs have different syntax for parameter markers and so this feature is necessarily database-dependent. We eschewed programming with bind variables in this chapter for this reason.

Working with Other Databases

SQL is an ANSI-standard language, and the Rexx/SQL interface follows standard API conventions for relational databases. This limits the differences in scripts that access different DBMSs. The changes you must make to point a script at one DBMS versus another when using Rexx/SQL are minimal. Usually, you need only change the `SqlConnect` statement.

The Rexx/SQL documentation at the Rexx/SQL SourceForge project at `http://rexxsql.source-forge.net/doc/index.html` includes a series of appendices, one for each DBMS the product supports. Read these appendices for DBMS-specific information. These appendices explain the minimal differences between database targets when using Rexx/SQL.

The one statement that does change when targeting different databases is `SqlConnect`. Database connections are inherently DBMS-specific. The next three brief sections describe the basic rules for encoding `SQLConnect` statements to access Oracle-, DB2 UDB–, and ODBC-compliant databases. The ODBC drivers, as explained earlier in this chapter, permit scripts to access almost any database, because ODBC is widely implemented as a universal interface for database access. You would use the ODBC drivers when connecting to Microsoft SQL Server databases, for example.

Connecting to Oracle

Here's how to connect to Oracle databases using the Rexx/SQL package. When connecting to Oracle databases via the `SQLConnect` function, all `SqlConnect` parameters are optional. Here are some sample connections. To connect to a database running on the local machine with an externally dentified `userid` and password:

```
rc = sqlconnect()
```

To connect to a local database with the default `userid` of `scott` with its default password of `tiger`:

```
rc = sqlconnect(,'scott','tiger')          /*  Scott lives! */
```

Now let's connect `scott` to a remote database on machine `prod.world` (as identified in Oracle's SQL*Net configuration files):

```
rc = sqlconnect('MYCON','scott','tiger',,'PROD.WORLD')
```

Connecting to DB2 UDB

This section describes how to connect to IBM's DB2 Universal database, better known as DB2 UDB. The DB2 UDB native interface uses the CLI provided by IBM Corporation.

The *database name* parameter is required for a DB2 connection. Here are some sample connections. To connect to the SAMPLE database and name the connection MYCON, encode this:

```
rc = sqlconnect('MYCON',,,'SAMPLE')
```

To connect as CODER with the password of TOPGUN, try a statement like this:

```
rc = sqlconnect(,'CODER','TOPGUN','SAMPLE')
```

The DB2 UDB database fully supports bind variables. DB2 bind variables are denoted by the standard marker, the question mark (?).

Connecting using ODBC

The Open Database Connectivity, or ODBC, standard is a generalized interface that is supported by a very broad range of relational databases. Use the ODBC driver for data access if Rexx/SQL does not support a direct or native driver for your database. The ODBC driver is especially popular in connecting to Microsoft's SQL Server database.

In making the ODBC connection, the *userid*, *password*, and *database name* arguments are required on the SqlConnect function. Here is an sample connection:

```
rc = sqlconnect('MYCON','scott','tiger','REXXSQL')
```

The connection is named MYCON and the login occurs using userid scott and its password tiger. The fourth argument is the ODBC Data Source Name, or DSN. Under Windows systems, this is created using the Window's ODBC Data Sources Administration tool. The DSN in the preceding sample statement is named REXXSQL.

Connecting to MySQL

MySQL is the most popular open-source database in the world. Like Rexx itself, it is freely downloadable and highly functional. As a result, it has become very popular as a fully featured, low-cost alternative to expensive commercial database management systems.

When connecting to MySQL databases, the *database name* is the only required parameter on SqlConnect. The sample programs in this chapter all connected to a MySQL database named test and showed how to connect to that database. These two statements from those sample scripts illustrate the connection in the SQLConnect function, and the selection of the MySQL test database in the second statement:

```
if SQLConnect(,,,'mysql')    <> 0 then call sqlerr 'On connect'
if SQLCommand(u1,"use test") <> 0 then call sqlerr 'On use'
```

One way in which MySQL differs from many other database management systems is that only certain kinds of MySQL tables support transactions. The SqlCommit and SqlRollback functions only provide transactional control against tables that support transactions. You must use the proper kind of table to write transactional programs. Another difference of which you should be aware is that MySQL does not support bind variables.

Ot\her database differences

Beyond the SqlConnect statement, what other aspects of Rexx/SQL will be coded differently according to which DBMS you use? *Bind variables* are one area. Bind variables allow you to dynamically place variables into SQL statements. The syntax for the placeholders varies between DBMSs.

The `SqlDefault` and `SqlDescribe` functions operate slightly differently under various databases. The `SqlVariable` and `SqlGetInfo` functions return slightly different information for different databases.

Finally, the way in which SQL statements themselves are encoded will sometimes vary. This is due to the databases themselves, not because of the Rexx/SQL interface. While most DBMSs support various ANSI SQL standards, most also support keywords and features beyond the standards. Oracle is an example. Oracle SQL is one of the most powerful database languages, but it achieves this power at some cost in standardization. Be aware of variants from SQL standards if retargeting Rexx/SQL scripts toward different DBMSs.

Other Database Interfaces

This chapter focuses on Rexx/SQL because it is the most popular open-source database interface and because it accesses all important DBMSs. Other Rexx database interfaces are also available.

One example is IBM's commercial interfaces for its DB2 Universal Database (DB2 UDB). DB2 UDB runs on a variety of operating systems including Linux, Unix, Windows, and mainframes. The mainframe product has a different code base than that sold for Linux, Unix, and Windows. Writing Rexx-to-DB2 scripts on the mainframe is popular because scripting offers an easy way to customize database management activities. Rexx is an easier language to program with than the alternatives in tailoring and managing the database environment.

This discussion focuses on DB2 UDB for Linux, Unix, and Windows (LUW). We discuss the LUW product because more readers will likely have access to one of these operating systems than a mainframe platform. But the Rexx scripting for data manipulation language, or DML, statements we present here for DB2 UDB under LUW is essentially the same as you would code when using mainframe DB2.

As opposed to a generic database interface like Rexx/SQL, the IBM Rexx / DB2 interfaces give much greater control over DB2 UDB, including all its administrative functions and utilities. The downside is that the Rexx/DB2 interfaces are DB2-specific. They are nonportable and come bundled with a purchased commercial database. They only operate against DB2 databases, whereas Rexx/SQL operates on nearly any relational database.

Among IBM's programming interfaces for managing and controlling DB2 UDB databases, the Rexx/DB2 interfaces are easier to program than the alternatives (those for compiled languages like C/C++, COBOL, or FORTRAN). They bring the power and productivity of Rexx scripting to the administration and management of DB2 UDB. Check IBM's interface documentation to see which Rexx interpreters their interfaces currently support.

Let's take a look at the Rexx/DB2 package. Three Rexx/DB2 interfaces come bundled with DB2 UDB for Linux, Unix, and Windows:

DB2 UDB Interface	Use
SQLEXEC	The SQL interface. Use this to access databases and issue SQL statements. This interface supports the kinds of SQL processing illustrated in this chapter with Rexx/SQL, for example, DML statements, cursor processing, and parameter markers.
SQLDB2	An interface to DB2's *command-line processor* (CLP). Use it to run any of the hundreds of commands the CLP supports, including those for attach, connect, backup, restore, utilities, an the like.
SQLDBS	An interface to DB2's *Administrative APIs*. Use this to script administrative tasks for DB2 databases.

These three interfaces give Rexx scripts complete control over DB2 UDB. Not only can you program DML and DDL statements, but you can also script database administration, utilities, configuration changes, and the like. Rexx scripts can even run database stored procedures on most platforms.

The Rexx statements that access the Rexx/DB2 interfaces vary slightly by operating system. Under Windows, for example, Rexx scripts use the SAA standards to register and load these three DB2 interfaces. This is the same standard for access to external functions illustrated previously with Rexx/SQL. For example, these statements set up the three DB2 interfaces for use within a Windows Rexx script:

```
if  RxFuncQuery('SQLEXEC')  <> 0  then
       feedback = RxFundAdd('SQLEXEC','DB2AR','SQLEXEC')

if  RxFuncQuery('SQLDB2')   <> 0  then
       feedback = RxFundAdd('SQLDB2','DB2AR','SQLDB2')

if  RxFuncQuery('SQLDBS')   <> 0  then
       feedback = RxFundAdd('SQLDBS','DB2AR','SQLDBS')
```

Once access to the DB2 interfaces has been established, scripts can connect to databases and issue SQL calls. Here is an example of how to embed SQL statements in scripts using the SQLEXEC interface. This code sequence updates one or more rows in a table by issuing the DML `update` statement:

```
statement = "UPDATE STAFF SET JOB = 'Clerk' WHERE JOB = 'Mgr'"
CALL SQLEXEC 'EXECUTE IMMEDIATE :statement'
IF ( SQLCA.SQLCODE < 0) THEN
   SAY 'Update Error: SQLCODE = '  SQLCA.SQLCODE
```

This example builds a SQL `update` statement in a variable named `statement`. It immediately executes the statement by the SQLEXEC function. The *host variable* named `statement`, identified by its preceding colon (:), contains the SQL statement to execute. The script checks the return code in special variable `SQLCA.SQLCODE` to see whether the SQL statement succeeded or failed. As in the Rexx/SQL interface, the Rexx/DB2 interface sets a number of variables that pass status information back to the script through the SQLCA.

In this example, note the use of uppercase for Rexx and SQL statements, and lowercase for literals and other parts of the code. This is the informal "standard" to which Rexx scripts often adhere in IBM environments and in mainframe programming. It's a popular way of coding that serves to identify different parts of the code. Of course, since Rexx is not case-sensitive, you can use whatever case or mix of case you feel comfortable with or find most readable. The only exception is the data itself (in character string literals within Rexx scripts and character data residing in the database). These are case-sensitive.

Here's another coding example. These statements show how to set up cursor processing using the SQLEXEC interface:

```
prep_string = "SELECT TABNAME FROM SYSCAT.TABLES WHERE TABSCHEMA = ?"
CALL SQLEXEC 'PREPARE S1 FROM :prep_string';
CALL SQLEXEC 'DECLARE C1 CURSOR FOR S1';
CALL SQLEXEC 'OPEN C1 USING :schema_name';
```

This time the script builds the SQL statement in the variable named prep_string. The question mark (?) is a *parameter marker* or *placeholder variable* for which values will be substituted.

The SELECT statement is dynamically prepared. The SQLEXEC interface first PREPAREs the SELECT; then it DECLAREs and OPENs the cursor. After executing the preceding code, a FETCH loop would then process each row returned in the result set, and a CLOSE statement would end the use of the cursor.

One issue in cursor processing is how to detect null values. Null values are data elements whose values have not been set. Whether a column can contain nulls depends on the column and table definitions, and also whether any column values have not been loaded or inserted. To detect null values, the Rexx/DB2 interface uses *indicator variables*. The keyword INDICATOR denotes them, as in this example:

```
CALL SQLEXEC 'FETCH C1 INTO :cm INDICATOR :cmind'
IF ( cmind < 0 )
   SAY 'Commission is NULL'
```

If the indicator variable cmind is set to a negative value by the interface, then the column variable cm is null. A null variable indicates that a column entry has not yet been assigned a value in the database.

Calls to the Rexx / DB2 SQLDB2 and SQLDBS interfaces are coded like those we've discussed in illustrating the SQLEXEC preceding interface. Here are the generic templates for invoking the SQLEXEC, SQLDB2, and SQLDBS interfaces. Each names the interface, then follows it with a SQL statement or command string representing the function desired in the call:

```
CALL SQLEXEC 'sql statement'

CALL SQLDB2  'command string'

CALL SQLDBS  'command string'
```

These three code examples appear in the IBM manual, *IBM DB2 UDB Application Development Guide, SC09-2949*. See that manual and also *IBM DB2 UDB Administrative Reference API, SC09-2947* for complete information on the Rexx/DB2 interfaces. Both manuals can be freely downloaded from the online IBM Publications Center, as described in Appendix A.

You can see from the code examples in this section that coding the Rexx/DB2 interface is slightly different from coding SQL calls with the Rexx/SQL package. Nonetheless, if you know one of these two interfaces, it is quite easy to learn the other. The principles that underlie how to code data manipulation and data definition statements are the same in both products.

Summary

This chapter overviews of the features of the Rexx/SQL interface in accessing relational databases. Rexx/SQL is an open-source product that accesses almost any type of SQL database.

The examples showed how quick and convenient Rexx/SQL coding is. It allows single-statement execution of SQL statements, including `select`'s and DDL. Yet it also supports statement preparation, bind variables, auto-commits, and all the other features programmers might want in their call-level database interface.

We discussed five sample scripts that use the Rexx/SQL interface. The first illustrated the basic mechanisms of creating and terminating database connections. It also retrieved and displayed database version and release information. The second script showed how to create and load a database table. Two scripts showed how to read all the rows of a table. The first used Rexx/SQL's "array" notation to refer to individual table rows, while the second illustrated the more standard but cumbersome approach called cursor processing. An update script showed how to retrieve and update individual rows within a table. It also illustrated the value of explicitly committing data from within a script.

We also took a quick look at IBM's proprietary Rexx/DB2 interfaces. These exemplify the kinds of database-specific programming and administration possible in Rexx scripts. Scripting these tasks is much more productive than using traditional compiled programming languages. While we did not walk through complete sample scripts illustrating the Rexx/DB2 interfaces, we discussed several code snippets that show how these interfaces are coded.

This chapter just touches upon the broad topic of database programming. Our purpose is to describe Rexx database scripting and to demonstrate its coding in a simple manner. If you need more information about database programming, please obtain one of the many books on that topic.

Test Your Understanding

1. What are the key advantages to the Rexx/SQL interface? What are the advantages to using a DBMS in your scripts?

2. What Rexx/SQL functions must every script start with?

3. How to you initiate and terminate database connections? How can you check the status of a connection?

4. Describe how you would write a single routine to process SQL errors. What are the advantages to such a routine? What SQLCA variables are set by the interface, and what do they tell your script?

5. SQL statement syntax is complex. Tell how you can code to quickly identify and reduce syntax errors.

6. What is the purpose of the `SqlDispose` function? How does it differ from `SqlDisconnect`?

7. Compare the use of Rexx/SQL to the bundled Rexx/DB2 interfaces for scripting with DB2 UDB. What are the advantages of each toolset?

16

Graphical User Interfaces

Overview

This chapter explores *graphical user interface*, or *GUI* packages. It gives you an overview of the major packages, explains when to use each, and explores how to design scripts that use them.

GUI development is a detail-oriented process and scripts that create and manage GUIs typically require many lines of code. We cannot cover all the ins and outs of GUI programming in a single chapter. GUI programming is a study in its own right. It means learning the many functions, parameters and attributes involved in windows programming. Our goals here are to describe the different GUI interfaces available to Rexx programmers and offer guidance on the advantages and drawbacks of each. We also give you an idea of the structure and design of typical GUI-based scripts. The sample scripts are quite basic, yet studying them should equip you to move into more serious GUI scripting.

As a universal scripting language, Rexx runs on every imaginable platform. One advantage of this versatility is that several GUI packages interface with Rexx. These include Rexx/Tk, Rexx/DW, Rexx Dialog, OODialog, GTK+, Dr. Dialog, VX*Rexx, and VisPro/REXX. The downside to this variety is that no single GUI interface has established itself as the de facto standard for Rexx developers.

In this chapter, we'll first briefly characterize the major GUIs available for Rexx scripting. For each, we'll mention some of its advantages and uses, and we'll list the environments in which it runs or is typically used. These brief product profiles orient you to which interface product might be most appropriate for your own applications. Following these short product profiles, we'll look at three packages in greater detail: Rexx/Tk, Rexx/DW, and Rexx/gd. The first two packages aid in scripting Rexx GUIs, while the latter is for creating graphical images. We've selected these three packages for detailed, coding-level coverage for specific reasons. All three are:

- ❑ Open-source products that are freely downloadable
- ❑ Popular, widely used, and well proven
- ❑ Run across the major operating systems families

Let's start with the brief sketches of the major GUI interfaces.

Rexx/Tk

Rexx/Tk allows Rexx scripts to use the Tk, or "ToolKit," GUI made famous by the Tcl/Tk scripting language. This package enables the development of portable, cross-platform GUIs. Tk supports all important *widgets* or window elements. Its dozens of functions categorized as Menus, Labels, Text, Scrollbars, Listboxes, Buttons, Text Entry, Sliders, Frames, Canvas, Window Design, Event Handlers, and Convenience functions.

To use Rexx/Tk, you must install both it and the Tcl/Tk scripting language. Your Rexx scripts invoke Rexx/Tk external functions, which then run their corresponding Tcl/Tk commands. The names and purposes of the Rexx/Tk functions are similar to their corresponding Tk commands, so if you know one, you know the other.

The advantage to Rexx/Tk is that Tk is the most widely used cross-platform GUI toolkit in the world. It runs on all major platforms. Tk became popular because it makes the complex, detail-oriented process of creating GUIs relatively easy. Sharing Rexx's goal of ease-of-use makes Tk a nice fit for Rexx scripting. Those who already know the Tk interface experience little learning curve with Rexx/Tk. You could read a Tcl/Tk book to learn Rexx/Tk. Plenty of documentation and tutorials are available.

The downside to Rexx/Tk is that it requires Tcl/Tk on your system and has the performance penalty associated with a two-layer interface. If problems arise, you could find yourself dealing with two levels of software — the Rexx/Tk interface with its functions, and the corresponding Tcl/Tk commands.

Rexx/Tk is open-source software distributed under the *GNU Library General Public License*, or *GNU LGPL*. Information on Rexx/Tk and downloads are `http://rexxtk.sourceforge.net/index.html`.

We discuss Rexx/Tk in more detail later in this chapter.

Rexx/DW

This GUI package is based on *Dynamic Windows*, or *DW*, a GUI framework hosted by Netlabs.org in Switzerland. DW is modeled on the GTK toolkit of Unix (GTK is also known as *GTK+* and the *Gimp Toolkit*). GTK is open source under the GNU LGPL license. With Rexx scripts, Rexx/DW presently runs under the Windows, Unix, Linux, and OS/2 environments.

Widgets are the basic display items placed on GUI windows. The Dynamic Windows package supports a wide variety of widgets, including: Entryfield or Editbox, Multiline Entryfield or Editbox, Combobox, Button, Radio Button, Spin Button, Checkbox, Container or Listview, Treeview, Splitbar, Bitmap/Pixmap/Image, Popup and Pulldown Menus, Notebook, Slider, Percent or Progress meter, Listbox, Render/Drawing Area, Scrollbar, and Text or Status Bar.

Rexx/DW differs slightly from the Dynamic Windows framework in that it offers a few special functions beyond what DW contains, while it lacks a few others DW has. So, while Rexx/DW closely follows Dynamic Windows' functionality, it is not an exact match.

The main advantage to Rexx/DW is that it is a lightweight interface. Compared to Rexx/Tk, Rexx/DW provides a cross-platform GUI, while eliminating the overhead of Tcl/Tk that Rexx/Tk requires. Rexx/DW addresses the performance concerns that sometimes arise when programming GUI interfaces. Sometimes it's simpler not to have the Tcl/Tk system installed on the computer and involved as an intermediate software layer.

Rexx/DW is a newer project than Rexx/Tk. As this book is being written, it is being developed and enhanced more than Rexx/Tk, so programmers who compare the two may wish to compare the level of ongoing effort behind the two projects when deciding which to use. An easy way to do this is to access the Web pages for the respective products at SourceForge.net.

Rexx/DW is open-source software distributed under the GNU LGPL. Information on Rexx/DW and downloads are at `http://rexxdw.sourceforge.net/`. Netlabs.org can be found at `www.netlabs.org`, and the GTK+ project homepage is located at `www.gtk.org/`.

We discuss Rexx/DW in more detail later in this chapter.

Rexx Dialog

This GUI is specifically designed for Windows operating systems with either the Reginald or Regina Rexx interpreters. Reginald is a Rexx interpreter based upon Regina, and was extended and enhanced with Windows-specific functions. It specifically targets Windows platforms. Rexx Dialog is the component added to support the typical kinds of GUI interactions users expect from Windows-based applications. It optimizes the GUI for Windows. Where portability is not a concern, Rexx Dialog brings Windows "power programming" to Rexx developers.

Chapter 23 covers Reginald and its Windows-oriented features. That chapter provides further information on Rexx Dialog and its functions, as well as information on where to download the package. It also offers examples of a few of Reginald's Windows-oriented functions.

OODialog and the Object REXX GTK+ Project

OODialog is the GUI for Object REXX on Windows systems. It is a set of classes and methods designed to provide graphical user interfaces for object-oriented Object REXX scripts. Object REXX was developed by IBM and is today maintained and enhanced by the Rexx Language Association as an open-source product named Open Object Rexx. Chapter 27 provides information on Open Object Rexx and how to use to script object-oriented applications. Chapter 28 presents a complete tutorial to get you started with Open Object Rexx and scripting object-oriented systems. OODialog runs only on Windows systems.

A similar product for Linux and other Unix-derived operating systems is available from the *Object REXX GTK+ Project*. This software provides "a modal dialog manager interface to the GTK+ library from IBM's Object REXX. The project consists of a set of REXX external functions and an Object REXX class library which wraps those functions." This quotation is from the product description at SourceForge at `http://sourceforge.net/projects/gtkrxdlg/`. Note that while the project documentation refers to "IBM Object REXX" at the time of publication, Open Object Rexx is essentially the same interpreter (see Chapter 27 for full details). Full documentation and the GUI product are available at the SourceForge Web site.

Dr. Dialog, VX*Rexx, VisPro Rexx

These interfaces were popular under OS/2 and have faded along with OS/2. The latter two were commercial. Searching under the names of any of these products in a common Internet search engine such as Google or AltaVista provides more information on them if you need it.

Rexx/Tk

Now that we've profiled the major GUI interface packages, let's explore three of the most popular in greater detail. We start with Rexx/Tk, a popular, portable interface modeled on the Tk interface popularized by the Tcl/Tk scripting language.

Rexx/Tk is an external function library that provides Rexx scripts interface to the Tcl/Tk command language. Rexx/Tk has well over 100 functions. Each directly corresponds to a Tcl/Tk GUI command. The Rexx/Tk documentation maps the Tcl/Tk graphics commands to their equivalent Rexx/Tk functions. This means that you can learn Rexx/Tk programming from Tcl/Tk graphics books. Or, to put it another way, to program in Rexx/Tk you must know something about Tcl/Tk GUI programming.

Rexx/Tk includes another 50 plus "extensions," extra functions that map onto Tcl code that is dynamically loaded during Tcl programming. This provides all the GUI facilities Tcl/Tk programmers have access to, whether or not those functions are dynamically loaded.

The Rexx/Tk function names correspond to their Tcl/Tk equivalents. For example, Tk's `menu` command becomes `TkMenu` in the Rexx library; `menu post` becomes `TKMenuPost`. This makes it easy to follow the mapping between the Tcl/Tk command and Rexx/Tk functions.

Tcl/Tk is case-sensitive. Quoted commands or widgets must be typed in the proper case. The special return code `tkrc` is set by any Rexx/Tk function. `tkrc` is 0 when a function succeeds, negative on error, or a positive number for a warning. The `TkError` function makes available the full text of any error message.

Appendix G lists all the Rexx/Tk functions and extensions and their definitions. It gives you the complete overview of the functions provided with the product.

Downloading and installing

First you must download and install Tcl/Tk on your system. Searching on Google provides a list of several download sites. Among them are ActiveState at `www.activestate.com/Products/ActiveTcl` and the Tcl Developer Exchange at `http://dev.scriptics.com/software/tcltk/`. Both sites provide the product along with documentation and set up information. Downloads come in both source and binary distributions for all major platforms. Tcl/Tk is free software. Read the license that downloads with the product for terms of use.

Under Windows we did nothing more than download the `*.zip` file, decompress it, and run the installer program. For first time users of Rexx/Tk, we recommend the "default install" of Tcl/Tk to avoid any problems.

After installing Tcl/Tk, be sure to run one or more of its "demo" programs. These reside in a subdirectory to the product directory and have the extension `*.tcl`. Running a demo program ensures that your installation succeeded.

The next step is to download and install the Rexx/Tk package. Rexx/Tk can be freely downloaded from SourceForge.net. The Rexx/Tk Web page documents the package at `http://rexxtk.sourceforge.net/`. The Web page includes a link to download the product, or go to `http://sourceforge.net` and enter keywords `Rexx/Tk` into the search panel.

The product is available in source and binaries for various platforms. After downloading and decompressing the appropriate file, read the README and the setup.html files that describe product installation. You must set environmental variables and the PATH to reflect the product and library location. To use the external function library, your scripts must be able to load the Windows DLL named rexxtk.dll or the Linux or Unix shared library file named librexxtk*.

Rexx/Tk is an external function library, as is Rexx/DW. Either is usable from any Rexx interpreter that supports standard access to external functions. Both are always tested with the Regina interpreter, so if you experience problems that appear to be interpreter-related, verify your install by testing with Regina.

Basic script design

Rexx/Tk scripts are *event-driven*, or activated by user interaction with the top-level window and its widgets, so scripts share a common structure. The logic of their main routine or driver is typically:

1. Register and load the Rexx/Tk external function library.

2. Create the top-level or main window, including all its widgets. Display the main window to the user.

3. Enter a loop which manages user actions on the widgets.

4. Specific routines are invoked within your script depending on user actions (mouse-clicks and inputs).

5. The script terminates when the user exits the top-level window.

Figure 16-1 diagrams this logic.

Rexx/Tk GUI Scripting

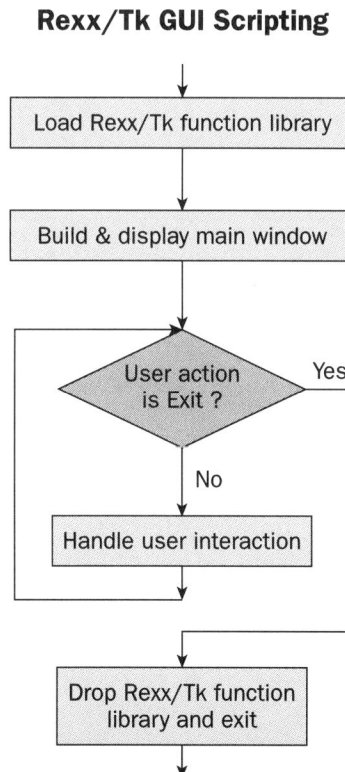

Figure 16-1

A simple example

Let's review a very simple sample script. We've kept it minimal so that you can see the basic script structure. The goal here is not to explore Tk widgets, of which there is a very full universe. It is simply to orient you to the typical design of Rexx/Tk scripts.

The script was developed under Microsoft's Windows operating system, but Rexx/Tk's portability means it could have been developed for several other operating systems, including Linux and Unix, as well.

All the sample script does is display a small GUI window with a menu bar. The sole option on the menu bar in the window is labeled File. When the user clicks on File, a drop-down menu appears. It contains three items labeled Open ... , Dir..., and Quit. So the drop-down menu structure is:

```
File
    Open...
    Dir...
    Quit
```

If the user selects Open..., the standard Windows panel for File Selection appears. The user selects a file to "open," and the script simply confirms the user's selection by displaying that filename in a Message Box. The user clicks the Ok button in the Message Box and returns to view the original window.

Similarly, if the user selects Dir..., the standard Windows dialog for Directory Selection appears. After the user picks a directory, the script displays the directory name in a Message Box to confirm the user's selection. The user clicks the Ok button in the Message Box and returns to the original window.

If the user selects Quit, a Message Box asks him or her Are You Sure? with Yes and No buttons below this question. Selecting the No button takes the user back to the original window and its menu bar. Clicking Yes makes the window disappear and the script ends.

Here's the main routine or driver of the script:

```
/*****************************************************************/
/* REXX_TK EXAMPLE:                                            */
/*                                                             */
/* A very simple example of the basics of Rexx/TK.             */
/*****************************************************************/

/* load the Rexx/Tk external function library for use          */

call RxFuncAdd 'TkLoadFuncs','rexxtk','TkLoadFuncs'
if TkLoadFuncs() <> 0 then say 'ERROR- Cannot load Rexx/Tk library!'

call top_window            /* create and display the main window */

do forever                 /* the basic loop in this program    */
   interpret 'Call' TkWait() /* wait for user action, then respond */
end

call TkDropFuncs           /* drop the library functions        */
exit 0                     /* end of script                     */
```

The first line of the script uses the SAA function RxFuncAdd to register the function TkLoadFuncs, which will be used to load the Rexx/Tk library:

```
call RxFuncAdd 'TkLoadFuncs','rexxtk','TkLoadFuncs'
```

The key parameter is the second one, rexxtk, which matches the filename for the external library. In Windows, for example, the file's name would be rexxtk.dll. Under Linux, Unix, or BSD, the parameter identifies the shared library file.

The installation of the Rexx/Tk library ensures that the Rexx interpreter can find this library through the proper environmental variable. If this line fails in your script, review the install README* files for how to set the environmental variables Rexx requires to locate external libraries.

Once the RxFuncAdd function has registered the TkLoadFuncs function, execute TkLoadFuncs to load the entire external library. Now all the Rexx/Tk functions are available for the use of this script:

```
if TkLoadFuncs() <> 0 then say 'ERROR- Cannot load Rexx/Tk library!'
```

This example assumes that we're using the Regina Rexx interpreter, which bases its access to external function libraries on the SAA standard. Other Rexx interpreters that follow the SAA interface standards to external libraries would use the same code as this script. Some Rexx interpreters accomplish access to external function libraries in a different manner.

Now the script creates a top-level window:

```
call top_window          /* create and display the main window */
```

The code in the top_window internal subroutine can establish all sorts of widgets (or controls) and attach them to the topmost window. We'll look at the code of the subroutine in a moment. The point here is that the script creates and then displays a window with which the user will interact.

Having displayed its initial window, this code is the basic loop by which the script waits for user interaction with the widgets or controls on the top-level window:

```
do forever                 /* the basic loop in this program          */
   interpret 'Call' TkWait()   /* wait for user action, then respond   */
end
```

The script ends when the user selects the action to end it from the top-level window. The following code should therefore never be reached, but just in case, always drop the Rexx/Tk functions and code an exit instruction to end the main routine:

```
call TkDropFuncs           /* drop the library functions              */
exit 0                     /* end of script                           */
```

That's all there is to the main routine. Pretty simple! The real work in most GUI scripts is in the definition of the widgets or controls and the development of the routines that handle the events prompted by user interaction with those controls.

Chapter 16

Here's the internal subroutine that creates the top-level window and all its widgets:

```
top_window:      /* create/display top-level window ****************/

menubar = TkMenu('.m1')      /* make a menubar for the top window  */

/* create drop-down menu, add it to the top-level menubar          */

filemenu = TkMenu('.m1.file','-tearoff', 0)    /* create drop menu */
call TkAdd menubar, 'cascade', '-label', 'File', '-menu', filemenu

/* now add items to the File menu */

call TkAdd filemenu, 'command', '-label', 'Open...', '-rexx', 'getfile'
call TkAdd filemenu, 'command', '-label', 'Dir...' , '-rexx', 'getdirectory'
call TkAdd filemenu, 'command', '-label', 'Quit'   , '-rexx', 'exit_window'

call TkConfig '.', '-menu', menubar  /* attach menubar to window   */

return                               /* end of routine TOP_WINDOW  */
```

The first line creates a menu bar for the top-level window. In Tk, the topmost window is denoted by a period (.), and all widgets on that window derive their name from this. This line creates the menu bar we have named .m1 for the topmost window:

```
menubar = TkMenu('.m1')      /* make a menubar for the top window  */
```

After creating the menu bar, the script can create a drop-down menu to attach to it. These two lines create the drop-down menu at the far left side of the menu bar in the main window. The invocation of the TkAdd function attaches the drop-down menu to the menu bar:

```
filemenu = TkMenu('.m1.file','-tearoff', 0)    /* create drop menu */
call TkAdd menubar, 'cascade', '-label', 'File', '-menu', filemenu
```

With the drop-down menu in place, the script needs to add items to this menu. Three more calls to TkAdd add the three items in the drop-down menu:

```
call TkAdd filemenu, 'command', '-label', 'Open...', '-rexx', 'getfile'
call TkAdd filemenu, 'command', '-label', 'Dir...' , '-rexx', 'getdirectory'
call TkAdd filemenu, 'command', '-label', 'Quit'   , '-rexx', 'exit_window'
```

A single call to the TkConfig function completes the set up by attaching the menubar to the window:

```
call TkConfig '.', '-menu', menubar  /* attach menubar to window   */
```

The routine has completed its task of building the top-level window and its widgets. It ends with a return instruction.

Now we need to create three routines, one for each of three actions the user can select from the drop-down menu. The TkAdd functions above show that the labels the user will view for these three actions are Open..., Dir..., and Quit. Those lines also show that the corresponding routines we need to create for the three actions must have the names of getfile, getdirectory, and exit_window. So the

`TkAdd` function associates the label the user selects with a routine in the script that will be run when he or she selects the label from the drop-down list.

Here is the code for the `getfile` routine, the routine that displays the typical Windows panel from which users select filenames (the Windows' File Selection panel). The `TkMessageBox` call displays back the filename the user selects in a Message Box and allows the user to exit back to the main window by pressing the `Ok` button:

```
getfile:      /* get a filename from user   **********************/

filename = TkGetOpenFile('-title','Open File')

if TkMessageBox('-message',filename,'-title', ,
   'Correct?','-type','ok','-icon','warning')  = 'ok' then nop

return
```

The `TkGetOpenFile` function sets up the Window's File Selection dialog. You can see the power of a widget or Windows control here: a single line of code presents and manages the entire user interaction with the File Selection dialog.

The code to implement the directory selection routine is nearly the same as that for the routine above, except that a Windows-style Directory Selection panel appears instead of a File Selection panel. Once again, the `TkMessageBox` call echoes the user's choice back to him or her inside a Message Box. The user acknowledges the Message Box and continues interaction with the script by clicking on the message `ok` displayed inside that Message Box:

```
getdirectory: /* get a directory name input **********************/

dirname = TkChooseDirectory('-title','Choose Directory')

if TkMessageBox('-message',dirname,'-title', ,
   'Correct?','-type','ok','-icon','warning')  = 'ok' then nop

return
```

Lastly, here is the code that executes if the user selects option `Quit` from the drop down menu. It displays a Message Box that asks `Are You Sure?` If the user pushes the `No` button, he or she again sees the top-level window because of the `return` instruction in the code below. If he presses the `Yes` button, he exits the script and its window. This executes the `TkDropFuncs` function below, which drops the Rexx/Tk function library from memory and further use by the program:

```
exit_window:   /* exits top-level window-END!**********************/

if TkMessageBox('-message','Are you sure?','-title', ,
   'Quit?','-type','yesno','-icon','warning')  = 'no' then Return

call TkDropFuncs               /* drop the library functions      */

exit 0                         /* end of script                   */
```

This sample script is very minimal. It just displays a small window with a drop-down menu and manages user interaction with the window and its menu selections. Nevertheless, the script does illustrate the basic structure of GUI scripts and how they manage user interaction. You could take this "skeletal script" and expand it into a much more robust and complex window manager.

Your next steps

The sample script shows that most GUI scripts have the same basic structure. The logic of the driver is simple. It is in the nearly 200 functions to create and define widgets in which complexity lies. And in writing the procedural logic to animate the actions the user selects by interacting with the controls. Learning the function library and how to program all the widgets or controls are the challenge.

Start by perusing the sample scripts shipped with Rexx/Tk. You can learn a lot from them. And consider learning more about the Tcl/Tk commands that underlie Rexx/Tk. Two good sources of information are the Tcl/Tk Developer's home page, listed earlier, and any of several popular books on how to program the Tcl/Tk GUI. Among those books are *Graphical Applications with Tcl and Tk* by Eric F. Johnson (M&T Books, ISBN: 1-55851-569-0) and *Tcl/Tk in a Nutshell* by Raines and Tranter (O'Reilly, ISBN: 1-56592-433-9). You can find many other books on the Tk toolkit by searching online at www.amazon.com or www.barnesandnoble.com.

Rexx/DW

Rexx/DW offers an alternative GUI toolkit to that of Rexx/Tk. Rexx/DW's main advantage is that it is a lightweight interface, offering potential performance improvements over Rexx/Tk.

Rexx/DW provides external functions that enable Rexx scripts to create and manage GUIs through Netlabs.org's *Dynamic Windows*, or *dwindows*, package. Rexx/DW scripts define *widgets*, elements placed in windows, such as check boxes, radio buttons, and the like. Widgets are assembled into the window layout by a process called *packing*. Internal subroutines you write called *event handlers* or *callbacks* are associated with particular actions the user takes on the widgets.

Scripts typically present a window or screen panel to the user and wait for the user to initiate actions on the widgets that activate the callback routines. Interaction continues as long as the user selects an action from the window. At a certain point, the user closes the window. This ends interaction and terminates the program.

Components

To set various layout and behavioral *attributes*, Rexx/DW has about 30 *constants*. Each constant has a default and can be set by the script to some other value to change behavior.

Rexx/DW contains over 175 functions. These categorize into these self-descriptive groupings:

- ❑ ProcessControl
- ❑ Dialog
- ❑ CallbackManagement

- ❏ Browsing
- ❏ ColourSupport
- ❏ ModuleSupport
- ❏ MutexSupport
- ❏ EventSupport
- ❏ ThreadSupport
- ❏ PointerPosition
- ❏ Utility
- ❏ PackageManagement

Rexx/DW supports 17 different *callbacks* or events that scripts can be programmed to handle.

Downloading and Installing Rexx/DW

Like Rexx/Tk, Rexx/DW can be freely downloaded from SourceForge.net. The Rexx/DW Web page documents the package at `http://rexxdw.sourceforge.net/`. The Web page includes a link to download the product, or go to `http://sourceforge.net` and enter keywords `Rexx/DW` into the search panel.

Download either compressed source or binaries for your operating system. The installation follows the typical pattern for open-source software. If you downloaded binaries, after decompression all you must do is set environmental variables and the PATH to reflect the product and library location. To use the external function library, your scripts must be able to load the Windows DLL named `rexxdw.dll` or the Unix/Linux/BSD shared library file named something similar to `librexxdw*`. The README* file that downloads with the product gives installation instructions and details on how to set environmental variables.

Basic script design

Rexx/DW scripts are *event-driven*, activated by user interaction with the top-level window and its widgets. Their logical structure is similar to that of Rexx/Tk scripts and those developed with other prominent GUI packages. The basic outline of user-driven interaction provided in Figure 16-1 applies to Rexx/DW programming as well (except that Rexx/DW functions are used in place of Rexx/Tk functions).

The basic structure of the typical Rexx/DW script is:

1. Register and load the Rexx/DW external function library. Use code such as this:

```
call  RxFuncAdd  'DW_LoadFuncs', 'rexxdw', 'DW_LoadFuncs'
if  DW_LoadFuncs()  <>  0  then say 'ERROR-- Unable to load Rexx/DW library!'
```

The first line uses the SAA-based function in Regina Rexx named `RxFuncAdd` to register the `DW_LoadFuncs` external function. It resides in the external library named named by the second parameter, `rexxdw`.

In Windows, `rexxdw` refers to the file `rexxdw.dll`. In Linux or Unix, it refers to the root part of the name of the shared library file. In either case, the proper environmental variable must be set to indicate the location of this file for the `RxFuncAdd` call to succeed. The second line invokes the `DW_LoadFuncs` function to load the rest of the DW external library.

2. Initialize the dynamic windows interface by invoking the Rexx/DW `dw_init` function. Initialize various attributes in the constants to set interface behaviors and defaults.

3. Create the topmost panel or window. This screen may consist of a set of packed widgets, each having various attributes and behaviors. Events are mapped into *callbacks* or event-handling routines for the various actions the user might take on the window, based on the widgets it contains. This mapping is achieved through the function `dw_signal_connect` and potentially other `CallbackManagement` functions. When all is ready, the script displays the top-level window to the user.

   Now the script driver runs an endless loop that receives actions from the user. Depending on the capabilities of the Rexx interpreter, this loop might use either of the functions `dw_main` or `dw_main_iteration`. This loop is similar to that of the `TkWait` function loop in Rexx/Tk.

4. The user ends interaction with the script by closing its top-level window.

In summary, you can see that the skeletal logic of Rexx/DW programs is the same as the sample Rexx/Tk script we discussed earlier in the chapter. So, scripting Rexx/DW interfaces is rather similar to scripting Rexx/Tk. The difference is that you use Rexx/DW functions to bring the logic to life. The real work in Rexx/DW scripting is in writing the callback routines to handle user interaction with the widgets on the window.

Your next steps

As with other forms of GUI programming, the program logic of Rexx/DW scripts is straightforward. The trick lies in learning the many attributes and functions the package contains. This powerful package contains some 175 functions!

Fortunately, Rexx/DW comes with complete documentation and sample scripts. Use these as models with which to get started. Take the sample scripts, look them over until you understand them, then copy them and adapt them to your own needs. This will get you up and running quickly.

Graphical Images with Rexx/gd

Rexx/gd is an external function library designed for the creation and manipulation of graphical images. It is not intended for the creation, manipulation and control of GUIs in the same manner as are Rexx/Tk and Rexx/DW. Rather, it creates images stored in `*.gif`, `*.png`, and `*.jpeg` files. These could be displayed within a GUI or Web page, for example, but the emphasis is on graphic images, not on controlling user interaction through a GUI.

Rexx/gd draws complete graphic images with lines, arcs, text, color, and fonts. Images may be cut and pasted from other images. The images that are created are written to PNG, GIF, JPEG, or JPG files.

Rexx/gd is based on *GD*, an open-source, ANSI C-language library. Rexx/gd is essentially a wrapper that gives Rexx scripts access to the GD library code. To use Rexx/gd, you need to download and install the GD library to your machine. Then download and install Rexx/gd.

The GD library is available at `www.boutell.com/gd`. Or enter the keywords `gd library` into any Internet search engine for a list of current download sites. Rexx/gd can be downloaded off the same master panel as Rexx/SQL and Rexx/DW at `http://regina-rexx.sourceforge.net/` or more specifically `http://rexxgd.sourceforge.net/index.html`.

The logic of a Rexx/gd routine

Rexx/gd is embedded within all kinds of Rexx scripts and used in a wide variety of applications. But the logic of an internal routine that creates an image is predictable. Here is its basic structure:

1. Register and load the Rexx/gd library for use. Following the same style we used with Rexx/Tk and Rexx/DW, this code looks like this:

   ```
   call  RxFuncAdd  'GdLoadFuncs', 'rexxgd', 'GdLoadFuncs'
   if  GdLoadFuncs()  <>  0  then say 'ERROR-- Unable to load Rexx/gd library!'
   ```

   This code registers and loads the GD function library for use according to the standard approach of the SAA registration procedures for external function libraries.

2. Allocate a work area to develop an image in by invoking the `gdImageCreate` function.

3. Assign background and foreground colors to the image by calling the `gdImageColorAllocate` function.

4. Use one or more of the *drawing functions* to draw graphics in the image area. For example, to draw a line, call `gdImageLine`. To create a rectangle, invoke `gdImageRectangle` or `gdImageFilledRectangle`. The script might also invoke styling, brushing, tiling, filling, font, text, and color functions in creating the image.

5. The script preserves the image it created in-memory by writing it to disk. Among useful externalization functions are `gdImageJpeg`, to write the image as a JPEG file, and `gmImagePng`, to store the image as a PNG file.

6. End by releasing memory and destroying the in-memory image by a call to `gdImageDestroy`.

Figure 16-2 pictorially summarizes the logic of a typical Rexx/gd script.

Rexx/gd Graphics Scripting

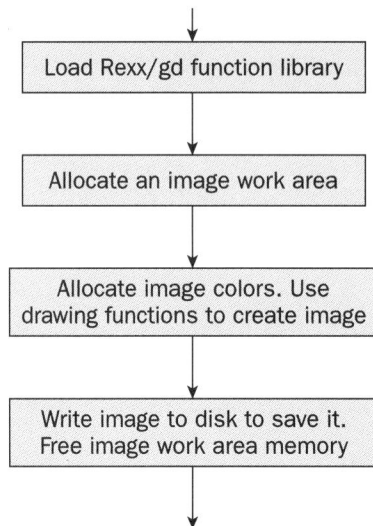

```
        ┌─────────────────────────────────┐
        │  Load Rexx/gd function library  │
        └─────────────────────────────────┘
                        │
        ┌─────────────────────────────────┐
        │   Allocate an image work area   │
        └─────────────────────────────────┘
                        │
        ┌─────────────────────────────────┐
        │  Allocate image colors. Use     │
        │  drawing functions to create image │
        └─────────────────────────────────┘
                        │
        ┌─────────────────────────────────┐
        │  Write image to disk to save it. │
        │  Free image work area memory     │
        └─────────────────────────────────┘
                        │
```

Figure 16-2

Rexx/gd provides over 75 functions. They are divided into these categories:

❑   Image creation, destruction, loading, and saving

❑   Drawing

❑   Query

❑   Font and text handling

❑   Color management

❑   Copying and resizing

❑   Miscellaneous

Rexx/gd can be combined with GUI tools like Rexx/Tk or Rexx/DW to create graphical user interfaces. It is also useful in building parts of Web pages. In fact, let's look at a sample script that does exactly that.

A sample program

This sample script draws the buttons that appear on a Web page. Each button contains one word of text. Figure 16-3 displays the Web page, which is the home page for Rexx/gd at SourceForge.net at `http://rexxgd.sourceforge.net/index.html`. The buttons created by the program appear down the left-hand side of the Web page. The script appears courtesy of its author, Mark Hessling, developer/maintainer of Regina Rexx as well as many other key open-source Rexx tools.

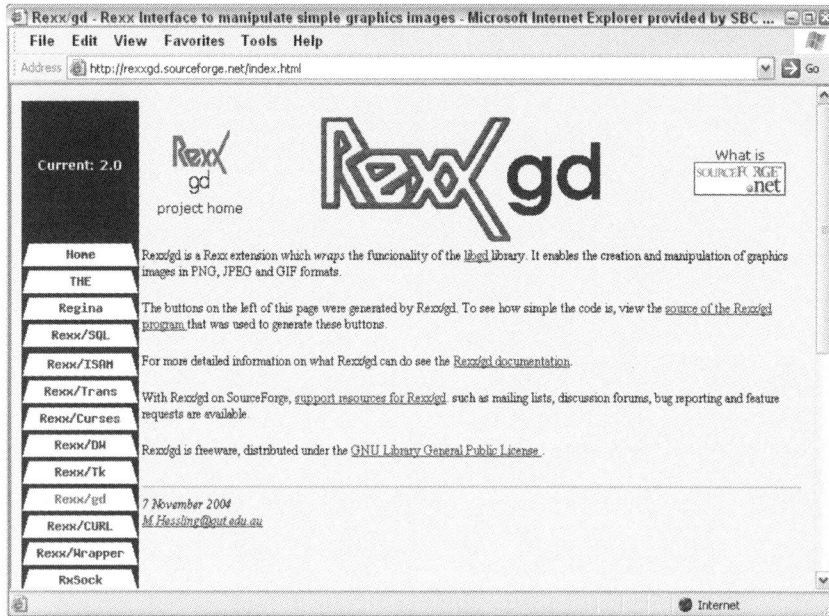

Figure 16-3

Here is the program. (A few lines in the program wrap around onto the next line due to the margin size.)

```
/*
 * This Rexx/gd script creates all of the buttons for my Web page
 */
Trace o
Call RxFuncAdd 'GdLoadFuncs', 'rexxgd', 'GdLoadFuncs'
Call GdLoadFuncs

text = 'Home Links Downloads Bug_Report Rexx/Tk Rexx/SQL Regina THE PDCurses
Rexx/Wrapper Documentation Rexx/ISAM Rexx/gd Rexx/Trans Rexx/Curses'
/*
 * Find the maximum length of any of the button texts
 */
maxlen = 0
Do i = 1 To Words(text)
    if Length(Word(text,i)) > maxlen Then maxlen = Length(Word(text,i))
End
/*
 * Image size is based on size of largest text
 */
font = 'GDFONTMEDIUMBOLD'
x = ((1+GdFontGetWidth( font )) * maxlen) + 8
y = GdFontGetHeight( font ) + 8
Say 'Image size:' x 'x' y

Do i = 1 To Words(text)
    img = GdImageCreate( x, y )
```

```
    /*
     * First color allocated is the background - white
     */
    white = GdImageColorAllocate( img, 245, 255, 250 )
    background = GdImageColorAllocate( img, 0, 0, 102 )
    blue = GdImageColorAllocate( img, 0, 0, 255 )
    yellowgreen = GdImageColorAllocate( img, 73, 155, 0 )
    /*
     * Although most browsers can't handle transparent PNGs,
     * set the transparent index to the background anyway.
     */
    call GdImageColorTransparent img, background
    /*
     * Determine text position - centered
     */
    xoff = (GdImageGetWidth( img ) % 2 ) - (((Length(Word(text,i)) *
(GdFontGetWidth( font )))-1) % 2)
    /*
     * Draw our borders for the fill of the top left and right corners.
     */
    call GdImageLine img, 6,   0, 0,   y-1, background
    call GdImageLine img, x-7, 0, x-1, y-1, background
    call GdImageFillToBorder img, 0,0, background, background
    call GdImageFillToBorder img, x-1,0, background, background
    /*
     * Write the string in blue, and save the image . . .
     */
    call GdImageString img, font, xoff, 3, Translate(Word(text,i),' ','_'),
yellowgreen
    call GdImagePNG img, makename(Word(text,i),'green')
    /*
     * . . . then overwrite the string in yellow-green, and write this image.
     */
    call GdImageString img, font, xoff, 3, Translate(Word(text,i),' ','_'), blue
    call GdImagePNG img, makename(Word(text,i),'blue')

    call GdImageDestroy img
End

Return

makename: Procedure
Parse Arg text, color
text = Translate(text,'abcdefghijklmnopqrstuvwxyz','ABCDEFGHIJKLMNOPQRSTUVWXYZ')
text = Changestr( '/', text, '' )
text = Changestr( '_', text, '' )
Return color||text'.png'
```

The logic of the script follows the straightforward steps listed in the preceding code. First, the script loads the gd function library:

```
Call RxFuncAdd 'GdLoadFuncs', 'rexxgd', 'GdLoadFuncs'
Call GdLoadFuncs
```

The script next determines the size of the buttons, based on the size of the longest word that will be displayed within them. This is the code of the do loop and some code that calculates the image size.

Now the script is ready to invoke the Rexx/gd function GdImageCreate to allocate the image. The image will be developed in a work area in memory:

```
img = GdImageCreate( x, y )
```

The script issues several GdImageColorAllocate functions to set up colors for the image and its background:

```
/*
 * First color allocated is the background - white
 */
white = GdImageColorAllocate( img, 245, 255, 250 )
background = GdImageColorAllocate( img, 0, 0, 102 )
blue = GdImageColorAllocate( img, 0, 0, 255 )
yellowgreen = GdImageColorAllocate( img, 73, 155, 0 )
```

Now, the script draws the borders of the buttons with this code:

```
call GdImageLine img, 6,   0, 0,   y-1, background
call GdImageLine img, x-7, 0, x-1, y-1, background
call GdImageFillToBorder img, 0,0, background, background
call GdImageFillToBorder img, x-1,0, background, background
```

These statements write the image in blue and yellow-green, and save it to PNG files:

```
/*
 * Write the string in blue, and save the image . . .
 */
call GdImageString img, font, xoff, 3, Translate(Word(text,i),' ','_'),yellowgreen
call GdImagePNG img, makename(Word(text,i),'green')

/*
 * . . . then overwrite the string in yellowgreen, and write this image.
 */
call GdImageString img, font, xoff, 3, Translate(Word(text,i),' ','_'), blue
call GdImagePNG img, makename(Word(text,i),'blue')
```

Now that the image has been allocated, developed, and saved to a file, the script can exit. Before terminating, the program destroys the allocated image and releases its memory with this statement:

```
call GdImageDestroy img
```

This script illustrates the straightforward logic of most Rexx/gd programs. As with Rexx/Tk and Rexx/DW, this logic is simple; the trick is in learning the details of the many available functions and how to combine them to meet your needs.

The graphical images created with Rexx/gd can be used for a variety of purposes. As shown by this program, the images can be combined with other logic to create sophisticated Web page designs.

Summary

This chapter describes the most popular GUI interface packages for Rexx scripting. It discusses Rexx/Tk, Rexx/DW, and Rexx/gd in detail. These are all open-source products that are widely used and well proven. New releases are tested with Regina and the products work with other Rexx interpreters as well.

We explored the basics of GUI programming at a very high level, showing the essential nature of event-driven programming. We presented a Rexx/Tk script, albeit a very simple one. Then we looked at Rexx/DW scripting. These scripts follow the same basic event-driven logic as the Rexx/Tk program, but of course use the functions of the Rexx/DW library.

GUI programming is necessarily detail oriented, and scripts tend to be lengthy, even if they are logically rather straightforward. If you are not an experienced GUI developer, this is the challenge you face. Rexx provides all the requisite tools.

Finally, we investigated Rexx/gd and how it can be used for creating graphic images. We looked at the Web page for the product and related the graphics on that Web page to the script that created them. Rexx/gd is a generic graphical image tool that can be combined with other Rexx interfaces and tools to create the graphical components of Web pages or for many other uses.

Test Your Understanding

1. What are the essential differences between Rexx/Tk and Rexx/DW? What are the advantages to each?

2. When would you use Rexx Dialog? For which operating system was it designed and customized?

3. What's a widget? How are widgets associated with top-level windows in Rexx/Tk versus Rexx/DW?

4. What is the basic logic of the driver in most GUI scripts? What are the differences between Rexx/Tk and Rexx/DW scripts in this regard?

5. Why has the Tcl/Tk GUI toolkit become so popular?

6. Does Rexx/gd create GUIs? How could it be used with Web pages? Where does Rexx/gd create its images?

17

Web Programming with CGI and Apache

Overview

Rexx is well-suited to Web programming because it excels at string manipulation. Web programming requires reading and interpreting string input and creating textual output. As in the next chapter on XML, the emphasis is on string processing. Rexx string processing strengths recommend it as a highly productive, easy-to-maintain language for Web programming.

There are many ways to program Web servers and build Web pages with Rexx. Two popular technologies are the *Common Gateway Interface*, or *CGI*, and Apache's *Mod_Rexx* interface.

First, we describe some of the tools available for CGI programming. CGI was one of the first popular Web server interfaces because it is easy to use and fully programmable.

Then we describe scripting Apache through its Rexx interface, Mod_Rexx. Apache is the world's most popular Web server. Mod_Rexx gives you complete scripting control over Apache. With it you can efficiently and effectively serve Web pages created by Rexx scripts. You can also dynamically create Web pages through a feature called *Rexx Server Pages*, or *RSP*. *Dynamic Web pages* are created and tailored in real time to meet user needs.

Common Gateway Interface

The *Common Gateway Interface*, or *CGI* specification lets Web servers execute user programs to produce Web pages containing text, graphics, forms, audio, and other information. The CGI interface allows Rexx scripts to control and drive the Web server in its provisioning of Web pages to the user's browser. Several free external function libraries are available to support CGI programming in Rexx.

The cgi-lib.rxx library

The Stanford Linear Accelerator Laboratory, or SLAC, offers a library of CGI programming functions called *cgi-lib.rxx*. Its two dozen functions are designed to simplify Rexx/CGI programming. It also includes a tutorial and sample scripts. Find the SLAC Web pages at `www.slac.stanford.edu/slac/www/resource/how-to-use/cgi-rexx` or search for the keywords `Rexx CGI` in any Web search engine. The complete function library and examples are at `www.slac.stanford.edu/slac/www/tool/cgi-rexx` and are accessible off the main SLAC Web page.

To give you an idea of what this library contains, here is a quick list of its functions. The package itself includes both the technical descriptions and full Rexx source code for these functions.

Function	Use
cleanquery	Removes unassigned variables from CGI query string
cgierror	Reports the error message and returns
cgidie	Reports the error message and "dies" or exits
chkpwd	Verifies username and password
delquery	Removes an item from CGI query string
deweb	Converts ASCII hex code to ASCII characters
formatdate	Converts date expression to Oracle format
fullurl	Returns complete CGI query URL
getowner	Returns a file's owner
getfullhost	Returns fully qualified domain name of the local host
htmlbreak	Breaks a long line into lines for HTML parsing
htmlbot	Inserts standard information ("boiler plate") at page end
htmltop	Inserts title and header at page top
httab	Converts tab-delimited file into HTML table
methget	Returns TRUE if the Form uses METHOD="GET"
methpost	Returns TRUE if the Form uses METHOD="POST"
myurl	Adds the script's URL to the page
oraenv	Establishes SLAC's Oracle/Rexx environment
printheader	Inserts the Content-type header
printvariables	Adds the Form's name-value variable pairs to the page
readform	Reads a Form's GET or POST input and returns it decoded
readpost	Reads a Form's standard input with METHOD="POST"

Function	Use
slacfnok	Identifies a file's visibility
striphtml	Removes HTML markup from a string
suspect	Returns an error message if an input string contains a suspect character
webify	Encodes special characters as ASCII hex
wraplines	Breaks long lines appropriately for terminal output

The `cgi-lib.rxx` package comes with several sample scripts. Here's a simple one that illustrates several of the functions. It simply reads form input from the user and echoes it to a Web page. It appears here courtesy of its author Les Cottrell and the SLAC:

```
#!/usr/local/bin/rxx
/*  Minimalist http form and script           */
F=PUTENV("REXXPATH=/afs/slac/www/slac/www/tool/cgi-rexx")
SAY PrintHeader(); SAY '<body bgcolor="FFFFFF">'
Input=ReadForm()
IF Input='' THEN DO  /*Part 1*/
  SAY HTMLTop('Minimal Form')
  SAY '<form><input type="submit">',
      '<br>Data: <input name="myfield">'
END
ELSE DO               /*Part 2*/
  SAY HTMLTop('Output from Minimal Form')
  SAY PrintVariables(Input)
END
SAY HTMLBot()
```

In this script, this first line accesses the `cgi-lib.rxx` package:

```
F=PUTENV("REXXPATH=/afs/slac/www/slac/www/tool/cgi-rexx")
```

The line is coded for *uni-REXX*, a commercial Rexx interpreter from The Workstation Group (see Chapter 19 for information on uni-Rexx and other major commercial Rexx interpreters). Your statement for library access would be coded differently if you use a different Rexx interpreter. For example, using Regina and most other interpreters you could code this statement with the `value` built-in function. The first parameter in the statement below is the symbol to change, the second is the value to set it to, and the third is the variable pool in which to make the change. The result is to update the environmental variable properly for access to the function library:

```
call value 'REXXPATH','/afs/slac/www/slac/www/tool/cgi-rexx','ENVIRONMENT'
```

The `cgi-lib.rxx` package provides full source code for the functions, so you can set them up however you need to as an external library for your version of Rexx. Or, use them as internal routines.

Next, the script writes the *Content Type header* by the `PrintHeader` function. The content type header must be the first statement written to the browser. It tells the browser the kind of data it will receive in subsequent statements:

```
SAY PrintHeader(); SAY '<body bgcolor="FFFFFF">
```

The next line reads the input form with the `ReadForm` function:

```
Input=ReadForm()
```

If there is no input, the script writes a minimal HTML page using the `HTMLTop` function. The `HTMLTop` function inserts a title and header at the top of a Web page:

```
IF Input='' THEN DO  /*Part 1*/
   SAY HTMLTop('Minimal Form')
   SAY '<form><input type="submit">',
       '<br>Data: <input name="myfield">'
END
```

If there was form input, the script echoes it back to the user by the `PrintVariables` function. The `PrintVariables` function adds the form's name-value variable pairs to the Web page:

```
ELSE DO              /*Part 2*/
   SAY HTMLTop('Output from Minimal Form')
   SAY PrintVariables(Input)
END
```

The program ends by writing a standard footer to the Web page with the `HTMLBot` function:

```
SAY HTMLBot()
```

You can see that developing Rexx scripts that interface to CGI is just a matter of following CGI rules regarding how input is read into the script and written to the interface. CGI scripts typically read user forms input, perform some processing, and write textual output that defines the Web page the user sees in response. A library of functions like those provided by the `cgi-lib.rxx` package makes the whole process easier. They offer convenience and higher productivity than manually coding everything yourself.

In concluding, we mention that this Rexx/CGI function library is also the basis for the CGI interface package offered with the Reginald Rexx interpreter. See Chapter 23 further information on Reginald and for example Reginald scripts.

The Internet/REXX HHNS WorkBench

The CGI / Rexx library function package described in the above section helps you develop scripts that interact with the Common Gateway Interface. Using it reduces the level of effort required in writing CGI programs. Another free external library of Web programming functions is downloadable from Henri Henault & Sons, Paris, France. It too, is designed for Web server programming through controlling the Common Gateway Interface.

The purposes of this package are to help you:

❏ Quickly create dynamic Web pages, tables and forms

❏ Easily handle forms results

❏ Run Rexx-CGI scripts without change across the supported platforms

The Internet/REXX HHNS WorkBench consists about 40 functions. This function library comes with about a dozen sample programs. English documentation and the library are available at the Henri Henault & Sons Web site at www.hhns.fr/fr/real_cri.html.

The library runs under Windows, Linux, and IBM's AIX operating systems. It is tested with the Regina, IBM Object REXX, and NetRexx interpreters. It supports two Web servers: Microsoft's Internet Information Services (or IIS) and the Apache open-source Web server.

Setting up the product requires several steps:

1. Download and install the product.

2. Ensure PATH or environmental variables point to the product's shared library.

3. Configure either IIS or Apache.

4. If you're using NetRexx, ensure you have installed a servlet container engine (such as JServ or Tomcat).

The product documentation describes these steps in detail.

To give an idea of what the library contains, here are its functions and their uses (all functions are described in full detail in the product documentation):

Function	Use
delay	Wait (in seconds and milleseconds)
inkey	Keyboard scan
getkwd	Parse a keyword parameter list
getenv	Return the value of an environmental variable
getpid	Returns the current process ID
getwparm	Returns a parameter value from an *.ini file
filesize	Returns file size
parsefid	Parses a Windows/DOS/Unix/Linux filename
popen	Issues an operating system command
cgiInit	Initializes, sets up CGI header
cgiSetup	Initializes CGI, sets up Rexx variables only

Table continued on following page

277

Function	Use
CgiEnd	Ends CGI script
CgiWebit	Processes nonalphanumeric characters in a string
TblHdr	Generates a table header
TblRow	Generates a table row
FrmHdr	Generates a `<FORM ACTION=`... tag
FrmInp	Generates an `INPUT` tag within a form
CgiImg	Generates an `<IMG>` tag
CgiHref	Generates a hypertext link
r4Sh	Unescape a string
CgiRefr	Goes to another URL
GetCookie	Extracts a value from the current cookie
Tags	Generates a pair of tags

Beyond the Web programming functions, the package includes other useful functions. The following table shows that they are divided into three categories: mathematical functions, CMS-like functions, and date functions:

Function Group	Purpose	Functions
Mathematical	These functions support advanced or transcendental mathematics.	atan, atan2, cos, sqrt, exp, fact, log, pow, sin
CMS	These functions support conversion between filenames and variables and stems.	stm2file, stm2var, file2stm, var2stm, makefid
Date	These functions convert between Julian day numbers and dates	d2date, date2d

Let's take a look at a sample program using this package. This script writes a Web page that lists program names and their descriptions. The programs it lists are the sample scripts that come with the Internet/REXX HHNS WorkBench. The output of this program can be viewed at the product Web site, www.hhns.fr/fr/real_cri.html, and is also depicted in Figure 17-1. The script appears here courtesy of Henri Henault & Sons.

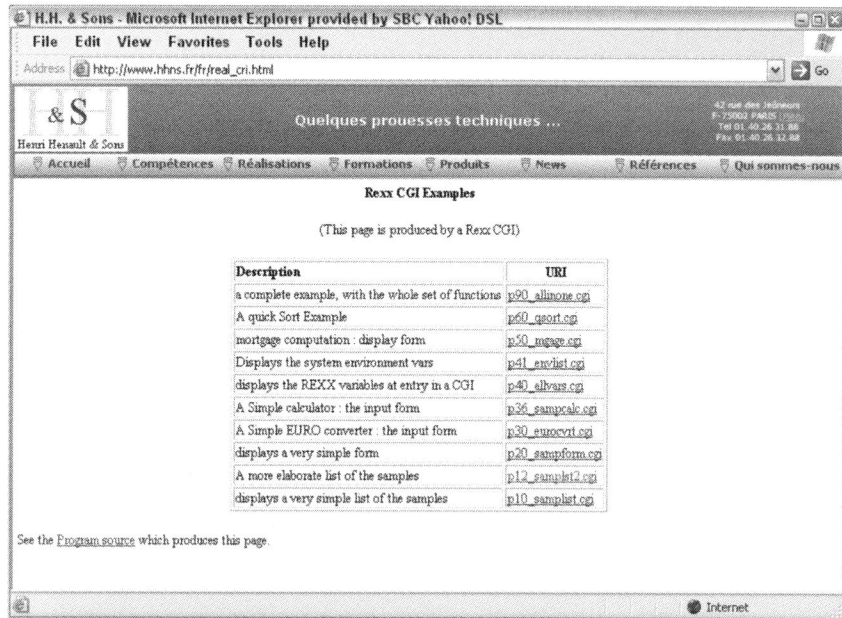

Figure 17-1

Here's the program:

```
#! /usr/local/bin/regina
/*   A more elaborate list of the samples                         */
/*----------------------------------------------------------------*/

call setdll   /* loads the HHNS shared lib */

call CgiInit "TITLE='Another List of samples' BGCOLOR=FFFFFF"

say "<center><h4>Rexx CGI Examples</h4></center>"
say "<center>(This page is produced by a Rexx CGI)</center><p>"

if left(translate(webos), 3) = "WIN" then
    call popen "Dir /b /o p*.cgi"
else call popen "ls -1 p*.cgi"
/* the above 3 statements may be replaced by :
    call popen webdir "*.cgi"
*/

say "<center>"
say "<table border=1>"
say tblHdr("Description",  " URI")

do queued()

    /*--- get the next program name ---*/
```

```
    parse pull z
    /*--- assume that 2nd line of the program is its brief description  --*/
    call linein z; desc = linein(z); call lineout z
    parse var desc '/*' desc '*/'
    /*--- Now, write a table Row with the description and the Web link ---*/
    say tblRow(strip(desc),  cgiHref(z, z))

end

say '</table>'
say '</center>'

say "<p>See the "cgiHref("r00_showsrc.cgi?p12_samplst2.cgi", "Program source")
"which produces this page."

call cgiEnd
return 0
```

The program starts by accessing the shared function library by its first statement:

```
call setdll    /* loads the HHNS shared lib */
```

Then it initializes by invoking the CgiInit function to write the page title:

```
call CgiInit "TITLE='Another List of samples' BGCOLOR=FFFFFF"

say "<center><h4>Rexx CGI Examples</h4></center>"
say "<center>(This page is produced by a Rexx CGI)</center><p>"
```

The next several lines get the list of program names (filenames) to place into the list of programs in the table on the Web page. This code first determines whether the operating system is Windows or a version of Unix; then it uses the popen function to issue either a dir or ls command to get the directory listing into the stack. This is a good example of how scripts can be written to operate across platforms through OS-aware programming:

```
if left(translate(webos), 3) = "WIN" then
    call popen "Dir /b /o p*.cgi"
else call popen "ls -1 p*.cgi"
/* the above 3 statements may be replaced by :
    call popen webdir "*.cgi"
*/
```

Now, the program writes the table header, using the tdlHdr function:

```
say "<center>"
say "<table border=1>"
say tblHdr("Description",   " URI")
```

Next, the program executes a do loop to read each program name from the stack. For each one it retrieves, it uses the tblRow function to write a row into the tabular listing. Each line in the output listing contains the program name, followed by the URL hyper-link to its code. The link is produced by the cgiHref function:

```
/*--- Now, write a table Row with the description and the Web link ---*/
    say tblRow(strip(desc),  cgiHref(z, z))
```

After it has created the table of program names and hyperlinks to their corresponding scripts, the program closes the table:

```
say '</table>'
say '</center>'
```

The program concludes by writing a message with a URL link by the cgiHref function. Then it terminates by invoking cgiEnd:

```
say "<p>See the "cgiHref("r00_showsrc.cgi?p12_samplst2.cgi", "Program source")
"which produces this page."

call cgiEnd
```

The Internet/REXX HHNS WorkBench makes CGI programming easier because you can leverage its set of Web-programming-specific functions for higher productivity. The scripting example employs only a small number of the package's functions, yet you can see how these functions make for a higher-level, more powerful script.

There are many more coding examples at the HHNS Web page at www.hhns.fr/fr/real cri.html. You can run the examples at the Web site and view their Web page output while viewing the code simultaneously in another browser panel. This makes it very easy to learn how to use this package.

Programming Apache with Mod_Rexx

The Apache Web server is the most widely used host system on the Internet. Its open-source download includes several *language processor modules*. These are designed to allow developers to process any part of an Apache request including the creation of Web pages. The modules are available for Rexx, Perl, and other languages, with names like Mod_Rexx, mod_perl, and mod_php, respectively. Each module has the same capabilities but supports a different scripting language.

The Apache Web server directly executes your Rexx scripts through its Mod_Rexx interface. Apache offers a more efficient way of writing Web server code than the Common Gateway Interface. Web server *extensions* like CGI typically suffer from performance overhead because they spawn separate processes to handle new requests. The Apache server handles new requests by executing within a new thread, rather than spawning a new process. Threads are a more efficient mechanism than processes on most operating systems. This also means that Mod_Rexx requires a *thread-safe interpreter*. Examples of thread-safe Rexx interpreters include Regina and Open Object Rexx (formerly known as Object REXX or IBM Object REXX).

Mod_Rexx gives Rexx developers full control over all aspects of the processing of Apache server requests. The product comes in two flavors. One is a traditional, function-based interface, while the other is an object-oriented interface. The procedural interface contains roughly 50 functions, all of which start with the letters www. The object-oriented interface consists of three classes and their accompanying 40-odd methods. This chapter focuses on the function-based interface.

Functions and special variables

Mod_Rexx is very complete and handles almost any requirement. To give you an idea of what's included, let's briefly discuss the functions for the traditional, function-based interface, and their uses. The functions are grouped into four categories:

- ❑ *General Functions* — This set of functions provides a base level of services necessary to work with the Apache Web server. They manage cookies and the error log, retrieve environmental information, and handle URLs.

- ❑ *Apache Request Record Functions* — These functions provide information about and manage the request record pointer, information coming into the script from Apache and the Web.

- ❑ *Updatable Apache Request Record Functions* — These functions manage the request record pointer and allow updating values as well as retrieving them.

- ❑ *Apache Server Record Functions* — These functions manage server-side concerns pertaining to Apache and its environment.

Appendix J lists all the functions in the Mod_Rexx package along with descriptions of their use.

Mod_Rexx uses a set of three dozen *special variables* to communicate information to Rexx scripts. The names of these variables all begin with the letters www. These special variables are set either before the script starts, or after the script executes a function call. Their purpose is to communicate information to the script either about the environment or the results of function calls. The sample program we discuss later creates a Web page and displays the values of these variables. Appendix J contains a complete list of all the Mod_Rexx special variables.

Installation

Mod_Rexx is distributed with Apache. Download Apache from www.apache.org. Or, obtain Mod_Rexx by separate download from SourceForge at http://sourceforge.net/projects/modrexx.

Mod_Rexx is distributed under the Common Public License. The license agreement downloads with the product. Be sure to read it and agree to its terms before using the product. Mod_Rexx runs under Windows, Linux, AIX, and OS/2. It is tested with the Regina and Open Object Rexx interpreters.

Installing Mod_Rexx is similar to installing the Rexx interfaces described in the last few chapters. Be sure that the Mod_Rexx shared library named mod_rexx.dll or mod_rexx.so is present and that it can be located through the PATH or the proper shared-library environmental variable. The installation instructions explain this in detail.

One additional step is required: configuring the Apache Web server to execute your Rexx scripts. To configure Apache, just edit its configuration file and restart the server for the changes to take effect. Apache's configuration file is typically named `http.conf` and is located in the Apache `conf` (configuration) directory. You must add lines to this file that:

❑ Load the Mod_Rexx module.

❑ Ensure that scripts with file extensions `*.rex` and `*.rexx` are processed by Mod_Rexx.

❑ Optionally define *Rexx Server Page*, or *RSP*, support.

The lines you add to the Apache configuration file should look similar to these:

```
# The following line needs to be added to the end of the appropriate
# httpd.conf LoadModule list.
#
LoadModule rexx_module modules/mod_rexx.dll

# The following lines should be added at the end of the http.conf file.
#
AddType application/x-httpd-rexx-script .rex .rexx
AddType application/x-httpd-rexx-rsp .rsp

# Add these for REXX Server Page support
#
RexxTempFileNameTemplate "c:/temp/execrsp?????.rex"
RexxRspCompiler "c:/Program Files/Apache Group/Apache2/bin/rspcomp.rex"
```

After reconfiguring this file, shut down and restart the Apache Web server so that the new directives take effect.

To test the install, start your browser and enter this line into its "address entry box:"

```
http://your.domain.com/test.rex
```

Replace the text `your.domain.com` with the name of your own server. This test runs a Rexx test script under Mod_Rexx and displays a simple Hypertext Markup Language (HTML) page.

Should you have any difficulty, Mod_Rexx comes with documentation that covers both installation and the relevant Apache directives. The documentation also gives complete information on the Mod_Rexx function library, the alternative object-oriented interface, special Rexx variables, and how to use Rexx Server Pages.

A sample script

Let's discuss how to write scripts that manage Apache through the Mod_Rexx interface. First, we'll describe the kinds of processing these scripts can perform; then we'll look at an sample program. The sample script reads input from a user of the Web server, and writes a Web page to his or her browser in response. It is a typical program in that it serves Web pages.

You can write scripts that take control from Apache at any point in its request processing. These are the processing phases during which your script might run:

1. Request
2. Post-read request
3. URI translation
4. Header parser
5. Access control
6. Authentication
7. Authorization
8. MIME type check
9. Fixup
10. Response
11. Logging
12. Cleanup
13. Wait
14. Post-read request

Most scripts are *response handlers* — they run during the Response phase of Step 10. Response handlers receive the user's input and write a Web page to his or her browser in response.

This scripting example is a response handler. The script creates a Web page that displays the value of the Mod_Rexx special variables. Appendix J lists the Mod_Rexx special variables. Each has a name that starts with the letters WWW. This script is one of the sample scripts distributed with the Mod_Rexx package. Here is the script:

```
/* these are some typical Apache return codes */
DECLINED  = -1    /* Module declines to handle */
OK        = 0     /* Module has handled this stage. */

/* get the Apache request record ptr */
r = arg(1)

/* set content-type and send the HTTP header */
call WWWSendHTTPHeader r, "text/html"
call WWWGetArgs r

/* start sending the html page */
say "<html>"
say "<head>"
say "<title>Sample HTML Page From Rexx</title>"
say "</head>"
say "<body>"
```

```
say "<h1>Sample HTML Page From Rexx</h1>"

say '<p>The Mod_Rexx version string is "'WWWGetVersion()'"'

say "<p>The following is the list of standard Rexx CGI variables and their values:"
say '<table border="1"><tr><th>Name</th><th>Value</th></tr>'
say "<tr><td>WWWAUTH_TYPE</td><td>"vorb(wwwauth_type)"</td></tr>"
say "<tr><td>WWWCONTENT_LENGTH</td><td>"vorb(wwwcontent_length)"</td></tr>"
say "<tr><td>WWWCONTENT_TYPE</td><td>"vorb(wwwcontent_type)"</td></tr>"
say "<tr><td>WWWGATEWAY_INTERFACE</td><td>"vorb(wwwgateway_interface)"</td></tr>"
say "<tr><td>WWWHTTP_USER_ACCEPT</td><td>"vorb(wwwhttp_user_accept)"</td></tr>"
say "<tr><td>WWWHTTP_USER_AGENT</td><td>"vorb(wwwhttp_user_agent)"</td></tr>"
say "<tr><td>WWWPATH_INFO</td><td>"vorb(wwwpath_info)"</td></tr>"
say "<tr><td>WWWPATH_TRANSLATED</td><td>"vorb(wwwpath_translated)"</td></tr>"
say "<tr><td>WWWQUERY_STRING</td><td>"vorb(wwwquery_string)"</td></tr>"
say "<tr><td>WWWREMOTE_ADDR</td><td>"vorb(wwwremote_addr)"</td></tr>"
say "<tr><td>WWWREMOTE_HOST</td><td>"vorb(wwwremote_host)"</td></tr>"
say "<tr><td>WWWREMOTE_IDENT</td><td>"vorb(wwwremote_ident)"</td></tr>"
say "<tr><td>WWWREMOTE_USER</td><td>"vorb(wwwremote_user)"</td></tr>"
say "<tr><td>WWWREQUEST_METHOD</td><td>"vorb(wwwrequest_method)"</td></tr>"
say "<tr><td>WWWSCRIPT_NAME</td><td>"vorb(wwwscript_name)"</td></tr>"
say "<tr><td>WWWSERVER_NAME</td><td>"vorb(wwwserver_name)"</td></tr>"
say "<tr><td>WWWSERVER_PORT</td><td>"vorb(wwwserver_port)"</td></tr>"
say "<tr><td>WWWSERVER_PROTOCOL</td><td>"vorb(wwwserver_protocol)"</td></tr>"
say "<tr><td>WWWSERVER_SOFTWARE</td><td>"vorb(wwwserver_software)"</td></tr>"
say "</table>"

say "<p>The following are some additional variables provided to the Rexx program:"
say '<table border="1"><tr><th>Name</th><th>Value</th></tr>'
say "<tr><td>WWWDEFAULT_TYPE</td><td>"vorb(wwwdefault_type)"</td></tr>"
say "<tr><td>WWWFILENAME</td><td>"vorb(wwwfilename)"</td></tr>"
say "<tr><td>WWWFNAMETEMPLATE</td><td>"vorb(wwwfnametemplate)"</td></tr>"
say "<tr><td>WWWIS_MAIN_REQUEST</td><td>"vorb(wwwis_main_request)"</td></tr>"
say "<tr><td>WWWRSPCOMPILER</td><td>"vorb(wwwrspcompiler)"</td></tr>"
say "<tr><td>WWWSERVER_ROOT</td><td>"vorb(wwwserver_root)"</td></tr>"
say "<tr><td>WWWUNPARSEDURI</td><td>"vorb(wwwunparseduri)"</td></tr>"
say "<tr><td>WWWURI</td><td>"vorb(wwwuri)"</td></tr>"
say "</table>"

say "</body>"
say "</html>"
return OK

/* vorb: return the value or a required space */
vorb:

if length(arg(1)) > 0 then return arg(1)
else return ' '
```

The first few lines in the script define two of the standard Apache return codes:

```
/* these are some typical Apache return codes */
DECLINED = -1    /* Module declines to handle */
OK       = 0     /* Module has handled this stage. */
```

The next line gets the main argument Apache always passes to every Rexx script. It contains a *request record pointer* used as an argument in the coding of subsequent Mod_Rexx functions:

```
/* get the Apache request record ptr */
r = arg(1)
```

Using this pointer, we can assign a *content type* to the responses that will be sent to the browser. This tells the browser how to interpret the Web page information it will receive next:

```
/* set content-type and send the HTTP header */
call WWWSendHTTPHeader r, "text/html"
```

Then this required statement gets the query string arguments from Apache:

```
call WWWGetArgs r
```

Now, the program can start creating its response to the user. This means writing HTML text to the browser. All the Rexx script really has to do is issue `say` instructions to send appropriate text strings. It begins by writing the page header information:

```
/* start sending the html page */
say "<html>"
say "<head>"
say "<title>Sample HTML Page From Rexx</title>"
say "</head>"
say "<body>"
say "<h1>Sample HTML Page From Rexx</h1>"
```

The next line invokes the `WWWGetVersion` function to get the Mod_Rexx version under which the script is running. The script displays this information on the Web page:

```
say '<p>The Mod_Rexx version string is "'WWWGetVersion()'"'
```

Now, the program issues a long series of `say` instructions. We won't repeat them all here, but here are the first few `say` statements:

```
say "<p>The following is the list of standard Rexx CGI variables and their values:"
say '<table border="1"><tr><th>Name</th><th>Value</th></tr>'
say "<tr><td>WWWAUTH_TYPE</td><td>"vorb(wwwauth_type)"</td></tr>"
say "<tr><td>WWWCONTENT_LENGTH</td><td>"vorb(wwwcontent_length)"</td></tr>"
```

Each `say` instruction displays the value of a different Mod_Rexx special variable on the Web page. These variables all begin with the letters `WWW`.

The program ends by closing the HTML tags and sending a return code string of `OK` to the caller:

```
say "</table>"

say "</body>"
say "</html>"
return OK
```

The code for a short internal function called `vorb` ends the program. This internal function is used in some of the `say` instructions to space output in a more attractive way.

That's all there is to it. Knowing just a few Mod_Rexx functions, you can take control of Apache to better customize Web pages and generate tailored output. This sample script shows how easy it is to get started. As your knowledge grows, the Mod_Rexx interface gives you the functions required to gain full scripting power over the Apache Web server.

Example — Rexx Server Pages

Rexx Server Pages, or *RSPs*, are similar to Java Server Pages or embedded PHP scripting. They allow you to embed Rexx code right into your HTML code. The benefit is that HTML pages can be dynamically created and altered at runtime. This customizes the Web page's response to the user.

To set up RSPs, you must configure Apache properly by giving it the appropriate directives and rebooting Apache. The install instructions above included the lines necessary to configure Apache to enable RSPs.

Just like server pages coded in other scripting languages, place your Rexx code directly within the HTML, and frame it between special markers. The delimiters must occur on their own line (without any other code). They identify the start and end points of Rexx code within the HTML. There are two kinds of delimiters: short and long. Use either within the HTML to identify your Rexx code:

Delimiter Type	Starts With	Ends With
short-form markers	<?rexx	?>
long-form markers	<script type="rexx">	</script>

Here is a sample RSP coded with *short delimiters* that show where the Rexx code starts and ends:

```
<p>The current date and time is
<?rexx
/* the following is a REXX statement */
say date() time()
?>
```

You can see that the Rexx code is embedded between the markers `<?rexx` and `?>`. This embedded code is simply standard Rexx. It enables programmability within the HTML code. The delimiter markers serve to identify the Rexx code and isolate it as opposed to native HTML code.

Here is the exact same example coded with *long delimiters*:

```
<p>The current date and time is
<script type="rexx">
/* the following is a REXX statement */
say date() time()
</script>
```

As in the example using short delimiters, this example shows how you can embed Rexx code directly within your HTML code that defines Web pages.

When RSP-enabled code is referenced, Mod_Rexx takes these steps to run it:

1. It creates a temporary file.

2. The *RSP compiler* compiles the RSP file into a Rexx program and places it in the temporary file.

3. It runs the compiled Rexx program.

4. It erases the temporary file.

Rexx Server Pages allow you to capitalize on your knowledge of Rexx in creating dynamic server pages. They present an alternative to coding in languages like Java Server Pages or PHP.

Further Information

For further information, visit the Mod_Rexx project pages hosted by SourceForge at http://source forge.net/projects/modrexx. Also, there is an excellent article on Mod_Rexx entitled "Harnessing Apache for REXX Programming" by W. David Ashley. It is available at IBM's DeveloperWorks site at the URL www-128.ibm.com/developerworks/opensource/library/os-modrexx/index.html. If the Web address has changed, locate the article by searching under its name either at IBM's Web site at www.ibm.com, or in any common search engine such as Google or AltaVista.

Summary

Two popular ways to script Web servers are CGI and the Mod_Rexx interface into Apache. This chapter describes both. Rexx scripts can manage almost any aspect of these popular Web server products, but most scripts run in response to a user request. These scripts serve Web pages to users.

We looked at three tools: the CGI/Rexx library from Stanford Linear Accelerator Laboratory, the Internet/REXX HHNS WorkBench from Henri Henault & Sons, and Apache's Mod_Rexx interface. The sample script for the first package read a user's form input and simply echoed it back to a Web page. It illustrates all the basics of CGI programming, and showed how the functions of the CGI/Rexx library simplify Web serving. The sample script for the second function library writes a Web page that includes a list of programs and their descriptions. It illustrates a little more advanced CGI programming, this time based on the package from Henri Henault & Sons. The final programming example uses Apache's Mod_Rexx interface. It serves a Web page that lists all of the Mod_Rexx package's special variables.

The sample programs were very brief and are intended to show how to get set up and started with these tools. For further information and complete documentation, visit the Web sites listed during the discussions where these tools can be freely obtained.

Test Your Understanding

1. Could you write Rexx/CGI scripts without using any of the packages this chapter describes? What would be the downside to this?

2. In the cgi-lib.rxx library, what functions do you use to write standard headers and footers on Web pages? What is a Content Type header and what function do you use to write it? What function(s) read user inputs?

3. In the Internet/REXX HHNS WorkBench, what functions typically begin and end scripts? What function do you use to write the Content Type header? What function inserts a hyperlink into the output Web page?

4. What is Mod_Rexx and what does it do? Does Mod_Rexx have all the same capabilities as mod_perl and mod_php? Compare Apache and Mod_Rexx to CGI. Which yields better Web server performance? Why?

5. What are Rexx Server Pages? Why are they useful? How do you create them?

6. What are short-form and long-form delimiters? Is there any functional difference between them?

7. You need to customize Apache's log processing. How can this be accomplished?

18

XML and Other Interfaces

Overview

There are more free and open-source Rexx interfaces and tools than one book can possibly cover, so this book just introduces a few of the most popular. This chapter describes XML programming with a package called *RexxXML*. It tells how to write scripts that manipulate XML and HTML data files and how to accomplish other XML-related tasks.

To start, we'll define what XML is, and what related terms like XSLT, XPath, and HTML mean. Then we'll look at the kinds of processing you can accomplish using the RexxXML package. After that, we'll briefly discuss the functions in RexxXML, including those for document tree parsing, document tree searching, XSLT processing, and schema validation. After we discuss how to download and install RexxXML, we'll illustrate specific XML operations, such as how to load and process XML documents, how to process documents, how to validate documents, and how to process them against an XSLT stylesheet. With this background, we'll review a script that uses RexxXML to read a Web page, identify a specific data element within that Web page, and compare the value of the data element to the version of RexxXML used within the script. The script uses the Web page to determine if a more recent version of RexxXML is available than the user has installed.

The chapter concludes by mentioning many other free and open-source Rexx tools, packages, and interfaces. Most can be found on the Web and freely downloaded just by entering their name into a popular search engine like Google, Yahoo!, or AltaVista.

XML with RexxXML

Extensible Markup Language, or *XML*, is a data description language. *XML files* are text files that contain both data and descriptive tags for that data. XML files offer a self-explanatory way to store, transport, and communicate data. They are often used for standardized data interchange between different organizations or between different application systems within the same company.

XPath is a standard for identifying and extracting parts of XML documents. *Extensible Stylesheet Language Transformations*, or *XSLT*, applies definitional templates called *stylesheets* to XML files. XSLT separates data from the format in which it appears. *Hypertext Markup Language*, or *HTML*, is the language in which many Web pages are defined. It is a predecessor technology to XML and XSLT.

XML and its related technologies have become popular as a way to provide self-descriptive, self-validating data. They underlie the construction of the internet and data transfer between many organizations.

RexxXML is an external function library that supports common XML operations. Rexx scripts use it to parse, transform, analyze and generate XML files. RexxXML goes well beyond XML itself to support HTML, XML dialects, XPath, and XSLT.

RexxXML is built on top of `libxml` and `libxslt`. These two free products are part of the XML C parser and toolkit of the Gnome open-source project. Based on every imaginable XML-related standard (and there are quite a few of them!), these function libraries give programmers a full range of XML capabilities. RexxXML brings most of these functions to Rexx programmers.

RexxXML has a wide range of features. Here are a few of the things you can do with it:

- ❑ Process XML, XML dialects, and HTML data from within Rexx scripts
- ❑ Access documents through URLs or Rexx variables
- ❑ Search and modify document contents
- ❑ Extract data from within documents
- ❑ Convert non-XML data into XML documents
- ❑ Validate XML documents via Schemas
- ❑ Scan Web pages (HTML files) and identify or extract information
- ❑ Transform XML data via XSLT
- ❑ Extend XSLT
- ❑ Use arbitrary precision arithmetic in XSLT transformations
- ❑ Use it as a macro language for an application based on `libxml`
- ❑ Send data to an HTTP server and retrieve non-XML data from HTTP and FTP servers
  The RexxXML library contains roughly 50 functions. They can be categorized into these self-descriptive groups:

- ❑ Housekeeping routines
- ❑ Document tree parsing
- ❑ Document tree searching
- ❑ XSLT processing
- ❑ Schema validation
- ❑ Communications with HTTP and FTP servers
- ❑ C-language interface

Here are the RexxXML functions along with brief descriptions (see the RexxXML documentation for more detailed code-oriented descriptions):

- ❏ *Housekeeping* — The housekeeping functions load the RexxXML library for use by a script, delete the library from memory when a script finishes using it, and returns version and error information to scripts:

  - ❏ `xmlLoadFuncs` — Register RexxXML functions, initialize ML/XSLT libraries

  - ❏ `xmlDropFuncs` — Ends the use of RexxXML functions, frees library resources

  - ❏ `xmlVersion` — Returns the version of the XML and XSLT libraries

  - ❏ `xmlError` — Returns error message text since the most recent call

  - ❏ `xmlFree` — Releases object's memory

- ❏ *Document Tree Parsing* — RexxXML uses the *document tree* as its underlying processing paradigm. The functions in this group allow scripts to create or retrieve document trees, to perform various parsing and update operations on them, and to save them to disk when done:

  - ❏ `xmlParseXML` — Parses XML data, returns 0 or a document tree

  - ❏ `xmlNewDoc` — Creates a new, empty XML document tree

  - ❏ `xmlParseHTML` — Parses HTML data, returns 0 or a document tree

  - ❏ `xmlNewHTML` — Creates a new HTML document tree

  - ❏ `xmlSaveDoc` — Writes a document tree to a URL, or returns it as a string

  - ❏ `xmlFreeDoc` — Frees a document tree

  - ❏ `xmlExpandNode` — Puts data from *node* into a stem

  - ❏ `xmlNodeContent` — Returns the content of *node* as a string

  - ❏ `xmlAddElement` — Creates a new element and adds it as a node

  - ❏ `xmlAddAttribute` — Creates a new attribute and adds it to a node

  - ❏ `xmlAddText` — Creates a text node and adds it as a child to a node

  - ❏ `xmlAddPI` — Creates a processing instruction and adds it as a child to a node

  - ❏ `xmlAddComment` — Creates a comment and adds it as a child to a node

  - ❏ `xmlAddNode` — Creates a new node and adds it as a child of another node

  - ❏ `xmlCopyNode` — Creates a new node as a copy of another

  - ❏ `xmlRemoveAttribute` — Removes attribute(s) from a node

  - ❏ `xmlRemoveContent` — Removes children of node(s)

  - ❏ `xmlRemoveNode` — Removes node(s) from a document tree

- ❑ *Document Tree Searching* — These functions are specifically concerned with parsing and analyzing document trees. They give scripts the ability to inspect documents and better understand their contents, without having to program these operations explicitly or at length in scripts:

  - ❑ `xmlEvalExpression` — Evalutes XPath expression and returns result as a string

  - ❑ `xmlFindNode` — Evaluates XPath expression and returns result as a nodeset

  - ❑ `xmlNodesetCount` — Returns number of nodes in a nodeset

  - ❑ `xmlNodesetItem` — Returns specified node from a nodeset

  - ❑ `xmlCompileExpression` — Converts an expression to a quick ("compiled") form

  - ❑ `xmlFreeExpression` — Frees a compiled expression

  - ❑ `xmlNewContext` — Allocates a new context

  - ❑ `xmlSetContext` — Changes or sets the context node

  - ❑ `xmlFreeContext` — Frees the context(s)

  - ❑ `xmlNodesetAdd` — Adds specified nodes to a nodeset.

- ❑ *XSLT Processing* — These functions work with and apply XSLT stylesheets to documents:

  - ❑ `xmlParseXSLT` — Parses and compiles an XSLT stylesheet

  - ❑ `xmlFreeStylesheet` — Free compiled stylesheet(s)

  - ❑ `xmlApplyStylesheet` — Applies the XSLT stylesheet to a document

  - ❑ `xmlOutputMethod` — Reports the output method of a stylesheet

- ❑ *Schema Validation* — These functions automate the process of schema validation, that is, ensuring that documents correctly match the specifications embodied in their related schemas:

  - ❑ `xmlParseSchema` — Parses a document schema

  - ❑ `xmlValidateDoc` — Validates a document according to a stylesheet

  - ❑ `xmlFreeSchema` — Frees schema document(s)

  - ❑ `xmlDumpSchema` — Writes schema(s) to a file (ususally for debugging)

- ❑ *HTTP and FTP* — These two functions retrieve data from URLs:

  - ❑ `xmlPost` — Sends an HTTP `post` command to a URL and returns result

  - ❑ `xmlGet` — Retrieves data from a URL

- ❑ *C-language Interface* — These two functions implement the C-language interface for the RexxXML library. The function library can be used as a set of callable routines from C programs, as well as from with Rexx scripts:

  - ❑ `rexxXMLInit` — Registers the XML library and initializes

  - ❑ `rexxXMLFini` — Ends XML library usage, frees resources

Licensing, downloading, and installation

RexxXML runs under operating systems in the Windows, Linux, Unix, and OS/2 families. It is free software, distributed without charge or warranty, under the Mozilla Public License. The terms of the license are explained in the documentation that downloads with the product. As licensing terms sometimes change, be sure to read the license prior to using the product.

RexxXML is tested with the Regina Rexx interpreter. It can be used with other Rexx implementations that can register and load external functions but is not formally tested with them.

RexxXML downloads as a single compressed file containing either binaries or source. Downloads include a complete guidebook in Adobe `*.pdf` format. Entitled *RexxXML Usage and Reference*, it is written by the author of the product, Patrick T. J. McPhee. The guide offers an excellent introduction to XML and related subjects like XPath, XSLT, and schemas. It also contains the complete function reference manual and a quick reference guide.

The first step in installing RexxXML is to download and install its prerequisites, the `libxml` and `libxslt` products. These free products are distributed under the MIT License and are downloadable at `http://xmlsoft.org`. They are available for almost any operating system as either binaries or source. The decompressed files include installation instructions that follow typical procedures for Windows, Linux, or Unix. Documentation for the products is at `http://xmlsoft.org/docs.html`. That Web site also offers good tutorials and introductory information on XML programming, the XML standards, dialects, related standards, and the like.

Download and install RexxXML. Download sites include `www.interlog.com/~ptjm` and `www.interlog.com/~ptjm/software.html`. As with `libxml` and `libxslt`, if any Web addresses have changed, merely enter the product name into a popular search engine such as Google or Yahoo! to locate other download sites. RexxXML installs in the same manner we've seen in previous chapters covering interfaces such as Rexx/SQL, Rexx/Tk, Rexx/DW, and Rexx/gd. The RexxXML Windows Dynamic Link Library, or DLL, is named `rexxxml.dll`; the Linux or Unix shared library has the same root name. As always, ensure that the proper environmental variable points to the library directory so that the interpreter can find and load the external functions.

Common operations

We've mentioned the wide variety of operations scripts can perform using the RexxXML functions. In this section, we'll review short code snippets that show how to perform several of the most common operations. The specific operations we'll explore include:

- ❑ How to load the RexxXML library for use
- ❑ How to load, transform, and save XML documents
- ❑ How to verify if a document is well formed and how to validate it
- ❑ How to create XML documents
- ❑ Simple ways to parse documents
- ❑ How to apply a stylesheet to a document

First, let's look at how to load the RexxXML external function library for use. A script must register and load the RexxXML library prior to using any of its functions. This is accomplished in a manner similar to registering and loading the Rexx/Tk, Rexx/DW, or Rexx/gd libraries:

```
call RxFuncAdd 'xmlloadfuncs','rexxxml','xmlloadfuncs'
if xmlloadfuncs() <> 0 then say 'ERROR- Cannot load RexxXML library!'
```

All RexxXML functions are now available to the script. Invoke the xmlDropFuncs function to deregister the library and free resources when all XML processing is complete.

Many scripts load, process or transform, and save an XML document. Figure 18-1 diagrams how this interaction typically occurs.

Processing Documents

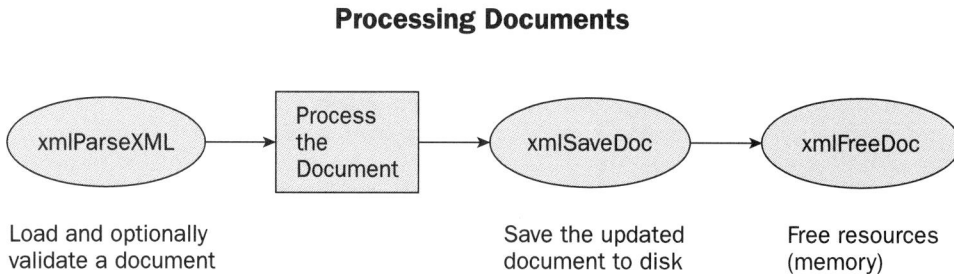

Figure 18-1

The xmlParseXML function accesses or loads a *well-formed* (syntactically correct) document:

```
document = xmlParseXML('test_file.xml')          /* document must be well formed */
```

An optional argument specifies whether the *Document Type Definiton*, or *DTD*, should be referenced and the XML file validated. Here are a couple examples:

```
document = xmlParseXML('test_file.xml', , 'V') /* validate the file            */
document = xmlParseXML('test_file.xml', , 'D') /* load the DTD, do not validate */
```

Applying xmlParseXML to a document that is not well formed returns 0. The same return code indicates an attempt to validate an invalid document.

After processing or transforming the file, the script can write it to disk:

```
call xmlSaveDoc  'test_file.xml', document      /* save the document for later  */
```

Always free resources after finishing with the data by calling the xmlFreeDoc function:

```
call xmlFreeDoc  document                       /* end processing, free reources*/
```

Now that we've seen how to load, validate, and save XML documents, let's see how to create them. This is just a matter of string processing—splicing and pasting data together with the proper descriptive tags. Assuming that the data is in the chunks array, here's how to build a simple, prototypical XML document. Each data item is written with the proper beginning and ending descriptive tags:

```
data = '<data>'
do j = 1 to number_of_chunks
    data = data || '<chunk>' || chunk.j || '</chunk>'
end
data = data || '</data>'                       /* add the end tag            */
```

Of course, building XML files can be much more complicated than our simple example. RexxXML provides the full set of required functions.

To add data to an existing document, a script creates the right type of node and inserts it into the proper location within the document tree. xmlAddElement is the function to use. Other useful functions for adding information to documents include xmlAddAttribute, xmlAddText, xmlAddPI, xmlAddComment, xmlAddNode, and xmlCopyNode. Figure 18-2 summarizes how scripts can add or remove data from documents through appropriate RexxXML functions.

Updating Documents

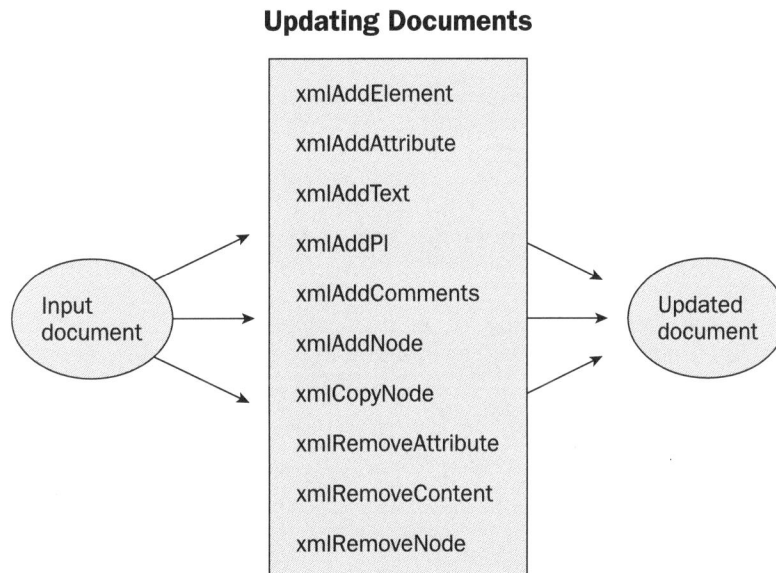

Figure 18-2

Processing an XML document means understanding and parsing its tree structure. This allows scripts to search, analyze, and transform XML documents. One approach to processing a document is to expand its document tree into a Rexx array or *stem* containing all the relevant data. The xmlExpandNode function accomplishes this. After issuing this function, scripts can traverse the data in the tree and analyze the document. You can access attribute values by using a tail for the stem that names the attribute.

XPath is another option for searching document trees and analyzing data. Figure 18-3 below diagrams how programs use XPath to process documents.

XPath for Document Processing

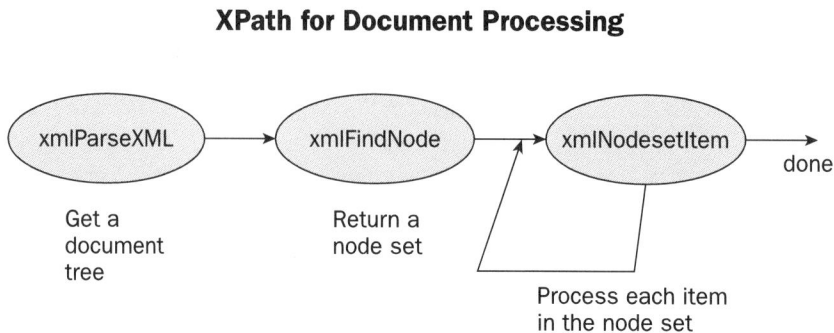

Figure 18-3

The xmlFindNode function returns a *node set* representing a document subtree, from which individual items can be extracted by xmlNodesetItem. xmlNodesetCount tells how many items are in a node set. Look at this example:

```
document = xmlParseXML(filename)                 /* yields a document tree   */
nodeset = xmlFindNode('//Root_Element', document) /* returns a node set       */
do j = 1 to xmlNodesetCount(nodeset)             /* while a node to process */
   call process xmlNodesetItem(nodeset, j)       /*    process a node        */
end
```

This code starts with the document tree or nodeset off the root element. It converts each eligible node in the document into an array and calls the routine named process to work with these nodes.

Validating documents against *schemas* (or data definitions) is another important operation. Schemas are read from files, Rexx variables, or the XSD environment. The four main functions applied to them are xmlParseSchema, xmlValidateDoc, xmlFreeSchema, and xmlDumpSchema.

To validate a document, use the xmlValidateDoc function. xmlValidateDoc validates a document against a schema and returns the string OK if the document matches it. Otherwise it returns a character string describing the problem. Here's an example that validates the document named document against a schema named xsd_to_use:

```
status = xmlValidateDoc(xsd_to_use, document)
if  status <> 'OK' then do
    say 'Document did not validate ok, status is:'  status
    say 'Here is more information:' xmlError()
end
```

The xmlError function returns the accumulated error and warning messages since the last time it was called. Use it as a generic function to return further information when an error occurs.

Applying XSLT stylesheets is as easy as document validation, in that it only involves four functions: `xmlParseXSLT`, `xmlFreeStylesheet`, `xmlApplyStylesheet`, and `xmlOutputMethod`. XSLT data can be read from a file, read from a Rexx expression, or taken from the environment. Figure 18-4 diagrams how scripts can apply stylesheets to documents.

Applying a Stylesheet to a Document

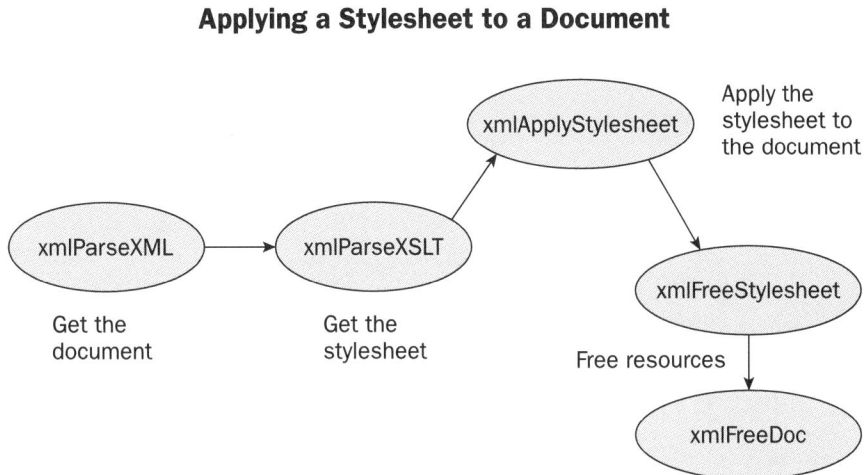

Figure 18-4

Here is an example that shows how to apply stylesheets to documents. It applies the stylesheet named in the first parameter of the `xmlApplyStylesheet` function to the document named in the second. That function returns the result tree:

```
document = xmlParseXML('test_file.xml')    /* get the document to process    */
stylesht = xmlParseXSLT('style_sheet.xsl') /* get the stylesheet to use on it */

new_document = xmlApplyStylesheet(stylesht, document)

call xmlFreeStylesheet stylesht            /* free the Stylesheet when done   */
call xmlFreeDoc document                   /* free the Document when done     */
```

The final two statements in this example free the stylesheet and the document after processing is complete. In working with XML it's a good idea to always free resources after the script has completed processing the items.

A sample script

RexxXML ships with a couple dozen sample programs. All come complete with appropriate `*.xml`, `*.xsd`, `*.xsl`, and `*.html` input files. The bundled manual *RexxXML Usage and Reference* discusses several of the examples in detail.

Let's take a look at an sample script. It appears courtesy of the author of RexxXML, Patrick T. J. McPhee. This sample script is called `iscurrent.rex`. It reads an HTML Web page. It scans the Web page and extracts a data element from items in a table in that Web page. The data item it extracts is the most current version for the RexxXML software package. The script compares that version to the one the script itself is using. If the Web version is newer, the script informs the user that a newer version of RexxXML than the one he or she is using is available.

This script demonstrates how to access an HTML Web page, how to scan it, and how to extract information from it.

Here is the script:

```
/* check software.html to see if we're up-to-date
 *
 * $Header: C:/ptjm/rexx/rexxxml/trip/RCS/iscurrent.rex 1.3 2003/10/31 17:16:45
ptjm Rel $
 */

rcc = rxfuncadd('XMLLoadFuncs', 'rexxxml', 'xmlloadfuncs')

if rcc then do
  say rxfuncerrmsg()
  exit 1
  end

call xmlloadfuncs

software.html = 'http://www.interlog.com/~ptjm/software.html'

parse value xmlVersion() with myversion .
package = 'RexxXML'

sw = xmlParseHTML(software.html)

if sw = 0 then do
  say xmlError()
  exit 1
  end

/* software.html has a single table. Each row of the table has the
   package name in the first column, and the version number in the second.
   The first occurrence of the package is the most current one. */

prow = xmlFindNode('/html/body/table/tbody/tr[td[1] = $package][1]', sw)
if xmlNodesetCount(prow) \= 1 then do
  say 'unexpected row count' xmlNodesetCount(prow)
  exit 1
  end

curver = xmlEvalExpression('td[2]', xmlNodesetItem(prow, 1))

if curver \= myversion then do
    say 'My version is' myversion
    say 'Current version is' curver
    say 'which was released'  xmlEvalExpression('td[3]', xmlNodesetItem(prow, 1))
    end
else
    say 'All up-to-date!'
```

The script initializes by registering and loading the RexxXML library:

```
rcc = rxfuncadd('XMLLoadFuncs', 'rexxxml', 'xmlloadfuncs')

if rcc then do
  say rxfuncerrmsg()
  exit 1
  end

call xmlloadfuncs
```

This initialization code would typically appear at the start of any RexxXML script. It is very similar in design to the code in previous chapters that loads and registers other external function libraries, for example, those for Rexx/SQL, Rexx/Tk or Rexx/DW. Note that the `rxfuncerrmsg` function is specific to Regina Rexx. It returns the most recently occurring error message. If you're not using Regina, leave this statement out your code. We recommend replacing it with your own error message concerning the problem.

Following initialization, this line specifies the URL (or Web page address) of the HTML Web page to analyze:

```
software.html = 'http://www.interlog.com/~ptjm/software.html'
```

This next line retrieves the version of RexxXML the script is running under:

```
parse value xmlVersion() with myversion .
```

The version this statement retrieves will later be compared to that on the Web page. If they differ, the script knows that a newer version of the RexxXML package is available and reports that finding in its concluding statements.

This code parses the HTML Web page into a variable as a document tree. A return code of 0 means that parsing failed, and results in a call to `xmlError` for more information:

```
sw = xmlParseHTML(software.html)

if sw = 0 then do
  say xmlError()
  exit 1
  end
```

Now that the code has retrieved the Web page HTML and parsed it into a document tree, it must inspect a table within the HTML that lists software packages and their versions. The header of the table describes its contents:

```
<thead>
<tr>
<td width="20%">Package</td>
<td width="10%">Version</td>
<td width="20%">Date</td>
<td width="50%">Notes</td>
</tr>
</thead>
```

The next program statement retrieves the row from the table that refers to the most recent version of the RexxXML package. The program knows that the first occurrence of the package in the table in the most recent one. It uses the following statement, with its XPath expression, to retrieve the appropriate information from the table:

```
prow = xmlFindNode('/html/body/table/tbody/tr[td[1] = $package][1]', sw)
```

Now, this statement extracts the `Version` data element from the row just retrieved. Together with the previous statement, this operation requires coding that is a bit detailed. For right now, just concentrate on what the statements do. They retrieve the appropriate data element, the RexxXML version, from the HTML table:

```
curver = xmlEvalExpression('td[2]', xmlNodesetItem(prow, 1))
```

The final lines of the program compare this version to that under which the script runs. It displays a message as to whether they differ:

```
if curver \= myversion then do
    say 'My version is' myversion
    say 'Current version is' curver
    say 'which was released'  xmlEvalExpression('td[3]', xmlNodesetItem(prow, 1))
    end
else
    say 'All up-to-date!'
```

This sample script illustrates how easy it is to process and analyze a Web page or document with the RexxXML functions. The package offers much more capability than can be shown here. It saves a lot of string processing work that scripts would otherwise have to perform themselves in order to process XML. Readers are urged to download the RexxXML product, review its examples, and read the documentation.

Other Rexx Tools, Interfaces and Extensions

While no one knows how many Rexx users there worldwide, IBM Corporation has estimated that there are up to one million. Such a large user base inevitably spawns a large collection of open-source and free tools. There are literally too many Rexx tools, utilities, extensions and interfaces to track them all. Appendix H lists some of the available tools and hints at their breadth. All are either open-source or free software.

You can locate most of these tools simply by entering their names as search keywords in any prominent search engine, such as Google, Yahoo!, or AltaVista. Many of the tools are also accessible from the home pages of the various Rexx interpreters discussed in Chapters 20 through 30. Just go to one of the Rexx product home pages, as provided in Chapters 20 through 30, and you'll often see lists of add-on products that run with that interpreter.

Summary

This chapter explores the free RexxXML package for processing XML files. RexxXML provides almost any function needed to work with XML, HTML, XPath, XSLT, and related data description languages. Combined with the string manipulation strengths of Rexx scripts, RexxXML makes XML processing quick and straightforward.

This chapter defined what terms like XML, XSLT, XPath, and HTML mean. We investigated the kinds of XML processing that the RexxXML package makes possible. We briefly discussed the functions in RexxXML, including those for document tree parsing, document tree searching, XSLT processing, and schema validation. And we discussed specific XML operations, such as how to load and process XML documents, how to process documents, how to validate documents, and how to process them against XSLT stylesheets. We reviewed one of the sample scripts that ships with the RexxXML package. The sample script demonstrates how to access a Web site, download an HTML page for processing, and how to scan that Web page and extract a relevant data element. In all, we saw that RexxXML is a comprehensive package that makes working with XML and its related technologies much simpler.

There are dozens of other add-in interfaces and tools for Rexx developers. In Chapters 15 through 18, we discussed a few of the most widely used packages and demonstrated how to use them. While we could only skim the surface of these products in the limited space available, the material did provide an introduction sufficient to get you started with the tools. Appendix H lists several dozen more free and open-source Rexx interfaces and tools along with brief functional descriptions. Most can be found for free download on the Internet merely by entering their names into any popular search engine, such as Google, AltaVista, or Yahoo!. New Rexx function libraries and utilities are continually being produced.

Test Your Understanding

1. What is the relationship between HTML, XML, XPath, and XSLT? What role does each play? Why is self-describing data useful? What language is used to build Web pages?

2. How can you validate a document against a schema? What RexxXML functions do you use to load documents and save them?

3. If you wanted to write a script to automatically scan Web pages and extract information, what RexxXML functions would you use? How do you ensure that the script dynamically connects to the Web page to analyze?

4. Does Rexx include regular expressions? If you wanted to add regular expressions to your scripts, how would you do this?

5. What RexxXML functions would you use to apply a stylesheet to a document?

Part II

Evolution and Implementations

Overview

You have reached the point in this book and in your understanding of Rexx that you know the core language. Now it is time to explore more deeply the many platforms, problems, and situations to which Rexx applies. Let's expand our knowledge into advanced Rexx.

This chapter outlines the history and evolution of Rexx. Discussing the evolution of the language shows how it has migrated across platforms and addressed new developer needs over time. This is useful in analyzing where Rexx fits into your own organization and how you can capitalize on its strengths as a universal scripting tool.

This chapter analyzes the roles Rexx fulfills, as a scripting language, macro language, shell extension, application programming interface, object-oriented scripting tool, mainframe command language, and vehicle for programming handheld devices. It discusses where different Rexx implementations fit into this picture. It describes the "personalities" of the various Rexx intepreters and when and where you might want to use each. It also introduces a methodology for comparing Rexx interpreters to one another. The methodology can be used, too, for comparing Rexx against other scripting and programming language alternatives. Different projects and different organizations have different needs. No one interpreter is best for every situation. This chapter helps you compare and contrast interpreters and discusses some of the roles of the various Rexx products.

This chapter also introduces the remainder of the book. The chapters that follow, Chapters 20 through 30, discuss specific Rexx interpreters. Each describes the strengths of an interpreter, where it runs, how to download and install it, and its features that extend beyond the Rexx standards. The upcoming chapters offer sample scripts that demonstrate many of the interpreter extensions and how they can be leveraged on specific platforms. The goal is to provide you with interpreter- and platform- specific information.

Rexx interpreters run the gamut of platforms and applications. Some emphasize portability, while others emphasize platform-specific extensions and leverage platform-unique features. Some target handhelds, while others target mainframes. Some are object-oriented, while one offers an alternative to Java programming (it runs under the Java Virtual Machine and even generates Java code!). The upcoming chapters in this book explore all these applications. This chapter lays the groundwork by giving you background on how these products evolved, and by briefly profiling the different Rexx interpreters and their uses.

The upcoming chapters go beyond the fundamentals of classic Rexx covered to this point and expand into the extended features of Rexx as it runs on different platforms. Now that you have a good grasp of the Rexx language, it is time to explore further the many ways in which Rexx can be applied to various problems in different environments. But first, we take a step back. We need to understand how Rexx evolved, why different interpreters are available, and some of the differences among them.

The Evolution of Rexx

Let's start by discussing how Rexx was invented and how it has evolved. This helps us understand why there are many different Rexx interpreters today, and how they came to be. Understanding the larger picture is useful in assessing the various uses of Rexx and the differences among Rexx interpreters.

Rexx was invented in 1979 by Michael Cowlishaw at IBM's UK laboratories. It evolved into its present form in the early 1980s. Rexx stands for *REstructured eXtended eXecutor*. Rexx is sometimes written in all-uppercase as REXX.

Rexx was designed to fulfill the promise of *scripting languages* — as general-purpose, high-productivity, easy-to-use vehicles for the quick solution of programming problems. Rexx was designed to be easy to use, yet powerful and flexible. These two design goals — ease of use and power — normally conflict. The specific goal in Rexx was to bring them together. This contrasts with the goals of many other scripting languages, which include:

❑ Addressing a specific problem space

❑ Fulfilling the personal goals or tastes of their inventors

❑ Compatibility with earlier languages

❑ Optimizing machines resources (CPU cycles or memory)

❑ Ease of interpreter writing

The goal with Rexx was to develop a general-purpose language that would be used by the widest possible cross-section of people and would fit their needs. Presciently anticipating how the Internet would drive cooperative software development more than a decade later, inventor Cowlishaw offered free use of Rexx within IBM's network and solicited suggestions and recommendations. He got it in abundance, frequently answering hundreds of emails with ideas every day. This feedback was critical in shaping the language as user-friendly yet powerful. The result is that Rexx distinguishes itself in its design and capabilities from other scripting languages, such as Perl, Tcl/Tk, Python, VBScript, shell languages, and Ruby.

Any programming language ultimately faces the popularity test. As Rexx spread throughout IBM, IBM's customers became aware of the language and demanded it. IBM complied by shipping Rexx as the scripting language for its VM mainframes. Soon IBM bundled Rexx with all versions of its mainframe operating systems, including OS and VSE.

In the early 1990s, IBM developed a strategy for common software across all their computers. They called it *Systems Application Architecture*, or *SAA*. IBM selected Rexx as its official *command procedure language* across all its operating systems. The result was that IBM has bundled Rexx with all its operating systems ever since, including i5/OS (previously known as OS/400), and OS/2.

Others soon picked up IBM's enthusiasm for the language. Microsoft offered Rexx as the Windows scripting language in the Windows 2000/NT Resource Kits. (The company later dropped Rexx in order to proprietarize Windows scripting. It did this by promoting its own nonstandard tools such as VBScript). Several other systems, including the Amiga, bundled Rexx as their main OS scripting language.

By the 1990s, Rexx had become quite popular. But it was still widely considered an IBM product — even if this view was not entirely accurate. Two events transformed Rexx from an IBM language into a universal scripting language:

❑ The American National Standards Institute (ANSI) standardized Rexx in 1996. This gave it international imprimatur and prestige and transferred control of the language from IBM to a recognized standards organization.

❑ The free software movement.

The result is that today free Rexx runs on virtually every known platform, from handhelds, to laptops and desktops, to midrange servers of all kinds, to the largest mainframes. There are very few platforms on which Rexx does not run. There are at least eight free Rexx interpreters, and IBM has estimated that there are up to one million Rexx programmers worldwide.

Figure 19-1 pictorially displays the cross-platform versatility of the free Rexx interpreters.

A survey by the Rexx Language Association indicated that half of Rexx users resided in the United States, while the other half were distributed over some 40 other countries.* Rexx users were well distributed among operating systems in the Windows, Unix, Linux, BSD, mainframe, and DOS families. What was once a mainframe-only language is no longer. Today, less than 20 percent of the users were on the mainframe. There were also users on many important "second tier" systems such as BeOS, VMS, eCS, OS/2, the Amiga, AROS, AtheOS/Syllable, the Macintosh, QNX, and many others. Rexx seems especially well suited to small devices like handhelds and smart phones. It runs natively on the three predominant handheld operating systems, Palm OS, Windows CE, and Symbian OS/EPOC32.

For a language to achieve this success, its *language definition* must coalesce at the right time. If a language is locked into definition too early, it may not evolve sufficiently and can ossify into a stunted form. On the other hand, if a language fails to acquire formal definition in time, it can fragment into a tower of babble. Or, when a formal definition does come along, there may be so many incompatible versions in use that the standard does not mean anything. (The BASIC language is an example. There are so many nonstandard versions of BASIC that the official language definition means little.)

Free Rexx Implementations

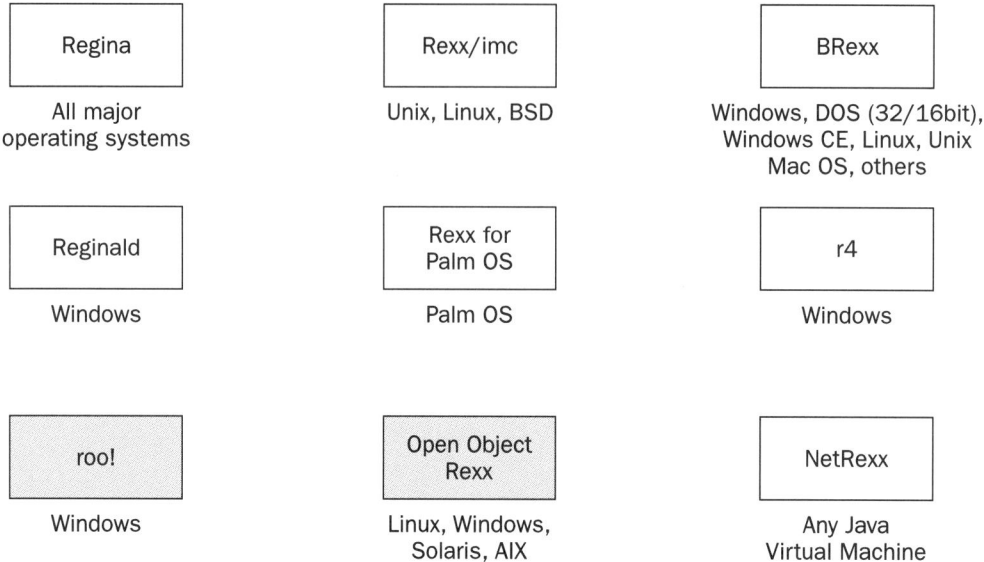

Regina	Rexx/imc	BRexx
All major operating systems	Unix, Linux, BSD	Windows, DOS (32/16bit), Windows CE, Linux, Unix Mac OS, others
Reginald	Rexx for Palm OS	r4
Windows	Palm OS	Windows
roo!	Open Object Rexx	NetRexx
Windows	Linux, Windows, Solaris, AIX	Any Java Virtual Machine

Figure 19-1

Rexx was lucky. Its inventor wrote a book to provide an informal language definition early on. *The Rexx Language* by Michael Cowlishaw (Prentice-Hall, 1985) crystalized the language and provided de facto direction for various implementations. With minor revisions, it was republished as a second edition in 1990. This edition is commonly referred to as *TRL-2* or *TRL2*.

American National Standards Institute promulgated their ANSI Rexx standard in 1996. The standard follows TRL-2 very closely and ties up a few minor loose ends. The ANSI-1996 standard finally gave Rexx the imprimatur and prestige of an international standards body. It is formally known as X3.274-1996 and was developed by ANSI technical committee X3J18. Chapter 13 enumerates the exact differences between the TRL-1, TRL-2 and ANSI-1996 standards.

Rexx is both *well documented* and *highly standardized*. This makes possible portable programming across the extremely wide variety of platforms on which Rexx runs. Chapter 13 made some recommendations about how to maximize the portability of Rexx scripts. These fundamentals also make skills transferable. If you can program Rexx on one platform, you can program it on any platform.

With the rise of object-oriented programming in the 1990s, two free object-oriented Rexx interpreters came out. IBM developed Object REXX and Kilowatt Software created roo! Both are supersets of classic Rexx; they run standard Rexx scripts without alteration. IBM's Object REXX became an open source product in early 2005. It is now called Open Object Rexx and is managed as an open source project by the Rexx Language Association.

As Java became a popular language for developing Web-based applications, IBM also developed NetRexx, a Rexx-like language that runs in the Java environment on the Java Virtual Machine (JVM). NetRexx scripts synergistically coexist with Java code. NetRexx scripts use Java classes and NetRexx can be used to create classes usable by Java programs. NetRexx can be used to write applets, servlets, applications, and Java Beans. NetRexx is also a free product.

Free Rexx Implementations

As you know, the examples in this book were tested using the Regina Rexx interpreter under Windows and Linux. We recommended that you start with Regina because it is an excellent open source Rexx that will run on any platform. Regina meets all Rexx standards and is the most popular free Rexx interpreter. It enjoys the largest user community and more interfaces are tested with Regina than any other Rexx interpreter.

The other Rexx interpreters offer benefits, too. It is time to explore them. There are at least six free "classic" Rexx interpreters:

- ❏　Regina
- ❏　Rexx/imc
- ❏　BRexx
- ❏　Reginald
- ❏　Rexx for Palm OS
- ❏　r4

There are also two free object-oriented versions of Rexx. Both are supersets of standard Rexx with additional object-oriented features. These are:

- ❏　roo!
- ❏　Open Object Rexx

Finally there is NetRexx, a Rexx-like language for programming in the Java environment. NetRexx is the only language listed here that does not meet the Rexx standards. It is best described as a "Rexx-like" language for the Java environment.

The following table lists the platforms, costs and licensing terms for all these products. Some are free regardless of the use to which you put them, while others are free for personal and nonprofit use but require a license fee for commercial use. Some are open source, while others are free but not open source. The license terms listed in the table are subject to change, so read the license for any free Rexx you download and agree to its terms before using the product. A convenient, one-stop list of most free software licenses is maintained by the Open Source Initiative or OSI at www.opensource.org/licenses.

Interpreter	Platforms	Cost/Licensing	Distribution	By
Regina	All platforms	Free. Open source. GNU Library or Lesser General Public License (LGPL)	Binaries or source	Original author Anders Christensen (Norway). Now Mark Hessling (Australia) and Florian Große-Coosmann (Germany)
Rexx/imc	Unix, Linux, BSD	Free. Copyrighted freeware. No warranty, distributed as is.	Binaries or source	Ian Collier (UK)
BRexx	Windows, Windows CE, 32-bit DOS, 16-bit DOS, Linux, Unix, Mac OS, Amiga, others	Freeware. Free for personal and nonprofit use; fee for commercial use.	Binaries or source	Vasilis Vlachoudis (Switzerland/France)
Reginald	Windows	Freeware. No warranty, distributed as is.	Windows Installer binaries	Jeff Glatt (USA)
r4	Windows	Freeware. Limited warranty.	Binaries	Kilowatt Software (USA)
Rexx for Palm OS	Palm OS	Shareware. Free for personal use, fee for commercial use.	Binaries	Jaxo (France)
Open Object Rexx (previously known as Object REXX)	Linux, Solaris, Windows, AIX	Free. Open source. Common Public License (CPL)	Binaries or source	Originally: Simon Nash, et al, IBM (UK). Today: Rexx Language Association
roo!	Windows	Freeware. Limited warranty.	Binaries	Kilowatt Software (USA)
NetRexx (A nonstandard Rexx-like language)	Any Java Virtual Machine (JVM)	Free. IBM License Agreement for Employee-Written Software.	Binaries for JVM	Michael Cowlishaw, IBM (UK)

Which Rexx?

Given that there are so many free Rexx interpreters, an important question is which one should you choose? The answer varies by project and by organization because different projects and organizations each have their own criteria. The *weighting* or relative importance of those criteria vary. For example, one organization might rank Windows GUI programming as their primary concern. r4, Reginald, or Regina might be their choice. Another organization might cite object-oriented programming as their goal. roo! and Open Object Rexx are their candidates.

No one interpreter is best for all situations — different projects have different criteria and will result in different "best" decisions. To determine which Rexx interpreter(s) are right for you, follow these steps:

1. List the selection criteria.

2. Rank the relative importance of the criteria to your project or organization.

3. Review the Rexx offerings in view of the ranked criteria.

The following series of tables starts the process. They list various criteria and suggest which Rexx interpreters fit each best. The lists are *not* definitive. They merely offer a starting point for your own analysis, as are the product characterizations in the rest of this chapter.

Criteria	Which Rexx?
Runs on nearly all platforms	Regina
Most widely used free Rexx	Regina
Largest user community	Regina
Meets 5.00 standard (ANSI-1996)	Regina
Meets 4.00 standard (TRL-2) OS, roo!, Open Object Rexx	Rexx/imc, BRexx, Reginald, r4, Rexx for Palm
Supports SAA API	Regina, Reginald, Rexx/imc (partial)
Longest record of support	Rexx/imc, BRexx, Regina, r4
Excellent tutorials	Reginald, r4, roo!, Rexx/imc
Most comprehensive documentation	Regina, Reginald
Fastest	BRexx
Smallest footprint	BRexx, Rexx for Palm OS, Regina
Can run in the shell	Regina
Has the most tested interfaces (Tk, DW, gd, SQL, XML, and many others)	Regina

Extensions for . . .	Which Rexx?
Windows	Reginald, r4, roo!, Regina
Linux/Unix/BSD	Rexx/imc, BRexx, Regina
Windows CE	BRexx
DOS	BRexx
Palm OS	Rexx for Palm OS
Compatibility with all other Rexx interpreters	Regina

Runs Natively on Handhelds	Which Rexx?
Palm OS	Rexx for Palm OS
Windows CE	BRexx
Symbian / EPOC32	Regina

Bundles	Which Rexx?
Bundled Windows GUI — most powerful	Reginald
Bundled Windows GUI — easiest	r4, roo!
Bundled database extensions	Reginald, BRexx
Bundled full-screen I/O extensions	BRexx

Object-Oriented	Which Rexx?
Object-oriented (OO) superset of classic Rexx	roo!, Open Object Rexx
Free OO Rexx for Windows	roo!, Open Object Rexx
Free OO Rexx for Linux, Solaris, and AIX	Open Object Rexx

Many organizations take a *weighted-ranking approach* to evaluating software. List all selection criteria in a spreadsheet and assign each criterion a rank (such as High, Medium, or Low, or a number between 1 and 10). Give each interpreter a rank for how well it fulfills each criterion. Multiply all criteria ranks by the weightings to derive an overall number for each product. The interpreter with the highest number best fits your requirements.

The next table shows how the weighted ranking approach works. Criteria for the project or organization are listed on the left-hand side of the chart, along with the priority for each. These will vary by project or company, as will their relative importance. Of course, your ranking chart will probably list more criteria than shown here; this is just an example of how to create the chart.

Criteria / –Rank–	Regina	Rexx/ imc	BRexx	Reginald	r4	Rexx for Palm OS	Open Object Rexx	roo!	NetRexx
Runs on our platforms/ --10--									
Performance / --5--									
Windows Extended / --1--									
Meets TRL-2 Standards/ --10--									
Total Weighted Scores =									

The free Rexx interpreters are listed across the top. Each column reflects the score for the interpreter versus the criteria. Multiply the score for each box times the rank or weight and add all rows to score a cumulative weighted ranking for each interpreter. This cumulative ranking is written for each interpreter in the last row of the chart.

Weighted-criteria comparison is useful for other kinds of evaluations in computer projects. For example, use it to determine which scripting language is most appropriate for a project or an organization. Rank Rexx versus other general-purpose scripting languages such as Perl, Tcl/Tk, Python, VBScript, the shell languages, Ruby and others. Just as in the comparison of different Rexx interpreters, different criteria and weightings tend to promote different tools as most the suitable for different projects.

Rexx Intepreters

The following table supplies more background on the free Rexx interpreters. All meet the TRL-2 standard except for NetRexx. Regina is the only interpreter that adds the improvements required to meet the ANSI-1996 standard. The differences between the ANSI-1996 and TRL-2 standards are very minor — see Chapter 13 for specifics.

The goal of this chart is to briefly summarize the Rexx interpreters. Following the chart, we sketch high-level profiles of each in separate paragraphs. Chapters 20 through 30 offer much more detail on the specific interpreters, their platforms, applications, and language extensions.

Interpreter	Language Level	Extra Functions and Features
Regina	5.00	Runs on every platform. The most popular free Rexx. The large user community means good support. *Many* extra functions from CMS, SAA, OS/2, and ARexx. Includes extensions from other Rexxes for compatibility with them. Compatibility documentation with detailed manual. Advanced C-like I/O. SAA interface to external function libraries. Tested with a wide variety of external function libraries and interfaces, including database I/O, Tk GUI, DW GUI, gd graphics, RexxXML, ISAM I/O, many others.
Rexx/imc	4.00	Unix- and Linux- oriented. Functions for C-like I/O, math, Unix environmental info. Includes other "C-like" and Unix-friendly extensions. Well adapted to Unix/Linux/BSD. Proven track record for long-term support.
BRexx	4.00	Extremely fast and runs on many platforms including resource-limited systems like Windows CE, DOS, tiny Linuxes. Functions for VM/CMS buffer control, math, C-like I/O, Windows CE, MySQL database interface, low-level PC control (view and change memory, for example). External function libraries for console I/O, ANSI-terminal I/O, DOS interface, PC file I/O, date/time, CGI scripting, ASCII-EBCDIC conversion. Runs natively on Windows CE.
Reginald	4.00	Customizes Rexx for Windows programmers. Includes many tools such as a Windows installer, GUI script launcher, and Rexx-aware editor. GUI dialog plus IDE, MIDI, file and directory functions, TCP/IP socket, speech, and math functions and interfaces. The "power platform" for Windows developers — supplies all the functions Windows developers need. Very nicely documented.
r4	4.00	Rexx tweaked for Windows with many tools for developers such as a GUI forms tool, color text file viewer and editor, over 135 windows command tools, visual accessories, XML to HTML auto-converter, GUI widgets, and so on. The only free classic Rexx from a company that also offers an upwardly compatible object-oriented Rexx. Excellent tutorials and sample scripts.

Interpreter	Language Level	Extra Functions and Features
Rexx for Palm OS	4.00	Rexx for the Palm OS. Glues applications and databases together in scripts that run without leaving the current application. Scripts can access all Palm data and resources, including TCP/IP, Infrared, and serial communications, console, clipboard, etc. Runs natively. Good sample scripts and easy-to-follow tutorials.
Open Object Rexx	superset of 4.00	Adds all object-oriented features to classic Rexx, including full class library and support for all object programming principles. Developed by IBM Corporation, it became open source in early 2005. Now enhanced and maintained by the Rexx Language Association. The most widely used object-oriented Rexx interpreter. Runs on Linuxes, Unixes, and Windows.
roo!	superset of 4.00	Adds all object-oriented features to classic Rexx, including full class library and support for all object programming principles. Upwardly compatible with r4, and uses all the same tools. Good tutorials bridge the gap between classic Rexx and object-oriented programming. An excellent free object-oriented Rexx for Windows.
NetRexx	nonstandard	A Rexx-like language that integrates with Java and runs on any Java Virtual Machine (JVM). Creates applets and applications. Uses the Java class library, and can be used to create classes used by Java programs as well as Java Beans. Brings Rexx's ease of use to the Java environment.

We emphasize that the material in this chapter is merely a starting point for your own investigations. Different projects and organizations have different needs. There is no one answer for everyone. Only you know what your needs are, so only you can select the right tool for the purpose you have in mind. With this background, let's briefly profile the different Rexx interpreters.

Regina

Regina is the most popular free Rexx, and it runs on almost all platforms. Its large user community guarantees good support and means that more interfaces and tools are tested with Regina than any other Rexx. Regina is an open source product distributed under the GNU Library General Public License. It includes a very wide variety of extensions: some to duplicate what other Rexx interpreters offer and others to support platform-specific features. Regina is one of the few free Rexx interpreters that fully implement the SAA application programming interface, or API. This provides a well-documented interface between Rexx and other languages and allows Regina to be employed as a set of callable routines.

Regina's documentation is very detailed and contains perceptive insights on Rexx interpreters and the finer points of the language. It explains Rexx standards and compatibility issues, how to use the SAA API, error conditions, I/O, the stack and language extensions. Chapter 20 discusses Regina in detail.

Rexx/imc

Rexx/imc runs on Unix, Linux, and BSD operating systems. It includes extra functions for C-like I/O, higher mathematics, Unix environmental info, and other C-like and Unix-friendly extensions. Rexx/imc is a partial implementation of the SAA API. It is a respected product with a proven track-record of support for over a decade. Chapter 21 describes Rexx/imc and offers a few sample scripts that illustrate its extended capabilities.

BRexx

BRexx is the fastest Rexx interpreter and it features a tiny disk footprint. It is especially well suited to systems with limited resources, such as handheld devices and smaller or older systems. It runs natively under Windows CE. It also runs under Linux, Unix, Windows, 32- and 16- bit DOS, the Mac OS, and other systems. BRexx comes bundled with a number of external function libraries that go beyond the Rexx standards and tailor it specifically for PCs and Windows CE. These include built-in and external functions for Windows CE, DOS interfaces, PC file I/O, ASCII-EBCDIC conversion, C-like I/O, console I/O, and ANSI-terminal screen I/O. BRexx allows you to view and change PC memory. It also includes functions for VM/CMS-like buffer management, a MySQL database interface, date/time conversions, and CGI scripting. Like Regina and Rexx/imc, BRexx features a long, proven support history. Chapter 22 describes Brexx and presents sample BRexx scripts.

Reginald

Reginald was originally based on Regina. It adds tools and functions that tailor Rexx specifically for Windows programmers. For example, it includes a Windows installer, a GUI script launcher, and a Rexx-aware text editor. Its tools and libraries help developers to create Windows GUI interfaces. It has many other interfaces including those for MIDI files, computerized speech synthesis, Windows file and directory I/O, and TCP/IP sockets. Its function libraries support transcendental math, regular expressions, and various utilities. For developers wishing to create Rexx scripts that mold seamlessly into Windows, Reginald fits the bill. It offers a free "power tool" for Windows programmers. Chapter 23 describes Reginald in detail and presents a few sample scripts.

Rexx for Palm OS

This interpreter runs under the Palm OS. It runs natively (no emulator required) and gives the Rexx programmer full access to all Palm resources. The product capitalizes on Rexx's strengths as a personal programming language by bringing Rexx to handhelds running any version of the Palm OS. Developers can hyperlink and glue Palm OS applications and databases together through *Rexxlets*, applications that cross-link information and pop-ups. Rexxlets can run without leaving the current Palm application so they're highly integrated and conveniently run. Rexx for Palm OS supports I/O to the console, databases, files, TCP/IP, serial interfaces, beaming and sound. If you're programming the Palm OS, this product addresses your needs. Chapter 24 discusses the topics of handheld and embedded systems programming, while Chapter 25 discusses Rexx for Palm OS.

r4

r4 is a product of Kilowatt Software, which also offers the upwardly compatible, fullly object-oriented roo! Both are Windows-only interpreters customized for Windows, with easy installation and developer tools specifically designed for that operating system. The support tools and utilities work with both r4 and roo! r4 and roo! offer GUI tools and accessories that are simpler to use than many Windows GUIs. The products each include some 50 sample scripts and introductory tutorials that bring to life the spirit of Rexx as an easy-to-learn language. This documentation helps beginners learn the languages quickly and experienced developers to become immediately productive. Like Regina, Rexx/imc, and BRexx, r4 has a proven track-record of long-term support. Chapter 26 describes both r4 and roo!

Object-Oriented Rexx

The two free object-oriented Rexx interpreters are both supersets of classic Rexx. They run standard Rexx scripts without alteration. In addition they support all the features of object-oriented programming (OOP) through their additions to standard Rexx. Both support inheritance and derivation, encapsulation, polymorphism, and abstraction. Both come with complete class libraries. There is one major difference between them — they are completely different implementations of object-oriented Rexx. Their class libraries, new instructions and functions, and even their object-oriented operators differ. Those interested in object-oriented Rexx programming should look closely at both products and compare them against their requirements.

We might add that there is no ANSI standard for object-oriented Rexx. A standard would give object-oriented Rexx greater importance as a universal language, encourage wider use, and might increase its availability on other platforms.

Object-oriented Rexx is popular both for classic Rexx programmers who wish to transfer their skills to object-oriented programming, and for those who know OOP but seek an easier-to-use language than many of the alternatives. Like classic Rexx, object-oriented Rexx combines its ease-of-use with power. But in this case, the power is based on extensive class libraries.

roo!

Kilowatt Software offers their object-oriented extension of classic Rexx called roo! roo! is a companion product to their classic Rexx interpreter r4. Both are tailored for Windows and come with many utilities specific to Windows, including easy-to-use GUI tools and accessories. r4 and roo! are the only two interpreters from a single source that support migration from classic Rexx to object-oriented Rexx. Chapter 26 describes roo! in detail.

Open Object Rexx

A product called Object REXX was originally developed by IBM Corporation in the mid-1990s. In early 2005, IBM open-sourced Object REXX and turned its continued development and support over to the Rexx Language Association. The Rexx Language Association renamed the product *Open Object Rexx*, sometimes referred to as *ooRexx*. Like roo!, Open Object Rexx is 100 percent upwardly compatible with classic Rexx and extends the procedural language into the object-oriented world. But ooRexx has a different set of class libraries than roo! So while roo! and Open Object Rexx are both object-oriented supersets of classic procedural Rexx, they take very different approaches to implementing object-oriented programming.

Open Object Rexx runs on Windows, Linux, Solaris, and AIX. Chapter 27 describes Open Object Rexx in detail, while Chapter 28 contains a complete object-oriented scripting tutorial for Rexx developers based on Open Object Rexx.

NetRexx

NetRexx runs wherever Java runs; it typically runs under a *Java Virtual Machine*, or *JVM*. NetRexx offers an alternative way to script Java applets and applications with a language that is closely modeled on Rexx. You can code NetRexx scripts that call Java programs, or vice versa, or you can use NetRexx as a complete replacement or alternative to Java programming. You can even code Java Beans in NetRexx and use it for server-side programming as well. NetRexx is an easier-to-learn and use scripting language than Java that jettisons Java's C-language heritage for the clean simplicity of Rexx.

NetRexx is not a superset of classic Rexx. It is best described as a Rexx-like language for the Java environment. Since NetRexx is not upwardly compatible with classic Rexx, there is a free standard Rexx to NetRexx converter program available called *Rexx2Nrx*. Find it at www.rexx2nrx.com or enter keyword Rexx2Nrx in any Internet search engine.

IBM offers a free license to download and use NetRexx for all Java environments. Chapter 30 describes NetRexx in detail.

Mainframe Rexx

Rexx was originally developed in the early 1980s to run under the VM family of operating systems. Later in the decade IBM released Rexx for OS- and VSE-family mainframe systems as well.

Rexx has now been the dominant mainframe scripting and command language for over 20 years. It integrates with nearly all mainframe tools and facilities and is the primary mainframe macro language. Mainframe Rexx is not free or open source but comes bundled with the operating system. Chapter 29 discusses mainframe Rexx. It lists the differences between it, the ANSI-1996 standard, and the free Rexx implementations. This helps those who are transferring either their skills or their code from mainframes to other platforms. It may also prove useful to those who know systems like Windows, Unix, or Linux and have occasion to work with mainframes.

IBM also offers Rexx for a number of specialized mainframe environments. An example is *Rexx for CICS*. Customer Information Control System, or CICS is the transactional teleprocessing monitor used on many mainframes. CICS is notoriously difficult to program, and programmers who know the system on a detailed level are difficult to find. Rexx for CICS brings Rexx's ease of use to this environment. It is especially useful for end-user computing, prototyping, and quick application development. It comes with its own CICS-based editor. Appendix A on resources provides sources for further information.

Other IBM Rexxes

IBM has bundled Rexx with nearly every one of its operating systems since the early 1990s. Here are a few examples beyond mainframe operating systems in the VM, OS, and VSE families.

❑ *iSeries(tm) OS/400 Rexx* — IBM bundles Rexx with the i5/OS and OS/400 operating systems for its proprietary midrange machines. Traditionally referred to as *Rexx/400*, it interfaces to the Integrated Language Environment, or ILE, C compiler, and supports the Double-Byte Character Set (DBCS), an external data queue, intermingling of CL commands, and the OS/400 security system. Rexx/400 follows the Rexx standards, while adding interfaces appropriate to the I-Series.

❑ *OS/2 Rexx* — OS/2 came with Rexx as its bundled procedure language. This gained the language many new adherents and resulted in the development of a large variety of Rexx packages and interfaces. OS/2 today has faded from the scene but its impact on Rexx's development remains. One of OS/2's descendants, called the *eComStation*, or *eCS*, carries both OS/2 and Rexx forward. See www.ecomstation.com or www.ecomstation.org for further information on the eComStation. An open source project called *osFree* is also based on OS/2 and uses Rexx as its command and scripting language. See www.osfree.org for information on osFree.

❑ *PC-DOS Rexx* — IBM has bundled Rexx with their version of DOS, called PC-DOS, since version 7. For example, PC-DOS 2000 comes with Rexx as its command and scripting language. PC-DOS Rexx includes a variety of PC-oriented and general-purpose utilities in external function libraries.

❑ *Commercial IBM Rexxes* — In addition to the Rexx interpreters IBM bundles with its operating systems, the company has also vended Rexx for such operating systems as Netware and AIX. While these are sold as stand-alone products, the license fees for these Rexx interpreters have typically been very modest.

Rexx for Handhelds and Embedded Programming

Small computing devices include personal digital assistants (PDAs), pocket PCs, palm PCs, PC tablets, mobile and smart phones, handheld keyboard PCs, and other programmable handheld consumer devices. They also include *dedicated devices* requiring *embedded programming*. Examples include consumer devices like real-time processors for control of automobile engines and industrial devices like robots, assembly line machinery, and numerical control systems.

For consumer-oriented devices, the key requirements for a programming language are:

❑ Limited resource consumption

❑ Ease of learning and ease of use

Memory, disk, and CPU resources are likely to be limited in handheld computers. And, handhelds are often programmed by hobbyists and casual users, not by IT professionals or professional software developers.

Embedded programming adds a third criterion for a programming language: the software must be 100 percent reliable. If a program fails in an embedded or dedicated device, the device itself is considered faulty or defective. Since the software must be as reliable as the hardware on which it runs, programmers must use an interpreter that helps them develop the most reliable code possible.

Rexx is ideally suited to these requirements. Several Rexx interpreters feature small footprints and have extremely modest resource requirements. Examples include Regina, BRexx, and Rexx for Palm OS. Of course, Rexx is also famous for its ease of use. Ease of use greatly increases the reliability of Rexx scripts in embedded programming — especially when the alternatives are apt to be languages like C++ or Java with its C-heritage syntax. Simplicity yields reliability.

There are three major operating systems families for consumer handheld computers: Windows CE, Palm OS, and Symbian OS/EPOC32. Rexx interpreters run under each. BRexx runs under Windows CE, Rexx for Palm OS runs under Palm OS, and Regina runs under Symbian/EPOC32.

Rexx interpreters also run under *DOS emulators* for these environments. Emulators make the underlying hardware and operating system appear like a personal computer running 16-bit DOS. This brings thousands of old PC applications to modern handhelds. Rexx interpreters that run under DOS emulators include the 16-bit version of BRexx.

Dedicated and embedded programming often employs 16- and 32- bit DOS and "tiny Linuxes," as well as specialized real-time operating systems. Several Rexx interpreters support free DOS and tiny Linux environments. BRexx is notable for its DOS extensions and it supports both 16- and 32- bit DOS. Regina, r4, roo!, and Reginald can run from the 32-bit Windows' DOS command line. Several Rexx interpreters run under resource-constrained Linux environments including Rexx/imc, Regina, and BRexx.

To summarize, Rexx makes a great fit in programming handheld consumer devices. It is small, easy to learn and use for casual programmers, and portable, yet powerful. It runs natively on the three major operating systems for handhelds: Windows CE, Palm OS, and Symbian/EPOC32. Rexx also fits the requirements of dedicated devices and embedded programming. Its ease of use increases the probability of completely reliable programs. Its smallness and ability to run under free DOS and small, specially configured Linuxes add to Rexx's appeal.

Chapter 24 discusses Rexx for handheld and embedded programming in detail. That discussion maps out the whole field, and also zeroes in on Rexx scripting for DOS emulation. It also briefly describes native Regina scripting under Symbian/EPOC32. Chapter 25 covers the Rexx for Palm OS interpreter and gives a tutorial on programming the Palm Pilot with Rexx. Chapter 22 describes BRexx for Windows CE and also includes a sample BRexx script for 16-bit DOS (as might run under a DOS emulator or in an embedded device).

While the information on handheld and embedded scripting is split between several chapters, in the aggregate it will give you a good background on how to program handheld PCs with Rexx.

Commercial Rexxes

Given Rexx's popularity, it comes as no surprise that there are many commercially vended Rexx interpreters. This book does not discuss them in detail as they fall outside its focus on free, bundled, and open source software. Here we mention some of more widely used commercial Rexxes, where to get further information, and where they can be purchased.

uni-Rexx by The Workstation Group

uni-Rexx is an ANSI-standard Rexx implementation for Unix. It includes a Rexx interpreter, a Rexx compiler, OS-related extensions, application programming interfaces and a sample scripts library. uni-Rexx is the macro language for editors and other tools from the same vendor including uni-SPF, uni-XEDIT, netCONVERT, and Co/SORT. Uni-Rexx is a rock-solid product: the author developed an application of over 10,000 lines of code in uni-Rexx and never encountered a single bug or issue. Find The Workstation Group at www.wrkgrp.com or in Rosemont, Illinois, at 1-800-228-0255.

Personal Rexx by Quercus Systems

Quercus vends their Personal Rexx for Windows, DOS, and OS/2. All versions include numerous functions for file access, operating system control, and screen management. Personal Rexx for Windows was once also known as WinRexx. Quercus evolved from the earliest vendor of Rexx for personal computers, called The Mansfield Software Group. Find Quercus Systems at www.quercus-sys.com or in Pacific Grove, California, at 1-831-372-7399.

S/Rexx by Treehouse Software Inc.

S/Rexx is a Rexx for Unix and Windows that offers compatibility with mainframe Rexx and enables scripts to be migrated from the mainframe to Unix and Windows computers. S/Rexx includes the S/Rexx Debugger, supports Motif and OpenLook dialog programming, and supports SEDIT (an XEDIT- and ISPF/PDF-compatible editor for Unix and Windows). It provides other improvements that allow Rexx scripts to take advantage of the Unix and Windows environments. Find Treehouse Software at www.treehouse.com/srx.shtml or in Sewickley, Pennsylvania, at 1-412-741-1677.

Amiga Rexx

Also known as ARexx and AREXX, this interpreter came bundled with the Amiga personal computer. While the Amiga is today little known, it was considered a very innovative machine for its time and had quite a mindshare impact. Amiga's success was based on its offering the first popular multi-tasking operating system for a personal computer. The OS coupled these advanced features with the easy programming provided by Rexx as its primary scripting language.

ARexx is mentioned here for primarily for its historical importance. Both ARexx and the Amiga continue to have a small band of loyal enthusiasts. A free, portable, Amiga OS–compatible operating system called *AROS* continues the Amiga OS tradition. See its home page at www.aros.org for further information. Rexx is also the scripting language of AROS.

Rexx Compilers and Tokenizers

Rexx is an interpreted scripting language, but Rexx compilers are also available. *Compilers* convert an entire source code program into a machine-language executable. Scripts are then run in a second, separate step. Compilers offer two advantages. Since the conversion step is separated from program execution, the program usually executes faster. This is especially beneficial when a compiled program is repeatedly run. Second, developers can distribute the executable without exposing their original Rexx source code. This keeps code proprietary.

In addition to compilers, there are also Rexx *tokenizers*. These convert Rexx source code into an intermediate, tokenized form that is then executed by the interpreter. Tokenizers don't go quite as far as compilers in that they convert source to an intermediate form but not machine code. They represent another of the several technologies that can potentially increase scripting performance and protect source code.

IBM offers a Rexx compiler for its mainframe platforms. Chapter 29 on mainframe Rexx programming provides further information on the mainframe Rexx compiler. Among free Rexx packages, r4, roo!, and Reginald offer tools to convert scripts into stand-alone executables. Appendix H also lists several tools, such as Rexx/Wrapper, that convert Rexx source into nonviewable forms.

Running Rexx in the Shell

Like other scripting languages, Rexx scripts run as a separate process than the one that invokes them. Run a Rexx script from the operating system's command line (or by clicking an icon), and the operating system spawns a separate process for the script.

Shell language scripts can run in the same process as the command interpreter. The advantages to this are:

❑   Environment variables set by the script remain in effect after its termination.

❑   The current working directory can be altered permanently by the script.

❑   The numeric return code of the script is available in the return code variable identified by the special shell variable named $?.

One packaging of Regina Rexx enables it to run in the same process as the Z-shell (zsh). This yields the previously listed advantages. This is useful for scripts that need to alter the user's environment, for example, for scripts that perform product setup, installation, or customization. If you need to run a script within the shell itself, Regina will fulfill your requirements.

Rexx As an API

Several Rexx interpreters are implemented as a library suitable for linking into other applications. This allows programs written in other languages to employ Rexx as a set of callable routines that provide the functionality inherent in Rexx.

Rexx interpreters use a consistent interface standard, called the *SAA API* or sometimes the *Rexx API*. These include Regina, Open Object Rexx, Reginald, and with partial compliance, Rexx/imc. The Regina Rexx documentation manual has a complete section that explains how this works. The documentation is written from the standpoint of C/C++ programmers. The IBM Rexx SAA manual may also be of interest to those using the Rexx API. See Appendix A for details on how to obtain these sources of API information.

Rexx As a Macro Language

Macro languages are used to provide programmability within a product. Rexx is a popular macro language for a variety of products. For example, Rexx can be used as a macro language to tailor and customize various text editors, including THE (The Hessling Editor), the Rexx Text Editor (RexxED), and the primary mainframe editors, ISPF and XEDIT. Rexx has found its greatest popularity as a macro language in the mainframe environment. On mainframes, Rexx is the "universal" macro language, embedded in a very wide range of tools and products.

Multiple Rexx Interpreters on One Computer

Given that there are so many Rexx interpreters, you might wonder: can I install more than one on the same computer? Absolutely. Chapters 20 through 30 describe various free Rexx interpreters and show how to install each.

In most cases, you can install more than one Rexx interpreter on the same machine without experiencing any conflicts. Just follow the normal installation procedures, then use the products in the usual manner.

There are a few situations of which to be aware. First, you'll need to ensure that each interpreter's executable has a unique name. This is important because a few of the products use the same name for their interpreter. For example, versions of Regina, Rexx/imc, and IBM's Object REXX all call their executable rexx. If you install these these interpreters into a shared directory this creates an obvious conflict. Secondly, when you install more than one interpreter on a single computer, you'll want to ensure you are running the interpreter you think you are in any particular situation. It is possible, for example, to implicitly run a script, and have that script executed by a different interpreter than the one you thought ran it! For example, if you install several Rexx intepreters on a Windows machine, you'll want to know which interpreter runs a particular script when you double-click on it.

The solution to the first problem is simply to ensure that each Rexx executable has a unique name. Installing the interpreters under different directories resolves this issue because the fully qualified path name is the filename for the executable. This approach works fine if you want to place each interpreter in its own unique product directory.

If you want to place multiple Rexx interpreters in the same directory, you'll have to rename any executables whose names conflict. An example where this might be an issue is if you use Unix-derived operating system and want to install all language interpreters into the same shared executables directory. The solution is simply to ensure that each Rexx interpreter in that directory has a unique name for its executable. For example, versions of Regina and Rexx/imc both call their executable rexx. You might change Regina's to regina and Rexx/imc's to rexximc to avoid conflict between their unqualified names.

Once you have installed multiple Rexx interpreters, any standard Rexx script will run under any of the interpreters. (Refer to the list of interpreters and the standards they meet in the table in the section entitled "Rexx Interpreters.") Still, you'll probably want to know (or ensure) which interpreter executes when you run a script. One solution is to *explicitly* invoke scripts. Name the interpreter to run on the command line with the name of the Rexx script to execute as its input parameter. For example, this command runs a script under the r4 interpreter on a Windows machine. r4's executable is named r4:

```
r4  rexxcps.rexx
```

This command runs the same script on the same computer under BRexx. The BRexx executable is named rexx32:

```
rexx32  rexxcps.rexx
```

If necessary, use the full path name to uniquely identify the executable to run. This technique is useful if the unqualified or "short" filenames of the interpreters are the same but their fully qualified path names differ. Here is an example that specifies the full path name of a Rexx interpreter on a Unix machine. The name of the executable is `rexx`, a potentially duplicate short filename, but the fully qualified pathname ensures that the interpreter you want runs:

```
/usr/local/bin/regina/rexx   rexxcps.rexx
```

If you don't fully qualify the executable name, the operating system's *search path* may dictate which binary runs. Take this command:

```
rexx rexxcps.rexx
```

Assuming that there are multiple `rexx` executables on the machine, the operating system has to choose which to run. Most operating systems have an environmental variable that tells which directories to search for the binary and the order in which those directories are searched. This environmental variable is named PATH (or `path`) under Windows, Linux, Unix, BSD, and other operating systems. In terms of the previous example, the first reference in the search path that resolves to a valid executable named `rexx` is the one the operating system runs. The path or search order determines which binary the operating system locates and runs.

Under the Linux, Unix, and BSD operating systems, you may direct which interpreter runs a script by coding this information on the first line of the script. The first line of the script begins with the characters `#!` and specifies the fully qualified name of the Rexx executable. For example, to run the Rexx/imc interpreter the first line in each script will typically be its fully qualified executable's name:

```
#!/usr/bin/rexx
```

The fully qualified path name and the name of the Rexx executable vary by the interpreter. If two interpreters use the same fully qualified name for their executable, change the name of one of them to distinguish it. This unique reference then becomes the first line in scripts that use that interpreter.

Under operating systems in the Windows family, the *file association* determines which Rexx interpreter executes a script when you click on that script. File associations are established for the interpreters automatically when they are installed. Here are the default file associations for some Rexx interpreters you might install under Windows:

Rexx Interpreter	Windows Default File Extension
Regina	.rexx (optionally others as well)
Reginald	.rex
BRexx	.r
r4	.rex
roo!	.roo
NetRexx	.nrx

You can also set the file associations manually (or alter them) through the Windows' file Explorer. Go to the top menu bar, select Tools | Folder Options... | File Types, and you can view and optionally change file associations. Or access this tool by searching for the keywords `associating files` in the Windows Help system. Managing the file associations allows you to avoid any conflicts in assigned file extensions among the Rexx interpreters.

The chance of a conflict when installing two or more Rexx interpreters on the same computer is low. In the preparation of this book, for example, the author installed a half dozen Rexx interpreters on each of four different computers. The simple points mentioned in this discussion resolved all problems except one. So a complex problem could occur, but the likelihood you'll confront such an issue is very low. The tips in this section should resolve most issues.

The Future of Rexx

Designed to combine ease of use with power, Rexx fills a niche other scripting languages ignore. It is as easy to work with as BASIC, the language whose very name declares its ease of use. Yet Rexx is as powerful as almost any procedural language: it is no "beginner's language." Rexx also enjoys the strong standardization that BASIC lacks. The eight free Rexx interpreters listed in the first table in this chapter all meet the Rexx standard. Rexx's unprecedented code portability and skills transferability present a key benefit to organizations selecting their software tools and to vendors bundling a command language with their products.

As the skills challenge continues, more organizations will appreciate the benefits of ease of use. With an easy language, new programmers come on line quickly. Experienced programmers also benefit. They are more productive. Their code contains fewer errors and is more maintainable than are programs developed in syntax-bound shell or scripting languages. A complex Perl or shell language program quickly becomes unmaintainable; a complex Rexx program outlives its creator.

Rexx has been the primary scripting language for many systems including VM, OS, and VSE family mainframes, Windows 2000 and NT servers, OS/400, i5/OS, OS/2, eCS, osFree, the Amiga, AROS, and others. It is likely that Rexx will be selected as the primary language for future systems, as yet undreamed of, based on its unique strengths. Perhaps this will occur with future handheld devices, where the combination of a small-but-powerful, easy-to-use interpreter has special appeal. Or Rexx may become the dominant scripting language for future operating systems that push the trends of ease of use and user-friendliness to new levels.

Meanwhile, the wide selection of free Rexx interpreters leads to expanding use of the language on existing platforms. Rexx enjoys wider use than many other languages and is especially popular as a free or open source offering outside the United States. The industry-wide trends toward scripting and open source software converge on Rexx in a way that ensures its expanding popularity.

Summary

In this chapter, we took a step back and described the invention and evolution of Rexx. The goal was to get a bit of perspective on the language's platforms, roles, and applications.

This chapter summarized the various Rexx interpreters that are available. It profiled their strengths, the platforms on which they run, and their major characteristics. We also presented a methodology for deciding which interpreter is most suitable for a particular project or application. Different projects and organizations have different needs, and the methodology helps structure decision-making when selecting a product. The methodology can be used either to compare Rexx to other scripting languages or to select a Rexx interpreter from among the several that are available.

This chapter also discussed the roles that Rexx scripts fulfill within organizations. These include using Rexx as a macro language, calling Rexx functions from other languages through the Rexx API, running Rexx in the shell, scripting handhelds and dedicated devices, and Rexx in its role as the mainframe command language. Two object-oriented Rexx interpreters are available. In an extended and altered version called NetRexx, the language also participates in the Java environment, providing both client- and server- side scripting that fits synergistically with Java.

Finally, this chapter addressed how to resolve any conflicts that might occur when installing more than one Rexx interpreter on the same machine. Conflicts rarely occur, but when they do, they can easily be resolved. This chapter explained how.

With this chapter laying the groundwork, let's discuss the organization of the remainder of the book. Chapters 20 through 30 describe different Rexx interpreters. Each chapter focuses on a different interpreter and describes its advantages, the platforms it supports, and its unique "personality." The chapters describe the features each interpreter offers beyond the Rexx standards and illustrate many of these extensions through sample scripts. The goal of these chapters is to take you beyond classic Rexx and into the realm of advanced scripting. If you follow the code examples in the chapters, you'll improve your scripting and also become privy to the advanced and interpreter- and platform-specific aspects of the language.

Several of the upcoming chapters cover specific kinds of programming. For example, three chapters address object-oriented Rexx scripting. They include an object-oriented tutorial that leverages your knowledge of classic Rexx to take you into the world of object-oriented programming. Two other chapters cover handheld programming. They include a complete tutorial on how to script handhelds with Rexx. Yet another chapter focuses on NetRexx, a Rexx-like language that complements Java. NetRexx fits into the Java environment and runs under the Java Virtual Machine. And one chapter summarizes Rexx as the predominant mainframe command language.

At this point in the book, you have a good working knowledge of standard Rexx. This chapter provided a little more perspective on the roles the language plays, where it runs, and the interpreters that are available. Let's go forward into the remaining portion of the book and learn about the various Rexx interpreters and how they apply to a wide range of platforms and programming problems.

Test Your Understanding

1. If you wanted a fast-running Rexx for Windows CE, which would you pick? Which interpreter runs on the most platforms? Which offers a complete set of Windows GUI functions? Which offers extensions for Linux, Unix, and BSD? Which is from a company that also offers an upwardly compatible object-oriented Rexx?

2. What are the major Rexx standards? To which do the free Rexx interpreters adhere? What is SAA and what was its impact on the standardization of Rexx?

3. What are roo! and Open Object Rexx and what are their benefits? Could you run a standard Rexx script under these interpreters? Would it make sense to do so? How do roo! and Open Object Rexx differ? Which is(are) free under: Windows? Linux? Solaris?

4. What is NetRexx and how is it used? Does NetRexx meet the Rexx standards? Can you access Java classes from NetRexx? Could you write Java classes in NetRexx?

5. Which open source Rexx not only meets all standards but includes the interpreter-specific extensions of the other free Rexx interpreters?

6. Which Rexx implementations run on handheld devices? On Windows CE? On Symbian/EPOC32? On Palm OS?

7. What is the difference between Rexx running natively on a handheld and running under an emulator? Which is better, and why?

Footnote:

* Rexx Language Association survey of 250+ users from 2001. Visit the Rexx Language Association at their homepage of www.rexxla.org. The Rexx Language Association is a key resource for community interaction and a great source for further information on the language.

Regina

Overview

Regina is the most widely used free Rexx interpreter. Its use is truly worldwide: it was originally developed by Anders Christensen of Norway in the 1990s and is today enhanced, maintained, and ported by Mark Hessling of Australia and Florian Große-Coosmann of Germany. Regina's popularity is well deserved. It meets all Rexx standards and goes well beyond them in the features and functions it offers. It runs on nearly any platform. Some of its many advantages were presented in the first chapter, when we described why it is an excellent choice of Rexx interpreter.

This chapter explores those aspects of Regina that go beyond the ANSI standards to give you a feel for the extra features of this product. Since Regina meets all Rexx standards, of course, everything from the tutorials of the earlier chapters of this book apply to your use of Regina. In fact, all the sample scripts to this point were tested with Regina in its role as a standards-compliant Rexx interpreter. The goal here is a bit different. This chapter specifically explores the Regina features that go above and beyond the Rexx standards.

First, we'll cover the advantages of the Regina interpreter. Then we'll discuss when and why it may be appropriate to employ the features of Rexx interpreters that extend beyond the standards, and what the downsides of this decision are. Different projects have different goals, and you want to be appraised as to when using interpreter features beyond those of the Rexx standards is advisable.

This chapter describes Regina's extended features. These include its many operands for the `options` instruction, additional functions (for bit manipulation, string manipulation, environmental information, and input/output), facilities for loading external function libraries, the stack and its uses, and the SAA API. Let's dive in.

Advantages

In deciding whether to use any particular Rexx interpreter, you'll want to know what the benefits to the product are. Do its strengths match your project's needs? This section attempts to answer that question for the Regina Rexx interpreter. This chapter lists and discusses many of the product's stengths. The chapters that follow this one present the same information for other Rexx interpreters including Rexx/imc, Reginald, BRexx, Rexx for Palm OS, r4, and roo!, Open Object Rexx, mainframe Rexx, and NetRexx. A separate chapter covers each interpreter, and each chapter begins with a list of the product's special strengths, similar to the one given here. Use these lists as your "starting point" in deciding which Rexx interpreter is right for any particular situation or project.

With this said, let's discuss the strengths of Regina. Figure 20-1 pictorially summarizes many of Regina's advantages as a Rexx interpreter.

Regina Rexx...Built on Strengths

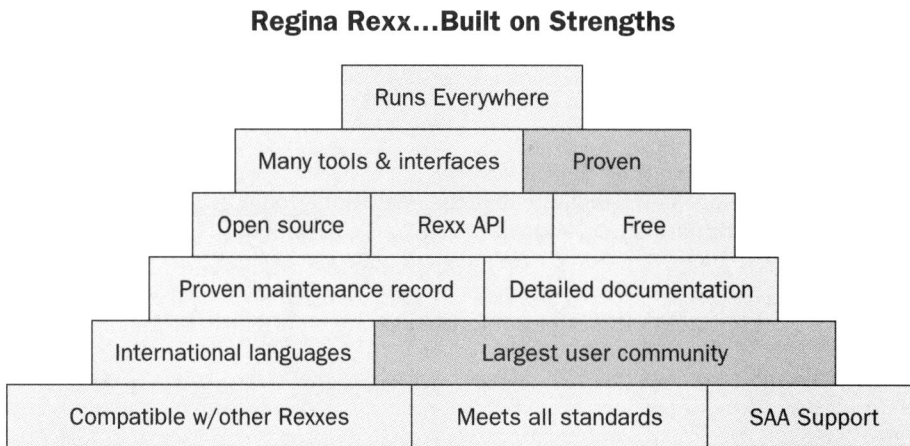

Figure 20-1

Let's discuss these advantages in more detail.

❏ *Regina runs anywhere* — Rexx is a platform-independent language, and Regina proves the point. Regina runs on any operating system in these families: Windows, Linux, Unix, BSD, 32- bit DOS, and Mac OS. It also runs on Symbian/EPOC32, BeOS, OS/2 and eCS, OpenVMS, OpenEdition, AmigaOS, AROS, AtheOS/Syllable, QNX4 and QNX6, and others. Regina runs on most of the platforms listed for Rexx interpreters in the tables in Chapter 1.

❏ *Regina meets all standards* — Regina fully meets the ANSI-1996 standards and conforms to the SAA, TRL-2, and TRL-1 standards as well. The product's detailed documentation provides precise explanations of the differences between these standards.

❏ *Regina has a large support community* — Regina's large worldwide user base means that this implementation has the largest support community. If you post a Rexx question on the Internet, chances are the response will come from someone using Regina. Also, Regina has a strong, proven track record for support.

❑ *Regina boasts tools and interfaces* — As the most popular free Rexx, most Rexx tools are written for and tested with Regina. Open-source interfaces that work with Regina include those for relational databases, the Tk and DW GUI toolkits, the gd library for graphics, the THE editor, ISAM access method, Curses for standard screen I/O, CURL for URL support, and many others.

❑ *Regina offers compatibility with other Rexxes* — Regina includes features and functions that go beyond the standards to provide compatibility with other Rexx implementations. We call this Regina's *supercompatibility*. Take issuing operating system commands, for example. Regina supports ANSI-standard redirected I/O via the `address` instruction. It also allows the `address` instruction to use the stack, as in mainframe and other Rexxes. Where Rexx implementations differ, Regina supports all the approaches and lets the developer choose which to use.

❑ *Regina includes functions from other Rexxes* — As part of its supercompatibility, Regina includes implementation-specific functions matching those supplied by VM mainframe Rexx, the SAA standard, Amiga AREXX, and OS/2 Rexx.

❑ *Regina offers detailed documentation* — Regina's documentation is probably the most comprehensive and detailed of any free Rexx interpreter. Its documentation goes far beyond the required and includes detailed discussions of conditions, I/O, extensions, and the stack. It includes a large section on the Rexx SAA API, which explains to developers how they can call Regina as a set of external routines.

❑ *Regina is open source.* Regina is open source and is distributed under the GNU Library General Public License. Not all free Rexx interpreters are also open source.

❑ *Regina supports the REXX API* — Regina is implemented as a library based on the standard Rexx *application programming interface*, or *API*. It interfaces to programs written in other programming languages based on this clean, well-documented interface. With this interface, for example, you could code C or C++ programs that employ Regina as a set of Rexx functions.

❑ *Regina is international* — Regina supports several spoken languages, including English, German, Spanish, Portuguese, Turkish and Norwegian.

❑ *Regina uses DLLs and shared libraries.* Regina includes the *Generic Call Interface*, or *GCI*, which allows scripts to call functions in Windows DLLs or Linux/Unix/BSD shared libraries as though they were Regina built-in functions. This gives Regina scripts full access to external code of all kinds for Windows, Unix-derived, and OS/2 platforms (even though that code was not specifically written to be invoked from Rexx scripts).

❑ *Regina is thread-safe* — This allows it be used by applications like the Apache Web server which use threads for superior performance.

❑ *Regina supports "superstacks"* — Regina's stack services extend way beyond the required or expected. As described in Chapter 11, Regina's external queues can be used for communications between different processes on the same computer, different processes on different computers, or even between different processes across the Internet.

Regina's Extras

Chapter 1 discusses where to download Regina from and how to install the product. The chapters following Chapter 1 presented a progressive tutorial on how to script with standard Rexx. All this material applies to Regina, and all the sample programs up to this point were tested using Regina. But now it's time to explore the extended features of Regina. The remainder of this chapter enumerates and discusses the major features Regina adds beyond the Rexx standards. Figure 20-2 summarizes these features.

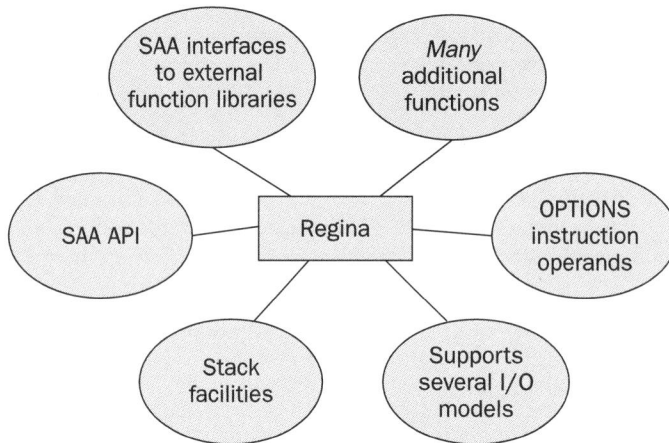

Figure 20-2

The extended Regina features include interpreter options, additional functions, and features for compatibility with other Rexx interpreters and platforms. These additions beyond the Rexx standards offer great power and are a strong advantage to Regina. But always carefully consider whether you wish to code beyond the Rexx standards. Coding within the standards ensures the highest degree of code portability. It ensures that others who know Rexx will be able to work with your code. Coding outside the standard subjects your scripts to a greater risk of desupport. Standard Rexx will enjoy use and support forever, whereas the extensions of any specific interpreter will always be subject to greater risk. We generally recommend always coding with the Rexx standards. Including this extended material in this and subsequent chapters on Rexx interpreter extensions is not meant to promote the use of these extensions. It is, rather, intended to provide introduction and reference to the extensions for those who may need them and understand both their benefits and their drawbacks.

There are very good reasons for Rexx interpreter extensions. They offer platform-specific features and power that can be very useful for scripts that will run in specific environments. They also support cross-platform portability in ways not possible otherwise. As one example, porting mainframe scripts to other platforms may be easier when the interpreter on the target platform supports mainframe Rexx extensions. As another example, programmers familiar with the I/O model of other programming languages may prefer the C-like I/O offered in many Rexx extensions to the standard Rexx I/O model.

The bottom line is this: use nonstandard Rexx extensions if you need them for some reason, and you have considered any potential downsides and have judged them acceptable. With this said, let's enumerate and discuss Regina's extended features.

Interpreter options

Recall that the `options` instruction allows you to issue commands to the Rexx interpreter. These options dynamically alter the interpreter's behavior. What options are available depend strictly on the Rexx interpreter. Regina's `options` instruction includes about two dozen parameters that scripts set to alter or direct the interpreter's behavior. These key ones dictate compatibility with various platforms and standards:

Option	Result
CMS	Enables the set of extensions expected in the VM/CMS mainframe environment
UNIX	Enables Unix command interface functions. This increases performance over using the command interface to issue shell commands
VMS	A set of interface functions to the VMS operating system. This makes it possible to script the same kinds of actions in Regina Rexx on VMS as one writes in VMS's DCL language
BUFFERS	Makes all VM-based buffer functions available to manipulate the stack
AREXX_BIFS	Makes all ARexx built-in functions available
REGINA	Language level 5.00 plus Regina extensions are available
ANSI	Conform to language level 5.00
SAA	Conform to SAA standards
TRL2	Conform to TRL-2 standards
TRL1	Conform to TRL-1 standards

Regina includes other options beyond those listed. We do not mention them here because most direct the interpreter in very specific ways or towards implementing very specific features. Often these control the internal behaviors of the interpreter. The options listed in the table manipulate the more specific options as groups of behaviors in order to gain compatibility with specific environments or standards. If you need to investigate the low-level options, the Regina documentation spells them out in detail.

Functions

As an ANSI-1996 compliant Rexx, Regina has all standard Rexx instructions and functions. Appendices B and C list these language elements in reference format with a coding level of detail. In addition, Regina offers functions that go beyond the standards. Regina's extra functions naturally group into several categories:

- ❑ Bit manipulation
- ❑ String manipulation
- ❑ Environmental
- ❑ Input/output
- ❑ SAA interface to external function libraries
- ❑ Stack manipulation

These functions originated from a number of platforms and other Rexx interpreters. The following table lists Regina's extended functions and shows from which version of Rexx each is derived:

Origin	Functions
AREXX	b2c, bitchg, bitclr, bitcomp, bitset, bitttst, c2b, close, compress, eof, exists, export, freespace, getspace, hash, import, open, randu, readch, readln, seek, show, storage, trim, upper, writech, writeln
SAA standard	rxfuncadd, rxfuncdrop, rxfuncerrmsg, rxfuncquery
Regina	cd, chdir, crypt, fork, getenv, getpid, gettid, popen, uname, unixerror, userid
VM (aka CMS)	buftype, desbuf, dropbuf, find, index, justify, makebuf, sleep, state
OS/2 Rexx	beep, directory, rxqueue

Appendix D alphabetically lists all Regina-specific functions with detail suitable for reference and coding. It includes coding examples of the use of each function.

In the next several sections, you'll learn about each group of functions. The goal here is simply to familiarize you with the names of the functions and what they do. For a complete alphabetical list of functions with full coding details, see Appendix D.

Bit manipulation

Bit manipulation refers to the ability to inspect and alter individual bits. Usually, the bits are manipulated in groups of 8 (one character or byte) or 4 (one hexadecimal character). Chapter 6 on strings briefly considered why bit string manipulation can be useful, while Chapter 7 offered a sample script that performed key folding based on bit strings.

Standard Rexx offers a set of bit manipulation functions that include `bitand`, `bitor`, and `bitxor`. These are backed up by bit conversion functions like `b2x` and `x2b`. Regina extends this power by adding another group of bit functions, all derived from Amiga Rexx, a Rexx interpreter that was the bundled standard with the Amiga personal computers. These functions are very useful when intense bit-twiddling is called for.

To access all of these functions, you must enable the `options` instruction string `AREXX_BIFS`, like this:

```
options arexx_bifs
```

Here are the extra functions available:

Bit Manipulation Function	Use
b2c	Returns a character string for a binary string input
bitchg	Toggles a given bit in the input string
bitclr	Sets a specified bit in the input string to 0
bitcomp	Compares two strings bit by bit, returns –1 if identical or the bit position of the first bit by which the strings differ

Bit Manipulation Function	Use
bitset	Sets the specified bit to 1
bittst	Returns the state of a specified bit in the string (either it is 1 or 0)
c2b	Converts the character string into a bit string

String Manipulation

String manipulation is even more vital than bit manipulation, as amply pointed out in Chapter 6. Regina offers a grab-bag of extra string functions. A few, like find, index, and justify, have mainframe origins. These all have more standard equivalents, yet their inclusion is useful for mainframe compatibility or for rehosting mainframe scripts.

Others of the string functions are just very useful and one wishes they were part of standard Rexx. hash returns the hash attribute of a character string, while crypt returns the encrypted form of a string.

This table lists the extended Regina string manipulation functions. Where a function has a direct standard Rexx equivalent, we have cited that equivalent. One should always code the standard Rexx function if feasible:

String Function	Use	Standard Alternative Function
compress	Compresses a string by removing any spaces, or by removing any characters not in a given list	—
crypt	Takes a string and returns it encrypted	—
find	Finds the first occurrence of a word in a string	wordpos
hash	Returns the hash attribute of a string	—
index	Returns the position of the needle string in the haystack string	pos
justify	Spaces a string to both right- and left-justify it	right or left or space
lower	Translates the string to lowercase	—
trim	Removes trailing blanks from a string	strip
upper	Translates string to uppercase	translate

Environmental functions

The environmental functions offer a plethora of operating system services and also retrieve information about the environment. Some of these functions are inspired by the PC platform, such as `beep`, `cd` or `chdir`, `import`, `export`, `rxqueue` and `storage`. Others obviously come from Unix, such as `fork`, `getenv`, `getpid`, `gettid`, `popen`, `uname`, `unixerror`, and `userid`. In all cases, the goal is the same: to provide operating system services to Rexx scripts.

Here are the environmental functions Regina adds to standard Rexx:

Environmental Function	Use
beep	Sounds the alarm or a "beep"
cd and chdir	Changes current process's directory to the specified directory
directory	Returns the current directory, or sets it to the given directory
export	Copies data into a specific memory address
fork	Spawns a child process
freespace	Returns a block of memory to the interpreter; inverse of getspace
getenv	Returns the value of the input Unix environmental variable
getpid	Returns the scripts process ID, or PID
getspace	Gets or allocates a block of memory from the interpreter
gettid	Returns the thread ID, or TID of the script
import	Reads memory locations
popen	Execute a command and capture its results to an array; superceded by the address with instruction
randu	Returns a pseudo-random number between 0 and 1
rxqueue	Controls Regina's queue function; creates, deletes, sets, or gets queues
show	Shows items in Amiga or AROS resource lists
sleep	Script sleeps for the designated number of seconds
state	Returns 0 if the steam exists, 1 otherwise
storage	With no arguments tells how much memory a system has, or it can return contents or even update (overwrite) system memory
uname	Returns platform information, including OS name, machine name, nodename, OS release, OS version, and machine's hardware type
unixerror	Returns the textual error message that corresponds to a Unix operating system error number
userid	Returns name of the current user

Input/output

Regina Rexx supports several I/O models. First, there is standard Rexx steam I/O, embodied in such built-in functions as `chars`, `charin`, `charout`, `lines`, `linein`, and `lineout`. This model is simple, standardized, compatible and portable.

Since some Rexx interpreters are actually implemented as C-language programs, they have added C-like I/O. The "C-language I/O model" provides a little better control of files because they can be explicitly opened, closed, positioned, and buffer-flushed. The *mode* a file is opened in (read, write, or append) can be specified. Direct access and explicit control of the read and write file positions is provided through the `seek` function.

AREXX on the Amiga and the portable, free BRexx interpreter (see chapter 22) are known for supporting the C-language I/O model. Regina does too. Regina offers it as a more powerful but less standard alternative to regular Rexx I/O. Here are these additional built-in, C-like I/O functions:

I/O Function	Use
close	Closes a file
eof	Tests for end of file; returns 1 on eof, 0 otherwise
exists	Tests whether a file exists
open	Opens a file for appending, reading, or writing
readch	Reads the specified number of characters from the file
readln	Reads one line from the file
seek	Moves the file pointer to an offset position, and returns its new position relative to the start of the file
writech	Writes the string to the file
writeln	Writes the string to the file as a line

Regina's `stream` function supports all the ANSI-mandated information options, as discussed in Chapter 5 on input/output. The ANSI-1996 standard also permits implementation-specific commands to be executed through the `stream` function. In Regina these commands include the full range of options to control file modes, positioning, flushing, opening, closing, status, and other operations.

In addition to standard stream I/O and C-like I/O, Regina can take advantage of several external packages for sophisticated data storage needs. For example, the Rexx/SQL package supports connections to a wide variety of databases including Oracle, DB2, SQL Server, MySQL, PostreSQL, and others. Chapter 15 illustrates Regina with the Rexx/SQL interface to relational databases. Another example is the open-source Rexx/ISAM package, which supports an indexed access method (ISAM).

Access to function libraries

Many free and open-source interface packages come in the form of external function libraries. Examples include the products discussed in Chapters 15 through 18, such as Rexx/Tk, Rexx/DW, Rexx/gd, RexxXML, and others. Many of the Rexx tools and interfaces listed in Appendix H also come in the form of external function libraries.

Chapter 20

Let's discuss how Rexx interpreters access these libraries of external functions. Regina makes a good example of how to do this because it uses the Systems Application Architecture, or SAA, standards for this purpose. Several other Rexx interpreters use the SAA standards as their interface mechanism, too.

Rexx external function libraries come in the form of *shared libraries* for Unix, Linux, and BSD operating systems. For Windows systems they are *Dynamic Link Libraries* (DLLs).

Let's discuss Unix-derived operating systems such as Linux, Unix, and BSD first. For Unix-derived operating systems, external function libraries typically have names in one of these forms:

Library Name Pattern	System
lib_____.so	All Linuxes and most Unix-derived operating systems other than those specified below
lib_____.sl	HP/UP
lib_____.a	AIX
lib_____.dylib	Mac OS X

The underscores are replaced by the name of the library. For example, under Linux for a library called funpack, it would be in the file libfunpack.so. Be sure to read the documentation for any product you download, as library names can vary.

You configure your system for access to the external function libraries by setting an environmental variable. This specifies the directory that contains the function library to use. Here is the name of this environmental variable for several popular Unix-derived operating systems:

Environmental Variable that Points to Shared Library Files	System
LD_LIBRARY_PATH	All Linuxes and most Unix-derived operating systems other than those specified below
LIBPATH	AIX
SHLIB_PATH	HP/UX
DYLD_LIBRARY_PATH	Mac OS X
LD_LIBRARYN32_PATH	SGI

The "install notes" for Regina and the external library products typically list the names of this environmental variable for all Unix-derived operating systems, as needed. Be sure to consult the documentation that downloads with the product for any changes or product-specific information.

The meaning of all this is, if you get a "not found" error of some sort when first setting up Rexx under Unix, Linux, or BSD, or when first trying to access an external function library, make sure that the proper environmental variable is set correctly.

On Windows operating systems, the DLLs are the equivalent of Linux/Unix/BSD shared libraries. Windows DLLs reside in folders specified in the PATH environmental variable. The system shared DLL folder is typically either C:\Windows\System or C:\Windows\System32, depending on the version of Windows. The external function library DLL can alternatively reside in any other folder, as long as you make the folder known to Windows through the PATH specification.

You install the Windows DLL or Linux/Unix/BSD library file and point to it with the proper environmental variable by interacting with the operating system. Then, from within Regina scripts, you use the SAA-defined standard functions to give scripts access to these shared libraries or DLLs containing external functions. The built-in functions to use are:

SAA Function	Use
rxfuncadd	Registers an external function for use in the current script
rxfuncdrop	Removes the external function from use
rxfuncquery	Returns 0 if the external function was already registered (via rxfuncadd) or 1 otherwise
rxfuncerrmsg	Returns the error message that resulted from the last call to rxfuncadd This function is a Regina-only extension.

Here's an example that uses these functions to register external functions for use by a script. In this example, the script sets up access to the external Rexx/SQL function library. The first line below uses the RxFuncAdd function to load (or "register") the external function named SQLLoadFuncs. The next statement then executes the SQLLoadFuncs function, which loads the rest of the Rexx/SQL external function library.

```
if RxFuncAdd('SQLLoadFuncs','rexxsql', 'SQLLoadFuncs') <> 0 then
   say 'rxfuncadd failed, rc: ' rc

if SQLLoadFuncs() <> 0 then
   say 'sqlloadfuncs failed, rc: ' rc
```

The name of the external library is encoded in the second parameter of RxFuncAdd. In this case it is rexxsql. rexxsql is the root of the filename of the file containing the external functions. For example, under Windows, the full filename is rexxsql.dll. Under Linux it would be librexxsql.so. SqlLoadFuncs is the name by which this script will refer to that external library file.

The preceding code loads the Rexx/SQL external function library for use, but the same pattern of instructions can be used to load a wide variety of other external libraries for use by scripts. For example, Chapter 16 described how this code applied to Rexx/Tk, Rexx/DW, Rexx/gd, and other interfaces. Here is how the sample Rexx/Tk script in Chapter 16 coded access to the external Rexx/Tk function library.

Stylistically, the code varies a little from the preceding example, but the same pattern of two functions is coded in order to access and load the external function library:

```
call RxFuncAdd 'TkLoadFuncs','rexxtk','TkLoadFuncs'
if TkLoadFuncs() <> 0 then say 'ERROR- Cannot load Rexx/Tk library!'
```

To summarize, we've discussed how to set up an external function library for use from within Regina scripts. Then, we've seen the SAA functions you encode from within the Regina scripts to set up their access to the external function library. Other SAA-conformant Rexx interpreters access external packages in this same manner.

The stack

Regina supports all ANSI-1996 keywords on the `address` instruction for performing input/output to and from commands via streams and arrays. These keywords include `input`, `output`, and `error` for specifying redirection sources and targets, and `stream` and `stem`, to define whether the I/O goes to a file or array.

Regina also permits the use of the stack for command I/O. In this it follows the lead of mainframe Rexx and many other implementations.

The script in the section entitled "Using the Stack for Command I/O" in Chapter 11 showed how to send lines to a command through the stack and retrieve lines from the stack using Regina. In addition, these Regina built-in functions can be used to create or destroy new stack buffers:

Stack Function	Use
makebuf	Create a new stack buffer
dropbuf	Removes buffer(s) from the stack
desbuf	Destroys all stack buffers
buftype	Displays all stack buffers (usually used for debugging)

To use these function, a script would normally begin by creating its own stack area through the `makebuf` function. This function could be called repeatedly if there were a need for more than one stack buffer. The script would invoke the `dropbuf` function to release any buffer after it is no longer needed. Or if stack processing is complete, the `desbuf` function will destroy all extant stack buffers. The `buftype` function is used mainly for debugging if problems occur. It displays the contents of all the stack buffers extant at the time it is called.

As mentioned in Chapter 11, Regina permits an innovative use of the stack, through its "external queue capability." The stack can function as an interprocess communication facility between different processes on the same machine, or between different processes on different machines. The facility even supports communication between processes across the Internet. This goes well beyond the role of the stack as an external communications data queue as supported by many other Rexx interpreters.

To use Regina's extended external queue capabilities, install and start its stack service. Check out the `rxstack` and `rxqueue` executables. Use the `rxqueue` extended function to manage and control the stack from within Regina scripts.

Regina's SAA API

Regina fully meets the SAA application programming interface, or API definition. It is implemented as a library of routines that can be invoked from an external program. This library module could be either statically or dynamically loaded. What this means is that you could develop code in some other language, say C or C++, then link into Regina and use Rexx as a library of functions and subroutines.

Regina's documentation provides a full explanation of how to do this. It tells programmers what they need to know to use the Regina API. Of course, because it is written for programmers, the guide is technical. It uses C-language syntax to explain the interface.

Sample Scripts

Subsequent chapters on other Rexx interpreters include sample scripts that demonstrate the specific features of those interpreters and were run using them. We felt it was not necessary to include Regina-specific scripts in this chapter for two reasons:

❑ The sample scripts in all chapters to this point were run and tested with Regina

❑ Subsequent chapters that demonstrate interpreter-specific features are often coded in a similar manner to how those features would be coded using Regina. Regina's *supercompatibility* means that many of the special features and functions in those scripts are included and available from within Regina

Subsequent chapters give many examples of how extended functions can be used in Rexx scripts. Appendix D provides a complete coding-level reference to all of Regina's extended functions.

Summary

This chapter summarizes the features of Regina that go beyond the Rexx language standards. Regina provides functions that duplicate most of the extensions found in other Rexx implementations. Specific features we described in this chapter include Regina's extra operands for the options instruction, its additional functions, how one accesses external function packages using Regina, and the SAA API and its role with the Regina interpreter. Regina's extra functions are extensive, covering bit manipulation, string manipulation, environmental information and control, and input/output. We also described Regina's external queue facility, or stack, and how it can be used as a generalized communications vehicle between processes regardless of their location.

When considering whether to use the extended features of Regina (or those of any other Rexx interpreter), one must be fully cognizant of both the benefits and the drawbacks of this decision. Power and flexibility are the advantages, but the loss of standardization can be the downside. Each project or organization has its own goals. These must be measured against the benefits and costs of using the extended features.

Regina is one of the world's premier Rexx interpreters. It is the most popular open-source Rexx. It runs on almost any platform. More developers use Regina than any other free Rexx interpreter, with the result that more tools are tested with it and its support community is larger.

The next several chapters take a look at other Rexx intepreters. Those chapters spell out the strengths and applications of the other interpreters. Some of the interpreters specialize in certain operating systems or platforms, while others extend Rexx in entirely new directions. Examples of the latter include roo! and Open Object Rexx, which support object-oriented scripting, and NetRexx, which brings Rexx into the world of Java and the Java Virtual Machine. Stay tuned. . . .

Test Your Understanding

1. What are Regina's major advantages? What platforms can it run on? Can it run on any version of Windows, Linux and Unix? Does it run on DOS machines? Under which handheld OS does it run natively?

2. What are the uses of the stack in Regina? Can you use it to send input to and receive output from operating system commands? Can you send input to and receive output from OS commands using ANSI-standard keywords?

3. What functions are available in Regina's C-like I/O model? Which do you use to read and write strings with linefeeds, as opposed to those that read and write strings without line terminators? How do you:

   ❏   Explicitly close a file

   ❏   Test for end of file

   ❏   Move a file pointer to a specific position

4. What is the SAA API? Of what value to programmers is it that Regina fulfills the SAA API? What SAA-based functions do you use to register an external function for use? How do you terminate use of an external function?

5. What compatibility parameters can you set on the `options` instruction?

Rexx/imc

Overview

Rexx/imc is a standard Rexx for Unix, Linux, and BSD environments. Written by Ian Collier of England, some of the systems it is used on include Solaris, AIX, HP/UX, Digital Unix, IRIX, Red Hat Linux and other Linux distributions, FreeBSD, and Sun OS.

Rexx/imc is at language level 4.00 and meets the TRL-2 standard. This chapter covers product installation and the extended Rexx/imc features that go beyond the Rexx standards. These features give you power beyond the confines of standard Rexx but are, of course, less portable across interpreters and platforms.

This chapter lists and discusses the strengths of Rexx/imc. Then it details how to install the product using the Red Hat Package Manager. After this we describe the extended features of the product. These include functions for retrieving environmental information, higher mathematics, SAA-based access to external function libraries, and C-language-style file I/O. We illustrate the special features of Rexx/imc within the contexts of two sample scripts. The first demonstrates some of the product's functions for retrieving environmental information, while the second shows how to use its C-like I/O functions. Let's start by reviewing Rexx/imc features.

Advantages

As we've mentioned, each chapter that covers a particular Rexx interpreter begins by listing and discussing the unique aspects of that interpreter. Here are some key points about Rexx/imc:

- ❑ *Meets standards* — Rexx/imc is at language level 4.00 and meets the TRL-2 standard.

- ❑ *Unix-oriented extras* — Rexx/imc offers a number of Unix-oriented features beyond the standard. These include C-like I/O functions and Unix-specific environmental-information functions.

❏ *Additional functions* — Rexx/imc includes a set of a dozen mathematical functions and the SAA-based functions to load and manage external functions.

❏ *Clear documentation* — Rexx/imc includes clear, complete documentation. It comes with a nice Rexx tutorial for beginning programmers. It includes a useful reference summary as well as a complete reference manual.

❏ *Reliable, well proven* — The interpreter has been used for a decade and is well proven. It has a long track record of support and is well known and respected in the Rexx community.

Installing Rexx/imc

Rexx/imc can be freely downloaded from several sites. These include that of its developer at `http://users.comlab.ox.ac.uk/ian.collier/Rexx/`. Other sites are `www.netsw.org/softeng/lang/rexx/rexx-imc` and `www.idiom.com/free-compilers/LANG/REXX-1.html`. Since Web addresses change, simply search for the keyword `Rexx/imc` on Google at `www.google.com` or any other search engine to list additional sites from which to download the product.

Rexx/imc is distributed in either Zip (`*.zip`) or "gzip" (`*tar.gz`) compressed formats. Red Hat Package Manager (`*.rpm`) files are also available for systems that support the RPM product for Linux installs. The files are either source code or compiled binaries.

Chapter 1 described how to install Rexx interpreters under Linux, Unix, or BSD. These procedures apply to Rexx/imc. Here we show how to install Rexx/imc under Linux using the *Red Hat Package Manager*, or *RPM*. RPM automates and simplifies product installation. It eliminates the need to enter any Linux commands beyond that of the `rpm` command itself. Originally developed for the Red Hat distribution of Linux, it is now used in other Linux distributions as well. The Red Hat Package Manager is an easy way to install Rexx interpreters (and other products) on many Unix-derived operating systems. While the discussion that follows is specific to Rexx/imc, the general approach it describes also applies to installing other Rexx interpreters when using the RPM.

Start the installation by downloading Rexx/imc from one of the Web sites listed above. The file to download will be an `*.rpm` file. In this case, the RPM package file was named:

```
rexx-imc-1.76-1.rh7.i386.rpm
```

Using the `root` user ID, make a new directory where you place this file, and change the current directory to that directory. You can name this new directory anything you choose. Here, we have named it `/rexximc`:

```
cd /
mkdir /rexximc
cd /rexximc
```

Copy the RPM package file into this new directory. Use the `cp`, or copy, command to do this from the command line, or use a GUI interface drag-and-drop approach if you prefer.

Now you are ready to use the `rpm` command to install the Rexx/imc package. Several of the most useful options for this command follow. Of course, these switches are case-sensitive, so a lower-case v is different from an uppercase V:

- ❏ `-i` — Install the package
- ❏ `-v` — Verbose install (provides information during the install)
- ❏ `-vv` — Very Verbose install (provides *lots* of information during install)
- ❏ `-q` — Query the status of the package
- ❏ `-V` — Verify the package

Go ahead and install the Rexx/imc package, using the "very verbose" (`-vv`) option to view feedback on what's happening:

```
rpm  -ivv  rexx-imc-1.76-1.rh7.i386.rpm       # install with feedback
```

If everything worked, you're done! It's that simple. The `rpm` command replaces the series of commands that are required in traditional product installs for Unix-derived operating systems.

The output from the `rpm` command provides a lot of useful information. It lists any errors so you can scroll through them to find further information if any problems occurred. It also shows the size of the installed package.

The output lists where it puts various Rexx/imc components. These vary by distribution, but typically they include components and directories similar to those shown in the following table:

Directory	Contains
`/usr/bin`	Location of Rexx/imc interpreter
`/usr/lib`	Shared library location
`/usr/man/man1`	Location of the help files and documentation
`/usr/share/doc`	Documentation, tools, services, libraries, and so on
`/usr/share/doc/rexx-imc-_.__`	Documentation for Rexx/imc including installation info

Verify that the installation worked by either querying or verifying the package name:

```
rpm  -q  rexx-imc-1.76-1              # Query the package
```

Another way to verify the status of the package is to enter this query:

```
rpm  -V  rexx-imc-1.76-1              # Verify the package
```

The best way to verify the package installed correctly is to run a test program. Start your favorite editor and enter this three-line test program:

```
#!/usr/bin/rexx
/*  a simple Rexx test program for Rexx/imc */
say 'hello'
```

The first line should refer to the fully qualified directory name where the Rexx/imc executable is installed. Save this code under the filename testme.rexx, then change the permission bits on that file such that it is executable:

```
chmod +x  testme.rexx
```

Now you can execute the script implicitly:

```
./testme.rexx
```

If you add the current directory to your PATH environmental variable, you can exclude the leading two characters ./ and just run the script by entering its name:

```
testme.rexx
```

If you do not have the Red Hat Package Manager available, or choose not to use it, follow the generic instructions for installing Rexx interpreters under Unix, Linux, and BSD given in Chapter 1.

Features

Rexx/imc fully conforms to the language level 4.00 standard defined by TRL-2. Beyond this, it includes additional functions, instructions, and features specifically oriented towards the Unix, Linux, and BSD environments.

Rexx/imc extends standard Rexx by adding a number of extra built-in functions. Figure 21-1 pictorially represents the categorization of these extra functions.

Let's enumerate and discuss the extended functions with their coding formats so that you can see what they offer. First, the Rexx/imc Unix-specific functions provide scripts information about their environment. All provide features Unix- and Linux- based programmers expect:

Environmental Function	Use
chdir(directory)	Change the current directory to a new directory
getcwd()	Returns the current working directory
getenv(name)	Get the value of the specified environmental variable
putenv(string)	Set the value of an environmental variable
system(s)	Return the output of a shell command
userid()	Get the process owner's login name

Rexx/imc's Additional Functions

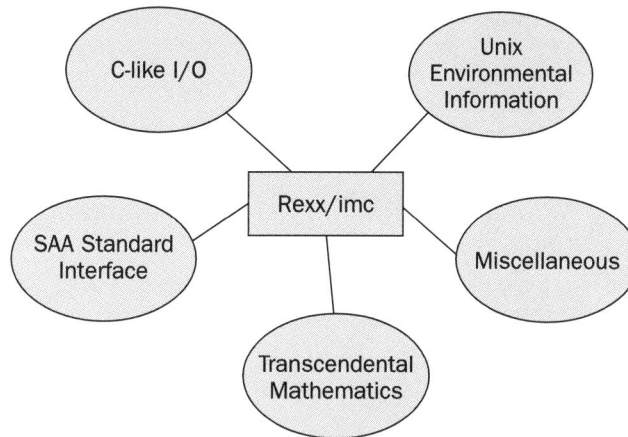

Figure 21-1

The Rexx/imc mathematical functions support transcendental mathematics. These functions are very similar to those you'll find in other extended Rexx interpreters, for example, BRexx, and Reginald. Recall that several add-on packages also include higher math functions. These include the Internet/REXX HHNS Workbench, discussed in Chapter 17, and several of the packages listed in Appendix H. Here are the Rexx/imc higher math functions:

Mathematical Function	Use
acos(n)	Arc-cosine
asin(n)	Arc-sine
atan(n)	Arc-tangent
cos(n)	Cosine of n radians
exp(n)	The exponential of n
ln(n)	The natural log of n
sin(n)	Sine
sqrt(n)	Square root
tan(n)	Tangent
topower(x,y)	Raise x to power y

Rexx/imc supports the three IBM Systems Application Architecture (SAA) functions for loading the using external functions. These are the same functions included in other Rexx interpreters, for example, Regina:

SAA Interface Function	Use
rxfuncadd(rexxname,module,sysname)	Load (register) an external function
rxfuncdrop(function)	Drop an external function
rxfuncquery(function)	Query whether a function is loaded

Code these functions in the same manner shown in the examples in Chapters 15 through 18 in order to access external functions from Rexx/imc. The standard SAA calling interface makes a wide variety of open-source interfaces available for use with Rexx/imc.

Rexx/imc offers a few additional miscellaneous functions. These support mainframe Rexx-style text justification and conversions between binary and decimal:

Miscellaneous Function	Use
justify(s,n [,pad])	This function justifies text to a given width. (It is similar to the mainframe VM/CMS Rexx justify function).
b2d(binary)	Convert binary to decimal
d2b(decimal)	Convert decimal to binary

In addition to its extra built-in functions, Rexx/imc enhances several instructions with additional convenience features:

❑   sayn instruction writes a line without a carriage return (i.e., no *linefeed* or *newline*)

❑   select *expression* instruction implements the Case construct, depending on a variable's value

❑   parse value instruction parses multiple strings (separated by commas) in one instruction

❑   procedure hide instruction explicitly hides global variables from an internal routine

❑   Arrays may be referenced by calculations. For example, you can code stem.(i+1), whereas in standard REXX you must write j=i+1 followed by stem.j.

Rexx/imc accepts any nonzero number for TRUE (not just 1). This means you can code C-style operatorless condition tests, where a function that returns any nonzero value evaluates to TRUE:

```
if my_function()  then
   say  'The function returned TRUE (any nonzero value)'
```

Recall that under standard Rexx, a condition must evaluate to either 1 (TRUE) or 0 (FALSE). In standard Rexx, a nonzero value other than 1 is not acceptable and causes a runtime error.

Finally, Rexx/imc includes a stack that is used in traditional Rexx fashion. It can be used to communicate data between Rexx programs and between routines within a program. It supports all the stack manipulation instructions (queue, push, pull, and parse pull), and the queued function to retrieve the number of items on the stack.

The C-language I/O Model

Like other open-source Rexx interpreters, Rexx/imc offers several functions beyond the Rexx standard to implement C-language style input/output. In the *C I/O model*, you explicitly open a file for use by the open function. The *mode* in which the file is opened determines whether it is used for reading, writing, or *appending* (adding data on to the end of a file). After use, explicitly close the file by the close function.

Here are the additional Rexx/imc functions for C-language I/O. We have included their coding formats so that you can see what parameters each function requires:

I/O Function	Use
open(file [,[mode] [stream]])	Explicitly opens a file in the specified mode
close(stream)	Closes a stream
fileno(stream)	Returns the *file descriptor* (or fd) number of a stream
ftell(stream)	Returns the current file pointer
fdopen(fd [, [mode] [,stream]])	Open a fd number. Used for accessing files which have already been opened by another program.
popen(command [,[mode] [,stream]])	Opens a pipe to a shell command
pclose(stream)	Closes a pipe (opened by the popen function)
stream(stream [,[option] , [command]])	Directly control file or stream operations through some 15-plus commands. Among them are flush, advanced open modes, and query for information.

The C I/O model offers greater control of file input/output, at the cost of less standardized code. Explicit control could be useful, for example, to close and reopen a file within a script, or when a script opens so many files it needs to close some to reclaim memory. Of course, Rexx/imc supports standard Rexx I/O as well.

Rexx/imc allows you to open a *pipe* to a shell command through the popen function and to close the pipe by the pclose function. The pipe is an in-memory mechanism for communication between the Rexx script and the shell command. Along with the system function this offers another mechanism for communication with operating system commands.

Interfaces and Tools

Since Rexx/imc is a standard Rexx interpreter that uses the SAA-standard functions for access to external function libraries, it interfaces to many packages and tools. One of the best known is The Hessling Editor (or THE), a Rexx-aware text editor that uses Rexx as its macro language. Another is Rexx/Curses, a library for screen I/O that gives applications a portable text-based user interface.

Other packages include Rexx/Tk, the cross-platform GUI toolkit, and RegUtil, an external function library. More information on these interfaces and tools is available at the Rexx/imc homepage at `http://users.comlab.ox.ac.uk/ian.collier/Rexx/`. Appendix H lists many additional free and open-source packages, tools, and interfaces.

A Sample Program — Environmental Information

The sample programs in this chapter were run under Linux (Red Hat). The first program illustrates several of Rexx/imc's environmental functions that extend beyond the Rexx standards. These include `getcwd`, `chdir`, `getenv`, `system`, and `userid`. The program also shows the results of the `parse source` and `parse version` instructions for Rexx/imc running under Linux.

Here is the output of the script named Environment:

```
[root /rexximc]$ ./environment.rexx
The initial directory is: /rexximc
The current directory is: /
The current directory is: /rexximc
The value of environmental variable USERNAME is: root

Uname is: Linux
Userid is: root
Default command environment is: UNIX
System: UNIX  Invocation: COMMAND  Filename: /rexximc/environment.rexx
Lang: REXX/imc-beta-1.75  Level: 4.00  Date: 25 Feb 2002
```

The full code of the program is shown here:

```
#!/usr/bin/rexx
/*******************************************************************/
/* ENVIRONMENT                                                     */
/*                                                                 */
/* This script uses some of Rexx/imc's unique environmental functions*/
/* It also shows results of PARSE SOURCE and PARSE VERSION.        */
/*******************************************************************/

/* change current directory to '/', display it, and change it back   */

current_dir = getcwd()                     /* save current dir.      */
say 'The initial directory is:' current_dir /* show current dir.     */
rc = chdir('/')                            /* change directory       */
say 'The current directory is:' getcwd()   /* display current dir.   */
rc = chdir(current_dir)                    /* change directory back  */
```

```
say 'The current directory is:' getcwd()    /* display current dir. */


/* display the value of environmental variable USERNAME              */

say 'The value of environmental variable USERNAME is:' getenv('USERNAME')


/* Capture UNAME command result, display it, display owner's login   */

uname_result = system('uname')              /* capture UNAME results */
sayn 'Uname is:' uname_result               /* display UNAME results */
say 'Userid is:' userid()                   /* display user login    */


/* display PARSE SOURCE, VERSION, for Rexx/imc under Red Hat Linux   */

say 'Default command environment is:' address()

parse source system invocation filename .
say 'System:' system ' Invocation:' invocation ' Filename:' filename

parse version language level date month year .
say 'Lang:' language ' Level:' level ' Date:' date month year
exit 0
```

The first block of code in the script retrieves and displays the current directory with the `getcwd` function, changes the current directory to the root directory with the `chdir` function, then changes it back to the original directory with `chdir`. The script's output shows that the current directory was changed, and then altered to its original setting, through these special functions:

```
current_dir = getcwd()                      /* save current dir.     */
say 'The initial directory is:' current_dir /* show current dir.     */
rc = chdir('/')                             /* change directory      */
say 'The current directory is:' getcwd()    /* display current dir.  */
rc = chdir(current_dir)                     /* change dir. back      */
say 'The current directory is:' getcwd()    /* display current dir.  */
```

The script uses the `getenv` function to retrieve and display the value of the USERNAME environmental variable:

```
say 'The value of environmental variable USERNAME is:' getenv('USERNAME')
```

Rexx/imc also has a corresponding `putenv` function to set an environmental variable.

The script issues the Linux `uname` operating system command through the Rexx/imc `system` function, and captures and displays its output. This shows how to capture command output into the script via the `system` function. The special `sayn` instruction writes a string without a newline or linefeed character.

This avoids an extra blank line in the program output, because the Linux uname command output contained a newline character:

```
uname_result = system('uname')                    /* capture UNAME results */
sayn 'Uname is:' uname_result                     /* display UNAME results */
```

Rexx/imc alternatively allows you to code the system command and capture its feedback in this manner:

```
uname_result = 'uname'()        /* capture the result of the UNAME command */
```

The script retrieves and displays the user's login id through the userid function:

```
say 'Userid is:' userid()                         /* display user login    */
```

Finally, the script displays the default command environment by the address function, and issues the parse source and parse version instructions to display their results. The last three lines of the output disclose how Rexx/imc, and indeed, all standard Rexx interpreters, report on their environment and the language version.

A Sample Program — I/O

This sample program demonstrates the C-language-like input/output functions of Rexx/imc. The program accepts input and output filenames as command-line arguments, then simply copies the input file to the new file specified by the output filename. While copying, the script displays the read and write file pointer positions after each I/O operation.

Here is the input file of test data:

```
this is line 1
this is line 2
this is the last line
```

The program copies this file as is to the output and displays these lines on the screen while doing so:

```
[root /rexximc]$ ./fcopy.rexx  fcopy_in.txt  fcopy_out.txt
Input  file position after read  # 1: 16
Output file position after write # 1: 16
Input  file position after read  # 2: 31
Output file position after write # 2: 31
Input  file position after read  # 3: 54
Output file position after write # 3: 54
```

The output shows both the read and write file pointer positions after each I/O operation. Pointer positions include the line termination characters that occur at the end of lines. (Sometimes these are referred to as the *newline character* or as *linefeeds* or *LF*.) Remember that file positions always point to the *next* character position to read or write. Here is the script:

```
#!/usr/bin/rexx
/***************************************************************/
/* FCOPY                                                     */
```

```
/*                                                                    */
/* Uses Rexx/imc I/O functions to copy a file.                        */
/* Reports file positions by the FTELL function.                      */
/**********************************************************************/
parse arg source target          /* get filenames, retain lower-case  */

/* open input & output files, establish STREAM names                  */

rc_in  = open(source,'r','in')          /* open input file            */
rc_out = open(target,'w','out')         /* open output file           */
if rc_in <> 0 | rc_out <> 0 then        /* check for errors on open   */
    say 'File OPEN Error!'

/* perform the file copy, display file pointers as copying occurs     */

do j=1 while lines('in') > 0
    line = linein('in')
    say 'Input  file position after read  #' j || ': ' ftell('in')
    call lineout 'out',line
    say 'Output file position after write #' j || ': ' ftell('out')
end

/* close the files and exit                                           */

rc_in  = close('in')                    /* close input file           */
rc_out = close('out')                   /* close output file          */
if rc_in <> 0 | rc_out <> 0 then        /* check for errors on close  */
    say 'File CLOSE Error!'

exit 0
```

The script accepts two command-line input parameters. They specify the names of the input and output files. These lines open the two files for use.

```
rc_in  = open(source,'r','in')          /* open input file            */
rc_out = open(target,'w','out')         /* open output file           */
```

The second parameter on the open function is the *mode* in which the file will be processed. The options are:

OPEN Parameter	Processing Mode
r	Read.
w	Write. If the file already exists, its contents are overwritten. If the file does not exist, it is created.
a	Append. If the file already exists, add new lines to the end of the file. If the file does not exist, create it.

The third parameter on open is optional. If specified, it supplies the name by which the stream can be referred to in subsequent file-oriented functions (such as linein, lineout, and close). This parameter works whether quoted as in the example, or just supplied as an unquoted symbol. Either 'in' or in will work. Consider this a *file handle*, or reference name, for the file.

The `do-while` loop copies the lines from the input file to the output file. These lines in the loop show the use of the `ftell` function to retrieve and print the current read and write file pointers:

```
say 'Input  file position after read  #' j || ': ' ftell('in')
say 'Output file position after write #' j || ': ' ftell('out')
```

`ftell` is useful to programs that explicitly manipulate the file pointers. It gives them a way to verify the current file positions. This could be useful, for example, for scripts that perform *direct* or *random* file I/O. It's also useful in scripts that read data from the same file more than once or in programs that update data within a file. The standard `charout` and `lineout` functions can also explicitly position a file pointer. The `stream` function allows you to open a file in advanced modes for special processing.

Finally, these lines `close` the two input files:

```
rc_in  = close('in')            /* close input file             */
rc_out = close('out')           /* close output file            */
if rc_in <> 0 | rc_out <> 0 then /* check for errors on close    */
    say 'File CLOSE Error!'
```

The script checks the return codes from the `close` operations just as it did from the `open` functions. This small step goes a great way to increasing program reliability. We have not included such error checking in the examples of this book out of concern for program length and clarity. But in industrial programming, the small effort required to check I/O return codes yields big dividends in program reliability.

We recommend checking return codes from *all* input/output operations, whether using C-like I/O or standard Rexx I/O functions.

Summary

This chapter summarizes some of the additional features offered by Rexx/imc beyond the TRL-2 standard. Several of these features are especially useful to Unix and Linux programmers, fitting the traditions and expectations of this programming community. Rexx/imc is a proven interpreter that runs on any Unix, Linux, or BSD operating system.

The specific areas we discussed were the strengths of Rexx/imc and why you might use this interpreter. Then, we illustrated the typical installation process, step by step, using the Red Hat Package Manager or RPM. While this chapter installed Rexx/imc using the RPM, the approach we discussed could be used to install other Rexx interpreters that support the RPM as well. We described Rexx/imc functions for retrieving environmental information, higher mathematics, SAA-based access to external function libraries, and C-language style file I/O. Finally, we illustrated some of the extended features of Rexx/imc in two sample scripts. The first demonstrated how to retrieve environmental information, while the second showed how to perform C-like input/output.

Test Your Understanding

1. Under what operating system families does Rexx/imc run? What are Rexx/imc's strengths? What Rexx language standards does it meet?

2. What extra I/O functions does Rexx/imc add beyond standard Rexx? What is this new I/O model and how do you use its functions? When would you use the extra C-like Rexx/imc I/O functions versus standard Rexx I/O?

3. How does Rexx/imc enhance the `select` instruction beyond its usual definition? How can this be useful?

4. How do you register or load an external function for use in a Rexx/imc script? How do you drop that function? How can you check to see if an external function is available from the script?

5. What values does Rexx/imc accept as TRUE in condition comparisons? How does this differ from traditional Rexx? Would a script that uses the standard truth value still run under Rexx/imc?

BRexx

Overview

BRexx is a free version of classic Rexx developed by Vasilis Vlachoudis of the Cern Laboratory in Switzerland. Written as an ANSI C-language program, BRexx is notable for its high performance. It also provides a nice collection of special built-in functions and function libraries that offer many extra features.

BRexx was originally written for DOS in the early 1990s. With the rise of Windows, it was revised for the 32-bit world of Windows and 32-bit DOS. BRexx also runs under Linux and Unix family operating systems, and it has a good set of functions specially written for Windows CE. Other operating systems it runs on include MacOS, BeOS, and the Amiga OS.

An outstanding feature of BRexx is its tiny footprint. The entire product, including full documentation and examples, comprises only a few hundred kilobytes. This is small enough to fit on a single floppy diskette. Installation is simple. Just download a file, decompress it, set an environmental variable, and voila! BRexx is ready to go.

This chapter describes BRexx's extended features and offers several sample programs. Specifically, we'll review the strengths of the product and how to download and install it under several common operating systems. Then we'll discuss some of its special features that extend beyond the Rexx standards. These include extra built-in functions, such as those for manipulating the stack, system information and control, higher mathematics, C-language style input/output, and MySQL database access. BRexx shines in supporting several I/O paradigms, including standard Rexx I/O, C-like I/O, and database I/O. We'll discuss when each is best used and the BRexx functions that support each I/O model.

We'll review the many function libraries that ship with BRexx, including the functions specifically designed for Windows CE. Then, we discuss several sample scripts designed to highlight BRexx features. The first script demonstrates C-like input/output, while the second shows how to perform random file access and ANSI-standard screen I/O. A third script further explores direct file input/output. The final script illustrates BRexx under DOS and how it provides information about the DOS environment. While no longer used as a desktop operating system, DOS survives and thrives in embedded device programming and on handhelds. The last sample program suggests how the BRexx interpreter provides a useful tool for handhelds and resource-constrained environments.

Advantages

As in previous chapters that examine specific Rexx interpreters, we need to know what BRexx features distinguish it from the alternatives. In this section, we briefly list and discuss some of the advantages to the BRexx interpreter. These are some of the key strengths of the product:

❑ *Performance* — Since it is written as a C program, this interpreter is fast. It consistently beats other Rexx interpreters in direct comparisons.

❑ *Small footprint* — Distributed as a single compressed file, the entire product requires only a few hundred kilobytes.

❑ *Proven support* — Product documentation shows a consistent, dedicated history of product improvements, bug fixes and upgrades for over a decade.

❑ *Extra functions for common tasks* — Bundled with the interpreter are about a dozen external function libraries for purposes like screen I/O, C-style file I/O, Unix and DOS functions and the like.

❑ *Special Windows CE features* — BRexx is specially customized for Windows CE by the addition of some 20 extra functions and appropriate documentation. It runs natively under Windows CE.

❑ *Commands and programs treated as functions* — Scripts can run commands or programs *coded as if they were functions* as long as those routines use standard I/O.

❑ *Good documentation with program examples* — The product comes with complete HTML-based textual documentation and three dozen programs that illustrate its unique features.

BRexx is especially suitable where machine resources are limited. For example, the author worked with a charity that collected donated personal computers, configured them, and shipped them to third-world countries. We needed to be able to write simple scripts that would run on almost any PC, without having the luxury of assuming that the PC had a working CD or DVD reader, Internet or LAN connection, or any minimum amount of internal memory. We quickly learned that the one working device every desktop PC has, no matter how old, is a floppy disk drive. BRexx is so compact we could put both our scripts and the entire BRexx distribution on a single floppy! Installation was as simple as copying floppy contents to the hard drive. No configuration or compatibility issues arose. BRexx is very fast so the scripts ran quickly even on older machines.

BRexx fully meets the TRL-2 standard and is at language level 4.00. It also goes well beyond the Rexx standards in offering many additional built-in functions, over a half-dozen external function libraries, and other extended features described in the following sections.

Downloading and Installation

BRexx can be downloaded from several web sites including that of its creator at `http://bnv.home.cern.ch/bnv/` and Twocows Inc. at `www.tucows.com`. It can also be obtained at `ftp://linux01.gwdg.de/pub/brexx` or `ftp://ftp.gwdg.de/pub/languages/rexx/brexx`. Or just access any search engine such as Google at www.google.com, and enter BRexx as the search term. Several download sites will pop up. Full product documentation downloads with the product, or access it online at http://ftp.gwdg.de/pub/languages/rexx/brexx/html/index.html.

Download a single compressed file that includes all code, documentation and sample scripts. The file contains either source code or is a binary. File extensions include *.zip, *.tar.gz, *.tgz, *.gz, and *.hqw (for the Mac OS).

The download files contain product licensing information. The produce is freeware, free for nonprofit and personal use. A modest fee is required for commercial use. Please read the product files for complete, current details on licensing and fees.

The product download comes with help information in browser-viewable files (HTML files). Among them is a file containing installation instructions, usually named install.html. These instructions tell you what you need to know to install BRexx under Windows, DOS, or Windows CE. For Linux, Unix, or BSD, perform the install as you would for any other product under those systems, adding the extra steps cited in the installation instructions.

Windows installation

Installing BRexx under Windows is quite simple and does not require the Windows Installer. Start by downloading the appropriate *.zip file. Double-click on the *.zip file to uncompress it. This effectively installs the product. No Windows installer program is needed.

There are three steps to complete installation:

1. Create and set a new environmental variable called RXLIB to point to the location of the library modules of BRexx (so that the interpreter can find its libraries).

2. Add the directory in which the BRexx interpreter resides to the PATH variable.

3. Optionally create a *file association* between Rexx script files and the BRexx interpreter. This allows you to run BRexx scripts just by double-clicking on them.

To set environmental variables under Windows versions such as Windows XP, right-click on the My Computer icon. Select Properties from the pick list; then select the Advanced tab. On the panel that appears, select Environmental Variables. Select New to create a new environmental variable. Call this new environmental variable RXLIB and set its value to the directory where the BRexx library modules reside:

```
RXLIB=C:\BREXX\LIB
```

The PATH environmental variable will likely already exist. Highlight it and select the Edit function. Add the BRexx home directory to the list of directories separated by semicolons. In this example, we added BRexx to the end of a PATH list that already contained several elements:

```
PATH=c:\perl;.;c:\pdksh;c:\brexx
```

An alternative way to set Windows environmental variables is by using the SET command in the autoexec.bat file. See the "Windows or DOS Installation" instructions that follow for information on how to do this.

To set the file association, open Windows Explorer. Select `Tools` from the top menu bar, and `Folder Options` from the `Tools` drop-down list box. Select the tab `File Types`. Select `New` to add a new file type for files having the extension `R`, and associate this extension with the BRexx interpreter executable. Most likely the interpreter executable will be named `rexx32.exe`. It will reside in the directory where you installed BRexx.

Windows or DOS installation

You could alternatively install BRexx under Windows just like you do under DOS-family operating systems. In other words, you can treat a Windows install as if you were performing a 32-bit DOS install. Here are the DOS install instructions.

After you download and optionally decompress the product file into an appropriate directory, set the `RXLIB` and `PATH` variables by adding lines to the `autoexec.bat` file. Place a statement like this in the `autoexec.bat` file to set environmental variable `RXLIB` to point to the directory in which BRexx's library modules reside:

```
SET RXLIB=C:\BREXX\LIB
```

Add the directory location to the `PATH` variable indicating where the BRexx executable resides. Here's an example where we added the BRexx directory to the end of an existing `PATH` list:

```
PATH=c:\perl;.;c:\pdksh;c:\brexx
```

These settings will automatically be established by the boot process every time you start up DOS or Windows. The OS boot process automatically executes the `autoexec.bat` procedure.

Linux installation

BRexx comes as a Red Hat Package Manager or `*.rpm` file. Follow the standard instructions on how to install products using RPM, as given in chapter 21. Or, download a compressed file and follow the instructions for installing under Unix in the next section.

Unix installation

To install BRexx under Unix-based systems, follow the same installation procedures you would for any product distributed as a compressed file. Chapter 1 described the generic procedures for Linux, Unix, and BSD installs.

Be sure to set environmental variable `RXLIB` (in capital letters) to point to BRexx's library directory.

Add a line like this as the first line of each script, assuming that the BRexx interpreter resides in directory `/usr/local/bin/`:

```
#!/usr/local/bin/rexx
```

Make any script file you create executable, so that you can run it:

```
chmod +x script_file_name          # set file permission bits to EXECUTABLE
```

Windows CE installation

For version 2.1 on, the download includes a `setup.exe` file. Just execute this program for a standard Windows CE install. Be sure to review the product documentation for any updates or additional details on how to install the product. The "Windows CE" section later in this chapter goes into more detail about installing BRexx under Windows CE.

Extra Built-in Functions

BRexx includes many built-in functions beyond those included in standard Rexx. These supply a lot of the power behind the BRexx interpreter and take it well beyond the features and capabilities of standard Rexx. This section describes these extended functions and their uses.

Three stack functions control the creation and destruction of stacks for the external data queue. All operate in the manner expected, as per the discussion of how stacks work in Chapter 11:

Stack Function	Use
`makebuf()`	Creates a new system stack
`desbuf()`	Destroys all system stacks
`dropbuf(n)`	Destroys the top n stacks

BRexx was originally written for DOS-based personal computers. Given this heritage, it offers several low-level PC-oriented functions that no other Rexx interpreter includes. These can be extremely useful for PC control and diagnostic programs of various kinds. Here is a brief list of these functions:

System Function	Use
`load(file)`	Loads a file of Rexx scripts to use as a library. This is the basic function by which scripts access external BRexx function libraries.
`import(file | dynamic library)`	New in version 2.1, this function imports a shared library using dynamic linking with Rexx routines. For example, to access the MySQL API library under Linux, code: `call import "librxmysql.so"` This function effectively supercedes the `load` function.
`intr(number,reg-string)`	Executes an x86 soft interrupt (works under DOS only).
`storage(address,length,data)`	Returns contents of the specified memory location, or returns the size of memory if no parms are encoded. Can also overwrite the contents of a storage location.
`vardump(symbol,option)`	Returns the tree of internal interpreter variables. Mainly useful for debugging purposes.

BRexx includes a full set of advanced mathematical functions. These are similar to those included in other Rexx interpreters and operate in the manner one would expect:

Math Function	Use
acos(number)	Arc-cosine
asin(number)	Arc-sine
atan(number)	Arc-tangent
cos(number)	Cosine
cosh(number)	Hyperbolic cosine
exp(number)	Exponentiation
log(number)	Natural log
log10(number)	Logarithm of base 10
pow10(number)	Power using base 10
sin(number)	Sine
sinh(number)	Hyperbolic sine
sqrt(number)	Square root
tan(number)	Tangent
tanh(number)	Hyperbolic tangent
pow(a,b)	Raise a to power b

Input/Output

BRexx supports the full set of ANSI-1996 input and output functions: charin, charout, chars, linein, lineout, lines, and stream. Standard Rexx scripts that run with any other Rexx interpreter will run under BRexx.

BRexx goes beyond standard Rexx I/O to give the developer alternatives. It offers a full set of C-language built-in functions for I/O. These allow programmers to explicitly open or close files, open files in specific modes by open and stream, flush file buffers, test for end of file through eof, read and write either characters or lines, and position the file pointers by seek.

This C-oriented I/O model offers a more full-featured alternative to traditional Rexx stream I/O. Some other Rexx interpreters offer such functions through stream function commands, and BRexx as well includes an extensive set of over a dozen stream function commands.

Here are the C-like I/O built-in functions:

Input/Output Function	Use
open(file,mode)	Opens a file for reading, writing, or appending in either binary or text modes; returns a file handle
close(file)	Explicitly closes a file
read(file,amount)	Reads data as characters, bytes, or lines
write(file,data,[newline])	Writes characters, bytes or lines of data
eof(file)	Tests for end of file
flush(file)	Explicitly flushes the file buffer
seek(file,offset,[option])	Explicitly positions the file pointer
stream(stream,[option],[command])	Supports ANSI stream options, plus permits issuing some 15 different file I/O commands

The C I/O model will be appreciated by those who require its powerful features or are familiar with the C++ or C languages.

BRexx also provides a set of functions that interface to the free database, MySQL. These are built-in functions, not an external library. The MySQL functions provide a third alternative for I/O, one based on the most popular open-sorce database. Here are these functions:

MySQL Function	Use
dbclose()	Terminates a database connection
dbconnect(host,[user], [password],database)	Establishes a database connection
dberror(["Alphanumeric"])	Returns the error number of the last error
dbescstr(string)	Escapes special characters for use in a string
dbfield[num|name [,"N","T","K","L","M","U", "A","F"]])	Returns info on fields from the previous query
dbget(row,col|name)	Returns the value of the specified data element
dbisnull(row,col|name)	Tells if a data element is null
dbinfo("Rows"|"Fields"|"Insertid")	Returns info about the previous database operation
dbsql(sqlcmd)	Executes the string as a SQL statement

For Windows users, the MySQL interface may not be part of the compiled Windows binary — check the release documentation to see. If you are using Windows and you require this feature, build BRexx from source code and link in your MySQL client software. For newer releases, you can dynamically access the MySQL functions by coding an `import` function to access the library.

To summarize, BRexx scripts have three alternative I/O methods, all based on built-in functions: standard Rexx I/O, C-like I/O, and MySQL database I/O. Each has its advantages. This chart contrasts them:

I/O Model	Advantages
Rexx I/O model	Simple, portable, standard
C I/O model	More explicit control over I/O
MySQL database I/O	Accesses the popular MySQL open-sorce database; yields all the benefits of full database I/O through built-in functions

The External Function Libraries

BRexx comes complete with about a dozen external function libraries. To use the library functions, first load the library with the `load` function:

```
call load "ansi.r"        /* loads the ANSI.R library functions for use */
```

Here is another example demonstrating how to encode the `load` function:

```
call load "files.r"       /* loads File function library for use        */
```

Once loaded, *all* the functions in the library are accessible in the normal manner. The `load` function is the rough equivalent of the `rxfuncadd` function used in other Rexx implementations, except that `load` makes accessible the full set of functions residing in the library by a single statement.

In newer releases of BRexx, the `import` function provides an alternative to `load`. This function imports a shared library using dynamic linking with Rexx routines. For example, to access the MySQL API library, code:

```
call import "librxmysql.so" /* access functions in the MySQL library    */
```

Here are the main external function libraries and what they offer.

❑ *ANSI screen I/O (for Unix and DOS* — A set of about a dozen functions that manipulate the cursor and control the attributes of text displayed on the screen. This provides the standard, terminal-independent set of ANSI screen control routines.

❑ *ANSI screen I/O (for Windows and 32-bit DOS)* — The 32-bit version of BRexx supplies the ANSI terminal emulation functions *as built-in functions* for higher performance.

❑ *Console I/O (for DOS* — About a dozen functions that control the I/O mode, manipulate the cursor and read keyboard input. These offer an alternative to ANSI Screen I/O modeled on the popular C language "console I/O' (or "conio") library.

❑ *Date functions (for Unix and DOS)* — A dozen functions that return and manipulate dates.

❑ *DOS functions (for DOS)* — 20 DOS functions that retrieve low-level information including segment, offset, and interrupt addresses, disk and directory information, machine name and more. These work with any form of DOS but may not be available under Windows (depending on your Windows version).

❑ *EBCDIC functions (for Unix and DOS)* — Functions that convert ASCII to EBCDIC and vice versa. This is useful because IBM and compatible mainframes use EBCDIC character encoding, while all midrange and desktop computers rely on ASCII. These functions prove useful in data transfer between machines using the two different data encoding schemes.

❑ *File functions (for Unix and DOS)* — A dozen file functions that read or write an entire file to/from a Rexx array, return file size and attributes, and so on.

❑ *HTML CGI-scripting functions* — These support CGI scripting and manage cookies.

Windows CE

Brexx has been specially customized to support the Windows CE family of operating systems for handheld computers. It includes built-in functions for Windows CE handhelds and an automatic installation program. It runs natively under Windows CE (it does not require a DOS emulator).

BRexx for Windows CE is downloadable in compressed binary form for a variety of popular handheld processors, including MIPS, StrongARM, and the Hitachi SH* series of 32-bit processors. The product includes an automatic installation program. To install BRexx on the handheld device:

1. Download the `*.zip` file containing the binaries for your particular handheld and its operating system to your desktop or laptop PC running Windows.

2. Decompress or unzip the downloaded file into an appropriate folder on your Windows PC.

3. Ensure that the Windows PC and the handheld are connected and that Microsoft ActiveSync is active and can transfer files between the two machines.

4. Double-click on the file `setup.exe`.

5. BRexx is automatically installed from the Windows PC to the handheld. When the installation is completed, the handheld will display a new desktop icon for `BRexxCE`.

6. Select the `BRexxCE` icon on the handheld, and you are interacting with BRexx.

Let's briefly take a look at the BRexx Windows CE functions. While more functions may be added and the workings of some of the existing ones altered, this list gives an idea of what is offered.

❑ *Console functions* — These functions manage the *console* or display. They help you manage cursor operations for character-oriented input and output:

    ❑ `clrscr()` — Clears main window

- ❏ `clreol()` —Clears from the cursor position to the end of the line
- ❏ `wherex(), wherey()` —Returns cursor position
- ❏ `gotoxy(x,y)` —Moves cursor to indicated screen coordinates
- ❏ `getch()` —Gets a character from the keyboard buffer
- ❏ `kbhit()` —Tells if a character is waiting in the keyboard buffer
- ❏ *File system functions* — These functions aid in using the file system. They support common file operations and directory navigation:
  - ❏ `copyfile(sourcefile,destfile)` —Copies a file
  - ❏ `movefile(sourcefile,destfile)` —Moves a file
  - ❏ `delfile(file)` —Deletes a file
  - ❏ `mkdir(directory)` —Makes a directory
  - ❏ `rmdir(directory)` —Eliminates a directory
  - ❏ `dir(filemask)` —Returns the complete directory list
- ❏ *Windowing functions* — The windowing functions set the window title, display message boxes, and manage the clipboard:
  - ❏ `windowtitle(title)` —Sets the title of the window
  - ❏ `msgbox(test, title, [option])` —Displays a message in a message box
  - ❏ `clipboard([type|cmd [,data]])` —Gets, sets, lists or clears data in the clipboard
- ❏ *Unicode functions* — The two unicode functions support two-way conversion between ASCII codes and unicodes:
  - ❏ `a2u(ascii_string)` —Returns the ASCII string as Unicode
  - ❏ `u2a(unicode_string)` —Returns the Unicode string as ASCII

Issuing Operating System Commands

BRexx issues commands to the operating system using the stack for command input and/or output. This example captures the output of the `dir` (directory) command into the stack:

```
'dir (STACK'
```

Access the command's output by issuing `pull` instructions to read the stack's contents. Chapter 4 provided examples of how to write a do loop using the `pull` instruction to read lines from the stack. Use that code to read lines output to the stack from commands like the preceding one when writing BRexx scripts.

BRexx recognizes the keyword strings (`STACK`, (`FIFO` and (`LIFO`, coded in the manner shown above. These permit scripts to specify stack input/output and the ordering involved. Remember that FIFO stands for "first-in, first-out," while LIFO specifies "last-in, first-out." These terms were defined and illustrated in the chapter on stack processing, Chapter 11. Please review that chapter if you need a refresher on how the stack works.

Here's a BRexx example of how to send data input into an operating system command by using the stack. This sample command sends input to the operating system's `time` command through the stack:

```
'STACK> time'
```

A BRexx feature that extends beyond the Rexx standards is that commands and programs can be invoked by coding them as if they were functions, *so long as they use standard I/O.* Here are examples:

```
say  'dir'()      /* displays a file list via the operating system DIR command */
say  'cd'()       /* displays the current working directory via the CD command */
directory = 'cd'()  /* capture results of the operating system's CD command   */
```

Be sure to encode the parentheses so that BRexx recognizes the "function call." This technique can be used with any command-line program (not just operating system commands), as long as they use standard I/O. It is a convenient and powerful way to access outside services.

Windows users may see varied results when using the redirection techniques, depending on their version of Windows. This is because operating systems in the Windows family do not treat standard I/O and redirection consistently. This is *not* a shortcoming of BRexx, but rather an aspect of how Windows operating systems redirect I/O. Different Windows versions redirect I/O inconsistently.

BRexx recognizes several environments as the target for operating system commands: COMMAND, SYSTEM, DOS, and INT2E. INT2E is the fast (but undocumented) way to issue `command.com` commands via Interrupt 2E. This is a DOS-only feature.

Example — C-like I/O

Let's take a look at a few sample scripts that demonstrate the extended features of Brexx. BRexx supports both standard Rexx I/O functions and a C-language-inspired I/O model. This program is similar to the I/O sample program of Chapter 21 on Rexx/imc. It illustrates the C I/O model and its functions. The script simply copies one file to another. The source and target files are specified on the command line when running the program. Here is the script:

```
/**********************************************************************/
/* FCOPY BREXX                                                    */
/*                                                                */
/* Uses BRexx I/O functions to copy a file.                       */
/**********************************************************************/
parse arg source target          /* get filenames, retain lowercase */

/* open input & output files, establish file Handles              */

in_hnd  = open(source,'r')              /* open input file         */
out_hnd = open(target,'w')              /* open output file        */
if in_hnd = -1 | out_hnd = -1 then      /* check for errors on open */
```

```
      say 'File OPEN Error!'

   /* perform the file copy                                    */

   line = read(in_hnd)
   do while eof(in_hnd) = 0
      bytes_written = write(out_hnd,line,newline)
      line = read(in_hnd)
   end

   /* close the files and exit                                 */

   rc_in  = close(in_hnd)              /* close input file        */
   rc_out = close(out_hnd)             /* close output file       */
   if rc_in <> 0 | rc_out <> 0 then    /* check for errors on close */
      say 'File CLOSE Error!'

   exit 0
```

In the script, these lines open the input and output files and check for errors:

```
   in_hnd  = open(source,'r')        /* open input file          */
   out_hnd = open(target,'w')        /* open output file         */
   if in_hnd = -1 | out_hnd = -1 then  /* check for errors on open */
      say 'File OPEN Error!'
```

The open function follows C-language protocol for the *mode*, or the manner in which the file will be used. These are the valid file mode flags that can be encoded:

open Function Mode	Use
r	Read
w	Write (overwrites any existing file)
a	Append (adds to the end of any existing file)
+	Read and write
t	Text mode
b	Binary mode

The Text and Binary modes are mutually exclusive. Use either one or the other on any open statement. The Text and Binary indicators are usually combined with one of the other flags. For example, you might open a file for Read in Text Mode, or for Write in Binary Mode. Later in this discussion sample scripts illustrate how this works.

The function returns a *file handle* that can be referred to in subsequent file operations. If the function returns −1, an error occurred during the open function.

The `do-while` group uses the `read` function to read the input file:

```
line = read(in_hnd)
```

`read` returns either a specific number of characters or line(s). It can also operate *on an entire file* by using the F parameter. In fact, we could have copied the entire file with one line of code instead of the `do-while` loop:

```
call  write  "new_file" ,  read("old_file","F")    /* copy entire file ! */
```

The `eof` function returns 1 at the end of file, or 0 if the file is open and there are still lines to read. As with the `read` and `write` functions, it takes the file handle returned from the `open` function as a parameter:

```
do while eof(in_hnd) = 0
```

The `write` function writes a line to the given file handle, optionally followed by a newline or line feed character(s). It returns the number of bytes written:

```
bytes_written = write(out_hnd,line,newline)
```

The `read` function does not provide the line-end character(s) to the script, so the script must add the new line to the output string through the `write` function `newline` parameter.

This code concludes the program. It closes both files based on their file handles, and checks for an error during closing. The return code of 0 means the files closed correctly:

```
rc_in  = close(in_hnd)          /* close input file            */
rc_out = close(out_hnd)         /* close output file           */
if rc_in <> 0 | rc_out <> 0 then   /* check for errors on close  */
   say 'File CLOSE Error!'
```

The C-like I/O model is powerful. The ability to work with files in *binary mode* simply by coding the b option on the `open` function is especially useful. This allows byte-by-byte file processing regardless of the manner in which the operating system separates lines or marks the end of file.

These file functions are all built-in. BRexx also provides an external function library for Unix and DOS that can, among other features, read or write an entire file to/from an array. Finally, BRexx offers an interface to the MySQL open-sorce database as a set of built-in functions.

Example — ANSI Screen I/O with Random Data Access

This sample script illustrates the American National Standards Institute (ANSI) standard commands for controlling a display screen. Using ANSI functions allows you to create portable programs with character-based, full-screen I/O. ANSI terminal emulation does not support graphical user interfaces, or GUIs.

In this era of GUIs, why would anyone code character-based, full-screen I/O? Some of the reasons include backward compatibility, hardware limitations, and legacy systems. Another reason is that this approach can be quick and convenient for "heads-down" data entry. This sample script illustrates this principle.

The sample program also shows another use for BRexx's C-like I/O. In this case, these functions create a *direct-access* (or *random-access*) file. This script writes records into that file. A separate script directly retrieves specified records from that file and displays them to the user.

The purpose of this script is to assign swimming pool passes to local pool patrons. The user enters each patron's first and last name and phone number. The script writes the patron information to the output file. The patron's Pool Pass Number is his or her relative record number within the output file. In other words, the first patron written to the file is implicitly assigned Pool Pass Number 1, the second person is assigned Pool Pass Number 2, and so on.

Here's how the script works. First it clears the screen; then it displays a data entry form similar to that depicted in Figure 22-1. The user fills in each data item, and presses the <ENTER> key for the cursor to skip to the next data entry position in the form. After the user enters the last data element on the form (the person's phone number), the script writes his or her record to the output file.

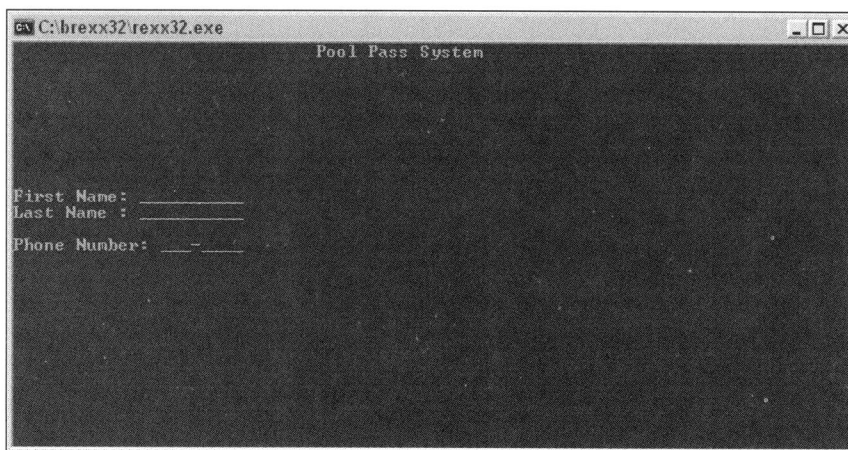

Figure 22-1

The script repeatedly displays the data entry form to collect information until the user enters the string exit into the first data entry position on the form (as the pool patron's last name). The script closes the output file and terminates.

Figure 22-2 shows what the data entry form might look like after the user enters information.

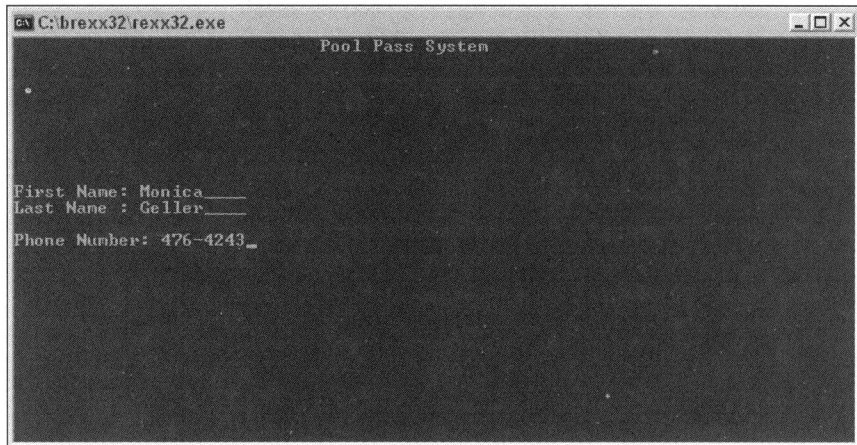

Figure 22-2

Here's the data entry script:

```
/*********************************************************************/
/* POOLPASS                                                          */
/*                                                                   */
/* Uses ANSI I/O to get Pool Pass info & build a random-access file  */
/*********************************************************************/

call AnsiColor 'LIGHTCYAN','BLUE'      /* set screen colors           */

recsize = 30                           /* length of each output record */
out_hnd = open('poolfile','ab')        /* append to binary output file */

do while first_name <> 'exit'

   /* Clear the screen and write the screen title                    */

   call AnsiCls
   call AnsiGoto 30,1
   call charout ,'Pool Pass System'

   /* Draw the form to gather first and last names, and phone number. */

   call AnsiGoto 1,10   ;   call charout ,"First Name: _____"
   call AnsiGoto 1,11   ;   call charout ,"Last Name : _____"
   call AnsiGoto 1,13   ;   call charout ,"Phone Number: ___-____"

   /* Read the information the user entered on the form              */

   call AnsiGoto 13,10    ;   parse pull first_name   .

   if first_name <> 'exit' then do      /* quit if user enters 'exit' */

      call AnsiGoto 13,11 ;   parse pull last_name    .
```

373

```
        call AnsiGoto 15,13  ;   parse pull phone_number .

        /* Build an output record, write user info to POOLPASS file    */

        outstr = first_name || ',' || last_name || ',' || phone_number
        outstr = left(outstr,recsize,' ')   /* ensure 30-byte record   */
        call write out_hnd,outstr           /* write the output record */
    end
end

call close out_hnd                          /* close pool pass file    */
call AnsiColor 'WHITE','BLACK'              /* set screen colors back  */
call AnsiCls                                /* clear screen            */
exit 0
```

The first line in the script sets the foreground and background screen colors by calling the `ansicolor` function:

```
call AnsiColor 'LIGHTCYAN','BLUE'           /* set screen colors       */
```

Since Rexx is a case-insensitive language, `ansicolor` is the same as `AnsiColor`. Code the function in whichever way you prefer. The script opts for bright light cyan letters on a blue background. The entire form (screen) will be dark blue over-written with cyan messages.

The next line opens the output file to which pool pass information is written. Since the file is used as a direct-access file, it is opened in *binary mode* (indicated by the b option). No line-termination characters will be written to the file. The option a stands for `append`. Every time this program runs it will append new data to the end of the file. The first time the script runs, the file will not exist, so the a option creates it:

```
out_hnd = open('poolfile','ab')             /* open binary output file*/
```

As in the prior sample program, the *output handle* (here called `out_hnd`) will be referred to in subsequent `read`, `write`, and `close` file functions.

These lines clear the screen with the `ansicls` function. They position the cursor at line 1, column 30 through the `ansigoto` function, then write the screen title at that position:

```
call AnsiCls
call AnsiGoto 30,1
call charout ,'Pool Pass System'
```

These lines invoke the `ansigoto` function to position the cursor and write lines to the display. The result is a full-screen data entry form:

```
call AnsiGoto 1,10   ;   call charout ,"First Name: _____"
call AnsiGoto 1,11   ;   call charout ,"Last Name : _____"
call AnsiGoto 1,13   ;   call charout ,"Phone Number: ___-____"
```

Position the cursor back at the first data entry position so that the user can enter the person's first name at the entry position labelled First Name:

```
call AnsiGoto 13,10     ;    parse pull first_name    .
```

If the user does not enter the string exit, continue collecting the form information:

```
call AnsiGoto 13,11  ;    parse pull last_name     .
call AnsiGoto 15,13  ;    parse pull phone_number  .
```

Now that the script has all the input information, concatenate it into an output record. Use the left function to ensure that output record is padded with blanks to the *record length*, the length of each record that is written to the output file. (The record length was set to 30 characters in the variable recsize at the start of the program.) Write the binary output record without any newline or end-of-line characters:

```
outstr = first_name || ',' || last_name || ',' || phone_number
outstr = left(outstr,recsize,' ')           /* ensure 30-byte record   */
call write out_hnd,outstr                    /* write the output record */
```

The program continues to display the data entry form, collect user information, assign pool pass numbers, and write records to the file. After the user enters exit, the program closes the output file, resets the screen colors to their usual setting, and clears the screen to terminate:

```
call close out_hnd                      /* close pool pass file  */
call AnsiColor 'WHITE','BLACK'          /* set screen colors back */
call AnsiCls                            /* clear screen           */
```

At the end of this script, the file named poolfile contains a number of 30-byte records, one per pool patron. The *relative record number* of each record represents its implicitly assigned Pool Pass Number. There are no line feeds between records. Since each record is padded with blanks to make a 30-byte record, the file might look like this:

```
    Monica,Geller,476-4243          Ross,Geller,476-1749          ...etc...
```

This script is a limited demo program. It does not error-check the user input or inspect return codes for I/O functions, as a production program would.

BRexx offers ANSI terminal emulation as built-in functions for Windows and 32-bit DOS. These built-in functions are faster than external functions. The sample scripts in this chapter all ran under Windows.

For some operating systems, you will need to use BRexx's external function library, called ansi.r, to support ANSI terminal emulation. In this case, encode this line at the top of the script to load the ANSI external functions prior to invoking them:

```
call  load  "ansi.r"    /* load all external ANSI terminal functions for use */
```

You will also need to ensure that your operating system uses the file ansi.sys. For example, under Windows or DOS, code a line in the config.sys file to reference the ansi.sys file. The config.sys file resides in the root directory, c:\ . Depending on where the file ansi.sys resides on your system, you would code one of the following lines in the config.sys file:

Windows Version	ANSI.SYS Reference
Windows XP	`device=c:\windows\system32\ansi.sys`
Windows 2003, 2000, NT	`device=c:\dos\ansi.sys`
Windows ME, 98SE, 98, 95	`device=c:\windows\command\ansi.sys`
DOS — all versions	`device=c:\dos\ansi.sys`

Typically, one reboots the machine to force the operating systems to access the `config.sys` file and pick up the new information on the `ansi.sys` driver.

Example — Direct Data Access

The preceding Pool Pass program created a file of 30-byte records, each having information on a swimming pool member. The script demonstrated two major groups of special BRexx functions: those for C-like I/O and those for ANSI-standard screen control.

The next sample script delves further into how to use the C-like I/O functions. This script shows their power in performing direct file access. The program goes to specific file locations to retrieve data elements, showing how the C I/O model can be used for direct or random file access.

This script prompts the user to enter a Pool Pass Number, then displays that patron's record on the screen. This sample interaction with the Pool Read program shows that the second record (Pool Pass Number 2) is assigned to Ross Geller, and Pool Pass Number 4 is assigned to Joey Tribiani. Pool Pass Number 17 is not yet assigned, because that relative record does not exist in the file. Pool Pass Numbers correspond to direct access positions or *slots* within the random-access file:

```
c:\brexx32\pgms> rexx32 poolread.r

Enter Pool Pass Number: 2

Pass Number: 2
Person          : Ross Geller
Phone           : 476-1749

Enter Pool Pass Number: 4

Pass Number: 4
Person          : Joey Tribiani
Phone           : 476-9876

Enter Pool Pass Number: 17
That Pool Pass number is not assigned.

Enter Pool Pass Number: exit
```

This script illustrates direct or random access to the pool pass records:

```
/*************************************************************************/
/*  POOLREAD                                                            */
/*                                                                      */
/* Reads random-access pool file records to display to the user.       */
/*************************************************************************/

in_hnd = open('poolfile','rb')                  /* open binary input file */

recsize = 30                                     /* size of 1 file record  */
filesize = seek(in_hnd,0,"EOF")                  /* returns file size      */
input_limit = filesize - recsize                 /* calculate last record  */

say ' '
call charout ,"Enter Pool Pass Number: "   /* get the user's request  */
pull pass_number .

do while pass_number <> 'EXIT'

   position = ((pass_number-1) * recsize)  /* read record at POSITION */

   if position > input_limit              /* POSITION > last record  */
      then say 'That Pool Pass number is not assigned.'

   else do
      call seek in_hnd,position            /* position to the record  */
      in_record = read(in_hnd,recsize)     /* read user's pool record */

      sep = ','                            /* parse & display record  */
      parse value in_record with first_name (sep) ,
                last_name (sep) phone_number
      say ' '
      say 'Pass Number:' pass_number
      say 'Person      :' first_name last_name   /* display the record */
      say 'Phone       :' phone_number
   end

   say ' '
   call charout ,"Enter Pool Pass Number: "     /* get user's request  */
   pull pass_number .
end

call close in_hnd
exit 0
```

The script opens the file for read access (r) and in binary mode (b). Binary mode is appropriate because there are no line-termination characters within the file:

```
in_hnd = open('poolfile','rb')                  /* open binary input file   */
```

This code uses the `seek` function to return the size of the file. The `EOF` parameter forces the file pointer to the end of file. The calculation for `input_limit` is used to tell if the user has entered a Pool Pass Number that does not yet exist (that is larger than the file size indicates has been stored):

```
recsize = 30                           /* size of 1 file record   */
filesize = seek(in_hnd,0,"EOF")        /* returns file size       */
input_limit = filesize - recsize       /* calculate last record   */
```

The script prompts the user to enter a Pool Pass Number. This code takes that `pass_number` and calculates the relative byte position where the record is located within the direct access file:

```
position = ((pass_number-1) * recsize)      /* read record at POSITION  */
```

If the `position` is too big, the script knows that there is no such record and tells the user so:

```
if position > input_limit                   /* POSITION > last record   */
    then say 'That Pool Pass number is not assigned.'
```

If the Pool Pass Number is valid, the script uses the `seek` function to position the file position pointer to read the proper record. Then the script reads that 30-byte record:

```
call seek in_hnd,position               /* position to the record   */
in_record = read(in_hnd,recsize)        /* read user's pool record  */
```

The `parse` instruction parses the record into its components, separated by commas:

```
sep = ','                               /* parse & display record   */
parse value in_record with first_name (sep) ,
                          last_name (sep) phone_number
```

Now the script displays the Pool Pass information on the screen. Then it prompts the user to input another Pool Pass Number. When the user enters the string `exit`, the script terminates.

This script demonstrates how to use BRexx's C-like I/O functions to open a direct-access file and randomly retrieve records. It shows that advanced I/O functions can be used to implement different approaches to data storage and retrieval. In this case, we stored fixed-length records within a standard operating system file and retrieved specific records based on their relative record positions within the file.

Example — DOS Functions

A DOS program? Who cares about DOS? Well, while desktop computer users long ago moved from DOS to Windows, DOS continues to be one of the most widely used operating systems in the world. Many applications require a completely stable, well-known operating system with a very small footprint. Examples include *embedded systems* and *device control programming*. The software on these systems must run error-free and without maintenance. If the software fails, the device is broken. DOS fits this need. It is so well known that even its quirks and bugs are documented. With many free versions available, DOS keeps prices down, important when programming consumer devices that sell in such large numbers that even a small fee becomes an important cost factor.

Another application where DOS is used is on handheld devices, such as personal digital assistants, or PDAs, and pocket computers. The PocketDOS emulator presents one example. PocketDOS provides a MS-DOS 6.2–compatible DOS environment for Windows CE, Pocket PC, Windows Mobile, or Psion/Symbian EPOC32–based pocket computers. It brings the huge world of DOS programs down to today's handhelds. It also supports DOS-based Rexx scripting for handhelds. DOS has not died. It has adapted and shifted its profile to new markets after it lost the desktop.

With its long-time support for 16- and 32-bit DOS and its many special DOS functions, BRexx offers a Rexx implementation specifically extended and customized for this world. This simple script demonstrates a few of BRexx's DOS-specific functions. Here's what the script does:

1. Retrieve system information about the PC on which the script runs.

2. Read in a filename from the user and:

    a. Display the file's size and attributes.

    b. Read the entire file into an array *in one statement*.

    c. Display the file's contents by writing out the array.

3. Issue an operating system command by five different methods.

Here's the script output. (We have removed extraneous blank lines from the output for readability.)

```
============= PC Information ===============
The machine name is : Not defined
The DOS version is  : 6.20
System memory is    : 201504
The current disk is : C
Freespace on drives : 112246784 211787776
Enter a filename: dos_info.txt
============= File Information =============
The filesize of the test file is: 48
The file attributes of test file: RHSVDA
Here is the contents of file: DOS_INFO.TXT
this is line 1
this is line 2
this is line 3
=========== DOS Command Tests =============
Method 1- DOS version is:
MS-DOS Version 6.20
Method 2- DOS version is:
MS-DOS Version 6.20
Method 3- DOS version is:
MS-DOS Version 6.20
Methods 4 and 5- DOS version is:
MS-DOS Version 6.20
MS-DOS Version 6.20
```

Here is the program:

```
/*****************************************************************/
/* DOS INFO                                                      */
/*                                                               */
/* Illustrates some DOS-specific functions of BRexx.             */
/*****************************************************************/
call load "dos.r"              /* load the DOS function library   */
call load "files.r"            /* load the FILES function library */

/* Display some PC system information                            */

say '============= PC Information ==============='
say 'The machine name is :'  machinename()
say 'The DOS version is  :'  dosversion()
say 'System memory is    :'  storage()
say 'The current disk is :'  getcurdisk()
say 'Freespace on drives :'  drivespace()

call charout ,'Enter a filename: '   /* get a filename from user  */
pull testfile .

if exist(testfile) then do            /* if the input file exists... */

   /* display file size and its attributes as a string          */

   say '============= File Information ============='
   say 'The filesize of the test file is:'  filesize(testfile)
   file_attr = fileattr(testfile)
   say 'The file attributes of test file:'  attr2str(file_attr)

   /* read the entire file in 1 statement into an array, display it */

   call readstem testfile,"filein."   /* read entire file into array */
   say 'Here is the contents of file:' testfile
   do j = 1 to filein.0               /* item 0 tells # in the array */
     say filein.j
   end
   end  /* if... then do */

else
   say 'File does not exist:' testfile

/* issue the DOS version (VER) command by many different techniques  */

say '=========== DOS Command Tests =============='

call charout ,'Method 1- DOS version is:'  /* the traditional method */
'ver'

version = 'ver'()                   /* capture "function" output   */
call charout ,('Method 2- DOS version is:' || version)

say 'Method 3- DOS version is:'
```

```
'ver (STACK'                          /* capture output via the Stack */
do while ( queued() > 0 )
   parse pull version
   say version
end
                                      /* use ADDRESS to issue command */
call charout ,'Methods 4 and 5- DOS version is:'
address SYSTEM  ver
address COMMAND ver

exit 0
```

The first statements in this program give the program access to all the functions in the two external function libraries in the files named `dos.r` and `files.r`:

```
call load "dos.r"            /* load the DOS function library   */

call load "files.r"          /* load the FILES function library */
```

Loading the entire function library in one command is as convenient as one can possibly imagine.

Now the script issues a series of functions to retrieve and display information about the machine on which it runs:

```
say 'The machine name is :'   machinename()
say 'The DOS version is  :'   dosversion()
say 'System memory is    :'   storage()
say 'The current disk is :'   getcurdisk()
say 'Freespace on drives :'   drivespace()
```

The `storage` function is particularly interesting. Without any operand, as in the preceding example, it displays the total amount of machine memory. It can also be coded to display the memory contents at a specific location. For example, this function displays 100 bytes of memory at machine location 500:

```
say  storage(500,100)
```

The function can also be used to change that memory. This changes 5 bytes of memory starting at decimal location 500:

```
say  storage(500,5,'aaaaa')
```

Next the script prompts for the user to enter a filename. This code tests whether the file exists:

```
if exist(testfile) then do               /* if the input file exists... */
```

Assuming that it does, the script uses BRexx functions to display its size and attributes. The `fileattr` function retrieves the file's attributes, and the `attr2str` function converts them to a displayable character string:

```
say 'The filesize of the test file is:'  filesize(testfile)
file_attr = fileattr(testfile)
say 'The file attributes of test file:'  attr2str(file_attr)
```

After displaying information about the file, the script reads the entire file into an array by this one statement:

```
call readstem testfile,"filein."          /* read entire file into array */
```

The script displays the contents of the file by reading through the array:

```
do j = 1 to filein.0                       /* item 0 tells # in the array */
   say filein.j
end
```

The zeroth item in the array (filein.0) tells how many elements the readstem function placed into the array. There is also a writestem function that corresponds to the readstem function. It writes an entire array in a single statement. The element stem.0 tells writestem how many lines to write. Here we've used a traditional do loop to display the contents of the array the script read in to the screen, but we could also have encoded writestem to store the entire array to disk in a single statement.

Finally, the program demonstrates several different ways to issue operating system commands from within BRexx scripts. In this case, the program issues the DOS ver (version) command. First the script issues this operating system command in the traditional fashion:

```
'ver'
```

The interpreter does not recognize this command, and so it sends it to the external environment for execution. Of course, the default environment for command execution is the operating system.

Next, the script treats the OS command as if it were a function and captures and displays its output. This technique works only if the command uses standard I/O:

```
version = 'ver'()                          /* capture "function" output   */
call charout ,('Method 2- DOS version is:' || version)
```

Now the script issues the command again and captures its output into the stack:

```
'ver (STACK'                               /* capture output via the Stack */
```

To retrieve the results, just pull or parse pull the stack items. The queued function tells how many lines are on the stack.

Finally, the script issues the ver command by the address instruction. First, it targets the SYSTEM environment for command execution, then the COMMAND environment:

```
address SYSTEM  ver
address COMMAND ver
```

While this script demonstrates a small number of the BRexx external functions, it suggests how useful they can be for OS-specific programming. The functions are easy to use, and the product documentation clearly and succinctly describes how to code them.

Summary

This chapter summarizes some of the extended features of BRexx. This goal is to give you a feel for the features BRexx offers for Windows, Windows CE, Linux, Unix, 32- and 16-bit DOS, Mac OS, and other platforms. This is only a brief summary of what is available. Interested readers should download the product and review its documentation for further information and product updates.

We demonstrated some of the extended features of BRexx in this chapter. These include additional built-in functions, such as those for manipulating the stack, retrieving system information, higher mathematics, C-language-style input/output, and MySQL database access. We looked at how BRexx installs under and supports Windows CE. BRexx runs in native mode under Windows CE and offers Rexx as an alternative scripting language for handhelds that run that operating system. We also discussed the many function libraries that come with BRexx. These include function libraries for ANSI screen I/O, C-like console I/O, date functions, ASCII-to-EBCDIC conversion, file management, and the like. While BRexx meets the TRL-2 standards, these additional functions give it the extra features beyond the standard that developers often find useful.

Finally, the sample scripts in this chapter demonstrated several BRexx features. These included C-like input/output, ANSI-standard screen input/output, and direct data access. Direct or random file processing is a useful tool that forms the basis for many kinds of applications. The last script illustrated a few of BRexx's extensions for DOS programming. While the average desktop user considers DOS a "dead product," DOS continues its worldwide popularity in embedded devices and handheld programming.

Test Your Understanding

1. Name three key advantages to BRexx. Why might you use it as opposed to other free Rexx interpreters?

2. How do you position a file pointer within a BRexx script? How do you determine what the position of the current file pointer is? How do you position the file pointer to the beginning of a file? To the end of the file? How can you determine the size of a file?

3. What is the purpose of the EBCDIC functions? Which function library would you use to perform "date arithmetic"?

4. Name the functions for managing stack buffers. What does each do?

5. What are the three *I/O models* BRexx supports? When would you use each?

6. What are the ways in which you can execute operating system commands from BRexx scripts? How do you send the command input and capture its output in each approach?

Reginald

Overview

Reginald Rexx was developed by Jeff Glatt of the United States. He took the Regina interpreter and heavily modified it to customize it, and added features especially oriented to the Windows operating system. The result is a well-documented product with features and tools that leverage Windows. Reginald supplies all the Windows-oriented "power tools" and functions Windows programmers expect. Reginald is a free product that provides an alternative to proprietary languages like Microsoft's Visual Basic and VBScript for Windows programming. Unlike Microsoft's Windows-only technologies, Reginald represents Rexx, a standards-based, free, and open-source language that runs across all operating systems and platforms.

This chapter provides an overview of the extended features and strengths of Reginald. The latter half of the chapter offers several sample scripts that illustrate some of these features. We'll start by listing and discussing some of the advantages of Reginald as a Rexx interpreter. After describing how to install the product, we discuss the extended functions of Reginald, how it supports Windows GUI programming, its advanced I/O features, and its other extended features and functions.

We present several sample scripts. The first illustrates functions for Windows device, file, and drive management. Two other short scripts show how to write Windows GUIs with Reginald. Another demonstrates speech synthesis, while the final script shows how to update the Windows Registry.

Advantages

As in previous chapters covering specific Rexx interpreters, we initiate the chapter by discussing a few of the reasons you might choose Reginald. Here are some of the benefits to Reginald:

❑   *Windows integration* — Reginald completely integrates Rexx into Windows. This extends from the high level (a Windows Installer and GUI script launcher) to the low level (good Windows error handling and internal memory management). Reginald fully leverages Windows.

❑ *Windows functions and features* — Reginald was written by a Windows developer because he saw a gap between portable Rexx interpreters and the Windows-specific features Windows developers require. Reginald eliminates this gap. For example, Reginald supports Windows GUI programming, interfaces to spreadsheets and Microsoft Access databases, runs Windows Dynamic Link Library files (DLLs), has built-in functions to support the Windows file system beyond the standard REXX functions, and fully accesses the Windows Registry. Reginald tools make typical Windows tasks easy, such as integrating sound into applications or developing sophisticated GUI interfaces.

❑ *Tools* — Reginald provides a full set of developer tools. We discuss them in the material that follows.

❑ *Documentation* — Reginald comes with comprehensive documentation. Whether seeking information about the interpreter, how-to's, or scripting examples, Reginald's "doc" provides the answer. Everything you need to learn about Reginald's many tools and Windows-specific functions comes right with the product. There is also an online forum dedicated to Reginald users at http://g.yi.org/forum/list.php?11.

❑ *Supports SAA API* — Reginald supports the SAA API interface into Rexx from any compiled Windows language (not just from C language).

❑ *Meets standards* — Reginald meets the Rexx TRL-2 standards and is at language level 4.00. It includes the new ANSI-1996 functions `changestr` and `countstr` functions, but not the ANSI-1996 `LOSTDIGITS` condition.

Download and Installation

Reginald, and its related tools, can be downloaded from the REXX User's Page at www.borg.com/~jglatt/rexx/rexxuser.htm. This Web page contains descriptions of Reginald and its tools and how to download them. They download as binary compressed files in either Zip (*.zip) or self-extracting (*.exe) formats for Windows. Simply download the files and double-click on them to initiate a typical Windows Installer interaction. Installation is similar to installing any other Windows products. The software can also be uninstalled via Control Panel's Add/Remove Programs option.

Reginald automatically creates a Windows file association between files with the extension *.rex and its Script Launcher. Double-clicking on a *.rex file runs Reginald through its Script Launcher. It is recommended that, at a minimum, you install the Reginald interpreter, the REXX Text Editor, REXX Dialog, and the online book *Learn REXX Programming in 56,479 Easy Steps*. Other tools and add-ons may be installed if you find a need for them.

Tools

Reginald offers a comprehensive set of tools for the Rexx programmer running Windows. Here are the major ones:

❑ *Installer* — A Windows installer for the Reginald package. Among other features it automatically associates Rexx files with the interpreter so that you can simply double-click on any Rexx script to run it.

- ❏ *Script Launcher* — A GUI panel that helps you easily run Reginald scripts. It also allows you to assign input arguments to scripts and to create autorun CDROMs with Rexx scripts.

- ❏ *Administration Tool* — A single-panel Programmer's GUI that aids in the development and debugging of Rexx scripts. It allows you to autoload external function libraries and exit handlers for your scripts, and to easily set Rexx options, `trace` levels, and script paths. This tool centralizes administrative tasks and is a snap to learn.

- ❏ *Documentation* — Explanatory documentation is a theme throughout Reginald. For example, there are Windows-style help systems for the Script Launcher, the Administrative Tool, and all the other components. There are extensive explanations of Reginald scripting and a full set of well-documented sample scripts. There are several online books containing tutorials on particular language features, and even a complete online book tutorial on Reginald. Everything you need to use Reginald comes with the product.

- ❏ *Rexx Text Editor (aka RexxED)* — An editor specifically designed for writing and testing Rexx scripts. The GUI tool features color-coded syntax, a full help system, and other aids specifically for Rexx programmers. It also features a built-in graphical debugger to debug your script by setting breakpoints and running or stepping through the actual source lines in the text editor window. It allows you to add your own macros written in REXX (which may use add-ons such REXX Dialog). You can therefore add new features and interfaces to the editor.

- ❏ *REXX Dialog* — Supports Windows GUI interfaces for Rexx scripts. Helps Rexx programmers develop complete, typical-looking Windows GUIs. The included online book fully documents the process and makes it easy to learn how to script Windows GUIs.

- ❏ *ODBC drivers* — Open Database Connectivity (ODBC) drivers for Reginald access Microsoft Access Databases, dBASE files, or Excel files. These are files of type `*.mdb`, `*.dbf`, and `*.xls`, respectively. The ODBC drivers also enable local or remote access to a variety of database management systems. These include both open-source databases such as MySQL and PostgreSQL, and commercial systems such as SQL Server, Oracle, and DB2.

- ❏ *SQLite driver* — SQLite is a self-contained, embeddable, zero-configuration SQL database engine. It is useful as a local SQL-compliant database. Reginald interfaces to this open-source product to provide a fast, embedded database engine.

- ❏ *Speech function library* — An external function library that allows scripts to use a synthesized voice to pronounce or speak text. Uses the sound card or speaker to "play" the text. Audio output complements the usual screen output.

- ❏ *MIDI Rexx function library* — An external library that allows scripts to read, write, play, and record MIDI files. MIDI files provide computerized control of musical equipment and are also used to play music on the PC. The included online book includes a full tutorial with sample scripts.

- ❏ *MIDI I/O function library* — An external library that enables input/output to MIDI ports. This connects the PC to electronically accessible musical instruments and related devices.

- ❏ *Rexx 2 Exe* — This utility converts a finished Reginald script into a self-running `*.exe` file. This allows distribution of Reginald programs without requiring distribution of the source script.

- ❏ *Math functions* — This library contains transcendental mathematical functions (e.g., cosine, sine, and so on).

- ❏ *RexxUtil* — Originally devised by IBM, these utilities manipulate stem variables and provide many other service functions. This is the Windows-based version of the IBM utility library that is widely distributed on many other platforms.

❑   *Regular expressions* — This library contains functions that parse regular expressions. *Regular expressions* are a precise way to describe string patterns. They can be very powerful when applied to pattern and string logic.

❑   *RxComm serial add-on* — An external function library that lets scripts access and control serial ports (the PC's COM ports).

❑   *RxSock* — TCP/IP sockets for communication between programs across the Internal or a local area network (LAN).

❑   *The FUNCDEF feature* — Allows scripts to register and then directly call any function in *any* DLL, regardless of whether that DLL was written to be used from a Rexx script.

❑   *Windows Internet API* — A function library for Internet communications that supports HTTP, FTP, and Gopher operations. Scripts can download and upload Web pages and files and use the remote file control functions of the FTP protocol.

❑   *CGI interface* — A function library for scripting the Common Gateway Interface, or CGI.

❑   *C Developer's Kit for Reginald* — Includes library files for C programmers who use Rexx as a scripting language for their programs, or for those writing Rexx function libraries or SubCom or exit handlers in C. Includes C source examples and "makefiles" for Microsoft Visual C++ tailored for Visual Studio. There is a Web page that contains tutorials for C developers wishing to use REXX as a scripting language. The REXX Developer's Page can be found at `www.borg.com/~jglatt/rexx/rexxdev.htm`.

Many of the above add-ons and tools support the Regina interpreter as well as Reginald. These include the REXX Dialog, Speech Function library, RexxUtil, Math Functions, Regular Expressions, RxComm Serial Add-on, RxSock, MIDI Rexx, MIDI I/O, and Rexx 2 Exe.

Windows GUI

One of the most important Windows-specific features of Reginald is the ability to create GUI dialogs for user interaction. Reginald calls this the *REXX Dialog*, or *RXDLG*, feature. REXX Dialog enables Reginald scripts to create and control the Windows graphical user interface.

The Reginald GUI functions are implemented as an external function library in a DLL file called `rxdlg.dll`. Once REXX Dialog is installed, Reginald can *autoload* these functions so that they are transparently available to any Reginald script you write. Reginald's *Administration Tool* makes this easy.

The REXX Dialog add-on will also work with the Regina interpreter, but it offers additional error-handling features under Reginald, as well as the ability to be autoloaded.

Alternatively, you can manually initialize (or "register") Rexx external functions for use from within any script that employs them. Do this by coding the function `RxFuncAdd` to register one external function for use. Better yet, code the special Reginald function `RxdlgLoadFuncs` to register *all* the REXX Dialog functions in the DLL with a single line of code. Call function `RxdlgDropFuncs` to drop all the functions once the script is done using them.

After making the dialog management functions available to the script, invoke function `RxErr` to establish how REXX Dialog will report any errors.

Next, set values for various *controls*, graphical objects that appear inside a window displayed to the user. Then invoke the RxCreate function to create and display the window that has those controls. Now the script issues RxMsg call(s) that allow the user to interact with the window's controls. With a RxMsg call, the script waits while the user manipulates the controls. RxMsg awakens the script when the user takes an action that needs to be handled by the script. The script then accesses information describing the user interaction and responds to it.

A script may repeatedly call RxMsg to interact with the user until the user takes an action to end the interaction. Or a script may invoke RxMsg only once, if the user interaction is a one-time event rather than an extended interaction through the window.

With these capabilities, scripts interact with users through one or more windows and through simple or extended interactions. Later in this chapter we present several scripts that show how to program basic GUI interfaces with REXX Dialog.

This table lists the major functions of REXX Dialog:

REXX Dialog Function	Use
RxCreate	Creates a new window with relevant controls
RxErr	Establishes the error-reporting protocol for REXX Dialog
RxMsg	Controls user interaction for a window
RxSay	Displays a pop-up message (a message box)
RxFile	Presents a file Dialog for the user to choose a filename
RxQuery	Returns the value or property attribute of an open window, group, or control
RxSet	Sets the value or property attribute of an open window, group, or control
RxInfo	Returns information about the REXX Dialog environment to a script
RxRunRamScript	Runs a series of Rexx instructions in memory (RAM)
RxRunScript	Runs a child REXX Dialog (RXDLG) script
RxDlgLoadFuncs	Makes *all* REXX Dialog functions available for a script
RxDlgDropFuncs	Terminates use of the REXX Dialog functions by a script
RxFuncAdd	Makes one specific external function available for use by a script
RxMakeShortcut	Creates a shortcut, an icon that links to a file

All dialog functions provide a return code. Check it for failure and to respond to any errors. Rexx conditions such as SYNTAX and HALT can also trap errors. The RxErr function customizes how Reginald handles errors via automatic message boxes and other techniques. Sample scripts later in this chapter show how RxErr displays a comprehensive set of error messages.

REXX Dialog supports the windowing concepts needed to create a typical GUI. Among them are controls, window moving and resizing, menus, accelerator keys, online help, timeouts, child dialog scripts, and window modal states.

REXX Dialog also supports a basic set of Windows controls. These include push, radio, and checkmark buttons; entry, list, and drop boxes; tree, spin, slider and text controls; a group box; and a menubar. REXX Dialog hosts Internet Explorer's rendering engine to allow your script to easily display any content that would appear upon a Web page, such as clickable Internet links, graphics, tables, scrolling banners, and so on.

In summary, Reginald's REXX Dialog package provides everything required to create professional Windows user interfaces.

GUI Development Aids

An independently developed Dialog Editor called *RxDlgIDE* works in conjunction with REXX Dialog. It allows you to use the mouse to graphically lay out a dialog with its controls, and then the tool generates a skeleton REXX script to create that dialog. This Dialog Editor is itself written in Rexx and uses REXX Dialog. It can run as a RexxEd macro, so it appears under RexxEd's macro menu and can output its skeleton script directly to a RexxEd editor window for manual editing.

The full name of RxDlgIDE is the *REXX Dialog IDE* (or *interactive development environment*). It was written by Kåre Johansson and may be downloaded from his Web site at www.sitecenter.dk/latenight/ nss-folder/rxdlgide. This Web site offers several other free productivity tools for Rexx developers. These help in the generation and reuse of Rexx code for GUIs, Web pages, and general use.

While this book was in preparation, Reginald's developer was creating a graphical add-on with a dialog/ resource editor. This will permit dragging and dropping graphical components onto a dialog template (much like Visual Basic or Visual C development). The resource editor will tightly integrate with RexxEd to automatically write Rexx code. Built-in ActiveX support for Reginald to directly control any ActiveX host or COM component is also in progress.

Input/output

Reginald supports the standard Rexx streaming I/O model and all the standard functions (charin, charout, chars, linein, lineout, lines, and stream). Reginald also offers many additional built-in functions and features pertaining to the Windows file system. These include opening a file in shared mode (i.e., allowing more than one program to access the one file simultaneously), creating and deleting directories: deleting, renaming, moving files; obtaining a directory listing, resolving paths, reading and writing numeric quantities from binary files; listing the drives and media on a system; and so on. Wildcard patterns can be used as arguments to many of these functions so that entire groups of files are affected in one function call (for example, to manipulate an entire directory of files with a single function call).

Here are some of the extra I/O functions in Reginald:

Input/Output Function	Use
Dir	Creates or deletes a directory or directory tree
Directory	Returns the current directory or changes it
ChDir	Changes the current directory
DeleteFile	Deletes one or more files
MoveFile	Moves (or renames) one or more files
CopyFile	Copies one or more files
State	Existence-tests a file or stream
MatchName	Finds the first or next file in a directory that matches the given pattern; also returns file information such as size, attribute bits, last write date and time, and so on
SearchPath	Finds a file or directory or gets the value of an environmental variable or returns the location of special folders such as the Windows directory
DriveMap	Lists all drives having specified attributes, such as all CD-ROM drives
DriveInfo	Retrieves drive information such as free space
Path	Gets a full path name from a filename, queries the current directory, and/or splits a path name into separate elements
Qualify	Returns a full path name from a filename
FileSpec	Returns part of a path name
EditName	Transforms a filename into a new name according to a template possibly containing wildcards
ValueIn	Reads binary values in as numeric values
ValueOut	Writes one or more numeric values as binary values
LoadText	Reads the lines of a text file into a stem variable, or saves a stem variable's lines to a text file

For those accustomed to Windows programming, the power of the Reginald's I/O functions should readily be apparent. They provide the functionality necessary to create Windows applications. They put Rexx scripting on competitive footing with any other approach to Windows programming.

Another alternative is to use Reginald's *Open Database Connectivity*, or *ODBC*, *drivers* to write scripts that connect to data sources such as Microsoft Access, Microsoft Excel, and Borland's dBASE database. ODBC also connects to commercial databases such as Oracle, DB2, and SQLServer, and to open-source databases like MySQL and PostgreSQL.

A third option is to use the *SQLite interface*. SQLite is an embedded, open-source, SQL desktop database. SQLite is a good tool for scripts that require data management but do not need a large, multiuser database. See `www.sqlite.org` for further information and downloads of SQLite.

Documentation and Tutorials

Reginald features comprehensive documentation. Each tool has a help system that you can use to learn how to code using the tool. Reginald offers a number of complete tutorials that are all freely download-able from the Web site:

- ❑ Learn REXX Programming in 56,479 Easy Steps
- ❑ Programming with REXX Dialog
- ❑ Using Reginald with a Common Gateway Interface (CGI)
- ❑ Using Reginald to Access the Internet
- ❑ Using Mailslots with Reginald

The package includes *Learn REXX Programming in 56,479 Easy Steps*, an easy-to-read tutorial. This online book downloads with Reginald, self-installs, and places an icon on the Windows desktop for quick access. Through it, Reginald's developer shares his comprehensive knowledge of Rexx programming in the Windows environment.

Reginald includes well-commented sample scripts for every one of its additional features. The kinds of coding techniques you can learn from them include how to:

- ❑ Create GUI windows and user dialogs with REXX Dialog
- ❑ Download a Web page or file from the Internet
- ❑ Send email, optionally with attachments
- ❑ Put text onto the Windows clipboard
- ❑ Create a Zip archive from several files
- ❑ Use the SQLite DLL to read rom and write to local SQL databases
- ❑ Manipulate the mouse pointer on the screen
- ❑ Play video and audio clips
- ❑ Place an icon in the Windows System Tray
- ❑ Play a MIDI file
- ❑ Recursively search a directory
- ❑ Read file attributes and information
- ❑ Read Windows Registry values
- ❑ Launch and run an independent "child" script

Reginald provides the hooks into the Windows operating system that other Rexx interpreters lack. If you need Windows-specific programming capabilities, Reginald provides them.

Other Features and Functions

This section describes other features or functions that represent Reginald extensions to standard Rexx. First, we'll take a look at how scripts issue Windows operating system commands. This is achieved in the same manner as with any other Rexx interpreter, but the topic is worthy of discussion from the standpoint of the Windows-specific programs one can launch. We'll also discuss operands on the `options` instruction, the Windows Registry, exception conditions, how to invoke Windows DLLs, and extended functions and instructions. Following this quick tour, subsequent sections introduce sample Reginald scripts that illustrate device, file, and drive management; GUI programming; speech synthesis; and how to update the Windows Registry.

Operating system commands

With Reginald, scripts can issue operating system commands to the CMD environment. This includes all Windows shell and command-line commands. Unless you frequently program under Windows, the range and power of Windows commands may not at first be evident. Keep in mind that you can invoke *any* Windows application. These bring broad power to your scripts. The examples that follow hint at the Windows-specific applications Rexx scripts can invoke by a single statement.

For example, this code sends a command to the CMD environment that invokes Microsoft Word:

```
address 'CMD'                         /* send OS commands to CMD environment */
'winword.exe  file_to_edit.doc'       /* invoke Microsoft Word editor        */
```

Windows file associations are active. This makes it easy to start various Windows applications. For example, to run a Windows Media Player on a *.mpg file, you could code:

```
'c:\videoplayer\my_clip.mpg'
```

Similarly, you can run an audio clip by issuing a command string like this from the Rexx script:

```
'c:\audioclips\my_audio_clip.wav'
```

A single statement brings up and displays a Web page:

```
'webpage.html'
```

You can also start up Notepad by issuing a single statement. Start Notepad with an empty panel, or place the user into editing a specific file by naming it on the statement, like this:

```
'c:\windows\notepad.exe  file_to_edit.txt'
```

Scripts gain complete power over Windows features when a knowledgeable Windows programmer integrates commands into his or her scripts. Here we've shown how to access Windows applications such as Microsoft Word, the Windows Media Player, the Internet Explorer browser, and Notepad. The same principles (and easy access) apply to any other Windows applications you want your Rexx scripts to start, manage, and control.

It is important to note that older Windows operating systems always give return codes of 0, regardless of whether the OS command succeeds or not. Error conditions FAILURE and ERROR are never raised. This is not a flaw in Reginald but rather an aspect of the Windows operating system that the interpreter does not control. This is an important fact to keep in mind when scripts issue operating system commands. Scripts may need to verify commands by some means other than just checking command return codes. Chapter 14 demonstrates some techniques to use to accomplish this.

You can run a series of programs or files from one directory by using Reginald's IterateExe function. This function launches an external program a number of times. Employ a filename pattern to select which files in a directory should run.

Reginald's POpen function is an alternative way to issue shell commands. Command output goes into the array specified on the POpen function, and variable position 0 (e.g., array.0) contains a count of how many lines were output into the array. Process the array to process the lines output by the command.

This sample code issues the operating system dir or directory command. The POpen function directs output from this command to the dir_list array (which must be specified in quotes). If the command return code were 0, the script would display the resulting directory listing:

```
feedback = POpen('dir', 'dir_list')    /* issue the DIR command to Windows      */

if feedback <> 0 then                  /* if return code <> 0, command failed   */
   say 'Error occurred in OS command'
else do
   do j = 1 to dir_list.0              /* element 0 tells number of array items */
      say dir_list.j                   /* display a line from the DIR command   */
   end
end
```

The extra I/O functions in Reginald perform many common OS tasks. Use them to move, copy, and delete files, get disk and OS information, and the like. Reginald reduces the number of OS commands scripts need to issue and provides better control over them. Built-in functions are also faster than sending commands to the operating system or using the POpen function.

Options

Reginald supports about two dozen Windows-oriented options for the Rexx options instruction. For example, the LABELCHECK option causes a SYNTAX condition to be raised if the same label name is used more than once in a script. This can help detect inadvertent errors due to cutting and pasting source code.

Another example is MSGBOX. Turned on by default, this option tells Reginald to display error messages in a Windows message box, rather than a console or command-line window. Options like these enable scripts to control Reginald's behavior in the Windows environment.

Windows Registry

Reginald scripts can query, read, write, create, and delete Windows registry keys and values. The `Value` function provides this access. By default, registry operations apply to the `Current User` directory, but they can also be applied to any other directory. Scripts read, write, create, or delete Registry files, and create or delete Registry directories. Later in this chapter, we present a sample script that retrieves and updates Registry information.

GUI trace panel

Reginald supports the standard Rexx trace facility, and adds a GUI interface. Its *Debugger Window* supports all the normal Rexx trace features. It displays two panels. The left panel shows trace interpretation, while the right one shows which lines in the script are running. The Debugger Window buttons for `Run`, `Step`, and `Redo` make it easy to step through scripts.

Error conditions

Reginald's `Raise` instruction allows scripts to manually raise error conditions. Reginald's `USER` condition allows scripts to define their own error conditions. This brings to Rexx a capability that many other programming languages support — the ability to define and raise your own exceptions.

This sample code enables a new error condition and then raises it:

```
signal on user 1 name  my_error_routine

    /*  ...  later in the program ...  */

raise user 1 description "Raised User 1 Error Condition!"

    /*  ...  later in the program ...  */

my_error_routine:

    /*  ...  code to handle the user-defined exception goes here ...          */

    say 'USER' condition('C') 'reports:'  condition('D')   /* write error msg */
```

The error condition is called `USER`, and its error number is 1. Reginald supports up to 50 different `USER` conditions, numbered 1 through 50. Use the `condition` function to retrieve information about the error:

❑   `condition('D')` — Retrieves the error message

❑   `condition('C')` — Retrieves the user number

❑   `condition('M')` — Displays a message box with the error message

Windows DLLs

Windows external function libraries are typically implemented as *DLLs*. These are like the *shared libraries* that provide external function libraries under Linux, Unix, or BSD operating systems.

For DLLs that were specifically written to be used with Rexx, register and load them through the SAA-compliant functions RxFuncAdd and RxFuncQuery. Or use Reginald's Administration Tool to autoload the external function library.

Reginald also allows script writers to access *any* DLL function from their Rexx scripts, even if those DLLs were not written with Rexx access in mind. This key feature extends to Reginald developers the full range of Windows functionality. Register DLLs that were not specifically designed to be used with Rexx through the FuncDef function. This requires a bit more information on the call but gives access to any Windows DLL.

Sorting

Reginald's Sort statement sorts items within an array. The format is:

```
sort   stemname. [template]
```

This statement sorts all items within the array stemname. The optional template is similar to the template used on a parse instruction. It controls matching string patterns, positional effects, and placeholders. The template allows for sophisticated sorts: by offset and length, on multiple values or criteria, in descending order, with or without case-sensitivity, and utilizing search strings.

Multiple stacks

Reginald scripts can have multiple stacks, of which one is active at any one time. The RxQueue function creates and deletes stacks. This function is also used to specify which stack is currently used. Reginald's Makebuf, Dropbuf, and Desbuf functions create, drop, and destroy all buffers within a stack. The Queued function returns the number of items in the current data stack. The BufType function returns information about the current stack for debugging purposes. One benefit to buffers is that you can easily delete all items placed on them by a single function call to Dropbuf.

Parameter passing

Reginald includes the Use Arg function to provide more sophisticated forms of parameter-passing between routines. This function makes it easier to pass multiple values between internal routines. It is especially useful in returning large amounts of data to a caller.

do over loop

Reginald includes the do over loop to allow enumerating all the compound variables that use a given stem. This is useful in processing all the variables that use a given stem name (even if you do not know how many there are or what tail names they use).

Here's an example. This code displays all the variable names used in the array named array.

```
do j over array.
   say 'array.' || j
end
```

If you initialize the array contents like this:

```
array.1 = 'a'
array.2 = 'b'
array.5 = 'c'
array.9 = 'd'
```

Then the code outputs the array element names in use:

```
array.1
array.2
array.5
array.9
```

This helps you keep track of which array elements are used, especially when you're working with a *sparse array* (an array in which only certain slots or positions are used). do over does not guarantee any particular order in enumerating the tails.

do over is useful in processing all elements in an array with a simple loop. This example sums all the numeric values in an array:

```
sum = 0        /* find the sum of all elements in the array B        */
b.1 = 1
b.2 = 2
b.5 = 5
do j over b.
    sum = sum + b.j
end
say sum        /* writes the sum of the array elements, which here is: 8  */
```

Here's another example that adds 5 to every element in an array:

```
do j over array.
    array.j = array.j + 5
end
```

do over is very convenient for quick array processing. While syntax may differ, the do over concept is implemented in several other Rexx interpreters including roo!, Open Object Rexx, and NetRrexx.

Array indexing

Reginald allows use of brackets to specify a compound variable as if it were a single tail name to be substituted. For example, execute these two statements in sequence:

```
MyVar.i = 5
MyStem.[MyVar.i] = 'hi'
```

Reginald treats MyVar.i (in MyStem.[MyVar.i]) as a single variable name whose value will be substituted. Therefore, Reginald substitutes the value 5, and the variable name becomes MyStem.5 after substitution.

Improved interpret instruction

Reginald's `interpret` instruction allows you to `signal` to some label outside of its string parameter. Reginald also allows a `return` or `exit` instruction within the string. A `return` aborts the execution of the interpret string and resumes at the instruction after the `interpret` statement. An `exit` aborts the script.

Other functions

Reginald includes many built-in functions beyond the ANSI standards. In addition to the extra I/O functions mentioned previously, there are many other functions to retrieve system information, access external libraries, perform bit manipulation, and perform other activities. Let's briefly take a look at these functions and what they have to offer.

❑ *System information functions*—This group of functions are based on those often seen in Unix systems. They return information about environmental variables, the process identifier (PID), the current user identifier (UID), and the operating system and CPU. The `unixerror` function is useful for debugging. It returns the textual error message for a specified error number. Here are the system information functions:

   ❑ `getenv`—Returns the value of an environmental variable

   ❑ `getpid`—Returns the process ID (PID) of the process that launched the script

   ❑ `uname`—Returns OS and CPU information

   ❑ `unixerror`—Returns the error message for an operating-system specific error `number`

   ❑ `userid`—Returns current username

❑ *External access functions*—These functions permit access to external function libraries. Four of the functions (`rxfuncadd`, `rxfuncdrop`, `rxfuncquery`, and `rxfuncerrmsg`) support the SAA interface to external function libraries. These allow Reginald scripts to access any of the open-source interfaces or tools described in Chapters 15 through 18 in the manner illustrated in those chapters. `funcdef` is a Reginald-specific function. It makes an external function library available to Reginald scripts even if that library is a DLL that was created without any knowledge or reference to Rexx. It makes any Windows DLL available to Rexx scripts.

   ❑ `funcdef`—Makes an external function in *any* DLL available to a script

   ❑ `querymacro`—Test if a Rexx macro is already loaded

   ❑ `rxfuncadd`—Make a Rexx-compatible external function available to a script

   ❑ `rxfuncdrop`—Drop availability of an external function

   ❑ `rxfuncquery`—Test if an external function is available for script use

   ❑ `rxfuncerrmsg`—Return the most recent error message from `rxfuncadd` or `funcdef` calls

❑ *Stack functions*—This group of functions is similar to those available in many other Rexx interpreters. They manipulate the external data queue, or stack, as described in Chapter 11:

   ❑ `buftype`—Prints debugging info about the stack

   ❑ `desbuf`—Deletes stack contents

- ❏ `dropbuf` — Deletes one or more buffers
- ❏ `makebuf` — Creates a buffer
- ❏ `queued` — Returns number of lines in the current stack
- ❏ `rxqueue` — Creates or deletes stacks

❏ *Miscellaneous functions* — Finally, Reginald offers a wide selection of miscellaneous functions. `steminsert` and `stemdelete` are of particular interest. These operate on any entire array (or stem variable) and serve to maintain that table as an ordered list during maintenance operations:

- ❏ `beep` — Makes a sound or can play a WAVE file
- ❏ `bit` — Performs bit operations on a value
- ❏ `convertdata` — Converts binary datatype to Rexx variables, or vice versa
- ❏ `expand` — Replaces tab characters with spaces in a string, or vice versa
- ❏ `iterateexe` — Runs non-Rexx programs multiple times, as selected by file matching criteria
- ❏ `justify` — Formats words in a string
- ❏ `sleep` — Suspends script execution for a specified number of seconds or milliseconds
- ❏ `steminsert` — Inserts elements into an ordered stem
- ❏ `stemdelete` — Deletes various elements of an ordered stem
- ❏ `random` — Returns a random number within a specified range

Leveraging Reginald

Before we discuss some sample Reginald scripts, let's ensure that you are familiar with and know how to leverage Reginald's development toolset. These GUI tools make scripting faster and easier. Here are a few key tools:

❏ *Script Launcher* — This GUI panel launches Rexx scripts. It presents a dialog panel that looks like the standard Windows file-selection panel. Pass arguments to scripts through the Launcher, and interact with scripts that issue `say` and `pull` instructions through the Launcher's console window.

❏ *Administration Tool* — This tool administers the scripting environment. Its GUI panel makes it easy to set `options` and `trace` levels, set paths so that scripts can locate unqualified filenames, and set values like `numeric digits`, `fuzz`, and `form`. It *autoloads* external function libraries, so the code that makes those libraries accessible does not have to appear in your scripts. It also autoloads *exit handlers*, functions written in other languages that modify Reginald's behavior. Using an exit handler, for example, you could change the way the `say` instruction works so that it pops up a message box instead of writing a line to the console.

❏ *Rexx Text Editor (aka RexxED)* — This editor is designed for writing and testing Rexx scripts. Its GUI features color-coded syntax, a full help system, a built-in macro language, and other features designed for Rexx scripting.

❑   *RxDlgIDE* — This independently developed dialog editor works in conjunction with REXX Dialog. It allows you to use the mouse to graphically lay out a dialog with its controls, and then the tool generates a skeleton REXX script to create that dialog. It can run as a RexxEd macro, so it appears under RexxEd's macro menu and can output its skeleton script directly to a RexxEd editor window for manual editing.

Sample Scripts — File, Directory, and Drive Management

Let's start with a simple script that uses some of Reginald's extended built-in functions to manage files and disks. These functions search through and manage files, manipulate filenames, and control folders and disks.

This program retrieves and displays information about the computer's disk drives, then lists specific information about the C: drive. Here's the script output:

```
List of disk drives     : C:\ F:\ G:\
List of CDROM drives     : D:\ E:\
List of removable drives: A:\
List of RAM drives       :
List of Network drives   :

Information about your C: drive...
Drive Type      : FIXED
Serial Number   : 548597677
Volume Label    :
Size            : 2785591296
Bytes Free      : 527294464
Filesystem      : NTFS
Filename length: 255
Drive Flags     : 0000000000000111000000001111111

Press <ENTER> to continue
```

Here's the script itself:

```
/****************************************************************/
/* DRIVES INFO                                                  */
/*                                                              */
/* Illustrates a few Reginald drive information functions.      */
/****************************************************************/

/* display information about the machine's disk drives          */

say 'List of disk drives     : ' DriveMap(,'FIXED')
say 'List of CDROM drives     : ' DriveMap(,'CDROM')
say 'List of removable drives: ' DriveMap(,'REMOVABLE')
say 'List of RAM drives       : ' DriveMap(,'RAM')
say 'List of Network drives   : ' DriveMap(,'NETWORK')
```

```
    say ' '


    /* display information about the C: drive                        */

    feedback = DriveInfo('drive_info')
    if feedback <> 0 then say 'Error on DriveInfo call'
    else do
        say 'Information about your C: drive...'
        say 'Drive Type      :' drive_info.4
        say 'Serial Number   :' drive_info.2
        say 'Volume Label    :' drive_info.3
        say 'Size            :' drive_info.1
        say 'Bytes Free      :' drive_info.0
        say 'Filesystem      :' drive_info.5
        say 'Filename length:' drive_info.6
        say 'Drive Flags     :' drive_info.7
        say ' '
    end

    say 'Press <ENTER> to continue'; pull .
    exit 0
```

This script relies on two built-in functions to accomplish its work: `DriveMap` to get information about disk drives and `DriveInfo` to get details about a specific drive.

The first block of code in the sample script issues the `DriveMap` function to retrieve information about the PC's drives. The script omits the first parameter in calling `DriveMap`, which specifies which drive to start the query with. Leaving this out prompts `DriveMap` to return a list of all drives matching the criteria. The second parameter is a keyword that specifies the kind of drives we're querying for. The example uses all possible keywords: FIXED, CDROM, REMOVABLE, RAM, and NETWORK:

```
say 'List of disk drives      : ' DriveMap(,'FIXED')
say 'List of CDROM drives     : ' DriveMap(,'CDROM')
say 'List of removable drives: ' DriveMap(,'REMOVABLE')
say 'List of RAM drives       : ' DriveMap(,'RAM')
say 'List of Network drives   : ' DriveMap(,'NETWORK')
```

The second code block makes a single call to `DriveInfo`. This function returns a several data items about one particular drive. This encoding omits the drive name, so it defaults to the C: drive. The quoted name `drive_info` is the array or stem variable that `DriveInfo` populates:

```
feedback = DriveInfo('drive_info')
```

The script displays the information returned in the array if this call succeeds and its return code was 0:

```
        say 'Information about your C: drive...'
        say 'Drive Type      :' drive_info.4
        say 'Serial Number   :' drive_info.2
        say 'Volume Label    :' drive_info.3
        say 'Size            :' drive_info.1
        say 'Bytes Free      :' drive_info.0
        say 'Filesystem      :' drive_info.5
        say 'Filename length:' drive_info.6
        say 'Drive Flags     :' drive_info.7
```

401

Example — display file information

The next sample script retrieves and displays information about a file. The program reads a filename from the user, opens that file, and displays basic information about the file: its full name, size, date of last modification, and attributes. Then the program reads and displays the several lines that make up the file.

Here's sample output for this script:

```
Enter file name:
file_info_input.txt             <= The user entered this line

File Name    : C:\Reginald\Reginald\hf\file_info_input.txt
File Size    : 82
Last Modified: 7 7 2004 22 34 33
Attributes   : 00000000000000000000000000100000

The file has 4 lines. Here they are:
line 1 of the file
line 2 of the file
line 3 of the file
last line of the file!

Press <ENTER> to end program...
```

In this example, the user enters the filename of file_info_input.txt , and the script lists some basic information about the file and displays the four lines that make up that file.

Here is the script:

```
/****************************************************************/
/* FILE INFO                                                    */
/*                                                              */
/* Lists information about a file and displays its contents.    */
/****************************************************************/

/* get the file name from the user, verify the file exists      */

say 'Enter file name:' ; pull filename
say

if state(filename) then do
   say 'File does not exist:' filename
   say 'Press <ENTER> to end this program' ; pull .
   return 1
end


/* retrieve and display information about the file              */

feedback = MatchName(,'FileInfo',filename,,'NFSDA')

if feedback = '' then do
```

```
      say 'File Name     :' FileInfo
      say 'File Size     :' FileInfo.0
      say 'Last Modified:' FileInfo.1
      say 'Attributes    :' FileInfo.2
      say
      end
else
      say 'Error on retrieving file info about:' filename


/* read and display all the file's lines by the LOADTEXT function */
/* IN_LINES.0 will be set to the number of lines that are read    */

if LoadText('in_lines.', filename) then do
      say 'The file has' in_lines.0 'lines. Here they are:'
      call LoadText('in_lines.',,'S')
end

say
say 'Press <ENTER> to continue...' ;  pull .

exit 0
```

The script prompts the user to enter a filename. After he or she does so, the script ensures that the file exists with this code:

```
if state(filename) then do
      say 'File does not exist:' filename
      say 'Press <ENTER> to end this program' ; pull .
      return 1
end
```

The `state` built-in function returns 1 if the file does not exist and 0 if it does. The script simply displays an error message and terminates if the file does not exist.

Next, the script uses the `MatchName` built-in function to retrieve information about the file. `MatchName` is quite flexible. It can test for the existence of a file or directory, based on either attributes or a wildcard file reference. It can also return information about the file, which is its use in the script. This shows one possible use:

```
feedback = MatchName(,'FileInfo',filename,,'NFSDA')
```

The variable name, `FileInfo`, represents a stem or array that will be populated with the results of the `MatchName` call. `filename` is simply the input filename (as entered by the user), while the string NFSDA requests the information the script requires:

❑   N — Returns the name of the matching item

❑   F — Returns the fully qualified name of the matching item

❑   S — Returns the file size

❑   D — Returns the date of last modification

❑   A — Returns the attribute string

403

So the string `NFSDA` tells `MatchName` to return the unqualified filename (`NF`), the file size (`S`), the date of last modification (`D`), and the file attribute string (`A`).

`MatchName` returns the null string if it succeeds. In this case, the script displays the file information:

```
if feedback = '' then do
   say 'File Name    :' FileInfo
   say 'File Size    :' FileInfo.0
   say 'Last Modified:' FileInfo.1
   say 'Attributes   :' FileInfo.2
   say
   end
else
   say 'Error on retrieving file info about:' filename
```

`MatchName` can do a lot more than shown here. You can specify file attributes as part of the file search mask. You can even specify wildcard filenames. This is useful for listing (and processing) all the files in a folder that match specified criteria. An upcoming example demonstrates this.

Finally, the script reads and displays the lines of the file. It reads the entire file into an array (a stem variable) in one statement by the `LoadText` function. It displays the entire file to the screen by a single call to `LoadText` as well. Here is the code:

```
if LoadText('in_lines.', filename) then do
   say 'The file has' in_lines.0 'lines. Here they are:'
   call LoadText('in_lines.',,'S')
end
```

The first parameter to the `LoadText` function is the stem variable name. It must end with the period that denotes an array name. The second parameter is the file to read or write. In the first call, this is `file-name`, the file to read. In the second invocation, it is not coded, which means to use the default device. In that second call, the final parameter (`'S'`) tells `LoadText` to save or write the data, rather than read it. Since the call specifies the default device, this displays the lines in the array on the user's screen.

This line shows that `LoadText` places the number of lines it reads into the 0th element of the array:

```
say 'The file has' in_lines.0 'lines. Here they are:'
```

The ability to read or write an entire file in a single statement is very convenient. It demonstrates the kind of power that Reginald functions add to standard Rexx.

Sample Scripts — GUIs

One of Reginald's big advantages is its support for Windows GUI development. The *REXX Dialog* external function library supports this through its dozen or so functions. REXX Dialog supports all kinds of Windows widgets including push, radio, and checkmark buttons; entry, list, text, and drop-down boxes; trees, spin counters, and sliders; groups, menus, and HTML pages. We show only a few very elemental examples here to demonstrate the basics of how to work with REXX Dialog.

This first script displays a text entry box to the user. The user enters some text into this box, as shown in Figure 23-1. Then the script reads and echoes this text to the user in a message box, as shown in Figure 23-2.

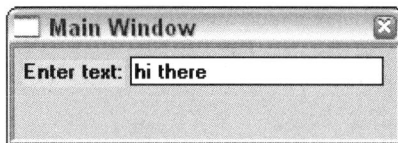

Figure 23-1

Figure 23-2

Here is the script:

```
/****************************************************************/
/* DISPLAY INPUT                                                */
/*                                                              */
/* Illustrates the basics of GUI interaction.                  */
/* Displays a text ENTRY box, writes back the user's input by  */
/* displaying it in a MESSAGE box.                             */
/****************************************************************/

/* trap errors for HALT/SYNTAX/ERROR, ask for ERROR raising    */

signal on halt
signal on syntax
signal on error
call RxErr 'ERROR|DISPLAY'    /* displays error messages       */


/* set values for the Text Entry box window                    */

Rx = ''                       /* "RX" will be our Window ID.   */

RxType.1  = 'MENU'            /* group type is MENU for a menu */
RxFlags.1 = ''
RxLabel.1 = 'MENU'

RxType.2  = 'ENTRY'           /* establish the ENTRY box       */
RxFlags.2 = 'REPORT'          /* through which the user will   */
RxLabel.2 = 'Enter text:|'    /* enter some text               */
RxPos.2   = '-1 5 5 150'
```

```
RxVal.2   = 'text'


/* now create the window (NOCLOSE keeps this window open)      */

call RxCreate 'RX', 2, 'Main Window', 'NOCLOSE'

do forever

   call RxMsg                   /* invokes user interaction      */

   if RxID == '' then signal halt /* exit if users clicks CLOSE*/

   /* display the text the user enters in the ENTRY text box    */

   if RxID == '2' then
      button = RxSay(text.1,'OK','You entered...')

end


syntax:                    /* handle errors here.           */
halt:                      /* RxErr with DISPLAY option     */
error:                     /* displays a nice error msg box */

   call RxMsg,'END'        /* close ENTRY box window, exit  */
   exit
```

The script issues several REXX Dialog functions, but it does not contain any code to access those external functions! Normally, you'd expect to see code like this to load the external function library:

```
feedback = RxFuncAdd('RxDlgLoadFuncs', 'RXDLG', 'RxDlgLoadFuncs')
if feedback <> 0 then say 'ERROR- Cannot load RxDlgLoadFuncs function!'

feedback = RxDlgLoadFuncs()
if feedback <> 0 then say 'ERROR- Cannot load Rexx Dialog library!'
```

Actually, the script *could* include this code to register and load the REXX Dialog external function library. But we've chosen to use the *Administration Tool* to *autoload* the rxdlg DLL instead. Just start the Administration Tool by double-clicking on it. The right-hand side of the panel allows you to autoload function libraries. rxdlg.dll may already be listed as autoloaded. If it is not, just press the Add button and add it to the list. Now, none of your scripts will need to include the code to register or load this external function library. This eliminates repetitiously coding these lines at the start of every script. It is a simpler approach, especially when a script accesses several external function libraries.

Because it does not include code to load the REXX Dialog external function library, the script starts by enabling error trap routines. This line is of special interest:

```
call RxErr 'ERROR|DISPLAY'    /* displays error messages       */
```

It is common to invoke RxErr at the start of a Reginald GUI program to establish error handling for the script. This automates error handling very nicely, and replaces explicit code in the script to manage errors. Figure 23-3 shows the kind of output RxErr displays when a programming error occurs. It is both complete and automated.

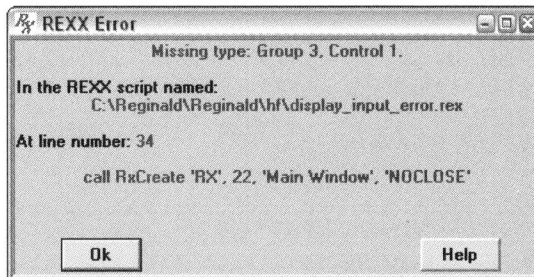

Figure 23-3

REXX Dialog works with *groups*, sets of identical *controls* or *widgets*. The major kinds of groups are listed earlier (Push Button, Entry Box, and so on). To create a window, first assign values to variables that define the appearance and operation of a group. This code, for example, sets the variables for the Menu group:

```
RxType.1  = 'MENU'              /* group type is MENU for a menu */
RxFlags.1 = ''
RxLabel.1 = 'MENU'
```

This code sets variables for the Entry group (the text entry box into which the user types the phrase the program echoes):

```
RxType.2  = 'ENTRY'            /* establish the ENTRY box       */
RxFlags.2 = 'REPORT'          /* through which the user will    */
RxLabel.2 = 'Enter text:|'    /* enter some text                */
RxPos.2   = '-1 5 5 150'
RxVal.2   = 'text'
```

The variables that must be set for each group are unique to the type of control. It's not necessary to go into them all here to understand the script. Reginald's comprehensive documentation describes them all and gives examples for each.

Every window must have a *Window ID*. Ours will be named RX. After all group variables have been set, invoke the RxCreate function to display the window:

```
call RxCreate 'RX', 2, 'Main Window', 'NOCLOSE'
```

The first parameter is the Window ID, the second is the number of groups in this window, and the third is the window title. NOCLOSE specifies that the script lets the user manually close the window, rather than automatically closing it for him or her.

With the window displayed to the user, the script enters a loop that repeats until the user manually closes the window and terminates the program. These lines start that loop:

```
do forever

    call RxMsg                    /* invokes user interaction    */
```

The call to the RxMsg function allows user interaction with the window. Here the call is simple. We just want the script to display the window and wait for user interaction. RxMsg has several parameters for more complicated interactions, for example, to manage interaction with multiple open windows or to clear pending messages for windows.

Control returns to the script after the user takes some action upon the open window. REXX Dialog sets variables so that the script can figure out what the user did: rxid and rxsubid. The simplified interaction in this script checks only for two values of rxid:

```
if RxID == '' then signal halt /* exit if users clicks CLOSE*/

/* display the text the user enters in the ENTRY text box    */

if RxID == '2' then
    button = RxSay(text.1,'OK','You entered...')
```

If rxid is the null string, the script knows the user clicked the close box in the window, so it exits.

If rxid is set to 2, the script knows the user entered a text string into the Entry box and pressed the <ENTER> key. This is the case the script needs to respond to. As shown earlier, the response is to display the text string the user entered in a message box. The RxSay function does this. Its first parameter, text.1, is a variable set to the text string by the user interaction. Figure 23-2 shows that OK is the label of the button the user presses to acknowledge the message box, and that the string You entered... is the title of the message box.

When the user decides to exit, the script terminates by closing the main window:

```
call RxMsg,'END'              /* close ENTRY box window, exit  */
```

To summarize, this simple example illustrates the basic logic many REXX Dialog scripts employ:

1. Establish error handling — through error traps and the RxErr function
2. Set variable values for groups. The variables that need to be set depend on the controls that are used.
3. Call RxCreate to display the window.
4. Call RxMsg to control user interaction with the open window.
5. Inspect variables set by REXX Dialog to determine how the user interacted with the window.
6. Close the window and exit with a final call to RxMsg.

More advanced scripts can employ more groups and controls and allow more sophisticated user interaction. This simple script shows how easy it is to get started with basic GUIs. Windows is a highly interactive environment. Along with Reginald's extensive tools and functions, this means you can start scripting Windows GUIs quite quickly.

Another GUI Example

Here's a more advanced GUI script. This one displays an Entry box for user data entry, just like the previous script. But this time, the user enters a wildcard filename with a filename extension. Figure 23-4 shows the user entering the extension *.rex. The script finds all files having that filename extension and displays them in a text box. Figure 23-5 below displays this output.

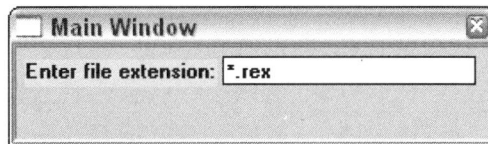

Figure 23-4

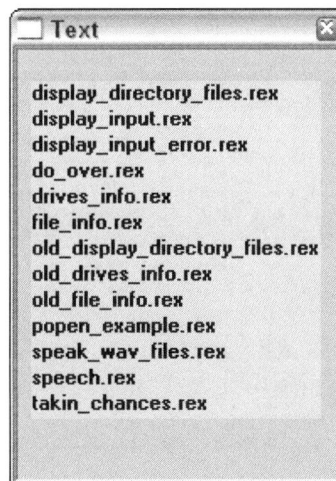

Figure 23-5

Here is the script:

```
/*******************************************************************/
/* DISPLAY DIRECTORY FILES                                         */
/*                                                                 */
/* Displays all files in a directory.                             */
/*******************************************************************/

    call setup_error_traps      /* set up the error trap routines*/
    call set_window_1_values    /* set up values for ENTRY box   */
```

```
call RxCreate 'RX', 2, 'Main Window', 'NOCLOSE'

do forever                    /* do until user closes window    */

   call RxMsg                  /* invokes user interaction       */

  if RxID == '' then signal halt /* exit if users clicks CLOSE */

  if RxID == '2' then do          /* continue if extension...    */

     result = '' ; list = ''

     do until result <> ''    /* get all files w/ the extension*/
        result = MatchName(, 'File', text.1)
        if result = '' then list = list || File || '|'
     end

     if list = '' then
        call RxSay 'No files with this extension', 'OK', 'Warning!'

     else do

        /* display results in 2nd window, a multiline TEXT box*/

        Rx2 = ''                      /* Window ID is 'RX2'    */
        Rx2Type.1  = 'TEXT'           /* use a TEXT box        */
        Rx2Flags.1 = 'NOBORDER'       /* how the text displays*/
        Rx2Label.1 = list             /* the text to display   */
        Rx2Pos.1   = '1 8 18'         /* display position      */
        call RxCreate 'Rx2', 1, 'Text', 'RESULT' /* make window*/
        call RxMsg                    /* do the interaction    */
     end
  end
end
```

The script starts by invoking two internal routines that (1) set up the error routines and invoke RxErr and (2) initialize all the variables required for the text Entry box:

```
call setup_error_traps        /* set up the error trap routines*/

call set_window_1_values      /* set up values for ENTRY box    */
```

These two internal routines are not shown in the preceding listing because their code is exactly the same as in the previous sample script. The line that displays the Entry box is also the same as that of the previous script:

```
call RxCreate 'RX', 2, 'Main Window', 'NOCLOSE'
```

When the user enters a filename extension into the text Entry box, the script identifies this by the fact that REXX Dialog sets the value of rxid to 2. The script enters a do loop that reads filenames with the extension the user requested via the MatchFile function:

```
result = '' ; list = ''

do until result <> ''    /* get all files w/ the extension*/
    result = MatchName(, 'File', text.1)
    if result = '' then list = list || File || '|'
end
```

The `MatchName` function should look familiar; the earlier sample script named `File Info` used it to retrieve file information. In this case, no options are encoded for the `MatchName` function, so it returns a filename that matches the search parameter. The variable `text.1` specifies the search parameter. In this case, this search string includes a wildcard. This parameter is the input the user entered into the text entry box. For example, the user might input:

```
*.txt
```

Or the user could input this information as the parameter:

```
*.rex
```

As `MatchName` retrieves the filenames that match the user's wildcard pattern, the script concatenates them into a list:

```
if err = 0 then list = list || File || '|'
```

Each element in the list is separated by the vertical bar (|). If the list has no elements, no filenames matched the user's search criteria. In this case, the script displays a message box telling the user that no filenames matched the pattern he or she entered:

```
if list = '' then
    call RxSay 'No files with this extension', 'OK', 'Warning!'
```

If some files are found, the script displays them to the user in a text box. This code sets the necessary values for the text box control:

```
Rx2 = ''                        /* Window ID is 'RX2'   */
Rx2Type.1  = 'TEXT'             /* use a TEXT box       */
Rx2Flags.1 = 'NOBORDER'         /* how the text displays*/
Rx2Label.1 = list               /* the text to display  */
Rx2Pos.1   = '1 8 18'           /* display position     */
```

Next, these two lines create the text box window, display it to the user, and control his or her interaction with it:

```
call RxCreate 'Rx2', 1, 'Text', 'RESULT' /* make window*/
call RxMsg                      /* do the interaction   */
```

When the user closes the text box, control returns to the script.

At this point, the user again sees the original text entry box. He or she can enter another wildcard filename pattern, or terminate the program by closing the window.

This simple program shows how you can integrate Reginald's built-in functions for file management with REXX Dialog GUI functions. Reginald provides a full set of GUI groups, controls, and techniques. We have shown only the basics here. See the REXX Dialog online book that downloads with Reginald for complete information and more scripting examples.

Let My Computer Speak!

The last example can easily be modified to do something other than displaying a list of matching files in a text box. For example, instead of building the list of files and displaying them, code this line as the sole action for each file that matches the user's extension criteria:

```
if err = 0 then File
```

Since `File` contains the complete filename, this line sends the filename to the default command environment (the operating system), and which executes the file. For example, if the user enters this into the entry box, the program would execute all `*.bat` files found in the directory.

```
*.bat
```

Similarly, if the user enters the following, the program would send each file in the directory with the `*.wav` extension to the operating system as a command.

```
*.wav
```

Windows recognizes the "Wave" file as an audio clip, and invokes the Windows Media Player to run it. In this case, the program would run the Media Player for each Wave file in the directory. So, this program could be used to play all the songs or audio clips in a directory, for example.

If you want your computer to talk to you, Reginald's extensive sound libraries can do the job. The external *Speech Function Library* allows scripts to use a synthesized voice to pronounce or speak text. It uses the sound card or speaker to "play" the text. Reginald's *MIDI Rexx Function Library* enables scripts to read, write, play, and record MIDI files. *MIDI*, or *Musical Instrument Digital Interface*, is a standard that allows computerized connection and control of musical instruments. Reginald's MIDI library enables input/output to MIDI ports. Of course, MIDI files are often used just to play music on the PC. They are another PC audio file format.

Let's discuss the Speech Function Library. It allows you to encode text strings in scripts that the sound card on the PC pronounces. What makes this interesting is that scripts can dynamically generate the text strings the sound card speaks. This provides computer-synthesized voice without the need to record audio clips in Wave files or other storage-consuming formats.

How could this be used? Since speech is a generalized computer/human interface, the potential is open-ended. Use it as complementary output to typical GUI interfaces or to help the visually impaired. In one IT project, the author used synthesized speech combined with a telephone autodialer to phone and read error conditions to support staff on their cell phones. (Well, maybe this was not the best use of this feature. . . .)

To set up Rexx Speech, simply download and install it from the Reginald Web site. Use the Administration Tool to add its DLL, named `rxspeech.dll`, to the list of autoloaded function libraries. You must also ensure that your Windows PC has a SAPI-compliant speech engine installed. For Windows XP and newer versions, the operating system comes with this facility installed by default. For older Windows versions, you may have to download and install the SAPI ActiveX control from Microsoft Corporation. The Rexx Speech documentation has the link to the module you require, or just access www.microsoft.com and search for the file named spchapi.exe or for the keywords SAPI speech engine. Once you locate the module, download it and double-click on it for automatic installation. Be sure that your PC's speakers are turned on and working before you verify the installation!

Using the Rexx Speech function library is easy. The library contains about 10 functions, and their use is straightforward and well-documented in the online book that automatically downloads with the library.

Take a look at this sample script:

```
/*****************************************************************/
/* SPEECH                                                        */
/*                                                               */
/* Shows how to have your PC speak from text.                    */
/*****************************************************************/

/* open the default speech engine, get ready to pronounce text */

voice = SpeechOpen()
if voice == "" then do
   say 'ERROR- could not initialize speech device!'
   return
end


/* Who says computers can't talk?                               */

error = SpeechSpeak(voice, "This is your computer talking.")
if error \== "" then say 'ERROR- trying to talk:' error


/* close the speech engine and exit the program                 */

call SpeechClose voice

exit 0
```

The script readies the speech engine by the SpeechOpen function:

```
voice = SpeechOpen()
```

This initializes the default engine with the default voice and readies it for use. If it returns the null string, it failed. Otherwise, it returns a voice parameter that is used during synthesis:

```
error = SpeechSpeak(voice, "This is your computer talking.")
```

The SpeechSpeak function should pronounce the string This is your computer talking. using the voice designated by the voice parameter. If it fails, it returns an error message. Otherwise it returns the null string.

When the program is done using the speech engine, it closes it by the `SpeechClose` function:

```
call SpeechClose voice
```

That's all there is to it. Let's look at some other features of the Rexx Speech Library. The `SpeechVoiceDlg` function, for example, automatically pops up a list of voices from the speech engine, from which the user can select the voice to use. You might invoke `SpeechVoiceDlg` at the start of the script to allow the user to select the voice the script employs:

```
id = SpeechVoiceDlg()
if id == "" then do
   say 'ERROR- could not get speech device ID!'
   return
end

voice = SpeechOpen(id)
if voice == "" then do
   say 'ERROR- could not initialize speech device!'
   return
end
```

In this case, `SpeechVoiceDlg` returns a value that indicates which voice the user selected from the automatic dialog. Feeding this parameter into the `SpeechOpen` call means that subsequent invocations of `SpeechSpeak` use this voice.

Prior to the calls to `SpeechSpeak` that synthesize the voice, you may want to make calls to:

❑ `SpeechVolume`—Controls the volume setting

❑ `SpeechPitch`—Sets the pitch

❑ `SpeechSpeed` —Sets the speed of the speaking voice

All three functions take the `voice` as their input parameter. The functions can be used to either set or retrieve current settings.

GUI scripts that use REXX Dialog have the special feature that they can *asynchronously* control speech synthesis. The reason is that scripts need to synchronize user actions with voice. Rexx Speech's *asynchronous speech* controls ensure that what is spoken matches the GUI interaction.

MIDI Rexx

Now let's discuss MIDI Rexx. This external function library allows scripts to create, edit, save, play, and record MIDI files. This could either be used by musicians to integrate computers into their instrumentation, or by the typical PC user to play music files.

To set up the PC environment, download and install the MIDI Rexx package from the Reginald Web site. It consists of two self-extracting files: `midifile.exe` and `genmidi.exe`. At the end of the installation, you will have these two new DLLs on your system:

❑ The MIDI file → `midirexx.dll`

❑ The GenMidi file→ `genmidi.dll`

As always, we recommend using Reginald's convenient autoload feature for access to the MIDI interface from your scripts.

The typical MIDI script operates in this manner. First, it either loads an existing MIDI file into memory (RAM), or it creates a new empty MIDI file in memory. Call the `MIDIOpenFile` function once to establish the existing or new MIDI file in memory. All subsequent MIDI operations apply to a file in memory.

MIDI files consist of *tracks* and *events*. Tracks are the larger entity, and multiple events occur within each track. MIDI Rexx allows scripts to add, modify, and delete events within tracks, add or delete tracks, and perform other kinds of processing.

When a script creates a new MIDI file, it adds tracks or events by invoking the `MIDISetEvent` function. If the script loads an existing MIDI file, it typically calls `MIDITrack` to set the search track. Then it accesses individual events by calls to `MIDIGetEvent`. Scripts typically access one event at a time by calls to `MIDIGetEvent` to perform their processing. `MIDISetEvent` allows scripts to change aspects of the currently selected event. When scripts are through processing a MIDI file, they save it to disk by the `MIDISaveFile` function.

In a manner very similar to the Rexx Speech Library, MIDI Rexx passes information to and from scripts through a set of variables. The documentation clearly explains what variables are relevant to each MIDI Rexx function and how they are used. Here's a list of the MIDI Rexx functions:

MIDI Function	Use
MIDICtlName	Returns the controller name
MIDICtlNum	Returns controller number for a controller name
MIDIEventProp	Returns information about an event
MIDIGetEvent	Searches for the next event matching some criteria
MIDIGetInfo	Returns information about the currently loaded MIDI file
MIDIGetGMDrum	Returns a MIDI drum key name or note number
MIDIGetGMPgm	Returns the MIDI program name
MIDINoteName	Returns the note name for a note number
MIDINoteNum	Returns the note number for a note name
MIDIOpenFile	Loads a MIDI file into memory, or creates a new MIDI file in memory
MIDIPortName	Returns the MIDI port name for a specified port number
MIDISaveFile	Saves a MIDI file from memory to disk
MIDISetEvent	Inserts a new event or updates an existing one; can also delete event(s) or tracks.
MIDISysex	Returns bytes from the currently selected Sysex event
MIDITrack	Sets or queries the track for searches

Accessing the Windows Registry

Reginald provides complete access to the Windows Registry. Directories and subdirectories can be accessed, created, and deleted. *Files* or individual entries can be read, updated, created, and deleted.

The Windows Registry is essential to Windows' operation. Before running any program against it, be aware that faulty updates can damage the operating system or even render it inoperable. Always back up the Registry before working with it. To do this, select the Run... option from the Windows Start button. Start one of the Registry editors, for example, by entering `regedit` as the command in the Run box. Within the Registry Editor, select File | Export... and export the entire Registry to a file.

Review how your particular version of Windows backs up and recoveries the Registry and other vital system information before running any test program against the Registry. Better yet, test any program that interacts with the Registry on a test instance of Windows.

For maximum safety, programs that manipulate the Registry should always verify return codes. The sample script omits error checking in the interest of brevity and clarity.

By default, Reginald functions work in the `Current User` section of the Registry (`HKEY_CURRENT_USER`). After discussing the sample script, we'll show how to access other portions of the Registry.

The sample script performs these Registry operations:

1. Creates a new directory and a new subdirectory to it in `Current User`
2. Creates a new file (entry) in the subdirectory
3. Retrieves and displays the value assigned to the new file in the Registry
4. Pauses so that the user can see the new directory, subdirectory, and file through the Registry Editor
5. Deletes the new file
6. Determines whether the new file was deleted and writes a confirming message
7. Deletes the subdirectory and directory
8. Pauses so that the user can confirm all deletions through the Registry Editor

The logic of the script is simple. It just performs one operation after another. It uses the `value` function to read and change Registry values. Here is the script:

```
/**************************************************************/
/* TAKIN' CHANCES                                           */
/*                                                          */
/* Illustrates Reginald's ability to work with the Registry.  */
/*                                                          */
/* CAUTION- Backup Registry before running this program!     */
/**************************************************************/

/* create a directory and a subdirectory to it              */

fd = value("My Dir\",                , "WIN32")
```

```
fd = value("My Dir\My Sub-Dir\", , "WIN32")


/* create and display a file within that subdirectory        */


fd = value("My Dir\My Sub-Dir\My File","TEST DATA ONLY","WIN32")

say 'Registry data:' value("My Dir\My Sub-Dir\My File", , "WIN32")

say 'Press <ENTER> to continue...' ; pull .


/* delete the registry file and prove that it is gone        */

fd = value("", "My Dir\My Sub-Dir\My File", "WIN32")

if value("My Dir\My Sub-Dir\", "My File", "WIN32") == 1
   then say 'Registry file exists'
   else say 'Registry file has been deleted'


/* delete the directory and subdirectory we created          */

fd = value("", "My Dir\My Sub-Dir\", "WIN32")
fd = value("", "My Dir\",              "WIN32")

say 'Registry directory and subdirectory have been deleted'
say 'Press <ENTER> to exit...' ; pull .
exit 0
```

In the script, these two lines create the directory, then the subdirectory:

```
fd = value("My Dir\",                , "WIN32")
fd = value("My Dir\My Sub-Dir\", , "WIN32")
```

The value call specifies the first parameter as a directory or subdirectory, which must end with the backslash (\). The second parameter is omitted and the third parameter is the environment, which will always be WIN32 when accessing the Registry. value returns a null string if successful. If the directory already exists, no error occurs.

Next, this line creates a new file entry within the new directory and subdirectory. The first parameter specifies the location and the second, the new value to insert. This script inserts a new file with the value: TEST DATA ONLY. If the file already exists, this action overwrites any previous entry:

```
fd = value("My Dir\My Sub-Dir\My File","TEST DATA ONLY","WIN32")
```

Next, this line retrieves the new file value the script just inserted and displays it on to the user. Because no second parameter or "new value" is specified, this value call retrieves information:

```
say 'Registry data:' value("My Dir\My Sub-Dir\My File", , "WIN32")
```

At this point, the script pauses so that the user can verify the new Registry information via the Registry Editor:

```
say 'Press <ENTER> to continue...' ; pull .
```

To verify the new Registry entries, just open a separate window while the script waits, and access the Windows Registry Editor from within this new window. Now you can inspect the Register to see the changes the script made. Assuming the new file value and its directory and subdirectory appear, the user presses the <ENTER> key to continue processing. If there is a problem, he or she can press Ctrl-C to abort the script.

Having made its Registry updates, the script cleans up after itself by deleting the information it added to the Registry. Next, this line deletes the file entry. The absence of the first parameter specifies deletion. No error occurs if there is no such file to delete:

```
fd = value("", "My Dir\My Sub-Dir\My File", "WIN32")
```

Then the script deletes the directory and subdirectory it previously created:

```
fd = value("", "My Dir\My Sub-Dir\", "WIN32")
fd = value("", "My Dir\",             "WIN32")
```

The script ends by pausing so that the user can use the Registry Editor to verify that the Registry has been properly cleaned up.

By default, Reginald functions work in the `Current User` section of the Registry (`HKEY_CURRENT_USER`). To work in other areas of the Registry, just specify the location as the first part of the directory name. This example retrieves a value from within `HKEY_LOCAL_MACHINE`:

```
seed = value("HKEY_LOCAL_MACHINE\HARDWARE\SYSTEM\WPA\PnP\SEED",,"WIN32")
```

To summarize, Reginald scripts can perform any desired Registry operation. Reginald provides a simple, straightforward set of functions for this purpose. Back up your Registry before testing or running any programs that alter it.

Summary

This chapter gives a quick summary of Reginald's comprehensive Windows programming environment. It delves into a bit of detail in only the areas of GUI management and file management. These epitomize the OS-specific features Reginald offers Windows programmers.

Reginald distinguishes itself by its integration into Windows, its ability to program the Windows environment, and its comprehensive self-teaching documentation. Reginald presents an easy-to-use, yet powerful, alternative to proprietary Windows-programming technologies.

This chapter also presented several sample scripts that demonstrate the extended features of Reginald Rexx. They demonstrate several file functions, and also a bit about how to create GUI interfaces with REXX Dialog. We looked into speech synthesis and the MIDI interface, and finally presented a script that accessed and updated the Windows Registry.

These sample scripts only suggest the wide-reaching functionality of the Reginald package. While Reginald is powerful, its complete documentation makes it easy to get started. Windows developers are urged to download and investigate the tools for themselves.

Test Your Understanding

1. What are some of Reginald's key advantages?

2. What kinds of documentation come with Reginald? Would you need any documentation beyond what downloads with the package in order to use it?

3. What functions do you use to give Reginald access to external function libraries (DLLs)? Do you need to code these functions in every script that uses external libraries?

4. Can Reginald scripts access Microsoft Excel spreadsheet data or Microsoft Access databases? If so, how? How do Reginald scripts access MySQL and PostgreSQL databases?

5. Your boss has told you that you'll be developing Web site code using the Common Gateway Interface (CGI). You have to start on it by Monday! Where can you get a tutorial on how to do this and get up to speed in a hurry?

6. What two functions provide information about disk drives? What function do you code to retrieve file attribute information? Does the file have to be opened before you can retrieve this information?

7. What function would you use to read binary information written to a file by a C++ program?

8. How does Reginald read and/or write arrays in one statement?

9. If you've never written a GUI using REXX Dialog, what package might you use to help generate skeletal code?

10. What do these key REXX Dialog functions do: RxErr, RxCreate, RxMsg? How do they fit together in the basic logic of many REXX Dialog programs? What variables do REXX Dialog scripts analyze to discover what the user did?

11. Compare the purposes of the Speech and MIDI Function Libraries. How do they differ? Which would you use to send control information to a keyboard instrument? Which would you use to read a document aloud?

Handhelds and Embedded Programming

Overview

One of the amazing features of Rexx is that it runs on computers ranging from the world's largest mainframes down to the smallest handheld devices. And it works very effectively on that wide range of computers.

This chapter takes a look at Rexx scripting on handheld computers and for embedded, or dedicated-device, programming. First, we describe exactly what handheld computers, or handhelds, are. They are categorized into groups that describe their physical characteristics and uses as well as the operating systems they run. We discuss the two major ways to program handhelds: natively and through DOS emulation. Then we talk specifically about how to program handhelds using Rexx. We discuss native programming using the example of Regina Rexx under the Symbian/EPOC32 operating system. Then we discuss running BRexx under DOS emulation using various DOS emulation products. Of course, if these terms are not clear, don't worry . . . that's the purpose of this chapter. We'll explain the different types of handhelds, the operating systems they run, and the various ways they can be programmed using Rexx.

We conclude the chapter with a discussion of embedded-device programming. Embedded programming considers software to be an integral part of the hardware, or "device." Rexx's ease of programming leads directly to the reliability that makes it a good technology for embedded programming. Software reliability is critical to embedded devices because if the software fails, the device itself is considered "broken." As with handhelds, the small size and limited resource requirements for certain Rexx intepreters also render them useful for this purpose.

The next chapter focuses on a particular handheld operating system, Palm OS. The chapter presents a complete, progressive tutorial on how to program "the Palm" with the Rexx interpreter called Rexx for Palm OS. At the end of the next chapter, you'll not only know how to script Palm devices, but you'll also have a very real understanding of handheld programming.

But that's for the next chapter. Right now, let's define handhelds, describe their major characteristics, and discuss how they can be scripted with Rexx.

Programming Handhelds

Rexx implementations support many small devices. These include personal digital assistants, or PDAs, pocket PCs, Palm PCs, mobile and smart phones, and other programmable handheld consumer devices. They also include *dedicated devices* requiring *embedded programming*. Dedicated devices come with hard-coded programs that are burned into the device. Examples include machine-control systems such as embedded automobile tuning diagnostics. Embedded systems are common in industrial settings, for example, in machinery, robots, and numerical control systems. They are also found in consumer devices that require hard-wired intelligence. Examples here range from sophisticated refrigerators to home security systems to dedicated email and Internet stations.

Whether consumer-oriented or industrial, interactive or embedded, the key characteristic of all these environments is their limited resources. Memory, CPU, and persistent storage — any of the three may be in short supply. Rexx interpreters fit this requirement perfectly. Several feature very small footprints and low memory requirements. For example, the runtime for 16-bit BRexx is well under 100 kilobytes. Regina's 32-bit runtimes for several platforms are similarly small. If you need a small, lightweight, fast language, Rexx fits the bill.

Programming languages for consumer devices such as pocket PCs, palm PCs and smart phones must be also be easy to learn and use. Scripts are often developed by casual users and hobbyists rather than professional programmers. With its emphasis on ease of learning and ease of use, Rexx meets this requirement. Rexx is especially useful when the alternatives are languages like C++ and Java, with its C-heritage syntax. These are great languages for professional developers but they make little sense for the user scripting a small utility for his or her palm or pocket PC.

There are many different kinds of interactive consumer handhelds. Most fall into one of these three categories:

Category	Style	Examples
Tablet PC	Small handheld computers in tablet shape or form factor. These are taller than they are wide, with displays that dominate the face of the device. They typically do not have full keyboards (though some do).	Palm Pilot and its many competitors from NEC, Fujitsu, Casio, others
Keyboard handhelds	Small handheld computers shaped like small keyboards, wider than they are tall. They open to reveal a miniature keyboard on the bottom half and a flip-up screen on the top half. The screens often display up to 80 characters per line horizontally with up to two dozen lines vertically.	HP Jornada, Psion organizers, NEC, Nokia Communicator, others

Category	Style	Examples
Smart phones	Programmable mobile phones. Telephony is the central feature around which other uses are added. New consumer features are continually being added, including text messaging, digital photography, Internet access, and so on. As this occurs, programmability becomes increasingly important and the familiar mobile phone morphs into the powerful smart phone.	Ericsson, Nokia, Motorola, others

What we have called *tablet PCs* some refer to generically as *palm PCs* or *palms. Smart phones* are also referred to as *smartphones, mobile phones,* or *cell phones*. The terminology for handhelds is not consistent. *Handheld PCs* and *pocket PCs* are common terms in the field but they lack precise definition. Our categorization is simplified: some devices are hybrids and new forms of devices continually come out.

For interactive consumer devices, three families of operating system predominate:

❑   *Windows CE* — This Microsoft operating system appears in many versions and under many names including Windows CE .Net, Windows Pocket PC, Windows Mobile, Windows Handheld/PC or H/PC, and Windows for Pocket Personal Computer or Windows P/PC, Pocket PC Phone Edition, and Microsoft Smartphone. Windows CE is quite popular for all three categories of consumer devices.

❑   *Palm OS* — While most often identified with Palm Pilot and competing tablet computers, Palm OS also runs on smart phones and other consumer devices.

❑   *Symbian OS* — This family of operating systems includes Symbian OS and EPOC32. While primarily identified with smart mobile phones, these OSs also run on other handheld devices.

As shown in Figure 24-1, programming languages that run on these devices can run in either of two ways, natively or under an emulator.

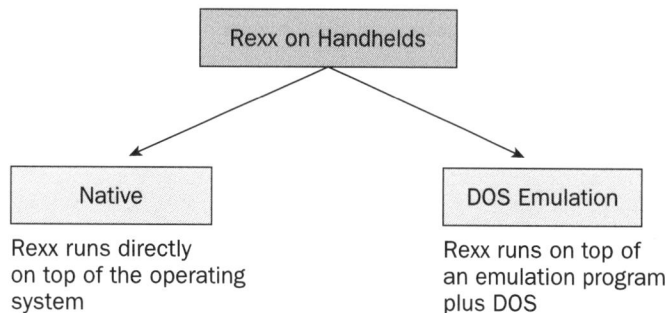

Figure 24-1

To run *natively* means to run directly under the host operating system. To run with an *emulator* means to run under an intermediate translation layer. The emulator makes the host system look like another operating system or platform to the program.

Figure 24-2 below further details how emulators work. The emulator makes the hardware look like a DOS environment running on a personal computer, then DOS runs on top of the emulator, and Rexx runs on top of DOS. Each lower layer of software supports the one running above it.

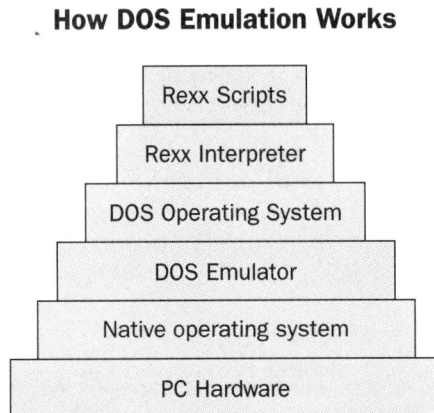

How DOS Emulation Works

| Rexx Scripts |
| Rexx Interpreter |
| DOS Operating System |
| DOS Emulator |
| Native operating system |
| PC Hardware |

Figure 24-2

Native programming is faster because it involves no intermediate software. Native programming is also simpler because the script runs directly under the operating system. If difficulties occur, you don't have to work through the emulator or confirm that the emulator is emulating correctly.

Emulators are an intermediate, software translation layer, which simulates the environment of another platform and/or operating system. Emulators allow you to run a program written for one environment, under another. Most emulators simulate DOS and the 8x86 processor. This permits the thousands of DOS applications to run on the handheld device. While DOS applications for desktop PCs are considered obsolete, emulation provides a huge library of service routines, games, and applications ready to run on the handheld operating system—without any effort or changes required to port them. Of course, DOS programs fit the handheld environment because they assume limited resources.

Examples of popular commercial emulators include *PocketDOS* for Windows CE-derived systems, and *XTM* for Symbian OS/EPOC32 devices. Both simulate a DOS/8x86 environment and make the handheld appear to be a 1980s-era PC.

Examples of free emulators include *PocketConsole* and the *Bochs* emulator. PocketConsole runs under Windows for Pocket PC and Windows for Pocket PC 2002 and works with handhelds that use the ARM, SH*, and MIPS processors. It can be found at `http://mamaich.kasone.com/` and `www.symbolictools.de/public/pocketconsole`. The Bochs emulator is a C++ program that runs on the Pocket PC with MIPS processors. It is open source, distributed under the GNU LGPL, and can be found at `http://bochs.sourceforge.net/`.

DOS emulators support 16-bit Rexx interpreters with small footprints and memory requirements. An example is 16-bit BRexx. The BRexx interpreter requires less than 100K of memory to run.

DOS emulators have especially become popular under Windows CE because these systems typically have limited or no built-in DOS compatibility. Windows CE has no *command line* or *DOS box*. Or, the set of commands the command line supports are limited or not compatible with DOS. Microsoft, the company that once vended DOS, purposely refused prohibited DOS applications from being used on handhelds running Windows CE. Their motive was planned obsolescence. DOS emulators from other companies remedy this situation.

Rexx runs natively on all the major handheld operating systems. The three native Rexx interpreters and their targeted operating systems are:

❑   Windows CE → BRexx

❑   Palm OS → Rexx for Palm OS

❑   Symbian OS/EPOC32 → Regina

Figure 24-3 details how Rexx runs on handheld operating systems in native mode and contrasts this to Rexx interpreters running under DOS emulation.

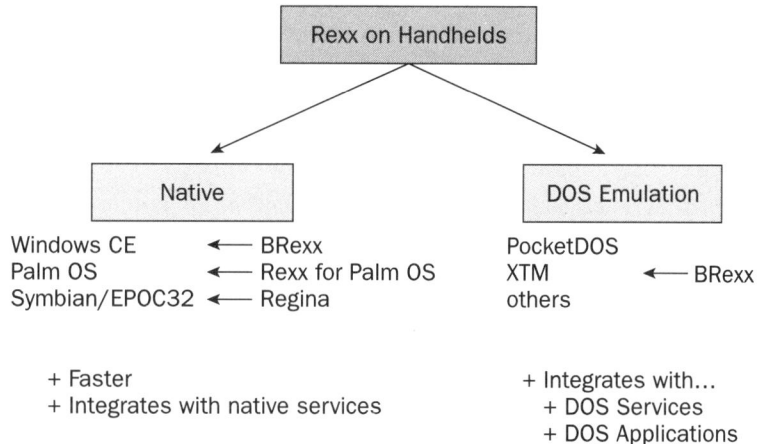

Figure 24-3

Chapter 22 discusses the Windows CE features of the BRexx interpreter and how to install it to run natively on Windows CE-based handhelds. Chapter 25 describes Rexx for Palm OS and presents a tutorial on Palm programming. We discuss native programming for Symbian/EPOC32 with Regina Rexx below.

Both BRexx and Rexx for Palm OS are standard TRL-2 Rexx interpreters. BRexx adds a couple dozen functions specific to Windows CE. Rexx for Palm OS adds a URI-based "resource reference" so that scripts can access Palm OS resources like databases, files, and communications.

The benefit to standard Rexx is that your Rexx knowledge transfers to the handheld environment. If you're a Rexx programmer, regardless of the platform on which you normally work, even if you've never touched a handheld, you can be up and programming handhelds almost immediately. No special training required — just add Rexx.

Running Native — Symbian/EPOC32

Chapters 22 and 25 discuss native Rexx scripting for Windows CE and Palm OS devices, respectively. Let's briefly discuss running Rexx natively under the Symbian family of operating systems.

The Symbian family of operating systems includes EPOC32, EPOC, and various releases of Symbian OS. Symbian is primarily associated with smart phones, but it runs on keyboard and tablet handhelds as well. To a great degree, what programs can do when running under Symbian depends on the nature of the handheld. For some mobile phones, for example, the capability and modes of user interaction are so limited that scripting does not add much value. In other cases, for example, when EPOC32 runs on keyboard handhelds, scripting vastly enhances the utility of the device.

Regina Rexx is distributed for Symbian/EPOC32 as a compressed file. This includes installation instructions and a *.sis file, the file format used for distribution and easy installation of applications under Symbian. Users install *.sis files either from a PC using connectivity software or from the Symbian OS handheld using an on-board installation program. *.sis files have an embedded mechanism that enables deployment of shared libraries and application upgrades.

The size of Regina for EPOC32 varies by release. At the time of writing, the complete distribution was only about 60K, which included the 58K *.sis file. This very easily fits on any EPOC32-based device.

Rexx presents an easy-to-use, standardized scripting language for programming under Symbian. The alternatives are C++, Java, and OPL. Rexx's ease of use distinguishes it from C++ and Java, which are mainly of interest to professional Symbian developers. OPL is a simpler language for Symbian, often described as BASIC-like. It is an open-source language that was specifically built for Symbian OS. The downside is that OPL is a little-known language that runs only under Symbian. Rexx offers a standardized, portable, widely used and well-known alternative. And developer skills transfer across platforms with Rexx.

For more information on natively programming handhelds, see Chapter 22 on BRexx for Windows CE, and Chapter 25 for Rexx for the Palm OS.

DOS Emulation

Since other chapters discuss running Rexx natively under Windows CE and Palm OS, let's talk about DOS emulation here. As mentioned previously, DOS emulation is a boon because it brings thousands of working DOS applications to the handheld without requiring any changes to the applications. The cost is the performance penalty extracted by the extra layer of emulation software.

For Rexx to run on a handheld via DOS emulation, the emulated environment must simulate:

❏ The DOS operating system (including its file system for access to storage)

❏ The memory architecture (and other hardware compatibility features beyond the processor)

❏ The 8x86 CPU

The last requirement is critical: Most handhelds run processors like the Hitachi SH* series, MIPS, ARM, or StrongARM. These are not compatible with Intel 8x86 or Pentium processors. The emulator must make these totally different CPUs appear like the Intel 8x86 processor series.

A variety of free and commercial emulation products are available to address these needs. Let's discuss two nicely packaged commercial products: PocketDOS and XTM. These two packages are representative of how emulators work and how they can underlie Rexx scripting. We chose these particular products simply because they are widely used and well proven.

PocketDOS

PocketDOS is a commercial product that emulates MS-DOS 6.22 for various versions of Windows CE. It allows you to run programs on Windows CE handhelds that run normally run under DOS. These programs require such typical DOS PC hardware as:

❏ 16-bit CPUs (i.e., 8088/8086/80188/80186 CPUs)

❏ CGA/EGA/VGA Screens

❏ Mice (as supported via the handheld's stylus or other pointing device)

❏ Serial and parallel ports

❏ DOS memory restrictions (recall that 16-bit DOS supports under 1 meg of RAM)

These programs also require DOS software. They run with:

❏ The DOS operating system

❏ The DOS file system

PocketDOS installs an icon on the handheld that produces a complete DOS box or DOS command line. The full DOS command set is available along with the simulated environment of 1980s-era DOS computer. PocketDOS maps the Windows CE file system onto traditional DOS drive letters to provide full read and write access. Rexx scripts run in this simulated environment. Specific components PocketDOS installs on the handheld include PocketDOS DOS File System Driver, PocketDOS DOS System Files, PocketDOS Online Help, and PocketDOS Virtual PC Environment.

Downloading and installing PocketDOS is easy. Go to the product Web site at www.pocketdos.com. Select the file for your handheld's version of Windows CE. Download the free demo version of the product to your Windows PC. Link your handheld to the Windows PC, and ensure that Microsoft's ActiveSync connection is up and working. Then double-click on the PocketDOS file you downloaded. The product will automatically self-extract and install itself on the attached handheld.

After installation, the PocketDOS icon appears on the handheld. Select it to enter DOS command mode. At the prompt, you can create or run any Rexx script designed for the 16-bit DOS environment.

As an example, the author downloaded PocketDOS for an HP keyboard handheld to his Windows PC. He attached the handheld to the desktop PC and started Microsoft's ActiveSync program. Then he double-clicked on the PocketDOS download file, which seamlessly installed itself on the handheld. The PocketDOS icon popped up on the handheld, showing that a successful install occurred.

Next, he downloaded the version of BRexx for 16-bit DOS to the Windows PC and used ActiveSync to install the interpreter and its libraries to the HP keyboard handheld. He used the DOS `edit` command in the PocketDOS window to create new Rexx scripts. He also transferred existing scripts over from the desktop PC. He ran the Rexx benchmark script `rexxcps.rex` as a test. Performance results were similar to a PC from the 1980s. The entire process — downloading and installing PocketDOS on the handheld, transferring over BRexx and a few sample scripts, verifying the installation, and playing around — took under 2 hours.

In exchange for this effort, you gain a powerful, flexible scripting language for your handheld. Scripts can use all the DOS capabilities of the handheld to provide applications, utilities, service routines, special functions, and the like. They provide the glue to control, manage, and combine traditional DOS applications in new ways and to tailor the handheld environment to a custom fit.

Finally, a technical note: PocketDOS is an emulator, but it is not DOS — it requires a DOS to run on top of it. PocketDOS comes bundled with a DOS called Datalight ROM-DOS v6.22. The product install is so convenient that it appears as if the emulator and DOS are seamlessly integrated. (You could install PocketDOS and run it without ever realizing that PocketDOS and the Datalight DOS it runs are actually two separate products.) PocketDOS supports many DOS operating systems. These include MS-DOS, OpenDOS, DR-DOS, PTS-DOS, CEDOS, MS-Windows 3.0, GEOS, and others. According to personal preference, you can run any of these DOSs with PocketDOS.

At the time of writing, PocketDOS is porting their product to Symbian OS/EPOC32. This will provide a similar, seamless DOS command line for this operating system. Today you can script Symbian/EPOC32 handhelds natively, with Regina for EPOC32. PocketDOS's port will add a DOS emulation alternative that supports any 16-bit Rexx interpreter.

XTM

XTM is a commercial product from NB Information Ltd. at www.nb-info.co.uk/index.htm. XTM is a DOS emulator for Symbian OS/EPOC32. The DOS environment it supports has these characteristics:

❑   80186 CPU and instruction set

❑   Math co-processor emulation (the 8087 MPU)

❑   MCGA display with all text and graphics modes

❑   Native code BIOS (for performance)

❑   Full access to the EPOC32 file system

❑   Access to serial ports

❑   Supports several spoken languages including English, French, German and Dutch

XTM does not include DOS. You must supply a DOS. DOS's tested with XTM include MS-DOS and DR-DOS. The latter is a free product for noncommercial use.

While XTM runs on any version of EPOC32 or Symbian OS, it is most effective on handhelds with landscape format screens and full keyboards — what we have termed the keyboard handheld. The PC emulation experience on a phone based platform that lacks these characteristics is not always sufficient to usefully run DOS applications. Examples of hardware on which XTM runs and offers good value-added includes various Nokias, Psions, netBooks, Diamond Mako, and Geofox One.

As with PocketDOS, you must transfer a 16-bit DOS-based Rexx interpreter to your handheld. BRexx is a good candidate.

The NB Information Ltd. Web site provides benchmark statistics on the relative speed of the DOS emulation environment on several Symbian OS handhelds, measured against the power of the original IBM PC/XT. This table includes a few of these benchmark numbers:

Benchmark	IBM PC/XT	XTM on Psion 5	XTM on 5mx	XTM on netBook
Sieve	1.0	0.64	1.43	9.65
Integer Math	1.0	1.28	2.72	21.73

Data courtesy of the NB Information Ltd Web site at www.nb-info.co.uk/index.htm posted during 2004.

Of course, you can establish your own relative Rexx benchmark. Just transfer the rexxcps.rex benchmark program to the handheld and run it. Compare your results to those in the first table appearing in Chapter 1. Performance is typically the equivalent of a PC from the 1980s.

The author's own Rexx benchmarks for PocketDOS and XTM confirmed those in the table. Rexx ran faster than on the original IBM PC but at speeds reminiscent of PCs in the late 1980s — altogether appropriate for a 16-bit DOS environment. Of course, if performance is the major concern, run Rexx natively. Rexx runs natively under all three of the major handheld operating systems.

If native mode is always faster, why would anyone use DOS emulation? The answer is that DOS provides an environment, a set of services, that might be useful to Rexx scripts. DOS emulation opens the door to integrating with thousands of existing DOS applications, which were used worldwide by consumers and to run businesses, prior to the advent of 32-bit Windows in 1995. You can use Rexx as a "glue language" to launch these applications, manipulate their results, and perform other services.

Embedded Device Programming

Embedded and dedicated device programming is similar to handheld programming in that limited hardware resources may be available. CPU, memory, storage, and other resources may be in short supply.

These systems also present another criterion: code must be 100 percent maintenance-free. If this requirement is not met, the device is considered defective. A software error means a broken device. Rexx's clean, simple syntax reduces errors and makes it ideal for this purpose. It is easier to develop error-free code with Rexx than it is in most other languages. Simplicity yields reliability.

A number of operating systems are used in embedded and dedicated device programming. These include specialized operating systems, for example, various *real-time operating systems*, or *RTOS*.

Embedded programming also employs *tiny Linuxes*—Linux kernels built for small systems. Tiny Linuxes strip out utilities and services superfluous to dedicated programming environments, retaining only the kernel and minimal services. Some refer to tiny Linuxes as *embedded Linux*. Embedded Linux is quite popular for dedicated device programming because it is both free and highly configurable. Royalty-free software is an important consideration in low-margin, mass-produced products, where profit margins may be thin.

16- and 32- bit DOS are also very popular for embedded- and dedicated-device programming. DOS is popular because it is so well known and documented that every possible behavior can be planned for. Even the bugs are all well known! This is a major advantage for systems requiring 100 percent reliability. There are also a number of free DOS implementations available, holding down costs and offering multiple sources for the product. Finally, the small size of DOS is a major advantage, conserving memory and resources from the operating system and making it available to the application.

Several Rexx interpreters support free DOS and tiny Linux environments. BRexx is notable for its DOS extensions and it supports both 16- and 32- bit DOS. Chapter 22 includes an example of a 16-bit DOS program that illustrates some of BRexx's DOS-specific extensions. Of course, Windows-oriented interpreters like Regina, r4, and Reginald can run from the 32-bit Windows' DOS command line. Several Rexx interpreters run under resource-constrained Linux environments. These include Rexx/imc, Regina, and BRexx.

Summary

Rexx fits the scripting requirements of handheld consumer devices perfectly. It is small, easy to learn and use for casual programmers, portable, yet powerful. It runs natively on the three major operating system families for handhelds, Windows CE, Palm OS, and Symbian OS. It also runs on almost any consumer device through DOS emulation. Rexx under DOS emulation runs more slowly, but sometimes DOS services can be useful for programming Rexx utility scripts. Rexx can also be used as a glue language to integrate, tailor or control DOS applications on handhelds.

Rexx also supports dedicated device or embedded programming. Its ease of use makes it easier to develop completely reliable, maintenance-free programs. Its small size and ability to run under free DOS and Linux add to its appeal.

For further information on handheld consumer devices, visit *Pocket PC Magazine* at www.pocketpcmag. com and *Handheld PC Magazine* at www.hpcmag.com. Or, search any major search engine on the operating system name (Windows CE, Palm OS, or Symbian OS), and you'll find several major Web sites dedicated to each. For embedded programming, see *Embedded Systems Programming Magazine* and its Web site at www.embedded.com, or check out *Embedded Computing Design* magazine at www.embedded-computing.com.

Test Your Understanding

1. What are the three major families of operating systems used on handhelds? Which Rexx interpreter runs natively on each?

2. What are the differences between running scripts natively versus under a DOS emulator? Why might you want to use the emulator? What is the advantage to running natively?

3. What is a "tiny Linux"? Why would someone create one?

4. If you run a DOS emulator such as PocketDOS or XTM, do you need to supply DOS? Are there free versions of DOS? (Hint: search for keywords `free DOS` in your favorite Internet search engine).

5. Why is it important that Rexx for handhelds and embedded programming support the language standards?

6. What are the advantages of Rexx for handheld and embedded programming versus C++ and Java?

Rexx for Palm OS

Overview

Palm OS is an operating system that runs on a wide variety of handheld, tablet-style computers, such as the Palm Pilot and its many competitors. It also runs on other small devices including mobile and smart phones. Palm OS is among the most popular operating systems for handheld consumer devices.

Rexx for Palm OS is a Rexx interpreter that runs natively under the Palm OS operating system. It enables the creation of scripts and utilities for handheld PCs that extends their usefulness. It accesses all Palm resources and integrates them in unique fashion. This chapter describes the product and presents a brief tutorial with sample scripts.

First, we start by listing and discussing the features of the Rexx for Palm OS interpreter. We describe how to download and install the product. Then, the tutorial takes you through progressive examples that show how to use the product to script Palm handhelds. The first script simply displays a memo on the screen of the handheld. It shows how to access Palm resources. Subsequent scripts search and copy databases, and demonstrate stream I/O and how to control, manage, and search for files. Several scripts present information on how to communicate with the Palm using infrared, USB, and serial ports, and TCP/IP communications. Finally, a rather ambitious script selects and plays a song. This script searches for a music file and plays it through MIDI output.

By the end of the chapter, you'll be able to script almost any Palm function or feature. Even if you are not specifically interested in programming the Palm OS with Rexx for Palm OS, you'll have a very good idea of how to go about scripting handhelds. What you'll find is that handheld programming is more about a change in perspective than anything else, because the Rexx language is the same as that employed on Linux servers, Windows PCs, and IBM mainframes.

Advantages

As with all of the previous chapters that cover individual Rexx interpreters, we first list and discuss the features of the Rexx for Palm OS interpreter. Rexx for the Palm OS runs on all versions of the Palm OS from version 3.0 on up and on any Palm OS hardware. Some of the key benefits of the product are:

❑   *Easy scripting* — Many script writers for handhelds are hobbyists or occasional developers, not professional programmers. Bringing Rexx to handhelds capitalizes on its advantages for easy script writing and offers an easy-to-learn and easy-to-use scripting language for everyone.

❑   *Runs natively* — Rexx for Palm OS runs directly under the Palm OS operating system. It does *not* require an emulator or other intermediate software layer that compromises performance.

❑   *Concurrency* — Rexx for Palm OS allows you to create Rexxlets, Rexx scripts that run concurrently with applications. You can launch a Rexxlet while in another application, by a simple pen stroke, for example, while not leaving the original application. This integration between Rexx scripts and applications fulfills the promise of Rexx as an easy-to-use, all-purpose utility language for the Palm OS.

❑   *A "glue" language* — Integration makes Rexxlets the "glue" that tie together the resources of the Palm. Rexxlets cross-link information, applications, and pop-up utilities without leaving the current application. They can read, write, and transfer data among applications and databases. Run them by pen strokes, menus, or icons.

❑   *Accesses all resources* — Rexx for Palm OS accesses all resources of the Palm including console I/O, databases, files, TCP/IP communications, the MIDI interface and sound, the USB and serial interfaces, and beaming (infrared communications). Rexxlets can read and write all Palm data, including record-oriented databases and files. They can access the console and the clipboard. (At the time of writing the product does not support forms-based GUI applications.)

❑   *Integrate applications* — Rexx for Palm OS supplies a universal macro language for the Palm OS. It extends the Palm's capabilities by tying together the thousands of Palm applications and your own data.

❑   *Standard Rexx* — Rexx for Palm OS meets the TRL-2 standard. All your Rexx knowledge applies. Only two things are new: setting up and configuring the product for the Palm, and the way in which scripts address Palm resources. Adherence to Rexx standards means that Rexx for Palm OS presents no learning curve to Rexx programmers.

❑   *It's easy!* — If you've never programmed a handheld before, this is the product to use. It comes with about 20 sample scripts and good documentation. As the tutorial that follows demonstrates, no experience programming handhelds is needed.

Downloading and Installation

Rexx for Palm OS is a product of Jaxo Inc. It can be downloaded from several sources, including the Jaxo Inc. home pages at www.jaxo.com/rexx or through the Palm Gear Web site at www.palmgear.com. If Web addresses change, enter the keywords Rexx for Palm OS or Jaxo Inc into any search engine to locate the product.

The Rexx for Palm OS online forum and a Web log are also accessible from the Jaxo Inc. Web site. Learn about the product by visiting the Jaxo Inc. Web site at `www.jaxo.com` and reading the documentation and examples posted there.

Rexx for Palm OS is a shareware product. The runtime module and integrated development environment, or IDE, are free. Developers who intend to develop and commercialize their Rexx scripts and Rexxlets must purchase a developer's license. Personal use is free, but corporate or commercial use requires purchasing a license. Check the license that downloads with the product for current details.

Rexx for Palm OS runs on all versions of the Palm OS from 3.0 on up and runs on any Palm OS hardware. It requires only 320K of memory. The product downloads as a single compressed file of file type `*.pgz`. If your decompression utility does not recognize files of this type, just change the file type to `*.zip` and run the Winzip utility.

Among the unzipped files is a `readme` file that provides installation instructions. Installation is easy and straightforward. The key decision in installing the product is whether you have Palm OS version 5.*x* or newer. If you do, you do *not* need to install a *system extension product* or *"hack manager."* This capability is built into the operating system.

If you have the older Palm OS 3.*x* or 4.*x*, you need to install a hack manager such as HackMaster or its equivalent. This is provided in the download file in the form of *X-Master*, a freeware product that manages Palm system extensions. It resides in the file `X-master.prc` and instructions on how to use it are in the file `xmaster-readme.txt`.

After installing the hack manager, if required, load the several `*.prc` and `*.pdb` files of Rexx for Palm OS onto the Palm. To test the install, launch Rexx and press the Edit button; then enter:

```
say "hello world!"
```

Press the Run button, and the `hello world!` message should appear on the console. Then press the Return and Exit buttons to end the test.

If you're using a hack manager (if you're using an operating system older than Palm OS 5.*x*), launch X-Master and enable the `RexxletHack` extension by checkmarking the box next to it. Configure Rexxlets through the `RexxletHack` preference screen. The installation instructions give full details on how to configure Rexxlets.

Now try another test. Launch the Palm OS `Expense` application. Press the `New` button. Swipe your pen from the App soft-button to the Grafitti area. In the Rexxlet Script window, enter: `return 2+2`.

Press the Run button, and the result 4 appears as a new expense item.

A Tutorial

Let's explore Palm OS programming by taking a look at a few sample scripts. All the examples appear here courtesy of their authors, Pierre G. Richard and Joseph A. Latone of Jaxo Inc., and are distributed with the product.

Here's the first complete script:

```
input = "dm:///MemoDB/Personal/1"
do while lines(input)>0
  say linein(input)
end
```

This script reads the first entry in the `Personal` category of your `MemoPad` and writes it to the display or *console*. We've seen everything in this script before; it is all standard Rexx. The only new code is:

```
input = "dm:///MemoDB/Personal/1"
```

This line refers to the first record in the `Personal` category of the `MemoDB` database. It shows that Rexx for Palm OS uses *Universal Resource Locators*, or *URLs*, to access Palm resources such as databases, files, the console, and the clipboard. URLs are also called *Universe Resource Identifiers*, or *URIs*. Rexx for Palm OS adheres to the URI standard "RFC2396, Uniform Resource Identifiers." These are sample resources that Rexx for Palm OS uses this notation to address:

Identifier	Palm Resource
dm:	Record-oriented databases (such as MemoPad, Expense, ToDo List, and others)
file:	Palm file streams
console:	The Palm display screen
clipboard:	The clipboard

Each type of resource has a simple URI naming convention. Remember that resource names in the Palm OS are case-sensitive (`MemoDB` is different from `Memodb`). Here are a few more resource naming examples:

❑   `dm:///RexxDB/Personal` — The first Memo in the `Personal` category of the `RexxDB` database

❑   `dm:///RexxDB/Personal/2` — The second Memo in the `Personal` category

❑   `dm://Rexx.data@localhost:0/MemoDB//1` — Same as the previous, but uses the full, explicit name

We'll see many more examples of how to access resources in the examples that follow. Just about every script illustrates how to access some sort of resource. These include databases, files, memos, or communication devices such as infrared communcations, the serial port, or TCP/IP.

Now that we've seen how to access resources, here's a script that searches the `RexxDB` database for the script named `ShowMemo`:

```
/* SearchARexx
Look for a Rexx in the RexxDB.
*/
SearchARexx:
    input = "dm:///RexxDB/REXX/"
```

```
DO i=1 BY 1
path = input || i
IF Stream(path) \= 'READY' THEN DO
    SAY "Sorry! ShowMemo was not found."
    LEAVE
    END
IF Linein(path) = "/* ShowMemo" THEN DO
    SAY "Yes: I know about ShowMemo"
    LEAVE
    END
    END
```

The script searches for the word ShowMemo, which occurs at the top of the script in its initial comment, much as in the preceding example. These lines identify ShowMemo if the script finds it:

```
IF Linein(path) = "/* ShowMemo" THEN DO
    SAY "Yes: I know about ShowMemo"
```

The script uses a do loop to append a number to the input filename and look for the ShowMemo script:

```
input = "dm:///RexxDB/REXX/"
DO i=1 BY 1
path = input || i
```

If the script cannot find ShowMemo, it invokes the stream function to identify and report that fact:

```
IF Stream(path) \= 'READY' THEN DO
    SAY "Sorry! ShowMemo was not found."
```

This script shows how the resource name can be dynamically created and used in a search function. All the regular rules of Rexx stream input/output apply: Files are automatically opened when they are first referenced, and they are closed when the script ends. The only way in which this script differs from all the other Rexx scripts in this book is in its resource reference.

Here's an example that shows how to create a new memo. It writes a single line to the Memo database:

```
/* WriteMemo
Add a new record with "Hello World!" in the Biz cat.
*/
WriteMemo:
    output="dm:///MemoDB/Business"
    CALL Lineout output, "Hello World!"
    CALL Charout output, '00'x
```

The line is written to the *default write position*, as a new record that follows the last record in the category.

The script writes one byte, hexadecimal '00', immediately following the output line. This is required because Palm OS ends each MemoDB record with that character. This is why the previous script that displayed a memo to the screen was followed by a small empty rectangle. That was actually the x'00' appearing in the display.

What this shows is that in order to work properly with Palm resources, you must be aware of the rules or conventions they follow. Fortunately, they are few and simple. www.palmos.com describes them in its public Web page at www.palmos.com/dev/support/docs/fileformats/FileFormatsTOC.html.

Here's a script that copies an entire database, the RexxDB, and writes it into the Memo database, MemoDB. This demonstrates the power of short scripts in managing, processing, and rearranging Palm resources:

```
/* Rexx2Memo
Read the entire Rexx database into the Memo database.
*/

Rexx2Memo:
output = "dm:///MemoDB/REXX"
   DO i=1
      input = "dm:///RexxDB/REXX/" || i
      IF Stream(input) \= 'READY' THEN LEAVE /* all done! */
      DO Lines(input)-1
         CALL Lineout output, Linein(input)
         END
      CALL Charout output, LineIn(input)     /* write the last line */
      CALL Stream output, 'C', 'CLOSE'       /* done with this record */
      END
```

As in the search script shown previously, this script dynamically builds the input name using a subscript:

```
input = "dm:///RexxDB/REXX/" || i
```

Because more than one item could be copied, the script must explicitly close the output stream after each:

```
CALL Stream output, 'C', 'CLOSE'        /* done with this record */
```

Rexx for Palm OS follows all Rexx standards, so user interaction is through the say and pull instructions. This example asks the user to enter the name of a Rexx script. It then accesses and runs that script from the RexxDB database:

```
/* RunARexx
Look for a Rexx in the RexxDB and execute it
This requires that the Rexx to run starts with a label
that has the same value as its first word
(e.g "RunARexx:" for this script).
*/
RunARexx:
SAY "Enter the name of a Rexx Script:"
PARSE UPPER PULL title
DO i=1 BY 1
   input = "dm:///RexxDB/REXX/" || i
   IF Stream(input) \= "READY" THEN DO
      SAY "Sorry!" title "was not found."
      LEAVE
```

```
        END
    line1 = Linein(input)
    IF Translate(Word(line1,2)) = title THEN DO
        SAY "Yes: I know about " title
        SAY "Do you want it run? (Y/N)"
        PULL answer
        IF answer \= 'N' THEN DO
            CALL Load input
            INTERPRET "call " title
            END
        LEAVE
        END
    END
END
```

As with the previous examples, this script relies on the programming convention that the script starts with a label naming it in order to identify the proper script.

Something new in this script is its use of the load function to load the user's script:

```
CALL Load input
```

The load function is an extension in Rexx for Palm OS. It works in a manner analogous to this function in other Rexx interpreters, for example, as in BRexx.

The interpret instruction that immediately follows executes the script that was just loaded:

```
INTERPRET "call " title
```

This script shows how to find, then dynamically load and execute, another Rexx script. It is easy to refer to, alter, and run other scripts residing on the Palm in this manner.

Databases are record-oriented files under the Palm OS. They are the most popular form of storage in the operating system because their record orientation matches the format of structured Palm data for Memos, ToDo Lists, and the like. But *files* are also useful. Files are stream-oriented; they consist of character streams rather than discrete records. Their main advantages are that they have no size limitations, and their structure matches traditional Rexx I/O. They can be useful in Rexx scripts on the Palm.

To get started with files, these two scripts show how to write a line to the FileStream named TempFile, then read it back and display it. This script writes one line to the file stream:

```
/* Append2File
Append "Hello World!" to the FileStream "TempFile".
*/
Append2File:
output="file:///TempFile"
CALL Lineout output, "Hello World!"
```

This script reads back the line and displays it:

```
/* ShowFile
Display a File
*/
ShowFile:
input = "file:///TempFile"
DO Lines(input)
   SAY Linein(input)
   END
```

The one key difference in these two scripts is the reference to a resource of the type file in these two lines:

```
output="file:///TempFile"    /* in the output script          */
input = "file:///TempFile"   /* in the read-and-display script */
```

With this knowledge we can easily write a short script that deletes a FileStream in just one instruction:

```
/* DeleteFile
Delete the Filestream "TempFile"
*/
DeleteFile:
CALL Charout "TempFile", "", 1
```

The trick to this script is this line:

```
CALL Charout "TempFile", "", 1
```

This statement positions the pointer to the first position in TempFile. It does not actually write anything to that file, since the second argument is the null string. This pointer repositioning effectively deletes the file.

Mixing files and databases within a script requires no special coding. Just refer to each resource as indicated previously. For example, this script reads the second record in the Personal category of the Memo database and writes it to the temporary file named MemoPers2. Note that it strips out the hexadecimal x'00', or *sentinel*, that follows the database record:

```
/* Memo2File
Read a memo and write it to a file.
*/
Memo2File:
input = "dm:///RexxDB/Personal/2"
output = "file:///MemoPers2"
CALL Charout output, '', 1  /* technique to reset output */
linesCount = Lines(input)
SAY input "has" Chars(input) "bytes in" linesCount "lines."
DO linesCount-1               /* forget the sentinel! */
   CALL Lineout output, Linein(input)
END
```

Rexx for Palm OS database and file functions duplicate what the Palm OS offers in its application programming interfaces, or APIs, called the *Database Manager API* and the *File Manager API*.

We've seen how Rexx for Palm OS scripts can create, alter, read, and write databases and files. Let's move on to other resources. One is IrDA communications, also referred to as infrared communications or *beaming*. Following the same rules of reference we've seen thus far, the Beamer is referred to simply as `beamer://` or `beamer:`. For convenience, the two slashes may be omitted.

How are IrDA communications implemented? Data sent by the Beamer is encapsulated into a file named `RexxData.REX`. Similarly, the Beamer reads files with the extension `.REX`. Beamer files with different extensions are read by applications other than Rexx scripts.

This script shows how the Beamer is easily accessed from Rexx. This program writes one line to the IrDA communications:

```
/* Talk2Beamer
Simple demo of the beamer (aka IrDA / exg) stream
*/
Talk2Beamer:
    beamer = "beamer:"
    IF Stream(beamer) \= "READY" THEN DO
        SAY "Cannot access the Beamer port"
        EXIT
        END
    CALL Lineout beamer, "Hello Beamer! Say something..."
    SAY "Beamer said:" Linein(beamer)
    EXIT
```

Another resource is the serial port. This sample script writes a line to the serial port:

```
/* Talk2Serial
Simple demo of the serial (aka rs232) stream
*/
Talk2Serial:
    serial = "serial:?bauds=19200"
    IF Stream(serial) \= "READY" THEN DO
        SAY "Cannot access the Serial port"
        EXIT
        END
    CALL Lineout serial, "Hello Serial! Say something..."
    SAY "Serial said:" Linein(serial)
    EXIT
```

This script refers to the serial port as `serial:`   Here are the options for naming this resource:

Identifier	Means
`serial://`	A generic serial port; refers to either the USB or the RS-232 port
`serial:`	Same as previous item
`rs232://`	Explicitly designates the RS-232 port
`usb://`	Explicitly designates the USB port

The URI designator may optionally be followed by a *query part* that specifies the baud rate of the serial port. As per the URI standard, this takes the form of a question mark followed by the speed. In the script, it is coded as:

```
serial = "serial:?bauds=19200"
```

Another Palm resource is TCP/IP communications. Writing Rexx scripts to harness this resource can automate various kinds of communication between the handheld and other devices. For example, the script that follows writes a line from the handheld to a personal computer via infrared communications. So, a wireless link is implemented between the two dissimilar computers.

The script is simple, varying little from the examples of infrared and serial communications seen earlier. The main difference is that the script dynamically builds the reference to the TCP/IP resource based on user input. Here is the script:

```
/* Talk2TcpIp
Simple demo of the tcpip (aka net) stream
*/
Talk2TcpIP:
    SAY "What host do you want to talk to?"
    PULL host
    IF host == "" THEN host = "10.110.2.36"
    SAY "And on what port?"
    PULL port
    IF port == "" THEN port = "6416"
    tcpip = "tcpip://" || host || ":" || port
    IF Stream(tcpip) \= "READY" THEN DO
        SAY "Cannot access to " tcpip
        EXIT
        END
    CALL Lineout tcpip, "Hello TcpIP! Say something..."
    SAY "TcpIP said:" Linein(tcpip)
    EXIT
```

The identifier for the TCP/IP resource is: `tcpip://`.

The script concatenates user input to the resource identifier to build a complete TCP/IP address. For example, this address might appear something like this: `tcpip://10.110.2.36:6416`.

Of course, for this script to work properly some setup must be done on both the server and the Palm (or handheld). This involves:

1. Installing an infrared communications program on the server
2. Configuring the server
3. Configuring the handheld (the client)
4. Setting up and starting the listener on the server's TCP/IP port

These steps are outside our scope here, but are fully described in the Rexx for Palm OS documentation.

Let's look at one last resource, the MIDI interface. This interface plays audio, such as voice or music. It is referred to as the resource: `midi://` or `midi:`.This sample script asks the user to enter a song to play from within a MIDI database. It shows how the song is referred to within the database. The script dynamically builds the song or file reference. The script also shows the use of two internal routines, `PlayASong` and `GetTitle`. The former plays the song that the user selected, while the latter searches for the song prior to playing it.

Here is the script:

```
/* PlayMidi
Play a Standard Midi FIle (SMF) out of a MIDI sound DB
*/
PlayMidi:
PARSE ARG dbName songNumber
if dbName == "" THEN DO
    SAY "Name the MIDI Database: (default System MIDI Sounds)"
    PARSE PULL dbName rest
END
IF dbName == "" THEN dbName = "System MIDI Sounds"
if songNumber == "" THEN DO
    SAY "What song number? (default gives a list)"
    PARSE PULL songNumber rest
END

IF songNumber <> "" THEN DO
    maxSong = 1
    input = "dm:///" || dbName || "//" || songNumber
    IF Stream(input) == "READY" THEN maxSong = songNumber + 1
    CALL PlayASong
    END
ELSE DO
    /* Collect titles */
    DO maxSong=1
        input = "dm:///" || dbName || "//" || maxSong
        IF Stream(input) \= "READY" THEN LEAVE
        SAY maxSong "->" GetTitle()
        END

    DO UNTIL answer <> 'Y'
        SAY "Please, choose a title number:"
        PULL songNumber
        CALL PlayASong
        SAY "Play another? (Y/N)"
        PULL answer
        END
END

RETURN

PlayASong: PROCEDURE EXPOSE dbName songNumber input
```

```
      IF Datatype(songNumber) <> 'NUM' |,
         songNumber < 1 | songNumber >= maxSong THEN DO
         SAY songNumber "is not valid."
         EXIT
         END
      input = "dm:///" || dbName || "//" || songNumber
      SAY "Now playing..." GetTitle()
      CALL Charin input, 1+C2d(Charin(input,5)), 0  /* start of the Midi rec */
      CALL Charout "midi:", Charin(input,,Chars(input)) /* play it */
      RETURN

   GetTitle: PROCEDURE EXPOSE input
      IF Charin(Input, 1, 4) <> "PMrc" THEN DO
         SAY dbName "doesn't appear to be a MIDIDatabase."
         EXIT
         END
      CALL Charin input, 7, 0
      DO titleLen = 0 WHILE Charin(input) \= '00'x; END
      RETURN Charin(input, 7, titleLen)
```

This concludes our quick tutorial on scripting with Rexx for Palm OS. To explore further, download the product or visit its Web site at www.jaxo.com. The product documentation provides a nice tutorial and includes more detail and examples.

Summary

The Palm OS operating system is very popular on tablet PCs, smart phones, and other handheld devices. The Rexx for Palm OS interpreter brings the simplicity and power of Rexx to this platform.

Rexx for Palm OS is a full implementation of the Rexx the TRL-2 standard. This makes it easy for Rexx programmers from other platforms to transfer their skills to the Palm OS. The package is well documented and includes many sample scripts. Combined with Rexx's ease of learning and ease of use, Palm hobbyists and casual users are able to write scripts to automate Palm operations and extend the value of the handheld. Professionals leverage the product to develop sophisticated, integrated applications.

Rexx for Palm OS provides a "glue language" that ties together thousands of Palm applications with user data and the programmability of scripting. *Rexxlets* run concurrently, as if they were simply extensions of applications, seamlessly extending them. The integration of Rexx as a Palm macro language brings power that only becomes apparent with use. Interested readers are urged to download Rexx for Palm OS from the Jaxo Inc. Web site and explore how it addresses their needs.

Test Your Understanding

1. What is a Rexxlet? How do Rexxlets integrate Palm applications and resources?

2. What are URLs and URIs? How are they used to refer to Palm OS resources? Name four of those resources.

3. How does a Rexx script open a database? A file? A USB serial port? An RS-232 serial port?

4. What are the differences between Palm databases and files? When do you use each?

5. Could you develop Rexxlets on your Windows desktop or laptop computer and port them to the Palm OS and Rexx for Palm OS? What, if any, changes would be required to the scripts?

6. What is a hack manager? Why would you need it? Do you need it if your handheld runs Palm OS 5.x or later? What is X-Master? How much does it cost and where can you get it?

7. Is I/O the same in Rexx for Palm OS as in standard Rexx?

26

r4 and Object-Oriented roo!

Overview

Kilowatt Software offers two free Rexx interpreters. r4 is a classic Rexx interpreter that meets the TRL-2 standard and is at language level 4.00. roo! is an object-oriented superset of r4. It offers a complete object-oriented Rexx programming language. Both r4 and roo! run under all modern versions of Windows and are complemented by many add-on tools for the Windows environment. This chapter briefly overviews both.

We'll discuss the advantages to r4 and roo! as a pair of Rexx interpreters from the same company. Then we'll briefly describe the installation process for the products. After this, we'll describe some of the tools that Kilowatt Software provides for both r4 and roo! These help developers leverage Windows features with much less effort than would otherwise be required.

The heart of the chapter is the quick overview of roo!'s object-oriented scripting features. Object-oriented programming is an approach many feel dramatically raises developer productivity. roo! supports all object-oriented features, while retaining full compatibility with standard Rexx. We'll describe the additions roo! makes to classic Rexx and explain how they support object-based scripting.

Advantages

r4 and roo! are two different products from the same vendor. Nevertheless, they share many of the same tools and charcteristics. Here are some key features of r4 and roo!:

❑ *Windows-oriented* — The products are customized for Windows, with easy installation and developer tools specifically designed for Windows. roo! is a free object-oriented Rexx that is tailored and configured for Windows.

❑ *Introductory material* — The Web site features several tutorials and presentations on classic Rexx and roo!. The r4 and roo! documentation is easy to read, fun, and informal. Beginners can learn the languages quickly, while experienced developers become immediately productive.

❑ *Sample scripts* — r4 and roo! each ship with about 50 sample scripts. The examples perform useful, real-world tasks such as HTML processing, managing sockets, processing comma-separated value (CSV) files, statistical functions, file conversions, and the like. These scripts can be used as models or a starting point for your own.

❑ *Support* — The products are supported by an established company with a track record extending back to 1988. Kilowatt Software is the only company that offers both a free classic Rexx interpreter and a free, upwardly compatible object-oriented Rexx.

❑ *Tools* — r4 and roo! come with a number of useful developer utilities. We describe them later.

❑ *Windows GUI development* — Windows GUI tools often include hundreds of functions and dozens of widgets with hundreds of attributes. This provides flexibility but confronts developers with a steep learning curve. For beginners it can be downright bewildering. Kilowatt Software offers a smaller, more focused tool set that makes Windows GUI development a snap.

❑ *Object-oriented migration* — r4 is 100 percent upwardly compatible with the object-oriented roo! You can ease into object-oriented programming with roo! while maintaining backward compatibility with your existing classic Rexx scripts. Whether the legacy scripts were written for r4 or any other classic Rexx interpreter, as long as they stay within the Rexx standards, they will run under roo!

❑ *The OOP alternative* — roo! presents an object-oriented Rexx alternative to the Open Object Rexx interpreter (developed by IBM Corporation and today enhanced and maintained by the Rexx Language Association). roo! features completely different design and class libraries. Windows developers enjoy a choice of two strong object-oriented Rexx interpreters for their platform.

Downloading and Installation

This section describes how to install both r4 and roo!. While they two are sister products from the same company, they require two separate downloads and installs. r4 and roo! run under all versions of Windows (newer than Windows 95 and 3.1). Both can be freely downloaded from Kilowatt Software's Web site at `www.kilowattsoftware.com`. Access the company's Web site to install the products. You perform one installation for each product.

Preinstall

The installs require a *preinstall step*. Enable the ActiveX permissions in your browser by setting them to `prompt`. Then click the *pre-install* step button on the Kilowatt Software Web site, and you will be prompted by the InstallShield product to permit a *Web install*, a remote installation across the Web.

If your browser does not already have the InstallShield browser plug-in or ActiveX control named *InstallFromTheWeb*, you may be prompted to allow its installation. (Or, you can manually install this plug-in as a separate step, from InstallShield at `www.installshield.com/client`.)

After the preinstall step is completed, reset your browser's ActiveX permissions back to their original settings, if you changed them. Then simply download the two `*.zip` files for r4 and roo! and unzip them. Installation is complete.

Verification

Verify that the install succeeded by running a few of the sample scripts in the product directory. For starters, run the scripts from the Windows command line. Just change to the product directory and enter the interpreter followed by the script name:

```
c:\r4>  r4  lottery.rex          <= Runs the r4 program: lottery.rex
```

or

```
c:\roo>  roo blueMoonGenie       <= Runs the roo! program: blueMoonGenie.rooProgram
```

Environmental variables can be set to customize program execution. All are described in the product documentation. You will also want to add the r4 and roo! installation directories to your PATH variable.

Documentation

After installation, read the `readme.txt` file. This contains the licensing terms. r4 and roo! are free for both personal use and corporate customers and come with a limited warranty.

A number of `*.htm` files in the product directories contain the documentation. Just double-click on any file to read it. The r4 documentation includes these two key documents:

Document	File
User's Guide	r4.htm
Syntax Summary	r4SyntaxSummary.htm

roo! documentation includes these major files:

Document	File
User's Guide	roo.htm
Syntax Summary	rooSyntaxSummary.htm
Language Specification	rooLang.htm
Scripting Examples	rooExamples.htm

There are also `*.htm` files that describe each of the tools. For example, to learn about some of the GUI accessories, just click on any of the files `FileDlg.htm`, `msgbox.htm`, `prompt.htm`, or `picklist.htm`. Each contains an explanation of the associated command and a complete sample script. Any of the add-in tools you install, such as AuroraWare!, Poof!, and Revu follow the same approach. An `*.htm` file explains each command. Let's discuss these tools now.

Tools

Kilowatt Software supplies a full set of Windows-oriented tools to complement r4 and roo! Figure 26-1 pictorially summarizes them.

R4 and roo! Tools

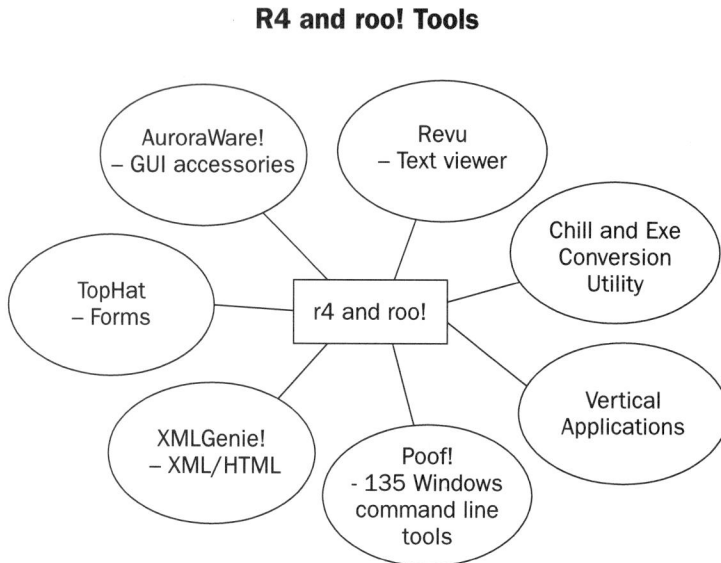

Figure 26-1

Let's describe the tools in more detail.

❑ *AuroraWare!* — This is a tool set of GUI accessories. Here are its components:

   ❑ CheckList — Visual checklist management facility

   ❑ Counter — A timer for activity, ticking clock, or count down

   ❑ Ticker — Time-keeping accessory

   ❑ TopClick — Action buttons

   ❑ TopClip — Text-clipping management accessory

   ❑ TopCue — Scrolling marquee accessory

   ❑ TopList — Drop-down lists

   ❑ TopNote — Note-editing accessory

   ❑ TopSort — Clipboard text sorting

   ❑ VuHtml — HTML-file-viewing accessory

❑ *TopHat* — A fill-in-the-blanks form accessory. Presents a tabbed GUI panel for data display, entry, and update. Related GUI tools include:

    ❑ `FileDlg` — File selection dialog

    ❑ `MsgBox` — Message boxes

    ❑ `Prompt` — Prompts for user responses

    ❑ `PickList` — Selection lists

These GUI tools are more readily learned than more comprehensive but complex GUI development tools. They transfer the Rexx ease-of-use philosophy to the world of Windows GUI development. If an advanced GUI interface is required, roo! and Java can used together to create it.

❑ *XMLGenie!* — A utility that automatically converts XML to HTML.

❑ *Poof!* — This provides more than 135 Windows command-line tools. Some of the areas they cover include:

    ❑ Batch-scripting aids

    ❑ Binary file utilities

    ❑ Clipboard utilities

    ❑ Command launching

    ❑ Task control

    ❑ File management (for many different file formats)

    ❑ HTML preparation

    ❑ Mathematical and conversion routines

    ❑ Software development

    ❑ File aids

    ❑ Many miscellaneous utilities

❑ *Revu* — Colorful text viewer. Highlights text appropriately for different programming languages.

❑ *Chill* — This utility converts an r4 or roo! program into an unreadable, closed-source file. This allows you to give others the use of your scripts without exposing the source code.

❑ *EXE Conversion Utility* — This converts scripts to stand-alone Windows executables, `*.exe` files.

❑ *CFLOW* — C/C++ flow analyzer.

❑ *Vertical applications* — Kilowatt software also ships several vertical applications for the educational sector and for Java development.

Object-Oriented Programming with roo!

roo! is derived from the first letters of the words *Rexx Object-Oriented*. It is a complete object-oriented interpreter. It presents a free alternative to Open Object Rexx for Windows. This section lists the basic elements of object-oriented programming (or OOP) in roo!

roo! supports all object-oriented concepts:

❑ Classes and methods

❑ Inheritance and derivation

❑ Encapsulation

❑ Abstraction

❑ Polymorphism

Classes and methods give roo! complete object orientation. It is through these that the language provides a class hierarchy, inheritance of behaviors and code and attributes, and the ability to derive new objects from existing ones. *Encapsulation* means that any interaction between objects is well defined. Data owned by one object, for example, is hidden from others. Communication between objects occurs only through messages, because an object's data and logic (or methods) are encapsulated together. Object orientation also provides *abstraction*, the ability to define programming problems through the higher-level paradigm of interacting objects. Finally, roo! supports *polymorphism*, the ability for operators to apply as appropriate to the kind of data and messages involved. Figure 26-2 summarizes how these new concepts expand classic Rexx into the realm of full object orientation.

Object-Oriented Rexx Means...

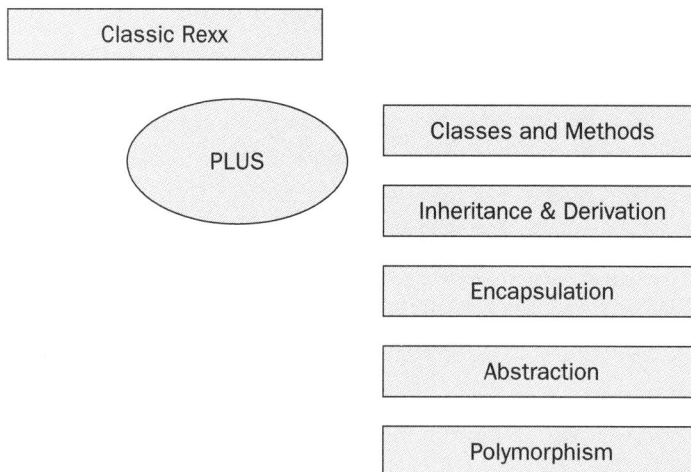

Figure 26-2

If you are not familiar with object-oriented programming, we introduce it in the tutorial on object-oriented Rexx programming in Chapter 28. That chapter uses Open Object Rexx as a basis for explanation.

For those who are familiar with object programming and terminology, let's describe how roo! achieves object orientation. To start with, roo! extends classic Rexx with a set of object-oriented features. Figure 26-3 expresses how roo! extends classic Rexx into the world of object orientation.

roo! Adds to Classic Rexx...

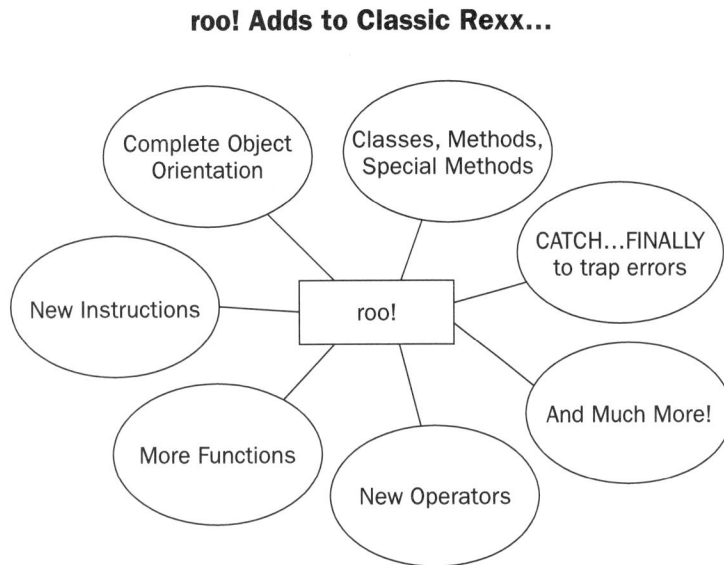

Figure 26-3

Here is a quick summary of these object-oriented features:

❑ class and method instructions

❑ Class variables are defined as local, shared, or static

❑ Built-in class library

❑ Special methods preinitialize, initialize, finalize, and terminate

❑ self and base references

❑ New operators:

    ❑ ^^ *(double caret)* — Instance creation

    ❑ ^ *(caret)* — Method invocation prefix operator

    ❑ ~ *(tilde)* — Method invocation infix operator

    ❑ [ ] *(brackets)* — Arraylike reference operator

- ❏   *{ } (braces)* — Vector class reference

- ❏   *! (exclamation)* — Identifies a command

❏   The new error condition `OBJECTION` traps when the `initialize` method returns an error string.

❏   `Instance` keyword for the `datatype` built-in function performs actions only on properly created object instances. This enables error-checking.

❏   The trace is extended to objects.

❏   New built-in functions:

- ❏   `callback` — Transfers control to a *callback routine* under certain conditions

- ❏   `nap` — A sleep or wait function

- ❏   `raiseObjection` — Raises the `OBJECTION` condition

- ❏   `split` — Splits a delimited string into a vector

- ❏   `squareRoot` — Returns the square root of a number

❏   Adds stack commands `makebuf`, `dropbuf`, `newstack`, and `delstack` for compatibility with other Rexx implementations

❏   A `roo.dll` module allows using roo! capabilities from C and C++, while *Java Native Interface* or *JINI* provides Java integration.

roo! also includes several extensions based on NetRexx (which is described in chapter 30), the ANSI-1996 standard, and Java:

❏   Comments on a line may start after a double-hyphen (--).

❏   New built-in functions:

- ❏   `changestr` — Replaces all substrings within a string (ANSI-1996 standard)

- ❏   `counstr` — Counts how many times a substring occurs (ANSI-1996 standard)

- ❏   `exists` — Returns 1 if a compound variable has a value

- ❏   `lower` — Converts a string to lowercase

- ❏   `upper` — Converts a string to uppercase

❏   Java-like `catch... finally` instructions capture exceptions in `do` and `select` instructions.

❏   `loop over` instruction processes all elements of objects or compound stem groups.

From this list, you can see that roo! adds the key elements required for object orientation. These are the class library, with the means to code classes and methods, the new operators for OOP, the special methods, and reference objects. Most of the other language additions extend roo! to cover the kind of extensions found in other Rexx interpreters. These include, for example, the new built-in functions, better exception handling, and the like. roo! offers a nice combination of object orientation plus key convenience features to round out the toolset.

The power of roo! resides in its extensive class library. In the world of object-oriented programming, the bigger and more powerful the class library, the easier scripting becomes. More classes and methods directly translate into less work for the developer.

Of course, each class has its own group of built-in methods appropriate to the class. The methods are too extensive to list, but you'll get an idea of their range from this alphabetical class list. Skim the class list and you'll understand the power of classes and what roo! has to offer:

Class	Use
Aggregate	Collection base class
BitVector	Vector of Boolean values
Callback	Callback class associated with external programs
CharacterVector	Vector of character values
Clipboard	Clipboard text
Comparator	Compares items
Console	The console stream
ContextVector	System call vector access class
DriveContext	Disk drive reference context
Emitter	Output stream emitter
Exception	Exception information caught by `catch` routines
ExternalClass	Class supported by external program
File	File information
FolderContext	Directory reference context
InLineFile	Line-oriented input file
InOutLineFile	Line-oriented update file
InStream	Standard input (default input stream)
List	Collection of heterogeneous items
Map	Collection of heterogeneous items indexed by strings
Math	Higher math functions
Object	Object base class
OrderedVector	Collection of ordered items (nonunique values)
OutLineFile	Line-oriented output file
OutStream	Standard output (default output stream)
Pattern	Regular expression pattern

Table continued on following page

Class	Use
PatternMatch	Matching regular expressions
Queue	Collection of heterogeneous items accessed at start or end
Set	Collection of ordered, unique items
Socket	TCP/IP socket class
Stack	Collection of heterogeneous items accessed at the end
System	System information
SystemPropertyMap	Collection of system properties (environmental variables) indexed by string values
Table	Table of rows and columns
Tree	Hierarchical tree object
Vector	Collection of heterogeneous items
WideCharacterVector	Vector of 2-byte wide characters

Learning roo! means learning the class hierarchy and their associated methods. Leveraging this built-in power reduces the code you write because it utilizes the object-oriented tools. This is the power of an object-oriented Rexx interpreter. The product documentation and sample scripts provide the information you need to build your knowledge as you go. The roo! tutorials are especially designed to help classic Rexx programmers transition to object-oriented scripting in an easy manner.

Summary

r4 and roo! are free Rexx interpreters from Kilowatt Software. Both are Windows-based products that conform to the TRL-2 language standards. This chapter discusses some of the unique features of these products beyond the language standards, concentrating especially on roo! and its unique object orientation. roo! is a powerful free object-oriented Rexx for Windows systems that offers an alternative to Open Object Rexx.

The specific features we covered in this chapter included the strengths of r4 and roo! as Rexx interpreters, how to download and install them, and where to find the product documentation. We then described the toolset that works with both the interpreters and is also freely downloadable. After briefly discussing the basic characteristics of object-oriented programming, we listed and describe the major object-oriented features of roo!. The idea was to give experienced object-oriented programmers a quick summary of roo!'s object features.

The next chapter introduces Open Object Rexx, another object-oriented Rexx interpreter. Chapter 28 provides a full tutorial on object-oriented scripting. It leverages your knowledge of standard Rexx scripting to introduce object-oriented programming through program examples.

Test Your Understanding

1. What are some of the advantages of the r4/roo! package? Name some of the tools that come with these interpreters.

2. Can r4 scripts be run under roo!? Can roo! scripts run under r4? Are r4 scripts portable? Are roo! scripts?

3. Which r4/roo! tools would you use to develop Windows GUIs? How do the r4/roo! GUI tools differ from those discussed in the chapter on "Graphical User Interfaces (such as Rexx/Tk and Rexx/DW)? Compare the r4/roo! GUI tools to Rexx/Tk and Rexx/DW. Which best satisfies each of these differing criteria:

   ❏ Best customization for Windows

   ❏ Most portable

   ❏ Easiest to use

   ❏ Most powerful (has the most widgets, attributes and functions)

   ❏ Can be learned most quickly

   ❏ Is most easily maintained by a programmer other than the one who wrote the script

   Are there trade-offs among these criteria? Does their relative importance vary in different programming projects?

4. How does the installation of r4 and roo! differ from that of other Rexx interpreters?

5. What principles of object-oriented programming does roo! support?

6. Name the new operators that roo! introduces to support object-oriented programming. What is the function of each?

7. Which roo! built-in classes would you use for line-oriented file I/O? Which would you use for screen I/O? Which would you use for TCP/IP sockets for client/server?

Open Object Rexx

Overview

Standard Rexx is a procedural language. In contrast, Open Object Rexx is a fully object-oriented superset of standard Rexx. With very minor exceptions, every Rexx script will run under Open Object Rexx without change. This means that all you have learned about Rexx applies directly to Open Object Rexx. Rexx developers find Open Object Rexx (or ooRexx) an easy way to leverage the power of object-oriented programming. It provides easy entry into the world of object-oriented programming, or OOP. The big benefit is that Rexx is an easy language to learn and grow with, and Open Object Rexx retains these advantages while supporting object-oriented scripting.

Since standard Rexx scripts typically run under Open Object Rexx without any changes, ooRexx makes it easy to migrate to object-oriented programming while preserving investment in traditional Rexx code. Existing code can run as is, while new programs are coded to take advantage of new object-oriented features. Developers may still code in classic, procedural Rexx while adding object-oriented features at a rate they find comfortable.

In comparison to other object-oriented languages, such as C++ or Java, Open Object Rexx emphasizes Rexx's traditional strengths in simple syntax and ease of use and combines them with power. If you have experience in other object-oriented languages, the overview in this chapter may be of interest to you so that you can see how ooRexx compares.

Leveraging Open Object Rexx means using its object-oriented features. This chapter describes ooRexx and those features. The following chapter presents a complete tutorial on object-oriented scripting using Open Object Rexx. This tutorial assumes no background in object-oriented programming, so if you don't know object-oriented programming, this lesson will launch you toward writing your own object-oriented scripts. The goal is to leverage your knowledge of classic Rexx to launch you into the world of object-oriented scripting.

Background

IBM developed a product they named *Object REXX* in the mid-1990s. In recent years, they offered the product for free under Linux, Solaris, and OS/2, while they charged a license fee for the product on the Windows and AIX platforms.

In late 2004, IBM and the Rexx Language Association finalized arrangements for the transfer of Object REXX from an IBM supplied product to an open-source project. The open-source product is named *Open Object Rexx*, or *ooRexx*. It is managed by the Rexx Language Association, often referred to as the RexxLA.

Since one of the principle goals of the ooRexx project is to provide a smooth transition for users of IBM Object REXX to Open Object Rexx, the functionality of the two products at the time of transition from IBM to RexxLA was identical. The language features this chapter covers are common to both products. Any references to Object Rexx in this book will cover both products.

This chapter focuses on Open Object Rexx as it runs under Linux. A brief section toward the end of the chapter profiles the Windows version of Open Object Rexx and highlights some of its differences and unique features. Of course, Open Object Rexx interpreters all behave consistently on the platforms on which they run. The differences come merely in the form of extended environmental features unique to various operating systems.

More information on ooRexx and how to download the product can be obtained at several sites, including that of the Rexx Language Association at www.rexxla.org and the Open Object Rexx Web site at www.oorexx.org. The product downloads with complete installation instructions and full documentation.

Features

While known to academics during the 1980s, object-oriented programming did not become widely popular in business computing until the mid-1990s. Many feel it is a superior approach to traditional, procedural programming. The benefits to object-oriented programming are:

❑   Greater code reuse.

❑   Greater quality assurance and a lower error rate through reusing proven components.

❑   Lower cost and maintenance by leveraging existing objects.

❑   Applications can be designed by modeling objects and their interactions.

❑   Rapid prototyping and development.

Open Object Rexx completely extends Rexx into OOP. It has all the features OOP requires including:

❑   Objects, classes, subclasses and superclasses, meta classes, mixin classes

❑   Comprehensive class libraries

❑   Online reference facility

- ❏ Public and private methods, class and instance methods
- ❏ Inheritance
- ❏ Multiple inheritance
- ❏ Encapsulation
- ❏ Polymorphism
- ❏ Method chaining
- ❏ Many interfaces to databases such as DB2, screen builders, applications written in C and C++, and others

Open Object Rexx can be used in place of shell scripts. The advantages to Open Object Rexx include:

- ❏ Ease of use and high productivity
- ❏ Adds a complete set of OO features
- ❏ Upwardly compatible with classic procedural Rexx
- ❏ Portability
- ❏ Key features including concurrency, queuing, and interactive debugging
- ❏ Extra utilities and interfaces

Figure 27-1 summarizes some of the major features of Open Object Rexx that go beyond the Rexx standards and the typical classic Rexx interpreter. It shows that ooRexx is a superset of classic Rexx that adds many new features.

Open Object Rexx Adds to Classic Rexx...

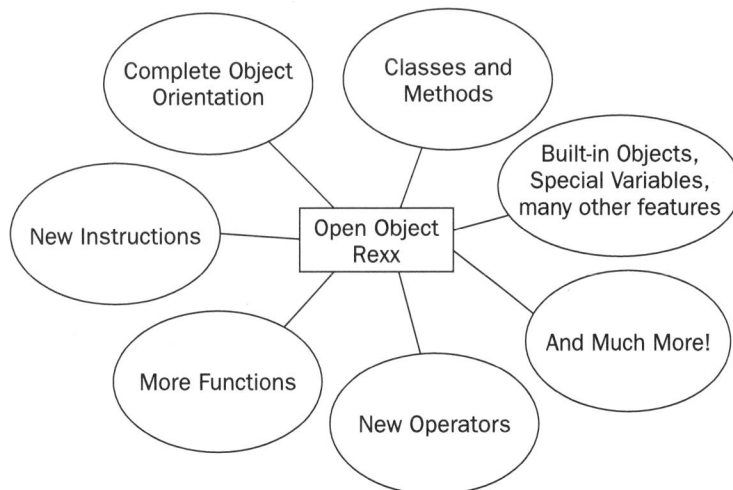

Figure 27-1

Open Object Rexx for Linux

As mentioned in the earlier "Background" section, Open Object Rexx for Linux has been available as a free product for several years under IBM's original moniker Object REXX for Linux. We'll discuss the details of this product as representative of Open Object Rexx as it runs on a variety of platforms. Specifically, we'll look at how to install the product under Linux, either by using the Red Hat Package Manager or by a more traditional install for Unix-derived operating systems. Then, we'll describe the fundamentals of object-oriented scripting in the section entitled "The Basics." This section defines various object-oriented terms and concepts and shows how they are embodied in Open Object Rexx. Next, the section "Class Libraries" describes the general structure of the class hierarchy in ooRexx, and discusses the role of the various classes in the language. This section explains the language's class hierarchy, while Appendix I lists all the classes and their methods in detail. Finally, the section "Other Open Object Rexx Additions" lists the other features ooRexx adds to the standard Rexx language. The section briefly describes what these features are and what they add to the language. The next chapter, Chapter 28, provides a full tutorial in object-oriented programming with Open Object Rexx. Even if you have never programmed in an object-oriented language before, the tutorial should get you up and running quickly with the language. It leverages your knowledge of classic Rexx to launch you into the world of object-oriented scripting.

First, let's discuss the Linux platforms on which ooRexx runs, and list its platform-unique extensions. The Linux version of Open Object Rexx runs under Red Hat, SuSE, and other Linux family operating systems. It supports Intel, PowerPC, and mainframe or zSeries hardware.

The special features of Open Object Rexx for Linux include:

❏ Regular expressions

❏ TCP/IP sockets

❏ FTP services

❏ Mathematical functions

❏ Security Manager facility

❏ Many extra utility functions

An *application programming interface*, or *API*, integrates Rexx scripts with programs developed in other languages. To download Open Object Rexx for Linux, access the ooRexx home page at www.oorexx.org. The Rexx Language Association home page at www.rexxla.org also indicates where to obtain Open Object Rexx. Or, simply enter the search keywords Object Rexx for Linux or Open Object Rexx in a public search engine such s Google at www.google.com.

To download the product, choose your hardware platform (Intel, PowerPC, or zSeries mainframe). Then download either the Red Hat Package Manager file (*.rpm) or a compressed file for Linux/Unix/BSD or Windows. The download includes the product manual set, which automatically installs as part of the product installation process.

Installation under Linux is the same as that shown for other Linux-based Rexx products in this book. The downloaded product includes a README file that describes installation in detail. (This file also includes licensing information you should read and agree to prior to using the product). Open Object Rexx is provided under the Common Public License, or CPL.

The installation instructions below are current at the time of writing. Due to the transfer of the product from IBM Corporation to the Rexx Language Association, it is possible that installation procedures may change in minor details. Review the downloaded files and their installation instructions for the final word on current installation procedures, filenames, and directory locations.

Installation using Red Hat Package Manager

To install Open Object Rexx, download the `*.rpm` file into a newly created directory. Install the product and specify that you want to see "very verbose" messages when issuing the `rpm` command. The right-most operand on the `rpm` command shown here is the name of the product's `*.rpm` file:

```
rpm  -ivv  ooRexx-3.0.0-1.rpm
```

The output from this command shows the directories RPM creates, where it places the Open Object Rexx files, and the links created by installation. Depending on the version and release, the default directories the install creates and populates will likely all begin with `/usr`, and the default executable will be named `/usr/bin/oorexx`.

Installing Open Object Rexx with the Red Hat Package Manager is very similar to installing any other language product with the RPM, such as the sample RPM installation of the Rexx/imc interpreter described in Chapter 21. The particulars may vary slightly, depending on the version and release of the product. For example, when the product was previously distributed by IBM Corporation as IBM's Object REXX, the `rpm` command looked like this:

```
rpm  -ivv  orexx-2.3.3.0-1.rpm
```

The directories that the install created and populated all began with `/opt/orexx`. The default name of the interpreter executable in this case is `/opt/orexx/bin/rexx`.

Installation without Red Hat Package Manager

To install Open Object Rexx if you do not have Red Hat Package Manager or choose not to use it, download the `*.tgz` file. Copy this file into the root directory (/), and decompress it with this command:

```
tar  -zxvf  ooRexx-3.n.n-n.i386.tgz
```

The final operand is the name of the file you downloaded (the n's will be replaced with digits for the version of Open Object Rexx you downloaded). After the `tar` command, you must create a series of links or symbolic pointers. The README file lists the exact commands you need to execute. The install is similar to the other Rexx on Linux installs with which you are already familiar, such as the examples in Chapter 1.

Of course, the name of the download file may vary slightly according the release of the product. For example, when the product was previously distributed by IBM Corporation as IBM's Object REXX, you would run a `tar` command similar to this one to decompress the product files:

```
tar  -zxvf  orexx-2.3.n.0-n.i386.tgz
```

Postinstall steps

If you did not use Red Hat Package Manager to perform the installation, complete the installation by setting the necessary environmental variables for Open Object Rexx. The names referred to below may vary slightly by version or release of the product.

Finish the installation by running one of the shell scripts you'll find in the `/usr/share/ooRexx` directory:

❏   `rexx.sh`—For Bourne, Bourne-Again, and Korn shell users

❏   `rexx.csh`—For c-shell users

For Bourne, Bourne-Again, and Korn shell users, run the script as a source file, like this:

```
. /usr/share/ooRexx/rexx.sh
```

The period that precedes the command is separated from it by at least one space (blank). This indicates that the file is *sourced* (run in the same process as the shell, rather than in a separate subshell). Sourcing is necessary because the script sets various environmental variables. These will only apply to the user's session if set in the current shell by sourcing. Setting these variables without sourcing means that they will be set by a program running in a subprocess and that they therefore would not apply to the user's shell when that program completes and the command prompt again appears.

For c-shell users, source the file like this:

```
source  /usr/share/ooRexx/rexx.csh
```

In either case, you might want to add the appropriate script given here to your *login* or *profile* script. Then it will automatically execute whenever you log in. This way the Open Object Rexx environmental variables will always be set for your use when you login to the system.

Of course, the naming of the files may vary slightly by release. For example, when the product was distributed by IBM Corporation as IBM's Object REXX, the scripts to run to create the required environmental variables resided in the `/opt/orexx/etc` directory. They were named and run as follows:

```
. /opt/orexx/etc/rexx.sh         #-- Bourne, Bourne-Again, Korn shells
source  /opt/orexx/etc/rexx.csh  #-- C-shell users
```

The Basics

The next chapter presents a complete tutorial on Open Object Rexx scripting. Here we discuss some of the basics to show how the language supports object-oriented programming. We define classes, methods, messages, attributes, abstract classes, instance classes, public and private methods, directives, and other object-oriented terms. We present brief code snippets to make these terms clear. If you follow this chapter, but do not know how to use these concepts in developing object-oriented scripts, don't worry. This is the purpose of the next chapter, Chapter 28. That chapter provides a full, step-by-step tutorial on how to write object-oriented scripts. Here the idea is just to introduce a few key object-oriented concepts and to show how Open Object Rexx implements these concepts in code.

Rexx *objects* contain *methods* and *variables*. Variables are more accurately called *attributes*. Object methods are actions that are invoked by sending a message to the object. Rexx uses the tilde operator (~) to send the message to the object and run its method. For example, in classic Rexx, you might "check in" a library book by coding a function called `check_in`. Then invoke the function like this:

```
feedback = check_in(book)          /* run user-defined CHECK_IN function */
```

In Open Object Rexx, send a message to the object `book` to run its `check_in` method:

```
feedback = book~check_in           /* run user-defined CHECK_IN method   */
```

Rexx runs the method that matches the message name following the *tilde* or *twiddle*. Note that the method is encoded to the right of the object to which it applies. Thus the ordering of `object~method` varies from the traditional ordering of `function(parameter)`.

Object variables or attributes are exclusively owned by the object. Attributes are *encapsulated* in that they are not visible or accessible by other objects and their methods; only the object's methods can change its variables. Each method in the object specifies which variables it accesses by coding them on its `expose` instruction. Any changes a method makes to an exposed variables remains after the method terminates.

Objects are created by the `new` method. For example, to create a new book in the library system:

```
new_book = .book~new
```

The `new` method creates the object and automatically invokes the `init` method (if it is defined) to initialize object variables from parameters and defaults. Here's an example that adds a newly acquired book to the library and sets some attribute values:

```
new_book = .book~new('The Third Reich','MacMillan Publishing',1970)
```

The *parameters* for a method immediately follow the name of the method and are enclosed in parentheses. The preceding statement encodes three parameters inside of the parentheses for the method.

To later delete the book permanently from the library system, use the `drop` instruction. This instruction needs only a single operand, the name of the object instance to delete:

```
drop new_book
```

A group of related objects compose a *class*. An individual object created from the class, such as the book referred to earlier, is called an *instance* or *instantiation* of that class.

To identify classes and methods in Open Object Rexx code, use *directives*. Directives are denoted by leading double-colons (::). This example creates the `book` class and methods to check books in, check them out, and initialize a new `book` instance. The class and each of its methods are denoted by the appropriate directive:

```
::class book
  ::method  check_in
        . . .
  ::method  check_out
```

```
        expose  title  book_id  patron_id
        . . .
::method  init
      use arg  title,  publisher,  pub_date
        . . .
```

This example also shows how the new `expose` instruction makes attributes available to a method that can change them. If the method alters any values listed in the `expose` instruction, these new values persist even after the `return` or `exit` from the method. So, the `check_out` method shown here can change the three arguments listed in its `expose` instruction. If an `expose` instruction is coded, it must appear as the first instruction in the method.

The new `use arg` instruction shown here retrieves the argument objects passed in to the method. It differs from the `arg` and `parse arg` instructions in that it allows nonstring arguments. The `use arg` instruction performs a direct, one-to-one assignment of arguments to variables. So, the `init` method in the example accesses three arguments through its `use arg` instruction.

Methods may be either *public* or *private*. Those that may be invoked from the main program or other classes are public. Those available only to the methods within the class are private. By default, methods are public. Use the keyword `private` to define a private method. In the example that follows, the method `replacement_cost` can only be invoked by other methods in the `book` class. The method can access and update any of the three attributes listed on its `expose` instruction. As shown here, it updates the `replacement_amount` value:

```
::class book
  ::method  check_in
    . . .
  ::method  check_out
    . . .
  ::method  replacement_cost  private
      expose  pages  cost_per_page  replacement_amount
      replacement_amount = pages  * cost_per_page
      return
```

Methods can be invoked by either of two operators: the tilde (~) or the double tilde (~~). Using ~ returns the result of the method, while using ~~ returns the object that received the message. Most situations call for returning the result of the method, so the tilde (~) appears more commonly in code.

Several methods may be applied to an object, one after another, by a technique referred to as *method chaining*. This example applies two methods to the `book` object, with the `check_out` method returning the result:

```
book~~loan_out~check_out
```

Open Object Rexx supports several kinds of methods. *Instance methods* perform an action on a specific object or instance of a class. They handle the data of a specific object. *Class methods* are more global. They apply to the class as a whole. For example, class methods might count the number of objects in the class or manage all the objects together as a collection.

Classes are organized into *class hierarchies*. These describe inheritance relationships in a hierarchical manner. A *subclass* inherits all the attributes and methods of its *parent class* or *superclass*. As well, the subclass adds its own attributes and methods as needed. For example, `hardback_book` and `paperback_book` could be subclasses to the book class. Each inherits all the behaviors of the book class (defined by its attributes and methods) but adds additional behaviors as well:

```
::class  book
  ::method  check_in
         . . .
::class hardback_book    subclass book
  ::method bind_it
         . . .
::class paperback_book  subclass book
  ::method rebind_it
         . . .
```

An *abstract class* is one for which you would not normally create instances, but whose definition could be useful to define common generic behavior. For example, along with the book class there might also be a magazine class. Both could be subclasses of the abstract class library_resource. This superclass might include some generic behavior common to any library resource, be it a book, magazine, video, or whatever. It is an abstract class that we choose never to create an instance of, as we only use it as a superclass to define some behaviors for its subclasses:

```
::class library_resource                /* abstract class with generic behaviors */
   . . .
::class book      subclass library_resource     /* a class to create instances */
   . . .
::class magazine subclass library_resource      /* a class to create instances */
   . . .
```

Some object-oriented languages only allow subclasses to inherit attributes and methods from a single superclass or parent class. Open Object Rexx permits *multiple inheritance*. An object can inherit from both its direct parent and also from other classes called *mixin classes*. Instances are not generated from mixin classes. Instead mixin classes are just containers of attributes and methods that subclasses can inherit. A subclass can inherit behaviors both from its single parent class and from one or more mixin classes.

In this example, the book class inherits variables and methods from both its abstract parent class library_resource and the mixin class named printed_resources:

```
::class library_resource                /* abstract class with generic behaviors */
   . . .
::class printed_resources mixinclass Object   /* MIXIN class for more behaviors */
   . . .
::class book    subclass library_resource    inherit  printed_resources
   . . .
```

Open Object Rexx supports *polymorphism*, the ability to send the same message to different kinds of objects and invoke the appropriate method in each. For example, the library might require different actions to check out reference books as opposed to regular books:

```
book~check_out

reference_book~check_out
```

In each case, Open Object Rexx runs the different check_out method appropriate to the object to which it is applied.

Rexx objects interact *concurrently*. Multiple objects may be active at any one time, sending messages and executing methods. It is also possible to permit concurrency *within an object* when that makes sense to the application. In this situation multiple methods within an object run at the same time. An example script in the next chapter shows how to implement concurrency.

The Class Libraries

Just as the power of a procedural language correlates to its set of functions, the power of an object-oriented language rests on the strengths of its *class libraries*. A class library is simply a set of predefined or built-in classes. How much work developers must perform to create their applications varies inversely to the size and power of the class libraries: the more extensive the class libraries that come with the product, the less work developers must do. ooRexx's class libraries are quite comprehensive, meaning that they support high developer productivity. This section lists the major Open Object Rexx classes and describes their uses.

Collection Classes refer to groups of objects. They may be compared to data structures in traditional (non-object-oriented) programming languages. Their power lies in their methods. With these methods, you can manipulate the entire group of items in a collection class in a single operation. Each collection class, of course, comes with a complete set of operations appropriate to that class.

Take, for example, the Array class. This class is similar to one form of a classic Rexx array, in that it is a collection of elements indexed by positive whole numbers. The Array class offers about 18 methods to manage the collection, plus it inherits another 18 from the Object class. The result is that the combination of a collection class plus its methods offer a lot of power with little programming required to use it.

Here is a quick list of the collection classes and their uses:

Collection Class	Use
Array	A sequenced collection
Bag	A nonunique collection of objects (subclass of Relation)
Directory	A collection indexed by unique character strings
List	A sequenced collection which allows inserts at any position
Queue	A sequenced collection that allows inserts at the start or ending positions
Relation	A collection with nonunique objects for indexes
Set	A unique collection of objects (subclass of Table)
Table	A collection with unique objects for indexes

Beyond the collection classes, Open Object Rexx includes another 10 or so classes. These do everything from implement I/O (the Stream class) to managing messages (the Alarm class). Each comes with a full set of methods — too many, in fact, to list here. Appendix I lists all the methods for each Open Object Rexx class. To give you the general idea as to what is involved, here is a quick list of the other classes:

Class	Use
Alarm	Generates messages at specified times in order to provide timing and notification
Class	The class that allows the creation of new classes
Message	Asynchronous or deferred sending of messages
Method	The class that allows dynamic creation of new methods
Monitor	Manages message forwarding
MutableBuffer	Allows fast editing of strings (append, insert, delete)
Object	The class that manages all objects (the root of the class hierarchy)
Stem	A collection with unique indexes that are character strings
Stream	Allows external communications and I/O. Goes beyond classic Rexx to include reading/writing entire arrays, binary and text I/O, shared-mode files, direct I/O, and so on
String	Operations on character strings supplier. Supplies the elements of a collection, one at a time
Supplier	Allows iterating over a collection supplying the index and its associated object

Each class has its own set of methods. The number and kinds of methods depend on the class. For example, the Message and Monitor classes have just a few methods, while the String class has several dozen. Appendix I lists all Open Object Rexx classes and their methods.

Other Object Rexx Additions

Beyond its full set of object facilities, Open Object Rexx makes other additions to standard or "classic" Rexx. We describe them in this section. Figure 27-1 diagrammatically illustrates these differences. The next chapter, Chapter 28, discusses examples of scripts that show how to use many of these new language features. Read that chapter for a tutorial explanation of how to use ooRexx classes and methods. The goal here is to summarize the language features that extend ooRexx beyond the realm of classic Rexx. We describe these language features to prepare you for the tutorial in the next chapter. These brief descriptions also allow you to compare Open Object Rexx to any other object-oriented programming language with which you may be familiar.

New operators

Open Object Rexx introduces several new operators. The first two listed below allow scripts to send a message to an object, thereby running the method associated with the message name. The difference between the two operators is in what is returned. The tilde returns a method result, while the double-tilde returns the object of the message. The final operator, the brackets, allows easy reference to objects within a collection. Brackets can be used in place of the formal message descriptors to add or retrieve an object to or from a collection. The table below lists these new operators and their meanings:

Operator	Use
~	Send a message to invoke a method and return its result
~~	Send a message to invoke a method, return the object of the message
[ ]	Add or retrieve objects to/from a collection

Directives

Directives set up a program's classes, methods, and routines. The ::class and ::method directives identify the beginning of classes and methods in your code. These underlie how you define new classes and methods in your scripts. Code the directive for a new class or method, then code the class or method right after the keyword identifier.

Directives are placed at the end of the source file containing them. There are just four directives. The two you will use most often are those for ::class and ::method. The other two are typically used less frequently. Here is a list of the four directives:

❑   ::class — Defines a class

❑   ::method — Defines a method

❑   ::routine — Defines a callable subroutine

❑   ::requires — Specifies access to another source script

Built-in objects

Open Object Rexx offers a set of built-in objects that are always available to scripts. These help scripts interact with their environment, perform input and output, view environmental parameters, and inspect return codes. This table lists the built-in objects and their functions:

Built-in Object	Use
.environment	The public environment object (a directory of global environmental info)
.nil	An object that does not contain any data (used for testing existence)
.local	The local environment object (a directory of process-specific information)
.error	The error object for Rexx's error and trace outputs (a monitor object for the default error stream)
.input	The input object (a monitor object for the default input stream)
.output	The output object (a monitor object for the default output stream)

Built-in Object	Use
.methods	Methods defined in the current program defined using ::method directives
.rs	Return code from any executed command. 0 is success, 1 is error, -1 is failure
.true	The Boolean value '1'
.false	The Boolean value '0'
.stdin	The default input stream
.stdout	The default output stream
.stderr	The default error stream

Special variables

Open Object Rexx adds two new special variables. They are used for referencing objects because object-oriented programming requires a convenient way to refer to certain objects. self refers to the currently executing method, while super refers to the parent of the current object:

❑   self — The object of the current executing method

❑   super — The superclass or parent of the current object

New instructions

Open Object Rexx enhances several instructions that exist in classic Rexx and also introduces a few new instructions. Among these instructions, expose and guard are concerned with variable scoping and control access to an object's variables or attribute pool. raise is especially interesting in that it allows scripts to explicitly raise an exception or error condition. This supports a more flexible and generalized error trap facility than classic Rexx offers.

The new and enhanced instructions include those in the following table:

Instruction	Use
expose	Permits a method to access and update specified variables
forward	Forwards the message that caused the active method to execute
guard	Controls concurrent execution of a method
raise	Explicitly raises error conditions or traps
reply	Sends an early reply from method to caller, allowing concurrency
use	Retrieves arguments into a program, routine, function, or method

New functions

Open Object Rexx introduces a handful of new functions and enhances a few existing ones. Among the new functions are the ANSI-1996 standard string functions, `changestr` and `countstr`. Of course, the emphasis in ooRexx is not on functions (which are central to classic Rexx), but rather on methods. Methods are the key to object-oriented scripting. For this reason, we don't discuss the new functions in detail here.

New condition traps

Open Object Rexx includes several new exception conditions, including `ANY`, `NOMETHOD`, `NOSTRING`, and `USER`. The ANSI-1996 standard `LOSTDIGITS` is also included. Users can define their own exception conditions and raise conditions manually (explicitly) via the new `raise` instruction. This provides a more generalized and flexible error-handling mechanism than classic Rexx. It also conforms to the philosophy of many object-oriented programming languages (such as Java) that encourage managing errors through consolidated exception routines. Of course, because ooRexx is a superset of classic Rexx, whether you choose to handle exceptions through this newer approach or in a more traditional fashion is up to you. Either approach works; either is accepted by Open Object Rexx.

New utility functions

Open Object Rexx includes a package that is often referred to as *RexxUtil*, which includes roughly 100 *utility functions*. Exactly which functions are included varies slightly by platform. The names of these functions all begin with the letters `Sys`. The utility functions retrieve system information, manage events, pipes, files, processes, and arrays. The product documentation describes their uses.

Chapter 13, "Writing Portable Rexx," described the RexxUtil package (as used by classic Rexx scripts). One of its main benefits is that it divorces scripts from operating system or environmental dependencies, because it is an intermediate layer of software between scripts and the operating system. Figure 13-4 diagrammed how RexxUtil functions in this role. See Chapter 13 for further details. There are several versions of the RexxUtil package for classic Rexx interpreters. Appendix H lists free and open-source Rexx software packages including RexxUtil and its variants.

Rexx API

The *application programming interface*, or *API*, allows you to interface applications to Open Object Rexx or extend the language. *Applications* are programs written in languages other than Rexx, such as C language. The Open Object Rexx manuals provide all the details on how to interface other languages to ooRexx or extend the product's capabilities. Full documentation downloads with the product, and advanced sections explain the use of the API.

Open Object Rexx for Windows

Open Object Rexx for Windows is also an open-source product enhanced and supported by the Rexx Language Association. It is basically the same as the Linux product described in this chapter, but it offers its own additional set of operating system unique features. Here is a high-level summary of those unique features:

❑ Product is the same as ooRexx for Linux, but with additional Windows-specific features

❑ Supports Windows Scripting Host (WSH)

❑ Supports OLE/ActiveX automation

❑ Can be an ActiveX script engine, which permits embedding of Open Object

❑ Rexx code into HTML, XML, and so on

❑ Unicode support reads/writes files with Unicode data

❑ Conversions between Unicode and non-Unicode character strings

❑ File system encryption/decryption

❑ Scripts can be converted into *tokens* so that it is not necessary to distribute original source code (this feature is also available with the Linux version)

❑ Tokenized scripts run via the *Runtime module*

❑ Integrated debugger

In its prior incarnation, as IBM Object REXX for Windows, this product came bundled with a GUI interface package called OODialog. At the time of writing it is unclear whether the new Open Object Rexx for Windows will include this component. Entering `OODialog` as a keyword into any Web search engine can provide current information.

Open Object Rexx for Windows features a high level of integration into Windows in its support of ActiveX and Windows Scripting Host. Along with its other features this constitutes a complete, Windows-based object-oriented scripting language. It can be used either as a Windows utility language or to build complete, stand-alone applications.

Summary

IBM developed a product they called Object REXX in the mid-1990s. They offered it for several operating systems including Linux, Windows, Solaris, AIX, and OS/2. Today the product is named Open Object Rexx and is managed as an open-source project by the Rexx Language Association. This chapter described that product, which is also referred to as ooRexx.

This chapter summarized the features of Open Object Rexx, how they support object-oriented programming, and how they extend beyond the standard of classic Rexx. It concentrates on the Linux version of the product, but the features are nearly the same in Open Object Rexx on other platforms. Each version of ooRexx includes a few extra classes specific to that operating system.

Open Object Rexx is a powerful, object-oriented language that retains the ease of use of classic Rexx. The product lies at the intersection of three of today's key software trends:

❑ High-level scripting

❑ Object-oriented programming

❑ Open-source software

With the open sourcing of the language in early 2005, many believe that Open Object Rexx will find increased popularity in the future. That the language seamlessly melds its object-oriented features onto the core of classic Rexx gives it broad appeal.

The next chapter presents a complete tutorial on Open Object Rexx scripting. It starts by showing how to integrate just a few simple classes into a traditional Rexx script. Then, it proceeds more deeply into the built-in classes and methods of the product. Eventually, the examples lead to our developing our own classes and using them to solve problems such as developing a stack data structure and implementing a video check-out system. The tutorial is designed so that, even if you have no object-oriented programming experience, you'll be able to quickly adapt your classic Rexx knowledge to learn object-oriented scripting.

Test Your Understanding

1. Is Open Object Rexx a superset of classic Rexx? Will classic Rexx scripts run under ooRexx without change? What are inheritance and multiple inheritance? How are they implemented in Open Object Rexx?

2. What are encapsulation and polymorphism, and how does Open Object Rexx support them?

3. Which class do you use to perform I/O? What advanced I/O features does this class's methods offer?

4. What are the new special variables of Open Object Rexx, and how are they used?

5. What are the four kinds of directives, and what are their functions?

6. What are collections and the collection class? Name five of the collection classes, and describe their definitions.

7. How do you define and manually raise a new error condition?

8. What is the function of the `expose` instruction? How is it coded and used?

28

Open Object Rexx Tutorial

Overview

For those who practice object-oriented programming, the summary of Open Object Rexx provided by the previous chapter is all you need. Install the product, look over the sample scripts that come with it, review the class libraries and their methods, and you're ready to program. If you are familiar with object-oriented programming from languages like Java, C++, or Python, review the class libraries and start programming.

For everyone else, something's missing. The previous chapter discussed *the basics* of OO programming with Open Object Rexx, but more to describe its capabilities than to teach you how to use it. This chapter tries to fill that gap. For those new to object-oriented programming, it presents a simple tutorial. Assuming that you know classic Rexx, it bootstraps you into the world of object-oriented programming with simple, complete program examples.

Open Object Rexx is ideal for learning OOP because it retains full compatibility with classic Rexx; everything you've learned about classic Rexx still applies. You can tip-toe into the object-oriented world at your own pace by learning ooRexx. For example, you can still manipulate strings with the string functions of classic Rexx. Or, you can start using Open Object Rexx's string class methods in their place. You can still perform traditional Rexx I/O. Or, you can use the object-oriented stream class methods. Code with either approach in Open Object Rexx.

Open Object Rexx retains the advantages of simplicity and clear syntax from classic Rexx. It adds the classes, methods and all the other features of object-oriented programming with a minimum of new syntax. Concentrate on solving the problem at hand, and leverage Open Object Rexx's new features in the quest.

Let's quickly discuss the sample scripts in this chapter. The first is very short; it merely tests for the existence of a file. It illustrates how to use a stream object and a few of its methods perform I/O. The next two scripts show you how to create your own classes and methods. Then, a more ambitious script implements a video checkout application for a DVD library. The final example demonstrates concurrency, where methods within a class run at the same time.

The examples in this chapter were all tested under Linux. Open Object Rexx runs on several platforms including Linux, Windows, Solaris, and AIX.

A First Program

Open Object Rexx features a *class library*, a built-in set of classes and methods that adds a wide range of capability to traditional Rexx. The *methods* in this library perform actions, much like the built-in functions of classic Rexx. One easy way to start object-oriented programming with Object Rexx is just to program as in classic Rexx, but to replace function calls with object methods.

Here is an example. This simple script reads one input parameter from the command line, a filename. The program determines whether the file exists and displays a message with its result:

```
[root /usr/bin/oorexx]$ ./oorexx file_exist.orex  square.orex
File exists
[root /usr/bin/oorexx]$ ./oorexx file_exist.orex  nonesuch.txt
File does not exist
[root /usr/bin/oorexx]$
```

The program is called File Exist. In the first preceding run, the input file exists. In the second run, the file did not exist in the current directory. All the script does is write a message indicating whether the file specified on its command line exists. Recall that the syntax ./oorexx is merely a way of ensuring, on Unix-derived operating systems, that the module named oorexx in the current directory will be invoked to run the script.

Here is the code for the first program:

```
/*******************************************************************/
/*   FILE EXIST                                                   */
/*                                                                */
/*   Tells if a specified file exists.                            */
/*******************************************************************/
parse arg file .                              /* get user input file  */

infile = .stream~new(file)                    /* create stream object */

/* Existence test returns either full filename or the null string     */

if infile~query('exists') = ''   then         /* test if nonexistent  */
    .output~lineout('File does not exist')    /* no such file exists   */
else
    .output~lineout('File exists' )           /* found the filename    */

exit 0
```

To work with file I/O in Open Object Rexx, you can either use classic Rexx instructions such as say, pull, parse pull, charin, charout, chars, linein, lineout, and lines, or you can use the new object-oriented methods. This script uses the methods.

The first action when using OO input/output is always to create a *stream instance*:

```
infile = .stream~new(file)                    /* create stream object    */
```

This object manages I/O for one input or output file. To create it, we send the message new to the built-in .stream class. The .stream class is denoted by the period immediately prior to the keyword stream. We passed the filename from the user to the new method as its input parameter. Now we have an object created representing an I/O stream for that file.

The following code invokes the query method on the new stream object. The method returns the null string if the file does not exist in the current directory. If the file does exist, it returns the fully qualified name of the file:

```
if infile~query('exists') = ''   then        /* test if nonexistent */
   .output~lineout('File does not exist')    /* no such file exists */
```

The lineout method is invoked with the character string to write as its input parameter. .output is one of the special *built-in objects* described in Chapter 27. It is a *monitor object* that forwards the messages it receives to .stdout, the stream object representing standard output.

Of course, if the file does exist, the script writes the appropriate message:

```
else
   .output~lineout('File exists' )           /* found the filename  */
```

This script uses the built-in object-oriented classes and methods for I/O. This same program could be coded using classic Rexx instructions such as say and pull, and it would have run under Open Object Rexx as well. All classic Rexx functions have object-oriented counterparts (methods) in Open Object Rexx.

The trick to learning ooRexx is to learn its class library. Remembering what it offers as built-in classes and methods is as important as knowing what functions are available in classic Rexx. This knowledge is the lever that enables you to exploit the language fully and let its built-in capabilities do the work for you.

Squaring a Number — Using Our Own Class and Method

The previous example shows how to leverage Open Object Rexx's large class library. This is especially useful when performing tasks that would otherwise require a lot of work, for example, in creating graphical user interfaces or performing database I/O. Now let's look at how to create and use our own classes and methods within ooRexx scripts.

This simple script squares a number. The user enters the number as a command-line argument, and the script writes back its squared value:

```
[root /opt/orexx/pgms]$  square.orex  4
The original value: 4  squared is: 16
```

Here is the code for this script:

```
/********************************************************************/
/* SQUARE                                                           */
/*                                                                  */
/* Returns the square of a number                                  */
/********************************************************************/
parse arg input .            /* get the number to square from user  */

value = .squared~new         /* create an object for a squared value */
sqd = value~square(input)    /* invoke SQUARE method on INPUT value  */

say 'The original value:' input 'squared is:' sqd

exit 0

::class squared              /* Here is the class.                  */

   ::method 'square'         /* Class SQUARED has 1 method, SQUARE.  */
   use arg in                /* get the input argument               */
   return ( in * in )        /* square it and return that value      */
```

In this script, the first task is to create an instance to square the value. Depending on what school of OOP you follow, this instance might also be called an *object instance*, the *instantiation of an object class*, or just an *object*. We're not concerned with formal terminology here; you don't need to be to use ooRexx. This statement creates the object:

```
value = .squared~new         /* create an object for a squared value */
```

The next line in the script invokes the `square` method to perform the work of squaring the number. It does this by sending the appropriate message to the object:

```
sqd = value~square(input)    /* invoke SQUARE method on INPUT value  */
```

Look down further in the code to see the code of the `square` method and its class, called `squared`. All classes and methods must follow the procedural code located at the top of the program. New classes and methods are always placed at the bottom of the script. Two colons indicate a *directive*, an identifier for a class, method, routine or external code block. This line defines our new class called `squared`:

```
::class squared              /* here is the class                   */
```

After the class directive, we place our methods and their code. This class has but a single method named `square`. This line defines this method:

```
::method 'square'            /* Class SQUARED has 1 method, SQUARE.  */
```

The name of a method is a character string. The interpreter matches this string with the message sent to the object (to invoke it) in the procedural code. Here the method name is coded within quotation marks, as many programmers prefer. You can also define a method name without the quotation marks:

```
::method  square            /* class SQUARED has 1 method, SQUARE   */
```

The method's code immediately follows this *method directive*. Its first line reads its input argument:

```
use arg in                  /* get the input argument               */
```

In Open Object Rexx, you code `use arg` instead of `arg` or `parse arg` to retrieve one or more input arguments. The method squares the number provided in the input argument and returns it as its return string through the `return` instruction:

```
return ( in * in )          /* square it and return that value      */
```

That's it! You can create your own classes and methods in this fashion. Run the methods in those objects in the same way that you run the built-in methods provided by ooRexx.

In many ways, creating objects and methods is similar to creating subroutines and functions in classic Rexx. The difference is in the hierarchical structure of object-oriented programming. The ability to inherit behaviors (attributes and methods) through the class hierarchy minimizes the amount of new coding you have to do. This advantage becomes most pronounced in large programming projects, where the chances for code reuse are higher. It becomes significant in any situation in which you can optimally leverage ooRexx's built-in class library.

Another Simple OO Program

Here's another simple OO script. This one allows the user to enter a shell name and responds with the full name of the shell or the operating system. Here's an example interaction with the program:

```
Enter the shell name:
csh
OS is: C Shell
```

The user enters a shell name, csh, and the script responds with its full name. Here's another interaction:

```
Enter the shell name:
COMMAND
OS is: Windows 2K/2003/XP
```

The user enters the shell for his or her operating system, COMMAND, and the program responds that the shell is used under several versions of the Windows operating system. The program recognizes a couple other inputs (ksh and CMD), but comes back with this message for any other input:

```
Enter the shell name:
pdksh
OS is: unknown
```

Here is the code for the script:

```
/*********************************************************************/
/* WHICH OS                                                        */
/*                                                                 */
/* Tells which operating system you use depending on the command shell. */
/*********************************************************************/
os = .operating_systems~new      /* create a new object              */

os~write_command_shell           /* invoke the method to do the work  */

exit 0

::class operating_systems        /* class with 2 methods following it */

  ::method init                  /* method INIT prompts for shell name */
    expose shell                 /* EXPOSE the shared attribute      */
    say 'Enter the shell name:'  /* prompt for and read user input   */
    parse pull shell .
    return

  ::method write_command_shell   /* This method determines the OS.   */
    expose shell
    select                       /* determine the OS for this shell  */
      when shell = 'CMD'      then string = 'DOS or Windows 9x'
      when shell = 'COMMAND'  then string = 'Windows 2K/2003/XP'
      when shell = 'ksh'      then string = 'Korn Shell'
      when shell = 'csh'      then string = 'C Shell'
      otherwise string = 'unknown'
    end
    say 'OS is:' string          /* write out the OS determined      */
    return 0
```

This script only contains three lines of procedural code. The first line creates a new instance of the class
.operating_systems. Send the class the new method message to create a new instance of the class:

```
os = .operating_systems~new              /* create a new object         */
```

The second line in the program runs the method write_command_shell in the class. This method does
all the real work of the program:

```
os~write_command_shell                   /* invoke the method to do the work  */
```

The last line of procedural code, the exit instruction, ends the program. Class and method directives
follow, along with the code that defines them. The class(es) and their method(s) are always placed at the
bottom of the code in the script. This line defines the .operating_systems class:

```
::class operating_systems                /* class with 2 methods following it */
```

This class is followed by its two methods. The first is the init method:

```
::method init                            /* method INIT prompts for shell name */
```

The `init` method is a specially named method. Open Object Rexx always runs the `init` method (if there is one) whenever its creates a new instance via the `new` message. So, the first line in the script not only created a new instance of the `operating_systems` class but also automatically ran the `init` method.

In the `init` method, the first line of code uses the `expose` instruction to access the variable named `shell`. By using `expose`, the method has read and update capability on any variables or attributes it names. The `expose` instruction is the basic technique by which attributes can be shared among methods in a class:

```
expose shell                           /* EXPOSE the shared variable       */
```

After accessing this variable, the `init` method prompts the user to enter a shell name, reads that user input, and returns:

```
say 'Enter the shell name:'            /* prompt for and read user input   */
parse pull shell .
return
```

The second line of code in the driver runs the `write_command_shell` method. This method also accesses the attribute `shell` by its `expose` instruction:

```
expose shell
```

Then, the method executes a `select` instruction to determine the full shell name or associated operating system, and its writes this response to the user:

```
select                          /* determine the OS for this shell   */
  when shell = 'CMD'       then string = 'DOS or Windows 9x'
  when shell = 'COMMAND'   then string = 'Windows 2K/2003/XP'
  when shell = 'ksh'       then string = 'Korn Shell'
  when shell = 'csh'       then string = 'C Shell'
  otherwise string = 'unknown'
end
say 'OS is:' string             /* write out the OS determined       */
```

When this method returns, the main routine or procedural code terminates with an `exit` instruction.

This script shows how user interaction can be encapsulated within classes and methods. The procedural code in the main routine or driver can be minimal. The classes and their methods perform all the work. Once you start thinking in object-oriented terms, you'll develop the knack of viewing problems and their solutions as groups of interacting objects with their logical methods.

Implementing a Stack through Objects

Object Rexx provides a large set of *collection classes*, built-in classes that provide a set of data structures and for data manipulation. The collection classes are:

❑ Array — A sequenced collection

❑ Bag — A nonunique collection of objects (subclass of Relation)

481

❑   Directory — A collection indexed by unique character strings

❑   List — A sequenced collection which allows inserts at any position

❑   Queue — A sequenced collection that allows inserts at the start or ending positions

❑   Relation — A collection with nonunique objects for indexes

❑   Set — A unique collection of objects (subclass of Table)

❑   Table — A collection with unique objects for indexes

You'll rarely have to create your own data structures with all this built-in power available. But for the purpose of illustration, we use the List collection class as the basis to implement a stack in the next sample script.

Here is a sample interaction with the stack script:

```
Enter items to place on the stack, then EXIT
line1
line2
line3
line4
exit
Stack item # 1 is: LINE4
Stack item # 2 is: LINE3
Stack item # 3 is: LINE2
Stack item # 4 is: LINE1
```

The script prompts the user to enter several lines and then the keyword exit. Here the user entered four lines plus the keyword exit. Then the script pops the stack to retrieve and print the items. Since a stack is a last-in, first-out (LIFO) data structure, the items display in the reverse order in which they are entered.

How do we design this script? First, identify the stack as the entity or *object* with which the script works. This should be a class that we can instantiate by creating an object.

Second, try to identify which operations or *methods* need to be executed on that object. Push and pop are two key stack operations, so we'll need a method for each of these. Further reflection leads to the realization we also require an initialization method (init) and a method to return the number of items on the stack.

Identifying objects and their methods are the basic steps in object-oriented design. One other step (not relevant to this simple example) is determining the relationships or interactions between objects.

So, the script will have one class, called stack, and four methods in that class. Here are the methods and their functions:

❑   init — Initializes the stack

❑   push — Places an item (or line) onto the stack (*pushes* the item)

❑   pop — Retrieves an item from the stack (*pops* the item)

❑   number_items — Returns the number of items on the stack

With this understanding of what objects and methods are required, we can write the program:

```
/***********************************************************************/
/*   STACK                                                           */
/*                                                                   */
/*   Implments a Stack data structure as based on the LIST Collection */
/***********************************************************************/
the_stack = .stack~new                  /* create a new stack object   */

.output~lineout('Enter items to place on the stack, then EXIT')
stack_item = .input~linein~translate    /* read user's input of 1 item */

do while (stack_item <> 'EXIT')          /* read all user's items to    */
   the_stack~push(stack_item)            /*    push onto the stack and   */
   stack_item  = .input~linein~translate /* translate to upper case */
end

do j=1 by 1 while (the_stack~number_items <> 0)  /* pop and display   */
   say 'Stack item #' j 'is: ' the_stack~pop     /*    all stack items */
end

exit 0

::class stack                        /* define the STACK class       */

  ::method init                      /* define INITIALIZATION method  */
    expose stack_list                /* STACK_LIST is our stack.      */
    stack_list = .list~new           /* create a new STACK as a LIST  */

  ::method push                      /* define the PUSH method        */
    expose stack_list
    use arg item
    stack_list~insert(item, .nil)    /* insert item as 1st in the LIST */

  ::method pop                       /* define the POP method         */
    expose stack_list
    if stack_list~items > 0 then     /* return item, remove from stack */
       return stack_list~remove(stack_list~first)
    else
       return .nil                   /* return NIL if stack is empty  */

  ::method number_items              /* define the ITEMS method       */
    expose stack_list
    return stack_list~items          /* return number of items in stack*/
```

As in previous scripts, the first action is to create an instance of the class object. Here we create a stack to work with:

```
the_stack = .stack~new                           /* create a new stack object    */
```

The program prompts the user to enter several lines of data:

```
.output~lineout('Enter items to place on the stack, then EXIT')
stack_item = .input~linein~translate             /* read user's input of 1 item    */
```

The script reads a line with the `linein` method applied to the default input stream via the `.input` monitor object. This input line is then acted upon by the `translate` method. The code chains these two methods so that they execute one after the other. This reads and translates the input to uppercase.

For each line the script reads, it places it into the stack. This runs the `push` method with the `stack_item` as input:

```
the_stack~push(stack_item)                          /*   push onto the stack and        */
```

After all user-input lines have been read and placed onto the stack, this loop retrieves each line from the stack via the `pop` method and writes them to the user:

```
do j=1 by 1 while (the_stack~number_items <> 0)   /* pop and display    */
   say 'Stack item #' j 'is: ' the_stack~pop      /*   all stack items  */
end
```

The loop invokes our method `number_items` on the stack to determine how many items are in the stack. All the methods `expose` the stack so that they can work with it and read and alter its contents. Here is the code that exposes the program's shared attribute:

```
expose stack_list                    /* STACK_LIST is our stack.          */
```

Let's discuss each of the methods in this program. The `init` method automatically runs when the stack object is first created; it merely creates a new List object. Recall that we selected the built-in *collection class* of type List with which to implement our stack. This line in the `init` method creates the new List object:

```
stack_list = .list~new                /* create a new STACK as a LIST    */
```

The `push` method grabs its input argument and places it into the stack. It uses the List class's `insert` method to do this. The first argument to insert is the line to place into the list, while the second is the keyword `.nil` which says to place the item first in the list:

```
use arg item
stack_list~insert(item, .nil)          /* insert item as 1st in the LIST    */
```

The `pop` method checks to see if there are items in the stack by executing the List class's method `items`. If the List contains one or more items, it returns the proper item from the List by the `remove` method:

```
if stack_list~items > 0 then            /* return item, remove from stack   */
   return stack_list~remove(stack_list~first)
else
   return .nil                          /* return NIL if stack is empty     */
```

If there are no items in the List, the `pop` method returns the NIL object. Coded as `.nil`, this represents the absence of an object (much in the same manner the null string represents the string with no characters).

The method `number_items` simply returns the number of items currently on the stack. It does this by running the `List` method `items`:

```
return stack_list~items                 /* return number of items in stack   */
```

To summarize, this script shows how you can use an object and Open Object Rexx's built-in collection classes and methods to create new data structures. With its built-in collection classes, ooRexx is a rich language in terms of its support for data structures.

A Video Circulation Application

The next script controls videos for a store that rents movie DVDs. It is a more ambitious script that demonstrates how a number of methods can be applied to a Directory collection class object. The program presents a menu like the following one to the user. After the user makes a selection, the script performs the action the user selected. Here's an example, where the store employee adds a new DVD title to the collection:

```
1. Add New DVD
2. Check Movie Out
3. Check Movie In
4. Show Movie Status
5. Remove Lost DVD
X. Exit
Enter Your Choice  ==> 1

Enter Movie TITLE  ==> Titantic
Movie added to titles: TITANTIC
```

After each action is complete, the script clears the screen again and redisplays the menu. The program terminates when the user selects the option: X. Exit.

The program error-checks for logical mistakes. For example, it will not let the user check out a video that is already checked out, nor will it allow the user to check in a movie that is already on hand. The script always ensures the title the user refers to is in the collection. If not, it writes the appropriate message to the user.

As in the stack program, the Videos program implements an in-memory data structure to control the videos. This script uses the Directory built-in collection class to make an indexed list of videos. The film title is the index into the Directory; the sole data item associated with the video's title is its status. The status can either be IN LIBRARY or CHECKED OUT. For simplicity, the program assumes that there is only a single copy or DVD for each movie title.

The Directory of videos will be the class called movie_dir. The methods for this class are:

❏   init — Initialize the Directory

❏   add_movie — Add a film to the circulating collection

❏   check_out_movie — Check a movie out

❏   check_in_movie — Check a movie back in

❏   check_status — List the status of a movie (IN LIBRARY or CHECKED OUT)

❏   lost_or_destroyed — Remove a lost or destroyed DVD from the circulating collection

Here is the script:

```
/******************************************************************/
/*  VIDEOS                                                      */
/*                                                              */
/*  An in-memory circulation system for films on DVD.          */
/******************************************************************/
movie_list = .movie_dir~new     /* create new Directory object   */

do while selection <> 'X'

   /* display menu of options                                  */

   'clear'
   say "1. Add New DVD"   ;  say "2. Check Movie Out"
   say "3. Check Movie In" ;  say "4. Show Movie Status"
   say "5. Remove Lost DVD" ;  say "X. Exit"

   /* prompt user to enter his choice and the movie title       */

   call charout ,'Enter Your Choice  ==> '
   pull selection .     ;  say " "
   if (selection <> 'X') then do
      call charout ,'Enter Movie TITLE  ==> '
      pull title .
   end

   /* perform user selection                                   */

   select
      when selection = '1' then movie_list~add_movie(title)
      when selection = '2' then movie_list~check_out_movie(title)
      when selection = '3' then movie_list~check_in_movie(title)
      when selection = '4' then movie_list~check_status(title)
      when selection = '5' then movie_list~lost_or_destroyed(title)
      when selection = 'X' then exit 0
      otherwise say 'Invalid selection, press <ENTER> to continue...'
   end
   pull .                   /* user presses ENTER to continue    */
end
exit 0

::class movie_dir           /* define the MOVIE_DIR class        */

  ::method init             /* INIT - create the DIRECTORY       */
     expose mv_dir          /* expose the DIRECTORY of interest*/
     mv_dir = .directory~new  /* creates the DIRECTORY class     */

  ::method add_movie        /* ADD_MOVIE                         */
     expose mv_dir
     use arg title          /* if title is new, add it by PUT   */
     if .nil = mv_dir~at(title) then do
        mv_dir~put('IN LIBRARY',title)    /* add  by PUT method */
        say 'Movie added to titles:' title
```

```
            end
        else                    /* if title is not new, err message*/
           say 'Movie is already in collection:' title

   ::method check_out_movie     /* CHECK_OUT_MOVIE                   */
      expose mv_dir
      use arg title             /* if title doesn't exist, error    */
      if .nil = mv_dir~at(title)  then
         say 'No such title to check out:' title
      else do                   /* if ALREADY checked out, error    */
         if 'CHECKED OUT' = mv_dir~at(title) then
            say 'Movie already checked out:' title
         else do                /* if no error, check out the title*/
            mv_dir~setentry(title,'CHECKED OUT')    /* alters data*/
            say 'Movie is now checked out:' title
            end
         end

   ::method check_in_movie      /* CHECK_IN_MOVIE                    */
      expose mv_dir
      use arg title
      if .nil = mv_dir~at(title) then /* if no title, error         */
         say 'No such title to check in:' title
      else do                         /* if not checked out, err */
         if 'IN LIBRARY' = mv_dir~at(title) then
            say 'This title is ALREADY checked in:' title
         else do                      /* otherwise check it in     */
            mv_dir~setentry(title,'IN LIBRARY')   /* alters data */
            say 'The title is now checked back in:' title
            end
         end

   ::method check_status        /* CHECK_STATUS                     */
      expose mv_dir
      use arg title             /* if no such title, error          */
      if .nil = mv_dir~at(title) then
         say 'Title does not exist in our collection:' title
      else                      /* if title exists, show its status*/
         say mv_dir~at(title)   /* retrieve data by the AT method   */

   ::method lost_or_destroyed   /* LOST_OR_DESTROYED                */
      expose mv_dir
      use arg title
      if .nil = mv_dir~at(title) then /* if no such title, error   */
         say 'Title does not exist in our collection:' title
      else do                   /* if title exists, remove it       */
         mv_dir~remove(title)   /* REMOVE method deletes from Dir. */
         say 'Title has been removed from our collection:' title
         end
```

The first line of procedural code creates the instance or object the script will work with. This is the same approach we've seen in previous example scripts, such as the Stack and Which OS programs:

```
movie_list = .movie_dir~new     /* create new Directory object    */
```

The next block of code clears the screen, displays the menu and reads the user's selection. The `select` instruction runs the proper method to perform the user's selection. The `.movie_dir` class and its six methods follow the procedural code. Let's briefly discuss each of the methods.

The `init` method creates the Directory instance:

```
mv_dir = .directory~new          /* creates the DIRECTORY class    */
```

The `add_movie` method checks to see if the title the user entered is in the circulating collection. It uses the `at` method on the Directory object to do this:

```
if .nil = mv_dir~at(title) then do
```

If `.nil` is returned, the script adds the title to the circulating collection (the Directory) with the status IN LIBRARY:

```
mv_dir~put('IN LIBRARY',title)      /* add  by PUT method          */
```

The `put` method places the information into the Directory. To check out a DVD, the method `check_out_movie` uses the `setentry` method on the Directory to alter the DVD's status:

```
mv_dir~setentry(title,'CHECKED OUT')      /* alters data           */
```

Method `check_in_movie` similarly runs the `setentry` built-in method to alter the DVD's status:

```
mv_dir~setentry(title,'IN LIBRARY')       /*  alters data          */
```

Method `check_status` executes method `at` to see whether or not a film is checked out:

```
if .nil = mv_dir~at(title) then
```

It then displays an appropriate message on the status of the video by these lines:

```
        say 'Title does not exist in our collection:' title
    else                      /* if title exists, show its status*/
        say mv_dir~at(title)  /* retrieve data by the AT method   */
```

Finally, the method `lost_or_destroyed` removes a title from the circulating collection by running the Directory `remove` method:

```
mv_dir~remove(title)          /* REMOVE method deletes from Dir. */
```

Like most of the collection classes, Directory supports alternative ways of invoking several of its methods. Here are a couple alternative notations:

❑   [ ]—Returns the same item as the `at` method

❑   [ ]=   —Same as the `put` method

For example, we could have written this line to add the new title to the Directory:

```
mv_dir[title] = 'IN LIBRARY'
```

This statement is the direct equivalent of what we actually coded in the sample script:

```
mv_dir~put('IN LIBRARY',title)     /* add  by PUT method        */
```

Similarly, we could have checked for the existence of a title by referring to mv_dir[title] instead of coding the at method as we did. This is another way of coding that reference:

```
if  .nil  =  my_dir[title]  then
```

This statement is the same as what was coded in the script:

```
if .nil = mv_dir~at(title) then    /* if no such title, error   */
```

This script employs simple say and pull instructions to create a simple line-oriented user interface. Most programs that interact with users employ graphical user interfaces or GUIs. How does one build a GUI with Open Object Rexx? This is where the power of built-in classes and methods comes into play. The menu becomes a *menu object* and the built-in classes and methods activate it. Creating a GUI becomes a matter of working with prebuilt objects typically referred to as *widgets* or *controls*. Chapter 16 discusses graphical user interfaces for object-oriented Rexx scripting. Besides a GUI, the other feature that is missing from the Videos script is *persistence*, the ability to store and update object data on disk. This simple script implements the entire application in memory. Once the user exits the menu, all data entered is lost. Not very practical for the video store that wants to stay in business!

Object-oriented programmers typically add persistence or permanence to their objects through interfacing with one of the popular database management systems. Among commercial systems, Oracle, DB2 UDB, and SQL Server are popular. Among open-source products, MySQL, PostgreSQL, and Berkeley DB are most popular.

GUI and database capability are beyond the scope of our simple example. Here the goal was to introduce you to object-oriented programming, not to get into the technologies of GUIs and databases. Of course, these interfaces are used by most real-world object-oriented Rexx programs. Using class libraries and methods reduces the work you, as a developer, must do when programming these interfaces.

Concurrency

Object-oriented programming with Open Object Rexx is *concurrent* in that multiple objects' methods may be running at any one time. Even multiple methods within the same object may execute concurrently.

The following sample script illustrates concurrency. Two instances of the same class are created and execute their single shared method concurrently. To make this clearer, here is the script's output. The intermixed output shows the concurrent (simultaneous) execution of the two instances:

```
Repeating the message for object #1 5 times.
Object #1 is running
Object #2 is running
Repeating the message for object #2 5 times.
Object #1 is running
Object #2 is running
Driver is now terminating.
Object #1 is running
Object #2 is running
Object #1 is running
Object #2 is running
Object #1 is running
Object #2 is running
```

Object #1 and Object #2 are two different instances of the same class. That class has one method, called repeat, which displays all the messages seen above, from both objects (other than the one that states that the Driver is now terminating.)

Here is the code of the script:

```
/**************************************************************************/
/*   CONCURRENCY                                                          */
/*                                                                        */
/*   Illustrates concurrency within an object by using REPLY instruction  */
/**************************************************************************/
object1 = .concurrent~new            /* create two instances,       */
object2 = .concurrent~new            /* both of the CONCURRENT class */

say object1~repeat(1,5)              /* get 1st object running       */
say object2~repeat(2,5)              /* get 2nd object running       */

say 'Driver is now terminating.'
exit 0

::class concurrent                   /* define the CONCURRENT class  */

::method repeat                      /* define the REPEAT method     */
  use arg who_am_i, reps             /* get OBJECT_ID, time to repeat */
  reply 'Repeating the message for object #' || who_am_i reps 'times.'
  do reps
    say 'Object #'|| who_am_i 'is running'   /* show object is running */
  end
```

The script first creates two separate instances of the same class:

```
object1 = .concurrent~new            /* create two instances,       */
object2 = .concurrent~new            /* both of the CONCURRENT class */
```

The next two lines send the same message to each instance. They execute the method repeat with two parameters. The first parameter tells repeat for which object is it executing (either 1 for the first object or 2 for the second). The second parameter gives the repeat method a loop control variable that tells it how many times to write a message to the display to trace its execution. This example executes the method for each instance five times:

```
say object1~repeat(1,5)              /* get 1st object running    */
say object2~repeat(2,5)              /* get 2nd object running    */
```

Following these two statements, the driver writes a termination message and exits. The driver has no further role in the program. Almost all of the program output is generated by the `repeat` method, written to show its concurrent execution for the two instances.

Inside the `repeat` method, this line collects its two input arguments. It uses the `use arg` instruction to read the two input arguments:

```
use arg who_am_i, reps               /* get OBJECT_ID, time to repeat */
```

The next line issues the `reply` instruction. `reply` immediately returns control to the caller at the point from which the message was sent. Meanwhile, the method containing the `reply` instruction keeps running:

```
reply 'Repeating the message for object #' || who_am_i reps 'times.'
```

In this case, `reply` sends back a message that tells which object is executing and how many times the `repeat` method will perform its `do` loop. Now, the `repeat` method message loop continues running. This code writes the message five times to demonstrate the continuing concurrent execution of the `repeat` method:

```
do reps
   say 'Object #'|| who_am_i 'is running'   /* Show object is running */
end
```

This simple script shows that objects and methods execute concurrently, and that even methods within the same object may run concurrently. Open Object Rexx provides a simple approach to concurrency that requires more complex coding in other object-oriented languages.

Summary

This chapter introduces classic Rexx programmers to Open Object Rexx. It does not summarize or demonstrate all the OO features of ooRexx. Instead, it presents a simple tutorial on the product for those from a procedural-programming background.

We started with a very simple script. That first script created a stream instance and demonstrated how to perform object-oriented I/O. Two more advanced scripts followed. These showed how to define and code your own classes and methods. The Stack sample program was more sophisticated. It defined several different methods that demonstrated how to employ the List collection class to implement an in-memory stack data structure. The Videos application built upon the same concepts, this time using the Directory collection class to simulate a video circulation control system. Finally, the Concurrency script illustrated the use of two instances of the same class and the concurrent execution of their methods.

Open Object Rexx is ideal for learning object-oriented programming. It retains all the simplicity and strengths of classic Rexx while surrounding it with a plethora of OO features and the power of an extensive class library.

Test Your Understanding

1. Will every classic Rexx program run under Open Object Rexx? When might this be useful? Does this capitalize on ooRexx's capabilities?

2. Are all classic Rexx instructions and functions part of Open Object Rexx? Which additional instructions and functions does ooRexx add?

3. What is a collection and how are they used?

4. Convert these two functions in classic Rexx to ooRexx method calls:

```
reversed_string = reverse(string)
sub_string = substr(string,1,5)
```

5. Do the `stream` class methods offer a superset of classic Rexx I/O functions? What additional features do they offer?

6. What are the four kinds of directives and what is each used for? Where must classes and methods be placed in a script?

7. What symbols commonly express `at` and `put` in many collections?

8. What are the error (`.error`), input (`.input`), and output (`.output`) monitor objects used for?

IBM Mainframe Rexx

Overview

IBM bundles Rexx with all its mainframe operating systems. These include operating systems in what we generically refer to as the VM, OS, and VSE families. IBM mainframe Rexx is not an open-source product but rather is bundled with commercial mainframe operating systems. The name of the product is typically written in uppercase, as REXX. For consistency, we'll continue to refer to it as we have previously in this book, as Rexx.

Mainframe Rexx is important for several reasons. Rexx was originally offered on the mainframe (specifically for VM/CMS). VM influenced early development of the language, leaving its imprint in various ways. For example, the stack is a VM/CMS feature, and many VM/CMS commands send their output to the stack. The stack remains a popular means for command I/O in Rexx today, and the free Rexx interpreters support the stack in this role.

Another important reason to discuss mainframe Rexx is the key role mainframes continue to play in many IT organizations. While the mainframe has a low profile in the trade press and in industry buzz, thousands of sites worldwide continue to rely on mainframes for their most vital business operations. Mainframes remain critical to organizations around the world. Rexx is the predominant mainframe scripting language. No other scripting language comes anywhere close to Rexx's usage level on the mainframe.

Many readers will face the prospect of porting Rexx code from the mainframe to other platforms. This often means changing IBM mainframe scripts into free Rexx scripts that run under Linux, Unix, or Windows. Briefly comparing the differences between mainframe Rexx and open-source Rexxes may be useful.

IT professionals will want to apply their skills across many platforms. They may have learned Rexx on the mainframe and now wish to script on some other platform (say Windows, Linux, or Unix). Or, they may be from the Windows, Linux or Unix background and are unfamiliar with mainframes. Rexx offers a quick means to become instantly productive across many platforms. Programmers can easily transfer their Rexx skills from Windows, Linux, or Unix to the mainframe environment or vice versa.

This chapter provides an overview of the differences among IBM mainframe Rexx, the Rexx standards, and the free Rexx interpreters this book discusses. The goal is to sketch the major differences between IBM mainframe Rexx and the free Rexxes, as well as outline the extended features of mainframe Rexx. We emphasize that this chapter is just a brief summary of mainframe Rexx. Space is too limited to really explore the products here other than by way of contrast with what you already know about Rexx and its standards from the rest of the book. A section towards the end of the chapter, entitled "Further Information," tells where you can get more information on mainframe Rexx.

Rexx differs in slight ways across the three mainframe operating system families, which we refer to as VM, OS, and VSE. All IBM mainframe Rexx implementations meet the TRL-2 standard (with one or two very minor exceptions, which we'll discuss). All offer many extensions and additional features, but what these extras are differ by mainframe platform.

IBM's official, cross-platform definition for Rexx is contained in its manual *Systems Application Architecture Common Programming Reference, SC24-5549*. If you need to assess detail-level differences between the various IBM Rexx implementations, you should review that document and its SAA Rexx definition. Appendix A on Resources shows where to access and download this manual at no cost.

VM Rexx Differences

Almost all of the special features of mainframe Rexx are language extensions. This section summarizes them for VM Rexx. The information is based on the *REXX/VM Reference, SC24-6113 (Version 5 Release 1)*. Where they fit in, we add a few comments on OS/TSO Rexx, based on *TSO/E REXX Reference, SC28-1975* (version 2 release 10) and *TSO/E REXX Reference, SA22-7790* (version 1 release 6). The next section, "OS/TSO Rexx Differences," explores the extended features of OS/TSO-E Rexx in greater detail.

This section compares VM Rexx to the ANSI-1996 standard and also enumerates many of its differences from free Rexx interpreters for other operating systems such as Linux, Windows, and Unix. Figure 29-1 summarizes many of the major differences:

Let's now discuss these extended features of VM/CMS Rexx.

First line

The first line of a VM/CMS Rexx script must be a comment. The first line of an OS TSO/E Rexx script normally must contain the word REXX. We recommend the first line of any mainframe script contain this first line, which satisfies both requirements:

```
/* REXX */
```

This first line is portable across almost all Rexx interpreters on all systems. The primary exceptions are those Linux, Unix, or BSD environments in which the first line of code traditionally indicates the location of the Rexx interpreter (such as: `#!/usr/local/bin/regina`). Running scripts explicitly on these systems avoids the need for a first line that indicates where the Rexx interpreter resides, in most cases.

How VM Rexx Differs

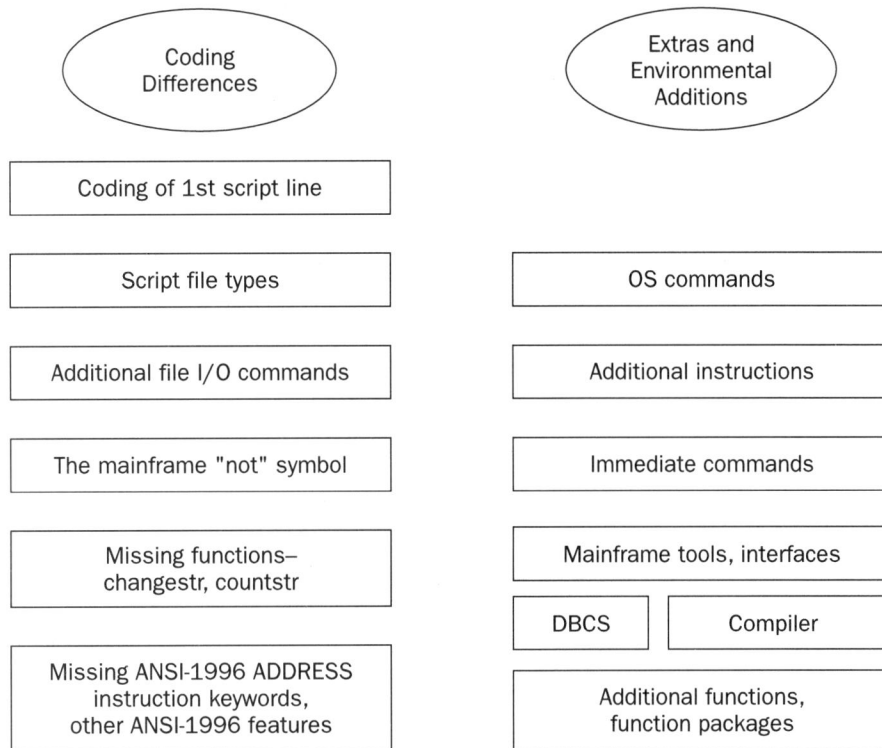

Coding
Differences

Extras and
Environmental
Additions

Coding of 1st script line

Script file types		OS commands

Additional file I/O commands		Additional instructions

The mainframe "not" symbol		Immediate commands

Missing functions– changestr, countstr		Mainframe tools, interfaces

DBCS	Compiler

Missing ANSI-1996 ADDRESS instruction keywords, other ANSI-1996 features		Additional functions, function packages

Figure 29-1

Online help facility

The help facility is a VM feature that distinguishes it from other platforms because the VM help facility includes Rexx documentation. For example, you can display information about Rexx instructions and functions via the help facility. Let's look at a few examples. To get information about the say instruction, you could enter:

```
help rexx say
```

To get information about a Rexx error message, enter help with that message id. Here is the generic command template:

```
help msgid
```

For example, for help on message ID dmsrex460e, enter that message ID as the operand on the help command:

```
help  dmsrex460e
```

File types

Mainframes use different file-naming conventions than other platforms. These differences apply to files containing Rexx scripts in several ways. Under VM, Rexx scripts typically reside in files of type EXEC. For this reason, Rexx scripts are often referred to as *EXECs* or *REXX EXECs*.

VM Rexx scripts designed to run as editor *macro commands* (or editor scripts) have the file type of XEDIT. These are referred as *edit macros*. Edit macros issue commands to the XEDIT Editor and can automatically drive the editor. Or, they can extend the editor's functionality or tailor or automate its use.

CMS pipelines use the file type REXX to identify a stage or program in the pipeline. CMS pipes are an alternative to the stack and provide a general-purpose communications vehicle popular on VM mainframes. Each stage in the pipeline manipulates or processes data.

In OS (or TSO) environments, Rexx scripts may either be sequential data sets or members of partitioned data sets (PDSs). PDS libraries of scripts are most common. Filenames for Rexx scripts under TSO/E normally end in EXEC.

"Not" symbol

Mainframe scripts often use this symbol ¬ as the "not" operator, for example, as in "not equal" ¬=. We recommend using the universally accepted, ANSI-standard backslash instead. For "not equal," for example, use: \=. The backslash appears on all keyboards and is more transportable than the traditional mainframe "not" symbol. Other portable alternatives available on all keyboards for "not equal" include <> and ><. This principle also applies to the other operators, such as "not greater than" (\>) and "not less than" (\<).

OS commands

VM Rexx scripts can issue both CMS and CP commands. CMS has its own command and function search order. Scripts can also issue subcommands. As always, limiting the number of OS-specific commands leads to more portable code, but there are techniques to limit the impact of OS-specific commands even when they must be included. For example, isolate OS-specific code in particular routines, or code if statements that execute the commands appropriate to the OS under which the script runs. Chapter 13 explores these techniques for code portability.

Instructions

VM Rexx adds a few new keywords for the options and parse instructions, as well as the upper instruction. These extended features are of relatively minor importance, but we mention them here for completeness. Note that mainframe Rexx thoroughly supports the Double-Byte Character Set (DBCS). The DBCS supports spoken languages that require more bits for proper representation of their symbology. For example, DBCS can be used to support languages based on ideographic characters, such as Asian languages such as Chinese, Japanese, or Korean. Here is a brief list of the mainframe-extended Rexx instructions:

Instruction	Use
OPTIONS	Several options specify how strings and the Double-Byte Character Set (DBCS) are handled.
PARSE	Two new keywords are added to standard Rexx:
	The external keyword parses the next string from terminal input.
	The numeric keyword retrieves the current numeric settings.
UPPER	This translates a string to uppercase.

Functions

VM Rexx provides a grab-bag of extended built-in functions. The FIND, INDEX, and JUSTIFY functions have largely been superceded by standard Rexx functions. Use WORDPOS, POS, RIGHT, and LEFT instead of the mainframe functions for more portable, standardized scripts. The EXTERNALS and LINESIZE functions manage I/O to the terminal (or the desktop computer emulating a terminal). Here are the extended VM functions:

Function	Use
EXTERNALS	Returns the number of elements in the terminal input buffer
FIND	Returns the word number of a specified word within a string (similar to the wordpos function in ANSI-standard Rexx)
INDEX	Returns the character position of one string within another (similar to the pos function in ANSI-standard Rexx)
JUSTIFY	Justifies a string by adding pad characters (use the right, left, and space ANSI-standard functions instead)
LINESIZE	Returns the current terminal line width
USERID	Returns the system-defined user identifier

VM Rexx also adds over a dozen functions to handle the DBCS. All begin with the letters DB. We have not listed the DBCS functions in the preceding chart.

Some standard Rexx functions are enhanced with mainframe-unique parameters. For example, the STREAM function includes specifications for LRECL and RECFM. These specifications describe the way files are structured in the mainframe environment.

Appendix E provides function formats and a usage description for the additional built-in mainframe functions.

Function packages and external functions

The VM Rexx language processor knows about and automatically loads any or all of these three named packages if any function within them is invoked from within a script: RXUSERFN, RXLOCFN, and RXSYSFN. Users may add their own functions to these libraries. These additional VM Rexx external functions are also automatically loaded if invoked:

External Function	Use
APILOAD	Includes a binding file in a Rexx program
CMSFLAG	Returns the setting of certain characters
CSL	Invokes callable services library (or CSL) routines
DIAG	Communicates with CP through the DIAGNOSE instruction
DIAGRC	Similar to the DIAG instruction
SOCKET	Provides access to the TCP/IP socket interface
STORAGE	Inspects or alters the main storage of the user's virtual machine

CMS immediate commands

The CMS *immediate commands* can be used to dynamically halt and restart script execution or the Rexx trace facility from outside the script. Since these commands operate from outside of scripts, you could, for example, start a script, then type in a TS immediate command while it runs. This dynamically turns on the trace facility in real time. Entering the TE command would immediately turn off the trace. Immediate commands act like toggle switches that you access from outside the script without making any code changes.

The immediate commands include:

❑ HI — Halt Interpretation

❑ TS — Trace Start

❑ TE — Trace End

❑ HX — Halt Execution

❑ HT — Halt Typing

❑ RT — Resume Typing

Compiler

IBM provides Rexx compilers for both VM and OS. To be more precise, IBM provides one compiler that generates code suitable for the operating system platform on which it runs. This compiler allows you to quickly develop scripts with the interactive interpreter, then convert finished programs to object code by compiling them. This approach yields the benefits of an interpreter in quick development and interactive debugging along with the compiler advantage of faster program execution for finished programs.

We note that the relative performance gain one experiences from compiling varies according to the environment and the nature of the script itself. A good example of a script that might benefit from compilation is a computationally intensive program. As another example, systems that do not execute much code outside of the Rexx environment might also see significant benefits. Yet there are situations where the compiler underperforms the Rexx interpreter. So, while compiled scripts are generally faster, we don't wish to oversimplify the relative performance of compiled versus interpreted scripts in the mainframe environment.

As in other environments, the mainframe compiler can be used as a mechanism to hide source code. Some organizations use the compiler, for example, where audit or security rules forbid the presence of source code in the production environment. The compiler can also aid in better syntax checking. For example, it checks all logic branches in a program, whereas the Rexx interpreter only verifies branches that execute.

Useful CMS commands

A number of CMS commands are especially useful from within VM Rexx scripts. These have no special relationship to Rexx; they are part of the CMS operating system and are CMS commands. But since they are commonly issued from within scripts, we list them here:

CMS Command	Use
DESBUF	Clears (drops) all stack input/output buffers
DROPBUF	Deletes the most recent stack buffer or a specified set of them
EXECDROP	Deletes EXECs residing in storage
EXECIO	Performs I/O, or issues CP commands and captures results
EXECLOAD	Loads an EXEC, readies it for execution
EXECMAP	Lists EXECs residing in storage
EXECSTAT	Provides EXEC status
FINIS	Closes files
GLOBALV	Saves EXEC data or variables
IDENTIFY	Returns system information
LISTFILE	Lists files
MAKEBUF	Creates a new buffer in the stack
PARSECMD	Parses EXEC arguments
PIPE	Calls CMS Pipelines to process a series of programs or stages; each stage manipulates or processes data
QUERY	Queries SET command information
SENTRIES	Tells how many lines are in the program stack
SET	Modifies the function search order; controls screen I/O or tracing
XEDIT	The XEDIT editor may be controlled by Rexx scripts called *edit macros*

OS/TSO Rexx Differences

As with VM Rexx, almost all of the special features of mainframe Rexx for OS/TSO are language extensions. This section summarizes the major differences. The information is from *TSO/E REXX Reference, SC28-1975 (version 2 release 10)* and *TSO/E REXX Reference SA22-7790 (version 1 release 6)*. The intent is to point out the extended features of OS/TSO Rexx versus ANSI-standard Rexx and the free Rexx interpreters available for environments such as Linux, Unix, and Windows. This section adds to some of the comments made in the earlier section entitled "VM Rexx Differences." We will not repeat the information already discussed in that section.

Figure 29-2 summarizes some of the major differences between Rexx under OS/TSO versus other platforms. The additional features and facilities of Rexx for TSO/E outweigh the few language elements that it lacks.

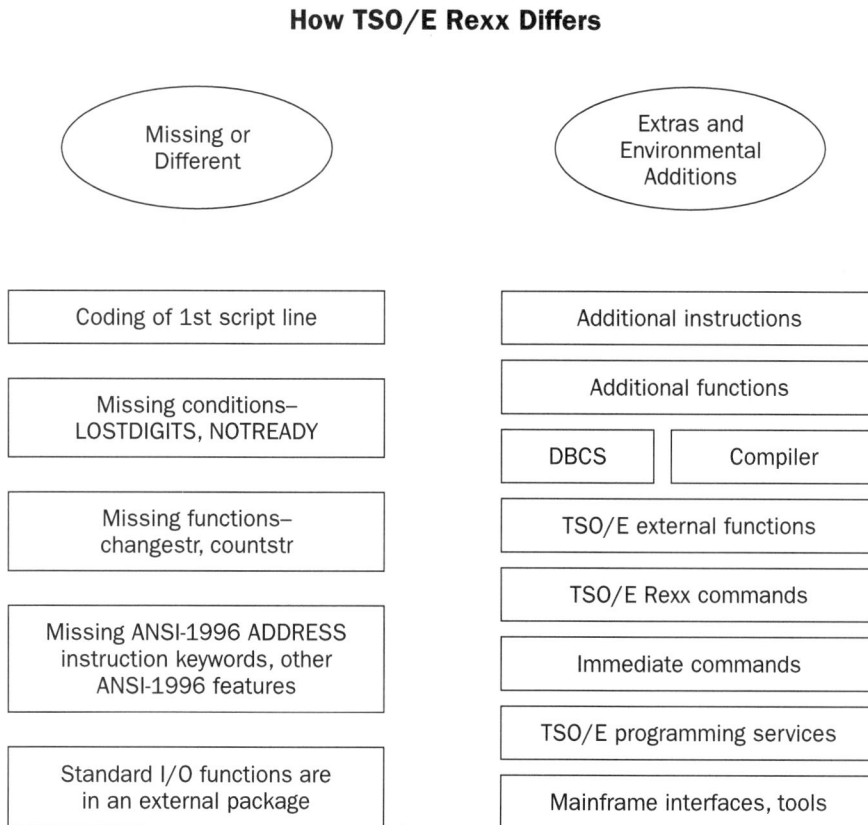

How TSO/E Rexx Differs

Missing or Different	Extras and Environmental Additions
Coding of 1st script line	Additional instructions
Missing conditions– LOSTDIGITS, NOTREADY	Additional functions
Missing functions– changestr, countstr	DBCS / Compiler
Missing ANSI-1996 ADDRESS instruction keywords, other ANSI-1996 features	TSO/E external functions
Standard I/O functions are in an external package	TSO/E Rexx commands
	Immediate commands
	TSO/E programming services
	Mainframe interfaces, tools

Figure 29-2

Let's discuss the details of the differences between programming Rexx in OS environments versus other platforms.

Additional instructions and functions

OS/TSO Rexx adds the exact same instructions and functions as does VM Rexx. See the two tables in the previous VM description labeled "Instructions" and "Functions" for complete lists and descriptions of these additions.

TSO/E external functions

While its extra instructions and built-in functions are very nearly the same as those for VM, OS/TSO Rexx differs almost totally from VM Rexx in its additional external functions. These are the OS TSO/E Rexx extensions:

External Function	Use
GETMSG	Returns a message issued during the console session. Since this affects the system console, most sites only authorize using this function in special situations.
LISTDSI	Returns information about a data set, including its allocation, protection, and directory.
MSG	Tells whether TSO/E messages are being displayed while the script runs. This status will be either ON or OFF.
MVSVAR	Returns information about the current session or security labels.
OUTTRAP	Either returns the name of the variable in which trapped output is stored, or returns OFF if trapping is turned off.
PROMPT	Returns the prompt setting for the script, either ON or OFF.
SETLANG	Returns a three-character code that tells the spoken language in which Rexx messages are displayed.
STORAGE	Reads a given number of bytes of storage from a specified address.
SYSCPUS	Returns information about active CPUs in a stem variable.
SYSDSN	Returns information about whether a given dsname is available for use.
SYSVAR	Returns information about the current session, including software levels, the logon procedure, and user id.

TSO/E Rexx commands

Another important extension to OS/TSO Rexx are its set of over 15 *commands*. These commands perform services such as controlling I/O processing and script execution characteristics, managing the stack, executing immediate commands, and checking for the existence of host command environments. This table lists the commands by their functional area:

Functional Area	Commands
Controlling I/O processing	EXECIO
Control script execution characteristics	EXECUTIL
Stack services	MAKEBUF, DROPBUF, QBUF, QELEM, NEWSTACK, DELSTACK, QSTACK
Check for existence of host command environments	SUBCOM
Immediate commands	HE, HI, HT, RT, TE, TS

Many of these commands duplicate functionality of the VM command environment, such as the stack services, the immediate commands, and the EXECIO command for input/output.

Here is a complete list of the commands along with descriptions of how they are used:

TSO/E Rexx Command	Use
DELSTACK	Deletes the most recently created stack and all its elements
DROPBUF	Drops the most recently created stack buffer
EXECIO	Controls and performs data set I/O; employs either the stack or stem variables for the I/O.
EXECUTIL	Changes script execution characteristics
HE	Halt execution; immediately halts the script
HI	Halt interpretation; immediately halts script interpretation
HT	Halt typing; immediately suppresses a script's terminal output
MAKEBUF	Creates a new buffer on the stack
NEWSTACK	Creates a new data stack (hiding the current data stack)
QBUF	Returns the number of buffers on the stack
QELEM	Returns the number of data stack elements in the most recently created stack buffer
QSTACK	Returns the number of data stacks for a script
RT	Resume typing; continues or resumes a script's terminal output
SUBCOM	Tells whether a specified host environment exists
TE	Trace end; immediately ends tracing
TS	Trace start; turns on tracing

These TSO/E commands are not Rexx functions, nor are they regular operating system commands. They are special operating system commands that can only be run from with Rexx scripts.

Code them in the same manner that scripts issue commands to the operating system. For example, this series of commands manipulates buffers and shows how Rexx scripts issue commands:

```
"MAKEBUF"               /* create one buffer            */
"MAKEBUF"               /* create a second buffer       */

"DROPBUF"               /* delete the second buffer     */

"QBUF"                  /* ask how many buffers we have */

SAY 'The number of current buffers is:' RC        /* displays: 1 */
```

Here is a similar example that issues some of the stack commands. Note that stacks differ from buffers in that one already exists prior to issuing the first NEWSTACK command:

```
"NEWSTACK"              /* create a second stack        */
                        /* (one already exists by default) */
"NEWSTACK"              /* create a third stack         */

"DELSTACK"              /* delete the most-recent stack */

"QSTACK"                /* ask how many stacks we have  */

SAY 'The number of data stacks is:' RC        /* displays: 2 */
```

TSO/E programming services

OS/TSO provides a range of extended "programming services" available to Rexx scripts. These are OS- and TSO-specific services that are typically used for controlling aspects of the mainframe environment or in using its facilities and subsystems.

The services available to Rexx scripts depend on the address space in which they run. Available services further depend on whether the scripts are run in the *foreground* (interactively) or in the *background* (as a noninteractive batch job).

These topics become very OS-specific and extend beyond the scope of this book. Please see the mainframe Rexx reference manuals for information on programming services and interfaces. Appendix A tells how to freely download them.

Mainframe Rexx and the Language Standards

Both VM and OS TSO/E Rexx conform to the TRL-2 Rexx language standard. There are a very few minor differences between VM and OS Rexx and the TRL-2 standard, which we'll discuss momentarily.

In contrast, mainframe Rexx makes little attempt to conform to the newer ANSI-1996 standard. Like many of the free and open-source Rexx interpreters available on other platforms, mainframe Rexx has not been upgraded to include the ANSI-1996 features.

First, let's discuss how mainframe Rexx conforms to the TRL-2 standard. Scanning the VM Rexx manuals, we were unable to find any TRL-2 standard feature or function that VM/CMS Rexx lacks. In contrast, TSO/E Rexx differs in several small ways from TRL-2. One minor difference is that TSO/E Rexx lacks the NOTREADY condition. Another difference is that TSO/E Rexx does not include the standard Rexx I/O functions in the core language. Recall that these standard I/O functions are CHARS, CHARIN, CHAROUT, LINES, LINEIN, LINEOUT, and STREAM. These functions are available to OS programmers through the external function package commonly called the *Stream I/O Function Package*. This includes all the standard I/O functions for TSO/E Rexx users. The IBM manual *Stream I/O For TSO/E REXX* (version 1.3, dated 2002, no SC number assigned) covers all aspects of this external function package, from installation, to describing the functions themselves, to integration into the TSO/E Rexx environment.

VM and TSO/E Rexx developers thus have a choice between the "traditional" mainframe I/O model supported by the EXECIO command, and the standard Rexx I/O model. EXECIO is widely used and understood and fits well with mainframe file systems and allocation methods. Standard Rexx I/O is simpler, portable, and conforms to the Rexx standard. Developers can use either model, or both, as they choose. The two may be intermixed within scripts.

While VM and OS Rexx conform to the TRL-2 standard, they lack the features introduced by the ANSI-1996 standard. Let's briefly list of these missing elements:

- ❑ *Instructions* — A couple standard instruction keywords are missing. They include:
  - ❑ ADDRESS — Does not support ANSI-1996 keywords INPUT, OUTPUT and ERROR — Command I/O is always through the stack.
  - ❑ SIGNAL — No LOSTDIGITS condition for error trapping
- ❑ *Functions* — Mainframe Rexx does not support the new ANSI-1996 string functions CHANGESTR and COUNTSTR. The TIME function allows only a single argument and does not support the ANSI-1996 conversion features. The DATE function supports date conversions but does not appear to strictly conform to the ANSI-1996 definition.
- ❑ *Condition Trapping* — The new ANSI-1996 condition trap LOSTDIGITS is absent. Recall that this exception condition is raised when the loss of significant digits occurs during computation.

In summary, both VM/CMS and TSO/E Rexx meet the TRL-2 standard, but omit nearly all of the ANSI-1996 standard's additions. This fits right in with the majority of free and open-source Rexx interpreters, most of which follow the same pattern at the time of writing.

Interfaces

Since IBM declared Rexx its official *command procedures language* (or scripting language), the company has interfaced or integrated practically every one of its other products into Rexx. Many different subsystems can be programmed with Rexx. Rexx has become the general-purpose default programming language for interfacing to and controlling mainframe services.

Here is a partial list of some of the Rexx mainframe programming interfaces:

Mainframe Rexx Programming Interfaces
EXEC interface
CMS assembler macros and functions
CP assembler macros (such as IUCS and APPC/VM)
Group Control System or GCS interface and GCS assembler macros
Callable service library routines (CSL routines)
OS and VSE simulation interfaces
CP DIAGNOSE instructions
Interface into some VM control blocks
CP system services
Data record formats intended for processing by applications (e.g.: accounting records)
Calls to Rexx scripts from programs written in languages like Assembler, C, COBOL, FORTRAN, Pascal, and PL/I
Rexx Exits — these allow applications to tailor the Rexx environment
XEDIT editor — you can write editor macros in Rexx
Interactive System Productivity Facility Editor (the ISPF Editor)
Interactive System Productivity Facility Dialog Manager (ISPF Dialog Manager)
`address cpicomm` — calls program-to-program communications routines that participate in the Common Programming Interface (CPI)
CPI Resource Recovery Routines
Netview — customization using Rexx
`address openvm` — invokes OPENVM routines
Rexx Sockets — a full set of functions and API to interface to TCP/IP
Customer Information Control System, or CICS — Customer Rexx offers easier programming with this teleprocessing monitor
VSAMIO interface to manipulate VSAM files (ESDS, KSDS, and RRDS)
VM GUI interface
MQ-Series Rexx interface
Information Management System or IMS Rexx interface (also called the DL/I Interface)
DB2 UDB SQL programming and database management and administration interfaces
Command environments CPICOMM, LU62, APPCMVS, CONSOLE, ISPEXEC, and ISREDIT

Describing these interfaces and showing how to use them is beyond the scope of this book (indeed, of any single book!). The point is that you can interface Rexx to almost any tool, language or facility under VM, OS or VSE. Rexx is the lingua franca of the modern mainframe. See the IBM documentation in Appendix A on resources for more information.

Rexx's dominance is such on mainframes that many third-party vendors also use the language in their products. For example, the setup and installation scripts for products may be coded in Rexx. Or, the products may support a Rexx scripting interface for customers. Candle Corporation's performance monitoring and automated operations products exemplify this trend. From the vendor's standpoint, of course, Rexx makes a nice fit. It is ubiquitous on mainframes and every customer will have it installed. Customers can be assumed to have Rexx expertise. The language is a powerful enough general-purpose language that it can accomplish any task. Yet it is an easy language to decipher if a customer has to understand the vendor's scripts.

Sample Scripts

Let's look at a few simple scripts to illustrate aspects of mainframe scripting. The scripts are from the VM environment and were developed and tested under various releases of that operating system. The purpose of these scripts is to demonstrate a few of the basic techniques of mainframe Rexx programming. To this end, we demonstrate how to issue VM's CMS and CP commands, how to retrieve operating system command output from the stack, how to send input to OS commands through the stack, and how to use the EXECIO command for file I/O. These sample scripts highlight a few of the typical techniques one would use in mainframe Rexx scripting. We've kept these scripts bare bones to hone in on the mainframe-specific aspects. So, we purposely exclude error checking, analyzing return codes, and the other essentials of robust, real-world scripts.

Let's take a look at the first sample script. Under VM, scripts can issue CMS commands or CP commands (among others). This script demonstrates how. In VM environments, CMS commands are those issued as if they came from the interactive command line, while CP commands control various aspects of the environment or one's virtual machine. By default, Rexx scripts send non-Rexx commands to CMS. Prefacing a command with the letters CP sends it to CP.

This sample script illustrates how scripts issue both CMS and CP commands. It links to another user's A-disk. To run the script, the user enters the userid of the other user, a virtual address for the device, and a disk letter. Here's the script:

```
/*  This Exec links to another user's A-disk                        */
/*                                                                  */
/*  Enter:   LINKTO  userid vaddr diskletter                        */
/*  Example: LINKTO  ZBPD01 201   E                                 */

arg  userid vaddr diskletter .

if diskletter = "" then
    say 'Wrong number of arguments, error!'
else do
    cp link to userid 191 as vaddr r
    access  vaddr  diskletter
end
```

To run this script, the user enters a line like this: `linkto   ZBPD01 201    E`

The script starts by reading the user's input parameters through the `arg` instruction. If the correct number of input arguments appear to have been encoded, the script issues the CP `link` command to link to the other user's minidisk in this line of code. The letters `cp` ensure that the command is sent to CP for execution:

```
cp link to userid 191 as vaddr r
```

This statement issues the CMS `access` command to make the minidisk accessible:

```
access   vaddr   diskletter
```

This simple example shows how scripts issue both CMS and CP commands. But it differs from many of the scripts you'll encounter in mainframe environments in one important way. We've written this script in the same style as most of the other scripts in this book. The mainframe has its own stylistic traditions and conventions. These are not required by any means, but they tend to reflect how mainframe Rexx scripts differ from those on many other platforms. When encoding operating system commands, mainframe developers often:

❑   Encode OS commands in uppercase

❑   Enclose all hardcoded (unevaluated) portions of commands in quotes

❑   Use double-quotation marks rather than single quotation marks

❑   Encode the `address` instruction to directly send commands to the desired environment

For example, we coded the two key commands in the preceding script like this:

```
cp link to userid 191 as vaddr r
access   vaddr   diskletter
```

While individual styles vary, many mainframe professionals would code the same two lines like this:

```
ADDRESS CP "LINK" userid "191 AS" vaddr "R"
"ACCESS" vaddr diskletter
```

The `address CP` instruction sends the LINK command directly to CP for execution. The capitalization and double-quotation marks visually separate the hardcoded portions of OS commands from the substitutable variables encoded in the statements. Some mainframe professionals prefer to capitalize both commands and variables, as in this example:

```
ADDRESS CP "LINK" USERID "191 AS" VADDR "R"
"ACCESS" VADDR DISKLETTER
```

When viewing these different ways to encode these two statements, remember that the difference is mainly stylistic. The rules on how Rexx determines whether or not to send command strings to external environments, whether or not it evaluates expressions in those commands and performs variable substitution, and the uppercasing of command strings is exactly the same in mainframe Rexx as in all other standard Rexx interpreters. Hopefully, ardent mainframers will forgive the author if he remains consistent with the rest of this book and continues its lowercase, minimal quotation mark style in the upcoming examples.

Let's move on to the next sample script. This sample script shows how programs typically interact with operating system commands through the external data queue, or stack. This script issues the CMS `identify` command, from which it retrieves a line of information about the environment. The script accesses this line from the stack and displays the output to the user:

```
/*  This procedure directs output from the CMS IDENTIFY command to the   */
/*  program stack. It then reads that information by the PULL instruction */
/*  and displays it.                                                      */

'identify (stack lifo'

pull userid at node via rscsid date time zone day

say  'The virtual machine userid is:' userid
say  'The RSCS node is:' node
say  'The userid of the RSCS virtual machine is:' rscsid
say  'The date, time, and day are:' date time day
exit
```

The script issues the CMS `identify` command through this line. The `stack` option directs CMS to place the command's output on the stack:

```
'identify (stack lifo'
```

The script then retrieves a line of output from that command off the stack through a `pull` instruction:

```
pull userid at node via rscsid date time zone day
```

The script concludes by displaying the various items of information to the user.

Many other CMS commands besides the `identify` command can place their output onto the stack for script processing. Here are a few others:

CMS Command	Use
EXECIO	Uses the stack for a variety of input/output operations; can execute CP commands and collect their output into the stack
IDENTIFY	Retrieves the user ID, node name, and other environmental information
LISTFILE	Retrieves file information
NAMEFIND	Retrieves communications information from the `names` file
QUERY	Retrieves information about CMS status

Here is another example of how scripts can use the stack. In this case, the script acquires a minidisk for an interactive user and then issues the `format` command to format the disk for use. The `format` command, of course, requires several input parameters. The script provides these parameters (or subcommands) by placing them on the stack *prior* to issuing the `format` command. That command then reads these input parameters from the stack. Here is the script:

```
/*  This procedure acquires a temporary 3390 minidisk. It places    */
/*  responses to the FORMAT command on the stack prior to issuing that */
/*  command to format the new disk for use.                          */

arg  cyls  vaddr  diskletter .

if diskletter = '' then exit 10

cp define t3390 as vaddr cyls
if rc \= 0 then exit 20

queue 'YES'
queue 'TDISK'
format  vaddr  diskletter
if  rc \= 0 then exit 30
exit
```

This script first specifies the minidisk characteristics with the CP `define` command. Then, it places the words `YES` and `TDISK` onto the program stack via the `queue` instruction. So, when the subsequent `format` command asks whether to format the disk, it reads the word `YES` from the stack, and when it prompts for a minidisk label, it reads the word `TDISK` from the stack. In this way, the program issues a CMS command and provides input to the command through the program stack. It issues what are often called *subcommands* to the CMS `format` command using the stack as its communications vehicle.

The next sample script retrieves a list of files, sorts it, and presents the sorted list to the user. Here is the program:

```
/*  This procedure lists 'script' files sorted by size, smallest to   */
/*  largest.                                                          */

makebuf

'listfile  *  script  a (exec  date'

push  47  51

set  cmstype  ht
sort  cms  exec  a  sortlist  exec  a
set  cmstype  rt

type  sortlist  exec  a

dropbuf

exit 0
```

This program first creates its own stack buffer, through the `makebuf` command. This ensures that the program works only with its own memory area.

After the CMS `listfile` command retrieves a list of files, the script issues the `set cmstype ht` command to ensure that the `sort` command does not prompt the user to input the sort positions used in sorting the CMS EXEC file. Instead, the script inputs the sort positions desired through its `push` instruction. After suppressing any prompt from the `sort` command, the script resumes display output by the `set cmstype rt` command. Finally, the script displays the sorted file list on the screen, and concludes by dropping the stack buffer it created when it started.

This is our second sample script that feeds input into an external command via the stack. This table lists a few common CMS commands which accept stack input:

CMS Command	Use
EXECIO	Uses the stack for a variety of input/output operations
COPYFILE	With the `specs` option, reads stack information that specifies how the copy is to occur
FORMAT	Requires input for formatting a minidisk
SORT	Requires input information in sorting a file

The final sample script illustrates the `execio` command, the CMS command that reads and writes lines to and from disk, the stack, or other virtual devices. It is very common to see mainframe scripts use the `execio` command instead of the standard Rexx I/O functions. This script simply prompts the user to enter lines via his or her keyboard. It then writes these lines to disk, and reads and displays them back to the user. This script has little practical value, but it does illustrate how mainframe scripts often use the `execio` command as a basic vehicle for I/O. Here is the script:

```
/*  This procedure prompts the user to enter lines, then writes them to  */
/*  a disk file by EXECIO. It then reads all the lines back via EXECIO   */
/*  and displays them to the user on his or her display screen.          */
/*                                                                       */
/*  If the file already exists, the input data is appended to it.        */
/*                                                                       */
/*  Enter:   INOUT  fn      ft                                           */
/*  Example: INOUT  NEWFILE  DATA                                        */

arg  fn  ft  .

conwait                                      /* clean up the environment */
desbuf

/*  Access input lines and write them to the disk file            */

say 'Enter lines of data, enter a null line when done'
parse pull line
do while line \= ''
   'execio 1 diskw' fn ft a '(string' line
   if rc \= 0 then say 'Bad RC on file write:' rc
   parse pull line
```

```
    end

    finis  fn ft a

    /*  Read the file lines back and write them to the user's display.          */

    say 'The following is typed courtesy of EXECIO reads:'
    'execio 1 diskr' fn ft a
    do while rc = 0
        parse pull line
        say line
        'execio 1 diskr' fn ft a
    end

    if rc \= 2 then say 'Bad RC on file read:' rc

    finis fn ft a

    exit 0
```

The two new lines in this script are those that write and read a disk file via the `execio` command. Here is the write statement:

```
    'execio 1 diskw' fn ft a '(string' line
```

And, here is the statement that reads the lines from the disk:

```
    'execio 1 diskr' fn ft a
```

In both cases, notice that the script explicitly closes the file after it is done using it through the CMS `finis` command:

```
    finis  fn ft a
```

Of course, mainframe Rexx for VM supports all the standard Rexx I/O functions and instructions, such as `chars`, `charin`, `charout`, `lines`, `linein`, and `lineout`. So, why would one use the `execio` command? In a word: compatibility. Many mainframe scripts are legacy systems, which were written using `execio` and other mainframe-only commands. Some programmers like the way `execio` fits with mainframe file system concepts, such as file allocation with blocking and record length specifications. Too, TSO/E Rexx only supports `execio`, unless your system has the Stream I/O package installed. Either I/O approach works fine, so use whichever you feel best fits your needs.

This concludes the sample mainframe scripts. Please see the mainframe manuals for further information. The two IBM user's guides offer good introductory tutorials for mainframe Rexx scripting. See the *REXX/VM User's Guide, SC24-6114* and its equivalent for z/OS, the *TSO/E REXX User's Guide, SC28-1974*. The section entitled "Further Information" lists some other good sources of information on mainframe Rexx programming.

Migrating Mainframe Scripts to Other Platforms

Many mainframe shops are rehosting their programs on downsized platforms. Some of the alternatives include Windows, Linux, and Unix. The goal is usually to reduce platform costs, although sometimes the goal is to redistribute machine resources or migrate to a new platform for strategic reasons.

To port mainframe Rexx scripts, follow the recommendations in Chapter 13 on portability. Code within the Rexx standards. Avoid mainframe Rexx extensions (for instructions and internal and external functions). Avoid using nonportable interfaces for databases, screen I/O and the like. Limit the number of operating-system-specific commands scripts issue. Isolate OS-specific instructions to their own routines when you must code them, or include logic that figures out which platform the script is running on and issue the appropriate OS commands based on that.

Of course, rehosting means working with legacy code. As far as following these portability suggestions, it's often too late — the deed is done, the code already exists. The real question is: how do you port existing scripts?

The first step in porting legacy code is to identify the kinds of machine-specific Rexx code we mention here. This can be a slow, manual process, requiring skilled personnel to look through the scripts to rehost.

Sometimes it is possible to speed the process and increase its accuracy by writing a Rexx script to scan the migrating scripts. This script identifies potential problems simply by printing the lines and/or line numbers in which nonportable code occurs. The script would scan for the extended language features of mainframe Rexx listed above. These would include mainframe-specific:

- ❑ Instructions
- ❑ Functions
- ❑ External functions
- ❑ Commands
- ❑ Interfaces
- ❑ I/O (such as the EXECIO command)
- ❑ "Not" symbol ¬
- ❑ Coding that depends on the EBCDIC character encoding scheme
- ❑ The Double-Byte Character Set

Computer-assisted rehosting through a scanning script can be faster and more accurate than manual script rewrites. Different Rexx interpreters offer different degrees of compatibility with mainframe Rexx. If you are rehosting mainframe scripts, pick an interpreter that has extensions that support mainframe Rexx features. Whatever approach you take, the scope of the porting effort ultimately depends on the degree to which the scripts employ mainframe-only Rexx features.

Applying Your Rexx Skills to Other Platforms

Another aspect of migrating to a new platform concerns how much training personnel require to make the change. Rexx presents a major benefit. Mainframe professionals almost always know Rexx or are familiar with it. The strong Rexx standard and the language's ease of use give mainframers a great tool that they can immediately use in their new environment. Instead of learning an entirely new language that mainframers most likely do not use (like Perl, the Unix shell languages, Python, or Tcl/Tk), Rexx presents a point of commonality between the mainframe and the new platform. Leveraging Rexx lessens training needs and reduces the impact of migrating to the new environment. Mainframers who know Rexx can be instantly productive on any new platform simply by installing and using free Rexx.

"Skills portability" works in both directions. Few colleges today teach their computer science students about mainframes. Rexx presents a point of commonality whereby those who know it on Windows or Linux also know the language of mainframe scripting. Knowing how to script Rexx on Windows or Linux provides an immediately usable mainframe skill and provides an "access point" to the mainframe environment for these individuals.

Further Information

There are many good sources of additional information on mainframe Rexx scripting. We've already mentioned the key IBM manuals in this chapter. Appendix A tells where you can download these manuals at no cost from IBM's Web site. The appendix also lists some online sources for further information on mainframe Rexx, including Web-based discussion groups where you can post questions and interact with peers.

Most mainframe Rexx books were published years ago, yet they are still quite useful today. They can easily be purchased through an online used book site, such as www.amazon.com. Useful books include those by authors Gabe Goldberg and Gabriel Gargiulo, among others. Some good titles to look for include *The Rexx Handbook* (G. Goldberg, McGraw-Hill, ISBN 0070236828), *REXX in the TSO Environment* (G. Gargiulo, QED, ISBN 0-89435-354-3), *Rexx: Advanced Techniques for Programmers* (P. Kiesel, McGraw-Hill, ISBN 0070346003), and *REXX Tools and Techniques* (B. Nirmal, QED, ISBN 0894354175).

Summary

This chapter summarizes some of the extended features of IBM mainframe Rexx. The goal was to give you background in case you need to:

❑ Transfer your skills across mainframe and other platforms

❑ Port or rehost scripts between mainframes and other platforms

❑ Assess the differences between free and mainframe Rexx implementations

❑ Assess the differences between mainframe Rexx and the ANSI Rexx standard

The chapter concentrates on VM and OS TSO/E Rexx. If you are interested in VSE Rexx, please see the resources listed in Appendix A.

This chapter also describes a few of the many interfaces with which Rexx interacts in the mainframe environment. IBM has long sought to leverage Rexx as its scripting language across all its mainframe tools and interfaces. On mainframes Rexx is truly a universal language that interfaces to all tools and products.

Test Your Understanding

1. What language standards does mainframe Rexx meet? What manual should you obtain if you want to know the details of IBM's SAA command procedure language specification?

2. What extra instructions does IBM mainframe Rexx add over the ANSI-1996 standard? What functions does it add? What features of the ANSI-1996 standard are missing from mainframe Rexx?

3. What is the Double-Byte Character Set, and why would you use it? Does mainframe Rexx support DBCS?

4. What are the extensions mainframe Rexx brings to file I/O? What functions support this?

5. What are CMS *immediate commands*, and how are they used when running scripts?

6. What are mainframe *function packages*, and how are they used from within scripts?

7. What is the advantage to a Rexx compiler? When do you typically compile a Rexx script?

8. What should you encode as the first line of a mainframe Rexx script?

9. What are the VM file types for Rexx scripts?

30

NetRexx

Overview

NetRexx is an object-oriented Rexx-like language designed to bring the ease of use associated with Rexx to the Java environment. Like Java, it can be used to create *applets*, scripts that run within a Web browser, and *applications*, programs run from the command line. It also brings Rexx to the world of server-side Java, in the form of *servlet programming* and dynamic *Java Server Pages*. You can even write *Java Beans* in NetRexx, components that fit into Java's reusable component architecture.

NetRexx scripts compile into Java byte code. They seamlessly use Java classes and create classes that can be used by either Java or NetRexx programs. NetRexx offers an alternative language in the Java environment, one that can be intermixed in any manner and to any degree with Java programs. The goal is to bring the ease of use, maintainability, and reliability of Rexx to the Java environment.

NetRexx is not a superset of classic Rexx. In this it differs from object-oriented Rexx interpreters like Kilowatt Software's roo! and the Rexx Language Association's Open Object Rexx. But NetRexx is similar enough to classic Rexx that programmers can pick it up quickly. To port classic Rexx scripts to NetRexx, use a utility like *Rexx2Nrx*, the free classic Rexx to NetRexx automated conversion tool.

This chapter briefly summarizes the purpose and highlights of the NetRexx language.

Why NetRexx?

NetRexx is very different in its goals as opposed to either classic or object-oriented Rexx interpreters. Let's look at the language's key advantages:

- ❑ *Ease of use and productivity* — NetRexx brings the ease of use and productivity associated with Rexx to the Java environment. NetRexx is clear, powerful, and simple.

❑ *Java integration*—NetRexx seamlessly integrates into the Java environment. NetRexx scripts use Java classes and can be used to create classes used by Java programs. You can write Java Beans in NetRexx. NetRexx also supports server-side development.

❑ *Portability*—Any platform that runs Java runs NetRexx. Like Java, NetRexx provides machine-independence through the Java Virtual Machine, or JVM.

❑ *Scripting*—NetRexx supports traditional scripting—quick, low-overhead coding—in Java environments. NetRexx automatically creates a class with a main method so that you can code simple scripts without overhead.

❑ *The Java alternative*—NetRexx fits into the Java environment and provides a fully compatible language alternative. NetRexx requires fewer keystrokes than Java and eliminates Java's C-heritage syntax. NetRexx can generate formatted Java code, including original commentary, if desired.

❑ *Easy migration*—Whether you're migrating classic Rexx scripts or transferring your skills, NetRexx eases migration into the Java environment.

❑ *Flexibility*—The NetRexx translator can be used as a compiler or an interpreter. As an interpreter, it allows NetRexx programs to run without needing a compiler or generating .class files. NetRexx programs can be both compiled and interpreted in just one command. This is easy to do and machine-efficient.

Do You Have to Know Java to Use NetRexx?

To install NetRexx, the need for Java background is minimal. It's quite simple to download and install Java on almost any machine, whether or not you know Java. The process is similar to that of any other download and install. The package contains complete instructions on how to install NetRexx in the Java environment for most major operating systems.

NetRexx runs in the Java environment and NetRexx programs compile into Java byte code. It helps to know the role of components like the Java Runtime Environment, or JRE, and the Java Software Development Kit, or SDK. Java should be installed on the machine in order for NetRexx to compile and run.

The big question is: are you familiar with the *Java class libraries*? These are the modules of reusable code that come with Java and provide its power. Java and NetRexx are both object-oriented programming languages. NetRexx can be used as a simple scripting language, but leveraging the true power of the product means becoming familiar with the reusable code supplied in the Java class libraries. NetRexx uses Java class libraries; it does not come with its own or supply alternatives.

For example, if you want to create a NetRexx script with a graphical user interface, you would typically use the prebuilt components of the Java class library. NetRexx does not provide its own GUI; it allows you to leverage what Java already supplies.

Java classes you might use in NetRexx scripts include those for I/O, utilities, GUIs, images, applets, TCP/IP connections, and wrappers. Java's collection classes are especially useful. Similar in function and purpose to the collection classes of the object-oriented Rexx interpreters, these provide for lists, maps, iterators, sorting and searching algorithms, and the like.

NetRexx is object-oriented. You need to know or learn object-oriented programming, just as you need to learn about the available class libraries. If you are comfortable with object-oriented programming (OOP) from roo! or Open Object Rexx, that's great. Experience with any other object-oriented programming language also provides a good background. The point is that NetRexx scripting means object-oriented programming.

If you know classic Rexx, NetRexx is a good vehicle by which to learn about the Java environment and pick up object-oriented programming. For example, if you work on mainframes and your site adopts Java, NetRexx presents a nice vehicle by which you can easily segue into the new environment and OOP. NetRexx is an easier entry point into the Java environment than Java, due to its simpler syntax and likeness to classic Rexx.

Downloading and Installation

To use NetRexx, you must first install Java on your computer. Java is free and downloadable from www.javasoft.com or from IBM's Java pages at www.ibm.com/java/jdk/download/index.html. You need the Java Runtime Environment, or JRE, if you just want to run NetRexx programs. If you want to compile and develop them, you'll need the software development toolkit. This toolkit is variously referred to as the Java Software Development Toolkit, or SDK, or as the Java Development Toolkit, or JDK. We recommend installing the toolkit, if space permits. The install is simple, and you'll have all the components you might want.

NetRexx will run on Java 1.1.2 or later, with 1.2 or above recommended. If Java is already installed on your machine, this statement confirms that by displaying the product version:

```
java  -version
```

NetRexx also requires an operating system that supports long filenames.

After installing and verifying the JRE or its SDK, download and install NetRexx. NetRexx is freely downloadable from IBM Corporation's Web site at www2.hursley.ibm.com/netrexx. Or just access www.ibm.com and search for keyword NetRexx.

The download includes a file containing the license terms you agree to by using NetRexx. It also contains a file named something like read.me.first that gives simple installation instructions. The complete *NetRexx User's Guide* is also bundled with it. It contains detailed installation instructions for all operating systems and explains everything you need to know about installing NetRexx. The included *NetRexx Language Supplement* provides further details on these topics.

In a nutshell, the steps for installing NetRexx are:

1. Decompress the NetRexx download file into an appropriate directory

2. Make the NetRexx translator visible to the Java Virtual Machine, or JVM. An easy way to do this is to copy the `NetRexx\lib\NetRexxC.jar` file to the JVM library subdirectory. This JVM directory will be underneath the Java install directory, and its name will end like this: `. . . jre\lib\ext`.

3. Make the file containing the `javac` compiler visible to the JVM. The file in which the `javac` compiler resides is under the Java install directory, and its name typically ends with: `. . . \lib\tools.jar`. Either copy this file to the Java installation subdirectory ending with: `. . . . jre\lib\ext`, or add the fully qualified filename to Java's `CLASSPATH` environmental variable.

4. Update the `PATH` variable to include the `\NetRexx\bin` directory.

5. Test the install by running these commands exactly as given:

```
java  COM.ibm.netrexx.process.NetRexxC  hello
java  hello
```

The first command runs the NetRexx compiler, which translates the NetRexx test script named `hello.nrx` into a Java program `hello.java`. Then the Java compiler javac automatically compiles the Java program into the binary class file named `hello.class`. The second command runs the program in the `hello.class` file, which displays: `hello world!`

The *NetRexx User's Guide* that downloads with NetRexx is very thorough and will resolve any issues should any arise during installation and testing.

Ways to Run NetRexx Programs

Once the environment is completely set up, there are several ways you can translate and run NetRexx scripts. For example, you can perform the script-translation and execution operations as separate steps, or you can run translate, compile, and run a NetRexx script in a single command. To get an understanding of what the NetRexx translator does, let's look at the multi-step approach first. From the operating system's command line, perform these actions:

1. Create a source file containing the NetRexx script (such as `hello.nrx`), and run the NetRexx translator against the NetRexx source script:

```
NetRexxC  hello
```

or

```
nrc  hello
```

2. Execute the program:

```
java  hello
```

As an alternative approach, here is how to translate, compile, and run a NetRexx source script in a single command:

```
nrc  -run  hello
```

Keep in mind that Java development is case-sensitive. So this statement:

```
nrc  -run  HELLO
```

is not the same as:

```
nrc  -run  hello
```

This might come as a surprise to developers used to the Windows operating system and classic Rexx. Neither of these environments recognizes case differences.

Figure 30-1 pictorially summarizes the multi-step process of converting a NetRexx source script into a runable module.

Developing and Running NetRexx Scripts

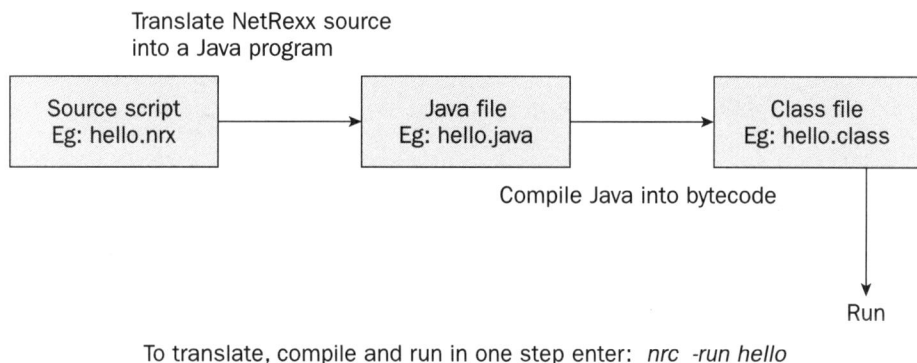

Translate NetRexx source
into a Java program

| Source script
Eg: hello.nrx | → | Java file
Eg: hello.java | → | Class file
Eg: hello.class |

Compile Java into bytecode

Run

To translate, compile and run in one step enter: *nrc -run hello*

Figure 30-1

Features

This section describes ways in which NetRexx differs from classic Rexx. This goal is to give you an idea of what NetRexx offers and how it extends classic Rexx into the world of JVM-based, object-oriented programming.

Figure 30-2 summarizes what NetRexx adds beyond classic procedural Rexx and indicates some key differences between the two.

NetRexx Goes Beyond Classic Rexx...

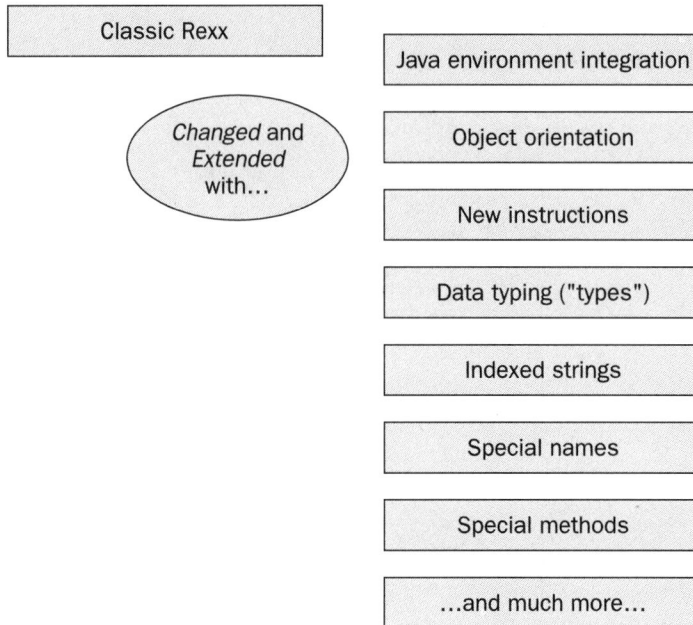

```
┌─────────────────────┐
│    Classic Rexx     │        ┌──────────────────────────────┐
└─────────────────────┘        │ Java environment integration │
                               └──────────────────────────────┘
        ╭───────────╮
       ╱  Changed and ╲        ┌──────────────────────────────┐
      │   Extended     │       │      Object orientation       │
       ╲   with...    ╱        └──────────────────────────────┘
        ╰───────────╯
                               ┌──────────────────────────────┐
                               │       New instructions        │
                               └──────────────────────────────┘

                               ┌──────────────────────────────┐
                               │    Data typing ("types")      │
                               └──────────────────────────────┘

                               ┌──────────────────────────────┐
                               │       Indexed strings         │
                               └──────────────────────────────┘

                               ┌──────────────────────────────┐
                               │        Special names          │
                               └──────────────────────────────┘

                               ┌──────────────────────────────┐
                               │       Special methods         │
                               └──────────────────────────────┘

                               ┌──────────────────────────────┐
                               │     ...and much more...        │
                               └──────────────────────────────┘
```

Figure 30-2

Let's discuss how NetRexx differs from classic Rexx in detail. Remember that NetRexx is not a superset of classic Rexx, but rather an entirely different, "Rexx-like" language that goes beyond standard Rexx and expands it into the world of Java.

First, NetRexx supports all object-oriented programming principles:

❑   Inheritance

❑   Abstraction

❑   Encapsulation

❑   Polymorphism

Methods are named routines or groups of instructions. They are always grouped into *classes*. Classes can be grouped into class libraries called *packages*. The variable definitions within classes are called *properties*.

The name and list of arguments for invoking each method is its *signature*. Overload operators by invoking the same method with different signatures. This ability to execute different code when referring to the same method name is also referred to as *polymorphism*.

NetRexx adds instructions for object-oriented programming. It also adds new instructions to provide "convenience features" beyond what's in classic Rexx. The new or enhanced instructions include:

New or Enhanced Instruction	Use
class	Defines a class
do	Enhanced with several new keywords:
	protect — gives the do loop exclusive access to an object
	catch and finally — Java-style exception handling
import	Simplifies references when using classes from other packages.
loop	The new instruction for looping. It includes catch and finally for Java-style exception handling.
method	Defines a method within a class.
options	New options are introduced, including one for faster binary arithmetic.
package	Defines the package to which class(es) belong.
properties	Defines the attributes of *property* variables, variables defined within classes.
select	Enhanced with several new keywords:
	protect — gives the construct exclusive access to an object
	catch and finally — Java-style exception handling
trace	Enhanced for OOP by the methods keyword.

All NetRexx values have associated *types*. For example, NetRexx strings are of type *Rexx*, which defines string properties and the methods that apply to them. NetRexx provides built-in methods for *Rexx* strings, which largely correspond to the functions of classic Rexx. NetRexx implementations may also provide *primitive types* such as boolean, char, byte, short, int, long, float, and double, and *dimensioned types*, or arrays. NetRexx automates *type conversions* whenever necessary in order to simplify programming.

In its addition of data typing, NetRexx departs from classic Rexx in order to be more Java-oriented. NetRexx is similar to Java in other ways, too. For example, array sizes must be declared in advance, and a new feature called the *indexed string* supports the associative array of classic Rexx. And NetRexx's exception handling is modeled on the Java catch . . . finally construct. Let's continue with the language description, and you'll discover other similarities between NetRexx and Java, as well.

Indexed strings are NetRexx strings by which subvalues are identified by an index string. This example shows how indexed strings work:

```
pname = 'unknown'              -- set a default value for the indexed string
pname['Monica'] = 'Geller'
shortn = 'Monica'
say pname[shortn]              -- displays:  Geller
say pname['Ross']             -- displays:  unknown
```

Multiple indexes create a hierarchy of strings. This can be used to create associative arrays or dictionary structures. Multiple indexes are referred to using comma notation:

```
valu = 'null'                  -- initialize
valu['a', 'b'] = 'Hi'         -- set the value of a multiple indexed variable
say valu['a', 'b']            -- displays:  Hi
valu_2 = valu['a']            -- set the value of another variable
say valu_2['b']               -- displays:  Hi
```

Arrays are tables of fixed size that must be defined before use. Arrays may index elements of any type, and the elements are considered ordered. Arrays can be single or multidimensioned. Elements are referenced by a bracket notation similar to that of indexed strings. Here's sample code that defines an array, then refers to elements within it:

```
my_array = int[5,10]   -- defines a 5 by 10 array of INT type objects
my_array[2,3] = 15     -- sets the value in array position '2, 3'
subb = my_array[2,3]   -- sets variable SUBB to the value of array position '2, 3'
```

NetRexx includes a number of *special names* and *special methods* for commonly used concepts. For example, the ask special name reads a line from the user and returns it to the script as a string of type *Rexx*. Here are the special names:

Special Name	Use
ask	Reads a line from the default input stream and returns it as a string of type *Rexx* (also called a *NetRexx string*)
digits	Returns the current setting of numeric digits as a NetRexx string
form	Returns the current setting of numeric form as a NetRexx string
length	Returns an array's length (the number of elements)
null	Returns the null value (used in assignments and comparisons)
source	Returns a NetRexx string that identifies the source of the current class
super	Used to invoke a method or property overridden in the current class

Special Name	Use
this	Returns a reference to the current object
trace	Returns the current setting as a NetRexx string
version	Returns the NetRexx language version as a NetRexx string

The special methods are used to refer to particular objects:

Special Method	Use
super	Constructor of the superclass
this	Constructor of the current class

NetRexx introduces back-to-back dashes for comments (--), and the continuation character for coding across lines is the single dash (-). By "dash" we mean the same character called a hyphen.

Sample Programs

Serious NetRexx scripting is beyond the scope of this book because it explores Java classes and methods more deeply than appropriate here. Nevertheless, here are a two very simple sample scripts. These will at least help you get started with NetRexx scripting. The first example shows how to create a simple NetRexx application, while the second illustrates a NetRexx applet.

The script we named Squared simply prompts the user to enter numbers, which the script squares and displays. Here is a sample interaction which prepares and runs the `squared.nrx` script:

```
c:\j2skd1.4.2_04\bin\nrc -run squared
NetRexx portable processor, version 2.02
Copyright (c) IBM Corporation, 2001. All rights reserved.
Program squared.nrx
Compilation of 'squared.nrx' successful
Running squared...
Please enter a number to square...
2
4
Please enter a number to square...
2.3
5.29
Please enter a number to square...
exit
```

The following command translates, compiles, and runs the `squared.nrx` script.

```
nrc -run squared
```

Chapter 30

The first line the script displays is its prompt:

```
Please enter a number to square...
```

The script continues prompting the user and displaying the squares of the numbers he or she enters until the user enters the keyword:

```
exit
```

Here is the code of the script:

```
/***************************************************************/
/* NetRexx - squared                                           */
/*                                                             */
/* Squares any number the user enters                          */
/***************************************************************/

loop label square_it forever
  say 'Please enter a number to square...'
  the_number = ask
  select
    when the_number.datatype('n') then say the_number * the_number
    when the_number = 'EXIT'        then leave square_it
    otherwise say 'Please enter a number!'
  end
end square_it
```

The first line of the script illustrates the new NetRexx loop instruction:

```
loop label square_it forever
```

loop is very similar to the do instruction in classic Rexx. It has many of the same keywords including while, until, for, to, by, and forever. It also has some new keywords, such as catch and finally, which implement Java-like error catching.

loop refers to a label name, which matches the label on the matching end keyword. In this code, the label's name is square_it:

```
loop label square_it forever
  .
  .
  .
end square_it
```

The prompt in this script employs the new ask *special name*. ask reads a line from the default input stream and returns it as a string of type *Rexx* (also called a *NetRexx string*):

```
say 'Please enter a number to square...'
the_number = ask
```

As `the_number` is an instance of the NetRexx string object, it has many methods that correspond to the string-related built-in functions of classic Rexx, such as the `dataype` function. This statement invokes the `datatype` method on `the_number` to check if `the_number` is numeric, and squares the value if so:

```
when the_number.datatype('n') then say the_number * the_number
```

This statement compares the NetRexx string to a literal value and terminates the script when the user inputs the string `exit`:

```
when the_number = 'EXIT'      then leave square_it
```

This simple script shows that NetRexx includes new instructions that are incompatible with classic Rexx, yet are quite as simple to use. NetRexx retains the spirit of classic Rexx, but it is not upwardly compatible. To port classic Rexx scripts to NetRexx, use a utility like *Rexx2Nrx*, the free classic Rexx to NetRexx automated conversion tool.

A simple sample applet

Java *applications* are complete programs run from the command line, such as the preceding sample script. NetRexx is also be used to write Java *applets*, scripts which run within Java-enabled browsers. An applet can run within Microsoft's Internet Explorer, for example.

Here is the code of a very simple NetRexx applet. This script simply displays the universal greeting of cartoon character Fred Flintstone within an Internet Explorer (IE) browser panel:

```
Yah-bah-dah-bah-DOOO!
```

To create the applet, first write the script's source code and save it in the file `Yaba.nrx`:

```
/****************************************************************/
/* NetRexx - Yaba                                               */
/*                                                              */
/* The simplest possible Applet: Fred Flintstone says "hi!"  */
/****************************************************************/

class Yaba extends Applet
   method init
      resize(250, 50)

   method paint(g=Graphics)
      g.drawString("Yah-bah-dah-bah-DOOO!", 50, 30)
```

This script uses the `init` and `paint` methods of the Applet class. These are, of course, provided by Java. They are not part of NetRexx. The NetRexx script uses Java classes and Java methods.

Next, create the Web page (the HTML file) that contains the tag that will invoke the applet we've named Yaba. Name the file `Yaba.html` and place this code in it:

```
<applet code="Yaba.class" width=250 height=50>
</applet>
```

This code simply runs the Yaba script from within the browser.

Now you must create a `.class` file from the `Yaba.nrx` source script. Do this by invoking the NetRexx translator:

```
nrc Yaba
```

This command outputs the CLASS file named `Yaba.class`.

Once you have created the NetRexx source for the applet and have developed the HTML code of the Web page, setup is complete. Now you can run the NetRexx applet. Under Windows, for example, you would double-click on the `Yaba.html` file. This invokes Internet Explorer, which recognizes the applet tag reference to the `Yaba.class` file, and runs this applet within the browser. The result is that Internet Explorer displays the Flintstone greeting in the top-left corner of the Web page:

```
Yah-bah-dah-bah-DOOO!
```

This simple script shows that most NetRexx scripts rely on the Java class library for their power. NetRexx is used for creating Java applets as well as Java applications. NetRexx can also be used to create Java Beans. And NetRexx can be used for server-side programming as well. All NetRexx scripts and components can be intermixed and used with Java code in any desired manner. The high degree of integration between NetRexx and Java is due to the flexibility of the NetRexx translator, which translates NetRexx source scripts into Java programs and `.class` files.

Summary

This chapter describes the purpose and features of NetRexx, a free Rexx-like language for developing applications, applets, servlets, and Java Beans that run in Java environments. Rely on NetRexx to any degree you like in intermixing its classes with those of Java. Invoke Java class libraries from NetRexx scripts, and write class libraries and Java Beans in NetRexx. NetRexx fully integrates into the Java environment and offers a 100 percent compatible language alternative.

This chapter described how to download and install NetRexx. Then we looked at the uses of the NetRexx translator and demonstrated a couple ways it can be invoked to translate and run NetRexx scripts. After a quick overview of various NetRexx features, we explored two very simple scripts. The first was a sample *application*, a script that would normally be run from the operating system's command line. This script just squared a number, but it did illustrate how NetRexx varies from classic Rexx in many small ways. For example, the script used the NetRexx `loop` instruction and the special name `ask`. The second script was a minimal *applet*, a script designed to run within a Java-enabled browser. While very simple, the script demonstrated the ability to use Java classes and methods from within NetRexx scripts. It also showed how to run a NetRexx script from within a browser.

The major benefit of NetRexx is that it makes available Rexx's ease of use and high productivity in Java environments. Those who know Rexx can learn NetRexx quickly. NetRexx eases the transition into the Java universe and makes you more productive once you get there.

Test Your Understanding

1. Why use NetRexx instead of Java? What are its advantages? Can you intermix NetRexx and Java classes within a single application?

2. What are the NetRexx translator's interpreter and compiler functions? Why is it useful to have both? Can you compile and run a NetRexx script in one command? Is it always necessary to have the Java Virtual Machine available to run NetRexx scripts?

3. Are NetRexx scripts portable? What is required to run them on different machines?

4. What are indexed strings and arrays? Describe how they differ. If you wanted to define the equivalent of an Open Object Rexx dictionary collection class in NetRexx, how could you do it?

5. How does NetRexx capitalize on the Java class library? Where can you learn what classes and methods are available in that library?

6. What are the roles of files with these extensions: `*.nrx`, `*.java`, `*.class`.

7. What are special names and special methods?

8. How do you migrate classic Rexx scripts to NetRexx?

Part III

A

Resources

User Groups

The primary user group that addresses Rexx in all its forms is the Rexx Language Association. The Rexx LA is an international organization with worldwide membership and is open to everyone. The Rexx LA home page is at www.rexxla.org. The home page provides a wealth of information on the Rexx language, including standards, FAQs, contacts, the newsletter, and the annual Rexx symposium. It also has many links to the home pages of various Rexx interpreters, tools, packages, books, technical articles, and other informational resources. The Rexx Language Association supports a mailing list, which is a mechanism to broadcast questions and view answers from Rexx users worldwide.

The IBM users group SHARE also covers Rexx scripting and related topics. Find it at www.share.org. Branches of SHARE/GUIDE in Europe also cover Rexx.

Web Forums

Rexx supports several active forums. These allow you to post any questions you might have and also learn from the postings of others.

To access the Rexx newsgroup forum at comp.lang.rexx through a Web browser, go through the site *DBForums* at www.dbforums.com/f135. You can also access the same forum by pointing your Web browser to the *Code Comments* community at www.codecomments.com/Rexx. This is one of the most active online Rexx communities covering all aspects of the language.

Another Rexx language forum is accessible through the Talkabout Network at www.talkaboutprogramming.com/group/comp.lang.rexx/. Or just access the Talkabout Network at www.talkaboutprogramming.com and search for the keyword Rexx.

Questions may be posted at the Regina Rexx language project pages at SourceForge.net at http://sourceforge.net/forum/?group_id=28102. Or access this forum from the main page for Regina Rexx at SourceForge at http://sourceforge.net/projects/regina-rexx/.

There are several other Rexx forums as well. They include:

- ❏ The Reginald Rexx Forum is at `http://g.yi.org/forum/list.php?11`.

- ❏ The Rexx for Palm OS Forum is at `www.jaxo.com/rexx/` or `www.jaxo.com`.

- ❏ Tek-Tips Rexx Forum is at `www.tek-tips.com/threadminder.cfm?pid=277` or just access their home page at `www.tek-tips.com` and search on the keyword `Rexx`.

- ❏ Several mainframe forums have discussion threads that cover Rexx. These include MVS Help at `www.mvshelp.com`, the MVS Forums at `www.mvsforums.com/index.html`, the WAVV Forum at `http://wavv.org/`, and Search390 at `www.search390.com`.

- ❏ For French speakers, a good Rexx forum is at `www.moteurprog.com/`, search on the keyword `Rexx`.

- ❏ For German speakers, your forum is at `http://f1933.siteboard.de`.

- ❏ There are forums at "Google Groups" for English, German, Russian, and Japanese speakers. Find Google Groups at `www.google.com`.

- ❏ Finally, for the dedicated band of Amiga followers still out there, the Amiga Forum often discusses ARexx scripting at `http://os.amiga.com/forums`. You might also check out the site for the open source AROS operating system at `www.aros.org`.

The Rexx Standards

The Rexx Language, second edition, by Michael Cowlishaw (Prentice-Hall, 1990) is known as TRL-2, and it defines the TRL-2 standard. The first edition is known as TRL-1, and it defines the TRL-1 standard.

The ANSI standard is entitled *Programming Language Rexx Standard X3.274-1996*, and is from the American National Standards Institute (X3J18 Technical Committee). It is available in draft form as a free download from the Rexx Language Association at `www.rexxla.org/Standards/ansi.html`. The final document is available for purchase from ANSI at their Web site `www.ansi.org`.

IBM's *Systems Application Architecture* or *SAA* defines common tools and interfaces across all IBM operating systems. The IBM SAA manual *SAA Common Programming Interface REXX Level 2 Reference, SC24-5549* is useful to developers who want to know the precise differences between different IBM Rexx implementations on different platforms. Download the manual for free from IBM Corporation. Go to `www.ibm.com` and search on the keyword `SC24-5549`. Or search for the keywords `IBM Publications Center` to access the Web site from which any IBM manuals may be freely downloaded.

Rexx Home Page at IBM

The Rexx Web site maintained by IBM has numerous Rexx links. It is an excellent place to mine for information about all aspects of the language on all platforms. Free downloads for NetRexx and Mod_Rexx are available from there as well.

The Rexx home page is located at www-306.ibm.com/software/awdtools/rexx/language/index. html. The home page for information on IBM Rexx interpreters and products is located at www-306.ibm. com/software/awdtools/rexx. If Web addresses change, just access www.ibm.com and search on the keyword Rexx.

Downloading IBM Rexx Manuals

The manuals for IBM Rexx on various platforms can be downloaded as Adobe *.pdf files at no cost from IBM Corporation. The easiest way to locate any particular manual is to go to www.ibm.com and search on the manual number. For example, to find the *REXX/VM User's Guide*, search on its manual number SC24-5962.

You'll find a full list of all IBM Rexx manuals and their manual numbers at www-306.ibm.com/ software/awdtools/rexx/library/index.html. This list covers all platforms including VM, OS, VSE, AIX, Windows, Linux, CICS, PC-DOS, and OS/2.

You can also search for and download manuals at the IBM Publications Center at www.elink.ibmlink. ibm.com/public/applications/publications/cgibin/pbi.cgi. Or, find the Publications Center by accessing www.ibm.com and searching on the keywords Publications Center. Your searches can be by keywords or the IBM manual number (these typically begin with the letters SC).

Rexx Books

Several of the Web sites mentioned in this appendix list Rexx books, including:

- ❏   IBM Rexx Family main Books page at: www-306.ibm.com/software/awdtools/rexx/library/published.html

- ❏   IBM Rexx Language main page at www-06.ibm.com/software/awdtools/rexx/language

- ❏   The Rexx Language Association's Links page at www.rexxla.org/Links/links.html

- ❏   Amazon's used book area. Search under the keyword Rexx

One motive for writing this book is that other Rexx books predate the free and open-source software movement. Most do not cover many of the interpreters, interfaces, and tools Rexx developers use today. Nevertheless, these books can be quite useful if you are interested in their specific topics, especially since the Rexx standards have remained stable for many years. These Rexx books cover such topics as mainframe programming, OS/2 programming, Amiga programming, or object-oriented scripting under early Windows or OS/2. Most can be had very inexpensively on Web sites that sell used books, such as www.amazon.com.

B

Instructions

This appendix provides a reference to all Rexx instructions, as defined by the ANSI-1996 standard. It also points out the major differences in the instructions between the ANSI-1996 standard and the earlier standard defined by TRL-2. This appendix is intended as a quick reference guide for developers, so please see the full ANSI-1996 and TRL-2 standards if more detailed information is required. Appendix A tells where to obtain the two standards.

Each entry is in this appendix identified by the instruction name. Entries contain the template for the instruction, which shows its operands, if any. The template is followed by a description of the instruction and its use, as well as an explanation of the operands. Coding examples show how to code each instruction.

In reading the instruction formats, operands that may optionally be encoded are surrounded by brackets ([ ]). The "or" bar (|) represents situations where you should encode either one set of operands or the other. Let's look at the address instruction template as an example:

```
ADDRESS    | environment  [ command ]   |
           | [ VALUE ]  expression       |
```

Brackets surround the command operand, so this means that its encoding on the instruction is optional. The same pertains to the VALUE keyword. Note that as a hardcoded keyword, VALUE appears in capital letters. The "or" bars vertically surround each of the two lines above, so you would code either one group of operands or the other. In this example, you would choose either one of these two basic formats in which to encode the address instruction:

```
ADDRESS    environment  [ command ]
ADDRESS    VALUE  expression
```

ADDRESS

```
ADDRESS    | environment  [ command ]   |
           | [ VALUE ]  expression       |
```

address directs commands to the proper external environments for execution.

An `address` instruction with both `environment` and `command` coded specifies to which external `environment` that `command` is sent. An `address` instruction with an `environment` but no `command` specifies the default external environment for subsequent commands. An `address` instruction with neither `environment` nor `command` coded toggles the target `environment` between the last two specified or used.

The `value` format defines the target `environment` by way of the resolved `expression` for subsequent commands. `value` and `command` cannot be coded in the same statement. The purpose of the `value` format is to provide for programmability in determining the target environment for subsequent commands.

The environments that may be specified for command execution are system-dependent. You may use the `address()` function to find out what the current `environment` is.

Example

```
say address()          /* displays the current command environment   */
address system dir     /* send DIR command to the SYSTEM environment  */
address command        /* send all subsequent commands to the COMMAND
                                                        environment    */
'dir'                  /* 'dir' is sent to the COMMAND environment     */
```

The ANSI-1996 standard added a new format for the `address` instruction. Here is the template for this new format:

```
ADDRESS     |   [ environment ]   [ command ]   [ redirection ] ]     |
            |   [ [ VALUE ]   expression   [ redirection ] ]          |

redirection is:    WITH INPUT     input_redirection
    and/or:        WITH OUTPUT    output_redirection
    and/or:        WITH  ERROR    output_rediection

input_redirection   is: [ NORMAL   |   STREAM   |   STEM  ]   symbol
output_redirection  is: [ APPEND   |   REPLACE ]
      plus a destination:     [ NORMAL   |   STREAM   |   STEM ]   symbol
```

Optional extensions for the ANSI standard are `fifo` and `lifo` for the `with input`, `with output` and `with error` options.

Any, all or none of the three clauses `with input`, `with output`, and `with error` may be specified. They may be specified in any order. `append` or `replace` specify whether an `output` or `error` file will be appended to or over-written. `replace` is the default.

`stream` or `stem` specify whether an I/O stream or compound variable stem (an array) will provide the `input` or be written to as `output` or `error`. When using an array, element 0 should state the number of elements for `input`. Element 0 tells how many lines of output there are for `output` or `error`.

Example

```
/* First, send an operating system SORT command to the SYSTEM environment.
   Use file sortin.txt for input with output going to file sortout.txt. */
address  SYSTEM  sort  WITH  INPUT  STREAM  'sortin.txt'  ,
```

```
                    OUTPUT STREAM  'sortout.txt'

  /* Now send the SORT command to the SYSTEM environment,
       but use arrays for input and output. Specify both arrays as compound
       variable stems (include the period after the array name). Before issuing
       the command, you must set Element 0 in the input array to the number
       of items in the input array. After the command, the number of elements
       in the output array will be in Element 0 of that array.
  */
  in_array.0 = 10            /* 10 items are in the input array called in_array.  */
                             /* They are in array positions in_array.1 thru .10.  */
  address  SYSTEM  sort  WITH  INPUT   STEM   in_array. ,
                              OUTPUT  STEM   sortout.
  say 'Number of output elements:'  sortout.0
```

ARG

```
. ARG  [ template ]
```

This instruction parses arguments in the template in the same manner as: `parse upper arg [ template ]`.

`arg` automatically translates all input arguments to uppercase.

Example

```
/* function invoked by:  testsub('a',3,'c')    */

arg  string_1, number_1, string_2

/* string_1 contains 'A',  number_1 contains '3', string_2 contains 'C' */
```

CALL

```
         | name [ expression ]   [, [ expression ] ] ...  |
  CALL   | ON condition  [ NAME trapname  ]               |
         | OFF condition                                  |
```

`call` either invokes a routine or enables an error condition. If `on` is specified, `call` enables the error condition and optionally specifies the `name` of the exception routine that will be invoked when it is raised. The `condition` must be one of `error`, `failure`, `halt`, and `notready`. Specifying `off` disables an error condition.

If neither `on` nor `off` is specified, `call` invokes an internal, built-in or external routine. Coding the routine name in quotes prevents searching for an internal routine. Zero, one, or more expression arguments may be passed to the routine.

If the routine returns a result, the special variable `result` is set to that value. Otherwise `result` is set to uninitialized.

537

Example

```
call on  error              /* enables ERROR trap with routine of ERROR:          */
call on  error   name  error_handler /* enables ERROR to ERROR_HANDLER:            */
call off error              /* dis-ables ERROR trap                               */

call my_routine  parm_1 , parm_2     /* call routine my_routine with 2 parameters*/
                                     /* if a result was returned, display it...  */
if  result  <>  'RESULT'  then say 'The returned result was:'  result
```

DO

```
DO   [ repetitor ]  [ conditional ]
        [ instruction_list ]
END  [ symbol ]

repetitor is:  symbol  = expression_i  [ TO expression_t ]
                             [ BY expression_b ]  [ FOR expression_f ]
                             expression_r
                             FOREVER

condition is:  WHILE expression_w
               UNTIL expression_u
```

The do-end instruction groups multiple instructions together and executes them 0, 1, or more times. to, by, and for are optional and can be coded in any order. by expression_b is an increment that defaults to 1. for expression_f sets a limit for loop iterations if not terminated by some other constraint. forever defines an endless loop that must be terminated or exited by some internal instruction. while is a top-driven structured loop, while until defines a bottom-driven unstructured loop. Loop control variables can be altered from within the loop and the leave, iterate, signal, return, and exit instructions may also modify loop behavior.

Example

```
if a = 2 then do      /* a simple do-end pair to group multiple         */
   say 'a is 2'        /* instructions into one for the IF instruction   */
   say 'Why?'
end

/* we assume all DOs below have a body and END. We just show the DO here.  */
do 40                  /* executes a loop 40 times                       */
do j = 1 to 40         /* executes a loop 40 times (BY 1 is implied)      */
do while counter < 30  /*  do-while with a condition specified            */
do while (counter < 30  & flag = 'NO')    /* multiple conditions specified */
do forever             /* codes an endless loop... better have an
                          unstructured exit inside the loop !             */
```

DROP

```
DROP  symbol  [ symbol ... ]
```

`drop` "unassigns" one or more variables or stems by setting them to uninitialized.

Example

```
a = 55
drop a
say a                    /* writes 'A' because this symbol is uninitialized */
```

EXIT

```
EXIT  [ expression ]
```

`exit` unconditionally terminates a program and optionally returns the single value defined by `expression` to the caller.

Example

```
exit  1                 /* unconditional termination, sends '1' to environment */
exit                    /* unconditional termination with no return code       */
```

IF

```
IF  expression [;]  THEN  [;]  instruction  [ ELSE [;]  instruction ]
```

`if` conditionally executes a "branch" of instruction(s). The `expression` *must* evaluate to either 0 or 1. The `else` always matches to the nearest unmatched `if`. To execute more than one instruction after the `then` or `else`, use a do-end pair: then do . . . end or else do . . . end. To code a branch with no instructions, use the `nop` instruction.

Example

```
if  b = 1 then say 'B is 1'      /* a simple IF instruction            */
        else say 'B is not 1'

if b = 1 then do                 /* THEN DO and ELSE DO are required    */
    say 'B is 1'                 /* to execute more than 1 instruction */
    say 'TRUE branch taken'      /* in a branch.                        */
    end                          /* END terminates a logical branch.    */
else do
    say 'B is not 1'
    say 'FALSE branch taken'
    end
```

INTERPRET

```
INTERPRET    expression
```

interpret executes instructions that may be built dynamically within the expression. The expression is evaluated, then executed. The expression must be *syntactically complete*; for example, a do must include a matched end. interpret is useful for creating *self-modifying scripts*. Set trace r or trace i if experiencing problems with interpret.

Example

```
interpret  say 'Hi there'      /* interprets (executes) the SAY instruction */
```

ITERATE

```
ITERATE    [ symbol ]
```

iterate alters the flow of control within a do loop by passing control directly back to the do instruction of that loop. This skips any subsequent instructions encoded south of the iterate instruction within that execution of the do loop.

Example

```
do j = 1 by 1 to 3          /* This displays 1 and 3, but not 2.          */
   if  j = 2  then  iterate  /* The ITERATE instruction skips displaying 2. */
   say  j
end
```

LEAVE

```
LEAVE  [ symbol ]
```

leave alters the flow of control within a do loop by immediately passing control directly to the instruction following the end clause. This causes an unstructured exit from the do loop. Whereas iterate sets the loop to start on a new iteration, leave exits the loop.

Example

```
do j = 1 by 1 to 3          /* This displays 1, then 'Hello.'  The LEAVE   */
   if  j = 2  then  leave   /* instruction exits the loop when j = 2.      */
   say  j
end
say 'Hello'
```

NOP

```
NOP
```

nop means *no operation*. It can be used within an `if` statement to code a branch with no action taken.

Example

```
if flag = 'YES'
    then nop                        /* no action taken when FLAG = 'YES'          */
    else say 'flag is NO'
```

NUMERIC

```
NUMERIC    DIGITS   [ expression ]
           FORM     [ SCIENTIFIC  |   ENGINEERING |   [ VALUE ] expression ]
           FUZZ     [ expression ]
```

The `numeric` instruction controls various aspects of numeric calculation. `digits` set the number of significant digits; it defaults to 9. `form` sets the form in which exponential numbers are written; it defaults to `scientific`. `fuzz` controls how many digits will be ignored during comparisons; it defaults to 0.

Use the `digits()`, `form()` and `fuzz()` functions to find out the current values for these `numeric` settings.

Example

```
numeric digits 12          /* Set precision to 12 significant digits.       */
say digits()               /* This will now display: 12.                    */
numeric form engineering   /* Display exponential numbers in engineering format. */
say form()                 /* This will now display: ENGINEERING.           */
numeric fuzz 1             /* 1 digit will be ignored during comparisons.   */
say fuzz()                 /* will now display: 1                           */
```

Note that the example code is run in sequence.

OPTIONS

```
OPTIONS  expression
```

`options` passes commands to the interpreter. It can be used to alter the behavior of the Rexx interpreter or its defaults. *The options allowable are strictly implementation-dependent.* Interpreters ignore any options they do not recognize. This is good because it means implementation-dependent coding on this statement runs under other interpreters. But it also means that you must check to see whether the options you coded were implemented or ignored.

Example

```
options  4.00  vm_compatible  /* The two options '4.00' and 'vm_compatible' */
                              /* may each be set, or ignored, depending    */
                              /* on whether the Rexx interpreter we are     */
                              /* using recognizes them.                     */
```

PARSE

```
PARSE    [ UPPER ]  type  [ template ]

type is: [   ARG   |   LINEIN   |   PULL   |   SOURCE   |   VERSION   ]
             VALUE   [ expression ]  WITH
             VAR   symbol
```

parse assigns values to one or more variables from various data sources according to parsing rules and its template. If upper is specified, all input values are translated to uppercase.

❏   ARG — Parses input values to this routine

❏   LINEIN — Reads a line from the default input stream and parses it into ariable(s)

❏   PULL — Reads a line from the stack, or it is empty, from the default input stream and parses this string into variable(s)

❏   SOURCE — Reads three words of system-dependent information:
    system   how_the_script_was_invoked   filename_of_the_script

❏   VERSION — Reads five words of system-dependent information:
    language   level   date   month   year

❏   VALUE expression WITH — Evaluates the expression and then parses it

❏   VAR symbol — Parses the string in symbol

Example

```
parse arg  a, b       /* internal routine reads its parameters   */
parse linein          /* reads a line from default input stream  */
parse pull a          /* reads A from the stack or input stream  */

                      /* parse the return from the DATE function  */
parse value date() with dd mmm yyyy
say  dd  mmm  yyyy     /* displays something like: 15 Jun 2005     */

string = ' a  b'      /* parses STRING, displays: a  b            */
parse var  string  c  d
say  c  d
                      /* retrieve and display system information   */
parse source  system how_called  filename
say system  how_called  filename
parse version  language  level  date  month  year
say  language  level date  month  year
```

PROCEDURE

```
PROCEDURE  [ EXPOSE  variable_list ]
```

The `procedure` instruction makes all variables of the caller unavailable to this one. If it is not coded, all the caller's variables are available to this routine (they are global). If `procedure` is coded with the `expose` keyword, only the variables listed after the `expose` keyword are available to this routine. Exposed variables are accessible for both reading and updating by the routine.

Example

```
my_sub: procedure           /* No caller variables are available to my_sub.  */
my_sub:                      /* ALL caller variables are available to my_sub. */
my_sub: procedure expose a b /* a and b only are available to my_sub.         */
```

PULL

```
PULL [ template ]
```

`pull` reads a line from the stack, or if none is available, reads a line from the default input stream. `pull` parses the input according to the template and always translates all arguments to uppercase. `pull` is equivalent to: `parse  upper  pull  [ template ]`.

Example

```
pull   input   /* reads one line from the stack, or reads      */
               /* input from the user if the stack is empty.    */
               /* waits for input to read if necessary.         */
               /* always translates to all uppercase letters    */
```

PUSH

```
PUSH  [ expression ]
```

Adds a line to the external data queue or stack, in the order last-in, first-out (LIFO). Use the `queued()` function to determine how many elements are on the stack at any time.

Example

```
push   line    /* pushes LINE onto the stack LIFO */
```

QUEUE

```
QUEUE  [ expression ]
```

Adds a line to the external data queue or stack, in the order first-in, first-out (FIFO). Use the `queued()` function to determine how many elements are on the stack at any time.

Example

```
queue  line     /* places LINE onto the stack FIFO */
```

RETURN

```
RETURN   [ expression ]
```

Returns control from a program or internal routine to its caller, optionally passing the single result of `expression`.

Example

```
return          /* return with no result   */
return 4        /* return with result of: 4 */
```

SAY

```
SAY  [ expression ]
```

Writes a line to the default output stream, after evaluating `expression`. Using `say` is the same as coding: `call  lineout , [expression]`.

Example

```
say 'Hi'          /* displays: Hi       */
say 'Hi'  'there' /* displays: Hi there */
```

SELECT

```
SELECT  ;  when_part  [ when_part ... ]   [ OTHERWISE  [;]
                                          [ statement  ... ]  ]   END  ;

when_part is:  WHEN  expression   [;]   THEN  [;]  statement
```

`select` implements the `Case` construct for determining the flow of control. Only the first `when` condition that evaluates to `true` (1) executes. `otherwise` executes if none of the `when` conditions are true. If no `otherwise` is provided and none of the `when` conditions is `true`, a syntax error results. We recommend always coding an `otherwise` clause.

Example

```
select
   when input = 'yes' then do
     say 'YES!'
     say 'branch 1'
   end
   when input = 'no'    then do
     say 'NO!'
     say 'branch 2'
   end
   otherwise
      say 'user is crazy'
      exit 99
end /* select */
```

SIGNAL

```
          |   label_name                          |
SIGNAL    |   [ VALUE ] expression                |
          |   ON condition  [ NAME trapname ]     |
          |   OFF condition                       |
```

signal either causes an immediate unstructured transfer of control to the label at label_name, or enables or disables an error condition. If on is specified, signal enables the error condition and optionally specifies the name of the routine invoked when it is raised. The condition must be one of error, failure, halt, novalue, notready, or syntax. The ANSI-1996 standard adds the new condition lostdigits. Specifying off disables an error condition.

If neither on nor off is specified, signal directly transfers control to the label of label_name, rather like the goto of other computer languages. Any active do, if, select, and interpret instructions are terminated. The value keyword allows transfer of control to a label whose name is determined at execution time.

Example

```
signal  on   error          /* enables ERROR trap with routine of ERROR:      */
signal  on   error   name   error_handler   /* enables ERROR to ERROR_HANDLER: */
signal  off  error          /* disables ERROR trap                            */

signal  goto_place          /* immediately goes to the label goto_place:      */
```

TRACE

```
TRACE    trace_setting    |    [ VALUE ] expression
```

`trace_setting` is any of these flags:

- ❏ A—All
- ❏ C—Commands
- ❏ E—Errors
- ❏ F—Failure
- ❏ I—Intermediates
- ❏ L—Labels
- ❏ N—Normal
- ❏ O—Off
- ❏ R—Results
- ❏ ? —Toggles *interactive tracing* on or off; can be followed by any letter in this list only.
- ❏ A positive whole number—If in interactive trace, skips the number of pauses specified
- ❏ A negative whole number—Inhibits tracing for the number of clauses specified

Sets the *trace level* for debugging. Multiple `trace` instructions may be placed within a script, altering the trace level at will. Setting it to a positive or negative whole number during interactive tracing skips or inhibits tracing for that number of pauses or clauses.

Use the `trace()` function to retrieve the current setting for the trace level.

Example

```
say trace()    /* displays the current trace setting      */
trace   a      /* turn on TRACE ALL                        */
trace   ?I     /* turn on interactive trace with setting of I */
```

Functions

This appendix provides a reference to all Rexx functions, as defined by the ANSI-1996 standard. It also points out the important differences between the ANSI-1996 standard and the earlier standard defined by TRL-2. As this appendix is intended as a quick reference guide for developers, please see the full ANSI-1996 and TRL-2 standards if more detailed information is required. Appendix A tells where to obtain the two standards.

Each entry is identified by the name of the function. Entries contain a template of the function, showing its arguments, if any. Optional arguments are enclosed in brackets ([ ]). The template is followed by a description of the function and its use, the function's arguments, and possible return codes. Coding examples show how to code each function.

ABBREV

```
ABBREV(information, info [,length])
```

Returns 1 if info is equal to the leading characters of information and info is not less than the minimum length. Otherwise returns 0. If not specified, length defaults to the length of info.

Example

```
abbrev('Hello','He')    ==   1
abbrev('Hello','Hi')    ==   0
abbrev('Hello','Hi',3) ==   0  /* INFO does not meet minimum LENGTH. */
```

ABS

```
ABS(number)
```

Returns the absolute value of number, formatted according to the current setting of numeric digits and without a leading sign.

Example

```
abs(-0.47)    ==    0.47
abs(0)        ==    0
```

ADDRESS

```
ADDRESS()
```

Returns the name of the environment to which commands are currently directed.

The ANSI-1996 standard allows a new format for this function that specifies an option. The option returns information on the targets of command output and the sources of command input. Here is the coding template with the option specified:

```
ADDRESS([option])
```

option may be any one of the following:

❑　N (Normal) — Returns the current default environment

❑　I (Input) — Returns the target details for input as three words: position type resource

❑　O (Output) — Returns the target details for output as three words: position type resource

❑　E (Error) — Returns the target details for errors as three words: position type resource

Example

```
address()      ==    SYSTEM          /* for example */
address()      ==    UNIX            /* for example */
address('I')   ==    INPUT NORMAL    /* for example */
address('E')   ==    REPLACE NORMAL  /* for example */
```

ARG

```
ARG([argnum [,option]])
```

If argnum and option are not specified, returns the number of arguments passed to the program or internal routine. If *only* argnum is specified, returns the *n*th argument string, or the null string if the argument does not exist. The option may be either:

❑　E or e (Exists) — Returns 1 if the *n*th argument exists.

❑　O or o (Omitted) — Returns 1 if the *n*th argument was omitted.

Example

```
/*  If issued from a routine invoked by: call routine  1, 2   */
arg()     ==     2
arg(1)    ==     1
arg(2)    ==     2
arg(3)    ==     ''    /* the null string */
arg(1,'e') ==   1
arg(1,'E') ==   1
arg(1,'o') ==   0
arg(3,'o') ==   1
```

BITAND

```
BITAND(string1 [,[string2] [,pad]])
```

Returns a string derived from logically ANDing two input strings, bit by bit.

If pad is omitted, ANDing terminates when the shorter string ends, and the remaining portion of the longer string is appended to the result. If pad is specified, the shorter string is padded on the right prior to the ANDing.

Example

```
bitand('00110011','00001111')   ==   00000011
```

BITOR

```
BITOR(string1 [,[string2] [,pad]])
```

Returns a string derived from logically ORing two strings, bit by bit.

If pad is omitted, ORing terminates when the shorter string ends, and the remaining portion of the longer string is appended to the result. If pad is specified, the shorter string is padded on the right prior to the ORing.

```
Examples: --    bitor('00110011','00001111')   ==   00111111
```

BITXOR

```
BITXOR(string1 [,[string2] [,pad]])
```

Returns a string derived from logically EXCLUSIVE ORing two strings, bit by bit.

If pad is omitted, EXCLUSIVE ORing terminates when the shorter string ends, and the remaining portion of the longer string is appended to the result. If pad is specified, the shorter string is padded on the right prior to the EXCLUSIVE ORing.

Example

```
bitxor('123456'x,'3456'x) ==  '266256'x
```

See this result on the display screen by entering:

```
say c2x(bitxor('123456'x,'3456'x))
```

B2X

```
B2X(binary_string)
```

Converts a binary string to its hexadecimal (base 16) equivalent. The hex string will consist of digits 0 to 9 and uppercase letters A through F.

Example

```
b2x('11000010')      == C2
b2x('111')           == 7
```

CENTER or CENTRE

```
CENTER(string, length [,pad])
--or--
CENTRE(string, length [,pad])
```

Returns a string of the length specified by length with the string centered within it. Characters of type pad are added to achieve the required length. pad defaults to blanks.

Example

```
center('HELP!',9)      == ' HELP! '     /* 2 spaces are on each side of HELP! */
center('HELP!',9,'x')  == 'xxHELP!xx'   /* 2 x's are added on each side.      */
```

CHANGESTR

```
CHANGESTR(needle, haystack, newneedle)
```

This function was added by the ANSI-1996 standard. It replaces all occurrences of string needle in string haystack with string newneedle. Returns the haystack if needle is not found.

Example

```
changestr('x','abcx','d')  ==  abcd
changestr('x','abcc','d')  ==  abcc        /* needle was not found in haystack   */
```

CHARIN

```
CHARIN([name] [,[start] [,length]])
```

Returns up to `length` characters from the character input stream `name`. The default length is 1, and the default character stream is the default input stream.

`start` may be coded to move the read pointer of a persistent stream and explicitly specify where to start the read. A start position of 1 is the first character in the persistent stream. To move the read pointer for a persistent stream without reading any input, specify a read `length` of 0.

If `length` number of characters cannot be returned, the program waits until they become available, or else the NOTREADY condition is raised and `charin` returns with fewer characters than requested.

Example

```
charin('text_file',5)     /* reads the next five characters from file text_file */
charin('text_file',1,5)   /* reads first five characters from file text_file    */
charin('text_file',1,0)   /* positions the read pointer to the start of text_file
                              and does not read in any characters                */
```

CHAROUT

```
CHAROUT([name] [,[string] [,start]])
```

Writes the characters of `string` to the output stream specified by `name`, starting at position `start`. Returns the number of characters remaining after the output attempt; a return of 0 means a successful write.

If `start` is omitted, characters are written at the current write pointer position (for example, appended to the end of the persistent stream or output file). If `name` is omitted, characters are written to the default output stream (normally the display screen).

To position the write pointer, specify `start` and omit `string`. A `start` value of 1 is the beginning of an output file.

The NOTREADY condition is raised if all characters cannot be written.

Example

```
charout('text_file','Hello')  /* writes 'Hello' to text_file and returns 0     */
charout(,'Hello')             /* writes 'Hello' to default output, the display */
charout('text_file',,1)       /* positions the write file pointer to start of
                                 the text_file (and does not write anything)    */
```

CHARS

```
CHARS([name])
```

Returns the number of characters remaining to be read in stream name. In the ANSI-1996 standard, chars may alternatively return 1 when *any number* of characters remain to be read. Always returns 0 if there are no characters left to read. If name is omitted, the function applies to the default input stream.

Example

```
chars('text_file')     ==  90   /* 90 characters left to read from text_file.  */
chars('text_file')     ==  0    /* end of file on text_file                    */
chars('text_file')     ==  1    /* Either there is exactly 1 character left to */
                                /* read from text_file, or this is ANSI-1996,  */
                                /*  and there may be 1 or more left to read.    */
```

COMPARE

```
COMPARE(string1, string2 [,pad])
```

Returns 0 if the strings are the same. Otherwise, it returns the position of the first character that is not the same in both strings. If one string is shorter, pad is used to pad it for comparison. pad defaults to blanks.

Example

```
compare('Hello','Hello')   ==  0
compare('Hello','He')      ==  3
compare('Hello','He','x')  ==  3
```

CONDITION

```
CONDITION([option])
```

Returns condition information concerning the current trapped condition, or the null string if no condition has been trapped. The option may be coded as follows:

❑   C (Condition name) — Name of the currently trapped condition

❑   D (Description) — Descriptive string for the condition

❑   I (Instruction) — Returns the invoking instruction, either call or signal. This is the default if no option is specified.

❑   S (State) — Returns state of the trapped condition, either ON, OFF, or DELAY.

Example

```
condition()    ==   CALL      /* if the trap was enabled by CALL      */
condition('C') ==   FAILURE   /* if the condition trapped was FAILURE */
condition('I') ==   CALL      /* if the trap was enabled by CALL      */
condition('S') ==   OFF       /* if the state is now OFF              */
```

COPIES

```
COPIES(string, times)
```

Returns a string copied the number of times specified by `times`.

Example

```
copies('Hello',3)   ==   HelloHelloHello
```

COUNTSTR

```
COUNTSTR(needle, haystack)
```

This function was added by the ANSI-1996 standard. It returns the count of the number of times `needle` occurs within `haystack`. Returns 0 if the `needle` is not found.

Example

```
countstr('a','abracadabra')   ==   5
```

C2D

```
C2D(string [,length])
```

Character to decimal conversion. Returns the decimal representation of a character `string`. Optional `length` specifies the number of characters of `string` to be converted. `length` defaults to the full string length, and `string` is considered an unsigned number.

Example

```
c2d('14'x) ==  20        /* hexadecimal 14 converted to decimal is 20 */
c2d('hi')  ==  26729     /* on ASCII machines only */
```

C2X

```
C2X(string)
```

Character to hexadecimal conversion. Returns the string of hex digits that represent `string`.

Example

```
c2x('123'x)  ==  0123
c2x('abc')   ==  616263   /* on ASCII machines only */
```

DATATYPE

```
DATATYPE(string [,type])
```

If `type` is omitted, returns NUM if string is a valid Rexx number; returns CHAR otherwise.

If `type` is specified, returns 1 if the `string` matches the `type`; returns 0 otherwise. Allowable `type` specifications are:

❑ A **(Alphanumeric)** — Returns 1 if `string` consists solely of alphanumeric characters 0–9, a–z, and A–Z

❑ B **(Binary)** — Returns 1 if `string` contains only 0's and 1's

❑ L **(Lowercase)** — Returns 1 if `string` consists solely of characters a–z

❑ M **(Mixed case)** — Returns 1 if `string` consists of characters a–z and A–Z

❑ N **(Number)** — Returns 1 if `string` is a valid Rexx number

❑ S **(Symbol)** — Returns 1 if `string` consists of characters valid in Rexx symbols

❑ U **(Uppercase)** — Returns 1 if `string` consists of characters A–Z

❑ W **(Whole number)** — Returns 1 if `string` is a Rexx whole number

❑ X **(HeXadecimal)** — Returns 1 if `string` is a hex number, containing only characters a–f, A–F, and digits 0–9

Example

```
datatype('  123  ')       ==   NUM   /* blanks are allowed within Rexx numbers */
datatype('  123  ','N')   ==   NUM   /* same test as omitting the 'N'          */
datatype('0011','b')      ==   1     /* yes, the string is binary              */
datatype('2f4a','x')      ==   1     /* yes, the string is hex                 */
```

DATE

```
DATE( [option_out [,date [,option_in]]] )
```

If all options are omitted, returns the date in the format dd Mmm yyyy, for example: 14 Jun 2005.

If the first argument is supplied, it defines the format of the return string. The list below shows possible encodings for the option_out parameter:

- ❑ B (**Base**) — Returns the number of complete days since the base date of January 1, 0001.

- ❑ D (**Days**) — Returns the number of days so far in the year (includes the current day)

- ❑ E (**European**) — Returns the date in EU format, dd/mm/yy

- ❑ M (**Month**) — Returns the full English name of the current month, for example: June

- ❑ N (**Normal**) — Returns the date in the default format (see above)

- ❑ O (**Ordered**) — Returns the date in a sort-friendly format yy/mm/dd

- ❑ S (**Standard**) — Returns the date in the sort-friendly format yyyymmdd

- ❑ U (**USA**) — Returns the date in American format, mm/dd/yy

- ❑ W (**Weekday**) — Returns the English name for the day of the week, for example: Monday

If the date option is encoded, the function converts that date. The parameter option_in specifies the format in which the date is supplied and option_out is the target format to which the date is converted.

The TRL-2 form of this function only allows for coding the first argument. ANSI-1996 adds the other two arguments.

Example

```
date('d')   ==  166      /* This is the 166th day of the year, including today. */
date('u')   ==  06/14/05 /* today's date in USA format      */
date('s')   ==  20050614 /* today's date in standard format */
```

DELSTR

```
DELSTR(string, start [,length])
```

Deletes the substring of string that starts at position start for the specified length. If length is omitted, the rest of the string is deleted from position start to the end.

Example

```
delstr('abcd',2)    ==  a
delstr('abcd',2,1)  ==  acd
```

DELWORD

```
DELWORD(string, start [,length])
```

Deletes the substring of string that starts at position start and is of length length blank-delimited words. If length is omitted, it defaults to removing the rest of the words in string.

Example

```
delword('Roses are Red',2)   ==  Roses      /* deletes from word 2 to end   */
delword('Roses are Red',2,1) ==  Roses Red  /* deletes 1 word at position 2 */
```

DIGITS

```
DIGITS()
```

Returns the current setting of numeric digits (which dictates the precision of calculations).

Example

```
digits()  ==  9        /* the default if NUMERIC DIGITS has not been altered */
```

D2C

```
D2C(integer [,length])
```

Decimal-to-character conversion. Returns the character string representation of integer. If length is specified, the returned string will be length bytes long with sign extension.

Example

```
d2c(127)  ==  '7F'x /* to display a result enter: say c2x(d2c(127))    */
d2c(0)    ==  ''     /* returns the null string */
```

D2X

```
D2X(integer [,length])
```

Decimal-to-hexadecimal conversion. Returns the hex representation of integer. length specifies the length of the resulting string.

Example

```
d2x(127)  ==  7F
d2x(0)    ==  0
```

ERRORTEXT

```
ERRORTEXT(error_no)
```

Returns the textual error message associated with the given error number, `error_no`. The ANSI-1996 standard adds the ability to retrieve the text from error submessages. For example, you could retrieve the textual equivalent of error submessage 14.1.

Example

```
say errortext(14)      ==      Incomplete DO/SELECT/IF
```

FORM

```
FORM()
```

Returns the current form in which numbers are exponentially represented, either `scientific` or `engineering`.

Example

```
say form() == SCIENTIFIC  /* this is the default if not altered by NUMERIC FORM */
```

FORMAT

```
FORMAT(number [,[before] [,[after]]])
```

Rounds and formats a number. `before` and `after` control the number of characters used for the integer and decimal parts, respectively.

Example

```
format('1',4)       ==  '   1'    /* 3 blanks precede the 1. */
format('1.22',4,0)  ==  '   1'    /* 3 blanks precede the 1. */
format('1.22',4,2)  ==  '   1.22' /* 3 blanks precede the 1. */
format('00.00')     ==  '0'
```

FORMAT

```
FORMAT(number [,[before] [,[after] [,[expp] [,expt]]]])
```

In this version of the `format` function, `expp` and `expt` control the formatting of the exponential part of the result. `expp` is the number of digits used for the exponential part, while `expt` sets the trigger for the use of exponential notation.

Example

```
format('12345.67',,,2,3)   ==   '1.234567E+04'
format('12345.67',,,4,4)   ==   '1.234567E+0004'
format('12345.67',,2,,0)   ==   '1.23E+4'
format('12345.67',,3,,0)   ==   '1.235E+4'
```

FUZZ

```
FUZZ()
```

Returns the current setting of numeric fuzz.

Example

```
fuzz() == 0    /* if the default of NUMERIC FUZZ was not altered */
```

INSERT

```
INSERT(string, target [,[position] [,length] [,pad]])
```

Returns the result of inserting string into the target string. position specifies where the insertion occurs, with a default of 0 (prior to any characters of the target string). length pads with the pad character or truncates string before it is inserted into the target string, as necessary.

Example

```
insert('J.','Felix Unger',6,3) ==  'Felix J. Unger'
insert('Happy!','I am',5)       ==  'I am Happy!'
```

LASTPOS

```
LASTPOS(needle, haystack [,start])
```

Returns the last occurrence of one string, the needle, within another, the haystack. The search starts at the last position within the haystack, or may be set by start. Returns 0 if the needle string is not found in the haystack.

Example

```
lastpos('abc','abcdef')      == 1
lastpos('abc','abcabcabc')   == 7
lastpos('abcd',abcabcabc')   == 0    /* The needle was not found in the haystack. */
```

LEFT

```
LEFT(string, length [,pad])
```

Returns the length leftmost characters in string. Pads with the pad character if length is greater than the length of string.

Example

```
left('Hi there',2)        == 'Hi'
left('Hi there',10)       == 'Hi there  '   /* 2 blanks trail */
left('Hi there',10,'x')   == 'Hi therexx'
```

LENGTH

```
LENGTH(string)
```

Returns the length of string.

Example

```
length('Me first!')   == 9
length('')            == 0        /* length of the null string is 0 */
```

LINEIN

```
LINEIN([name] [,[line] [,count]])
```

Returns lines from the input stream name. count may be 0 or 1, and it defaults to 1. name defaults to the default input stream. line positions to the given line number prior to the read. count may be specified as 0 with a line number to position the read pointer to a particular line in a persistent input file without reading data.

Example

```
linein('text_file')   /* reads the next line from the input file TEXT_FILE */
linein()              /* reads the next line from the default input stream */
linein('text_file',5,0)   /* positions read pointer to the 5th line in the file */
                          /* and reads no data due to the count of 0         */
```

LINEOUT

```
LINEOUT([name] [,[string] [,line]])
```

Writes string to output stream name and returns either 0 on a successful write or 1 on failure.

May be used to position the write pointer before a specified `line` number on persistent streams or files. If `string` and `line` are omitted, the write position is set to the end of stream. In most Rexxes, this closes the file specified by name.

Example

```
lineout(,'Hi!')    /* writes Hi! to default output stream, normally returns 0 */
lineout('text_file','Hi!')    /* writes Hi! to text_file, normally returns 0 */
lineout('text_file')    /* positions write pointer to end of file,    */
                        /* and closes the file in most Rexxes         */
```

LINES

```
LINES([name])
```

Returns 0 if no lines remain to be read from the `name` input stream. Otherwise, it returns 1 or the actual number of lines in the input stream.

Example

```
lines('text_file')    ==    0    /* end of file, no lines left to read */
lines('text_file')    ==    127  /* 127 lines left to read on input    */
lines('text_file')    ==    1    /* 1 (or more) lines left to read     */
```

This is a new format for the `lines` function added by the ANSI-1996 standard. This new format adds an `option` to control whether or not the user wants the interpreter to return an exact line count at the cost of performance overhead:

```
LINES([name] [,option])
```

In this format, the `option` may be either:

❏   c (Count) — Returns the exact number of lines left in the input stream

❏   n (Normal) — Default. Returns 1 if there are one or more lines left in input stream

Example

```
lines('text_file')        ==    1    /* 1 (or more) lines left to read */
lines('text_file','N')    ==    1    /* 1 (or more) lines left to read */
lines('text_file','C')    ==    1    /* EXACTLY 1 line left to read    */
```

MAX

```
MAX(number1 [,number2]...)
```

Returns the largest number from the list of numbers.

Example

```
max(-9,14,0)  ==  14
```

MIN

```
MIN(number1 [,number2]...)
```

Returns the smallest number from the list of numbers.

Example

```
min(-9,14,0)  ==  -9
```

OVERLAY

```
OVERLAY(string1, string2 [,[start] [,[length] [,pad]]])
```

Returns a copy of `string2`, partially or fully overwritten by `string1`. `start` specifies the starting position of the overlay, and defaults to the first position, 1. `length` truncates or pads `string1` prior to the operation, using `pad` as the pad character.

Example

```
overlay('not','this is really right',9,6,'.') == 'this is not... right'
overlay('eous','this is right',14)            == 'this is righteous'
```

POS

```
POS(needle, haystack [,start])
```

Returns the first position of the string `needle` within the string `haystack`. The scan starts at the first position in the `haystack`, unless `start` is coded as some number other than 1. Returns 0 if `needle` does not occur within `haystack`.

Example

```
pos('abc','abcdef')       == 1
pos('ab','abracadabra')   == 1
pos('abd','abracadabra')  == 0        /* needle was not found in the haystack */
```

QUALIFY

```
QUALIFY([streamid])
```

This function was added by the ANSI-1996 standard. It returns a name for the `streamid` that will be associated with the persistent stream or file and can be used in future references to that resource.

Example

```
qualify('text_file') == C:\regina\pgms\text_file
                        /* Text_file was located and its fully  */
                        /* qualified path name was returned.     */
```

QUEUED

```
QUEUED()
```

Returns the number of lines remaining in the external data queue (the stack).

Example

```
queued()    ==    5    /* five reads will process the stack */
```

RANDOM

```
RANDOM(max)      or      RANDOM([min] [,[max] [,seed]])
```

Returns a pseudo-random integer. In the first format, this number will be between 0 and `max`. The second format allows the dictating of the eligible range of numbers and the seeding of the operation.

Example

```
random(5)      /* returns a pseudo-random number between 0 and 5 */
random(1,6)    /* simulate the roll of one die                   */
```

REVERSE

```
REVERSE(string)
```

Returns a copy of a `string` with its characters reversed.

Example

```
reverse('abc')    ==    'cba'
```

RIGHT

```
RIGHT(string, length [,pad])
```

Returns a string of length `length` containing the rightmost characters of `string`, padded with the `pad` character or truncated to fit the `length`.

Example

```
right('abc',7)      ==    '    abc'    /* 4 spaces precede: abc */
right('abc',7,'x')  ==    'xxxxabc'    /* 4 x's precede: abc    */
```

SIGN

```
SIGN(number)
```

Returns 1 if the number is positive, 0 if the number is 0, and -1 if the number is negative.

Example

```
sign(-88)  ==   -1
sign(88)   ==   1
sign(+0)   ==   0
```

SOURCELINE

```
SOURCELINE([line_number])
```

With no argument, `sourceline` returns the number of lines in the script. If `line_number` is given, that specific line is returned from the script.

Example

```
sourceline(2)    /* returns the second line in the script */
sourceline()     /* returns the line number of the last line in the script */
```

SPACE

```
SPACE(string [,[length] [,pad]])
```

Formats a `string` by replacing internal blanks with `length` occurrences of the `pad` character. The default `pad` character is blank and the default `length` is 1. Leading and trailing blanks are always removed. If `length` is 0, all blanks are removed.

Example

```
space('abc   abc')       == 'abc abc'  /* reduces 3 internal spaces to 1      */
space('abc   abc',1,'x') == 'abcxabc'  /* reduces 3 internal spaces to one x */
space('abc   abc',0)     == 'abcabc'   /* LENGTH of 0 removes spaces          */
```

STREAM

```
STREAM(name [,option [,command]])
```

name is the stream to which to apply an option and optionally a command. The options are:

- ❑ c (Command) — Issues the command (implementation-dependent)
- ❑ D (Description) — Returns textual description of the stream's state
- ❑ S (State) — Returns the stream's state, which will be either: ERROR, NOTREADY, READY, or UNKNOWN.

The commands that can be encoded on the stream function depend on the interpreter. See your interpreter's reference guide to see what commands it supports. Many interpreters permit such operations as explicitly opening, closing, and flushing files; moving the file position pointers; returning detailed stream information; and setting and/or changing the file's processing mode.

Example

```
stream('text_file','s')    ==    READY  /* stream state is good for I/O     */
stream('text_file','c','open read')    /* issues a COMMAND on the stream    */
                    /* The allowable commands are implementation-dependent */
```

STRIP

```
STRIP(string [,option] [,char]])
```

Returns string stripped of leading and/or trailing blanks or any other char specified. Option values determine the action:

- ❑ L (Leading) — Strip off leading blanks or char if specified.
- ❑ T (Trailing) — Strip off trailing blanks or char if specified.
- ❑ B (Both) — Strip off both leading and trailing blanks or char if specified. This is the default.

Example

```
strip('   abc   ')        == 'abc' /* strip off both leading & trailing blanks */
strip('xxxabcxxx',,'x')   == 'abc' /* strip off both leading & trailing x's    */
strip('xxxabcxxx','t','x')== 'xxxabc'   /* strip off only trailing x's         */
```

SUBSTR

```
SUBSTR(string, start [,[length] [,pad]])
```

Returns a substring from `string`. `start` is the starting character position in `string`, defaulting to 1. `length` is how many characters to take, defaulting to the remainder of the string from `start`. If `length` is longer than the `string`, padding occurs with the `pad` character, which defaults to the blank.

Example

```
substr('Roses are Red',7,3)    == 'are'
substr('Roses are Red',55)     == ''        /* null string, START is too big */
substr('Roses are Red',11,5,'x') == 'Redxx' /* padded with x's */
```

SUBWORD

```
SUBWORD(string, start [,length])
```

Returns the substring that begins at blank-delimited word `start`. If `length` is omitted, it defaults to the remainder of the `string`.

Example

```
subword('Violets are due',3)   == 'due'
subword('Violets are due',4)   == ''        /* null string, no fourth word */
```

SYMBOL

```
SYMBOL(name)
```

Returns the state of symbol `name`. Returns:

- ❑ BAD — name is not a valid symbol.
- ❑ VAR — name is a symbol and has been assigned a value.
- ❑ LIT — name is valid symbol but is assigned no value (or it is a constant symbol).

Example

```
a = 'valid!'
symbol('a')    == VAR
symbol('b')    == LIT    /* b has not been assigned. */
```

TIME

```
TIME( [option_out [,time [option_in]] ] )
```

The TRL-2 form of this function allows for coding the first argument only. ANSI-1996 adds the other two arguments.

If only the first parameter is encoded, the function returns the system time in 24-hour clock format: hh:mm:ss, for example: 19:19:50. Options include:

- ❏   C (Civil) — Returns hh:mmxx civil-format time. xx is am or pm.
- ❏   E (Elapsed) — Returns elapsed time since the clock was started or reset, in the format sssssssss.uuuuuu
- ❏   H (Hours) — Returns the number of completed hours since midnight in the format hh. Values range from 0 to 23.
- ❏   L (Long) — Returns the time in long format: hh:mm:ss.uuuuuu
- ❏   M (Minutes)–Returns the number of completed minutes since midnight in the format mmmm
- ❏   N (Normal) — Returns the time in the default format (hh:mm:ss)
- ❏   R (Reset) — Returns elapsed time since the clock was started or reset in the format sssssssss.uuuuuu
- ❏   S (Seconds) — Returns the number of complete seconds since midnight

Example

```
time('C')   ==   7:25pm   /* for example */
time('m')   ==   1166     /* for example */
```

To use the elapsed timer, make a first call to time('e') or time('r'). This returns 0. Subsequent calls to time('e') and time('r') will return the elapsed interval since the first call or since the last call to time('r').

Example

```
time('e')   ==  0          /* first call always returns 0    */
time('e')   ==  46.172000  /* time elapsed since first call  */
```

In the ANSI-1996 version of this function, if the time option is encoded, the function converts that time. The parameter option_in specifies the format in which the time is supplied and option_out is the target format to which the time is converted.

TRACE

```
TRACE([setting])
```

Returns the trace setting. If `setting` is specified, it sets the trace to that level (and returns the old trace value). The settings are:

- ❏ A (**All**) — Trace all clauses before execution.
- ❏ C (**Commands**) — Trace all host commands before execution.
- ❏ E (**Errors**) — Trace host commands that result in error or failure.
- ❏ F (**Failure**) — Trace host commands that fail.
- ❏ I (**Intermediates**) — Trace all clauses before execution, with intermediate results.
- ❏ L (**Labels**) — Trace labels.
- ❏ N (**Normal**) — Default, trace only host commands that fail.
- ❏ O (**Off**) — Trace nothing.
- ❏ R (**Results**) — Trace clauses before execution and expression results.
- ❏ ? (**interactive**) — Toggles the interactive trace on or off. May precede any of the preceding letters.

Unlike the `trace` instruction, whole numbers may not be coded on the `trace` function.

Example

```
trace()            /* returns current trace setting        */
trace('I')         /* turns on the Intermediate-level trace */
```

TRANSLATE

```
TRANSLATE(string [,[tableout] [,[tablein] [,pad]]])
```

Returns a translated copy of `string`. Characters are translated according to the input translation table `tablein` and its output equivalent, `tableout`. If `tablein` and `tableout` are not coded, all characters in `string` are translated to uppercase. If `tableout` is shorter than `tablein`, it is padded with the `pad` character or its default, blanks.

Example

```
translate('abc')              ==  'ABC'  /* translates to uppercase */
translate('abc','xy','ab')    ==  'xyc'  /* a and b were translated */
```

TRUNC

```
TRUNC(number [,length])
```

Returns `number` truncated to `length` decimal places. If not specified, `length` is 0, meaning that a whole number is returned.

Example

```
trunc(27.33)      ==  27      /* returns a whole number      */
trunc(27.23,1)    ==  27.2    /* truncated to 1 decimal place */
trunc(27.23,3)    ==  27.230  /* 3 places past decimal place  */
```

VALUE

```
VALUE(symbol [,[newvalue] [,pool]])
```

Returns the value of the variable specified by symbol. If newvalue is specified, this value is assigned to the named variable. pool references an implementation-dependent variable collection or pool to search for the symbol. This function performs an extra level of variable interpretation.

Example

```
/* assume these statements are executed in sequence */
a = 2
b = 'a'
value('b')  == a   /* looks up b */
value(b)    == 2   /* looks up a */

/* this second example shows updating an environmental variable via VALUE */
/* The variable to update is called REXXPATH, and the value it will be    */
/* assigned is in the second argument. ENVIRONMENT is the pool name.       */

call value 'REXXPATH','/afs/slac/www/slac/www/tool/cgi-rexx','ENVIRONMENT'
```

VERIFY

```
VERIFY(string, reference [,[option] [,start]])
```

Verifies that all characters in string are members of the reference string. Returns the position of the first character in string that is not in reference, or 0 if all characters in string are in reference.

start specifies where in string to start the search, the default is 1. The option may be:

❑   N (Nomatch) — Default. Works as described earlier.

❑   M (Match) — Returns the position of the first character in string that *is* in reference.

Example

```
verify('ab12','abcdefgh')     ==  3  /* 1 is the first character not in REFERENCE */
verify('dg','abcdefgh')       ==  0  /* all STRING characters are in REFERENCE    */
verify('dg','abcdefgh','m')   ==  1  /* d is first character found in REFERENCE   */
```

WORD

```
WORD(string, wordno)
```

Returns the blank-delimited word number `wordno` from the string `string`, or the null string, if the word does not exist in `string`.

Example

```
word('tis the time',2)   ==   'the'
word('tis the time,4)    ==   ''        /* The null string is returned. */
```

WORD

```
WORDINDEX(string, wordno)
```

Returns the character position of the first character of the blank-delimited word given by word number `wordno` within `string`. Returns 0 if the word numbered `wordno` does not exist in the `string`.

Example

```
wordindex('tis the time',2)   ==   5    /* 'the' starts in position 5 */
```

WORDLENGTH

```
WORDLENGTH(string, wordno)
```

Returns the length of blank-delimited word `wordno` within the `string`. Returns 0 for a nonexistent word.

Example

```
wordlength('tis the time',2)   ==   3   /* 'the' has three characters */
```

WORDPOS

```
WORDPOS(phrase, string [,start])
```

If `phrase` is a substring of `string`, returns the word number position at which it begins. Otherwise returns 0. `start` is an optional word number within `string` at which the search starts. It defaults to 1.

Example

```
wordpos('time of','tis the time of the season')   ==   3
wordpos('never','tis the time of the season')     ==   0 /* phrase not found */
```

WORDS

```
WORDS(string)
```

Returns the number of blank-delimited words within the string.

Example

```
words('tis the time of the season for love')        ==  8
words('tis    the    time of the season  for    love') ==  8
```

XRANGE

```
XRANGE([start] [,end])
```

Returns a string composed of all the characters between start and end inclusive. start defaults to '00'x, and end defaults to 'FF'x.

Example

```
xrange('a','d')   ==   'abcd'
xrange()          /* returns the entire character set from '00'x thru 'FF'x */
```

X2B

```
X2B(hexstring)
```

Hexadecimal to binary string conversion.

Example

```
x2b('FF')    ==   '11111111'
x2b('ff')    ==   '11111111'
x2b('0d0a')  ==   '0000110100001010'
```

X2C

```
X2C(hexstring)
```

Hexadecimal-to--character string conversion.

Example

```
c2x('Hello')      ==  48656C6C6F
x2c(48656C6C6F)   ==  Hello           /* verify the result by inverting back */
```

X2D

```
X2D(hexstring [,length])
```

Hexadecimal-to-decimal conversion. Returns the whole number string that is the decimal representation of hexstring. Omitting length means hexstring will be interpreted as an unsigned number. Coding length means the leftmost bit of hexstring determines the sign.

Example

```
x2d('FFFF')      ==  65535
x2d('FFFF',4)    ==  -1     /* LENGTH means signed interpretation */
```

Regina Extended Functions

This appendix provides a reference to all functions Regina Rexx provides beyond the ANSI-1996 and TRL-2 standards. This appendix as intended as a quick reference guide for developers, so please see the Regina documentation if more detailed information is required. The Regina documentation is easily downloaded with the product itself, as described in Chapter 20.

Each of the following entries is identified by the name of the function. Entries contain a template of the function, showing its arguments, if any. Optional arguments are enclosed in brackets ([ ]). The vertical "or" bar (|) means to choose exactly one option from among the choices listed. The template is followed by a description of the function and its use, the function's arguments, and possible return codes. Coding examples show how to code each function.

To make some of the extended functions available, you must issue the options instruction with appropriate operands. Here are a few key examples.

To enable the VM buffer functions buftype, desbuf, dropbuf, and makebuf, encode:

```
options buffers
```

To enable the Amiga Rexx (AREXX) functions, encode this instruction. Note that *bifs* is a popular acronym that stands for "built-in functions:"

```
options  arexx_bifs
```

If you want the open, close, and eof functions to use AREXX semantics instead of standard Regina semantics encode:

```
options  arexx_semantics
```

B2C

```
B2C(binstring)
```

Converts a binary string of 0s and 1s into its corresponding character representation.

Example

```
b2c('01100011')   ==  c        /* displays the character the bitstring represents */
b2c('00110011')   ==  3
```

BEEP

```
BEEP(frequency [,duration])
```

Sounds a tone through the default speaker. The duration is in milliseconds.

Example

```
beep(40,1000)   /* generates a brief tone through the system speaker  */
beep(70,1000)   /* generates a higher pitched tone than example 1      */
beep(70,2000)   /* generates a tone for twice as long                  */
```

BITCHG

```
BITCHG(string, bit)
```

Toggles (reverses) the state of the specified bit in the string. Bit 0 is the low-order bit of the rightmost byte of the string.

Example

```
bitchg('0313'x,4)   ==   '0303'x
```

To display this result, encode:

```
say c2x(bitchg('0313'x,4))
```

BITCLR

```
BITCLR(string, bit)
```

Sets the specified bit in the string to 0. Bit 0 is the low-order bit of the rightmost byte of the string. This is the inverse of the bitset (bit set) function.

Example

```
bitclr('0313'x,4)  ==  '0303'x
```

To display this result, encode:

```
say c2x(bitclr('0313'x,4))
```

BITCOMP

```
BITCOMP(string1, string2, bit  [,pad] )
```

Bit-compares the two strings, starting at bit 0. Bit 0 is the low-order bit of the rightmost byte of the string. Returns the bit number of the first bit by which the two strings differ, or -1 if the two strings are identical.

Example

```
bitcomp('ff'x, 'ff',x)    ==   -1
bitcomp('aa'x,'ab'x)      ==    0
bitcomp('aa'x,'ba'x)      ==    4
bitcomp('FF'x,'F7'x)      ==    3
bitcomp('FF'x,'7F'x)      ==    7
```

BITSET

```
BITSET(string, bit)
```

Sets the specified `bit` in the `string` to 1. Bit 0 is the low-order bit of the rightmost byte of the string. This is the inverse of the `bitclr` (bit clear) function.

Example

```
bitset('0313'x,2) == '0317'x
```

To display this result, encode:

```
say c2x(bitset('0313'x,2))
```

BITTST

```
BITTST(string, bit)
```

Returns a Boolean value of 0 or 1 to indicate the setting of the specified `bit` in the `string`. Bit 0 is the low-order bit of the rightmost byte of the string.

Example

```
bittst('0313'x,4)   ==   1
bittst('0313'x,2)   ==   0
bittst('0000'x,1)   ==   0
```

BUFTYPE

```
BUFTYPE()
```

Displays stack contents (usually used for debugging).

Example

```
say buftype()    /* displays number of lines and stack buffers  */
```

C2B

```
C2B(string)
```

Converts the character string into a binary string (of 0s and 1s).

Example

```
say  c2b('a')  ==  01100001
say  c2b('b')  ==  01100010
say  c2b('A')  ==  01000001
```

CD or CHDIR

```
CD(directory) or CHDIR(directory)
```

Changes the current directory to the one specified. Return code is 0 if successful; otherwise, the current directory is unchanged and the return code is 1.

Example

```
cd('c:\')           /* changes to C:\ directory under Windows          */

rc = cd('xxxxx')    /* assuming directory 'xxxxx' does not exist, displays */
say rc              /* the return code of 1. Current directory not changed */
```

CLOSE

```
CLOSE(file)
```

Closes the file specified by the logical name `file`. Returns 1 if successful, 0 otherwise (for example, if the file was not open).

Example

```
close('infile')  ==  1  /* closes the open file */
close('infile')  ==  0  /* The file was not open when CLOSE was issued. */
```

COMPRESS

```
COMPRESS(string [,list] )
```

Removes all occurrences of the characters specified by `list` from the `string`.

If list is omitted, removes all blanks from the `string`.

Example

```
compress(' a  b  c    d')              ==  'abcd'
compress('12a3b45c6712d','1234567') ==  'abcd'
```

CRYPT

```
CRYPT(string, salt)
```

Returns `string` as encrypted according to the first two characters of `salt`. Not supported under all operating systems — in this case, the original `string` is returned unchanged. The encrypted string is not portable across platforms.

Example

```
say crypt('ABCD','fg') /* displays string ABCD encrypted as per seed: fg    */
                       /* If ABCD is returned, your operating system does not */
                       /*   support encryption.                              */
```

DESBUF

```
DESBUF()
```

Clears the entire stack by removing both lines and buffers. Returns the number of buffers on the stack after the function executes, which should always be 0.

Example

```
say desbuf()      /* all buffers are removed and 0 is returned */
```

DIRECTORY

```
DIRECTORY( [new_directory] )
```

If issued without an input parameter, this function returns the current working directory.

If the new_directory is specified, the current directory of the process is changed to it and the new_directory is returned. If the new_directory does not exist, the current directory is unchanged and the null string is returned.

Example

```
/* assume these commands are run in sequence                   */
say directory()        == c:\regina   /* displays the current directory   */
say directory('c:\') == c:\      /* changes current directory to c:\   */
say directory('xxx') ==          /* null string returns because there  */
                                 /* is no such directory to change to  */
say directory()        == c:\      /* directory was unchanged by prior call*/
```

DROPBUF

```
DROPBUF( [number] )
```

If called without a parameter, this removes the topmost buffer from the stack. If no buffers were in the stack, it removes all strings from the stack.

If called with a number that identifies a valid buffer number, that buffer and all strings and buffers above it are removed. Strings and buffers below the buffer number are not changed.

If called with a number that does not identify a valid buffer number, no strings or buffers in the stack are changed.

Returns the number of buffers on the stack, *after* any removal it performs. (This differs from CMS, where the return code is always 0).

Example

```
say dropbuf(3)   ==  2  /* assuming the highest buffer is numbered 4,   */
                        /* this would remove buffers 3 and 4            */
say dropbuf()    ==  1  /* assuming there were 2 buffers prior to this call  */
say dropbuf()    ==  0  /* assuming no buffers existed                  */
```

EOF

```
EOF(file)
```

Returns 1 if the file is at end of file, 0 otherwise. `file` is the logical filename assigned at `open`.

Example

```
say eof('infile')    == 1  /* file is open and at EOF */
say eof('infile')    == 0  /* file is at not at eof, or not open, etc */
```

EXISTS

```
EXISTS(filename)
```

Tests to see whether the file specified by `filename` exists. Returns 1 is it does, 0 otherwise.

Example

```
say exists('input.txt')      == 1  /* The file exists. */
say exists('none_such.txt')  == 0  /* The file does not exist. */
```

EXPORT

```
EXPORT(address, [string] , [length] [,pad] )
```

Overwrites the memory beginning at the 4-byte `address` in a previously allocated memory area with the `string`. Returns the number of characters copied.

If `length` is omitted, the number of characters copied will be the length of `string`. If `length` is specified, it determines the number of characters copied. If `length` is less than the `string` length, `pad` is used to specify the pad characters copied.

Be aware that this function attempts to directly overwrite memory at direct addresses. If used improperly it could cause unpredictable effects including program or even operating system failure (depending on the operating system).

> **WARNING — this function could overwrite and destroy memory contents if improperly used!**

Example

```
export('0004 0000'x,'new string')  == 10
/* The 10 bytes beginning at address '0004 0000'x are now set to: 'new string'.  */
```

FIND

```
FIND(string, phrase)
```

Returns the word number of the first occurrence of phrase in string. Returns 0 if phrase is not found. Multiple blanks between words are treated as one in comparisons. The standard function wordpos performs the same work and should be used instead if possible.

Example

```
find('now is the time','the')         == 3
find('now is the time','xxx')         == 0
find('now  is   the   time','the time') == 3
```

FORK

```
FORK()
```

Spawns a new child process, which then runs in parallel to the parent.

If successful, it returns the child process ID to the parent and 0 to the child process. If unsuccessful or unsupported on your operating system, it returns 1 to the parent.

Example

```
fork()   ==  1     /* unsupported on your operating system or failed    */

fork()   == 22287 /* This is the child process ID returned to the parent */
                  /* (the actual number will differ from this example).   */
                  /* 0 will be returned to the child process.             */
```

FREESPACE

```
FREESPACE(address, length)
```

getspace allocates a block of memory from the interpreter's internal memory pool. freespace returns that space to the system. Returns 1 if successful, 0 otherwise.

Example

```
/* this example assumes these two statements are run in sequence */

addr = getspace(12)        /* get a block of 12 bytes of space */
rc = freespace(addr,12)    /* free the 12 bytes of memory      */
```

GETENV

```
GETENV(environment_variable)
```

Returns the value of the `environment_variable` or the null string if the variable is not set. This function is obsolete, use the equivalent `value` function instead. Here is its template:

```
VALUE(environmental_variable,,'SYSTEM')
```

Example

```
/* these two examples retrieve and display the values of the PROMPT and   */
/* SYSTEMDRIVE environmental variables, respectively                      */

say value(PROMPT,,'SYSTEM')        == $P$G   /* for example              */
say value(SYSTEMDRIVE,,'SYSTEM') == C:       /* for example              */
```

The `value` function has some operating system dependencies. See system-specific documentation for any differences from the operation shown here.

GETPID

```
GETPID()
```

Returns the process id or `PID` of the currently running process.

Example

```
say getpid()   ==   588   /* displays the script's PID, whatever it might be   */
```

GETSPACE

```
GETSPACE(length)
```

`getspace` allocates a block of memory of the given `length` from the interpreter's internal memory pool. It returns the address of the memory block. `freespace` returns that space to the system.

Example

```
addr = getspace(12)        /* get a block of 12 bytes of space */
rc = freespace(addr,12)    /* free the 12 bytes of memory       */
```

GETTID

```
GETTID()
```

Returns the thread id or TID of the currently running process.

Example

```
say gettid()  ==  1756  /* displays the script's TID, whatever it might be  */
```

HASH

```
HASH(string)
```

Returns the hash value of the string as a decimal number.

Example

```
say hash('abc')  ==  38
say hash('abd')  ==  39
```

IMPORT

```
IMPORT(address [,length] )
```

Returns a string of the given length by copying data from the 4-byte address. If length is omitted, copies until the null byte is encountered. Coding the length is highly recommended.

Example

```
import('0004 0000'x,8)  /* returns the 8-byte string at address '0004 0000'x */
```

INDEX

```
INDEX(haystack, needle [,start])
```

Returns the character position of needle within string haystack. Returns 0 if needle is not found.

If specified, start tells where in haystack to initiate the search. It defaults to 1 if not specified.

The standard pos function should be used instead of index if possible.

Example

```
index('this','x')           == 0    /* not found                  */
index('this','hi')          == 2    /* found at position 2        */
index('thisthisthis','hi') == 2     /* first found at position 2 */
```

JUSTIFY

```
JUSTIFY(string, length [,pad])
```

Evenly justifies words within a string. The length specifies the length of the returned string, while pad specifies what padding to insert (if necessary). pad defaults to blank.

Example

```
justify('this is it',18)      == 'this     is    it' /* 5 blanks between words */
justify('this is it',18,'x')  == 'thisxxxxxisxxxxxit' /* 5 x's between words    */
justify('   this is it',18,'x')== 'thisxxxxxisxxxxxit'    /* 5 x's between words */
                                          /* ignores leading/trailing blanks    */
justify('this is it',3)== 'thi'           /* truncation occurs due to the LENGTH */
```

MAKEBUF

```
MAKEBUF()
```

Creates a new buffer at the top of the current stack. Buffers are assigned numbers as created, starting at 1. Returns the number of the newly created buffer.

Example

```
/* assume these two commands are executed in sequence      */
makebuf()  == 1   /* if there were no buffers before this call   */
makebuf()  == 2   /* creates the next (second) buffer            */
                  /*   and returns its buffer number             */
```

OPEN

```
OPEN(file, filename, ['Append' | 'Read' | 'Write'] )
```

Opens the filename for the specified processing type. Returns 1 if successful, 0 otherwise.

file is a logical name by which the opened file will be referenced in subsequent functions (for example, readch, readln, writech, writeln, seek, and close).

Example

```
open('infile','input.txt','R')    /* open an input file for reading  */
open('outfile','output.txt','A')  /* append to the output file       */
```

POOLID

```
POOLID()
```

Returns the current variable pool level at the same depth as the call stack. This function enables you to get directly at unexposed variables from a subroutine from the parent hierarchy using the `value` built-in function. Using it, you can get or set variables.

Example

```
/*  run these statements in sequence */
level = poolid()                          /* get current variable pool level/id */
say value('mystem.0',,level-1)
call value 'mystem.45','newvalue',level-1  /* mystem.45 is now changed in parent */
```

POPEN

```
POPEN(command [,stem])
```

Runs the operating system `command` and optionally places its results (from standard output) into the array denoted by `stem`. Note that the `stem` should be specified with its trailing period. `stem.0` will be set to the number of output lines in the array.

The ANSI-1996 `address` instruction should be used instead if possible. `address with` can also capture standard error from the command, which `popen` does not do.

Example

```
popen('dir', 'dir_list.')          /* returns DIR results in dir_list array */
```

Use instead:

```
ddress system 'dir' with output stem dir_list. /* stem name ends w/ period */

/* dir_list.0 tells how many items were placed in the array by the command  */
/* to process the command's output (in the array), run this code....        */
do j = 1 to dir_list.0
   say dir_list.j
end
```

RANDU

```
RANDU( [seed] )
```

Returns a pseudo-random number between 0 and 1. `seed` optionally initializes the random generator.

Example

```
randu()          /* returns a random number between 0 and 1
                    with precision equal to the current value
                    of NUMERIC DIGITS                      */
```

Use the ANSI-1996 function `random` instead for greater portability and standards compliance.

READCH

```
READCH(file, length)
```

Reads and returns `length` number of characters from the logical filename `file`. Fewer characters than `length` could be returned if end of file is reached.

Example

```
readch('infile',10)    /* returns the next 10 characters from the file */
```

READLN

```
READLN(file)
```

Reads the next line from the input file. The line read does not include any end of line character(s) (aka the *newline*).

Example

```
readln('infile')       /* returns the next of line data, sans newline */
```

RXFUNCADD

```
RXFUNCADD(external_name, library, internal_name)
```

Registers an external function for use by the script. `library` is the name of the external function library. Under Windows, this will be a *dynamic link library* or DLL. Under Linux, Unix, and BSD, this will be a *shared library* file.

Make sure that the operating system can locate the library file. For Windows, library must reside in a folder within the PATH. For Linux, Unix, and BSD, the name of the environmental variable that points to the shared library file will vary by the specific operating system. LD_LIBRARY_PATH, LIBPATH, and SHLIB_PATH are most common. Check your operating system documentation if necessary to determine the name of this environmental variable.

Returns 0 if registration was successful.

Example

```
/* this registers external function SQLLoadFuncs from REXXSQL library for use */
rxfuncadd('SQLLoadFuncs', 'rexxsql', 'SQLLoadFuncs')
```

RXFUNCDROP

```
RXFUNCDROP(external_name)
```

Removes the external function name from use. Returns 0 if successful.

Example

```
rxfuncdrop('SQLLoadFuncs')     /* done using this external library */
```

RXFUNCERRMSG

```
RXFUNCERRMSG()
```

Returns the error message from the most recently issued call to rxfuncadd.

Use this function to determine what went wrong in issuing a rxfuncadd.

Example

```
rxfuncerrmsg()             /* returns the rxfuncadd error message */
```

RXFUNCQUERY

```
RXFUNCQUERY(external_name)
```

If the external_name is already registered for use, returns 0. Otherwise returns 1.

Example

```
rxfuncquery('SQLLoadfuncs')    /* returns 0 if registered and usable    */
```

RXQUEUE

```
RXQUEUE(command [,queue])
```

Gives control commands to the external data queue or stack. This controls Regina's extended external data queue facility.

Commands:

- ❑ C — Creates a named queue and returns its name. Queue names are not case-sensitive.
- ❑ D — Deletes the named queue.
- ❑ G — Gets the current queue name.
- ❑ S — Sets the current queue to the one named. Returns the name of the *previously current* queue.
- ❑ T — Sets the timeout period to wait for something to appear in the named queue. If 0, the interpreter never times out . . . it waits forever for something to appear in the queue. Time is expressed in milliseconds.

Please refer to the Regina documentation for further information and examples.

SEEK

```
SEEK(file, offset, ['Begin' | 'Current' | 'End'] )
```

Moves the file position pointer on the logical file specified by file, specified as an offset from an anchor position. Returns the new file pointer position. Note that Rexx starts numbering bytes in a file at 1 (not 0), but AREXX-based functions like seek start numbering bytes from 0. The first byte in a file according to the seek function is byte 0!

Example

```
seek('infile',0,'E')  /* returns number of bytes in file    */
seek('infile',0,'B')  /* positions to beginning of the file */
seek('infile',5,'B')  /* positions to character 5 off the file's beginning */
```

SHOW

```
SHOW(option, [name] , [pad] )
```

Returns the names in the resource list specified by option. Or, tests to see if an entry with the specified name is available.

Possible `options` are:

- ❑ `Clip` — The Clip list
- ❑ `Files` — Names of currently open logical files
- ❑ `Libraries` — Function libraries or function hosts
- ❑ `Ports` — System Ports list

`Files` is available on all platforms; other `options` are valid only for the Amiga and AROS.

Example

```
say show('F')   ==   F STDIN infile STDERR STDOUT
/* this shows that the file referred to by the logical name INFILE is open */
```

SLEEP

```
SLEEP(seconds)
```

Puts the script to sleep (in a wait state) for the specified time in `seconds`. Useful to pause a script.

Example

```
sleep(3)    /* script sleeps for 3 seconds   */
sleep(10)   /* script sleeps for 10 seconds  */
```

STATE

```
STATE(streamid)
```

If the `streamid` exists, returns 0. Otherwise returns 1.

Better portability is possible with the command:

```
stream(streamid, 'C', 'QUERY EXISTS')
```

Example

```
state('xxxx')   == 1  /* assuming this STREAMID does not exist */
state('infile') == 0  /* assuming this STREAMID exists         */
```

STORAGE

```
STORAGE( [address] , [string] , [length] , [pad] )
```

With no arguments, returns the amount of available system memory. If `address` is specified (as a 4-byte address), copies the `string` into memory at that `address`. The number of bytes copied is specified by `length`, or else it defaults to the length of the `string`. `pad` is used if `length` is greater than the length of `string`. Returns the previous contents of the memory before it is overwritten.

Be aware that this function attempts to directly overwrite memory at direct addresses. If used improperly it could cause unpredictable effects including program or operating system failure (depending on the operating system).

Example

```
say storage()      /* displays the amount of available system memory */

storage('0004 0000'x,'new string')
/* the memory at location '0004 0000'x is overwritten with 'new string'
   and its previous contents are returned */
```

> **WARNING — this function could overwrite and destroy memory contents if improperly used!**

STREAM

```
STREAM(streamid, [,option [,command]])
```

`stream` is part of the ANSI-1996 standard, but Regina adds dozens of `commands` to it. These commands permit opening, closing, and flushing files; positioning read or write file pointers; setting file access modes; and, returning information about the file or its status. See the Regina documentation for full details.

TRIM

```
TRIM(string)
```

Returns `string` with any trailing blanks removed. The `strip` function can achieve the same result and is more standard.

Example

```
trim('abc     ')  ==  'abc'
```

UNAME

```
UNAME([option])
```

Returns platform identification information, similar to the uname command of Linux, Unix, and BSD.

Options:

❑ A (**All**) — Returns all information. The default.

❑ S (**System**) — Returns the name of the operating system

❑ N (**Nodename**) — Returns the machine or node name

❑ R (**Release**) — Returns the release of the operating system

❑ V (**Version**) — Returns the version of the operating system

❑ M (**Machine**) — Returns the hardware type

Example

```
/*  output will be completely system-dependent   */
/*  here's an example under Windows XP            */
uname() ==  WINXP NULL 1 5 i586            /* perhaps  */
```

UNIXERROR

```
UNIXERROR(error_number)
```

Returns the textual error message associated with the error_number. Since this function interfaces to operating system services, the error text returned is operating-system-dependent.

Example

```
unixerror(5)  ==  Input/output error   /* under Windows XP, */
unixerror(7)  ==  Arg list too long    /*    for example    */
```

UPPER

```
UPPER(string)
```

Returns string translated to uppercase. Duplicates the function of the standard function translate(string).

Example

```
say upper('abc')  == 'ABC'
say upper('AbCd') == 'ABCD'
```

USERID

```
USERID()
```

Returns the name of the current user (his or her userid). If the platform cannot provide it, this function returns the null string.

Example

```
/*  here's a Windows example, running under the Administrator */
userid()  ==  Administrator

/*  here's a Linux example for regular userid: bossman        */
userid()  ==  bossman
```

WRITECH

```
WRITECH(file, string)
```

Writes the `string` to the logical filename `file` and returns the number of bytes written.

Example

```
writech('outfile','hi')  /* writes string 'hi' to the file and returns 2  */
```

WRITELN

```
WRITELN(file)
```

Writes the `string` to the logical file specified by `file` with the end of line character(s) or *newline* appended. Returns the number of bytes written, including the newline.

Example

```
writeln('outfile','hi2')  /* writes string 'hi2' to the file and returns 4
                             (since this value includes the newline)    */
```

Mainframe Extended Functions

This appendix provides a reference to the extended functions of VM/CMS and OS TSO/E Rexx. It excludes the dozen or so Double-Byte Character Set (DBCS) functions. This appendix as intended as a quick reference guide for developers, so please see the IBM mainframe Rexx manuals for full details: *REXX/VM Reference, SC24-6113 (V5R1)* and *TSO/E REXX Reference SA22-7790 (V1R6)* or *TSO/E REXX Reference SC28-1975-05 (V2R10)*.

Each entry is identified by the name of the function. Entries contain a template of the function, showing its arguments, if any. Optional arguments are enclosed in brackets ([ ]). The template is followed by a description of the function and its use, the function's arguments, and possible return codes. Coding examples show how to code each function. We have noted where the functions differ under VM/CMS versus TSO/E Rexx.

EXTERNALS

```
EXTERNALS()
```

For VM, returns the number of lines (or elements) in the terminal input buffer. This is the number of logical typed-ahead lines.

Example

```
externals()    ==  0          /* if no lines are present         */
```

For OS TSO/E, this function has no meaning since there is no terminal input buffer. Under OS TSO/E, this function always returns 0.

Example

```
externals()    ==  0          /* Under OS/TSO, 0 is ALWAYS returned */
```

FIND

```
FIND(string, phrase)
```

Returns the word number of the first occurrence of phrase in string. Returns 0 if phrase is not found. Multiple blanks between words are treated as one in comparisons. The ANSI-1996 standard function wordpos performs the same work and should be used instead when possible.

Example

```
find('now is the time','the')          == 3
find('now is the time','xxx')          == 0
find('now  is   the   time','the time')  == 3
```

INDEX

```
INDEX(haystack, needle [,start])
```

Returns the character position of needle within string haystack. Returns 0 if needle is not found. If specified, start tells where in haystack to initiate the search. It defaults to 1 if not specified. The ANSI-1996 standard pos function is preferred over index.

Example

```
index('this','x')           == 0      /* not found   */
index('this','hi')          == 2
index('thisthisthis','hi')  == 2      /* returns position of first occurrence */
```

JUSTIFY

```
JUSTIFY(string, length [,pad])
```

Evenly justifies words within a string. The length specifies the length of the returned string, while pad specifies what padding to insert (if necessary). pad defaults to blank. The ANSI-1996 standard right and left functions can be used as alternatives to justify.

Example

```
justify('this is it',18)      == 'this     is     it'  /* 5 blanks between words */
justify('this is it',18,'x')  == 'thisxxxxxisxxxxxit'  /* 5 x's between words    */
justify('   this is it',18,'x') == 'thisxxxxxisxxxxxit'  /* 5 x's between words    */
                                   /* ignores leading/trailing blanks */
justify('this is it',3)       == 'thi'                 /* truncation occurs, LENGTH too short */
```

LINESIZE

```
LINESIZE()
```

Under VM, returns the current terminal line width (the point at which the language processor breaks lines displayed by the say instruction). It returns 0 in these cases:

- ❑ Terminal line size cannot be determined.

- ❑ Virtual machine is disconnected.

- ❑ The command CP TERMINAL LINESIZE OFF is in effect.

Example

```
linesize()         /* returns the current terminal width            */
linesize()  == 0   /* one of the three conditions listed above pertains */
```

Under OS TSO/E, if the script runs in foreground, returns the current terminal line width minus 1 (the point at which the language processor breaks lines displayed by the say instruction). If the script runs in background, this function always returns 131. In non-TSO/E address spaces, this function returns the logical record length of the OUTDD file (default is SYSTSPRT).

Example

```
linesize()        /* if the script is running in foreground, returns terminal width */
linesize()        == 131 /* script is running in background                          */
```

USERID

```
USERID()
```

Returns the name of the current user (his or her userid).

Example

```
userid()              ==      ZHBF01   /* if the login id were ZHBF01 */
```

Under OS, if the script is running in a non-TSO/E address space, this function returns either the userid specified, the stepname, or the jobname.

Rexx/SQL Functions

This appendix provides a reference to all Rexx/SQL functions, as defined by the product documentation for Rexx/SQL version 2.4. This appendix is intended as a quick reference guide for developers, so see the product documentation if more detailed information is required. Chapter 15 tells where to obtain this documentation.

Each of the following entries is identified by the name of the function. Entries contain a template of the function, showing its arguments, if any. Optional arguments are enclosed in brackets ([ ]). The template is followed by a description of the function and its use and the function's arguments. Coding examples show how to code each function. All Rexx/SQL functions return 0 upon success unless otherwise noted.

SQLCLOSE

```
SQLCLOSE( statement_name )
```

Closes a cursor. Frees associated locks and resources.

statement_name — The statement identifier

Example

```
if SQLClose(s1) <> 0 then call sqlerr 'During close'
```

SQLCOMMAND

```
SQLCOMMAND( statement_name, sql_statement [,bind1[,bind2[,...[,bindN]]]] )
```

Immediately executes an SQL statement.

Bind values may optionally be passed for DML statements, if the database permits them. Bind values may not be passed for DDL statements. The format for bind variables is database-dependent.

`statement_name` — Names the SQL statement. For SELECTs, names a stem for an array that will receive statement results

`sql_statement` — A SQL DDL or DML statement

`bind1...bindN` — The bind variables

Variable `sqlca.rowcount` is set by this function to the number of rows affected by DML statements.

Example

For a SELECT statement:

```
rc = sqlcommand(s1,"select deptno, dept_desc from dept_table")
```

Variables `s1.deptno.0` and `s1.dept_desc.0` will both be set to the number of rows returned. Variables `s1.deptno.1` and `s1.dept_desc.1` will contain values retrieved for these respective columns for the first row, variables `s1.deptno.2` and `s1.dept_desc.2` will contain values retrieved for these respective columns from the second row, and so on.

Example

For a DDL statement:

```
sqlstr = 'create table phonedir (lname char(10), phone char(8))'
if SQLCommand(c1,sqlstr) <> 0 then call sqlerr 'During create table'
```

SQLCOMMIT

```
SQLCOMMIT()
```

Permanently applies (or commits) the pending update to the database.

Example

```
if SQLCommit() <> 0 then call sqlerr 'On commit'
```

SQLCONNECT

```
SQLCONNECT( [connection_name], [username], [password], [database], [host] )
```

Creates a new connection to the database. This becomes the default database connection. Which parameters are required, and what their values are, is database-dependent.

connection_name — Names the connection. Required if more than one connection will be open simultaneously.

username — User ID for the connection.

password — User ID's password.

database — Name of the database to connect to.

host — Host on which the database resides. This string is system-dependent.

Example

Oracle — All parameters are optional:

```
rc = sqlconnect(,'scott','tiger')          /*  Scott lives!  */
```

DB2 — Only the database name is required:

```
rc = sqlconnect('MYCON',,,'SAMPLE')
```

MySQL — Only the database name is required:

```
if SQLConnect(,,,'mysql') <> 0 then call sqlerr 'During connect'
```

SQLDEFAULT

```
SQLDEFAULT( [connection_name] )
```

If connection_name is specified, sets the default database connection to it.

If connection_name is not specified, returns the current connection name.

connection name — The name of the database connection to set the default to. Optional.

SQLDESCRIBE

```
SQLDESCRIBE( statement_name [,stem_name] )
```

Run after a SQLPREPARE statement, describes the expressions returned by a SELECT statement. Creates a compound variable for each column in the select list of the SQL statement. The stem consists of statement_name, followed by the constant "COLUMN" and one of the following attributes:

❑   NAME — Column name

❑   TYPE — Column's datatype (a database-specific string)

- ❏ SIZE—Column's size

- ❏ SCALE—The overall size of the column

- ❏ PRECISION—Column's precision (the number of decimal places)

- ❏ NULLABLE—1 if the column is nullable, 0 otherwise

The values returned are database-dependent.

statement_name—The statement identifier

stem_name—Optional stem name for any variables created to return the information

 Note that the columns returned by this function can be determined by calling the SQLGETINFO function with the DESCRIBECOLUMNS argument.

Example

```
rc = sqlprepare(s1,"select deptno, dept_desc from dept_table")
rc = sqldescribe(s1,"fd")
```

This code sequence might result in the following Rexx variables:

```
fd.column.name.1        == 'DEPTNO'
fd.column.name.2        == 'DEPT_DESC'
fd.column.type.1        == 'NUMBER'
fd.column.type.2        == 'VARCHAR2'
fd.column.size.1        == '6'
fd.column.size.2        == '30'
fd.column.precision.1   == '0'
fd.column.precision.2   == ''
fd.column.scale.1       == '6'
fd.column.scale.2       == ''
fd.column.nullable.1    == '0'
fd.column.nullable.2    == '1'
```

SQLDISCONNECT

```
SQLDISCONNECT( [connection_name] )
```

Closes a database connection and all open cursors for that connection.

connection_name—The name of the connection specified in SQLCONNECT, if any.

Example

```
if SQLDisconnect() <> 0 then call sqlerr 'During disconnect'
```

SQLDISPOSE

```
SQLDISPOSE( statement_name )
```

Deallocates a work area originally allocated by a SQLPREPARE statement. Implicitly closes any associated cursor.

statement_name — The SQL statement identifier

Example

```
if SQLDispose(s1) <> 0 then call sqlerr 'During dispose'
```

SQLDROPFUNCS

```
SQLDROPFUNCS(['UNLOAD'])
```

Terminates use of Rexx/SQL and frees resources. The inverse of SQLLOADFUNCS. If the UNLOAD string is coded as the only argument, all Rexx/SQL functions are removed from memory. Use this function with caution as this can affect other running Rexx/SQL programs or other running threads in the current program.

Example

```
if SQLDropFuncs('UNLOAD') <> 0 then
    say 'sqldropfuncs failed, rc: ' rc
```

SQLEXECUTE

```
SQLEXECUTE( statement_name [,bind1[,bind2[,...[,bindN]]]] )
```

Executes a previously "prepared" INSERT, UPDATE, or DELETE statement. The sequence of Rexx/SQL functions to execute these SQL statements in discrete steps would therefore be: SQLPREPARE, SQLEXECUTE, and SQLDISPOSE.

statement_name — Identifies the SQL statement.

bind1...bindN — Bind variables. Notation is database-dependent.

Variable sqlca.rowcount is set to the number of rows affected by the DML statement.

SQLFETCH

```
SQLFETCH( statement_name, [number_rows] )
```

Fetches the next row for an open cursor. If `number_rows` is specified, it can return more than one row.

For one-row fetches, a compound variable is created for each column name identified in the SQL statement. The stem is the statement name, and the tail is the column name.

For multiple-row fetches, a Rexx array is created for each column name in the SQL statement.

`statement_name` — The statement identifier

`number_rows` — An optional parameter that specifies how many rows to fetch

Returns 0 when there are no more rows to fetch. Otherwise, returns a positive integer.

Example

Here is a complete example of preparing a cursor, opening the cursor, fetching all rows from the cursor `SELECT`, and closing the cursor:

```
sqlstr = 'select * from phonedir order by lname'
if SQLPrepare(s1,sqlstr) <> 0 then call sqlerr 'During prepare'

if SQLOpen(s1) <> 0 then call sqlerr 'During open'

/* this loop displays all rows from the SELECT statement     */

do while SQLFetch(s1) > 0
    say 'Name:'  s1.lname  'Phone:'  s1.phone
end
if SQLClose(s1)     <> 0 then call sqlerr 'During close'
```

SQLGETDATA

```
SQLGETDATA(statement_name, column_name, [start_byte], [number_bytes] [,file_name] )
```

Extracts column data from `column_name` in the fetched row. The data is returned in a Rexx compound variable, unless `file_name` is specified, in which case it is written to a file.

`statement_name` — Identifies the SQL statement

`column_name` — Specifies to column data to return

`start_byte` — Optionally specifies the starting byte from which to return column data

`number_bytes` — Optionally specifies the number of bytes to retrieve `file_name` — If specified, names the file into which complete column contents are written

Returns 0 when there is no more data to retrieve. Otherwise, returns the number of bytes retrieved.

You can usually code `SQLFETCH` and then reference columns by their compound or stem variable names without explicitly invoking `SQLGETDATA`. See the entry under "SQLFETCH" earlier in this appendix for a complete example. Please see the Rexx/SQL documentation to see an example of the `SQLGETDATA` function.

SQLGETINFO

`SQLGETINFO( [connection_name], variable_name [,stem_name] )`

Returns information about the database referred to by the connection identified by `connection_name`.

`connection_name` — The database connection name. If not present, uses the current connection.

`variable_name` — Specifies the data to return. Valid values are:

- ❏ `DATATYPES` — Lists column datatypes supported by the database.
- ❏ `DESCRIBECOLUMNS` — Lists column attributes supported by the database.
- ❏ `SUPPORTSTRANSACTIONS` — Returns 1 if the database supports transactions, 0 otherwise.
- ❏ `SUPPORTSSQLGETDATA` — Returns 1 if the database supports the `SQLGETDATA` function, otherwise returns 0.
- ❏ `DBMSNAME` — Returns the database name and version.

`stem_name` — If provided, the information is returned in variables that use this name as their stem. If the information is not provided, this returns a data string.

Example

Get the database version information:

```
if SQLGetinfo(,'DBMSVERSION','desc.') <> 0
   then call sqlerr 'Error getting db version'
   else say 'The database Version is: ' desc.1
```

SQLLOADFUNCS

`SQLLOADFUNCS()`

Loads all external Rexx/SQL functions. Call this function after loading it with `RXFUNCADD`.

Example

Here is a typical code sequence to load and execute the SQLLOADFUNCS function to access the entire Rexx/SQL function library. Be sure that the operating system can locate the external functions by setting the proper environmental variable first:

```
if RxFuncAdd('SQLLoadFuncs','rexxsql', 'SQLLoadFuncs') <> 0 then
    say 'rxfuncadd failed, rc: ' rc

if SQLLoadFuncs() <> 0 then
    say 'sqlloadfuncs failed, rc: ' rc
```

SQLOPEN

```
SQLOPEN( statement_name [,bind1[,bind2[,...[,bindN]]]] )
```

Opens and instantiates a cursor for SELECT processing. The statement must have previously been prepared by a SQLPREPARE statement.

statement_name — The statement identifier.

bind1...bindN — Bind variables. Notation is database-dependent.

Example

See the entry under "SQLFETCH"for a complete SELECT cursor-processing example.

```
if SQLOpen(s1) <> 0 then call sqlerr 'During open'
```

SQLPREPARE

```
SQLPREPARE( statement_name, sql_statement )
```

Allocates a work area for a SQL DDL or DML statement and prepares it for processing. A SELECT statement will subsequently be executed by cursor processing (SQLOPEN, SQLFETCH, and SQLCLOSE). All other statements are executed by a subsequent SQLEXECUTE.

statement_name — The SQL statement identifier.

sql_statement — The SQL statement to prepare. Bind variable notation is database-dependent.

Example

See the entry under "SQLFETCH" for a complete SELECT cursor-processing example.

```
sqlstr = 'select * from phonedir order by lname'
if SQLPrepare(s1,sqlstr) <> 0 then call sqlerr 'During prepare'
```

SQLROLLBACK

```
SQLROLLBACK()
```

Discards and does not apply (rolls back) any pending database updates.

Example

```
if SQLRollback() <> 0 then call sqlerr 'On rollback'
```

SQLVARIABLE

```
SQLVARIABLE( variable_name [,variable_value] )
```

Either returns or sets the specified variable. If `variable_value` is not present, returns the value of `variable_name`. If `variable_value` is present, sets `variable_name` to that value. Can be used to set various aspects of database behavior.

`variable_name` — The variable to be set or retrieved. May be implementation-dependent.

`variable_value` — If coded, the value to set the variable to.

Allowable `variable_name` codings are:

- ❏ VERSION (a read-only value) — The version of Rexx/SQL with:
    - ❏ Package name
    - ❏ Rexx/SQL version
    - ❏ Rexx/SQL date
    - ❏ OS platform
    - ❏ Database
- ❏ DEBUG — debugging level:
    - ❏ 0 — No debugging info (default)
    - ❏ 1 — Rexx variables are displayed when set
    - ❏ 2 — Displays function entry/exit info
    - ❏ The debugging feature traces internal Rexx/SQL functions and is only useful for Rexx/SQL developers.
- ❏ ROWLIMIT — Limits the number of rows fetched by SELECTs run via SQLCOMMAND. The default, 0, means no limit.
- ❏ LONGLIMIT — Maximum number of bytes retrievable via SELECT. Default is 32,786.
- ❏ SAVESQL — If 1, the variable `sqlca.sqltext` contains the text of last SQL statement. Defaults to 1

- ❑ AUTOCOMMIT — Sets database auto-commit ON or OFF (1 is ON, 0 is OFF). Results depend on how the database auto-commit feature works.

- ❑ IGNORETRUNCATE — Dictates what action occurs when a column value gets truncated. Default (OFF) results in function failure and error message. ON truncates data with no error.

- ❑ NULLSTRINGOUT — Returns a user-specified string instead of the null string for a NULL column value.

- ❑ NULLSTRINGIN — Enables a user-specified string to represent null columns. Defaults to the null string.

- ❑ SUPPORTSPLACEMARKERS (a read-only value) — Returns 1 if the database supports bind place-holders, 0 otherwise.

- ❑ STANDARDPLACEMARKERS — if 1, enables use of the question mark (?) as the placeholder for databases that support placeholders other than the question mark (?).

- ❑ SUPPORTSDMLROWCOUNT (a read-only value) — Returns 1 if the database returns the number of rows affected by INSERT, UPDATE, and DELETE statements, 0 otherwise.

Example

```
if SQLVariable('AUTOCOMMIT') = 1
   then say 'Autocommit is ON'
   else say 'Autocommit is OFF'

if SQLVariable('SUPPORTSPLACEMARKERS') = 1
   then say 'Database supports bind placeholders'
   else say 'Database does not support bind placeholders'

if SQLVariable('SUPPORTSDMLROWCOUNT') = 1
   then say 'Database supports SQL Row Counts'
   else say 'Database does not support SQL Row Counts'
```

Rexx/Tk Functions

The following table lists the standard Rexx/Tk functions. The table is reproduced from the Rexx/Tk documentation at `http://rexxtk.sourceforge.net/functions.html`. For further details, please see the Rexx/Tk home page at: `http://rexxtk.sourceforge.net/index.html`.

Rexx/Tk Function	Tcl/Tk Command
TkActivate(pathName, index)	activate command in various widgets
TkAdd(pathName, type [,options...])	menu add
TkAfter(time | 'cancel', 'command' | id)	after
TkBbox(pathName [,arg...])	bbox command in various widgets
TkBind(tag [,sequence [,[+ | *]command]]])	bind
TkButton(pathName [,options...])	button
TkCanvas(pathName [,options...])	canvas
TkCanvasAddtag(pathName, tag [,searchSpec [,arg])	canvas addtag
TkCanvasArc(pathName, x1, y1, x2, y2 [,options...])	canvas create arc
TkCanvasBind(pathName, tagOrId [,sequence [,[+ | *]command]])	canvas bind
TkCanvasBitmap(pathName, x, y [,options...])	canvas create bitmap
TkCanvasCanvasx(pathName, screenx [,gridspacing])	canvas canvasx
TkCanvasCanvasy(pathName, screeny [,gridspacing])	canvas canvasy
TkCanvasCoords(pathName, tagOrId [,x0, y0, ...])	canvas coords
TkCanvasDchars(pathName, tagOrId, first [,last])	canvas dchars
TkCanvasDtag(pathName, tagOrId [,deleteTagOrId])	canvas dtag

Table continued on following page

Rexx/Tk Function	Tcl/Tk Command
TkCanvasDelete(pathName [,tagOrId [,tagOrId...]])	canvas delete
TkCanvasFind(pathName, searchCommand [,arg...])	canvas find
TkCanvasFocus(pathName [,tagOrId])	canvas focus
TkCanvasImage(pathName, x, y [,option...])	canvas create image
TkCanvasLine(pathName, x1, y1, x2, y2 [xn, yn [,options...]])	canvas create line
TkCanvasOval(pathName, x1, y1, x2, y2 [,options...]])	canvas create oval
TkCanvasPolygon(pathName, x1, y1, x2, y2 [xn, yn [,options...]])	canvas create polygon
TkCanvasPosctscript(pathName [options...])	canvas postscript
TkCanvasRectangle(pathName, x1, y1, x2, y2 [,options...]])	canvas create rectangle
TkCanvasText(pathName, x, y [,options...]])	canvas create text
TkCanvasType(pathName, tagOrId)	canvas type
TkCanvasWindow(pathName, x, y [,options...]])	canvas create window
TkCget(pathName [,arg...])	*cget* command in various widgets
TkCheckButton(pathName [,arg...])	checkbutton
TkChooseColor(option [,options...])	tk_chooseColor
TkChooseDirectory(option [,options...])	tk_chooseDirectory
TkConfig(pathName [,options...])	configure command in most all widgets
TkCurSelection(pathName [,arg...])	curselection command in various widgets
TkDelete(pathName, start, end)	delete command in various widgets
TkDestroy(pathName)	destroy
TkEntry(pathName [,options...])	entry
TkError()	new command — return Rexx/Tk error details
TkEvent(arg [,arg] [,options...])	event
TkFocus(pathName [,arg...])	focus
TkFontActual(font [,'-displayof', window], arg [,arg...])	font actual
TkFontConfig(font [,options...])	font configure
TkFontCreate(font [,options...])	font create
TkFontDelete(font [,font...])	font delete

Rexx/Tk Function	Tcl/Tk Command
TkFontFamilies(['-displayof', window])	font families
TkFontMeasure(font [,'-displayof', window], text)	font measure
TkFontMetrics(font [,'-displayof', window], arg [,arg...])	font metrics
TkFontNames()	font names
TkFrame(pathName [,options...])	frame
TkGet(pathName)	get command in various widgets
TkGetOpenFile(option [,options...])	tk_getOpenFile
TkGetSaveFile(option [,options...])	tk_getSaveFile
TkGrab(type, pathName)	grab
TkGrid(pathName [,pathName...] [,options...])	grid configure
TkGridBbox(pathName [,x, y [,x1, y1]])	grid bbox
TkGridColumnConfig(pathName, index [,options...])	grid columnconfigure
TkGridConfig(pathName [,pathName...] [,options...])	grid configure
TkGridForget(pathName [,pathName...])	grid forget
TkGridInfo(pathName)	grid info
TkGridLocation(pathName, x, y)	grid location
TkGridPropagate(pathName [,boolean])	grid propagate
TkGridRowConfig(pathName, index [,options...])	grid rowconfigure
TkGridRemove(pathName [,pathName...])	grid remove
TkGridSize(pathName)	grid size
TkGridSlaves(pathName [,options...])	grid slaves
TkImageBitmap(pathName [,options...])	image create bit map
TkImagePhoto(pathName [,options...])	image create photo
TkIndex(pathName arg)	index command in various widgets
TkInsert(pathName [,arg...])	insert command in various widgets
TkItemConfig(pathName, tagOrId | index [,options...])	itemconfig command in various widgets
TkLabel(pathName [,options...])	label
TkListbox(pathName [,options...])	listbox

Table continued on following page

609

Rexx/Tk Function	Tcl/Tk Command
TkLower(pathName [,belowThis])	lower
TkMenu(pathName [,options...])	menu
TkMenuEntryCget(pathName, index, option)	menu entrycget
TkMenuEntryConfig(pathName, index [,options...])	menu entryconfigure
TkMenuInvoke(pathName, index)	menu invoke
TkMenuPost(pathName [,arg...])	menu post
TkMenuPostCascade(pathName, index)	menu postcascade
TkMenuType(pathName, index)	menu type
TkMenuUnPost(pathName [,arg...])	menu unpost
TkMenuYPosition(pathName, index)	menu yposition
TkMessageBox(message,title,type,icon,default,parent)	tk_messageBox
TkNearest(pathName, xOry)	nearest command in various widgets
TkPack(option [,arg, ...])	pack
TkPopup(arg [,arg...])	tk_popup
TkRadioButton(pathName [,arg...])	radiobutton
TkRaise(pathName [,aboveThis])	raise
TkScale(pathName [,options...])	scale
TkScan(pathName [,args...])	scan command in various widgets
TkScrollbar(pathName [,options...])	scrollbar
TkSee(pathName, index)	see command in various widgets
TkSelection(pathName [,args...])	selection command in various widgets
TkSet(pathName, value)	set command in various widgets
TkSetFileType(type, extension[s...])	sets the rtFiletypes Tk variable for use in both TkGetSaveFile() and TkGetOpenFile() as the -filetypes option
TkTcl(arg [,arg...])	any tcl command
TkText(pathName [,options...])	text

Rexx/Tk Function	Tcl/Tk Command
TkTextTagBind(pathName, tagName [,sequence [,[+ | *]command]])	text tag bind
TkTextTagConfig(pathName, tagName [,option...])	text tag configure
TkTopLevel(pathName)	toplevel
TkVar(varName [,value])	Tcl set command — set and retrieve Tk variables
TkVariable(varName [,value])	new command — set/query internal variables
TkWait()	new command — returns the Rexx "command" from widgets when pressed/used
TkWinfo(command [,arg...])	winfo
TkWm(option, window [,arg...])	wm
TkXView(pathName [,arg...])	xview command of various widgets
TkYView(pathName [,arg...])	yview command of various widgets
TkLoadFuncs()	N/A
TkDropFuncs()	N/A

The Rexx/Tk library is distributed under the LGPL.

Rexx/Tk Extensions

Rexx/Tk is supplied with a number of extension packages. These extensions enable access to additional Tk widgets written in Tcl and are dynamically loaded by Tcl programmers as required. These widgets are included in the base Rexx/Tk package. They are listed in the following tables.

The tables that follow are reproduced from the Rexx/Tk documentation at http://rexxtk.sourceforge.net/extensions.html. For further details, please see the Rexx/Tk home page at http://rexxtk.sourceforge.net/index.html.

Rexx/Tk Tree Function	Tree widget command
TkTree(pathName [,options...])	Tree:create
TkTreeAddNode(pathName, name [,options...])	Tree:newitem
TkTreeClose(pathName, name)	Tree:close
TkTreeDNode(pathName, name)	Tree:delitem

Table continued on following page

Rexx/Tk Tree Function	Tree widget command
TkTreeGetSelection(pathName)	Tree:getselection
TkTreeGetLabel(pathName, x, y)	Tree:labelat
TkTreeNodeConfig(pathName, name [,options...])	Tree:nodeconfig
TkTreeOpen(pathName, name)	Tree:open
TkTreeSetSelection(pathName, label)	Tree:setselection

Items marked with * are base Rexx/Tk functions that can be used with Rexx/Tk extensions.

Rexx/Tk Combobox Function	
TkCombobox(pathname [,options...])	combobox::combobox
*TkBbox(pathName, index)	combobox bbox
TkComboboxICursor(pathName, index)	combobox icursor
TkComboboxListDelete(pathName, first [,last])	combobox list delete
TkComboboxListGet(pathName, first [,last])	combobox list get
TkComboboxListIndex(pathName, index)	combobox list index
TkComboboxListInsert(pathName, index [,args...])	combobox list insert
TkComboboxListSize(pathName)	combobox list size
TkComboboxSelect(pathName, index)	combobox select
TkComboboxSubwidget(pathName [name])	combobox subwidget
*TkConfig(pathName [,options...])	combobox configure
*TkCurselection(pathName)	combobox curselection
*TkDelete(pathName, first [,last])	combobox delete
*TkGet(pathName)	combobox get
*TkIndex(pathName, index)	combobox index
*TkInsert(pathName, index, string)	combobox insert
*TkScan(pathName [,args...])	combobox scan
*TkSelection(pathName [,args...])	combobox selection

Items marked with * are base Rexx/Tk functions that can be used with Rexx/Tk extensions.

Rexx/Tk MCListbox Function	MCListbox widget command
TkMCListbox(pathname [,options...])	mclistbox::mclistbox
*TkActivate(pathName, index)	mclistbox activate
*TkBbox(pathName [,arg...])	mclistbox bbox
*TkCget(pathName [,arg...])	mclistbox cget
*TkConfig(pathName [,options...])	mclistbox configure
*TkCurSelection(pathName [,arg...])	mclistbox curselection
*TkDelete(pathName, start, end)	mclistbox delete
*TkGet(pathName)	mclistbox get
*TkIndex(pathName arg)	mclistbox index
*TkInsert(pathName [,arg...])	mclistbox insert
TkMCListboxColumnAdd(pathName, name [,options...])	mclistbox column add
TkMCListboxColumnCget(pathName, name ,option)	mclistbox column cget
TkMCListboxColumnConfig(pathName, name [,options...])	mclistbox column configure
TkMCListboxColumnDelete(pathName, name)	mclistbox column delete
TkMCListboxColumnNames(pathName)	mclistbox column names
TkMCListboxColumnNearest(pathName,x)	mclistbox column nearest
TkMCListboxLabelBind(pathName,name,sequence, [* | +]command)	mclistbox label bind
*TkNearest(pathName, xOry)	mclistbox nearest
*TkScan(pathName [,args...])	mclistbox scan
*TkSee(pathName ???[,options...])	mclistbox see
*TkSelection(pathName [,args...])	mclistbox selection
*TkXView(pathName [,arg...])	mclistbox xview
*TkYView(pathName [,arg...])	mclistbox yview

Items marked with * are base Rexx/Tk functions that can be used with Rexx/Tk extensions.

The Rexx/Tk Library Extensions are distributed under the LGPL.

H

Tools, Interfaces, and Packages

As a universal scripting language that enjoys worldwide use, Rexx has inevitably spawned a large collection of open-source and free tools. There are literally too many Rexx tools, utilities, extensions, and interfaces to track them all. This partial list shows some of the available tools and hints at their breadth. All those listed here are either open-source or free software. You can locate most of these tools simply by entering their names as search keywords in any prominent search engine, such as Google, Yahoo!, or AltaVista. Many of them can also be located through links found at the home pages of the Rexx Language Association, SourceForge, and those of the various Rexx interpreters. The Rexx Language Association is located at www.rexxla.org, SourceForge is located at www.sourceforge.net, and the Web addresses for the Rexx interpreters are found in Chapters 20 through 30 in the section of each chapter entitled "Downloading and Installing."

Package or Product	Uses
Administration Tool	A "programmer's GUI" and administration aid designed to assist in the development and debugging of Rexx scripts.
Associative Arrays for Rexx	Routines that manipulate associative arrays.
Bean Scripting Framework	Allows Java programs to call Rexx scripts, and for Rexx scripts to create and manipulate Java objects.
cgi-lib.rxx (also known as CGI / Rexx)	A library of Common Gateway Interface, or CGI, functions from Stanford Linear Accelerator Center (SLAC). These functions make it easy to retrieve and decode input, send output back to the client, and report the results of diagnostics and errors.

Table continued on following page

Package or Product	Uses
CUR for Rexx	A version of "ObjectCUR for Object REXX" for classic Rexx.
FileRexx Function Library	Functions with new file I/O commands specific to Windows.
FileUt	Scripting interface for standard I/O.
GTK+	Modal dialog manager for Object REXX.
Hack	Hexadecimal editor for Windows with Rexx script capabilities.
HtmlGadgets	Generates code snippets to support HTML coding.
HtmlStrings	Generates HTML code.
HtmlToolBar	Generates code snippets for HTML gadgets.
Internet/REXX HHNS Workbench	A Common Gateway Interface external function library from Henri Henault & Sons, France.
MacroEd	Manages RexxEd macros.
MIDI I/O Function Library	Enables input/output to MIDI ports.
MIDI Rexx Function Library	Read, write, play and record MIDI files.
Mod_Rexx	Applies Rexx to Apache Web page development. Controls all Apache features through Rexx scripts.
ObjectCUR for Object REXX	A cross-platform class library that includes functions for system information, logging, file system control, FTP, Win32 calls, and text file support.
ODBC Drivers	Open Database Connectivity (ODBC) drivers for Microsoft Access databases, dBASE files, or Excel files.
Regular Expressions	Regular expressions for Rexx scripts.
REXREF3	Produces Rexx script cross-reference listings.
Rexx 2 Exe	Converts scripts into a self-running `*.exe` files.
Rexx Dialog	Creates GUI interfaces for Windows.
Rexx Math Bumper Pack	Math libraries.
Rexx/CURL	Interface to the cURL package for access to URL-addressable resources.
Rexx/Curses	Interface to the `curses` library for portable character-based user interfaces.
Rexx/DW	Provides a cross-platform GUI toolset, based on the *Dynamic Windows* package.

Package or Product	Uses
Rexx/gd	Create and manipulate graphics images using the gd library.
Rexx/ISAM	Interface to Indexed Sequential Access Method (ISAM) files.
Rexx/SQL	Interface to all major open-source and commercial SQL databases.
Rexx/Tk	The Tk GUI interface toolkit for cross-platform GUIs for Rexx scripts.
Rexx/Trans	Translates Rexx API calls from an external function package into API calls specific to a particular Rexx interpreter.
Rexx/Wrapper	"Wraps" Rexx scripts into a closed-source, stand-alone executables.
Rexx2Nrx	Classic Rexx to NetRexx converter.
RexxED	A Rexx-aware editor.
RexxMail	Email client that uses only WPS and Rexx scripts.
RexxRE	Regular expression library for Rexx scripts.
RexxTags	Rexx Server Pages (RSP) compiler for prototyping XML tags in Rexx; an easy way to write XML tags in Rexx.
RexxUtil	IBM's function library for interaction with the environment.
RegUtil	Another implementation of RexxUtil (the Windows version of RexxUtil).
RexxXML	Provides support for XML and HTML files.
RxAcc	Generates code snippets through a keyboard accelerator.
RxBlowFish	Callable DLL implements Blowfish encryption.
RxCalibur	Creates a library of code snippets; aids in reusing this code.
RxComm Serial Add-on	Control/access serial ports from Rexx scripts.
RXDDE	DDE client functions for Rexx under Windows.
RxDlgIDE	An Interactive Development Environment (IDE) designed to work with Rexx Dialog under Windows.
rxJava	Rexx functions for Java.

Table continued on following page

Package or Product	Uses
RxProject	A Rexx script preprocessor that aids in managing scripting projects.
RxRSync	Callable DLL implements Rsync compession/ differencing.
RxSock	Interface for TCP/IP sockets.
RxWav	Create and manipulate audio files.
Script Launcher	GUI panel for launching Rexx scripts under Windows.
Speech Function Library	Pronounces synthesized voice.
THE	The Hessling Editor, a cross-platform, Rexx-aware text editor.
W32 Funcs	Functions for Windows Registry access.
Wegina	Windows front end for the Regina interpreter.

Open Object Rexx: Classes and Methods

These lists show the classes and methods in Open Object Rexx. For details see the manual *Open Object Rexx for Windows Reference* for Windows systems or the manual *Open Object Rexx for Linux Programming Guide* for Linux systems. The list below is based on the Windows reference manual, version 2.1. The classes and methods are largely similar between the Windows and Linux products. From the Windows standpoint, the one major exception is that the Windows product includes a number of additional Windows-specific classes and their methods.

Collection Classes and Their Methods

Array Class

NEW (Class Method), OF (Class Method), [ ], [ ]=, AT, DIMENSION, FIRST, HASINDEX, ITEMS, LAST, MAKEARRAY, NEXT, PREVIOUS, PUT, REMOVE, SECTION, SIZE, SUPPLIER

Bag Class

OF (Class Method), [ ], [ ]=, HASINDEX, MAKEARRAY, PUT, SUPPLIER

Directory Class

[ ], [ ]=, AT, ENTRY, HASENTRY, HASINDEX, ITEMS, MAKEARRAY, PUT, REMOVE, SETENTRY, SETMETHOD, SUPPLIER, UNKNOWN, DIFFERENCE, INTERSECTION, SUBSET, UNION, XOR

List Class

OF (Class Method), [ ], [ ]=, AT, FIRST, FIRSTITEM, HASINDEX, INSERT, ITEMS, LAST, LASTITEM, MAKEARRAY, NEXT, PREVIOUS, PUT, REMOVE, SECTION, SUPPLIER

Queue Class

[ ], [ ]=, AT, HASINDEX, ITEMS, MAKEARRAY, PEEK, PULL, PUSH, PUT, QUEUE, REMOVE, SUPPLIER

Relation Class

[ ], [ ]=, ALLAT, ALLINDEX, AT, HASINDEX, HASITEM, INDEX, ITEMS, MAKEARRAY, PUT, REMOVE, REMOVEITEM, SUPPLIER, DIFFERENCE, INTERSECTION, SUBSET, UNION, XOR

Set Class

OF (Class Method), [ ], [ ]-, AT, HASINDEX, ITEMS, MAKEARRAY, PUT, REMOVE, SUPPLIER

Table Class

[ ], [ ]=, AT, HASINDEX, ITEMS, MAKEARRAY, PUT, REMOVE, SUPPLIER, DIFFERENCE, INTERSECTION, SUBSET, UNION, XOR

Other Classes and Their Methods

Alarm Class

CANCEL, INIT

Class Class

BASECLASS, DEFAULTNAME, DEFINE, DELETE, ENHANCED, ID, INHERIT, INIT, METACLASS, METHOD, METHODS, MIXINCLASS, NEW, QUERYMIXINCLASS, SUBCLASS, SUBCLASSES, SUPERCLASSES, UNINHERIT

Message Class

COMPLETED, INIT, NOTIFY, RESULT, SEND, START

Method Class

NEW (Class Method), NEWFILE (Class Method), SETGUARDED, SETPRIVATE, SETPROTECTED, SETSECURITYMANAGER, SETUNGUARDED, SOURCE

Monitor Class

CURRENT, DESTINATION, INIT, UNKNOWN

Object Class

NEW (Class Method), Operator methods: =, ==, \=, ><, <>, \==, CLASS, COPY, DEFAULTNAME, HASMETHOD, INIT, OBJECTNAME, OBJECTNAME=, REQUEST, RUN, SETMETHOD, START, STRING, UNSETMETHOD

Stem Class

NEW (Class Method), [ ], [ ]=, MAKEARRAY, REQUEST, UNKNOWN

Stream Class

ARRAYIN, ARRAYOUT, CHARIN, CHAROUT, CHARS, CLOSE, COMMAND, DESCRIPTION, FLUSH, INIT, LINEIN, LINEOUT, LINES, MAKEARRAY, OPEN, POSITION, QUALIFY, QUERY, SEEK, STATE, SUPPLIER

String Class

NEW (Class Method), Arithmetic Methods: +, -, *, /, %, //, **, prefix +, prefix -, Comparision Methods: =, \=, ><, <>, >, <, >=, \<, <=, \>, ==, \==, >>, <<, >>=, \<<, <<=, \>>, Logical Methods: &, |, &&, Concatenation Methods: "" (by abuttal), | |, " " (with one intervening space), ABBREV, ABS, BITAND, BITOR, BITXOR, B2X, CENTER/CENTRE, CHANGESTR, COMPARE, COPIES, COUNTSTR, C2D, C2X, DATATYPE, DELSTR, DELWORD, D2C, D2X, FORMAT, INSERT, LASTPOS, LEFT, LENGTH, MAKESTRING, MAX, MIN, OVERLAY, POS, REVERSE, RIGHT, SIGN, SPACE, STRING, STRIP, SUBSTR, SUBWORD, TRANSLATE, TRUNC, VERIFY, WORD, WORDINDEX, WORDLENGTH, WORDPOS, WORDS, X2B, X2C, X2D

Supplier Class

NEW (Class Method), AVAILABLE, INDEX, ITEM, NEXT

Classes Unique to Windows

Capitalization for these methods is exactly as provided in the manual.

WindowsProgramManager Class

AddDesktopIcon, AddShortCut, AddGroup, AddItem, DeleteGroup, DeleteItem, Init, ShowGroup

WindowsRegistry Class

CLASSES_ROOT, CLASSES_ROOT=, CLOSE, CONNECT, CREATE, CURRENT_KEY, CURRENT_KEY=, CURRENT_USER, CURRENT_USER=, DELETE, DELETEVALUE, FLUSH, GETVALUE, INIT, LIST, LISTVALUES, LOAD, LOCAL_MACHINE, LOCAL_MACHINE=, OPEN, QUERY, REPLACE, RESTORE, SAVE, SETVALUE, UNLOAD, USERS, USERS=

WindowsEventLog Class

INIT, OPEN, CLOSE, READ, WRITE, CLEAR, GETNUMBER

WindowsManager Class

FIND, FOREGROUNDWINDOW, WINDOWATPOSITION, CONSOLETITLE, CONSOLETITLE=, SENDTEXTTOWINDOW, PUSHBUTTONINWINDOW, PROCESSMENUCOMMAND

WindowObject Class

ASSOCWINDOW, HANDLE, TITLE, TITLE=, WCLASS, ID, COORDINATES, STATE, RESTORE, HIDE, MINIMIZE, MAXIMIZE, RESIZE, ENABLE, DISABLE, MOVETO, TOFOREGROUND, FOCUSNEXTITEM, FOCUSPREVIOUSITEM, FOCUSITEM, FINDCHILD, CHILDATPOSITION, NEXT, PREVIOUS, FIRST, LAST, OWNER, FIRSTCHILD, ENUMERATECHILDREN, SENDMESSAGE, SENDCOMMAND, SENDMENUCOMMAND, SENDMOUSECLICK, SENDSYSCOMMAND, PUSHBUTTON, SENDKEY, SENDCHAR, SENDKEYDOWN, SENDKEYUP, SENDTEXT, MENU, SYSTEMMENU, ISMENU, PROCESSMENUCOMMAND

MenuObject Class

ISMENU, ITEMS, IDOF, TEXTOF(position), TEXTOF(id), SUBMENU, FINDSUBMENU, FINDITEM, PROCESSITEM

WindowsClipBoard Class

COPY, PASTE, EMPTY, ISDATAAVAILABLE

OLEObject Class

INIT, GETCONSTANT, GETKNOWNEVENTS, GETKNOWNMETHODS, GETOBJECT, GETOUTPARAMETERS, UNKNOWN

Mod_Rexx: Functions and Special Variables

This appendix lists the Mod_Rexx functions and special variables. Mod_Rexx is the package that permits Rexx scripts to control all aspects of the popular open source Apache Web server product. Chapter 17 describes Mod_Rexx and demonstrates how to script it. See that chapter for a full product description and sample program.

General Functions

These functions provide a base level of services necessary to work with the Apache Web server. They manage cookies and the error log, retrieve environmental information, and handle URLs.

General Function	Use
WWWAddCookie	Set a new cookie for the browser
WWWConstruct_URL	Return a URL for the specified path
WWWEscape_Path	Convert a path name to an escaped URL
WWWGetArgs	Get the GET/POST arguments
WWWGetCookies	Get the GET/POST cookies
WWWGetVersion	Get the Mod_Rexx version
WWWHTTP_time	Get the current RFC 822/1123 time
WWWInternal_Redirect	Create a new request from the specified URI
WWWLogError	Log an error message to Apache log file
WWWLogInfo	Log an informational message to Apache log file

Table continued on following page

General Function	Use
WWWLogWarning	Log a warning message to Apache log file
WWWRun_Sub_Req	Run an Apache subrequest
WWWSendHTTPHeader	Set the MIME content, and send HTTP header
WWWSetHeaderValue	Set a new value for a cookie.
WWWSub_Req_Lookup_File	Run subrequest on a filename
WWWSub_Req_Lookup_URI	Run subrequest on a URI

Apache Request Record Functions

These functions provide information about and manage the request record pointer, information coming into the script from Apache and the Web.

Apache Request Record Function	Use
WWWReqRecConnection	Return connection record pointer
WWWReqRecNext	Return next request record pointer
WWWReqRecPrev	Return previous request record pointer
WWWReqRecMain	Return main request record pointer
WWReqRecIsMain	Return 1 if this is the main request
WWWReqRecThe_request	Return the request
WWWReqRecProxyreq	Return 1 if this is a proxy request
WWWReqRecServer	Return the server record pointer
WWWReqRecHeader_only	Always returns 0
WWWReqRecProtocol	Return request HTTP protocol
WWWReqRecBytes_sent	Return bytes sent field
WWWReqRecArgs	Return args field
WWWReqRecFinfo_stmode	Return finfo stmode field
WWWReqRecUsern	Return user's login name
WWWReqRecAuth_type	Return authentication type

Updatable Apache Request Record Functions

These functions manage the request record pointer and allow updating values as well as retrieving them.

Updateable Request Record Function	Use
WWWReqRecStatus_line	Return or set status line field
WWWReqRecStatus	Return or set status field
WWWReqRecMethod	Return or set method field
WWWReqRecMethod_number	Return or set method number field
WWWReqRecAllowed	Return or set allowed field
WWWReqRecHeader_in	Return or set values in bytes headers in field
WWWReqRecHeader_out	Return or set values in bytes headers out field
WWWReqRecErr_header_out	Return or set values in bytes error headers out field
WWWReqRecSubprocess_env	Return or set values in subprocess environment
WWWReqRecNotes	Return or set values in the notes
WWWReqRecContent_type	Return or set content type field
WWWReqRecContent_encoding	Return or set content encoding field
WWWReqRecHandler	Return or set handler field
WWWReqRecContent_languages	Return or set content languages field
WWWReqRecNo_cache	Return or set no_cache field
WWWReqRecUri	Return or set URI field
WWWReqRecFilename	Return or set filename field
WWWReqRecPath_info	Return or set path_info field

Apache Server Record Functions

These functions manage server-side concerns pertaining to Apache and its environment.

Server Record Function	Use
WWWSrvRecServer_admin	Return server admin email address
WWWSrvRecServer_hostname	Return server hostname
WWWSrvRecPort	Return server listening port
WWWSrvRecIs_virtual	Return non-zero for a virtual server
WWWCnxRecAborted	Return non-zero for a virtual server

Special Variables

Mod_Rexx uses a set of three dozen *special variables* to communicate information to Rexx scripts. The names of these variables all begin with the letters WWW. These special variables are set either before the script starts, or after the script executes a function call. Their purpose is to communicate information to the script either about the environment or the results of function calls. Here are the Mod_Rexx special variables:

Special Variable	Use
WWWARGS.0	Number of arguments passed to the script for GET or PUT requests (set by invoking function WWWGetArgs)
WWWARGS.n.!NAME and WWWARGS.n.!VALUE	Argument list passed to the script, formatted as per GET or POST (set by invoking function WWWGetArgs)
WWWAUTH_TYPE	Authentication method
WWWCONTENT_LENGTH	Length of client data buffer
WWWCONTENT_TYPE	Content type of data
WWWCOOKIES.0	Number of cookies passed to the script (set by invoking function WWWGetCookies)
WWWCOOKIES.n.!NAME and WWWCOOKIES.n.!VALUE	List of name=value cookie pairs passed to the script (set by invoking function WWWGetCookies)
WWWDEFAULT_TYPE	Value of DefaultType directive or text/plain if not configured
WWWFILENAME	Fully qualified filename, translated from the server's URI
WWWFNAMETEMPLATE	Temporary filename template that will be passed to Mod_Rexx
WWWGATEWAY_INTERFACE	Name and version of gateway interface
WWWHOSTNAME	Hostname in the URI
WWWHTTP_USER_ACCEPT	List of acceptable MIME types
WWWHTTP_USER_AGENT	Client browser type and version
WWWIS_MAIN_REQUEST	Always 1
WWWPATH_INFO	Script's file name
WWWPATH_TRANSLATED	Script's fully qualified path and file name
WWWPOST_STRING	Unparsed name/value pairs from browser if POST request (set by invoking function WWWGetArgs)

Special Variable	Use
WWWQUERY_STRING	Unparsed QUERY_STRING portion of the URI for GETs
WWWREMOTE_ADDR	Host's TCP/IP address
WWWREMOTE_HOST	Host's DNS name (if available)
WWWREMOTE_IDENT	Remote user name
WWWREMOTE_USER	Authenticated username
WWWREQUEST_METHOD	Request method, either GET or POST
WWWRSPCOMPILER	REXX RSP compiler program name
WWWSCRIPT_NAME	Fully qualified URI path and name of the script or RSP file
WWWSERVER_NAME	Server host name
WWWSERVER_ROOT	Server's root path
WWWSERVER_PORT	Server's port number
WWWSERVER_PROTOCOL	Request HTTP protocol version
WWWSERVER_SOFTWARE	Name and version of the WWW server software
WWWUNPARSEDURI	Unparsed portion of the request URI
WWWURI	Full request URI

K

NetRexx: Quick Reference

This appendix provides a quick summary of NetRexx. For full authoritative reference, see the book *The NetRexx Language* by Michael Cowlishaw (Prentice-Hall, 1997). Also refer to the manuals that download with the product, all written by Michael Cowlishaw: *The NetRexx Language: Specification*; *NetRexx Language Supplement*; *NetRexx Language Overview*; and the *NetRexx User's Guide*.

NetRexx Special Names

Special Name	Function
ask	Reads a line from the default input stream and returns it as a string of type *Rexx* (also called a *NetRexx string*)
digits	Returns the current setting of `numeric digits` as a NetRexx string
form	Returns the current setting of `numeric form` as a NetRexx string
length	Returns an array's length (the number of elements)
null	Returns the null value (used in assignments and comparisons)
source	Returns a NetRexx string that identifies the source of the current class
super	Used to invoke a method or property overridden in the current class
this	Returns a reference to the current object
trace	Returns the current setting as a NetRexx string
version	Returns the NetRexx language version as a NetRexx string

Special Methods

Special Method	Use
super	Constructor of the superclass
this	Constructor of the current class

Instruction Syntax

This section lists the NetRexx instructions. Each consists of a coding template with allowable operands. Optionally coded operands are surrounded by brackets ([ ]). Operands in italicized boldface are to be replaced by an appropriate term or list. This is intended as a quick programmer's reference. For greater detail, please see the NetRexx documentation cited in the introduction to this appendix.

CLASS

```
class   name   [ visibility ]   [ modifier ]   [ binary ]
               [ extends   classname ]
               [ uses   classname_list ]
               [ implements   classname_list ]   ;
```

visibility is either *private* or *public*.

modifier is either *abstract*, *final*, or *interface*.

DO

```
do [ label name ]   [ protect term ] ;
   instruction_list
   [ catch [vare = ]   exception ; instruction_list ] . . .
   [ finally [;] instruction_list ]
end   [ name ]   ;
```

EXIT

```
exit   [ expression ]   ;
```

IF

```
if   expression [;]
   then [;]   instruction
   [ else [;]   instruction   ]
```

IMPORT

```
import   name ;
```

ITERATE

```
iterate  [ name ] ;
```

LEAVE

```
leave  [ name ]  ;
```

LOOP

```
loop  [ label name ]  [ protect termp ]  [ repetitor ]  [ conditional ]  ;
    instruction_list
    [ catch [vare = ] exception ; instruction_list ] . . .
    [ finally [;] instruction_list ]
end [ name ]  ;
```

repetitor is one of:

   $varc = expression\_t$ [to *expression_t*] [by *expression_b*] [for *expression_f*]

   varo over *termo*

   for *expression_r*

   forever

conditional is either: while *expression_w*   or   until *expression_u*

METHOD

```
method name [( [ argument_list ] )]
   [ visibility ]   [ modifier ]  [ protect ]
   [ returns termr ]
   [ signals signal_list ] ;
```

argument_list is a list of one or more assignments separated by commas

visibility is one of: *inheritable, private,* or *public*

modifier is one of: *abstract, constant, final, native,* or *static*

signal_list is a list of one or more *terms,* separated by commas

631

NOP

```
nop ;
```

NUMERIC

numeric digits [*expression_d*] ;

or

```
numeric  form   [ form_setting ]  ;
```

form_setting is either *scientific* or *engineering*.

OPTIONS

```
options  options_list  ;
```

PACKAGE

```
package  name  ;
```

PARSE

```
parse  term  template  ;
```

template consists of non-numeric *symbols* separated by blanks or *patterns*.

PROPERTIES

```
properties   [ visibility ]  [ modifier ]  ;
```

visibility is one of: *inheritable, private,* or *public.*

modifier is one of: *constant, static,* or *volatile.*

RETURN

```
return  [ expression ]  ;
```

SAY

```
say  [ expression ]  ;
```

SELECT

```
select   [ label name ]  [ protect termp ] ;
         when expression [;]  then  [;]  instruction . . .
         [ otherwise [;]  instruction_list ]
         [ catch [vare = ] exception ;  instruction_list ] . . .
         [ finally [;]  instruction_list ]
end [ name ] ;
```

SIGNAL

```
signal  term ;
```

TRACE

```
trace  trace_term  ;
```

trace_term is one of: *all, methods, off,* or *results*.

Interpreter System Information

Table L-1 parse source system Strings

This table lists some example *system information strings* returned by the instructions:

```
parse  source  system  .
say  'The system string is:'  system
```

Since this information is system-dependent and subject to change, readers should retrieve this information for their own environments by executing the preceding statements.

Interpreter	Platform	"System Information" String
Regina Rexx	Windows	WIN32
Regina Rexx	Linux	UNIX
BRexx	Windows	MSDOS
Reginald	Windows	WIN32
Rexx/imc	Unix	UNIX
Rexx/imc	Linux	UNIX
r4	Windows	Win32
roo!	Windows	Win32
Open Object Rexx	Linux	LINUX
IBM REXX	OS TSO/E	TSO
IBM REXX	VM/CMS	CMS
IBM REXX	VSE/ESA	VSE

Table L-2   Default Environment Strings

This table lists the *default command environments* for the Rexx interpreters and platforms listed.

Since this information is system-dependent and subject to change, verify the default command environment for your platform by running this Rexx statement:

```
say  'The default command environment is:'  address()
```

Interpreter	Platform	Default Environment String
Regina Rexx	All platforms	SYSTEM
BRexx	Windows	SYSTEM
Reginald	Windows	SYSTEM
Rexx/imc	Unix	UNIX
Rexx/imc	Linux	UNIX
r4	Windows	system
roo!	Windows	system
Open Object Rexx	Windows	CMD
IBM REXX	OS/TSO	TSO
IBM REXX	VM/CMS	CMS
IBM REXX	VSE/ESA	VSE

M

Answers to "Test Your Understanding" Questions

Chapter 1

1. Rexx is a *higher-level language* in that each line of code accomplishes more than does code written in traditional languages like C++, COBOL, or Pascal. Rexx derives its power from the fact it is a *glue language*—a language that ties together existing components such as other programs, routines, filters, objects, and the like. The industry-wide trend towards scripting languages is based on the higher productivity these languages yield.

2. Rexx is a *free-format language*. There are no requirements to code in particular columns or lines or in uppercase, lowercase, or mixed case.

3. Expert programmers sometimes mistakenly think that they don't need an easy-to-use language. Nothing could be farther from the truth. Expert programmers become wildly productive with easy-to-use languages. Their code lasts longer as well, because less skilled individuals can easily enhance and maintain it.

4. The two free object-oriented Rexx interpreters are roo! from Kilowatt Software and Open Object Rexx from the Rexx Language Association (formerly known as IBM's Object REXX). Both run standard or classic Rexx scripts without any alterations.

5. One outstanding feature of Rexx is that it runs on all sizes of computer, from handhelds to personal computers to midrange machines to mainframes. Rexx runs on cell or mobile phones, Palm Pilots, and mainframes.

6. One of the two current Rexx standards was established by the book *The Rexx Language*, second edition, by Michael Cowlishaw, published in 1990. The other was promulgated by the American National Standards Institute, or ANSI, in 1996. There is little difference between these two standards. Chapter 13 lists the exact differences between these two similar standards.

7. Rexx bridges the traditional gap between ease of use and power through: simple syntax; free formatting; consistent, reliable behavior; a small instruction set surrounded by a large set of functions; few language rules; support for modularity and structured programming; and standardization.

Chapter 2

1. Comments are encoded between the starting identifier /* and the ending identifier */. They may span as many lines as you like. They may also appear as *trailing comments*, comments written on the same lines as Rexx code.

2. Rexx recognizes functions as keywords immediately followed by a left parenthesis: `function _name()` or `function_name(parameter)`. The `call` instruction can also be used to invoke functions. In this case, the function is encoded just like a call to a subroutine, and parentheses do not immediately follow the function name. Chapter 8 fully discusses how to invoke functions and subroutines.

3. Variables do not have to be predefined or declared in Rexx. They are automatically defined the first time they are used or referred to. If a variable is equal to its name in uppercase, it is uninitialized.

4. The basic instruction for screen output is `say`. The basic instruction for keyboard input is `pull`. Rexx also offers more sophisticated ways to perform input and output, described in subsequent chapters.

5. *Comparisons* determine if two values are equal (such as character strings or numbers). *Strict comparisons* only apply to character strings. They determine if two strings are identical (including any preceding and/or trailing blanks). The strings are not altered in any way prior to a strict comparison. For example, the shorter string is not blank-padded as in regular or "nonstrict" character string comparison.

6. Define a numeric variable in the same way you define any other Rexx variable. The only difference is that a numeric variable contains a value recognized as a number (such as a string of digits, optionally preceded by a plus or minus sign and optionally containing a decimal place, or in exponential notation).

Chapter 3

1. Structured programming is recommended because it leads to more understandable code, and therefore higher productivity. The first table in the chapter lists the structured programming constructs and the Rexx instructions that implement them. Subroutines and functions support modularity, the key structured programming concept of breaking code up into discrete, smaller routines.

2. Rexx matches an unmatched `else` with the nearest unmatched `if`.

3. Test for the end of input by testing for the user's entry of a null string or by inspecting input for some special character string denoting the end of file in the input (such as end or `exit` or x). Chapter 5 introduces functions that can test for the end of an input file, such as `chars` and `lines`.

4. *Built-in functions* are provided as part of the Rexx language. The code of *internal routines* resides in the same file as that of the calling routine; *external routines* reside in separate files. A Rexx *function* always returns a single value; a *subroutine* may optionally return a value. Chapter 8 gives full details on how to pass information into and out of functions and subroutines.

5. TRUE tests to 1. FALSE tests to 0. Standard Rexx does not accept "any nonzero value" for TRUE. (However, some specific Rexx interpreters will accept any nonzero value as TRUE).

6. The danger of a do forever loop is that it will be an *endless loop* and never terminate. Avoid coding the do forever loop; use structured programming's do-while loop instead. If you do code a do forever loop, be sure to code a manual exit of some sort. For example, the leave, signal, and exit instructions can end the otherwise endless loop.

7. The signal instruction either causes an unconditional branch of control, or aids in processing special errors or *conditions*. signal differs from the GOTO of other languages in that it terminates all active control structures in which it is encoded.

8. do while tests the condition at the top of the loop, while do until is a bottom-driven loop (it tests the condition at the bottom of the loop). Only the do while is structured. Its use is preferred. Any do until can be recoded as do while.

Chapter 4

1. Any number of subscripts can be applied to array elements. An array may have any desired dimensionality. The only limit is typically that imposed by memory. Array elements do not have to been referenced by numbers; they may be referenced by arbitrary character strings also. This is known as an *associative array*.

2. All elements in an array can be initialized to some value by a single assignment statement, but other operations cannot be applied to an entire array. For example, it is not possible to add some value to all numeric elements in an array in a single statement. Use a simple loop to accomplish this. A few Rexx interpreters do allow additional or extended array operations. The chapters on specific interpreters in Section II of this book cover this.

3. Rexx does not automatically keep track of the number of elements in an array. To process all elements in an array, keep track of the number of elements in the array. Then process all array elements by a loop using the number of array elements as the loop control variable. Alternatively, initialize the entire array to some unused value (such as the null string or 0), prior to filling it with data elements. Then process the array elements using a loop until you encounter the default value. These two array processing techniques assume you use a numeric array subscript, and that contiguous array positions are all used. To process all elements in an array subscripted by character strings, one technique is to store the index strings in a list, then process that list against the array, one item at a time.

4. Arrays form the basis of many data structures including lists, key-value pairs, and balanced and unbalanced trees. Create a list with a one-dimensional array (an array in which elements are referenced by a single subscript). Create key-value pairs by matching subscripts with their corresponding values. Create tree structures by implementing an element hierarchy through the array.

Chapter 5

1. The two types of input/output are *line-oriented* and *character-oriented*. Use the former to read and write lines of information, and the latter to read and write individual characters. Line-oriented I/O is typically more portable across operating systems. Character-oriented is useful in reading all bytes in the input stream, regardless of any special meaning they might have to the operating system.

2. The `stream` function is used either to return information about a character stream or file, or to perform some action upon it. The `stream` function definition allows Rexx interpreters to offer many implementation-dependent file commands, and most do. Look the function up in your product documentation to learn what it offers for I/O and file manipulation. The statuses it returns are ERROR, NOTREADY, READY, and UNKNOWN.

3. Encode the I/O functions immediately followed by parentheses — for example, `feedback = linein(filein)` — or through a `call` instruction (for example, `call linein filein`). Capture the return code as shown in the example for the first method, or through the `result` special variable for the `call` method. It is important to check the return code for I/O operations because this informs your program about the result of that I/O and whether or not it succeeded.

4. Rexx does not require explicitly closing a file after using it. Program end automatically closes any open files. This is convenient for short scripts, but for longer or more complex scripts, explicitly closing files is a good programming practice. This prevents running out of memory (because each open file uses memory) and may also be necessary if a program needs to "reprocess" a file. The typical way to close a file is either to encode a `lineout` or `charout` function that writes no data, or to encode the `stream` function with a command parameter that closes the file.

5. Rexx offers several options beyond standard I/O for sophisticated I/O needs. One option is to use a database package, such as one of those described in Chapter 15. Another option is to use Rexx interpreter I/O extensions (discussed in Chapters 20 through 30 on the specific Rexx interpreters).

Chapter 6

1. String processing is the ability to process text. It is critically important because so many programming problems require this capability. Examples include report writing and the building and issuing of operating system commands.

2. Concatenation can be performed *implicitly*, by encoding variables with a single space between them; by *abuttal*, which means coding varaibles together without an intervening blank; or *explicitly*, by using the string concatenation operator: `||`.

3. The three methods of template parsing are: by *words*, in which case each word is identified; by *pattern*, which scans for a specified character or pattern; and by *numeric pattern*, which processes by column position.

4. The functions to use are: `verify`, `datatype`, `pos`, `delstr`, `right` and `left`, and `strip`. Given the flexibility of the string functions, you might choose other string functions and combine them in various ways to achieve these same operations.

5. `wordindex` returns the character position of the nth word in a string, while `wordpos` returns the word position of the first word of a phrase within a string.

6. Hex characters each represent strings of four bits; character strings are composed of consecutive individual characters of variable length, where each character is internally made up of 8 bits; bit strings consist solely of 0s and 1s. Rexx includes a full set of *conversion functions*, including: `b2x`, `c2d`, `c2x`, `d2c`, `d2x`, `x2b`, `x2c`, and `x2d`.

7. Bit strings can be used for a wide variety of tasks. Examples mentioned in the chapter include bit map indexes, character folding, and key folding.

Chapter 7

1. `numeric digits` determines how many significant digits are in a number. This affects accuracy in computation and output display. `numeric fuzz` determines the number of significant digits used in comparions. You might set `fuzz` in order to affect just a single comparison, while keeping the numeric precision of a number unchanged.

2. Scientific notation has one digit to the left of the decimal place, followed by fractional and exponential components. Engineering notation expresses the integer component by a number between 1 and 999. Rexx uses scientific notation by default. Change this by the `numeric form` instruction.

3. There are several ways to right-justify a number; one of them is the `format` function.

4. The `datatype` function allows you to check many data conditions, including whether a value is alphanumeric, a bit string, all lower- or uppercase, mixed case, a valid number or symbol, a whole number, or a hexadecimal number.

```
-22                    valid
'    -22    '           valid- the blanks are ignored
2.2.                   invalid- has a trailing period
2.2.2                  invalid- more than one decimal point
222b2                  invalid- contains an internal character
2.34e+13               valid
123.E  -2              invalid- no blanks allowed in exponential portion
123.2  E  + 7          invalid- no blanks allowed in exponential portion
```

Chapter 8

1. Modularity is important because it underlies *structured programming*. Modularity reduces errors and enhances program maintenance. Rexx supports modularity through its full set of structured control constructs, plus internal and external subroutines and functions.

2. A *function* always returns a single string through the `return` instruction. A *subroutine* may or may not return a value. Functions return their single value such that it is placed right into the statement where the function is coded, effectively replacing the function call. Get the value returned by a subroutine through the `result` special variable. Functions can be coded as embedded within a statement or invoked through the `call` instruction. Subroutines can only be invoked via the `call` instruction.

3. Internal subroutines reside in the same file as the main routine or driver. External subroutines reside in separate files. `procedure` can be used to selectively protect or expose variables for an internal routine. External routines always have an implicit `procedure` so that all the caller's variables are hidden.

4. The *function search order* determines where Rexx searches for called functions. It is: internal function, built-in function, external function. If you code a function with the same name as a Rexx built-in function, Rexx uses your function. Override this behavior by coding the function name as uppercase within quotes.

5. Information can be passed from a caller to a routine by several methods, including: passing arguments as input parameters, `procedure expose`, and using global variables. Updated variables can be passed back to the calling routine by the `return` instruction, changing `expose`'d variables, and changing global variables.

6. A `procedure instruction` without an `expose` keyword hides all the caller's variables. `procedure expose` allows updating the variables, whereas those read in through `arg` are read-only. (Argh!)

7. In standard Rexx condition testing, expressions must resolve to either 1 or 0, otherwise an error occurs. Some Rexx interpreters are extended to accept any nonzero value as TRUE.

Chapter 9

1. The default setting for the trace facility is `trace n` (or Normal). `trace r` is recommended for general-purpose debugging. It traces clauses before they execute and the final results of expression evaluation. It also shows when values change by `pull`, `arg`, and `parse` instructions. `trace l` lists all labels program execution passes through and shows which internal routines are entered and run. `trace i` shows intermediate results.

2. The trace facility is the basic tool you would use to figure out any problems that occur while issuing operating system commands from within a script. The trace flags C, E, and F would be useful for tracing OS commands.

3. To start interactive tracing, code the `trace` instruction with a question mark (?) preceding its argument. The ? is a toggle switch. If tracing is off, it turns it on; if tracing is on, it turns it off. The first `trace` instruction or function you execute with ? encoded turns tracing on. The next one that executes with the question mark will turn it off.

4. When in *interactive mode*, the Rexx interpreter pauses after each statement or clause. Use it to single-step through code.

Chapter 10

1. The purpose of error or exception trapping is to manage certain kinds of commonly occuring errors in a systematic manner. The conditions are ERROR, FAILURE, HALT, NOVALUE, NOTREADY, SYNTAX and LOSTDIGITS. The ANSI-1996 standard added LOSTDIGITS.

2. To handle a control interrupt, enable an error trap for the HALT condition. Enable this exception condition, then Rexx automatically invokes your error routine when this condition occurs.

3. `signal` applies to all seven error conditions. `call` does *not* apply to SYNTAX, NOVALUE, and LOSTDIGITS errors. `signal` forces an *abnormal change* in the flow of control. It terminates any `do`, `if` or `select` instruction in force and unconditionally transfers control to a specified label.

`call` provides for normal invocation of an internal subroutine to handle an error condition. The `result` special variable is not set when returning from a called condition trap; any value coded on the `return` instruction is ignored.

4. Use the `interpret` instruction to dynamically evaluate and execute an expression.

5. Enable a condition routine through a `signal` or `call` instruction. You can have multiple routines to handle a condition by coding `signal` or `call` multiple times, but only one condition routine is active for each kind of error trap at any one time.

6. If the error trap was initiated by the `signal` instruction, after executing the condition trap routine, you must reactivate the error condition by executing the `signal` instruction again.

7. Whether it is better to write one generic error routine to handle all kinds or errors, or to write a separate routine for each different kind of error, depends on what you're trying to do and the nature of your program. Both approaches have advantages. Sometimes it is convenient to consolidate all error handling into a single routine, other times, it may be preferable to have detailed, separate routines for each condition.

Chapter 11

1. All Rexx implementations covered in this book have a stack; however, how the stack is implemented varies. Review the product documentation if you need to know how the stack is supported within your version of Rexx.

2. Stacks are last-in, first-out structures, while queues are first-in, first-out. Instructions like `push` and `queue` place data into the stack, and instructions like `pull` and `parse pull` extract data from it. The `queued` built-in function reports how many items are in the stack.

3. The limit on the number of items the stack can hold is usually a function of available memory.

4. The answer to this question depends on the Rexx interpreter(s) you use and the platforms to which you wish to port. Check the documentation for the platforms and interpreters for which you intend to port.

5. Some Rexx interpreters support more than one stack, and more than one memory area or buffer within each stack. Functions or commands like `newstack` and `delstack` manage stacks, while `makebuf`, `dropbuf`, and `desbuf` manage buffers. Check the documentation for your specific Rexx interpreter regarding these features, as they do vary by interpreter.

Chapter 12

1. Consistency in coding is a virtue because it renders code easier to understand, enhance, and maintain.

2. Some programmers deeply nest functions because this makes for more compact code. Some developers find it an intellectually interesting way to code, and others even use it to demonstrate their cleverness. If overdone, it makes code indecipherable and result in slower execution of the program.

3.   A good comment imparts information beyond what the code shows. It explains the code further, in clear English. Rexx comments may appear on the end of a line, in stand-alone lines, or in comment boxes.

4.   Modularity and structured programming permit a limited number of entry and exit points from discrete blocks of code. This makes code easier to understand and follow, and restricts interactions between different parts of programs. The result is higher productivity, and more easily understood code that is easier to maintain.

5.   `do until` and `signal` are unstructured control instructions. Any code using them can be rewritten as structured code by use of the `do while` and `if` statements.

6.   A good variable name is descriptive. It is not short or cryptic but long and self-explanatory. It does not employ cryptic abbreviations but instead fully spells out words. Good variable naming makes a program much more readable.

7.   Global variables can be highly convenient when coding. But best programming practice limits their use in larger and more complex programs. Structured programming involves carefully defined interfaces between routines, functions, and modules. Variables should be localized to routines and their use across routines should be carefully defined and limited. Global variables do not follow these principles. Different programmers and sites may have their own standards or opinions on this matter.

Chapter 13

1.   No. Writing portable code typically takes more effort than writing nonportable code. In some cases, where the goal is quick coding, a nonportable solution may meet the goal more effectively.

2.   Scripts can learn about their environment in several ways. Key instructions for this purpose include `parse version` and `parse source`. The chapter also lists many other instructions and functions that help scripts learn about their environment.

3.   `arg` automatically translates input to uppercase, while `parse arg` does not.

4.   The `sourceline` function either returns the number of lines in the source script, or a specific line if a line number is supplied as an argument

5.   The appendix of the TRL-2 book lists all its differences from TRL-1.

Chapter 14

1.   Rexx sends a command string to the environment when it does not recognize it as valid Rexx code. The default environment, the environment to which external commands are directed by default, is typically the operating system's shell or command interface.

2.   Enclose commands in quotation marks when their contents will otherwise be incorrectly interpreted or evaluated by the Rexx interpreter. For example: `dir > output.txt` will not work because the carrot symbol will be interpreted as a "greater than" symbol by Rexx, rather than as a valid part of the OS command. So, this OS command would fail unless enclosed within quotation marks. Some developers like to enclose *all* of the OS command string in quotes, except the parts they specifically want Rexx to evaluate. Other developers quote only those parts of the

command that must not be evaluated. We generally follow the latter approach in this book. Either technique works fine; it is a matter of preference as to which you use.

To prepare a command in advance, assign the command string to a Rexx variable prior to issuing it to the operating system. You can easily inspect the variable's contents merely by displaying it.

3. Basic ways to get error information from OS commands include inspecting their command return codes, capturing their textual error output, and intercepting raised condition traps within error routines. Look up return code information for OS commands in the operating system documentation.

4. Two ways to redirect command input/output from within a script are the `address` instruction or through the operating system's redirection symbols. Command I/O redirection works on operating systems in the Windows, Linux, Unix, BSD, and DOS families, among others. Not all operating systems support I/O redirection.

5. Sources and targets can be specified as arrays or streams (files). They may be intermixed within the same `address` command.

6. To direct all subsequent external commands to the same interface, specify `address` with a system target only (without any external command encoded on the same instruction). Repeated coding of `address` without any environment operand effectively "toggles" the target for commands back and forth between two target environments.

Chapter 15

1. Rexx/SQL is free, open source, universal, and standardized. Database programming provides sophisticated I/O for multiuser environments. Advantages to database management systems include backup/recovery, database utilities, central data administration, transaction control, and many other features.

2. Scripts typically start by loading the Rexx/SQL function library for use through the `RxFuncAdd` and `SQLLoadFuncs` functions.

3. Connect to a database by `SQLConnect`, and disconnect through the `SQLDisconnect` function. Check connection status by `SQLGetInfo`. You can also check the return code for any Rexx/SQL function to verify its success or failure.

4. Consolidating error handling in a single routine is typical in database programming. It allows consistent error handling, while minimizing code. Here are the SQLCA variables set by Rexx/SQL:

❑   `SQLCA.SQLCODE` — SQL return code

❑   `SQLCA.SQLERRM` — SQL error message text

❑   `SQLCA.SQLSTATE` — Detailed status string (N/A on some ports)

❑   `SQLCA.SQLTEXT` — Text of the last SQL statement

❑   `SQLCA.ROWCOUNT` — Number of rows affected by the SQL operation

❑   `SQLCA.FUNCTION` — The last Rexx external function called

❑   `SQLCA.INTCODE` — The Rexx/SQL interface error number

❑   `SQLCA.INTERRM` — Text of the Rexx/SQL interface error

5. Assigning a SQL statement to a Rexx variable makes its coding clearer. It can also be verified simplying by displaying the variable's value via a simple `say` instruction.

6. `SQLDisconnect` terminates a connection with a database and closes any open database cursor(s) for that connection. `SQLDispose` releases the work area (memory) resources originally allocated by a `SQLPrepare` function.

7. Rexx/SQL is a database-neutral product that is free, open source, very capable, and widely used. It offers both generic and native database interfaces to nearly any available database. Database-specific Rexx interfaces are also available from a few relational database companies. These products are proprietary and support only that company's database. In exchange, they often offer access to database-unique features, for example, the ability to write Rexx scripts for database administration or for controlling database utilities. An example of a proprietary interface is IBM Corporation's DB2 UDB interface described in this chapter.

Chapter 16

1. Both Rexx/Tk and Rexx/DW are free, open source interfaces that allow you to create portable graphical user interfaces for Rexx scripts. Rexx/Tk is based on the widely used Tk toolkit and provides Rexx programmers entre into the Tcl/Tk universe. Rexx/DW is a lightweight protocol; it does not have the overhead that Rexx/Tk does. Both products offer very large libraries of GUI functions and features.

2. Rexx Dialog was designed specifically for scripting Windows GUIs. It works with both the Reginald and Regina Rexx interpreters.

3. A widget is a control or object placed on a window with which users interact. Widgets are added in Rexx/Tk by functions like `TkAdd` and `TkConfig and others`. Widgets are packed onto DW window layouts.

4. The basic logic of GUI scripts is the same, regardless of whether Rexx/Tk or Rexx/DW is used. Register and load the function library; create the controls or widgets for the topmost window; display the top-level window; wait for user interaction with the widgets, handle the interactions requested through event-handling routines; and terminate the window and the program when requested by the user.

5. Tcl/Tk GUI toolkit has achieved worldwide use because it renders inherently complex windows programming relatively simple. It is also portable and runs on almost any platform.

6. Rexx/gd creates graphical images, not GUIs. These images can be used as part of a GUI (for example, as components placed on a Web page). Rexx/gd creates its images in memory work areas. The images are typically stored on disk after developed, then the script releases the image memory area and terminates.

Chapter 17

1. Yes, you could write Web programs without using any of the packages described in the chapter. However, you would be doing a lot more work, and essentially duplicating code and routines that already exist and that you can freely use.

2. Functions `htmltop` and `htmlbot` write standard headers and footers, respectively. Scripts write the *Content Type header* by the `PrintHeader` function. The content type header must be the first statement written to the browser. It tells the browser the kind of data it will receive in subsequent statements. Read user input through the `ReadForm` function, among others.

3. Function `CgiInit` initializes and sets up the CGI header, while `CgiEnd` typically ends a script. `CgiHref` generates a hyperlink.

4. Mod_Rexx makes the Apache open source Web server completely programmable by Rexx scripts. Apache scales better than traditional CGI Web server programming because Apache handles incoming connections much more efficiently. Mod_Rexx gives the same capabilities to Rexx scripts as Perl programs get from mod_perl and PHP scripts from mod_php.

5. Rexx Server Pages are analogous to Java Server Pages or embedded PHP scripting, in that RSPs permit embedding Rexx code directly into the HTML of Web pages. This permits "dynamic pages" that are tailored or customized in real time.

6. Short- and long-form delimiters identify and surround Rexx code within HTML pages. They are used with Rexx Server Pages, or RSPs. There is no functional difference between short- and long-form delimiters.

7. To customize Apache's log processing, use the Mod_Rexx package. It enables you to code Rexx scripts that control any of the 14 or so processing steps of the Apache Web server, including the one that manages log processing.

Chapter 18

1. XML is a self-describing data language. XML files contain both data and tags that describe the data. They are textual files. XML is useful for data interchange between applications or companies. XPath is a standard for identifying and extracting parts of XML files. XSLT applies definitional templates called stylesheets to XML files. It can be used to transform XML files. HTML is a language that defines Web pages.

2. Function `xmlParseXML` can be used to load and optionally validate a document. Function `xmlSaveDoc` saves a document, while function `xmlFreeDoc` frees resources.

3. Function `xmlParseHTML` can parse or scan a Web page written in HTML. `xmlFindNode` and `xmlNodesetCount` may also be useful, as per the example in the chapter.

4. Rexx does not include regular expressions. However, many packages are freely available that add this facility to the language, including *RexxRE* and *Regular Expressions*. Appendix H lists many of the free and open source packages, tools, and interfaces for Rexx programmers.

5. Apply an XSLT stylesheet to a document by the `xmlApplyStylesheet` function. `xmlParseXSLT` parses and compiles an XSLT stylesheet, while `xmlFreeStylesheet` frees a compiled stylesheet. `xmlOutputMethod` reports the output method of a stylesheet.

Chapter 19

1. BRexx runs fast and runs natively on Windows CE. Regina runs under virtually any imaginable platform. Rexx interpreters that are extended specifically for Windows are r4, Reginald, and Regina. Several interpreters offer extensions for Unix, Linux, and BSD, especially Rexx/imc,

BRexx, and Regina. Kilowatt Software offers both their classic Rexx interpreter called r4 and an upwardly compatible, fully object-oriented interpreter called roo!

2. The major Rexx standards are TRL-1, TRL-2, SAA, and ANSI-1996. Most Rexx interpreters adhere to TRL-2, while Regina is the primary offering that implements full ANSI-1996. SAA was IBM's attempt to rationalize its diverse operating systems in the early and mid- 1990s. SAA declared Rexx its common procedures language. The practical effect was that IBM ported Rexx to all its operating systems and established more rigorous standardization for the language across platforms.

3. roo! and Open Object Rexx are fully object-oriented Rexx interpreters. Both are supersets of standard or classic Rexx. This means that you can take a standard Rexx script and run it under either roo! or Open Object Rexx without any changes to that script. roo! is free under Windows, while Open Object Rexx is free under Linux, Windows, Solaris, and AIX.

4. NetRexx runs under the Java Virtual Machine (JVM). So, it runs anywhere Java runs. It presents an easy-to-use alternative to Java and may be freely intermixed with Java scripts. So, for example, NetRexx can make full use of the Java class libraries. You can write applets, applications, classes, Java Beans, and Servlets in NetRexx. NetRexx is a Rexx-like language; it does not meet the Rexx standards such as TRL-2 or ANSI-1996.

5. Regina is the open source Rexx that it includes many of the extended functions offered in other Rexx interpreters.

6. Rexx runs in native mode and emulation mode under the three major handheld operating systems. BRexx runs natively under Windows CE, Regina runs natively under Symbian/EPOC32, and Rexx for Palm OS runs natively under the Palm OS.

7. Emulation is slower and less efficient than running in native mode. However, emulation has the immediate benefit that it ports thousands of DOS applications to the handheld device without any code changes. Rexx interpreters are one example of the kinds of programs that can run under DOS emulation. Specifically, BRexx runs under DOS emulation (as well as in native mode under Windows CE).

Chapter 20

1. Regina is open source, widely popular, well supported, and meets all standards. It runs on virtually every platform, including any version of Windows, Linux, Unix, and BSD. It also runs natively under the handheld operating system Symbian/EPOC32, as well as a variety of less used operating systems such as BeOS, OS/2, AROS and others. Regina does not run under 16-bit DOS, but it does run from the Windows command prompt.

2. Use the stack to manage command I/O and pass information between routines. Regina also has a unique stack facility that permits communications between different processes on the same machine, and even between different processes on different machines. Regina also supports sending and receiving I/O to/from commands using the address instruction with standard keywords like input, output, and error.

3. Use readch and writech to read and write character strings, and readln and writeln to read and write lines. Use open to explicitly open a file, close to explicitly close a file, eof to test for end of file, and seek to move the file pointers.

4. The SAA API is an interface definition that allows programs written in languages like C to use Regina as a set of services or a function library. Regina uses offers SAA-compatible functions for loading external function libraries. These include `rxfundadd` to register an external function and `rxfundrop` to remove external functions from use.

5. Regina supports a wide variety of parameters on the `options` instruction, including CMS, UNIX, BUFFERS, AREXX_BIFS, REGINA, ANSI, SAA, TRL2, and TRL1. See the `Regina` documentation for full details on these and other `options` instruction parameters.

Chapter 21

1. Rexx/imc runs under all forms of Linux, Unix, and BSD. Rexx/imc meets the TRL-2 standards. Its advantages include its strong Unix heritage and orientation, extra Unix functions, good documentation, and a strong track record of support.

2. Rexx/imc includes C-like I/O functions such as `open`, `close`, `stream`, and `ftell`. This I/O model provides more explicit control than Rexx's standard I/O. Use the standard I/O functions for portability and standardization, and use the the C-like I/O functions for more explicit file control.

3. `select` can key off the values in a variable in Rexx/imc, rather than requiring condition tests. This is useful in implementing a CASE construct based on the value of a variable.

4. Use `rxfuncadd` to load and register and external function for use, and `rxfuncdrop` to drop an external function. Use `rxfuncquery` to determine if a function is already loaded.

5. Rexx/imc accepts any nonzero value as TRUE, whereas standard Rexx only accepts 1 as TRUE. In this respect, any standard Rexx script will run under Rexx/imc, but a script written for Rexx/imc's approach to TRUE conditions might fail when run under standard Rexx.

Chapter 22

1. BRexx's advantages include its high performance, small footprint, wide array of built-in functions, and extra function libraries. It is effective for a wide variety of problems. It runs on a wide variety of platforms and in addition is uniquely positioned among Rexx interpreters to run on smaller, limited-resource environments (such as Windows CE), and older systems (like 16- and 32-bit DOS).

2. Position a file pointer through the `seek` function. Using `seek`, you can position to anywhere in the file including its beginning or end. The `seek` function can also return current file pointer positions. Use it to determine the size of a file by this statement: `filesize = seek(file_pointer, 0, "EOF")`.

3. The EBCDIC functions convert data between ASCII and EBCDIC (these are the two predominant coding schemes, with the former being used on PCs and midrange machines, and the latter being used for mainframes). The Date Functions external function library can handle date arithmetic.

4. The stack buffer functions include `makebuf` (create a new system stack), `desbuf` (destroy all system stacks), and `dropbuf` (destroy the top *n* stacks).

5. BRexx supports standard Rexx I/O, C-like I/O, and database I/O through MySQL. Standard Rexx I/O is for general use in standards-based, portable programs; C-like I/O is nonstandard but offers more explicit file control; and the MySQL functions provide the full power of a relational database.

6. Code operating system commands in the same manner as with any standard Rexx interpreter. You can also encode them as if they were functions, if they use standard I/O. Capture command output through the stack, or code a command as if it were a function and capture its return string through an assignment statement.

Chapter 23

1. Reginald's biggest advantage is that it is specifically tailored and customized for Windows. Furthermore, it offers many add-on tools, provides great documentation on how to use its extended features and functions, permits use of *any* Windows DLL, meets the Rexx TRL-2 standards, and supports the SAA API.

2. Reginald comes with complete documentation that includes examples of every new function and feature. You shouldn't require any information other than what comes with Reginald to use it.

3. Use Reginald's SAA-compliant functions like `rxfuncadd`, `rxfuncquery`, and `rxfuncdrop` to access external function libraries. Use `funcdef` to access DLLs that were not written to Rexx's specifications. You can autoload many function libraries through Reginald's Administration Tool and thereby avoid explicitly loading them in every script. This is very convenient and also reduces the amount of code you must write.

4. Reginald accesses virtually any external data source, including office products like Microsoft Excel and Access, and databases like SQL Server, MySQL, and PostgreSQL. The Open Database Connectivity or ODBC drivers are the means to accomplish this.

5. Reginald offers a freely downloadable tutorial on how to use Reginald with the Common Gateway Interface, or CGI. Other tutorials address subjects like mailslots, Internet access, sockets, and GUI programming.

6. `DriveInfo` and `MatchName` are two functions (among others) that supply information about disk drives. `MatchName` also provides attribute information. A file does not have to be open to retrieve information about it, but it must exist.

7. `Valuein` reads binary values in as numeric values.

8. The `LoadText` function reads lines of a text file into a stem variable, or saves a stem variable's lines to a text file.

9. The RxDlgIDE add-on product helps generate GUI code.

10. `RxErr` establishes how GUI-related errors will be handled; `RxCreate` creates a new window with its controls; `RxMsg` controls user interaction with a window. The key values scripts check to determine how a user interacted with a window and its controls are `rxid` and `rxsubid`.

11. The Speech library allows the computer to synthesize speech. The MIDI function library controls the MIDI interface, which connects a computer to external instrumentation. Use MIDI to send information to a musical instrument, and the Speech library to read a document aloud.

Chapter 24

1. The three major families of handheld operating systems are Windows CE, Palm OS, and Symbian/EPOC32. The Rexx interpreters that run under them natively are BRexx, Rexx for Palm OS, and Regina (respectively).

2. Native scripts run faster, because they require no intermediate layer of software (or emulator) to run. Emulators are mainly useful for reasons of compatibility. They allow thousands of old DOS programs to run on the handheld, without any upgrading or changes being necessary. DOS emulation provides another way to run Rexx scripts on the handheld. The main advantage here is that Rexx can function as a glue language to tie together existing DOS programs or customize their use.

3. Tiny Linux is a version of Linux (or "kernel build") that minimizes resource use by stripping out any unnecessary components. It is useful because it allows Linux to run on small embedded devices. Sometimes it is referred to as *embedded Linux*.

4. You need to supply a DOS with any emulator. PocketDOS ships with a free DOS, while XTM does not. Many free DOS operating systems are available on the Internet, includng DR-DOS, Free DOS, and others.

5. The fact that Rexx for handhelds supports Rexx standards is very useful for reasons of portability and ease of learning. The Rexx standards mean that the Rexx skills you may have learned on other platforms apply to handhelds as well.

6. Rexx offers several advantages for programming handhelds and embedded programming versus C, C++, and Java. Among them are ease of use, ease of learning, and the fact that an easy-to-use language yields more reliable code.

Chapter 25

1. Rexxlets run concurrently with applications. This empowers them as a glue language for control and customization of applications. They can be started by any single action, such as a pen stroke or keypad entry.

2. URLs and URIs are essentially the same thing: a standard way to reference a resource such as a Web site address or file. Rexx for Palm OS uses them as a standard means of naming and accessing resources, such as databases, files, the display screen, and the clipboard.

3. Scripts identify and access handheld resources by their URI names. Scripts open their resources implicitly, in the same manner as Rexx scripts running on any other platform.

4. Databases contain structured information. Files are stream-oriented. Databases are the most popular form of storage on the Palm, but files are also useful because their size is unlimited and they match the default concept of Rexx I/O.

5. You could develop Rexxlets in environments other than the handheld, but testing them really requires running them on the target (the handheld). Resources references might need to be altered if development occurs on a machine other than the handheld.

6. A hack manager enables and manages operating system extensions. It is only required if you use an older version of the Palm OS (older than version 5). X-Master is a free hack manager for versions of the Palm OS prior to version 5.

7. I/O is the same in Rexx for Palm OS as it is in any other standard Rexx. What sometimes make Palm scripting different are the different kinds of devices programmed on the handheld (for example, the beamer or a serial port). Rexx for Palm OS is a TRL-2 standard Rexx interpreter.

Chapter 26

1. Among the advantages to r4/roo! are that they are specifically tailored for Windows, they fit together as a classic Rexx/object Rexx pair, and they share a large set of Windows-specific tools. Among the tools are AuroraWare! (to create GUIs), TopHat (for creating fill-in-the-blank forms), Poof! (with 135 command-line aids and tools), Revu (to view text), XMLGenie! (to convert XML to HTML), Chill (to hide Rexx source code), and the Exe Conversion Utility (to convert scripts to stand-alone executable files).

2. r4 scripts run under roo! without any alteration. roo! scripts will typically not run under r4, because roo! is a superset of classic Rexx and r4. Since r4 scripts are classic Rexx, they are widely portable across operating systems. roo! scripts are portable only across varieties of Windows, because roo! is a Windows-specific product.

3. Several of the r4/roo! utilities aid in building GUIs, AuroraWare! being the most directly pertinent. In the list of attributes, the r4/roo! GUI tools offer the best customization for Windows, are easiest to use, can be learned most quickly, and are easiest to maintain. Competing tools such as Rexx/Tk and Rexx/DW are the most portable and the most powerful. These statements are generalizations that may not apply across the board to all projects, so always assess the available tools versus the criteria and goals of your own project.

4. Installation of r4 and roo! is simple and similar to other Windows installs. The one variant is that there is a preinstall step that Web-installs on the user's system.

5. roo! supports *all* the principles of object-oriented programming, including classes and methods, inheritance, an hierarchical class structure, encapsulation, abstraction, and polymorphism. As in all object-oriented systems, messages invoke methods in the various classes.

6. roo! supports a number of new operators in order to bring full object-orientation to classic Rexx. These include the following:

Operator	Symbols	Use
^^	Double caret	Instance creation
^	Caret	Method invocation prefix operator
~	Tilde	Method invocation infix operator
[ ]	Brackets	Arraylike reference operator
{ }	Braces	Vector class reference
!	Exclamation Point	Identifies a command

7. For line-oriented I/O, use classes such as `InLineFile` and `OutLineFile`. To manage the display screen, the `Console` class is useful. `InStream` and `OutStream` handle the default input and output streams. Use the `Socket` class to manage TCP/IP sockets.

Chapter 27

1. Open Object Rexx is a superset of classic Rexx. Classic Rexx programs typically run under Open Object Rexx without any alteration. ooRexx features *inheritance*, the ability to create subclasses that inherit the methods and attributes of their superclasses. *Multiple inheritance* allows a class to inherit from more than one superclass. Open Object Rexx's class hierarchy implements all this.

2. Encapsulation means that only an object can manipulate its own data. Send a message to the object to invoke its methods to manipulate that data. Polymorphism means that messages invoke actions appropriate to the object to which they are sent.

3. The `Stream` class has I/O methods. It goes beyond classic Rexx capabilities to include reading/writing entire arrays, binary, and text I/O, shared-mode files, direct I/O, and so on.

4. Open Object Rexx adds new special variables. Two are used for referencing objects: `Self` references the object of the current executing method, while `Super` references the superclass or parent of the current object.

5. The four directives are: ::CLASS (to define a class), ::METHOD (to define a method), ::ROUTINE (to define a callable subroutine), and ::REQUIRES (to specify access to another source script). Directives mark points within the script at which these definitions or actions apply.

7. Collection classes manipulate sets of objects and define data structures. A few of the collection classes are: Array (a sequenced collection), Bag (a nonunique collection of objects), Directory (a collection indexed by unique character strings), List (a sequenced collection which allows inserts at any position), and Queue (a sequenced collection that allows inserts at the start or ending positions).

8. The new `USER` condition trap allows user-defined error conditions. Explicitly raise an error condition (user-defined or built-in) by the new `raise` instruction.

9. As in classic Rexx, the `expose` instruction permits access to and updating of specified variables. In object programming, `expose` permits access to objects as well as string variables.

Chapter 28

1. Every classic Rexx program will run under Open Object Rexx, but this does not take advantage of any of the new object-oriented capabilities of Open Object Rexx. Compatibility both preserves legacy scripts and allows you to tip-toe into object-oriented scripting at a pace at which you are comfortable.

2. All instructions and functions of classic Rexx are part of Open Object Rexx. The latter adds a number of new and enhanced instructions and functions.

3. Collections are classes that implement data structures and allow manipulation of the objects in the class as a group.

4. Here are some solutions:

   ❑ To return a string with its character positions reversed, code: `string~reverse`

   ❑ To return a substring, code: `string~substr(1,5)`

5. The `stream` class offers a superset of the I/O capabilities of classic Rexx. Extra features it includes are: reading/writing entire arrays, binary and text I/O, shared-mode files, direct I/O, and so on.

6. The four directives are: ::CLASS (to define a class), ::METHOD (to define a method), ::ROUTINE (to define a callable subroutine), and ::REQUIRES (to specify access to another source script). Classes and methods are placed after the main routine or driver (towards the end of the script).

7. These symbols can be used to express `at` and `put` in many collections:

Operator	Use
[ ]	Same as the `at` method
[ ] =	Same as the `put` method

8. These monitor objects are applied against the default streams. The default streams are `.stdin`, `.stdout`, and `.stderr`.

Chapter 29

1. Mainframe Rexx generally meets the TRL-2 and SAA standards. There are slight differences between Rexx interpreters on the different mainframe platforms as well as between mainframe Rexx and the standards. See the manual *SAA Common Programming Interface REXX Level 2 Reference, SC24-5549* for SAA definition and information.

2. Mainframe Rexx enhances the instructions `options` and `parse` and adds the extended mainframe instruction `upper`. Mainframe extended functions include `externals`, `find`, `index`, `justify`, `linesize`, and `userid`. In addition, both VM and OS Rexx add their own external functions, but what is included in this list varies between VM and OS.

3. Mainframe Rexx supports the Double-Byte Character Set, which allows encoding for ideographic languages, such as Asian languages like Chinese and Korean.

4. I/O on the mainframe is often performed using `EXECIO`.

5. Immediate commands can be entered from the command line and they affect the executing script in real time. Immediate commands can turn the trace on or off, suspend or resume script execution, and suspend or resume terminal (display) output.

6. VM Rexx knows about and automatically loads any or all of these three named packages if any function within them is invoked from within a script: `RXUSERFN`, `RXLOCFN`, and `RXSYSFN`. Users may add their own functions to these libraries.

7. Rexx compilers separate the compile (or script preparation step) from its execution. This usually produces an executable that runs faster, purchased at the price of a two-step process. If a Rexx script is stable and unlikely to change, and is run frequently, compiling it might increase its run-time performance. Note that the mainframe compiler does not guarantee a performance increase.

8. VM Rexx requires a comment line, while OS TSO/E Rexx requires the word REXX. To satisfy both requirements, encode this as the first line in a mainframe Rexx script: `/* REXX */`.

9. VM Rexx scripts reside in files of type EXEC. XEDIT editor macros reside in files of type XEDIT. CMS pipelines use files of type REXX.

Chapter 30

1. NetRexx offers some of the traditional advantages of Rexx: easy syntax, ease of use, and ease of maintenance. You can intermix NetRexx and Java classes however you like.

2. The NetRexx translator can be used as a compiler or an interpreter. As an interpreter, it allows NetRexx programs to run without needing a compiler or generating .class files. As a compiler, it can compile scripts into .class files. NetRexx programs can be both compiled and interpreted in just one command. This is easy to do and machine-efficient. NetRexx can also generate formatted Java code, including original commentary, if desired.

3. NetRexx scripts run on any machine that offers a Java Virtual Machine (JVM). This makes them portable across all Java environments. As an interpreter, the NetRexx translator allows NetRexx programs to run without needing a compiler or generating .class files.

4. Indexed strings are NetRexx strings by which subvalues are identified by an index string. Arrays are tables of fixed size that must be defined before use. Arrays may index elements of any type, and the elements are considered ordered. To define a dictionary collection class, refer to the Java documentation. NetRexx uses all the Java classes and methods.

5. NetRexx uses all the Java classes and methods, so refer to the Java documentation for information.

6. *.nrx files contain the source of a NetRexx script. *.java files contain Java source code, and can be produced automatically from NetRexx scripts by the NetRexx translator. *.class files contain the binary or compiled form of a program.

7. Special names perform an action wherever they appear in the source. For example, ask reads a line from the default input stream and returns it as a string of type *Rexx* while length returns an array's length (the number of elements). The special methods include super, the constructor of the superclass, and this, the constructor of the current class.

8. To migrate classic Rexx scripts to NetRexx, download the free *Rexx2Nrx* classic Rexx to NetRexx automated conversion tool.

Index

SYMBOLS